Colin Wilson was born in Leicester in 1931. He left school at sixteen and spent several years working in a wool warehouse, a laboratory, a plastics factory and a coffee bar before *The Outsider* was published in 1956 to immense critical acclaim.

Since then he has written many books on crime, philosophy, the occult and sexual deviance, as well as a number of successful novels. His work includes *Encyclopaedia of Murder* (with Patricia Pitman), *A Criminal History of Mankind*, *Written In Blood: A History of Forensic Detection* and *The Mammoth Book of True Crime*.

Colin Wilson is well known as a lecturer and as a radio and television personality.

The Mammoth Book of
TRUE CRIME
2

The Mammoth Book of
TRUE CRIME
2

Colin Wilson

*Edited and with a Foreword
by
Damon Wilson*

Carroll & Graf Publishers, Inc.
New York

First published in Great Britain 1990
First Carroll & Graf edition 1990

Carroll & Graf Publishers, Inc.
260 Fifth Avenue
New York
NY 10001

ISBN: 0–88184–591–4

10   9   8   7   6   5   4   3   2   1

Printed by Wm. Collins Ltd., Glasgow

Contents

Foreword by Damon Wilson

Translyvanian apprentices. He insults the Turkish ambassadors. Capture of Guirgiu. War against Turks. He flees to Hungary. In captivity, he impales rats and mice. His death in battle. Bram Soker's *Dracula*. How it came to be written. Life of Ivan the Terrible. Murder of the Shuiskys. Fire of Moscow. Marriage and death of his wife. His abdication and return. Purge of the boyars. Destruction of Novgorod and torture of its inhabitants. His death. The crimes of Gilles de Rais. Joan of Arc. Murder of children. Practice of alchemy. His fatal mistake. Trial and execution. H.G. Wells on Gilles. Countess Elizabeth Bathory bathes in blood. Her capture and death. The witchcraft craze. Torture and rape of suspected witches. Death throes of the old religion. The life of the Marquis de Sade. His years in prison. *The 120 Days of Sodom*. His death in a lunatic asylum. The rise of pornography. The importance of the novel. The rise of sex crime. The case of the Hillside Stranglers.

3. Predators of the Seas 77
The history of piracy. The Greek pirates. Pompey stamps out Mediterranean piracy. Pirates of the Spanish Main. Red Beard. Lepanto. Pierre Legrand. Jean-David Nau. Henry Morgan. Henry Every. Blackbeard. The brief career of William Fly. The end of piracy after Napoleon.

4. Order of Assassins 90
Hasan bin Sabah and the Order of Assassins. Hasan's conversion. The resistance movement in Persia. Assassination of Nizam-al-Mulk. The Assassins in Syria. Assassins and crusaders. The fascination of the Assassins. The legend of human monsters. The Thugs of India – descendants of the Assassins? Thug methods. Their ceremonies. The Ismailis in India. Mighty Mahmud. The origin of sadism. The dark mother. Mr Evans and his 'worm' of violence. Dualism. The Axeman of New Orleans. The Ratcliffe Highway murders. Assassination of Lord Mayo. The murder of the Niebels. Charles Guiteau and the assassination of President Garfield. Ruth Ellis. The Zodiac murders. Van Vogt's theory of the Violent Man. Compulsive need to be 'in the right.' The rapist as woman-worshipper. Gorky's *Twenty Six Men and a Girl*. The changing patterns of murder. The crimes of Hans

van Zon. The Krays and the Richardsons. Arthur Hosein and the kidnapping of Muriel McKay. Raymond Morris, the Cannock Chase murderer. Norman Collins, the Ann Arbor sex killer.

5. Murder – Elizabethan Style 142

Why do certain crimes fascinate the public? The murder of William Weare. The Maria Marten case. Elizabethan domestic murders. Walter-Calverley. *Arden of Faversham*. The Max Garvie case. The murder of George Sanders. Francis Thorney. The murder of Christopher Marlowe. Was Marlowe Shakespeare? Execution of Dr Lopez. Amy Robsart. Sir Thomas Malory, rapist and bandit. Gesualdo, composer and wife murderer. Murder of Sir Thomas Overbury. Murder of Sir Edmund Berry Godfrey.

6. The Age of Gin 162

Gin and the rising crime rate. The Mohocks. Dick Turpin. Sarah Malcolm and Hogarth. Tyburn Tree. History of hanging. Jack Ketch. Marwood the executioner. 'Laughing' Jack Hooper. John Price. *The Newgate Calendar*. Catherine Hayes. Mrs Brownrigg. The Metyards. Trial of the smugglers for murder of Galley and Chater. Earl Ferrars, last nobleman to be publicly hanged. Captain John Pourteous. Criminals who survived hanging. Thomas Colley. Henry Fielding and the Bow Street Runners.

7. Cannibals and Rapists 190

Calhoun's criminal rats. The 19th century. Transportation to Australia. Jeffries the Monster. Cannibalism. Alexander Pierce. Dignum and Cornerford. The bushranger Morgan. Arthur Thistlewood and the Cato Street Conspirators. Abduction and rape of heiresses. Rape of Sarah Woodcock. Luke Dillon and Miss Frizell. George Cant and Jane Bolland. False Allegations of Rape. The Red Barn Murder. Ellie Hanley, the Colleen Bawn.

8. Into the Age of Violence 219

Motiveless 'joy murder.' Journals of the Nuremberg hangman Hans Schmidt. Andrew Bichell, the Bavarian ripper. Martin Dumollard, the mass murderer of Lyon. The Ratcliffe Highway murders. Burke and Hare, the body snatchers. Parisian crime – Vidocq, Balzac's Vautrin. Lacenaire. Thomas Griffiths Wainewright. Female Poisoners: Gesina Gottfried, Helene Jegado, Anna Zwanziger. Dr Palmer of Rugely. Thomas Neill Cream. George Chapman.

'Vanishings.' The Sheward case. The Adelaide Bartlett mystery.

12. The Century of Espionage   339

The capture of the German code books in 1914. Blinker Hall and Naval Intelligence. The murder of Szek. The Redl case. Ernst Wollweber, Russian master spy. Klaus Fuchs. The defection of Gouzenko. Nunn May. The Rosenbergs. Kim Philby. The first spies: Edward IV's 'espials.' Spying during the American civil war. Bismarck and Stieber. Richard Sorge. His downfall in Tokyo.

13. British Murder, 1900–35   356

The Hangman's Record. The murder of Mary Bennett. Samuel Herbert Dougal. Johan Hoch, American bluebeard. Landru. *The Crippen Case*. The truth about Dr Crippen and Ethel LeNeve. The Seddon poisoning case. The Brides in the Bath. Harold Greenwood. Herbert Rouse Armstrong. Bywaters and Thompson. Vacquier. John Donald Merrett is acquitted. Browne and Kennedy. Sidney Fox. *The Wallace Case*. The murder of Helen Priestly. *The Ruxton Case*.

14. An American Classic   400

The Lindbergh Kidnapping

15. The Rise of Sex Crime   411

The murder of Fanny Adams. Eusebius Pieydangelle. Vincent Verzeni. Thomas Piper the bellringer. Jesse Pomeroy. Louis Menesclou. The French Ripper, Joseph Vacher. Ludwig Tessnow. Theodore Durrant. The Gatton mystery. The lynching of Leo Frank. Why sex crime? Tolstoy's *Kreutzer Sonata*. Victorian prudery. Emile Zola's human beast and Barbusse's *Hell*. Bela Kiss. The Ypsilanti car burning case. The Cleveland Torso murders. The Black Dahlia. The Raymond Carney rape case. The murder of Ethel Little. Patrick Byrne, the YWCA killer. Vandalism. H.P.Lovecraft's *Call of Cthulhu*. Lovecraft's antisemitism. Houston Stewart Chamberlain's racism. Eddy's *Loved Dead*. Melvin Rees's murder of the Jackson family. The problem of beauty starvation. A botched civilisation. The Wimbledon 'queer bashing' case. Boredom and murder.

Sartre's theory of 'magical thinking.' Sergeant Bertrand the necrophile. The Christie murders. The Thames nude murders. The Jersey rapist. Ed Gein. Frederick Ducharme. The Moonlight murderer of Texarcana. Harvey Glatman, rapist. Mack Edwards, the child killer. Evolutionary blockage. The 'dominant 5%.' Overcrowding. Maslow and the three 'dominance groups.' Leopold and Loeb. Patrick and Jones. Fernandez and Beck, the 'lonely hearts killers.' The Moors Murder case.

Foreword
by Damon Wilson

I WAS brought up in a house purchased on the proceeds of crime. When my father was eighteen, he began a novel called *Ritual of the Dead*, based on the crimes of Jack the Ripper. Five years later, in the Reading Room of the British Museum, he was still working on the novel when the superintendent, Angus Wilson, looked over his shoulder and asked him what he was writing. Wilson himself was a novelist, and he offered to read the unfinished typescript and, if he liked it, show it to his publisher. This is why, during the Christmas holiday of 1954, my father sat in his room in south London and decided to keep himself occupied in the interval by writing another book. It was to be a non-fictional exploration of the themes of the novel: the pressures that drive the alienated "outsider" who feels himself cut off from the rest of society. It was intended to be a survey of every type of "outsider", from intellectual rebels like Nietzsche and Lawrence of Arabia to criminal rebels like Jack the Ripper and the Düsseldorf "vampire" Peter Kürten. He began the book as soon as the Reading Room opened in the new year. And when Angus Wilson returned from a prolonged Christmas holiday, the first two chapters were already written.

In fact, Wilson liked the unfinished novel; but my father decided to complete *The Outsider* before he went back to it. It was a lucky decision. After he had typed out the first few chapters, he sent off a summary of the book to a publisher, Victor Gollancz, who liked it and asked to see the typescript. When *The Outsider* appeared in May 1956, it became an international bestseller, and enabled my father (and mother) to move down to Cornwall, where they still live. The Jack the Ripper novel appeared in 1960, under the title *Ritual in the Dark*. But my father continued to be fascinated by crime, and immediately began work on *An Encyclopedia of Murder* in which the only surviving fragment of the "criminal outsider" chapter appeared as an appendix. (It had been dropped from *The Outsider* on Gollancz's advice.)

In due course, he passed on the fascination to me. Every morning before he drove us to school, he would read to me and my sister. The books ranged from *The Lord of the Rings* to the complete Sherlock Homes stories. He also whetted my appetite for real-life mysteries by talking to us about the *Mary Celeste* and the identity of Jack the Ripper. Which explains why, when I began to read, I found true crime as interesting as the fantasies of Tolkien and C.S. Lewis. And since a cupboard in my bedroom was full of *True Detective* magazines, and my father's study contained a thousand or so books on criminal cases, there was no shortage of reading matter. Many people would say that this sort of information is best kept out of the hands of children, but I certainly suffered no ill effects.

I once asked my father how he became interested in Jack the Ripper, and he told me that it started in his childhood when his father brought home a book called *The Fifty Most Amazing Crimes in the Last Hundred Years*. He and his brother were forbidden to read it – in case it gave them nightmares – so they naturally seized every opportunity. We still have a copy of the book in the house. Each article is headed with a picture of the criminal: Charlie Peace, Landru, and so on. But the article entitled: "The Fiend of East London: Jack the Ripper" has only a large black question mark. After reading this, my father seized upon everything he could find about the case. And when, in 1951, he went to live in London, the first thing he did was to cycle around Whitechapel, looking at the old Ripper murder sites, after which he went to the British Museum and read the accounts of the murders in *The Times* for 1888. All this went into *Ritual in the Dark*, which in turn spawned *The Outsider* and *An Encyclopedia of Murder*, as well as the various books and articles that I have drawn upon for the present volume.

When I was thirteen, our family became involved in a real life murder case. I had gone to school with a local girl named Genette Tate, and on one occasion she came to a children's party in our house. In 1975, Genette's family moved to Aylesbeare in Devon. On the afternoon of 19 August 1978, she set out on her bicycle to deliver newspapers, and disappeared. She had stopped in a narrow country lane to talk to two friends, then cycled on. A few minutes later, when they came round a bend in the road, her bicycle was lying on the ground, its wheel still spinning, the newspapers scattered around it. Her friends thought she was playing a joke and called her name. When there was no reply, they realised that something was wrong and ran to the village to raise the alarm. Her father and stepmother were in Exeter at the time, and when they returned, most of the village was already engaged in the search.

I heard about Genette's disappearance on the TV news the next day, and was shocked. You do not expect things like that to happen to people you know. When, two days later, there was still no sign of her, it had become obvious that she had been abducted, and was probably dead.

A few days before her disappearance, a "psychic" named Bob Cracknell had called at our house on his way to a holiday near Land's End. He had often helped the police to solve crimes, and he and my father were working on a book together. Soon after Genette's disappearance Bob rang us, and my father asked him if he had any "psychic impressions" about the missing girl. "What missing girl?" he asked. He had been on a remote caravan site without television or newspapers, and had not heard of the case. When my father explained what had happened, Bob said immediately that he felt Genette was dead, and that she had been taken away in a blue car. My father then rang the local BBC, and told a friend there what Bob had said. The result was that a radio journalist recorded Bob's impressions, and broadcast them on a news programme the next morning. A few hours later, the BBC rang us. The police had been so intrigued by what Bob had to say that they wanted to know if he would go to Aylesbeare. Witnesses *had* seen a blue car around the time of Genette's disappearance, but it had not been made public.

Two days later, my father and Bob Cracknell drove to Aylesbeare, and went to the police incident room. There Bob handled some of Genette's belongings – standard procedure with "psychics" – and again gave his impressions; Genette had been abducted by a stranger who had seen her name embroidered on her T-shirt and dragged her into his car. He also felt that her body would be found within ten days.

In this he was mistaken. But the search continued, and when the police decided to mobilise the army and hundreds of local volunteers to look for clues, my father decided that we should all join in. We drove up to Aylesbeare – my father, mother, sister Sally, brother Rowan and myself – and went into the incident room, which was also the village hall. I suppose I can be forgiven for finding the whole thing an exciting adventure and for daydreaming that I would find the vital clue. It was fascinating to be shown the site of the abduction, listen to the inspector in charge of the case describing the investigation, and then drive around the local lanes in a bizarre army vehicle called a Tomkat. It was a strange experience to join a long line of searchers walking through woodland, our eyes on the ground, wondering if we would see a foot sticking out of the undergrowth. In fact, a few interesting items of clothing were found, but they proved to have no connection with Genette. It made me realise that the difference between a detective story and a real life crime is that the world is full of millions of possible clues, and that there is no simple method for deciding which of them might be relevant. Genette vanished twelve years ago, and although there have been occasional newspaper stories about arrests of suspects, the police still know as little about Genette's disappearance as they did in August 1978.

In one respect I was more fortunate than my father. He was brought up in a working class background, and had no one with whom he could discuss his ideas. I, on the other hand, had him. Driving us to school, or into the local town, he would talk to us about philosophy, criminology and science (on one occasion he sketched out the theory of relativity), and listened with genuine interest to our opinions. There is nothing quite so fulfilling for a child as to have his ideas taken seriously. A few of my schoolfriends had tried *The Outsider* and found it too "difficult". But when I began to dip into his books, I kept coming across ideas he had already explained to us – for example, that we have two people living inside our heads, in the right and left hemispheres of the brain – and finding them immediately understandable. I also began to grasp why he found crime so interesting. The fundamental question which lies at the heart of all his work on the subject is: what causes a normal human being to become a criminal? His own attempt at an answer is contained in a section of the introduction to *An Encyclopedia of Murder* which begins: "Belief in the abnormality of the murderer is a part of the delusion of normality on which society is based".

He is not making the obvious point – that we are all capable of crime – but pointing out that there is no clear dividing line between the "normal" human being and the criminal. "*All our values are makeshift*; the murderer simply goes further than most people in substituting his own convenience for absolute values." This is the basic theme of *The Outsider*: that there is something oddly wrong with human consciousness. When faced with real crisis, human beings are magnificent. But as soon as the crisis is behind them, they tend to collapse into a kind of boredom. Dr Johnson said: "When a man knows he is to be hanged in a fortnight, it concentrates his mind wonderfully". Ideally, a life without crisis ought to be heaven on earth. In practice, it sends us to sleep, so we begin to look around for something "exciting" to do. A yachtsman decides to sail single-handed round the world. A bored housewife decides to go and buy herself a new hat. A serial killer decides to go out and find another victim. All are driven by the same impulse. They differ in degree, not in kind.

In 1961 two American psychologists, Samuel Yochelson and Stanton Samenow, inaugurated a programme to study criminals in St. Elizabeth's hospital in Washington DC. Both were liberals who believed that criminals are really "victims of society", people with deep psychological problems. The conclusions they reached dismayed them both. In their book *The Criminal Personality* they admit that they have found the chief characteristics of the criminal to be weaknes, immaturity and vanity, and an endless capacity for lying, both to themselves and others. Criminals lacked self-discipline and were often cowards – for example, preferring to let their teeth go rotten rather than face a dentist's drill. The greatest fear of these criminals was that others would see the weakness in them. They were hypersentitive to what was said to them, and reacted very angrily to being "put down". Yochelson and Samenow also discovered that the basis of most criminality was sex. A large percentage of criminals were obsessed by sex from an early age, trying to peep through the bathroom keyhole at sisters undressing, or making attempts at sexual assault on small girls. Their researches made it clear that criminality is a mixture of weakness and self-pity, and that it could be regarded as a long-standing habit or addiction, like smoking. In other words, it is a form of "defeat-proneness". And this is something from which we all suffer.

My father's books on crime make it clear that what fascinates him so much is the actual mechanism of defeat. When most of us open our eyes in the morning, we are in a more-or-less stable and optimistic condition, prepared to cope with whatever problems might arise. If we receive some sudden shock or disappointment, we experience a collapse of inner-pressure – literally "depression" – and slip backward to a lower stage of vitality. If minor problems continue to erode our sense of purpose, we may slip back several stages further. And the longer we remain in this condition, the more we are undermined by pessimism and self-doubt, and inclined to slip back further still. At this stage, it is easy to collapse into nervous breakdown.

Consider, on the other hand, what happens when you have an unexpected piece of luck, or some crisis you expected fails to materialise. Your vitality increases; your inner-pressure rises. If things continue to go well, you begin to feel that no problem is insoluble. Life is self-evidently wonderful, and you can see that if you want it to continue like that, you only have to remain in a state of optimism and determination. Suddenly it is perfectly obvious that the worst thing we can do is to allow ourselves to "slip backward" into a state of defeat. We feel like taking a solemn vow never to be such an idiot. Half our problem is self-pity, a tendency to "let go". In this basic respect, we are all like Yochelson and Samenow's habitual criminals.

What can we do to prevent ourselves from slipping back into that insidious state miscalled "normality"? One method of remaining aware of the insight is to contemplate the sheer stupidity of the criminal. We are all trapped in the "triviality of everydayness", but the criminal is more trapped than most of us. The result is that he gambles away his life or liberty in exchange for some purely momentary satisfaction. If he was the victim of a confidence swindler, we would feel sorry for him; but he swindles himself.

If you want to grasp the point I am making – and of which I have been continually aware as I have been compiling this volume – turn to its final section on the crimes of Ted Bundy, and try to imagine yourself into his state of mind on the evening before his execution. The judge who sentenced him recognised the appalling waste of human potential when he said: "You went the wrong way, pardner – take care of yourself". Bundy was an intelligent man; why did he not recognise that he was going the wrong way long before he began to commit murder? The answer seems to be that he was trapped in the same kind of defeat-proneness that afflicts most of us. As the executioner shaved his head, he must have become aware of something that we can experience simply by reading about him. In Bundy we contemplate the paradox of a man who possessed intelligence, but who never tried to develop it into awareness.

The lesson is that we can all "concentrate the mind wonderfully" without knowing we are to be hanged in a fortnight. Anyone who possesses imagination can do it merely by reading this book. . . which is my justification for bringing together such a gruesome collection of human cruelty and depravity.

Introduction

IN THE year 1910 there appeared in San Francisco a bulky volume entitled *Celebrated Criminal Cases of America* by Thomas S. Duke, a captain in the San Francisco police force. It was an epoch-making volume, for it was the first attempt at a comprehensive collection of crimes of one particular period – in this case, the past eighty years. It was, if you like, a criminal history of America in the nineteenth century. And, as such, it still remains a work of singular fascination. For many years now, together with the more famous *Newgate Calendar*, it has been one of my favourite bedside books. And not solely because of its "morbid" interest. It is the history of an epoch, and it gives you a better insight into the true nature of America in the nineteenth century than any number of history books about great statesmen and generals.

For we must face this fact: history, by its very nature, tells lies. History books deal with "important events", the rise and fall of kings and nations. You could read all about the age of Shakespeare in the great historians; yet if some time machine could transport you back to London in the time of Queen Elizabeth, you would realise instantly that you did not know the first thing about it. When Shakespeare got up in the morning, his mind was focused on dozens of minor details, not on great events. What kind of bed did he sleep in? What did an Elizabethan chamberpot look like? Did he use soap to wash his hands? Did he even bother to wash his hands when he got up? – in earlier ages, they often believed that too much washing was bad for you. What did he eat for breakfast? Did he drink tea? How often did he wash his socks? Did he comb his hair? (Did they have scissors then?) When he went to the lavatory, how did he wipe his behind? Paper would certainly have been too expensive, and probably too stiff. Unless we know the answer to hundreds of similar questions, we cannot even begin to create an accurate mental picture of the Elizabethan age.

But as you read Thomas Duke on American crime, you realise there is another kind of history that also gets left out of most history books. Of course, we know a little more about America in the nineteenth century than England in the sixteenth – to begin with, it is closer to our own age. It was visited by various English writers, like Charles Dickens, Fanny Trollope and Oscar Wilde, who have left us their impressions. It was a rough, turbulent and violent country, a land that paid scant attention to the genius of the author of *Moby Dick*, and that allowed Edgar Allen Poe to die as a result of some obscure bar room brawl. If you want to get a clear idea of what it was like to be Edgar Allen Poe, then you would do better to read Thomas Duke than even the most eminent historian. You can learn about the Vigilance Committees that were set up to do battle with squatters, about the Chinese tongs that sprang up in the gold fields, about Alfred Packer, the cannibal who ate five fellow prospectors, about marauding Indians who murdered settlers, about the assassination of the Mormon leader Joseph Smith, about various bomb outrages committed by Anarchists, as well as about such *causes celèbres* as the murder of Dr Parkman by Professor Webster, or the architect Stanford White by Harry Thaw. This was the America that Poe and Melville lived in and saw around them every day. In some ways – perhaps in most – it was a better and more innocent America than the one that exists today. One of Duke's stories describes "The Murder of Norah Fuller by a Degenerate". Norah was a fifteen year old girl who was lured to a house by means of an advertisement, and there strangled, raped and mutilated. A modern writer would call it "The Rape of Norah Fuller" and leave it at that. Duke obviously finds it a little difficult to understand such a crime; he is more at home chronicling robberies, assassinations and poisonings. In his world, human beings needed a *motive* for committing crime, usually cash.

(And, as we shall see in Chapter 2, sex crime was a rarity until the late nineteenth century.) And his reactions are always there, implicitly, in the writing. The chapter on the Bender family, who killed travellers in their tavern, is entitled "The Hideous Murders Committed at Bender's Tavern in Kansas". Then there is "The Diabolical Plot Concocted by Dr Hyde of Kansas City", and "Tom Bland the Desperado killed near Seattle." We are in a violent world, yet a world in which crime is never taken for granted. The underlying assumption seems to be that most of the population is law abiding, even virtuous, and that a few evildoers have backed out of their obligations to society.

In America, Duke's book was the beginning of a flood of anthologies of "true crime stories." In England – as we shall see in Chapter 4 – it had started rather earlier. The Elizabethans were fond of pamphlets describing the crimes and trials (and especially the executions) of various notorious characters, and around the year 1700 various compilations of such cases began to appear under such titles as *The Newgate Calendar* (although the most famous and comprehensive edition that that work appeared in 1774). This continued to appear, under various incarnations (such as *Chronicles of Crime*) until the late nineteenth century. In 1873, Luke Owen Pike produced a two volume *History of Crime in England*. In 1898, Major Arthur Griffiths published his popular two volume work *Mysteries of Police and Crime*, while in the same year, Matthew Worth Pinkerton, of the famous detective family, produced a massive work called *Murder in All Ages*. Both these are highly readable and deserve reprinting.

But I suspect that it was the Crippen case of 1910 that suddenly aroused the interest of the British public in true tales of gore and mayhem. (The latter word – meaning committing violence on the person – seems to be derived from the same source as maim.) Crippen – who dismembered his wife's body – was effectively condemned on the medical evidence given by an unknown young pathologist called Bernard Spilsbury. From then on, Spilsbury was famous, and any case in which he gave evidence was newsworthy. Many of his later cases involved gruesome dismemberments – Voisin, Norman Smith, Patrick Mahon (who scattered fragments of his mistress's body out of the window of a train.) The reading public soon developed an appetite for horrors. It is also worth bearing in mind that a new reading public had come into being since the late nineteenth century; workmen were learning to read, and enterprising publishers deliberately catered for them with cheap works of popular education. This was essentially the same public of "groundlings" for whom the Elizabethan dramatists wrote "shockers" like *The Spanish Tragedy*, and *Arden of Feversham*, and for whom Shakespeare wrote *Titus Andronicus*. A few of these workmen read Ruskin and Darwin; but the majority wanted their ha'penny newspapers to have plenty of tales of violence and scandal in high life. Since 1870, the best seller among Victorian tabloids had been the *Illustrated Police News*, which specialised in sensational sketches of hangings, floggings and decapitations. After the turn of the century, there was suddenly a market for books with titles like *Cavalcade of Justice* or *The Fifty Most Amazing Crimes of the Last Hundred Years*. (It was a copy of this latter – brought home by my father – that was responsible for my own early interest in crime.) In America, Munsey invented the "pulp magazine", and reached a new audience with its tales of incredible adventure. And then, some time in the 1920s (I have been unable to track down the date) some American publisher hit on the idea of a magazine-form of the old *Illustrated Police News*, with photographs taking the place of the drawings. "True detective" magazines caught on quickly; as the post-1918 crime rate soared, material was even more plentiful than in the Victorian era. "Troodicks" (as my friend the late John Dunning liked to call them) have never looked back.

And – perhaps unfortunately – there is no reason why they should. With the twentieth century, we have entered the new age of murder. This is apparent even to the most casual student of crime. The Crippen murder is basically the "old fashioned" type of crime; it might have been dramatised by an Elizabethan playwright. It is essentially a drama of good against evil, of a fairly decent human under the strain of temptation, giving way to "diabolic impulses" – like Macbeth. This element can be found in most classic murder cases – the Red Barn murder, Lizzie Borden, Crippen, William Herbert Wallace (all to be found in this book.) The Victorians found it necessary to apply the same explanation to the strange crimes of Jack the Ripper, who killed and disembowelled five prostitutes in 1888; the favourite theory was that he was some sort of religious maniac – perhaps also a surgeon – driven mad by brooding on sin and prostitution. Now, more than a century later, we can see that he was an ordinary sadist, a man who – probably when drunk – had an overwhelming urge to cut open women. And our knowledge of modern murderers of this type – we now call them "serial killers" – enables us to say with a fair degree of confidence that he was a member of the working class, not some unbalanced doctor or lawyer (or member of the royal family, as a recent theory has it).

In 1918, as we shall see, New Orleans had its own series of "Ripper murders": an individual who became known as "the Mad Axe Man" broke into houses and attacked sleepers with a hatchet; he also cut their throats with a razor. He was never caught; but, like the Ripper murders, this series of crimes suddenly ceased. The Axe Man crimes simply fail to fit the pattern of murder as it had been known up till then. He was not even a "degenerate" – at least, there were no sexual attacks on the victims. A new age of murder had begun.

And nowadays we look back on the older type of crime with a certain nostalgia. The American Modern Library series, which specialises in reprints of classics, has included Edmund Pearson's *Studies in Murder*, with its long study of the Lizzie Borden case. The Viking Portable Library – which has produced a portable Shakespeare, Nietzsche and James Joyce – has also published a Portable Murder book, consisting mainly of such classic mysteries as the murder of Julia Wallace and the crime of Constance Kent. We read such accounts as we read the Sherlock Holmes stories – as period pieces. We may deplore the violence, but we still read with a kind of fascinated detachment. But imagine an updated murder book (such as the present volume) that includes the Moors Murder case, the Manson murders, the mass homosexual killings by Dean Corll and John Gacy, and later cases like Herb Mullin, Ed Kemper, Ted Bundy and Leonard Lake. Could anyone – no matter how blasé – read such cases with detachment? They really belong in a textbook, of pathology, such as Krafft-Ebing's *Psychopathia Sexualis*. We try *not* to think about what the Moors Murderers did to their child victims or what Lake did to his captured "sex slaves" in the concrete bunker he had built as a kind of torture chamber. The new type of murder seems to be motiveless because it is fundamentally "psychological".

What has caused this change in the pattern of murder? Where America is concerned the answer is fairly straightforward. As Thomas Duke's book makes clear, America has always been a country with plenty of violence. But in the nineteenth century, it was also a country with plenty of freedom, in the purely physical sense. Life was hard for the under-privileged, but there were still inviting wide open spaces – out west. By the 1920s, most of this feeling of freedom had vanished. Living standards were higher, of course – industrialisation had seen to that – but cities were bigger, and more people felt trapped in them. A modern American is no longer in much danger of seeing his wife and children starve to death. But the children feel themselves regimented and controlled from the moment they are old enough to cross the street. The rich and famous, the people who have "made it", exist up there in a kind of Olympus; you are "down here", together with hundreds of millions of others, and nobody will ever see your name in the paper or your face on TV. You are an immeasurably small fragment of an anonymous mass. . . But since a high proportion of that anonymous mass is at least as intelligent as the TV stars and politicians, they feel resentment at this unfair scheme of things. Everybody would like to be Somebody – or at least, feel that the opportunity is there. Among the young, the natural reaction is to "drop out." The more idealistic talk about the preservation of human rights and protection of the environment. Others, like Charles Manson, dream of violent revolution and destruction of the "pigs". Others drift into the underworld of drugs. A youth like John Linley Frazer, who slaughtered the whole family of a successful eye surgeon in California, had become increasingly paranoid simply because Dr Victor Ohta was obviously well-to-do. The "Symbionese Liberation Army" kidnapped Patty Hearst and ordered her millionaire father to donate $2 million-worth of food to the poor, after which they "brain-washed" her into helping them hold up banks. "Squeaky" Fromme, a follower of Charles Manson, wrote letters to businessmen threatening them with death if they continued to pollute the environment, then attempted to shoot President Gerald Ford as a protest. . .

In European countries too the pattern of crime has been changing, although less drastically than in America. West Germany – the most prosperous country in Europe – has a flourishing urban guerrilla movement, which robs, murders and kidnaps the "capitalist oppressors"; in December 1989, it murdered Alfred Herrhausen, head of the Deutsche Bank, merely because he was a banker. In Italy, kidnapping has become almost a national sport. In England, Ian Brady and Myra Hindley, the Moors Murderers, kidnapped and murdered children simply as an expression of Brady's contempt for society and his admiration for the philosophy of the Marquis de Sade. In Japan, a group who called themselves the Japanese Red Army planted bombs and murdered policemen, then finally began to murder their own members in a kind of Stalinist purge. In the last quarter of the twentieth century, "philosophy" – or a kind of muddled idealism – seems to be playing an increasingly large part in crime. And while urban guerrillas and homicidal "drop outs" continue to make the headlines, organised crime quietly spreads and flourishes, without publicity, in almost every country in the world.

For many years now I have felt that these "patterns of crime" deserve closer study. Criminologists are inclined to confine themselves to statistical analyses and studies of the criminals' behaviour in prison. But the most interesting criminals are often "loners", and few of them are professionals. With the aid of Patricia Pitman, I compiled *An Encyclopedia of Murder* in 1960, and later *An Encyclopedia of Modern Murder* and a book on *The Serial Killers* with Donald Seaman. In the 1970s I drew up an outline scheme of of a twenty volume "encyclopedia of crime" which appeared under the title *Crimes and Punishment*, and although it makes many concessions to the tastes of "troodick" readers, it is still probably the most comprehensive general work on crime that has ever appeared.

In the 1980s, I decided to try and set down all my ideas on the subject in a vast work that would be called *A World History of Crime*. I sold the idea to my publisher and accepted an advance. But when I settled down to writing it, I realised that I had overlooked an important problem. Before you can describe –

let us say – the crimes of ancient Rome, you need to give the reader a rough outline of the history of ancient Rome, otherwise he would feel lost. And the same applies to every other period. In fact, such a book could easily turn into an even longer version of H.G. Wells's *Outline of History*. There was nothing for it but to change my plan, although the resulting work – *A Criminal History of Mankind* – still seems to me one of my best books.

Now, with the aid of books and articles written over the years, I have decided to try to go back to my original plan and compile a kind of world history of crime on a smaller scale. The backbone of the present book is a volume called *A Casebook of Murder*, written in 1968, and its sequel *Order of Assassins*; both of them were attempts to understand the change in "patterns of murder". The result is bound to be patchy – since whole periods of history are inevitably neglected – but I trust that the result is an interesting overall view of crime over the centuries.

1.
Planet of
the Killer Apes

LET ME ask you a serious question – erhaps the most serious
question that has ever been put to you.

Imagine that you are a superbeing from some distant star
system, and that your spacecraft is approaching the earth. Even
from beyond the orbit of Neptune, your scanners have made you
aware that the earth is the only planet in the solar system that
contains life. Its white clouds and its blue seas reflect an unusual
amount of sunlight, and this enables you to see that it is also
streaked with green and brown patches which indicate vegetation.
So there is obviously life; the question is, of what kind? You have
studied planets that are completely covered in water, and whose
inhabitants live in gigantic cities in the depths of the sea. You
have encountered a planet whose gravity is so immense that the
only intelligent beings take the form of mountains, whose living
flesh is harder than steel. You have even visited a planet made of
attenuated gas, whose highly intelligent life forms appear to be
gigantic clouds. But these creatures have evolved over hundreds
of millions of years, and your high energy probes inform you
that the planet you are now approaching is too young for such
advanced evolutionary products.

All living creatures are surrounded by their own vital aura, which is perceptible to other living creatures – particularly those who possess a high degree of intuition. As you approach the earth, you tune in to its aura, and are impressed by its sheer vitality; the creatures on this planet are obviously driven by an immense and enthusiastic will to live. But as you approach more closely, you become aware of a more disturbing vibration – the cosmic equivalent of an unpleasant smell. It tells you that some of the most dominant creatures on this planet are also possessed of an immense will to power. The aura of the planet reeks of tragedy. A week later, you have completed your case study of the blue and white planet, and you are in a sombre mood. The beings on your home planet are rational, benevolent and highly motivated, so that life there is almost totally free of conflict. By comparison, this planet seems to exist in a state of perpetual crisis. Many of its creatures have achieved a high degree of rationality, and this accounts for the technical achievements of their civilisation. But even they have failed to carry their insights to their logical conclusion, and trust themselves entirely to reason. In the face of all common sense, they continue to have a deep distrust of reason. It takes them an absurdly long time to learn from experience. Another complication is that these creatures are so short-lived – their life span is less than a century, so that they are only just beginning to achieve some kind of insight into the meaning of their lives when their faculties begin to decay.

But what troubles you most, as you study the historical records, is their capacity for sheer cruelty. It is true that the majority are well-meaning and good natured, but these tend to be lazy and passive, and to have little influence on history. The greatest single problem of this race is that those dominant individuals who are their natural leaders are often sadistic psychopaths. The result is that their history consists largely of wars, revolutions and massacres. And even at this fairly advanced stage in their civilisation, large numbers of their dominant individuals feel no social obligation towards their fellows, and spend their lives preying on them. You find it hard to imagine how a society with such a high level of antisocial behaviour can resist the forces of disintegration.

How did it all come about? As good a theory as any was put forward in 1953 by the palaeontologist Raymond Dart, in a paper called *The Predatory Transition from Ape to Man*. What Dart suggested, briefly, is that man is the only member of the ape species who is a born killer. About fifteen million years ago, an intelligent ape discovered that it could kill its prey by hitting it with a bone club. This made it a far more efficient killer than its fellows. But if it was going to carry a club, it had to learn to walk upright on two feet, so its hands were free to grasp. It was forced to learn to balance on its hind legs. Hitting an animal with its club – or hurling a stone from a distance – meant a new kind of co-ordination between the hand and the eye. So its brain began to develop. Within a few million years this killer ape had become the most dominant species on the surface of the earth. But because its dominance had been gained through violence, its deepest instinct was for killing. And even when it finally created a complex civilisation, it was unable to shake off the old habit.

H.G. Wells had a simpler theory: that man was a peaceable creature until he began to congregate in cities with other men. The unnatural pressure of living together with thousands of members of his own species made him irritable and aggressive. . . Whichever version we choose to accept, it amounts to the same thing: that man is the most violent creature on earth.

Now here is the question that I wish to put to you. You are, as I have said, a superbeing whose powers are almost limitless – what our ancestors would have called a god. You can do virtually anything you like to improve the condition of these human creatures, and to bring them to a higher level of understanding. So what exactly would you *do* to improve the human condition?

Let me make a few suggestions. You can see that one of their chief problems is criminality – from gangsters who make a fortune selling drugs to terrorists who think nothing of blowing up an aeroplane full of innocent passengers. There are even mass murderers who wander around torturing and killing at random, often choosing women and children as their victims. You can identify such people by the peculiar blood-coloured tinge of their aura – they suffer from "personality problems" which are as perceptible as body odour. So would it not be simpler to kill off all these degenerate individuals, so that they could no longer exercise their evil influence? This is certainly a solution that most of us would endorse. And obviously, the earth would be a better place without these murderous individuals. But before we decide that this is the answer, let us look at the problem a little more closely. In fact, the earth already has one highly efficient executioner; he is called Time. Without any help, he kills off vast numbers of criminals and degenerates every year. And yet there seem to be just as many in the next generation. Besides, as a superbeing, you recognise that this simplistic solution – to kill off the "degenerates" – is simply another version of the same criminal urge that you were trying to eradicate. H.G. Wells pointed out that when we hear of some appalling piece of cruelty, our reaction is to become angry and say, "Do you know what I should like to do to that brute?" – a revelation "that vindictive reaction is the reality of the human animal."

If you agree that the mass extermination of criminals is not likely to raise the intelligence of the human race, you may as well admit that we should be thinking in terms of less drastic solutions. Should we not, for example, be thinking in terms of the social conditions that incubate the criminal?

Our space visitor is interested to discover that the human race already has a long tradition of this type of constructive thinking. Ever since Plato, philosophers have been outlining their ideas for a perfect society. One such work, Sir Thomas More's *Utopia*, has become so famous that its name has become a synonym for an ideal society. In More's crescent-shaped island kingdom, all goods are communally owned, and each human being regards himself primarily as a "social animal." The result is that violence, bloodshed and vice have disappeared completely. Gambling is unknown. The people spend their days working in their gardens, attending lectures and listening to music. Meals are eaten in gigantic communal dining rooms, and everyone works willingly for six hours a day, which provides sufficient wealth for the whole community. The few criminals who exist are punished by slavery, and the same penalty is meted out to adulterers.

More's vision is seductive, and four centuries later many of his ideas were borrowed by H.G. Wells for his own "modern utopia." Yet by this time, many of them had been tried out, and found to be less practical than they seemed. The chief stumbling block was the communal ideal, and many "co-operatives" came to grief simply because they ran into the realities of human nature.

The basic problem was described by the American philosopher William James, who went to the famous Chautauqua community in New York State. This was basically a religious community founded by Methodist Episcopalians. James found the place so pleasant that he ended up staying for a week. He wrote:

> *The moment one treads that sacred enclosure, one feels oneself in an atmosphere of success. Sobriety and industry, intelligence and goodness, orderliness and ideality, prosperity and cheerfulness, pervade the air. It is a serious and studious picnic on a gigantic scale. Here you have a town of many thousands of inhabitants, beautifully laid out in the forest and drained, and equipped with means for satisfying all the necessary lower and most of the superfluous higher wants of man. You have a first-class college in full blast. You have magnificent music – a chorus of seven hundred voices, with possibly the most perfect open-air auditorium in the world. You have every sort of athletic exercise from sailing, rowing, swimming, bicycling, to the ball-field and the more artificial doings which the gymnasium affords. You have kindergartens and model secondary schools. You have general religious services and special club-houses for the several sects. You have perpetually running soda-water fountains, and daily popular lectures by distinguished men. You have the best of company and yet no effort. You have no zymotic diseases, no poverty, no drunkenness, no crime, no police. You have culture, you have kindness, you have cheapness, you have equality, you have the best fruits of what mankind has fought and bled and striven for under the name of civilisation for centuries. You have, in short, a foretaste of what human society might be, were it all in the light, with no suffering and no dark corners. . .*
>
> *And yet what was my only astonishment, on emerging into the dark and wicked world again, to catch myself quite unexpectedly and involuntarily saying: "Ouf! What a relief! Now for something primordial and savage, even though it were as bad as an Armenian massacre to set the balance straight again. This order is too tame, this culture too second-rate, this goodness too uninspiring. This human drama without a villain or a pang; this community so refined that ice-cream soda-water is the upmost offering it can make to the brute animal in man; this city*

*simmering in the tepid lakeside sun; this atrocious harmlessness
of all things – I cannot abide with them. Let me take my chances
again in the big outside worldly wilderness with all its sins and
sufferings. There are the heights and depths, the precipices and
the steep ideals, the gleams of the awful and the infinite; and
there is more hope and help a thousand times than in this dead
level and quintessence of every mediocrity."*

Such was the sudden right-about-face performed for me by my
lawless fancy! There had been spread before me the realisation –
on a small, sample scale of course – of all the ideals for which
our civilisation has been striving: security, intelligence, humanity
and order; and here was the instinctive hostile reaction, not of
the natural man, but of a so-called cultivated man upon such
a Utopia. There seemed thus to be a self-contradiction and
paradox somewhere, which I, as a professor drawing a full
salary, was in duty bound to unravel and explain, if I could.

So I meditated. And first of all, I asked myself what the thing
was that was so lacking in this Sabbatical city, and the lack
of which kept one forever falling short of the higher sort of
contentment. And I soon recognised that it was the element that
gives to the wicked outer world all its moral style, expressiveness
and picturesqueness – the element of precipitousness, so to call
it, of strength and strenuousness, intensity and danger. What
excites and interests the looker-on at life, what the romances
and the statues celebrate and the grim civic monuments remind
us of, is the everlasting battle of the powers of light with those
of darkness; with heroism reduced to its bare chance, yet ever
and anon snatching victory from the jaws of death. But in this
unspeakable Chautauqua there was no potentiality of death in
sight anywhere, and no point of the compass visible from which
danger might possibly appear. The ideal was so completely
victorious already that no sign of any previous battle remained,
the place just resting on its oars. But what our human emotions
seem to require is the sight of the struggle going on. The moment
the fruits are merely eaten, things become ignoble. Sweat and
effort, human nature strained to its uttermost and on the rack,
yet getting through alive, and then turning its back on its success
to pursue another more rare and arduous still – this is the sort of
thing the presence of which inspires us, and the reality of which

it seems to be a function of all the higher forms of literature and fine art to bring home to us and suggest. At Chautauqua there were no racks, even in the place's historical museum; and no sweat, except possibly the gentle moisture on the brow of some lecturer, or on the sides of some player in the ball-field . . .

With these thoughts in my mind, I was speeding with the train towards Buffalo, when near that city, the sight of a workman doing something on the dizzy edge of a sky-scaling iron construction, brought me to my senses very suddenly. And now I perceived, by a flash of insight, that I had been steeping myself in pure ancestral blindness, and looking at life with the eyes of a remote spectator. Wishing for heroism and the spectacle of human nature on the rack, I had never noticed the great fields of heroism lying round about me. I had failed to see it present and alive. I could only think of it as dead and embalmed, labelled and costumed, as it is in the pages of romance. And yet, there it was before me in the daily lives of the labouring classes. Not in clanging fights and desperate marches only is heroism to be looked for, but on every railway bridge and fire-proof building that is going up today. On freight trains, on the decks of vessels, in cattle-yards and mines, on lumber-rafts, among the firemen and the policemen, the demand for courage is incessant; and the supply never fails. There, every day of the year somewhere, is human nature in extremis *for you. And wherever a scythe, an axe, a pick or a shovel is wielded, you have it sweating and aching with its powers of patient endurance racked to the upmost during the length of hours of the strain".*

Was James saying that the human race *needs* rape and robbery and murder? Or was he merely saying that man needs adventure, purpose and excitement? In either case, the implications are disturbing. The world of the 1990s is certainly far less exciting and adventurous than William James's world of the 1890s, and the world of the 2090s will almost certainly be tamer still. Does this mean that the human race has to choose between violence and boredom?

Before we try to answer that difficult question, let us look a little more closely at the psychology of violence.

2.
A Gallery
of Monsters

ON 2 JUNE 1985, a security guard at South City Lumber in San Francisco observed a young Asian walking out with a vice without stopping at the check-out desk. The guard alerted a policeman, who caught up with the man just as he was putting the vice into the boot of a car. As soon as he saw the policeman, the Asian ran away, and disappeared among the parked cars. An older, bearded man who was bending over the open boot explained that it was all a mistake, and offered to pay for the vice. The policeman insisted on making a routine search of the car, and in a green holdall, discovered a hand gun with a silencer. Since this was against the gun laws of California, the policeman told the bearded man that he would have to accompany him to the station. There, the man handed over his documentation, which gave his name as Robin Stapley, and then asked for a glass of water. When it was handed to him, he popped a small capsule into his mouth, and swallowed it down with the water. A moment later, he slumped forward heavily onto the table. Rushed to hospital, it was discovered that he had taken a cyanide capsule. He died four days later without recovering consciousness. The Honda he was driving proved to be registered to a used car dealer called Paul

Cosner, who had disappeared seven months previously. But a check with the fingerprint records revealed that the name of the dead man was, in fact, Leonard Lake, and that he had a criminal record for burglary. Papers found in his wallet led the police to a small ranch at Wilseyville, Calaveras County, a hundred and fifty miles north east of San Francisco. There they discovered a bedroom equipped with chains, shackles, and hooks in the ceiling – it looked ominously like a torture chamber. And in an underground bunker with prison cells, they discovered video tapes that showed young women being sexually abused by Leonard Lake and by his partner, a young Chinaman called Charles Ng. In a trench nearby, police unearthed the remains of eight victims. Eventually, fragments of bone found on the property and photographed in the ranchhouse brought the total to twenty-four, including two small children. It eventually became clear that Lake and Ng had made a habit of luring men and women to the bungalow, and then murdering them. The women were held as "sex slaves", and made to cater to perverted sexual demands before they were murdered. Lake's voluminous journals described the rapes and murders in detail. He wrote: "The perfect woman is totally controlled. A woman who does exactly what she is told to and nothing else. There is no sexual problem with a submissive woman. There are no frustrations – only pleasure and contentment."

Lake przoved to be a Vietnam veteran who was also a "Survivalist" – that is, someone who is obsessed with the idea of the inevitability of a Third World War and who makes elaborate preparations to survive it – this was the original purpose of the underground bunker. The picture that finally emerged was of a man who spent most of his life living in a world of fantasy, who indulged in grandiose daydreams of success without any realistic attempt to put them into practice. He was also a man whose whole life had been dominated by sex – a man who, as a teenager, had obtained sexual favours from his sisters, in exchange for protecting them from a delinquent younger brother – whom Lake later murdered.

Charles Ng was arrested in Calgary, Canada, for shoplifting, and sentenced to four and a half years in prison. He also had a criminal record for theft, and had spent some time in prison. He insisted that he had played no part in the killings, and that the murders had all been carried out by Lake.

Lake is an example of a type of criminal who has been labelled "the serial killer". One of the first known examples in modern times was Jack the Ripper, who killed and mutilated five prostitutes in the East End of London in 1888. In the 1970s and 1980s, this total has been exceeded by many serial killers including Dean Corll (27), John Gacy (33), Patrick Kearny (28), Ted Bundy (23), Randall Woodfield (44), and Pedro Lopez (360). In 1983, a derelict named Henry Lee Lucas made headlines in America when he also confessed to killing 360 people, mostly women.

No criminologist has so far succeeded in explaining why so many serial killers have emerged in the second half of the twentieth century. One thing seems clear: that in the past, such crimes were almost invariably committed by tyrants like Ivan the Terrible, or wealthy perverts like the French child murderer Gilles de Rais. The explanation that suggests itself is that the advance of civilisation has raised the general level of comfort so that large numbers of people have a security that was almost unknown in the ancient world. Millions of people are now able to enjoy the kind of leisure that would have been envied by Greek tyrants or Roman emperors. The trouble is that leisure and comfort also produce boredom, a desire for sensation, and this seems to explain why an increasing number of criminals have come to behave like Ivan the Terrible or Gilles de Rais.

The study of tyrants in history makes one thing clear: that most of them were not sadists in the precise sense of that term – that is, someone who derives sexual pleasure from inflicting pain. The Greek tyrant Phalaris, who roasted people alive in a brazen bull, seems to be the exception rather than the rule. The first tyrants whose lives have been extensively chronicled are Roman emperors like Tiberius, Caligula and Nero, and none of these qualifies as a sadist in this sense of the word.

Tiberius was a bad-tempered, withdrawn, introverted man who was fifty-six when he became emperor, and whose early life had been soured when he was forced to divorce a wife whom he adored, to marry Julia, the nymphomaniac daughter of the emperor Augustus. He was an excellent but strict general who was disliked by his soldiers. He once said, "Let them hate me so long as they obey me". And this also seems to have been his attitude towards the people of Rome. Yet there is also evidence that he was a kindly and fair-minded man. The historian Suetonius tells how, in his days as a tribune, he visited the island of Rhodes, and expressed a wish to visit the local sick. His staff misunderstood him and all the patients were carried to a public cloister. Tiberius was shocked, and went among them apologising for the inconvenience, "even to the humblest".

After a dozen years as emperor, he retreated to the island of Capri where, according to Suetonius, "No longer feeling himself under public scrutiny, he rapidly succumbed to all the vicious passions which he had for a long time tried but not very successfully, to disguise." He was a voyeur, who organised a private brothel in which he could watch young men and women engaging in "unnatural practices". "Some aspects of his criminal obscenity", says Suetonius with obvious relish, "are almost too vile to discuss, much less believe. Imagine training little boys, whom he called his 'minnows', to chase him while he went swimming and get between his legs to lick and nibble him. Or letting babies not yet weaned from their mother's breast, suck at him – such a filthy old man he had become. . . . The story goes that once, while sacrificing, he took an erotic fancy to the acolyte who carried the incense casket, and could hardly wait for the ceremony to end before hurrying him and his brother, the sacred trumpeter, out of the temple and indecently assaulting them both. When they protested at this dastardly crime he had their legs broken." One Roman lady whom he summoned to his bed showed such a distaste for the things he wanted her to do that he persecuted her until she committed suicide.

Suetonius writes: "A few days after he came to Capri, a fisherman suddenly intruded on his solitude by presenting him with an enormous mullet, which he had lugged up the trackless cliff at the rear of the island. Tiberius was so scared that he ordered his guards to rub the fisherman's face with the mullet. The scales skinned it raw, and the poor fellow shouted in his agony: "Thank heaven I did not bring Caesar that huge crab I also caught!" Tiberius sent for the crab and had it used in the same way. Soon, Tiberius broke out in every sort of cruelty and never lacked for victims. . . Not a day passed without an execution; he even desecrated New Year's Day. Many of his male victims were accused and punished with their children – some actually by their children – and the relatives forbidden to go into mourning. Special awards were voted to the informers who had denounced them. . . An informer's word was always believed. Every crime became a capital one, even the utterance of a few careless words. . . The bodies of all executed persons were flung on the Stairs of Mourning, and dragged to the Tiber with hooks – as many as twenty a day, including women and children. Tradition forbade the strangling of virgins, so when little girls had been condemned to die in this way, the executioner began by violating them. . . In Capri, they still show the place at the cliff-top where Tiberius used to watch his victims being thrown into the sea after prolonged and exquisite tortures. An ingenious torture of Tiberius's devising was to trick men into drinking huge quantities of wine, and then suddenly to knot a cord tightly around their genitals which not only cut into the flesh, but prevented them from urinating."

Tiberius's chief aide Sejanus was now in almost sole control in Rome, and seems to have spent his time making accusations against knights and ensuring they were executed or committed suicide. In AD 23 he poisoned Tiberius's son Drusus, making it look like a disease. But with a master as pathologically suspicious as Tiberius, Sejanus was bound to make a mistake. He was arrested and accused of conspiracy; after execution, his body was thrown to the rabble, who abused it for three days. Sejanus's three children were also executed; the girl of fourteen was a virgin, so the executioner raped her before killing her. On hearing rumours that his son Drusus had been murdered, Tiberius instituted another reign of terror, that continued more or less unchecked until his death six years later. Citizens were tried and executed on the slightest of pretexts. When he finally died, at the age of seventy-eight – probably smothered by his chief henchman – the people of Rome went wild with joy.

The best that can be said of Caligula, Tiberius's grand nephew and successor, is that he was almost certainly insane. According to Suetonius, he loved watching tortures and executions, and Tiberius took a certain grim pleasure in appointing him his successor because he realised that he would spread ruin and chaos. "I am nursing a viper in Rome's bosom." He became Emperor at the age of twenty-five, and at first the Romans could hardly believe their luck. He showered gifts of money on the people, and organised gladiatorial contests on a fantastic scale. Because an astrologer had once said that he stood no more chance of becoming Roman emperor than he had of walking dry-shod across the Gulf of Baiae, he had ships anchored in a double line across the bay, extending for a distance of three miles, then had them covered with planks, and walked across several times.

It soon became clear that absolute power had driven him insane. He announced that he was a god and that Jupiter had asked him to share his home. He committed incest with his three sisters, on the grounds that it was the correct thing for a god to do – Jupiter having slept with his sister Juno. And he began to kill with total abandon, without any of Tiberius's pretence of legality. One day when he was fencing with a gladiator with a wooden sword, the man fell down deliberately; Caligula pulled out a dagger, stabbed him to death, then ran around flourishing the blood-stained weapon as evidence that he had won. One day when he was presiding at a sacrifice in the temple – at which he was supposed to stun a beast with a mallet – he swung the mallet at the priest who was supposed to cut its throat and knocked him unconscious; it was his idea of a joke. At one of his banquets, he began to laugh, and when politely asked the cause of his mirth, answered: "It just occurred to me that I have only to give one nod and your throats will be cut." When he was told the price of raw meat for the wild animals in the circus, he decided that it would be cheaper to feed them on criminals; he had a row of malefactors lined up and told his soldiers: "Kill every man between that bald head and that one over there." He called Rome "the city of necks waiting for me to chop them". And when he ran out of money, he adopted the time-honoured remedy of accusing rich men of various crimes and seizing their property. His favourite method of execution was what might be called "the death of a thousand cuts", in which hundreds of small wounds were inflicted.

It seems surprising that Caligula survived as emperor for as long as he did – it was partly because he surrounded himself with a specially picked bodyguard of German troops. One day at the arena, he took a brief stroll to the hallway under the grandstand, and one of his officers seized the opportunity to cut him down and then stabbed him, appropriately, in the genitals. Other guards went to the palace, killed Caligula's wife and dashed out the brains of his baby daughter against the wall.

His successor Claudius has become known as one of the better behaved of the twelve Caesars – largely because of the two Claudius novels by Robert Graves. Suetonius's account makes it clear that he was rather less saintly than Graves makes out. He enjoyed watching criminals being put to the torture, and witnessing "ancient style" executions in which a man was flogged to death. Like his predecessors, he was a sex maniac, and likely to order any attractive woman to his bed. He ordered dozens of executions of knights and senators, and had his two nieces condemned to death "without any positive proof of their crimes. . .or so much as allowing them to make a defence". When he discovered that his wife Messalina was a nymphomaniac – who on one occasion had organised a contest with a famous prostitute to see who could satisfy most men in one night – he not only ordered her execution, but that of more than three hundred men and women who had been present at her sexual orgies. He then married his niece Agrippina, who brought his career to an end in 54 AD by poisoning him with mushrooms.

But for criminal psychology, Claudius's successor Nero is by far the most interesting of the Roman emperors. He was neither a mad man nor a sadist, and when he came to the throne at the age of seventeen, seemed to be a thoroughly ordinary young man with a pleasant disposition. The only doubtful element in his character was the sheer intensity of his naive egoism; he found himself inexhaustibly interesting. As a child, he had been wildly applauded when he acted in a play about Troy, and the taste for applause – and the desire to be liked – had never left him. He began his reign by distributing largesse to the people, and followed this with some of the most spectacular games they had ever seen. But since – unlike his predecessors – he hated the sight of blood, no one was allowed to be killed in the contests. And since Nero was a cultured young man who loved music and poetry, it seemed probable that the Romans had at last found themselves a benevolent ruler. He certainly showed a desire to be just and humane. When sitting in judgement, he preferred to defer his decision to the following day and then give it in writing, so that he could be more certain of being objective. He was no imperialist – he felt that the Roman Empire was big enough, and considered withdrawing his forces from Britain, although he finally decided against it. In Greece, he tried to have a canal cut through the Isthmus of Corinth, and even dug the first basket of earth himself.

His basic problem was that he did not possess the strength of character to be emperor of Rome. He was childish, self-absorbed and easily flattered. His vanity, while rather absurd seemed quite harmless. He sent for a famous lyre player and decided to study it himself. When told that his voice was too light, he accepted advice to lie on his back with heavy lead weights on his chest to strengthen the breathing muscles. Then he began singing to his dinner guests, and so encouraged by their applause that he decided to make a stage appearance. In Naples, the theatre he chose for his debut was shaken by an earthquake, but he insisted on performing to the end – the theatre collapsed shortly after the audience had dispersed. The Roman crowds clamoured for their own performance, and applauded wildly when he complied. Soon he was appearing on stage in various tragedies. Because, like most cultured Romans, he regarded Greece as the home of music and drama, he began making regular excursions there to take part in lyre contests – which, of course, he invariably won. Because the Greeks always asked him to sing after dinner, Nero announced: "The Greeks alone are worthy of my genius. . ."

His first murder – which took place a year after he became emperor, in AD 54 – was of his half-brother Britannicus, the son of Claudius and Messalina, who might have been regarded as having a better claim to the throne than Nero. Nero hired a famous poisoner called Locusta – who is reputed to have supplied the mushrooms that killed Claudius – but the boy was understandably cautious, and had his food sampled by a taster. One day, at a banquet, Britannicus tried a drink after his taster had tried it, found it too hot and asked for water to be added. The water had been poisoned, and Britannicus promptly went into convulsions and died. Nero looked on unconcernedly and commented that such attacks often happen to epileptics.

Another problem was Nero's mother Agrippina. She was only twenty-two years his senior and he seems to have had a Freudian fixation on her. When Nero became emperor, Agrippina – who had been the real emperor in Claudius's last years – naturally expected to continue to play a leading role. At first Nero let her do as she liked; but he was finding his feet and soon began to resent the way she seemed to want to run the empire. Early coins of his reign show Nero and his mother facing each other; within a year they were facing in the same direction with his head almost eclipsing hers. Agrippina was inclined to lose her temper at snubs like this, then would obviously reflect that it was now Nero who held the reins and go to the opposite extreme, trying to win him over with flattery and affection. When Nero began a love affair with a freedwoman named Acte, Agrippina at first opposed it violently; then as Nero's smart young friends urged him on, decided to support the intrigue; and since Nero felt it had to be kept secret from the populace as he was already married, she offered her son the use of her bedroom and bed. Finally she seems to have decided on an even more drastic measure – to allow Nero to commit incest with her. Details are lacking, but Suetonius records that it occurred whenever he rode with her in an enclosed litter and that the disarranged state of his clothes when he emerged proved it. (The Roman toga was a rather complicated device compared to modern garments.) But the forbidden seems to have lost its charm the moment it ceased to be forbidden, and Nero turned to other sexual outlets, both male and female. Relations between mother and son once again soured. Since he undoubtedly knew that she was behind the poisoning of the emperor Claudius, Nero may have begun to worry that he might be next on the list. At all events, he decided that she had to be removed.

At this point, Nero's former tutor produced an ingenious suggestion. He had been appointed commander of the fleet and told Nero that it should not be too difficult to construct a boat that would fall to pieces when at sea. Accordingly, Nero invited his mother to join him at the festival of Minerva at Baiae on the Bay of Naples. The evening before, they dined at Bauli, not far from Baiae; the party was arranged by Nero's millionaire friend Otho, who was also his go-between with Acte. Nero seemed to have paid special attention to his mother and treated her with a kindness that suggested remorse; the aim was to lull any suspicion she might feel when he told her she was to travel by sea and he by land. Then the ship with Agrippina sailed for Baiae. It seems to have been fairly large – perhaps twenty or thirty feet long – and covered with a wooden roof. It was a still, starlit night, and Agrippina was in a good mood as she sat on a settee, with her feet in the lap of her friend Acerronia, and discussed the change in Nero's attitude towards her. At a signal, the roof suddenly caved in, under the pressure of heavy lead weights. One of Agrippina's friends, Crepereius Gallus, was standing, and caught the full force, which killed her immediately. But the back of the settee took the weight, and since Agrippina and Acerronia were reclining, they were untouched. The ship should then have fallen apart; but apparently it failed to do so. Oarsmen who were in the assassination plot tried to capsize it by throwing their weight on one side. Acerronia, in an attempt to save Agrippina – for by now it must have been obvious that this was a murder attempt – began to call out: "Help, I am the emperor's mother." At this, the crew beat her to death with oars. The real Agrippina slipped over the side in the confusion; in spite of an injured shoulder she managed to swim to some sailing boats, one of which took her back to Bauli. There she sent a message to Nero saying that by the grace of the gods she had escaped a serious accident. This was a mistake; she should have hurried back to Rome and allowed rumour of the murder attempt to circulate so that, if Nero tried again, no one would have any doubt about the instigator. When Agrippina's freedman arrived with the message, Nero did some quick thinking. He had to make it appear that it was *his* life that was in danger, and that his mother was responsible. He dropped a sword on the ground, and then cried out that the man had been sent to kill him.

News of the attempted drowning had spread in Bauli. Crowds gathered on the seashore, but were dispersed by troops. Meanwhile, Nero sent his ex-tutor, inventor of the collapsing ship, with two henchmen to kill his mother. As they forced their way into her bedchamber, she seems to have assumed that they had come to find out if she was well; then, when one of them struck her on the head with a club, she grasped the truth. The historian Tacitus says that, as one of the men drew his sword, she presented her belly and told him to strike her there – in the womb that had borne Nero. She was hacked to pieces.

Nero, typically, was now in a state of funk, probably expecting a general revolt when the news became public. He began to feel better when two of his praetorian guard came to congratulate him on his "narrow escape"; it had no doubt dawned on him for the first time that the emperor could do exactly as he liked. So he wrote a letter to the senate, accusing his mother of an attempt on his life; he added that, conscious of her guilt, she had paid the penalty, implying that she had committed suicide. Then he hurried to Bauli to make sure that his mother was dead and to remove the evidence that would prove she had not died by her own hand. He was reported to have viewed the body and admired its beauty, although in view of his dislike of blood, this was probably an invention. What is certain is that Agrippina was promptly cremated. Even so, Nero was unable to summon the courage to return to Rome, and face the senate and the populace; he stayed away from March AD 59 – when the murder took place – until September. When he finally arrived back in Rome, he was relieved to find that his popularity with the mob was unimpaired. Rome was far too accustomed to murder to be shocked at a little matricide; and an emperor who gave them such magnificent public spectacles was not to be antagonised.

Without the frowns of his mother to restrain him, Nero was able to fling himself into his amusements with total abandon. He began to spend his evenings in taverns with selected companions, such as Otho. They started to break into shops, and attack late night travellers. He seems to have lost his distaste for blood to the extent of stabbing them if they struggled. His banquets lasted from midday until midnight, and according to the *Satyricon*, a vast novel by his friend Petronius, aphrodisiacs played an important part in the menu.

Nero fell in love again; the new mistress was Poppaea, the wife of his friend Otho. At first they seemed to have shared her favours; then Nero grew jealous at the thought of her sleeping with her own husband. Otho would probably have died of poison; but Nero's tutor Seneca – a distinguished dramatist and philosopher – managed to persuade Nero to send his former friend to Portugal as a governor. Soon afterwards, to Nero's delight, Poppaea became pregnant. There was only one obstacle in the way of marrying Poppaea, Nero's wife Octavia. They had been betrothed as children – she was the daughter of Claudius and Messalina – and she was now only just out of her teens. Her conduct was irreproachable, so she had to be "framed". The commander of the guard, Tigellinus, was given the job of torturing her slaves until he had enough confessions to ensure a divorce. At this point, the unpredictable Roman populace suddenly decided to take the part of Octavia and demonstrated in front of the palace. More evidence was needed, so Nero's friend Anicetus – the one who had designed the collapsing ship – made a public confession that he had committed adultery with Octavia and that she had aborted a child. The divorce went through. Octavia was exiled to an island and then ordered to kill herself. When she protested, Nero's henchmen bound her and opened up her arteries. To hasten the process, she was placed in a steam bath. Tacitus states that her head was sent to Poppaea to convince her that her former rival was dead. It was something of an anticlimax when Poppaea presented Nero with a daughter.

In the following year, AD 64 Rome was devastated by a fire that lasted a week. The later rumour that Nero started this fire is undoubtedly false; on the other hand, there seems to be some evidence that he "fiddled" while Rome burned – in fact, he took his lyre and sang a tragic song of his own composition called "The Fall of Troy". Since the fire lasted so long, Nero can hardly be accused of callousness for singing during that period; but when the story became current, it caused a steep decline in his popularity. When the fire was finally halted by demolishing public buildings, Nero seems to have behaved rather well. He organized relief, had large quantities of corn brought in from Ostia, and cut its price to one sixteenth of normal.

Why should Nero have wanted to start a fire? According to the historians, because he wanted to clear a large area in the centre of the city for a new palace. In fact, Nero did build himself an immense and magnificent palace called the Golden House. He also rebuilt a great deal of the rest of Rome. But the rumours of his responsibility for the fire persisted, and Nero looked for scapegoats. This was no problem, since Rome was now full of members of a "deadly superstition" called Christianity. (Tacitus mentions that its prophet Jesus, had been executed in Tiberius's reign by Pontius Pilate.) Rumours of the "notoriously depraved Christians" spread. The Romans disliked Christians partly because they were associated with the Jews, and the Jews were regarded as religious fanatics who caused endless trouble. Tacitus also remarks that the Christians hated the human race. To the Romans, this foreign religious sect, with its belief in the imminent end of the world, must have seemed almost insane. If the Christians hated earthly things, then it seemed quite possible that they might have started the great fire. What struck the Romans as even more incredible and disgusting was that many of these Christians seemed to have no fear of dying for their religion and confessed to it willingly. So the Christians were killed with exceptional ferocity. They were smeared with tar and tied to posts, to be ignited as living torches after dark. They were dressed in animal skins and then set upon by wild dogs who tore them to pieces. They were thrown to wild beasts in the arena, and crucified in enormous numbers. And yet, paradoxically, Nero's good intentions backfired. He had overestimated the bloodthirstiness of the Romans. People were sickened by so much torture, and his popularity declined even further.

Nero's problem was that he was too self-absorbed to react to public opinion. It seemed to him that he was an excellent emperor who was always giving the public what it wanted. As to being bloodthirsty, he felt it was shockingly untrue. In AD 61, the prefect of the city had been murdered by one of his slaves – probably in a homosexual quarrel – and law decreed that every slave under the same roof be executed, including women and children. The populace rioted on behalf of the unfortunate slaves – four hundred of them – and Nero, who was a liberal in theory, agreed entirely with the people. The senate felt otherwise. They were afraid that, if murder by slaves was tolerated, they might all be murdered in their beds. So soldiers had to line the route when the four hundred men, women and children were taken to execution, and the populace put the blame on Nero. He felt that he was a misunderstood saint. His reaction to this latest problem was to spend more money, organize more games and entertainments, and to spend more time in the company of selected sycophants such as the elegant aesthete Petronius. (But Petronius eventually fell from favour; accused by Tigellinus of plotting against Nero's life, he committed suicide by severing his veins in his bath.)

In AD 65, Poppaea died; Nero had lost his temper and kicked her when she was pregnant. Her death shattered him; the funeral was of unparalleled lavishness, and the spices that were burned were the equivalent of a full year's supply from Arabia. Poppaea was pronounced a goddess; Nero's fancy fell upon a eunuch named Sporus, whose looks reminded him of Poppaea. Suetonius alleges that it was Nero who made Sporus into a eunuch by castrating him, attempting to turn him into a girl. He then went through a wedding ceremony with Sporus, dressed him in female clothes and treated him like a wife. The orgies became wilder, Nero seems to have discovered the pleasures of binding, and invented a new game. Men and women were tied to stakes, and Nero, dressed as a wild beast, came bounding at them and pretended to eat their genitals. The game ended with Nero being sodomized by his freedman Doryphorus. Apparently anxious to try every sexual experience, Nero had another "wedding ceremony" performed – according to the scandal-loving Suetonius – with himself as the bride and Doryphorus as the groom; while being deflowered he imitated the screams and moans of a girl.

Nero found it easy to slip into the Roman habit of ordering executions whenever he felt like it. A half-hearted conspiracy to murder him, led by an aristocrat named Piso, provided him with an admirable excuse in AD 65; Petronius was one of the victims on this occasion; so was Nero's old tutor Seneca. Unlike Claudius, Nero derived no pleasure from watching men die; instead, he preferred to order them to commit suicide. Soon he was adding disapproving senators to the list, in the best tradition of Tiberius and Caligula. It began to dawn on the senate that getting rid of Nero was a matter of self-preservation.

Meanwhile, Nero was preoccupied with grandiose schemes. He was rebuilding Rome, with wide streets and buildings of stone and marble. His own Golden House had an arcade a mile long, and his apartments were plated in gold set with jewels. The ceilings slid back so that showers of perfume could be sprinkled down, or a rain of flowers. (Flowers were a kind of status symbol in Rome – one rich man spent £100,000 – four million sesterces – on roses for one banquet.) At the entrance stood an immense statue of Nero, twelve storeys high.

In AD 67 – the twelfth year of his reign – Nero set off on a tour of Greece, taking part in various games and contests. He continued to be obsessed by the thought of plots against him and, while he was in Greece, sent for his greatest general, Corbulo, and ordered him to commit suicide; as he died, Corbulo murmured the ambiguous phrase "Serves me right". Nero also suspected the loyalty of his Rhine armies – completely without reason – and sent for the two brothers who commanded the provinces on the Rhine. Without being allowed to defend themselves or see Nero, these were also ordered to commit suicide.

But things were already drifting towards the point of no return. In Judea, the Roman prefect was causing deep offence by trying to force the temple treasury to pay enormous tax arrears, and when he allowed his men to plunder parts of Jerusalem, Jewish terrorists organized a revolt; the Roman population of Jerusalem was massacred. The governor of Syria tried to recapture Jerusalem and was driven back with heavy losses. Nero appointed a middle-aged general named Vespasian to suppress the revolt. Then, in March, he heard that the governor of Gaul, Gaius Vindex, had also rebelled, after issuing a proclamation denouncing Nero's extravagances. He was supported by Galba, the governor of Nearer Spain, and by Nero's one-time friend Otho, governor of Portugal. The neurotic emperor was thrown into a panic by the news, and it was obvious to his guards that he was totally incapable of dealing with the situation. He left the dining-room one day with his arms around the shoulders of two friends explaining that he intended to go to Gaul, stand in front of the rebel army and weep and weep until they felt sorry for him. Then, he said, he would stroll among his troops singing paeans of victory. What really seems to have cut him to the quick was a comment by Vindex that Nero played the lyre very badly.

On 8 June a report arrived stating that an army in northern Italy had decided to join the rebels. For Nero, this was the last straw; he decided to flee to Egypt. It was a scheme he had been considering for some time – he had remarked that, if he lost the throne, he could always live by his art. He left the Golden House and moved to his mansion in the Servilian gardens, en route for the port of Ostia, where ships had been ordered to get ready. When he woke from a short sleep to find that the Praetorian guard was no longer on duty, he seems to have realized that this was the end. In fact, the commander of the Praetorian guard had decided to go over to Galba and had bribed the men with an offer of 30,000 sesterces each (about £750) to proclaim Galba emperor. Nero hurried to the houses of various friends but could get no reply. Returning to his house, he found that his bodyguard had fled and had taken his bedclothes and his box of poison. Sounds of shouting and cheering from a nearby army camp convinced him that the revolt was spreading. With only four companions – including his "wife" Sporus – he set out for the house of his freedman Phaon nearby. There he crawled into a cellar, ordered his grave to be dug, and had hysterics, repeating over and over again: "What a loss I shall be to the arts". A runner arrived with a message; it declared that the senate had branded him a public enemy and decreed that he should be executed in the "ancient style", which meant being flogged to death. He asked one of his companions to commit suicide first, and then, when he showed reluctance, muttered: "How ugly and vulgar my life has become." When he heard the sound of approaching hooves, he placed the sword point to his throat; one of the others also placed his hand on it, and pushed it in. He was already dying when a centurion entered to arrest him; as the man tried to staunch the blood with his cloak, he murmured "How loyal you are," and expired.

The lesson of Nero is fairly simple. He was neither a sadist nor a tyrant; if he had lived out his life as a private citizen, he would probably have remained an amiable and decent human being. But he was allowed to do what he liked, and he did it. He was like a good-natured child who is spoilt by over indulgence until he becomes intolerable. In fact, most of Roman history seems to be a record of such individuals: men who would have made excellent private citizens, but who were turned into maniacs by the addictive drug of limitless power.

The historian John Addington Symonds was so puzzled by the

cruelty of tyrants that he invented his own word – haematomania, meaning "blood-madness" – to describe it. He devotes an appendix in his work *The Renaissance in Italy* to the subject, taking as an example the Dark Age tyrant Ibrahim ibn Ahmed, prince of Africa and Sicily in the second half of the ninth century. "This man, besides displaying peculiar ferocity in his treatment of enemies and prisoners of war, delighted in the execution of horrible butcheries within the walls of his own palace. His astrologers having once predicted that he should die by the hands of a "small assassin", he killed off the whole retinue of his pages, and filled up their place with a suite of negroes whom he proceeded to treat after the same fashion. On another occasion, when one of his three hundred eunuchs had by chance been witness of the tyrant's drunkenness, Ibrahim slaughtered the whole band. Again, he is said to have put an end to sixty youths, originally selected for his pleasures, burning them by gangs of five or six in the furnace, or suffocating them in the hot chambers of his baths. Eight of his brothers were murdered in his presence; and when one, who was so diseased that he could scarcely stir, implored to be allowed to end his days in peace, Ibrahim answered: "I make no exceptions". His own son Abu l-Aghlab was beheaded by his orders before his eyes; and the execution of chamberlains, secretaries, ministers and courtiers was of common occurrence. But his fiercest fury was directed against women. He seems to have been darkly jealous of the perpetuation of the human race. Wives and concubines were strangled, sawn asunder, and buried alive if they showed signs of pregnancy. His female children were murdered as soon as they saw the light; sixteen of them, whom his mother managed to conceal and rear at her own peril, were massacred on the spot when Ibrahim discovered whom they claimed as father. Contemporary Arab chroniclers, pondering upon the fierce and gloomy passions of this man, arrived at the conclusion that he was the subject of a strange disease, a portentous secretion of black bile producing the melancholy which impelled him to commit atrocious crimes." And Symonds goes on to make a comment that distinguishes between tyrants like Ibrahim and slaves of vanity like Nero. "Ibrahim was a great general, an able ruler, a man of firm and steady purpose; not a weak and ineffectual libertine whom lust for blood and lechery had placed below the level of brute beasts." He goes on to say: "The only way of explaining his eccentric thirst for slaughter is to suppose that it was a dark monomania, a form of psychopathy analogous to that which we find in the Marechal de Retz [Gilles de Rais] and the Marquise de Brinvilliers."

Symonds is prompted to these speculations after devoting a chapter to "the Age of the Despots", the period in the fourteenth and fifteenth centuries when Italy was dominated by small feudal lords whose power depended upon sheer brutality. The worst of these was a minor princeling called Ezzelino da Romano, who was born in 1184. In the previous century, one of his forbears had been given two estates near Padua as a reward for serving the German Emperor. In the Middle Ages, Italy was divided into two factions: supporters of the Pope, who were called Guelphs, and supporters of the Holy Roman Emperor who were called Ghibellines. The long rivalry between these two meant that most of Italy became a battlefield, dominated by the law of survival of the fittest. In fact, Ezzelino's father was a supporter of the Pope. After a long career of murder, pillage and rape, the elder Ezzelino became a monk in one of his own castles, and his son – who was to become known as one of the worst monsters of the Middle Ages – stepped into his shoes.

Ezzelino's great obsession was to capture Padua. By this time, he was fighting on the side of the Emperor Frederick II and had helped him fight the combined forces of Padua, Treviso and Vicenza – the latter was virtually reduced to rubble by the invaders. In 1226, the Emperor went back across the Alps, and in 1227 – when he was forty-three – Ezzelino besieged and finally entered Padua.

What happened now was what seems to happen so often in the careers of absolute despots. At first, he treated his new subjects well, and gained a measure of popularity. But he saw himself surrounded by enemies, since the Emperor was now back in Germany, and his most bitter enemy Pope Gregory, was in Italy. Frederick II has been called the first Renaissance man, and he had nothing but contempt for the old dogmatic religion of the Middle Ages. This is why the Pope regarded him with loathing and horror. And since Ezzelino was Frederick's ally, he came in for his share of the loathing. Padua had always been loyal to the Pope, so Ezzelino was in charge of what was virtually a nest of rebels. And as his spies and secret police discovered plots against him, his naturally suspicious temperament developed into paranoia. He began a reign of terror that made Rome under Tiberius look like a haven of peace and prosperity. Unlike Tiberius or Nero, who simply had people arrested and executed, Ezzelino seemed to have desire to terrify them into submission through torture. By 1250 – the year in which the Emperor died – he had turned into a sadistic madman. He erected eight prisons in Padua, each one of which contained hundreds of captives. These were executed, and the prisons filled again. The Papal Bull that excommunicated him in 1248 declared: "He blinds innocent youths, cuts adults to pieces with every variety of refined torment and, shameful to mention, horribly castrates men and women . . ." This was no exaggeration. In fact, Ezzelino seemed to have a peculiar horror of sex, which led to a kind of morbid obsession with organs associated with love or reproduction. He had young men castrated; girls had their breasts and lips removed. When he captured Friola he ordered a massacre accompanied by torture. Everybody was to be blinded, have their noses removed and have arms and legs chopped off. After this, they were left to die in the open. He walled up a whole family of his enemies in their castle, and left them to starve to death. It appealed to his grim sense of humour to leave corpses in the prisons, so that his captives had to live in an odour of rotting flesh. Chroniclers like Rolandino describe how he would walk through the city with a strange, mad look in his eyes, searching for victims. It is estimated that about a quarter of the population of Padua (5,000) were executed on his orders. Finally, after almost twenty years of domination by this madman, Padua was "saved" by the armies of the Pope. Ezzelino was fighting elsewhere when the crusaders finally burst into Padua to be met by cheering citizens. But the crusaders did not want to be welcomed. Part of the pleasure of war in the Middle Ages was pillage and rape, and the crusaders had no intention of forgoing their reward. So for the next eight days, they looted and burned the houses and ravished the women. Finally, they retreated with their spoils, and the citizens were able to come out of hiding and open the prisons. Hundreds of starving mutilated cripples staggered out into the sunshine, most of them unable to understand what was happening. And in spite of the devastation, the citizens of Padua went into a frenzy of celebration at being rid of the tyrant. When Ezzelino, who was in his other city of Verona, heard what had happened, he took his revenge by ordering every Paduan in his army to be thrown into prison, while survivors who had escaped from Padua to Verona were burnt alive.

Naturally, Ezzelino tried to re-take Padua. The Pope made sure he was unsuccessful. When he was told that one of his Paduan prisoners was an astrologer who had foretold that he would never re-take the city, he ordered that all ten thousand should be executed. Only two hundred survived. Ezzelino lived on for another three years, defying the Pope and proving himself to be a brilliant general. When he took the city of Brescia, he instituted another reign of terror, ordering that all the prisoners who had been taken in battle should be either beheaded or tortured. Those who escaped with their lives had their eyes gouged out, or limbs hacked off, while pregnant women had their bellies slit open. Families were tortured to death in one another's presence, priests were burned alive and disembowelled; most of the men who were killed were castrated, and their testicles thrown into a deep well, which he swore he would fill to the top. It was at this point that he devastated the town of Friola, which had been captured by a Paduan force, and ordered that every inhabitant should be mutilated. After that, he marched on Milan, looking forward to an orgy of torture that would surpass everything he had done so far. Fortunately, it was too well defended, and his enemies closed around him. In 1259, he was finally captured in battle, and taken to a castle in the small town of Somcino. The opposing army went wild with joy, but Ezzelino had no intention of giving them the pleasure of showing weakness or fear. When a man spat in his face, he stared grimly straight in front of him. In the castle of Somcino, he refused food and drink, and finally succeeded in killing himself by ripping off the bandages from his wounds, and bleeding to death. He was seventy-five years old, and had been torturing and murdering for twenty-two years.

Symonds talks about "blood madness" and moral insanity, but he seems to be missing the main point: that Ezzelino enjoyed watching his victims being *sexually* mutilated. All the chroniclers mention the interesting fact that in the last decades of his life, he seemed to be totally uninterested in women. The reason is obvious. He had no desire to express his sexuality in a normal act of "lovemaking." He had learned to derive his pleasure from the infliction of pain.

The same thing has been noted by criminologists who have studied modern "serial killers": that in case after case, rape, torture and murder became a habit. When the American sex killer Ted Bundy escaped from jail in Colorado, he made his way down to Tallahassee, Florida, and found himself a room in a student lodging house. Only two weeks later, he entered a sorority house for female students of Florida State University and made a frenzied attack on four girls in quick succession, killing two of them and seriously injuring the other two. An hour later, he broke into another lodging house and fractured the skull of a girl who was lying in bed – he was interrupted before he could complete the assault. A few weeks later, he was arrested after murdering and raping a twelve year old schoolgirl. Bundy was finally executed for these murders in January 1989. If he had chosen to live quietly in Florida, he might have spent the remainder of his life there without being recognised – no one even suspected he was there. But sex murder had become an incurable obsession.

Symonds raises the question "Whether such men are mad – whether in the case of a Nero or a Marechal de Retz or an Ezzelino, the love of evil and the thirst for blood are not monomaniacal perversion of barbarous passions which even in a cannibal are morbid. Is there in fact such a thing as Haematomania, Blood-madness? But if we answer this question in the affirmative, we shall have to place how many Visconti, Ssorzeschi, Malatesti, the Borgias, Farnesi and princes of the houses of Anjou and Aragon in the list of these maniacs. Ezzelino was indeed only the first of a long and horrible procession, the most terror-striking because the earliest, prefiguring all the rest."

A century after the death of Ezzelino, another "haematomaniac" spread terror from India to southern Russia. His name was Timur Lenk, Timur the Lame – better known in the west as Tamerlane – and he was a descendant of the Mongol conqueror

Genghis Khan, who had spread terror from China to the Mediterranean a century earlier. From 1362 to 1380, Tamerlane made himself master of what is now Russian Turkestan, fighting invading nomads. Then he spent another seven years conquering Persia. Unfortunately for the people he conquered, he was an obsessive killer, who felt that a conqueror's chief business was to murder on a massive scale. His violence was pointlessly sadistic; when he took Sabwazar in 1383 he had 2,000 prisoners built into a living mound, then bricked in. Later the same year, he had 5,000 captives beheaded at Zirih, and their heads made into an enormous pyramid. In 1386 he had all his prisoners at Luri hurled over a cliff. In Delhi, he massacred 100,000 prisoners. This extraordinary man invaded Anatolia (Turkey) in 1400, took the garrison of Sivas, and had its 4,000 Christian defenders buried alive. Yet since he lacked political good sense, and was more interested in conquest and murder than in consolidating his gains, his empire collapsed within half a century of his death in 1405.

If Tamerlane stands out as the most spectacular sadist in world history, the Wallachian ruler Vlad Tepes – which means Vlad the Impaler – born precisely one century later, probably deserves second place. He was eventually to be immortalised by Bram Stoker as Dracula, which means "son of the devil" (or of a dragon); in his brief reign – a mere six years – he is estimated to have killed 100,000 people, many by his favourite method of impaling on a sharp pole. His grandfather, Prince Mircea, has been described as a kind of Romanian Charlemagne; his father, Vlad II, was one of Mircea's bastard sons, and he was placed on the throne of Wallachia (southern Romania) in 1436 with the aid of the Hungarians. His problem was that he had to remain equally friendly with two powerful neighbours – the Hungarians and the Turks – and he found this difficult, losing his throne to the Hungarians in 1442, and regaining it with the aid of the Turks in the following spring. But neither the Hungarians nor the Turks entirely trusted him, and this is why, in 1444, he felt obliged to send his two younger sons, Dracula and Radu, as hostages to the Turks. Dracula was about twelve at the time, and his brother nine; their four years imprisonment was a period of gloom and stress, particularly when the Hungarians started a crusade against the Turks, and obliged Vlad II to send four thousand soldiers to help them. Vlad was convinced that he had condemned his sons to death; in fact, the Turks allowed them to live, largely because the sultan, Murad, had conceived lustful designs on Radu, who was handsomer than his elder brother. Radu resisted strenuously at first, holding the sultan at bay with a dagger. But, predictably, he finally gave way and became Murad's "protegé". His elder brother remained a difficult prisoner, and harsh treatment hardened his character and made him vengeful.

Meanwhile, the Hungarians had once again turned against Vlad II; betrayed by his boyars (noblemen) he was defeated near his capital Tirgoviste and his eldest son Mircea, his favourite, was buried alive. Vlad himself was hunted down and killed. When the Turkish sultan heard that Vlad had been killed by the Hungarians, he gave the two boys their liberty, and Dracula was made an officer in the Turkish army. Meanwhile, the Hungarian leader Janos Hunyadi seized Vlad's throne. But in new battles against the Turks, Hunyadi was defeated, and the seventeen year old Dracula entered Tirgoviste and appointed himself prince – Vlad III.

His first taste of power lasted less than two months; then the rightful prince, Vladislav II, returned and defeated him in battle, forcing him to flee. For the next eight years, Dracula was a wanderer; he spent some time at the court of the Turkish sultan Murad, where his brother was still living, then went to Moldavia, and the court of his step-uncle Bogdan II; he was forced to move on when Bodgdan was assassinated in 1451. At one point he even threw himself on the mercy of Janos Hunyadi, who promptly showed him the door; but Hunyadi eventually changed his mind, and appointed Vlad to a post of commander in his army. When Hunyadi died of the plague in 1456, Vlad made a second bid for the throne of Tirgoviste; this time his small army defeated Vladislas II, and for the second time, Dracula became a prince. During the next six years he perpetrated the horrors that caused him to be known as Vlad the Impaler.

His first act as ruler was to rebuild an ancient castle on the River Arges, twenty miles north of Tirgoviste; after years of insecurity, he wanted an impregnable stronghold. He made it clear to his subjects that he would be a firm and puritanical ruler. His four years in Turkey had made him aware that Moslem women were expected to keep their faces covered, and to guard their virtue. Possibly he was shocked to find that Christian women allowed themselves far more freedom. At all events, he announced that unfaithful wives were to have their sexual organs cut out, then they were to be skinned alive and exposed in a public square. Girls who lost their virginity before marriage were to meet the same fate. Lesser sexual offences were punished by cutting off a nipple. Another chronicler mentions that, in extreme cases of unchastity, he had a red hot iron stake inserted into the vagina and forced in until it came out of her mouth.

A chronicler describes how, when one of Vlad's mistresses declared that she was pregnant, he had her examined by a doctor, who found it to be untrue. Vlad felt that her lie had exposed him to ridicule, and ordered her to be cut open from the vagina to the breasts; then he looked at the dying woman's exposed womb and remarked: "Now everyone can see where I have been."

Like Haroun Al Raschid in the *Arabian Nights*, Vlad seems to have taken an intense interest in the private lives of his subjects. One story tells of how he met a peasant whose shirt and trousers were too short. Dracula asked him if he was married, and when the peasant admitted that he was, remarked that his wife must be a lazy slut. "I am satisfied with her", said the peasant, "She stays at home and is honest." "You will be more satisfied with another", said Dracula, and had the wife brought before him and impaled on a stake in the usual manner. After that, he presented the peasant with a second wife, but insisted that she should be shown the body of her predecessor, to make her aware of what would happen if she failed in her duties. He seems to have been sincerely convinced that he was doing the peasant a favour.

Those who received his hospitality must have found it a stressful experience. One Florentine merchant went to Dracula's palace in Tirgoviste to ask if he could borrow some servants to keep guard over his merchandise. He was invited to stay at the palace, leaving his merchandise and money in his carriage in the public square – Vlad had an obsession about honesty, and was convinced that no one would dare to commit theft. (He had a gold cup placed in the public fountain, and so great was the fear he inspired that it remained there during the six years of his reign.) In the morning, the merchant discovered that someone had stolen 160 gold ducats. Vlad told him that the thief would be found, and meanwhile ordered his treasurer to replace the money, and to add an extra ducat. When the merchant returned to his carriage he counted the money, and found he had a ducat too many.

Meanwhile, Vlad's soldiers had been told to announce the citizens of Tirgoviste that if the thief was not handed over the city would be destroyed. They hastened to investigate the matter, and the thief was soon apprehended. The merchant was summoned before Vlad to witness his execution. Asked if he had found his money, the merchant mentioned that he had one ducat too many. "Go in peace", said Vlad. "If you had not admitted to the extra ducat I would have had you impaled too."

Vlad was disturbed at the number of beggars in his realm – war had left hundreds of peasants homeless and sick. The beggars were all invited to a large dining hall in the palace complex, where they were provided with a generous meal of food and wine. In the midst of the merrymaking, Vlad entered the hall, and asked if they were satisfied; they roared their approval. "Would you all like to be without care?" Again, the answer was a shout of affirmation. Vlad then made his exit, ordered the dining hall to be locked and boarded up, and watched as it was set on fire. No one escaped. Vlad told his boyars that his intention was to make sure that the beggars ceased to be a burden on decent citizens.

Vlad's cousin Stephen of Moldavia, later known as Stephen the Great, shared Vlad's taste for impalement. In 1473 he had 2,300 Wallachian prisoners executed in this way; but at least he had them impaled through the navel. Vlad liked the stake to be inserted into the anus or vagina. It was greased, so that the victim's weight gradually caused him to slip down until the point came out of his throat or mouth. Vlad ordered that the stake should not be made too sharp, otherwise death came quickly and he liked to watch the victim suffering. On occasion, he added another refinement, attaching two horses to each of the victim's legs, and then making them gallop off in opposite directions.

When Vlad came to the throne in 1456, his two closest neighbours were Moldavia (to the northeast) and Transylvania (to the northwest.) To the south lay the Turks, who were masters of Bulgaria. A century earlier, the Turks had gained their first foothold in Europe, at Gallipoli, as a result of an appeal from the

Emperor of Byzantium for help against the Serbs. If the emperor had realised what he was doing, he would undoubtedly have cut off his hand rather than send the appeal; three years before Dracula's accession, Byzantium had fallen to the Turks; three quarters of a century later, by 1529, they were laying siege to Vienna. In 1443, the Pope had called for a crusade against the Turks, and this explains why Dracula's father, Vlad II, found himself so divided in his loyalties.

Dracula began his reign by strengthening trade links with Transylvania; but within a short time, relations had deteriorated, due to complicated political rivalries and to Dracula's dislike of the German merchants who dominated its commercial life. In the second year of his reign, 1457, he made a lightning raid into Transylvania, and wrought havoc. Various villages and castles were taken and their inhabitants massacred; even women and children were burned alive; others were taken back to Tirgoviste to be impaled. (There seems to be little doubt that Vlad derived sexual satisfaction from watching these impalements; his biographer Radu Florescu speculates that he had become incapable of normal sex.) After this he returned to Tirgoviste, and seems to have resumed normal trade relations with Transylvania, so that four hundred German trainees were sent to study in Wallachia.

In the spring of 1459, he seems to have learned – rather belatedly – that his brother Mercia had been buried alive, with the connivance of the boyars of Tirgoviste. Vlad made a secret search for the body, and found it lying face-down in the grave. A few weeks later, at Easter, five hundred of the older boyars were invited to a banquet, then seized and impaled in rows near the palace. Younger boyars and their families, who were preparing to celebrate Easter with feasting and dancing, were taken *en masse* to a half-ruined castle at Poenari, and made to dismantle it and transport its stones across the river, to help build Vlad's new castle above the River Arges. A chronicler records that they were forced to work until the clothes fell off their backs and they were left naked.

Political tensions continued, and in March 1459, he secretly recalled all the Wallachian merchants from Transylvania, then had the apprentices arrested and burned alive in a hall. It has been suggested that, with the pathological suspicion that characterised him, he regarded them as spies. The Transylvanians sent ambassadors to investigate rumours of the atrocity; Vlad had them arrested and imprisoned. They were all convinced that they were destined to be impaled. In fact, Vlad wanted to prevent them from betraying his preparations for another invasion of Transylvania. His first objective was the city of Brasov, one of its two main centres of commerce (the other being Sibiu.) Most of its inhabitants were impaled on a hill near the church of St Bartholemew, after which Vlad set up tables and gave a banquet among the corpses. One boyar found the smell of blood and entrails too much for him, and held his nose; Vlad immediately sent for a particularly long pole, and had him impaled. He then invaded Sibiu, a town that had offered him refuge in his early years of wandering, and there slaughtered 10,000 of his former fellow citizens. His campaign in Transylvania continued into the following year. Two more towns that had defied him – Fagaras and Amlas – were burned, and their citizens – more than 20,000 – impaled. Many surrounding villages were so totally destroyed that they simply vanished off the map. Vlad returned to Tirgoviste well satisfied with his triumphant campaign.

But his cruelty and vengefulness had overreached themselves. The real enemy was not Transylvania, but the Turkish forces to the south. It was the Turks who had replaced his father on the throne of Wallachia, and who had helped Dracula to ascend the throne in 1456. They expected loyalty and tributes – 10,000 gold pieces a year. He found all this intensely irksome; sooner or later, a war with Turkey was inevitable. And when that happened, he would need all the help he could get from his neighbours.

Turkish envoys were sent to his court, probably in the first year of his reign. They bowed before him but failed to remove their turbans. When Vlad enquired the reason (which he knew as well as they did), they explained that it was not the custom in their land. Thereupon Vlad perpetrated another of his celebrated acts of cruelty, and ordered that their turbans should be nailed to their heads. The nails used were short ones, and the envoys probably survived with damaged skulls. The atrocity seems oddly pointless – surely Vlad realised that it was almost a declaration of war? – but it affords us an important insight into his tortuous mind. He had been a prisoner of the Turks at the age of twelve, and had spent four years of humiliation. Now the least challenge to his authority, the least suggestion of an insult, was enough to drive him to lose all self-control.

It seems that, on this occasion, his Turkish masters swallowed the insult. But by 1461, they were becoming impatient about lack of tributes, which included children, whom they wanted for their armies. Vlad was also supposed to appear at the Turkish court in Byzantium once a year and kiss the sultan's robe. He had not kept his agreement since 1458. It struck the Turkish sultan, Mohammed II, that Vlad's younger brother Radu, who was still at the court in Byzantium and had become his "protegé", would make an altogether more satisfactory prince of Wallachia. They invited Vlad to come to Byzantium to discuss their differences; he refused, on the grounds that his enemies would seize the throne in his absence. The Turks decided to trap him in an ambush. He was invited to go to the port of Giurgiu to meet the Turkish governor of Nicopolis, Hamza Pasha. But Vlad knew the Turks too well to be taken in. To gain time, he pretended to agree. But when he arrived in Giurgiu, he was accompanied by his army of 20,000 men – the dense forests that covered the shores of the Danube enabling them to make their approach unseen. The garrison was overwhelmed, and the Turks were marched back to Tirgoviste, there to die in a meadow outside the town in a mass impalement – Hamza Pasha being impaled upside down.

It was a declaration of war. And as an old hand at warfare, Vlad understood the importance of striking the first blow. In the winter of 1461, his army burnt Giurgiu and massacred its Turkish garrison. He counted 23,809 heads, noses and ears. He then sent off messages to the Pope and to King Mathias of Hungary for help. He had every reason to expect it, since the Pope had called for a crusade against the Turks. In fact, he was ignored. By the following spring, he had recognised that his only hope was to fight on alone. He advanced along the Danube (which divides Wallachia from Bulgaria), then into Bulgaria, where he was joined by many peasants who were tired of Turkish oppression. But he was slowed down by the need to besiege Turkish forts. And in April, Mahommed II set out from Byzantium to meet him. Vlad appealed for help to his cousin Stephen of Moldavia; Stephen responded with treachery, joining with the Turks in an attack on the Wallachian fortress of Chilia. Historians have been at a loss to explain this treachery; the probable reason is that Vlad had come to inspire so much loathing with his sadism that no one wanted to be his ally. Vlad was forced to retreat into Wallachia, leaving scorched earth behind him. By mid-June, the Turkish sultan was approaching Tirgoviste. But on the way, in a narrow gorge, he came upon a forest of stakes, 20,000 of them, with rotting corpses impaled on them, many of them Turks. It turned his stomach, and he gave the order to retreat. It began to look as if Vlad was saved after all. Unfortunately, Vlad himself was unaware of this. He believed that his only chance of victory was a surprise attack on the Turkish camp, aimed at killing the sultan. It took place on the night of Friday 17 June, not far from Tirgoviste. Within minutes, Vlad's cavalry overran the Turkish janissaries, and slaughtered men who ran half naked out of their tents – thousands were killed. But when they were within sight of the sultan's golden tent, the Turks rallied and counter-attacked. Recognising the danger of being cut off, Vlad ordered a retreat. When Mahommed II advanced into Tirgoviste the next day, he found a city reduced to burning ruins, surrounded by bodies impaled on stakes. Mahommed is said to have groaned: "What can one do against a man like this?" And since plague had begun to make its appearance in his army, he decided to turn homeward.

Vlad retreated to his stronghold above the Arges river. His wife is said to have committed suicide by throwing herself from the battlements into the river. Vlad himself escaped over the Fagaras mountains. During the flight, his son fell from his horse; Vlad was in too much of a hurry to stop to search for him. In fact, the boy was found the next morning by a shepherd, and taken back to his hut. (When Vlad eventually returned to Tirgoviste, he was to reward him richly). The next morning, from the crest of the Fagaras range, they were able to look down on the Turkish assault on Castle Dracula.

His aim was to reach King Mathias of Hungary, whose forces were at Brasov. But his reception was cool, and within weeks, he had been taken prisoner. Again, historians debate why Mathias decided to betray a man he should have embraced as an ally; one explanation is that some forged letters which seemed to show that

Vlad was still offering alliance to the Turks. The more probable explanation can be that Vlad inspired so much disgust – after all, Brasob had been the scene of his most publicised atrocity, when he had eaten dinner among hundreds of impaled bodies.

Twelve of the remaining fourteen years of Dracula's life were spent in Hungary, first in Buda, then Visegrad, twenty miles away. His guards kept him supplied with small animals – birds, mice, rats and toads – which he could torture or impale. (He is said to have filled his cell with their impaled corpses.) Then, after only four years, Mathias not only decided to free him, but to allow him to marry one of his own relatives. In order to do this, Vlad was made to abjure the Orthodox faith and become a Catholic; he apparently did this without misgivings. He fathered two children, and was given a house in Pesth. Only one anecdote survives from this period – how a Hungarian officer pursued a thief into Vlad's house, and how Vlad was so indignant that he stabbed the officer to death for failing to ask permission. The thief, oddly enough, was pardoned.

Back in Tirgoviste, his brother Radu was now king. He was, of course, a faithful servant of his Turkish masters. Radu was defeated in battle by Stephen the Great in 1473; his successor, Basarab the Old, lasted only two years, before also being defeated by Stephen. Meanwhile, Vlad was sent to Transylvania to guard a frontier district – he must have felt that it was a humiliating loss of face. In an action against the Turks he displayed his usual sadism, killing prisoners with a spear, then dismembering them and impaling the separate limbs. Vlad may also have taken part in the battle of Vaslui (10 January 1475) in which Basarab the Old and a vast Turkish force were defeated. That winter Vlad lived in Sibiu, another town he had devastated.

In the summer of 1476, he set out to retake Wallachia, together with Hungarian armies led by Stephen Bathory, and a Moldavian army led by his cousin Stephen, with whom he was now reconciled. On 8 November, he re-entered Tirgoviste; Bucharest was captured a week later.

What happened in the final two months of Vlad's life is still uncertain. There are no records of further atrocities – no doubt he was still too busy trying to strengthen his position. But when the Hungarians and Moldavians went back home, it became impossible. Some time in January 1477, Vlad's small army of about 4,000 men were surprised near Bucharest by the Turks, and Vlad himself was killed in battle. A Slavic narrative claims that he was assassinated by his own men, but this is unconfirmed. We only known that his head reached Byzantium in February, where it was publicly exposed. Those who went to gaze on the "monster" must have been surprised to see an ordinary looking man with a full mouth under a huge handlebar moustache. The headless body had been buried in an unmarked grave in the monastery of Snagov, on an island in a lake near Bucharest.

Four hundred and ten years later, Vlad achieved a kind of dubious immortality as the villain of Bram Stoker's famous novel. The story opens with the diary of a solicitor's clerk, Jonathan Harker, who has been sent to Castle Dracula in Transylvania (Stoker got the country wrong, but no doubt felt that Transylvania sounds more romantic than Wallachia) to settle some business about Count Dracula's forthcoming move to England. After a hair-raising drive over the Borgo Pass, Harker is finally greeted by "a tall old man, clean shaven save for a long white moustache, and clad in black from head to foot, without a single speck of colour about him anywhere". An actual description of Vlad by the papal legate in Buda runs: "He was not very tall, but very stocky and strong, with a cruel and terrible appearance, a long straight nose, distended nostrils, a thin and reddish face in which the large, wide-open green eyes were framed by bushy black eyebrows, which made them appear threatening. His face and chin were shaven but for a moustache. A bull's neck supported the head, from which the black curly locks were falling to his wide shouldered person". So Stoker's description is totally unlike the real Dracula, both in detail and in spirit. Yet what is so interesting about the novel is that Stoker has displayed such a sound instinctive knowledge of the mind of a "vampire". Such insight was hardly to be expected, for Stoker was a prim Victorian Irishman of impeccable morals, who would certainly have been horrified at the suggestion that *Dracula* is basically a rape fantasy. The son of a Dublin clerk, he spent most of his life as a secretary to the actor Henry Irving, and died of exhaustion and overwork at the age of 59. His other horror novels, with titles like *The Lair of the White Worm* and *The Lady of the Shroud* show a depressing lack of literary talent. In 1890, he had met a Hungarian professor of Oriental languages named Arminius Vambery, who told him about Vlad the Impaler, and tales of Romanian vampires. Soon after this, Stoker had an appalling nightmare about a vampire king rising from his tomb. He began to study the history and geography of eastern Europe, and the eventual result was *Dracula* – which, unlike his other fiction, is a masterpiece, and perhaps the greatest novel of horror ever written.

Stoker's Dracula (a mere count, not a prince) comes to England while Harker is still a prisoner in his castle, and drinks the blood of Lucy Westenra, causing her to turn into a vampire. Harker returns to England, and with the aid of Dr Van Helsing (Arminius Vambery) destroys the undead Lucy and drives Dracula from the country. They then pursue Dracula back to his castle, and finally kill him in his coffin, which is then burned.

And yet it only emphasises the question: what turned Vlad Tepes into a sadist? It is true that many people have a certain innate sadism – we have all known boys who enjoy pulling wings off flies – but most case studies of sadists reveal that it is an acquired rather than a inborn trait. Perhaps the most typical case of the twentieth century is of Peter Kürten, the "Düsseldorf sadist", who committed a series of violent attacks in 1929; he used a knife, scissors or a hammer, and experienced orgasm as he stabbed or battered his victims (nine of whom died.) He was obsessed by the sight and smell of blood. On one occasion he even cut the head off a swan in a public park. Once he had experienced orgasm, he lost interest in the victim (although he had been known to dig up a corpse to commit further acts of outrage). This is what finally brought about his arrest; he raped and half-throttled a servant girl, then let her go; she was later able to lead police to his flat. Before his execution by decapitation, he remarked that his greatest wish was to hear the sound of his own blood running into the basket.

But Kürten became a sadist by slow stages. He was brought up in an overcrowded slum, and attempted incest with one of his sisters. (His father served a term in jail for attempting to rape the same girl). When he was eight, he became friendly with a sadistic dog catcher, who taught him to masturbate the dogs, and enjoyed committing acts of cruelty on them. As a teenager, Kürten used to practise bestiality with sheep, whom he would stab at the same time. But it was during long periods in prison for burglary that Kürten spent his days in sexual fantasy, until only the thought of blood or violence could induce a satisfactory orgasm. (He admitted that when he made love to his wife he had to imagine decapitating her).

Vlad also spent the most impressionable part of his life, the whole period of puberty, in prison. The result was an oversensitive ego that exploded into violence at the least suggestion of an affront. His subsequent history reveals the typically vengeful disposition of a man whose self-esteem was like a continually suppurating wound. Many of the stories of his cruelties reveal an oversensitivity amounting to paranoia.

But it would be a mistake to lose sight of the fact that in the fifteenth century, a man could commit acts of brutal sadism without arousing public condemnation. Because the "great" of the world were at a god-like distance from its peasants and beggars, their worst barbarities took on the unreality of legend, like the immoralities of the Greek gods. The chronicler who describes how Mohammed II was nauseated by the sight of thousands of impaled corpses near Tirgoviste goes on to say: "Even the emperor, overcome by amazement, admitted that he could not win the land from a man who does such great things. . ." The use of the word "great" causes a mild surprise; but in the fifteenth century, a man's "greatness" was judged by his power over the lives of others.

The circumstances that spawned the Russian tyrant Ivan the Terrible are curiously similar to those that produced Vlad Tepes.

Born in 1530, a century after Vlad, Ivan was the grandson of Ivan the Great. His father, Vassili III, died when he was three, and his mother – who became regent – when he was seven (probably poisoned). Until that time, Ivan had been spoilt and pampered; then, quite suddenly, he found himself ignored and treated with contempt. The government was taken over by a council of boyars, chief among whom were the Shuiskys; in retrospect, it seems amazing that Ivan and his younger brother were not simply murdered. Ivan had always been rather a brutal child. One of his favourite games was "splattering dogs", dropping them from the top of a high tower into the courtyard two hundred feet below. Now neglect and disdain turned him into a bully and a sadist, inflicting pain on anyone who was too weak not to fight back. He also enjoyed riding out with his friends and bodyguards into the streets of Moscow, then allowing the horses to ride at full gallop into crowds, trampling underfoot anyone who was too slow to get out of the way. (The teenage Shuiskys and their friends went one better: they enjoyed hunting human game and allowing their dogs to tear men to pieces.) Ivan, not unnaturally, believed that his chances of being crowned were minimal. When he was twelve, soldiers burst into his bedroom – they were pursuing a churchman who had defied the Shuiskys – but Ivan was totally convinced that he was about to die, and went on shaking uncontrollably for hours after the soldiers had left.

Finally, Prince Andrew Shuisky overreached himself. He and his partisans burst in on Ivan and his closest friend Fedor Vorontsov, and dragged Vorontsov outside to kill him; Ivan had to plead for his friend's life. Vorontsov was finally exiled.

In the Christmas of 1543, when he was thirteen, Ivan summoned the boyars before him, and delivered a lecture, telling them that they were misruling Russia and that they were utterly corrupt. This time, he said, only one of them would be punished, and he turned and pointed his finger at his pet detestation, Prince Andrew Shuisky. Shuisky fled, but was soon captured. Ivan then ordered that the hunting dogs should be set on him, and Shuisky was torn to pieces. After that, Ivan promptly broke his promise to confine himself to one victim, and ordered all Shuisky's supporters to be executed. From that time onward, no one doubted who ruled Russia.

One his his first acts as ruler was to recall his friend Vorontsov from exile. Two years later, Ivan suspected Vorontsov of plotting against him, and had him beheaded.

Yet he was not entirely a barbarian. He had a deep thirst for knowledge, and would often, to the disgust of his courtiers, lock himself away for days at a time, reading ancient books (many of which were Russian and Byzantine chronicles.) Yet there was a sense in which all this reading did him no good at all; hours of eye-strain left him tired, depressed, and prone to outbreaks of temper which resulted in more acts of cruelty and vengefulness.

As a recreation from too much reading, he pursued sexual pleasures, treating the wives and daughters of the merchants as his private harem. At seventeen he decided to have himself crowned, and instead of calling himself (like his predecessors)

Prince or Grand Duke, he chose the title Tsar, a word derived from Caesar, signifying that he was absolute ruler. He also decided to find himself a wife. Two thousand girls were summoned from all parts of Russia, and all were examined by doctors or midwives to ensure that they were virgins. As far as the parents were concerned, it was rather like a raffle, with the ultimate prize for the winning draw. It seems that Ivan's advisers and doctors were allowed to make the preliminary choices, and the other girls were sent home with presents. Ivan began to take an active part fairly late in the selection. When there were only ten girls left, he observed them privately, listened to their conversations, and often made his way into their bedroom to observe them asleep. Finally he settled on a tall, striking girl of gentle disposition called Anastasia Romanov; they were married on February 3, 1547. (In England at that time, Henry VIII had just died, and his ten year old son Edward crowned.)

His temper had not improved. While he was on honeymoon, burghers from the city of Pskov came to complain about a brutal governor. Ivan was so furious at having his honeymoon interupted that he ordered them all to be stripped naked and laid out on the ground, then poured spirits on them and personally set fire to their hair and beards. At that point he was interupted by a messenger – Moscow was on fire. Within twenty four hours, the greatest city in Russia was a heap of ashes. The mob blamed the Glinskys, the ruling family of boyars that had replaced the Shuiskys, and massacred all they could lay their hands on. Ivan, always a coward, hid in his palace, wondering if he would be next. Finally his courage came back, and he ordered his guards to seize the ringleaders and execute them on the spot.

The mob fled, but Ivan had learned his lesson. A deeply superstitious man, he believed this was a sign from God to tell him to mend his ways. For the next thirteen years he was an admirable Tsar, surrounding himself with good counsellors, many of lowly origin, inaugurating reforms, and conquering the Tartars of Kazan and Astrakhan. He established trade relations with England, now ruled by Bloody Mary. During this period many called him Ivan the Good.

It ended in 1560, with the death of his wife. The company of this sweet-natured girl had always soothed him; but she had borne seven children in ten years and her health had become poor. Ivan went almost mad with grief. All his natural paranoia revived, and he became convinced that she had been murdered. Inevitably, there was a bloody purge of those he suspected. He was to remarry five years later, but his new bride was an illiterate and half-savage Circassian princess, and she did nothing to restrain his increasing outbursts of fury. It is probably charitable to assume that he went insane after the age of thirty. From then until his death, his cruelty was unrestrained. No one in his court was allowed to express an opinion that was not the Tsar's. His two most reliable advisers were deposed. Many of his supporters fled to other countries, realising that any of them might be killed at any time if the Tsar conceived one of his insane suspicions. The defection of his childhood friend Prince Kurbsky hurt him most; Ivan transfixed the foot of the messenger to the earth when the news was brought to him, and after the man had read aloud Kurbsky's farewell message had him tortured.

In his mid-thirties he decided on a curious action that is somehow typically Russian. He wandered out of the capital with no announced destination, and went to the village of Alexandrov, a hundred miles from Moscow. After several weeks had passed in anxiety and bewilderment, he announced that he had abdicated. Instead of heaving a sigh of relief, his courtiers immediately sent a mission to implore him to return. He finally consented. It seems that there was genuine fear and alarm when he disappeared, as, in spite of his cruelties, he was regarded as the indispensible figurehead. As a condition for his return, Ivan specified that all his actions should in future be condoned by the church and the boyars (both of whom had often done their best to restrain him.) Back in Moscow, he immediately took advantage of his new license to begin a campaign of robbery and murder. Six friends of Kurbsky were beheaded; another was impaled. He went on to divide Russia into two parts: his own personal property, which he called the *Oprichina*, or widow's portion, and the Zemschina, which belonged to the nobles. He established a political security force to run the *Oprichina*, whose task was to spy on his enemies and destroy them; hence Ivan may be regarded as the inventor of the modern police state. His black-robed inquisitors toured the country executing the Tsar's vengeance, which in fact meant burning and torturing as they felt inclined.

His paranoia reached a climax in the destruction of the city of Novgorod. Ivan had an idea that Novgorod intended treason, so he marched there with an army, burning, raping and looting on the way. He arrived at the city in early 1570, and had a timber wall built around it to prevent any inhabitants from fleeing. Then, for the next five weeks, he directed an orgy of sadism worthy of Dracula. Every day several thousand inhabitants were tortured to death in the presence of the Tsar and his depraved son Ivan. All kinds of refinements were invented: husbands and wives were roasted alive or beaten to death in one another's presence; children were murdered in front of their mothers. More than 60,000 people were murdered – more than in any one of Dracula's orgies.

The Tsar then went on to Pskov with the intention of continuing the orgy of torture, but he altered his mind when he arrived, presumably because even his blood lust had been sated at Novgorod. The citizens received him kneeling, and assured him that his mercy was beyond belief.

The remainder of Ivan's life followed the same curious pattern as the earlier part. His sexuality was unremitting (and it has been suspected that his insanity was the result of syphilis), his murders and cruelties never ceased. He carried a pointed iron staff, and frequently impaled courtiers who irritated him; one day, in a rage, he killed his own son – no great loss, since Ivan was as evil as his father. But he also talked periodically of becoming a monk, and on one occasion actually placed his crown on the head of a Tartar prince in his retinue and allowed him to rule for a year. In the city of Wenden in Livonia, against which he conducted a war for a quarter of a century, hundreds of citizens preferred to blow themselves up in a castle rather than fall into his hands. He then tortured to death all the remaining citizens of the town. His own cousellors and favourites became his victims. One of the worst and most debauched was Prince Ivan Viscovaty. The Tsar had him hung upside down and sliced to death; then he and his son Ivan went to Viscovaty's house and raped the grief-stricken widow and daughter.

Ivan's death, at the age of fifty four, is somehow typical. He had become sexually incapable, and felt tired and ill. He summoned a number of soothsayers to the court, and they forecast his death for

March 18, 1584. Characteristically, Ivan told them that they would be burnt alive on that day if he was still alive. Towards midnight on the 17th, Ivan reminded the soothsayers that they were to die the next morning. They pointed out that the day could not be said to have ended until the setting of the sun. The next day he played chess with Boris Godunov, one of his advisers, but his king kept falling down. Then Ivan fell backwards, and a few minutes later, he was dead.

The greatest mystery is that no one assassinated him in the early years of his reign. Stranger still, there was genuine mourning for him when he died. Even the title by which he became known to history, Ivan the Terrible, is a mistranslation; in fact, *strozny* means awe-inspiring. Again, we have to accept this strange fact that in these remote times of general misery and hardship, a cruel emperor was regarded as a kind of scourge sent from God, and revered accordingly.

The lives of the tyrants we have considered so far seem designed as illustrations of Lord Acton's dictum that power corrupts. Yet this is an oversimplification. History is full of rulers who were not corrupted by power: Asoka, Hadrian, Marcus Aurelius, Charlemagne, Kubla Khan. The truth seems to be more straightforward. There is an uncontrolled element in all of us, a "spoilt child". If it is allowed too much freedom at an early stage, it becomes ungovernable, and the result is often sadism. This applies as much to western Europeans as to Roman emperors or Eastern tyrants. One of the strangest and most disturbing examples in western European history is the man John Addington Symonds referred to as Marechal de Retz; the commoner spelling of his name is de Rais.

The problem of Gilles de Rais was that he was the wealthiest man in Europe. His father had married a landed heiress, and Gilles was born in 1404 in the château of Machécoul, where he would commit so many of his atrocities. His father died when he was nine, and his mother immediately married again and abandoned her two children. And so once again we can observe the classic pattern – a child who had been treated as the lord of the manor suddenly finding himself in the position of a nobody. When his mother died two years later, Gilles and his brother René must have felt alone in the world. Their father's will made provision for them to be brought up by a cousin and educated by two priests; instead they were sent to live with their grandfather, Jean de Craon, who had a violent temper, but was too wrapped up in his own affairs to pay attention to his grandsons. His own son had been killed at the battle of Agincourt in 1415, so that Gilles became heir to the entire vast fortune. He was an intelligent child who read Latin fluently and loved music. But he had a taste for the "forbidden" and secretly devoured Suetonius, with his details of the sexual excesses of the Roman emperors. Since Gilles himself was homosexual, these stories must have encouraged the tendency to sexual fantasy, to which he admitted at his trial.

Gilles came from a family of mediaeval knights, and was himself trained as a soldier. The Hundred Years War with the English had been going on since 1338, so a training in arms was essential for any gentleman. When Gilles was sixteen, his grandfather married him off to a rich heiress, Catherine de Thouars, whose estates abutted those of the de Rais in Brittany and Poitou. Five years later, he went to the court of the Dauphin, the uncrowned heir to the throne, and made a considerable impression with his good looks and fine breeding. In 1429 he was at Chinon when a seventeen year old peasant girl named Jeanne, from the village of Domremy, demanded to see the Dauphin, and told him that she had been sent to defeat the English, who were now laying siege to Orléans. The Dauphin thought she was mad, but decided it was worth a try. He ordered Gilles to accompany "the Maid" (la pucelle) to Orleans, perhaps because he had noticed that Gilles was fascinated by the girl's boyish figure and peasant vitality. Gilles fought by her side when she raised the siege of Orléans, and again at Patay, when she once more defeated the English. At twenty four, Gilles was a national hero. When the Dauphin decided to have himself crowned, it was Gilles who was sent to collect the holy oil with which the king was to be anointed. After the coronation, Gilles was appointed Marshall of France and allowed to include the *fleur de lys* in his coat of arms. But after her military triumphs, Joan of Arc's career was soon undermined by jealous ministers, and the king was too weak and self-indulgent to withstand the pressure. In the following year she was captured by the English, and burned at Rouen in 1431; she was only nineteen.

Gilles still had one more martial exploit to come – the deliverance of Lagny from the English. Then he retired to his grandfather's estate. After the years of glory, he seems to have found life unbearably dull. And during the course of the following year, according to his later confession, he committed his first sex murder, that of a boy. His grandfather seems to have suspected what had happened; he willed his sword and cuirass to the younger brother René. The grandfather died in the following year, and Gilles was suddenly able to do what he liked.

What he liked, it seems, was to sodomize young boys, then cut their throats and disembowell them. The evidence at his trial makes it clear that he was a classic case of sexual sadism. Like Peter Kürten, he was obsessed by the sight of blood and the thought of violence. He had undoubtedly been fantasising about it since he was an adolescent. But unlike most sex criminals of the twentieth century, he was not obliged to hunt his own prey. His cousins Roger de Briqueville and Gilles de Sille were both homosexuals; so was his steward Henriet Griard; they were more than willing to procure boys for his pleasure. One of these was a youth called Poitou; he was brought to the château and raped, after which Gilles prepared to cut his throat. At this point, Gilles de Sille pointed out that Poitou was such a handsome boy that he would make an admirable page. So Poitou was allowed to live, and to become one of Gilles' most trusted retainers.

Gilles' attacks of sadism seem to have descended on him like an epileptic fit, and turned him into a kind of maniac. A boy would be lured to the castle on some pretext, and once inside Gilles' chamber, was hung from the ceiling on a rope or chain. But before he had lost consciousness, he was taken down and reassured that Gilles meant him no harm. Then he would be stripped and raped, after which Gilles, or one of his cronies, would cut this throat or decapitate him – they had a special sword called a *braquemard* for removing the head. But Gilles was still not sated; he would continue to sexually abuse the dead body, sometimes cutting open the stomach, then squatting in the entrails and masturbating. When he reached a climax he would collapse in a faint, and be carried off to his bed, where he would remain unconscious for hours. His accomplices would meanwhile dismember and burn the body. On some occasions, he later confessed, two children were procured, and each obliged to watch the other being raped and tortured.

Gilles was not merely sexually deranged; he was also a reckless spendthrift. He surrounded himself with a retinue of two hundred knights, for whom he provided. He loved to give banquets and fêtes; in 1435, when the city of Orléans celebrated its deliverance by Joan of Arc, Gilles presented a long mystery play about the siege, with enormous sets and a cast of hundreds, playing, of course, the leading role himself. He also provided food and wine for the spectators. Like a Roman emperor he must have felt that he was virtually a god.

Unfortunately, his money was already running out. In a mere three years he had spent what would now be the equivalent of millions of pounds. Even at Orléans, he realised that he did not possess enough ready cash to pay all the bills (including lodgings for his vast retinue), and had to pawn some of his possessions to pay hoteliers. Back at Machecoul, he had to sell some of his most valuable estates. His brother was so alarmed that he persuaded the king to issue an interdict forbidding any further sales of land.

For a man of Gilles' unbridled temperament, this was an intolerable position. He went into a gloomy and self-pitying retirement. And now, suddenly, he saw a possible solution. Years before, when he first went to court, he had borrowed a book on alchemy from an Angevin knight who had been imprisoned for heresy. Alchemy was prohibited by law, and for a man with Gilles' romantic craving for "the forbidden", this must have been an additional incentive to learn more about it. Now, ten years later, with his coffers empty, he realised that alchemy might be the answer to his problems. He asked a priest named Eustache Blanchet to find him a magician. Several were tried, but the results were poor – one of them, a man named Fontanelle, succeeded in conjuring up twenty crows. The others were not even able to conjure up a few birds. But Fontanelle also claimed he had conjured up a demon called Barron; and it was clear to Gilles that, if his magical operations were to succeed, he was going to need the active co-operation of Barron and his fellow demons.

At that time, it was taken for granted that "magic" was performed through the agency of the Devil, the ancient tradition of "white magic" having long ago been stamped out by the church. Now in spite of his taste for killing children, Gilles remained a devout Catholic; so deciding to invoke the Devil must have seemed a far more frightening step than murder. But finally, he and his cousin Gilles de Sille locked themselves in the basement of his castle at Tiffauges, together with a magician, and prepared to converse with demons. The magician warned them solemnly not to make the sign of the cross, or their lives would be in great danger. Sille stayed by the window, prepared to jump out; Gilles ventured fearfully into the magic circle and watched the beginning of the conjuration. Suddenly, a prayer to Our Lady came into his head, and he told the magician what had happened; the magician instantly ordered him to leave the magic circle. Gilles obeyed, making the sign of the cross from force of habit. Then he and his cousin hastened from the room. Fiascos like this were discouraging, but Gilles felt he now had no alternative.

Gilles now began to receive signs and portents that his soul was in danger; one magician drowned on his way to the castle, and another died soon after he arrived. Gilles was advised that his only way of learning to make gold was to agree to sell his soul to the Devil, but he refused to go this far. All the same, he needed money so badly that there seemed no other way than continuing with his magical experiments. In 1439, he sent the priest Blanchet to Italy to search for a more skilled magician; Blanchet returned with a "clerk in minor orders" called François Prelati, a young man of great charm – and also, apparently, a homosexual. It is hard to know whether he was simply a confidence trickster, or whether he had some genuine knowledge of the magic arts; it seems clear that Gilles found him immensely attractive and trusted him completely. Prelati told him that they would have to offer a child's blood and parts of its body as a sacrifice to the Devil; there was no problem about this, and Gilles hastened to sodomize and murder another young boy. But he still refused to take the final step, of selling his soul to the Devil. Prelati told him that in that case, he would have to continue the conjurations alone. During one of these sessions, Gilles and his cousin heard loud thumps from inside the room; they looked in and found Prelati "so hurt that he could hardly stand up". He explained that he had been beaten by the demon Barron, and had to take to his bed for several days, during which time Gilles nursed him tenderly. On another occasion, he rushed out to tell

Gilles that he had finally conjured up a heap of gold. Gilles rushed back to see it, but Prelati was there first; as he opened the door, he staggered back and shouted that it was guarded by a huge green serpent. Gilles fled. When he returned, the gold had vanished, leaving only piles of dust. . .

During all this time, he continued to murder children, girls as well as boys. In the case of girls, he rubbed his erect member against the stomach or between the thighs until he ejaculated, "saying he had more pleasure and less pain than acting in nature". Afterwards he would frequently play with the heads. It was the fear that excited him, the feeling of having the power of life and death over another human being. The records of the case contain a list of children who vanished:

"Lost, at La Rochebernart, the child of the woman Peronne, a child who did go to school and apply himself to his book with exceeding diligence." "Lost at St Etienne de Montluc, the son of Guillaume Brice, and this was a poor man and sought alms." "Lost at Machecoul, the son of Georget le Barbier, who was seen a certain day knocking apples from a tree behind the hotel Rondeau, and who since hath not been seen." "Lost at Thonaye, the child of Mathelin Thouars, and he had been heard to cry and lament, and the said child was about twelve years of age." At Machecoul, the day of Pentecost, mother and father Sergent leave their eight year old boy at home, and when they return from the fields "they did not find the said child of eight years. . ." "At Chantelou, two little children of the age of nine who were brothers and the children of Robin Pavot of the aforesaid place, and since that time neither have they been seen nor doth any know what became of them." A widow living close to the castle reported the disappearance of her eight year old son, "a comely lad, white of skin and very capable." Two weeks later another boy vanished, and there was an outcry in the village. Gilles decided that something had to be done, and sent his cousin to explain that the boys had been given as part of a ransom for his brother, who was being held by the English; they would be trained as pages. . .

During his years of murder, Gilles often came close to discovery. In 1437, his family heard that he intended to sell the castle of Champtoce, in spite of the royal interdict; they hastened to seize it. Gilles was terrified; he had left the mutilated bodies of dozens of children there. He was also afraid that the castle of Machecoul would be next – the remains of many children had been thrown into a locked tower. He and his companions removed about forty dismembered bodies from Machecoul. When he regained control of Champtoce in 1438 he hastened to remove another forty or so corpses, which had apparently remained unnoticed.

In July 1440, Gilles made his fatal mistake. He had sold a castle called Mermorte to Geoffroy de Ferron, treasurer to the Duke of Brittany, Gilles' suzerain. For some reason, Gilles decided that he was entitled to repossess the castle, which had not yet been occupied by its new owner. The keys, it seemed, were in the hands of Geoffroy's brother, a priest called Jean de Ferron. Here Gilles' impatience was his undoing. Instead of waiting until Jean de Ferron was in his home, he led his men into the church of St Etienne de Mermorte soon after mass, and had the priest dragged outside, where he was beaten. By entering a church and permitting violence, Gilles had committed sacrilege, a capital offence. The Duke of Brittany was delighted. If Gilles was convicted and executed, his lands would be forfeit. So the Duke lost no time in complaining to the Bishop of Nantes and starting proceedings for sacrilege, adding a charge of heresy for good measure. Gilles' companions later revealed that, even on this expedition to recover his castle, he had been overcome by his craving for rape and murder. After leaving the church, he had halted for the night in the town of Vannes and taken lodging in a house near the bishop's palace. One of the ex-choristers of his private chapel, André Bouchet, had brought him a ten year old boy. Since his present lodging was not private enough for rape and murder, the boy was taken to another house near the market, and there sodomised and decapitated; the body was thrown into the latrines of the house, where the smell was less likely to cause its discovery.

Meanwhile, the Duke of Brittany had imposed a huge fine on Gilles, aware that Gilles would be unable to pay. He also began an investigation into the disappearance of hundreds of children. Gilles committed his final murder in August 1440 – it is a reasonable assumption that he would have gone on indefinitely if he had not been arrested – but was arrested soon after, and brought before the judges on 13 October, 1440. The Duke of Brittany was so certain of the verdict that he disposed of his own share of Gilles' lands fifteen days before the trial began. His confidence was not unfounded. The indictment was forty-nine paragraphs long, and included many charges of child murder. Gilles was at first arrogant and defiant; but after being threatened with excommunication and torture, he suddenly gave way, and made a full confession. Some historians have suggested that Gilles was "framed", and that the duke and the bishop conspired to seize his lands. The detail of his confession makes this virtually impossible. He described the murders at length, and his accomplices gave damning evidence against him. He confessed to a hundred and forty murders. The actual number is almost certainly more than two hundred. Charged with him were his steward Henriet Griard and his page Etiène Corillaut, called Poitou. Many parents gave evidence about the disappearance of their children – a man named Ayse described how his ten year old son had gone to seek alms at the castle at Machecoul, and never returned. Ayse learned later from a serving maid that the child had been offered a meal and had entered the castle.

In court, Gilles sobbed, confessed his sins, and begged the parents for forgiveness. And they, oddly enough, also sobbed and declared that they forgave him. They knew that his real sin was heresy, and that this meant eternal damnation.

On 25 October, Gilles was excommunicated; the following day he was marched to the gibbet in Nantes, together with his two companions, and there strangled. His corpse was placed on a pyre, but his relatives were allowed to remove his body before the flames reached it, and he was interred in the nearby Carmelite church. His two companions were less lucky; they were burned alive.

H.G. Wells comments on the case in a book called *Crux Ansata*:

All this was the behaviour of an uncontrolled upper-form schoolboy with a belief in his luck . . . and an unanalysable disposition to torment fags . . . He was cruel; by all our standards, he was hideously cruel; he delighted in the tormenting of children; and the points best worth discussing about him here are, first, whether he was an exceptional sinner, or whether his crimes were the outcome of a mental disposition that has always been operative since that wretched congestion of mankind that is called civilisation began; and secondly, and

*more important for our present purpose, how far the religious
beliefs and practices of Catholic Christendom in the fifteenth
century really condemned his abominations.*

Wells's own answer to this second question becomes apparent
when he writes: ". . . his body was saved from being burnt by 'four
or five dames and demoiselles of great estate', who removed his
body from the pyre built so that he would fall into it. Manifestly
they thought no great evil of what he had done. . ."

Wells is making an interesting point. We find the crimes of Gilles
de Rais too horrible to contemplate; his contemporaries thought
them less important than the fact that his soul was damned. We
can observe much the same attitude in the contemporaries of
Vlad the Impaler and Ivan the Terrible. Our own century may
have produced an appalling number of sadists and serial killers,
but at least we regard them with horror rather than a sneaking
admiration.

In Hungary, the tradition of Vlad the Impaler was continued by a
female descendant of Stephen Bathory, the general who had helped
Vlad to reconquer Wallachia. Her name was Countess Elizabeth
Bathory, and until recent years there was little written about her
in English, and even these few accounts were inaccurate. In the
early 1970s, Raymond T.McNally and Radu Florescu, researching
a book on Dracula, went to Hungary and studied the original trial
documents. What they discovered was as follows.

Countess Elizabeth Bathory was born in 1560 in a part of
Hungary close to the Carpathians; she came of a distinguished
family. Her cousin Gyorgy Thurzo, was Prime Minister, and she
was related to Sigismund Bathory, Prince of Transylvania. There
seems to have been some degree of oddness in the family: her
brother was sexually insatiable, one uncle was a devil worshipper,
and an aunt was a witch and a lesbian.

At the age of fifteen Elizabeth was married to Count Ferencz
Nadasdy, and King Mathias sent them a wedding present. They
lived in Castle Csejthe, in the Nyitra country in northern Hungary.
The count was a soldier, and in those turbulent times spent much of
his time fighting, not only against the Turks but against Spanish and
Italian mercenaries employed by the Hapsburgs on the northern

frontier. His exploits made him a national hero, known as "The Black Hero of Hungary." But while the Count was away fighting, his passionate young bride was left alone in the castle, her newly awakened sexuality doomed to frustration.

Her childhood nurse, Ilona Joo, had some knowledge of witchcraft, but it seems to have been one of her husband's manservants, Thorko, who introduced her to practical "occultism". She wrote to her husband: "Thorko taught me a lovely new one. Catch a black hen and beat it to death with a white cane. Keep the blood and smear a little of it on your enemy. If you get no chance to smear it on his body, obtain one of his garments and smear that instead."

Life in the castle bored her, and she hated her mother-in-law. Like Gilles de Rais, she surrounded herself with astrologers and "magicians", including a "witch" named Dorottya Szentes and a "forest witch" named Darvula. And, inevitably, she was unfaithful to her husband. Little is known of the affair except that her lover was a young nobleman who was reputed to be a vampire, and that she briefly eloped with him. Further details are unknown, except that her husband forgave her, which would seem to indicate that he was under the spell of his young bride.

During the first ten years of her marriage Elizabeth bore no children, no doubt because her husband was seldom at home. But between 1585 an 1590, she gave birth to three boys and a girl. Then, in 1600, her husband died, and once again his bride was condemned to sexual frustration. On the other hand, as a widow, she was now mistress of the castle. She lost no time in sending away her hated mother-in-law. She also began to indulge in lesbian practices with her two maids, Barsovny and Otvos, chosen for their beauty. (One account of the case states that this had been going on for many years.)

According to McNally and Florescu, her sadistic practices began by accident when she lost her temper with a maid who pulled her hair while combing it, and slapped her so hard that she drew blood, probably making the girl's nose bleed. Her own hands became bloodstained, and she convinced herself that the skin where the blood had fallen had become fresh and white. This suggested that she had discovered the secret of eternal youth. So the maid was murdered by her servants Thorko and Johannes Ujvary, and her blood drained into a bath. Elizabeth then stripped and sat in the blood, rubbing it all over her body.

In effect, Elizabeth Bathory went on to become a female version of Gilles de Rais, except that she was not interested in disembowelling her victims or using them for sexual purposes. Her servants kidnapped children and teenage girls from the surrounding area, and some of these were kept in dungeons and fattened – Elizabeth believed that the fatter they were, the more blood they had in their veins. She was totally convinced that her baths in blood were keeping her young. In fact, she seems to have stayed remarkably youthful. During the course of ten years, she killed about fifty girls – at least, this is the number of corpses eventually discovered buried in the castle grounds.

Rumours of the murders came to the attention of King Mathias of Hungary long before he finally decided to take action. But the turning point in the countess's career came when one of her victims escaped and went to the authorities. Elizabeth's cousin, Count Gyorgy Thurzo, led a band of soldiers to Castle Csejthe on the night of 30 December, 1610; in the main hall they found a girl whose body had been drained of blood, and another who was covered with small punctures made by a sharp instrument. In the dungeons there were more girls in the same condition. It seems clear that the countess had decided to abandon her original method of killing the victim, and instead milked them like cows until they died.

Countess Bathory was placed under house arrest. Her trial took place at Bitcse in January and February 1611, although she herself never appeared in the courtroom, and refused to plead innocent or guilty. The major domo, Johannes Ujvary, testified that he knew of about 37 girls who had been killed, six of whom he had brought to the castle with promises of jobs as maids. Their veins were then pierced, and the blood drained into dishes; sometimes the countess did it herself, sometimes it was Dorottya Szentes and Ilona Joo.

At the conclusion of the trial, judge Theodosius de Szulo pronounced sentences of death on Thorko, Ujvary, Darvuka and the two maids Barsovnu and Otvos; all were to be beheaded. Ilona Joo and Dorottya Szentes were to have their fingers torn out one by one, then to be burned alive. The countess herself was not sentenced; although the king had demanded the death penalty, he finally agreed to Thurzo's demand that it should be delayed indefinitely. Instead, stonemasons were sent to Castle Csejthe, and Elizabeth Bathory was walled up in her own chamber, with only a small aperture through which she might receive food. She lived on for another three years, until she was fifty four. On 21 August 1614, a new guard who wanted to take a look at the famous beauty peeped through the aperture, and saw that the countess was lying still on the floor; the chamber was broken open, and Elizabeth Bathory was found to be dead. Discovered among her belongings was a curious document written on the eve of her arrest; it was an invocation to the Devil, who was asked to send her ninety nine demon cats, who were to tear out the hearts of King Mathias, Count Thurzo, and various other officials who were involved in her arrest. The document also seems to indicate that she knew the castle was going to be raided; yet she took no action to hide evidence of her crimes. It seems conceivable that, like so many other mass murderers, she had finally developed a curious indifference to her own fate.

Elizabeth Bathory was virtually "the last of the monsters" – at least in Europe. In effect, history was changing its rules, and the age of the old-fashioned tyrant was drawing to a close. In 1542, a canon of the Church named Nicholas Copernicus published a book called *On the Revolution of the Heavenly Bodies*, which suggested that the earth went around the sun, and not vice versa. By the time of the death of Countess Bathory, an astronomer named Galileo had virtually proved it. Mediaeval superstition, and the cruelty that went with it, were slowly giving way to the new spirit of science and enquiry. Before the end of the century, Isaac Newton's *Principia* was able to specify the mathematical laws that governed the heavens. The real monsters of the seventeenth century were "inquisitors" like Franz Buirmann of Bamberg and the Essex clergyman Matthew Hopkins, whose job was to seek out and burn witches; such men often raped as well as tortured their victims. In the 1630s, Buirmann burned 150 people in only two villages; Hopkins was probably responsible for several hundred deaths. But by the second half of the century, the tide had turned; a general revulsion set in, and many of the "witch finders", like Hopkins, had to flee from angry crowds. In America, in Salem, Massachusetts, the witchcraft "epidemic" of 1692 ended abruptly in the following year when common sense suddenly prevailed. In the dawning age of reason, the kind of ignorance and superstition that had nurtured the "monsters" of the Middle Ages was an anachronism.

As the new philosophy of materialism began to undermine religious faith, the Church itself began to experience a breakdown in morals. This was particularly evident in France. The notorious "Affair of the Poisons" of the 1670s revealed that priests had been performing Black Masses in which babies were sacrificed, while a number of disgusting old women who claimed to have supernatural powers sold poisons that enabled their customers to dispose of unwanted spouses. King Louis XIV finally decided to suspend the trial – held in a room called the "Chambre Ardente" (candlelit chamber) because he was afraid that the scandal would bring the monarchy into disrepute; in 1709 he also ordered that all the evidence should be destroyed, but a court transcript survived by accident. By the end of that century, Louis' grandson had been guillotined, and the age of absolute monarchs was at an end.

The death throes of the old dogmatic Christianity were to produce one more "monster" whose bloodthirsty fantasy was to eclipse all his predecessors; no one was to devise more horrific cruelties than Donatien Alphonse Francois de Sade, the man whose name became synonymous with torture and murder. It therefore comes as something of a surprise to learn that this incarnation of wickedness never actually committed a murder or indeed, any other sort of crime. All his cruelties took place in his imagination. He is nevertheless an important figure in the history of crime, since he is virtually a one-man textbook of criminology. He might also be regarded as the patron saint of serial killers like Leonard Lake, and the "Moors murderer" Ian Brady, who justified his murder and rape of children with arguments from de Sade.

De Sade's career also enables us to look more closely at the psychology of the kind of cruelty that has characterised the "monsters" described in this chapter. He was born in 1740, the son of a count in the dipomatic service and a lady in waiting to the Princess de Condé. Brought up by servants in the palatial Hotel de Condé, he soon developed into the most disagreeable kind of spoilt brat. He later remarked in a passage that is almost certainly autobiographical: "It seemed to me that everything ought to give

in to me, and that the whole universe should humour my whims",
a comment that applies to every sadist from Tiberius to Ivan the
Terrible. In spite of which, de Sade was not a bad natured youth.
His chief peculiarity was a fairly harmless desire to flog and be
flogged, preferably on the bare behind. As a young army officer,
he had many mistresses – he had a taste for actresses – and spent
much of his time in brothels, paying large sums to girls who would
permit themselves to be whipped and sodomized. All this was
relatively normal for an imperious young aristocrat of the time,
and would certainly not have prevented him from pursuing a
distinguished career in the diplomatic service. But Sade's downfall
was another peculiarity, which dated from his childhood in a Jesuit
boarding school – an almost pathological hatred of religion. Sade
was a philosopher as well as a libertine, and agreed entirely with
thinkers like Condillac, La Mettrie and Holbach, who regarded
God as one of the odder delusions of the human mind. Even that
would have done him no harm if he had kept it to himself. But
one day in October 1763, when he was twenty three, Sade spent a
night trying to convert a young prostitute to atheism, masturbated
on a crucifix, and made her trample on it at gunpoint. The girl
reported all this to the procuress, who passed it on to the police.
Sade was arrested for the first time. The king, Louis XV, had him
imprisoned for two weeks, after which he was allowed to return
in disgrace to his home in the country. Five years later he again
drew the attention of the law when he picked up a beggar woman,
lured her back to his house, then tied her up and whipped her. She
escaped through a window, and Sade's mother-in-law was forced
to buy her off with a sum that amounted to a fortune. Once again,
Sade returned to the country in disgrace.

Three years later, he spent a day in Marseilles with his
manservant, whom he paid to sodomize him. They picked up
some prostitutes and indulged in an orgy of sodomy and flogging,
then went to another prostitute and gave her an aphrodisiac; when
she refused to permit sodomy, they left. Soon after, the girl was
violently sick. Arsenic poisoning was suspected, and the police
informed. Since sodomy was a capital offence, Sade and his
manservant were forced to flee. He also took with him his
wife's younger sister, an apprentice nun who had fallen in love
with him. As far as his mother in law was concerned, this was

the last straw, and she became his most implacable persecutor, and used her influence to procure a warrant for his arrest. He was taken into custody, but after four months in prison, his wife arranged his escape. He was sentenced to death in his absence. Sade should now have learned his lesson, but he was incorrigible. Still in hiding, he filled the house with young female servants, whom he flogged so vigorously that they needed hospital treatment. And when his mother in law heard that he had even persuaded his wife to join in the orgies, decided to put an end to the scandal, and had him arrested again. And in spite of the fact that the death sentence had now been lifted, he was incarcerated for the next thirteen years.

For a man of Sade's imperious temperament, imprisonment was a nightmare. The ventilation in his cell was almost non-existent, and rats and mice ran over him when he tried to sleep. These conditions turned a spoilt but fairly well-meaning scapegrace into an implacable "enemy of society". He had nothing to do but brood and nurture his resentment. In Shaw's *Heartbreak House*, one of the characters asks Captain Shotover: "How long can you concentrate on a feeling without risking having it fixed in your consciousness all the rest of your life?", and Shotover answers: "Ninety minutes. An hour and a half." Sade brooded on his hatred for day after day, month after month, year after year. Not surprisingly, he went a little crazy. And since it was the only way in which he could express his resentment, he began writing books.

The first of his works, *A Dialogue Between a Priest and a Dying Man*, describes how the dying man scorns the priest's pleas for repentance. There is no God, he declares, only a mindless Nature which is indifferent to good and evil. Nature has created our bodies for pleasure, and this should be the main purpose of our lives. Since the sexual orgasm is the most intense pleasure man knows, it deserves to be our primary objective. The next room, says the dying man, is full of beautiful girls who are waiting to console his last hours, and if the priest has any sense, he will take his pick of them. Incredibly, the priest accepts this offer, "and in their arms became a man corrupted by nature because he had been unable to explain what corrupt nature was."

The dialogue typifies Sade's total lack of realism. A "dying man" would hardly be in a state to have an orgy. And a priest would certainly not be converted to atheism by such absurd and feeble arguments. But Sade was not concerned with realism. The very essence of the sadist, from Gilles de Rais to Leonard Lake, is that he focuses all his attention on a world of fantasy inside his own head, *and makes a determined attempt to convert external reality into fantasy*. But he is like a dreamer trying to stay asleep; consciousness supervenes whether he likes it or not. Sade's novels, with their total lack of realism, reveal a kind of grim determination not to wake up.

In his prison cell at Vincennes, and then in the Bastille, there was very little to anchor Sade's mind to the external world. Three years after writing the *Dialogue*, he began a work called *The 120 Days of Sodom* that was designed to be the most comprehensive sexual fantasy ever attempted. It is about four wealthy and influential libertines (one a bishop and another a Lord Chief Justice) who decide to spend four months at a château in the country, systematically indulging every form of sexual satisfaction. They hire four brothel madames, whose job is to procure a small army of men, girls and children (mostly kidnapped), and also to relate, in a kind of obscene parody of the *Arabian Nights*, their lifelong experiences of debauched clients. Also present are the four daughters of the libertines, all of whom have been deflowered anally by their own fathers at an early age. The plan of the book is to work up from minor perversions, such as a priest who likes to masturbate in front of seven year old girls while he mutters obscenities, to perverts who enjoy roasting children alive and shooting pregnant women out of cannons.

Sade wrote this vast novel in minute handwriting on a continuous roll of paper; but when he was finally freed, at the time of the French Revolution, it was left behind in his cell. It was discovered accidentally in the following century, and first printed in Germany.

By the time of the French Revolution, in 1789, Sade had written fifteen books, including the early version of the work by which he is best known, *Justine, or the Misfortunes of Virtue*. This is the story of an innocent girl who is thrown out upon the world after her father's bankruptcy. A rich banker makes a determined attempt to rape her, but she is saved when he ejaculates prematurely. Condemned to death for a crime she did not commit, Justine escapes and falls into the hands of robbers, who commit various perverted sex acts on her, but leave her virginity intact. After more hair-raising adventures with villains, perverts and libertines, she feels she has finally found safety in a monastery, only to discover that the monks are more depraved than anyone she has met so far. There, at last, she loses her virginity – with a great deal of pain – and is forced into sexual slavery. At last she is rescued by her sister Juliette, a highly successful courtesan who has lived a luxurious life of sin. But just as it looks as if Justine is about to live happily ever after, she is struck by lightning. In a later version of the book, her corpse is then ravished by necrophiles. Sade's point could hardly be clearer. His view of life resembles that of a demented Jonathan Swift: in this utterly corrupt and rotten world, the only successful people are those who embrace wickedness. The virtuous are trampled underfoot and finally destroyed. Moreover, their virtue causes providence to shower them with misfortunes. Sade's philosophy is an exaggerated version of Darwin's survival of the fittest.

When he was finally released from prison by the revolutionary mob, Sade became a kind of hero; he even wrote a pamphlet called *Frenchmen, One More Effort if You Wish to Become Republicans*, in which he argued that now the French had done away with the king, they had to take the final logical step and do away with God. In fact, even in revolutionary Paris no one was ready for Sade's totally antisocial attitudes. But they felt that his heart was in the right place, and he was even made a member of a revolutionary tribunal which had the power of life and death over "enemies of the people". One of the "enemies" who now fell into Sade's power was his mother-in-law. Incredibly, he behaved with Christian magnanimity and spared her life.

Now, at last, he was able to publish his works. Some of his plays were performed, and *Justine* quickly became a *succès de scandale*. He went on to write a second and far more violent and obscene version, in which Justine loses her virtue a great deal earlier when she helps a young traveller to escape from robbers who intend to kill him; he knocks her unconscious, rapes her, then takes her money and leaves her tied to a tree. All this was lavishly illustrated with obscene prints.

It took Sade's contemporaries very little time to recognise that his aim was not really satire or the denunciation of corruption of the old régime. A work called *Philosophy in the Bedroom* made it clear that he was basically a pornographer who was aroused to a frenzy of sexual excitement by the very idea of the "forbidden". The book is about an innocent young girl who is corrupted by an incestuous brother and sister, and introduced to every form of sexual pleasure. But even here, de Sade is more concerned to expound his philosophy of materialism and atheism than to describe sexual activities. He is a man with an obsession that knows no bounds; he loves to get into the pulpit and sermonise endlessly about the importance of abandoning all moral scruples.

In 1779, Sade's publisher brought out his most vast work to date: the ten volume novel that combined the story of the virtuous Justine with that of her totally immoral sister Juliette. The aim was to rewrite the endless catalogue of cruelty that Sade believed he had lost in *The 120 Days of Sodom*. Juliette describes how she was introduced to debauchery at her convent school by the lesbian mother superior, and the results are sometimes unconsciously funny. ('By Zues's crotch' said Mother Delbéne, lifting herself to her feet, 'That was an orgasm if ever I saw one!/) She then moves into a brothel, where she meets two libertines who guide her in the paths of debauchery. In the course of the novel she seduces (then murders) her father, engages in a sexual orgy with the Pope, and finally allows one of her lovers to burn her daughter alive while he brings her to orgasm.

Four years later, in 1801, de Sade and his publisher were arrested, and the publisher denounced him as the author of *Justine* and other anonymous works of sadistic pornography. Sade was incarcerated again, and spent the remaining fourteen years of his life in a kind of insane asylum. He wrote more novels, and it is interesting to observe that these contain a minimum of cruelty and obscenity. The reason may have been a desire to find a publisher; but one of the few that has survived, *The Marquise de Grange*, gives the impression that the sadistic orgies of imagination had left him drained of the desire to contemplate cruelty. He finally died, still in prison, in 1814, at the age of seventy four.

Now it is admittedly the reaction of any normal and healthy person to say: "Why do we bother with such a silly idiot? He is obviously a mental case". Even in our uncensorious age, Sade's ideas can never be absorbed and "normalised" – the day will never come when *The 120 Days of Sodom* is studied in sixth form colleges. Nevertheless, he affords us more important insights into the mind of the criminal than most textbooks on criminology. It is because he hides his violent irrationality under the guise of rationality that he could be regarded as the archetypal criminal. This alone would make him worth studying.

There is another reason: Sade had an interesting effect on the history of literature. Before his time, pornography, in our modern sense of the word, scarcely existed. There were many works that were technically obscene, particularly in France in the seventeenth and eighteenth centuries, but their purpose was mainly to satirise religion, and they were full of scenes of priests seducing their penitents and nuns giving themselves to monks. In 1747, the first work of true pornography, John Cleland's *Fanny Hill* (or *Memoirs of a Woman of Pleasure*) appeared in England, but the government gave its author a pension on condition he wrote no more dirty books, and he complied. After the death of the Marquis de Sade, his works were soon being printed by underground presses all over Europe. By the 1820s, hard-up writers had realised that they could make some kind of a living by writing pornography – works with titles like *The Lustful Turk* and *The Ladies' Telltale*, whose aim was to exploit "the forbidden" – schoolgirls engaging in lesbian relationships and being seduced by schoolmasters, virtuous young ladies losing their virginity to their brothers or fathers, and so on. Queen Victoria came to the throne in 1837, and the famous Victorian prudery was soon dominating social and cultural life in England; this gave pornography a new impetus, and it became an industry.

It is important to understand how all this came about. It was not simply due to the literary labours of Sade and his followers. We have to understand that the first "modern novel" appeared as late as 1740 – Samuel Richardson's *Pamela*. There *had* been novels before that, but they were usually travelogues, like *Robinson Crusoe*, or picaresque fantasies like *Don Quixote* or Lesage's *Gil Blas*. Samuel Richardson might be regarded as the inventor of the soap opera, the novel about everyday life, with which the reader (particularly the female reader) could identify. *Pamela* was about a virtuous servant girl who resists all the young master's attempts to seduce her (described in considerable detail) until he agrees to marry her. It was a vast novel, nearly as long as *War and Peace*, told in letters, and its readers could enter into it for days at a time; in effect, *Pamela* enabled them to take a journey into someone else's life. As incredible as it seems, our ancestors before 1740 scarcely knew how to use their imaginations; the theatre (and the Sunday sermons) were their only escape from reality. In our age of the cinema, radio and television, we can hardly grasp what this meant. Then Richardson came along, and it was as if someone had invented a kind of magic carpet. A century later, in the Victorian age, lending libraries proliferated, and every cultivated Victorian housewife took it for granted that she could spend hours of every day immersed in the imaginative worlds of Sir Walter Scott or Charles Dickens. The novel taught people how to dream, and it would be no exaggeration to say it marked a turning point in human evolution.

But, as we have seen, imagination can be negative as well as positive. Gilles de Rais learned his sadism from Suetonius and Tacitus; if he had never learned to read, he would undoubtedly been the typical stupid and rather brutal lord of the manor of the period. The rise of pornography in the nineteenth century made it inevitable that sex crime would also make its appearance in human history.

This may seem an astonishing statement – after all, what else has this chapter been about? But we can also see that sexual violence tended to be confined to members of society who had a great deal of power over the lives of other people. It was simply not committed by the ordinary criminal, who was more concerned to keep body and soul together by stealing money or food. In England in 1774, a vast compilation called *The Newgate Calendar* was published in London, containing over two hundred accounts of murders and robberies; there are only three cases of rape, and they involve what would now be called seduction rather than sexual violence. It was not that the people of that age were more virtuous than their descendants, merely that sex was not one of their priorities. Even in the Victorian era, most working class girls would yield their virginity for five shillings. So although there were a few rapes – usually committed by drunks – there was no sex crime in our modern sense of the word. And, as we have seen in the Introduction, when the unknown maniac known as

Jack the Ripper began murdering prostitutes in Whitechapel in 1888, the Victorians simply failed to recognise them as sex crimes. The Ripper was frequently described as "morally insane", and it was generally believed that he was a religious maniac who hated prostitutes. No one saw him as a direct descendant of Gilles de Rais and the Marquis de Sade. The Ripper murders began what might be called the "Age of Sex Crime", the age of the rapist, the sadist and the mutilator. We shall examine the "Age of Sex Crime" at a later stage in this book.

Meanwhile, what have we learned that helps us to understand the psychology of a "monster" like Leonard Lake? To begin with, that sadism seems to be a dangerously easy habit to acquire. As we shall see in later chapters of this book, many sex criminals have begun as rapists, then developed a certain pleasure in making the victim suffer. Most normal people may feel that they are in no danger of ever developing a taste for sadism; this is because they are unaware of how easily it can happen. The "Yorkshire Ripper", Peter Sutcliffe, began attacking prostitutes out of resentment, because one of them had swindled him out of £10, then held him up to ridicule when he approached her in a pub. At first he simply crept up behind them and struck them on the head; soon he was also disembowelling them. And at a certain point, he ceased to care whether or not the victim was a prostitute. Any woman or girl would serve to provide a release for his morbid sexuality.

In 1985, in a London taxicab being driven to Paddington Station, I mentioned to the driver that I was reading a book about the Yorkshire Ripper. The driver told me that, until fairly recently, he had been a butcher working in a slaughterhouse, and that the pay had been far better than what he now made as a taxi driver. But he realised one day that he was beginning to enjoy killing the animals, and found this so terrifying that he gave up the job. I cited this in a review of the book on the Yorkshire Ripper, but the editor cut it out, evidently feeling that it was irrelevant. To me it still seems to be the most relevant thing in the review.

Another case of the 1970s offers a vital insight into the development of the sadistic sexual criminal.

In October 1977, the naked corpse of a black prostitute was found near a Los Angeles freeway. The murder aroused little media attention in a city that has nine hundred a year. But in the period around Thankgiving, the fourth Thursday in November, seven more strangled women were found on hillsides in the Los Angeles area, and the popular press labelled the unknown killer "the Hillside Strangler". No less than three nude corpses, two of them schoolgirls, were found on 20 November 1977. By the time the violated body of a girl named Cindy Hudspeth was found in the trunk of her car in February 1988, ten murders had been attributed to the Hillside Strangler.

The crimes ceased, but in January 1979, a double sex murder occurred in the small town of Bellingham, in Washington state. Two students, Karen Mandic and Diane Wilder, had apparently been lured to an empty house in a prosperous area of the city, and there strangled and subjected to sexual attack. Their bodies were later found in Karen Mandic's car. The man who immediately came under suspicion was a young security guard named Kenneth Bianchi, who had the keys to the empty house, and who was known to have offered one of the dead girls a house-sitting job on the evening when they were last seen. Bianchi, a charming and plausible man in his twenties, seemed so bewildered by the charge that the police were at first inclined to believe in his innocence. But stolen goods found in the home he shared with his common-law wife and baby made them aware that they were dealing with a thief. A psychiatrist who examined Bianchi became convinced that he was a multiple personality, a kind of Jekyll and Hyde whose evil "alter ego" had committed the murders. Under hypnosis, this "alter ego", who called himself Steve, admitted that the Hillside murders had been committed by himself and Bianchi's cousin Angelo Buono, a Los Angeles car upholsterer. He confessed to the crimes in considerable detail. But it looked as if neither Bianchi nor Buono would ever stand trial for the murders; if Bianchi was a genuine "multiple", then he would be suffering from a mental disorder, and unable to testify against his cousin. Skilled psychiatric detective work finally proved that Bianchi was malingering, and he and Buono went on trial in Los Angeles.

The story that emerged seemed typical of the development of a sex killer. Buono, who was seventeen years older than his cousin, had been married four times. All his wives had left him because of his brutality and his penchant for sodomy. When one of them had refused him sex, he had hurled her on the floor and sodomized her in front of the children. Now living alone, he prided himself on his prowess as a stud – he liked to describe himself as "the Italian Stallion" – and on his ability to seduce teenage girls, of whom he had a harem.

Bianchi had come from the east coast and joined his cousin in Los Angeles. He was deeply impressed by Buono's sexual prowess and did his best to emulate him. But there was an element of weakness and vanity about Bianchi that tended to lead to the breakdown of long-term relationships. In 1976, Bianchi was looking for work, and he and his cousin decided that a simple way to make money would be to become pimps, and force young girls into prostitution. This venture proved fairly successful, until one of the prostitutes told her story to a Hollywood client who was also a lawyer. He felt so sorry for her that he put her on the next plane home. Buono began to make threatening telephone calls, until the lawyer sent a well-muscled bouncer to see him. The bouncer found Buono working in a car, and when he addressed him, Buono ignored him. The bouncer reached in through the window, dragged Buono out by his shirtfront, and asked: "Do I have your attention Mr Buono?" After that, the lawyer received no more threatening phone calls.

For a man who prided himself on his macho image, this incident was a stinging humiliation, and it engendered a deep and totally illogical resentment towards prostitutes. Not long after this, a professional prostitute swindled him when selling him a list of clients which proved to be useless. The cousins were unable to locate the woman herself, but knew where a friend of hers worked on Hollywood Boulevard. Yolanda Washington was picked up by Buono and Bianchi on October 16, 1977; she was raped, sodomized and strangled, and her body dumped near a freeway. She was the first victim of "the Hillside Strangler".

The killing gave the cousins a taste for rape and murder. Two weeks later they picked up a teenage runaway named Judy Miller, took her back to Buono's house, and there stripped and raped her. After this, the two of them strangled and suffocated her at the same time, placing a plastic supermarket bag over her head.

The next victim was an out-of-work dancer. Posing as policemen, they took her back to Buono's house. When she was naked, they decided they disliked her hairy legs; Bianchi violated her with a root beer bottle, then strangled her, repeatedly releasing the cord as she lost consciousness, so that she took a long time to die; meanwhile, Buono sat on her legs and shouted: "Die, cunt, die". Causing suffering had become part of the pleasure of rape. In the case of another victim, they tried to electrocute her with a live wire, but only succeeded in causing burns. Bianchi sodomized one girl as he suffocated her with a plastic bag, climaxing as she died.

Bianchi was twice questioned by the police as a suspect, but was never arrested. But his cousin began to regard him as a liability, and persuaded him to leave Los Angeles and follow a girlfriend, who had deserted him, to Bellingham. There Bianchi obtained a job as a security guard, and committed the double murder of Diane Mandic and Karen Wilder in a bravado attempt to show his cousin that he could kill just as efficiently on his own.

The trial of the Hillside Stranglers lasted from 1981 until 1983, and was the longest in American history. Both were eventually sentenced to life imprisonment with no possibility of release.

Here, once again, we can see the typical elements that go into the development of the sadist, from Tiberius to Leonard Lake and the Yorkshire Ripper. First of all, there is the sense of power over other people, of control over their lives, in this case, of the prostitutes in their "stable". These women were all treated as sex slaves – one had been sodomised so often that she had to wear a tampon in her rectum. Resentment caused by the episode of the bouncer, and the subsequent swindle by the professional prostitute, led to the first murder. The sense of power that came with killing proved to be addictive, and they went on to commit eleven more murders. Buono was unusual in that he then ceased to murder, but this was simply because he kept a harem of under-age mistresses, who satisfied the craving to feel himself "the conquering male". But Bianchi, who had achieved safety and anonymity in Bellingham, was unable to overcome the craving to rape and kill, and committed the crimes that led to their arrest and conviction.

It seems clear that the psychology of the sadist has remained unchanged over two thousand years. What is so disturbing is that in the second half of the twentieth century, he has ceased to be a rarity, and become a depressingly persistent feature of our crime statistics.

3.
Predators
of the Seas

As FAR as their subjects were concerned, the tyrants and monsters of the previous chapter had one thing in their favour: they maintained law and order. The real scourge of what Wells called "that wretched congestion of mankind that is called civilisation" were human predators, such as the brigands and outlaws who lurked in the wilderness between cities. But even they could be thwarted if merchants travelled in convoy. Far more dangerous, and often far more ruthless and sadistic, were the predators of the seven seas.

It was the great Hollywood dream factory that turned the pirate into a figure of romance. When Douglas Fairbanks senior leapt aboard a Spanish galleon with a cutlass between his teeth, or Errol Flynn bowed with elaborate courtesy to a captive lady in crinolines, who could believe that the original buccaneers were mostly criminal degenerates? But this is the unromantic truth. Throughout the history of civilisation, pirates, like brigands and highway robbers, have been a kind of vermin, as useless to the human race as the cholera germ. And soon as men decided to live in cities for their mutual protection, the bandits began to infest the roads between the cities. And as soon as enterprising merchants began to link the cities of the Mediterranean and North Africa, the bandits of the sea began to waylay their ships. There was one basic difference between the pirate and the brigand. If a brigand committed wholesale murder, he was likely to enrage the authorities into hunting him down at all costs. If a pirate killed everybody on board a merchant ship, then burnt the ship down to the waterline, he was lessening his chances of being detected. So piracy always made for a kind of sadistic criminality seldom met with among brigands.

Just as bandits are people who find it hard to make a success in honest business, so nations without commercial acumen often take to piracy. The earliest and most notorious of the pirates of the ancient world were Greeks – the people we now think of as the founders of European civilisation. The great Achilles himself was a pirate; so was Ulysses, who describes in the *Odyssey* how he landed at Ismaros and "sacked the city, killing the men and taking their wives and goods. . ." This underlines another point about piracy; one of its chief attractions is the opportunity for rape. They descended on a coastal village by night, slaughtered the men, then carried of all the women and casks of wine back to the ship for an orgy. It was a sadist's dream.

The Greeks lived in a rocky and barren land, and their national character did not include commercial brilliance. On the other hand, their neighbours the Phoenicians were born sailors and merchants. They exchanged the dyes and copper vessels of Tyre and Sidon for the tin of Cornwall, the ivory of Africa, the perfumes of Arabia. And the Greeks lay in wait for them in rocky inlets, and stole the results of their enterprise. A later French traveller referred to a "people who were cruel, wicked, faithless and without humanity – in a word, Greek". They had nature on their side. In the Mediterranean, the only practical trade routes were by sea. Inland, there were too many mountains. The early sailors stuck close to the coast, for fear of storms, so all a pirate had to do was conceal himself in an inlet, and keep watch.

The trade of piracy was still flourishing when the Romans came to power, and Rome finally decided it had to be got rid of at any price. The Rome of Julius Caesar depended on Egyptian wheat and there were finally so many pirates that the country was starving. The pirates were literally terrorists. They would often besiege a fortified city, then burn everybody in it; other cities would take warning, and everybody would flee before the pirates arrived, leaving them to pillage at leisure. They hated the Romans for their power and success; any Roman nobleman who was captured was likely to be held for a huge ransom, or killed in a disgusting manner.

A day came when the Romans decided it was time to forget internal squabbles and destroy the pirates. They selected their greatest general, Pompey. He approached the task with typical military genius. The Mediterranean was a big place; so he raised 270 ships and 120,000 men. Then, as soon as the winter storms were over, he sailed, and his fleet combed the seas. The pirates were still holed up in their winter strongholds, preparing their ships for another summer of looting and murder. Pompey's huge forces descended on them, and gave them a taste of their own medicine. There was mass slaughter; the strongholds were turned into smoking ruins, full of corpses. The sea wolves were no match for Roman legions. In forty days, all the major pirate villages had been destroyed. Then, having shown that he could be cruel and merciless, Pompey announced that Rome was prepared to pardon all pirates who surrendered voluntarily. Most of them had no alternative; forced off the major sea routes, they would have starved to death. They surrendered by the thousand. Pompey had cleared the Mediterranean for many years to come.

Pirates were like lice, who need to batten on to a host. When the Roman empire collapsed, there was no one for them to rob. So during the Dark Ages, the seas were relatively free of pirates. The Arabs controlled North Africa and Spain; life was stable and fairly safe. Then, in 1492, the year Columbus discovered America, the Spanish finally hurled the Arabs back into their own country. But North Africa was poor; it could hardly support its own people. In a vengeful mood, the Arabs decided to wreck the commerce of the Christian world. And that is exactly what they did. Overnight, the Mediterranean was full of fast, light vessels that could overtake most merchant ships. And suddenly, the Christians realised that their rejoicing about the conquest of the Infidels had been premature. Their ships were robbed and burned, their coastal towns were raided, their women were raped or sold to Arab brothels, their men were turned into galley slaves. It made no difference even if the ship was heavily armed; the Arabs could swarm over it like man-eating ants. In 1504, Pope Julius II sent two great warships loaded with treasure from Genoa to Rome. They lost sight of one another. Suddenly, a tiny, fast craft appeared, and within minutes, the unprepared Roman ship was overrun. It was as unexpected as an eagle being attacked by a flock of sparrows. The Arabs then made the prisoners strip, and dressed in their clothes. Then they caught up with the other treasure ship, and signalled it to wait. Suspecting nothing, the ship allowed its companion to draw alongside – and only realised there was something wrong when a storm of arrows killed most of the men on the decks. The slaves who rowed the Roman treasure ships were Arabs; they were released, and Christians put in their place. Then the three ships sailed for Tunis with a fortune in Vatican treasures.

The exploit reverberated throughout Europe. So did the nickname of the captain of the pirate ship, Red Beard – Barbarossa. His real name was Arouj, and he was the eldest of two brothers who both earned the nickname of Redbeard the Pirate. Arouj's career was bloody and fairly short. He persuaded the Emir of Tunis to give him protection, in exchange for a share of the booty. The Emir was delighted; Barbarossa was a national hero among the Arabs. Barbarossa repaid him by strangling him one day (with only one hand – he had lost the other in battle) then proclaiming himself Emir. Charles V of Spain sent an army of ten thousand against him, and Redbeard was literally hacked to pieces. But his younger brother remained, and he went on to make the name of Barbarossa as feared as that of Atilla or Genghis Khan. He decided it was too dangerous to be a king or sultan; so he approached the Turkish Sultan of Constantinople, and offered to re-take Tunisia and present it to him. The Sultan lent him a huge army with which Barbarossa II reconquered all the land his brother had lost. Then he went on to become the most successful pirate in world history. His pirates raided from Spain to the Black Sea. Majorca and Minorca were overrun so often that they moved their villages inland and fortified them. And the coastal towns of Italy were now subjected to a reign of terror like the one they had known sixteen hundred years earlier.

Because Barbarossa regarded this as a Holy War, he would have whole towns destroyed; everybody who was too old or too young to be carried off as slaves was murdered. On one occasion, he heard about a famous beauty, the Duchess of Trajetto in Italy. He decided that he would like to present her to his master, the Sultan of Constantinople, so his ships swooped on Calabria a fleet of sixty galleys. The Duchess was warned just in time, and fled in her night dress, riding until the horse dropped from exhaustion. When she returned a few weeks later, the town of Fondi was now a few smoking ruins, full of horribly mutilated and crucified corpses of women and children. Barbarossa was a man of violent temper, who did not like to be thwarted.

When he was finally tamed, it was not by the armies and fleets that the Europeans threw against him, but by a beautiful Christian girl. His fleet was sailing past Reggio, in Calabria, when someone in the shore battery was stupid enough to fire a defiant shot. Barbarossa had not intended to land, but this insult so enraged him that he took twelve thousand men, and besieged the town. The daughter of the governor was taken prisoner; she was eighteen, and very beautiful. Barbarossa was an old man in his sixties but he fell in love. He could have had her sent to his harem and raped her; instead, he begged her to marry him, offering to show mercy to the townspeople. She had no choice. And Barbarossa found married bliss so satisfying that he retired to Constantinople, built himself a magnificent mausoleum, and died happily in his bed.

Europe was getting sick of the corsairs. They had besieged Malta in 1565, and the garrison was only saved by the bravery of the Knights of St John, and false rumour that a Christian fleet was on its way to help them. Cyprus was captured by Ochiali, a Christian-turned-Moslem pirate, who used it as a basis for raids on Crete and the villages and town of the Adriatic. Christendom was shocked and outraged; something had to be done. And something was done. The Pope summoned all the knights of Europe to a great crusade – even the Protestant Queen Elizabeth of England sent one of her best seamen, Sir Richard Grenville. Spain supplied a large fleet and on one of its galleys sailed Miguel Cervantes, the future author of *Don Quixote*. On 7 October 1571, two enormous fleets of about 300 vessels each, commanded by Don John of Austria, faced one another in one of the great historic battles of the world, Lepanto. The Turkish fleet was bigger, but the Christians had muskets, while most of the Moslems had only bows and arrows. By the evening of that day, Moslem sea power in the Mediterranean had been broken as decisively as Pompey had broken the pirates so long before. The world's second great age of piracy was over.

And, strangely enough, the third age was just beginning, the age of the Spanish Main. The defeat of the Turks meant that Spain was now one of the leading nations of Europe. It might have gone on to become the master of Europe if it had not been for the defeat of the great Armada in 1588. But Spain was still a great power in the New World across the Atlantic. It held Cuba, Puerto Rico, Santa Domingo, and parts of the mainland, known as the Spanish Main. The Spaniards were determined to retain their new empire at all costs. A French settlement in Florida was wiped out in 1562; in 1604, two British ships were captured in the West Indies, and the Spaniards cut off the hands, feet, noses and ears of the men, smeared them with honey, then left them tied to trees to be bitten by flies and ants.

The same kind of ruthlessness had destroyed most of the native population of the West Indian islands. Various Europeans began to drift in, mostly French and English, escaping from religious persecution at home and hoping to make new lives. There was plenty of meat on Santa Domingo (Haiti) in the form of wild hogs; French settlers, many of them criminals fleeing from justice, made some kind of a living by killing and skinning the hogs. They dried their skins in smoking-huts called *boucans*, so they became known as "boucaneers" or buccaneers. When the Spanish got sick of these seventeenth century hippies living on their island, they drove them off, and the buccaneers retreated to a small island called Tortuga. And now they had no pigs to skin, they took to piracy for a living. Again, the Spaniards had made a rod for their own backs.

One of the first buccaneers of whom we have some details was Pierre Legrand, and he is unusual because he stayed in the business for such a short period. He managed to assemble a boat and a small crew in Tortuga, then set out to find ships to rob. For weeks they had no luck, until they were running short of food.

One day, they saw a heavily armed convoy of treasure ships sailing past, and Legrand decided to try and equal Barbarossa's feat with the Pope's galleys. Under cover of darkness, they sailed up to the last ship. The watch was asleep, as no one expected a warship to be attacked. Legrand found the captain and three Spanish grandees playing cards; and they were shot down when they resisted. Twenty of the crew were killed before the rest surrendered. Then the pirates turned the ship in the darkness and sailed off. The treasure on board was enough to make most of them rich, and Legrand retired to Normandy, where he lived in comfort until his death.

One of the most brutal and vicious of these pirates of Tortuga was Jean-David Nau, known as Lolonais, an ex-slave, who seems to have been motivated by a desire for revenge on the Spaniards. One chronicler describes how he became so enraged with one of his Spanish captives that he slashed open his chest with a cutlass, tore out his heart, and began to gnaw it with his teeth. It is certainly in character. Lolonais raided towns on the Spanish mainland – Maracaibo and Gibraltar – and inflicted horrible tortures on their inhabitants to force them to reveal where they had hidden their money. Captives were executed *en masse*.

The fortunes of the Spanish went from bad to worse. Charles I of England was a Catholic and friendly to Spain, but when he was executed, Oliver Cromwell sent an expedition to the West Indies, and captured Jamaica. Naturally, the British were glad to help anybody who made the lives of the Spaniards a misery, so they encouraged the buccaneers. They encouraged a man whose name has become almost synonymous with the history of piracy – Henry Morgan. Morgan was a Welshman, who went to sea as a cabin boy and landed in Jamaica. And it was with the aid and the blessings of the governor of Jamaica, Sir Thomas Modyford, that Morgan began his career as a pirate. There was actually a treaty of non-aggression with Spain in 1667, but Modyford heard that the Spaniards were preparing a huge expedition to conquer Jamaica. So he sent out Henry Morgan in charge of twelve ships to get in the first blow. Morgan marched fifty miles inland to the town of Puerto del Principe, took it by storm, then tortured the inhabitants until he extracted a confession that seventy men *had* been forced to join the army for an expedition against Jamaica. His men then tortured the inhabitants further to make them reveal their treasures. Delighted by success and eager for more treasure, they attacked the strongly fortified towns of Puerto Bello and La Gloria; they captured the latter by driving monks and nuns in front of them as living shields as they advanced with siege ladders on the walls.

Morgan's most daring raid was on Panama, which involved a nine day march through jungles and up rivers. This caused trouble with the British government, and Sir Thomas Modyford was ordered to arrest Morgan and send him to London. Morgan went voluntarily and arrived in London to find himself a national hero, like Drake. He spent three comfortable years in London, became a friend of the king, and was finally sent back to Jamaica with a commission to wipe out the buccaneers. Morgan didn't mind. He persecuted his former shipmates with the same ruthless ferocity he had shown towards the Spaniards. He was knighted, and died a rich man. The greatest of the buccaneers brought the era of buccaneers to a close.

But not the era of piracy. Now it had ceased to be profitable on the Spanish Main, the pirates moved across the Atlantic to the Indian Ocean. The East India Company had opened up the trade routes to India, and the seas around Africa were now as full of ships as the Mediterranean had been a few centuries earlier. The most famous of these Indian Ocean pirates was again an Englishman, Henry Every (sometimes spelt Avery). His most famous feat was the seizure of two ships of the "Mocha fleet" in 1695. Mocha used to be one of the greatest ports of south-western Arabia, and the ships that sailed from Mocha to India were usually laiden with treasure. According to a legend that made Every's name famous in England, one of these two ships contained the daughter of the Grand Mogul of India, who was so beautiful that Every married her. The truth is less romantic and more brutal. The ships *were* full of treasure, and beautiful Turkish girls who were being taken to a harem. All the women, young and old, were raped, some of them so sadistically that they died; a few escaped by jumping overboard. One old lady who was raped *was* a relative of an Indian king, which may have given rise to the story of the beautiful princess. The pirates obtained about

£1,000 each. Every took refuge in the Bahamas, and applied for a Royal Pardon. Unfortunately, his action had caused so much trouble in India that the British government offered a reward of £500 each for Every's crew. They split up and fled. Twenty four were caught and six of these hanged, but Every vanished completely, to become another of the great legends of piracy.

The pirate who has the most evil reputation of all, "Blackbeard", was, in fact one of the least vicious of all the pirates. He started his career round about 1700, serving on privateers against Spain. A privateer was a privately owned warship, permitted by its own government to prey on the ships of an enemy government. Blackbeard's real name was Edward Teach, and when the war with Spain ended in 1713, he continued as a pirate in a captured French ship. He plied his trade up and down the east coast of America, with the active support of the Governor of North Carolina. The reason for this support was simple. England tried to force her colonies to trade only with English ships, so the resentful Americans didn't mind English ships being attacked by pirates. Blackbeard was highly successful as a pirate, and he seems to have treated captives reasonably. Finally, the Governor of Virginia, a richer state with no liking for pirates, despatched Lieutenent Robert Maynard with two sloops to look for Blackbeard. Maynard finally cornered him in an inlet, drove his ship aground and captured it after fierce fighting. Blackbeard's head was cut off, and left to dry on the mainmast. He was one of the last of the great pirates.

"Captain" William Fly was hardly in the same league; yet his brief piratical career deserves mention for its sheer brutality. Fly came from Bristol, a port infamous for its slums and misery, and went to sea as a cabin boy. By 1726, he had worked himself up to the position of petty officer, and was known as a hard man with an incredible command of blasphemy and obscenity. In the early months of 1726, Fly was in Jamaica when he heard that another Bristol-man, Captain John Green, needed men for his boat the *Elizabeth*. The boat proved to be a small vessel called a "snow", and Captain Green's business was slave-trading. He would sail to the coast of Guinea, anchor in a quiet harbour, and make contact with a local tribe who specialised in raiding their neighbours and seizing prisoners. These prisoners were bought for the equivalent of a few dollars each, and chained in a narrow space below the decks, with a hundred or so men and women packed into the space intended for two dozen. Some slavers even economised on space by chaining slaves in the gangway, so it was almost impossible for the prisoners to move more than an inch or so. On the long voyage back to America, as many as fifty per cent were expected to die, sometimes more. Back in America, the emaciated blacks could be sold for a hundred times the price the slaver had paid for them.

This trade brutalised everyone involved in it, and Captain Green was no exception. He was as harsh and violent as the infamous Bligh of the *Bounty*. He expected to be treated as a kind of god on his own ship, and any sailor who seemed to lack respect might be literally flogged to death.

Now petty officer William Fly was also a dominant man, with a high opinion of himself. If Green had not been captain, their encounter would have been a clash like that of the irresistable force and the immovable object. But Green *was* captain, and he sensed the brutal dominance that was latent in Fly. A more sensible man would have got rid of Fly at the first opportunity; Green reacted by bullying and shouting at Fly. His chief mate, whose name is unrecorded, took his cue from the captain, and did the same. Fly decided they both had to die.

He talked to other members of the crew. They had also felt the lash, and hated Green. Half a dozen of them agreed to help him, and join him as pirates if they could take over the snow.

In the dark hours of the morning of 27 May 1726, Fly and the other mutineers walked up to the man at the wheel, placed a pistol against his head, and told him they were taking over the ship. The man agreed to keep quiet. And now came the moment Fly had looked forward to with sadistic delight. He seized a cutlass, and went to the captain's cabin, accompanied by a mutineer named Alexander Mitchell. The two of them shook the captain violently. He sat up, roaring: "What in hell's the matter?" It was Mitchell who answered: "Captain Fly is now commander. Get up on deck." Fly held the cutlass firmly; he was hoping Green would resist, and give him the pleasure of running him through. He was disappointed. The brutal bully collapsed, perhaps he saw death on Fly's face. Trying to control his voice, he asked to be put ashore as

soon as they sighted land. "What, so you can give evidence and
hang us all?", said Fly, and the captain knew suddenly that they
meant to kill him.

On deck, Green was asked whether he would prefer to jump
overboard or be thrown. The captain begged for his life. Fly
signalled to the men. "Over with him." They grabbed the captain
and lifted him. He reached out and grabbed the mainsheet. One
of the mutineers swung a hatchet, and cut off his hand at the
wrist. Then he was tossed over the side. The mate Jenkins
was next. He struggled in the water for a few minutes, then
sank. Two sailors who were regarded as "captain's men" were
thrown in irons. Then the successful mutineers celebrated with
a rum punch. They changed the name of the ship to *Fame's
Revenge*.

A week later, the pirate ship arrived off the coast of North
Carolina, and saw a sloop, the *John and Hannah*, anchored inside
the harbour bar. The captain, John Fulker, offered his services
as a pilot to take them into the harbour as the sand bar was
dangerous. Fulker and three companions were invited into the
cabin for punch, then Fly announced they were pirates, and that
they wanted Fulker's ship. Looking down the barrels of several
pistols, Fulker had no choice. But he explained that the wind was
in the wrong quarter for bringing out the *John and Hannah*. Fly
cursed him and told him he had better try. So Fulker went back
accompanied by six pirates and tried to sail his ship out to the
Fame's Revenge. He had been telling the truth; the wind was in
the wrong direction, and drove them towards the sand bar. In the
boat, they rowed back to the pirate ship. Convinced he was being
cheated, Fly fell into a foaming rage, and ordered Fulker to be
flogged. Fulker was stripped to the waist, tied to the gears, and
flogged with a cat o' nine tails until his back was hanging with
strips of flesh, and his blood soaked his trousers and filled his
shoes. Fly now sent Mitchell and a number of pirates to bring
out the *John and Hannah*. Mitchell could see it was dangerous,
but he tried. The wind caught them, and drove them across the
sand bar. There was a ripping of timbers, and the ship started to
sink. Everyone escaped. Fly almost foamed at the mouth seeing
what had happened, but there was nothing he could do about it
but curse, which he did for an hour or more.

Two days later, Fly took his first prize. They saw a ship called *John and Betty* and sailed after her. The captain ordered all sails to be hoisted, and they gained on the pirate ship. Fly tried hoisting a distress signal, but Captain Gale of the *John and Betty* declined to stop and investigate. Then his luck turned, the wind slackened, and the *Fame's Revenge* got within gun-shot. With the first volley from her cannons, the *John and Betty* surrendered. Fly went on board, helped himself to all the portable valuables, forced six of the sailors to join the pirates, and then allowed the ship to go.

Delighted with his success, Fly now made his mistake. A few days later, they sighted another ship, the *James*, and fired at it. The captain surrendered, and came aboard the pirate vessel. They were close to fishing grounds, and other unarmed schooners sailed across the horizon. Fly decided to use his own ship and the *James* to capture some of these. He saw himself as the captain of a whole pirate armada. He sent six of his pirates, under Alexander Mitchell, on board the *James*, and told them to sail towards the nearest fishing vessel; he would follow. What he was forgetting is that the men who remained aboard the *Fame's Revenge* were nearly all sailors who had been taken from the *John and Hannah* and *John and Betty*. Chief among these was Captain William Atkinson, who had been with Fulker when he rowed out to the pirate ship. Atkinson had already been planning mutiny with other "forced men", and now he saw his chance. Fly was on the bridge, a pistol in his belt and a cutlass in his hand. His arsenal of guns and swords was close by. Atkinson, standing in the bow with a telescope, called that there were several new vessels on the horizon, and that they seemed to be unarmed. Fly rushed forward, sat on the windlass, and seized the telescope. At a nod from Atkinson, two men grabbed him by the arms, and clamped a hand over his mouth. Atkinson rushed on to the quarter deck and grabbed a loaded pistol. One of the pirates down below heard the noise and came up on deck; Atkinson was waiting for him, and stunned him with a tremendous blow from the butt of the pistol. Fly and three other pirates were put in irons, and the *Fame's Revenge* sailed for Boston. There, on Tuesday 12 July 1726, a mere two months after he had become a pirate captain, Fly and two of the other pirates were hanged on the island of Nix's Mate. (The pirate cook was pardoned.) At least Fly died well. After listening to a sermon by Cotton Mather, he laughed and joked with the spectators until his body finally dangled from the gibbet.

There was another brief outburst of piracy after the Napoleonic wars, but finally most of the civilised nations banded together to outlaw piracy when they signed the Declaration of Paris in 1856, making it internationally illegal. It continued in the China seas until the coming of steamships put an end to it. It has taken mankind just over three thousand years to get rid of one of its most vicious habits.

4.
Order
of Assassins

THERE IS another type of killer who cannot be classified either with the criminal "vermin" of the previous chapter, or with sadistic monsters like Gilles de Rais. He kills out of conviction or out of revenge, and when his victim is a politician, we describe him as an assassin. Most modern terrorists belong to this type. But the terrorist of the twentieth century is usually a misguided patriot or a fanatical idealist. The founding father of terrorism was an altogether more strange and complex figure. In the year 1273, the Venetian traveller Marco Polo passed through the valley of Alamut, in Persia, and saw there the castle of the Old Man of the Mountain, the head of the Persian branch of the sect of Ismailis, or Assassins. By that time, the sect was two hundred years old, and was on the point of being destroyed by the Mongols, who had invaded the Middle East under the leadership of Genghis Khan.

According to Marco Polo, the Old Man of the Mountain, whose name was Aloadin, had created a Garden of Paradise in a green valley behind the castle, and filled it with "pavilions and palaces the most elegant that can be imagined", fountains flowing with wine, milk and honey, beautiful *houris* who could sing and dance seductively. The purpose of this Garden was to give his followers a foretaste of Paradise, so that they might be eager to sacrifice their lives for their leader. When the Old Man wanted an enemy murdered, he would ask for volunteers. These men would be drugged and carried into the secret garden, which, under normal circumstances, was strictly forbidden to all males. They would awake to find themselves apparently in paradise, with wine, food and damsels at their disposal. After a few days of this, they were again drugged and taken back to the Old Man's fortress. So when the Old Man would have any prince slain, he would say to such a youth: "Go thou and slay so and so; and when thou returnest, my angels shall bear thee to paradise. . ."

There is evidence that the story may have a foundation in fact. Behind the remains of the castle, which still exists in the valley of Alamut, there is a green enclosed valley with a spring. But it is hardly large enough to have contained "pavilions and palaces".

The Ismailis were a breakaway sect from the orthodox Moslems; they were the Mohammedan equivalent of Protestants. After the death of the prophet Mahomet in 632, his disciple Abu Bakr was chosen to succeed him, thus becoming the first Caliph of Islam. It is a pity that Mahomet, unlike Jesus, never made clear which of his disciples – or relatives – was to be the rock upon which his church was to be built. For other Moslems felt that the Prophet's cousin Ali was a more suitable candidate: the result was a dissension that split the Moslem world for centuries. The Sunni – the orthodox Moslems – persecuted and slaughtered Ali's followers, who were known as the Shi'a. In 680, they almost succeeded in wiping out their rivals, when seventy of them, including the prophet's daughter Fatima, were surprised and massacred. But the killers overlooked a sick boy, the son of Fatima; so the rebel tradition lived on.

All this murder and suffering produced powerful religious emotions among the Shi'a. They set up their own Caliph, known as the Imam, and they looked forward to the coming of a messiah (or Mahdi) who would lead them to final victory. Strange sects proliferated, led by holy men who came out of the desert. Some believed in reincarnation, others in total moral and sexual freedom. One sect believed in murder as a religious duty, strangling their victims with cords; these may be regarded as the true predecessors of the Assassins.

The Ismailis were a breakaway sect from the original breakaway sect. When the sixth Imam died, his eldest son Ismail was passed over for some reason, and his younger brother Musa appointed. The Ismailis were Moslems who declared that Ismail was the true Imam: they were also known as Seveners, because they believed that Ismail was the seventh and last Imam. The rest of the Shi'a became known as the Twelvers, for they accepted Musa and his five successors as true Imams. (The line came to an end after the twelfth.) The Twelvers became the respectable branch of the heretics, differing from orthodox Sunni only on a few points of doctrine. It was the Ismailis who became the true opposition, creating a brilliant and powerful organization with its own philosophy, ritual and literature. They were intellectuals and mystics and fanatics. With such drive and idealism they were bound to come to power eventually.

It was some time around the middle of the eleventh century that the greatest of the Ismaili leaders was born – Hasan bin Sabbah, a man who combined the religious fervour of Saint Augustine with the political astuteness of Lenin. He founded the Order of Assassins, and became the first Old Man of the Mountain.

By the time Hasan was born, the Ismailis had become one of the great political powers. The Sunni Caliphs were decadent: the Ismailis set up their own Caliph and their own dynasty. They called themselves the Fatimids (descendants of Fatima, the Prophet's murdered daughter). They conquered the Nile valley, then spread slowly across Egypt, Syria, North Africa, parts of Arabia, even Sicily. By the end of the tenth century, it looked as if nothing could stop them becoming rulers of all the Moslem lands. But at that point, a new force entered Middle Eastern politics – the Seljuk Turks – who swept across the Moslem world like the ancient Romans. And the Turks, as good Moslems, decided to lend their support to the Sunni Caliphs. By the time Hasan bin Sabbah was a young man, the Ismaili empire was already past its peak.

Hasan was born an orthodox Moslem – or at least, a Twelver, which was almost the same thing. His family lived in Rayy, near modern Teheran. We know little about his early life except that he became an avid student of every branch of learning. A strong religious impulse led him to look beyond the sect into which he had been born. He was impressed by the intellectual force and mystical fervour of the heretical Ismailis. It took him a long time to decide to join them – for the Ismailis were generally regarded as outcasts and cranks. A serious illness decided him; in 1072 he took the oath of allegiance to the Fatimid Caliph. Four years later he was forced to leave Rayy – no doubt for spreading Ismaili doctrines – and started to make his way towards Cairo, a new city that had been built by the Ismailis as their capital. The journey took two years. In Cairo, he impressed the Caliph, and became a supporter of his eldest son Nizar. He spent three years in the Fatimid court; then his ardent revolutionary temperament got him into trouble – history does not go into detail – and he left Egypt and became a wandering missionary for the Ismaili cause. Legend has it that he was sentenced to death, but that just before his execution, one of the strongest towers in the city collapsed suddenly; this was seen as an omen, so he was sent into exile instead. Another story tells how the ship on which he sailed ran into a violent storm; while the other passengers flung themselves on their knees and prayed, Hasan stood perfectly calm, explaining that he could not die until he had fulfilled his destiny. When the storm suddenly ceased, Hasan got the credit, and made several converts. "Thus," says von Hammer (a thoroughly hostile chronicler), "to increase his credit, did he avail himself of accidents and natural occurrences, as if he possessed the command of both." Von Hammer seems to regard Hasan as a kind of Rasputin figure, a trickster and a fraud who used religion to gain personal power (but then, he also describes the Ismaili religion as "mysteries of atheism and immorality").

Hasan bin Sabbah was a highly successful missionary, particularly among his own people of Daylam, a wild, independent race who loathed the Turks. The Daylamis had been among the last to be converted to Islam, and even now they tended to be rebellious and unorthodox. Hasan saw their value. Their country was an ideal stronghold. And if Nizar failed to become the next Fatimid Caliph – which seemed highly likely, in view of the intrigues at court – Hasan might well need a stronghold.

As the number of his converts increased, Hasan selected his fortress, the castle of Alamut (or Eagle's Nest), perched high on a rock in the Elburz mountains, above a cultivated valley about thirty miles long.

His method of acquiring the castle was typical of his strategy. First he sent "dais" – preachers – to the villages around the castle, and they made many converts. Then the dais got into the castle, and converted some of its garrison. The castle's owner, Alid – an orthodox Moslem – was not sure what to do about all this. At first he professed to be converted; then, one day, he persuaded the Ismailis to leave the castle, and slammed the gates. But he allowed himself to be persuaded to let them in again. At this point, Hasan was smuggled into the castle in disguise. One morning, Alid woke up to discover that his castle was no longer his own. He was politely shown the door and (according to one chronicler) given 3,000 gold dinars in compensation.

This was in 1090. From that time on, until his death thirty-four years later, Hasan lived in his castle. He studied, wrote books, brought up a family and planned conquests. Most of his followers never saw him. The religious rule in the castle was strict; they ate sparingly, and wine was forbidden. Hasan had one of his sons executed for drinking wine. (Another was executed on suspicion, false, as it later turned out, of having planned the murder of one of the dais.)

But if the aims were religious, the method was military. The Ismailis wanted to supplant the Sunni Caliphs of Baghdad. In order to do that, they first had to drive out the Turks who supported them. The Turks were the overlords of Persia. So Hasan's task was to extend his realm, village by village and castle by castle, until he could challenge the Turks directly. Where castles declined to be converted to the Ismaili faith, they were infiltrated or stormed. In towns and villages, Ismaili converts rose up and took control. Like Lawrence of Arabia, in his own battle to overthrow the Turks, Hasan's great advantage was the hatred of the conquered people for their overlords. When he had extended his control to all the area surrounding Alamut, he sent a missionary to the mountainous country called Quhistan in the south-east, where various heretical sects were oppressed by the Turks. There was a popular rising, the Turks were overthrown, and Quhistan became the second great Ismaili stronghold. Not long after, another area of mountain country in the south-west became an Ismaili stronghold when another of Hasan's followers seized two castles near Arrajan. The Turks now became aware of their danger, and decided it was time to crush the Ismailis; two great expeditions were sent out, one against Alamut, the other against Quhistan. They soon discovered how well Hasan had chosen his fortresses. Although there were a mere seventy defenders, the castle of Alamut was impregnable to direct attack; and the surrounding villages made sure the defenders were not starved into submission by smuggling food up to them by night. A surprise attack sent the Turkish armies flying. The expedition against Quhistan fared no better.

And it was at this point, in 1092, a mere two years after moving to Alamut, that Hasan made the great decision that may well have been his crucial mistake. He recognized that open war with the Turks was out of the question; his armies were too small. But his followers were fanatics who would give their lives for their cause. Why not use them to strike down his chief enemies, one by one? In 1092, the "assassins" claimed their first, and perhaps their most eminent victim, Nizam Al-Mulk, the Vizier of the Turkish Sultan.

Until recent years, it was accepted that Nizam Al-Mulk had been a fellow student of Hasan's. The story told by von Hammer – who repeats it from earlier Persian chroniclers – is that Hasan, Nizam Al-Mulk and the poet Omar Khayyam were fellow students, and Hasan suggested to the other two that if any of them should achieve eminence, he should share it with the other two. They all agreed. After some years, Nizam became the Vizier of the Turkish Sultan Alp Arslan, one of the great military geniuses of the period. When Alp Arslan died (1073) and his young son, Malik Shah, came to the throne, Nizam became the most powerful man in the land. At this point, his old schoolfellows presented themselves and reminded him of their agreement. Omar, being a poet and mathematician (one of the greatest of the Middle Ages), asked only for a quiet place to study; so Nizam gave him a pension and sent him back to his home town of Naishapur. Hasan wanted power, so Nizam found him a position at court. What happened then is not quite clear, except that Nizam realised that his old schoolfellow was supplanting him in the royal favour, and took steps to bring about his downfall. Hasan left Malik's court vowing vengeance; and that, says von Hammer, is why Nizam became the first victim of the Assassins.

By 1092, Nizam Al-Mulk was Hasan's chief enemy, the greatest single danger to the Assassins. Hasan asked for a volunteer to kill the Vizier. A man called Bu Tahir Arrani stepped forward. He disguised himself as a Sufia holy man, and during the feast of Ramadan, in October, 1092, was allowed to approach the litter of Nizam as he was carried out of his audience tent. He drove a knife into Nizam's breast, and was himself immediately killed by Nizam's guards. When he heard that the assassination had been successful, Hasan remarked: "The killing of this devil is the beginning of bliss." He meant it literally; his followers accepted that to die like Bu Tahir Arrani was an immediate passport to paradise.

It may be that this murder showed Hasan where his real power lay. He could capture a fortress by preaching, cunning and bribery. He could destroy an enemy by sending out a single assassin. It looked like the ideal formula for guerrilla warfare.

Where he made his mistake was in failing to grasp the ultimate consequences of such a method: that if his men destroyed their enemies like scorpions or cobras, they would arouse the same loathing and detestation as scorpions or cobras. And that sooner or later, the horror they inspired would cancel all their gains. It was this that eventually frustrated Hasan's plans for conquest.

But that lay far in the future. For the moment, Hasan's method was triumphantly successful. Not long after Nizam's death, the Sultan Malik also died, of a stomach complaint, apparently. One of Nizam's sons, Fakhri, was killed in Naishapur; he had been accosted by a beggar who said: "The true Moslems are no more and there are none left to take the hand of the afflicted." As Fakhri reached for alms, he was stabbed to the heart. Nizam's other son, Ahmed, laid siege to the castle of Alamut; the inhabitants suffered severe hardships, but again it proved impregnable. Ahmed was later stabbed by an Assassin, but he recovered.

The candidates for assassination were always carefully chosen. Hasan played his game like a master chess player. The death of Malik Shah brought on a struggle for power at court; the new Sultan, Berkyaruq, had to defend his throne against his half-brothers. Hasan lent his support to Berkyaruq, and assassinated a number of Berkyaruq's enemies. Berkyaruq's officers formed an uneasy liaison with the Assassins. So when Berkyaruq finally put down the rebellion, Hasan was allowed to operate in peace for a few years. But he continued to practise the arts of infiltration and intimidation; Ismailis joined Berkyaruq's army, and made converts. When officers opposed them, they were silenced with the threat of assassination. A point came where no one in authority dared to go out without armour under his robes. Leaders of rival religious sects were murdered. One opponent was stabbed in the mosque as he knelt at prayers, even though a bodyguard was standing directly behind him. Eventually – in 1101 – Berkyaruq lost his temper and decided it was time to destroy the Ismailis. He combined with his half-brother Sanjar to attack the stronghold at Quhistan; the armies laid waste the countryside, destroying the crops, and would have captured the main stronghold (Tabas) if the Ismailis had not bribed the enemy general to go away. Sanjar made other attempts to subjugate the Ismailis, but eventually came to tolerate them. The historian Juvanyi tells a story to explain this. Hasan managed to bribe one of Sanjar's guards to stick a dagger into the ground near his head, when Sanjar lay in a drunken sleep. Shortly thereafter, Sanjar received a message from Hasan that said: "That dagger could just as easily have been stuck in your heart." Sanjar saw the wisdom of tolerating the Ismailis.

Nevertheless, Hasan's dreams began to collapse within a few years of his greatest triumphs. In 1094, the Fatimid Caliph, spiritual head of the Ismailis, died in Cairo. Nizar, Hasan's patron, should have replaced him. Instead, the Vizier, Al-Afdal, put Nizar's younger brother on the throne. There was a war, and Nizar was killed. Hasan remained faithful to Nizar (in fact, his sect called themselves the Nizari); he refused to acknowledge the new Sultan. So he was now isolated from his own co-religionists. After Berkyaruq turned against him, it was all the Assassins could do to hold on to their territories. When Berkyaruq died in 1105, he was succeeded by his half-brother Muhammad Tapar, who was even more determined to destroy the power of the Ismailis. The castle at Isfahan was besieged and taken, and the Ismaili leaders flayed alive. Alamut was besieged, but managed to hold out. For several years, the Sultan sent his troops to destroy all the crops in the valley; then, when the defenders of Alamut were exhausted with hardship, the siege was started again. In 1118 the castle was on the point of surrendering when the army received news of the death of the Sultan. So they went home. The Ismailis were saved again.

The Assassins had been contained in Persia. But in the early years of the new century, Hasan sent out missionaries – and killers – to Syria. In 1103, they murdered Janah Al-Daulah, the Emir of Homs, as he prayed in the mosque. In 1106, they killed Khalaf, the ruler of a citadel called Afamiya. Their method here was again typical. Six Assassins got hold of the horse, shield and armour of a Frankish knight, and presented themselves at Khalaf's headquarters; they explained that they had killed one of his enemies, and had come to enter his service. Khalaf (himself an Ismaili, but a supporter of the present Fatimid Caliph) made them welcome. The Assassins watched for their opportunity, then murdered him. Then, with the help of other Ismailis, they seized the citadel. Their triumph was short-lived. The Crusader Tancred besieged the town and took the Assassins captive. (They were allowed to ransom themselves.) This is the first known encounter between Crusaders and Assassins. Later on, there were many more.

Back in the castle of Alamut, Hasan was getting old. He had seen his empire rise, and then crumble. For thirty years he had directed assassinations from his castle, yet nothing had changed very much. The Turks were as strong as ever; the Sunni Moslems were still in power. And, worst of all, the Ismailis of Cairo, the men who held the power, were the enemies of the Ismailis of Persia.

Hasan's chief grudge was against the Vizier Al-Afdal, the man who had plotted against Nizar and put Nizar's younger brother, Al Mustali, on the throne in 1094. Twenty-seven years later, Hasan got his revenge; three of his Assassins succeeded in murdering the Vizier. Strangely enough, the present Fatimid Caliph was delighted; he was sick of his overbearing Vizier. He ordered the new Vizier to write Hasan a letter, urging him to return to the fold. Hasan was willing enough. At eighty-seven, he was getting tired; he could not afford to defy the whole Arab world forever. But before the Caliph and the Old Man of the Mountain could make peace, the new Vizier discovered a plot by the Assassins to murder the Caliph. In all probability, there was never such a plot. Nizar and his children were dead; Hasan had no motive for wanting to kill the man who was now offering him peace and co-operation.

But the Vizier was a Twelver (not an Ismaili); he had good reason for wanting to prevent the reconciliation. And Hasan's reputation was such that any mud would stick. The Caliph took the "plot" so seriously that he ordered that all the citizens of Cairo should be registered, and that all strangers should be carefully watched. Many "agents of Hasan" were arrested and executed, including the tutor of the Caliph's children.

And so the last hope vanished. And in May, 1124 Hasan bin Sabbah, one of the most remarkable religious leaders of all time, died in his castle of Alamut, at the age of ninety. He appointed one of his generals to succeed him, demonstrating thereby that he had learned from Mahomet's chief mistake.

This was by no means the end of the Assassins. After initial difficulties, the Syrian branch took root, and it was the stories of the Syrian mission, carried back to Europe by Crusaders, that introduced the word "assassin" into the European languages. The event that caused this notoriety was the murder of the Christian knight Conrad of Montferrat in 1192; Conrad was stabbed by two Assassins – agents of the Syrian Old Man of the Mountain, Sinan – who were disguised as monks. (King Richard the Lion Heart of England is supposed to have been behind the murder; one of his protégés quickly married the widow, and became "King of Jerusalem" in his place.) After this, Assassins began to figure in every chronicle of the Third Crusade, and the legend captured the imagination of Europe. They were masters of disguise, adepts in treachery and murder. Their Old Man was a magician who surveyed the world from his castle like some evil spider, watching for victims. They were without religion and without morality (one early chronicler says they ate pork – against the Moslem law – and practised incest with their mothers and sisters). They were so fanatically devoted to their master that he often demonstrated their obedience to visitors by making them leap out of high windows. Their arts of persuasion were so subtle that no ruler could be sure of the loyalty of his own servants. A typical story illustrates this. Saladin, the Sultan of Egypt and the great enemy of the Crusaders, sent a threatening message to Sinan, the Syrian Old Man. The Assassin chief sent back a messenger, whose mission was to deliver a message in private. Aware of the danger, Saladin had him thoroughly searched, then dismissed the assembly, all except for two guards. The messenger turned to the guards and asked: "If I were to order you, in the name of my Master, to kill the Sultan, would you do it?" They nodded and drew their swords. Whereupon the messenger, having made his point, bowed and took his leave, taking the two guards with him. Saladin decided to establish friendly relations with the Assassins.

But by the time Marco Polo saw the castle of Alamut in 1273, the power of the Assassins was at an end. In Persia they had been slaughtered by the Mongols; in Syria, ruthlessly suppressed by Baybars, Sultan of Egypt. Some of the survivors remained in the area of Alamut, where they may be found to this day. Others scattered to distant countries, including India, the significance of which will appear in a moment.

What was it about the Assassins that made them the focus of so many legends? Something about them appealed to the mediaeval mind as Dracula or Jack the Ripper appealed to the late Victorians. In order to find an historical parallel, we have to turn to the semi-mythical figure of Rasputin, the "holy devil" who was assassinated in 1916. The truth about Rasputin, like the truth about Hasan bin Sabbah, was interesting but unspectacular. He was deeply religious; he had a "charisma" that attracted converts; he liked power, and was not free of human weaknesses. In short, he was 90 per cent ordinary, 10 per cent extraordinary. The legendary Rasputin is 100 per cent monster. Like the minotaur, he is a mythical archetype; he exists because people want him to exist. He has hypnotic powers and immense physical strength (in fact, Rasputin was not particularly strong); his "holiness" is a mask that hides cruelty and power mania; he is sexually insatiable and capable of drinking vodka by the quart; he manipulates politicians and princes as if they were puppets. . .

Why should people want to believe in such a legend? Because it symbolizes and objectifies a secret fear in which there is also an element of fascination. This is also true of the Assassins. "And in the night of Friday, 23 May, he hastened off to the fire of God and his Hell," says Juvayni, describing Hasan's death. Murder was a sin that involved eternal damnation – and the Middle Ages took this very seriously indeed; yet the Assassins committed this sin for purely political ends. This is why the Christian chroniclers preferred to gloss over the religious motivation, and to emphasize the trickery and chicanery and fanaticism; it made the damnation so much more certain, so much more frightening.

But this is not the whole explanation. The Old Man of the Mountain never ordered any deed of cruelty. If he had sent his soldiers to besiege a town and massacre the inhabitants, he would have aroused respect rather than horror. But he was doing something altogether more alarming. He was refusing to play the game according to the rules. The whole purpose of the social structure was to protect the citizens against evildoers. In *A Casebook of Murder* I quoted H. G. Wells: "The early civilizations were not slowly evolved and adapted *communities*. They were essentially jostling *crowds* in which quite unprecedented reactions were possible." Men came together into cities for protection; not from wild animals – for that purpose villages were as good as cities – but from their fellow human beings, the dispossessed who found it easier to rob and rape than to work. When the marauders were caught they were treated with unprecedented ferocity (after all, it is not so long ago that the bodies of highwaymen were allowed to rot on gibbets in England). A ruler might be cruel and arbitrary; but he was also the law-giver and protector, the foundation stone of social stability. By sending out his fanatics to murder viziers and princes, Hasan was touching a nerve of deep insecurity. It was as if some modern terrorist organisation held society up to ransom by threatening to bomb school nurseries. The Assassin produced a feeling of outrage by doing something that simply "wasn't done". It is difficult for us, in our relatively stable and law-abiding society, to understand the feeling aroused by the Assassins in a society where stability was newly acquired. They seemed to threaten a return to chaos and violence. They were creatures of nightmare.

By AD 1300, the Assassins had ceased to exist in the Middle East, at least as a political force. In 1825, the English traveller J. B. Fraser remarked that although the Ismailis no longer committed murder, they were still fanatically devoted to their chief. Fraser also commented that there were Ismailis in India too. This raises a fascinating question: whether the Assassins of the Middle East formed a liaison with their Indian counterparts, the Thugs. When William Sleeman was investigating the Thugs in the nineteenth century, he was puzzled why, although they were

Moslems, they worshipped the Hindu goddess Kali. One captured Thug explained that Kali was identical with Fatima, the murdered daughter of the prophet.

The Thugs (pronounced "tug") came to the attention of Europe after the British annexation of India in the late eighteenth century. At first, the conquerors noted simply that the roads of India seemed to be infested with bands of robbers who strangled their victims. In 1816, a doctor named Robert Sherwood, stationed in Madras, induced some of these robbers to talk to him about their religion. His article "On the Murderers Called Phansigars" appeared in *Asiatic Researches* in 1820, and caused some excitement. Sherwood alleged that the phansigars or Thugs (phansi means a noose; thug means cheat) committed murders as a religious duty, and that their aim was the actual killing, rather than the robbery that accompanied it.

The bizarre story caught the imagination of the English, and the word "thug" soon passed into the language. The Thugs, according to Sherwood, lived quietly in their native villages for most of the year, fulfilling their duties as citizens and fathers in a manner that aroused no suspicion. But in the month of pilgrimage (usually November–December) they took to the roads and slaughtered travellers, always taking care to be at least a hundred miles from home.

The method was always the same. The advance guard would locate a band of travellers, then one or two of the Thugs would approach the group and ask if they might travel with it – for protection. A few days later, a few more Thugs would make the same request. This would continue until there were more Thugs than travellers. The killing usually took place in the evening, when the travellers were seated around the fire. At a given signal, three Thugs would take their place behind each victim. One of them would pass the strangling cloth (or *ruhmal*) around the victim's neck; another would grab his legs and lift them clear of the ground; the third would seize his hands or kneel on his back. Usually, it was all over within seconds. The bodies of the victims were then hacked and mutilated to prevent recognition, and to make them decompose more quickly. The legs were cut off; if there was time, the whole body might be dismembered. Then it was buried. It was now time for the most important part of the ritual, the ceremony known as *Tuponee*. A tent was usually erected to shield the Thugs from the sight of travellers. The *kussee*, the consecrated pickaxe (their equivalent of the Christian cross), was placed near the grave: the Thugs sat around in a group. The leader prayed to Kali for wealth and success. A symbolic strangling was enacted, and then all who had taken an active part in the murder ate the "communion sugar" (*goor*), while the chief poured consecrated water on the grave. One of the captured Thugs told Sleeman: "Let any man once taste of that *goor* and he will be a Thug, though he know all the trades and have all the wealth of the world."

William Sleeman was a captain in the British army; born in St Tudy, Cornwall, he had served in India since 1809. He was fascinated by Sherwood's paper, and in the early 1820s, he began to study the Thugs in the Nerbudda Valley. The revelations he made in 1829 caused a sensation throughout India. Sleeman revealed that Thuggee was not a local religious sect, but a nationwide phenomenon that claimed the lives of thousands of travellers every year. Sleeman became the acknowledged authority on the subject, and in 1830, Lord William Bentinck appointed him to suppress the Thugs.

Fortunately for Sleeman, the organization had already become corrupt and degenerate. In its earlier days, the members of the sect had been strict in their observance of the rules. It was forbidden to kill women, because Kali was a woman; it was also forbidden to kill religious mendicants, carpenters, metal workers, blind men, pariahs, lepers, mutilated men, and men driving a goat or cow. Greed had caused a gradual relaxation of the rules (it must have been infuriating to let a rich caravan escape because it contained a carpenter or blind man); and it was to this disobedience that the Thugs attributed their decline in fortunes. In a sense, this was true. Haste and greed meant that bodies were sometimes left unburied, so a search could be instituted more quickly. And in some cases, lack of preparation meant that the killing was bungled; Sleeman mentions a case in which the Thugs were pursued back to their own village, and saved from arrest only by the intervention of the villagers (who had been well bribed). When Sleeman's researches were published, travellers became suspicious of "holy men" or poor Moslems who asked for protection. Better roads (built by the British) meant that Thugs could be pursued more easily. Many of them became informers (or "approvers") to save their own lives. Within a few years, thousands of Thugs had been arrested and brought to trial.

Sleeman was the first to understand the fundamentally religious nature of Thuggee: that the murders were sacrifices offered to the dark mother, Kali (also known as Durgha and Bhowani). Because he was deeply religious, the Thug was usually scrupulous, honest, kindly and trustworthy; Sleeman's assistant described one Thug chief as "the best man I have ever known". Many Thugs were rich men who held responsible positions; part of their spoils went to local Rajahs or officials, who had no objection to Thugs provided they committed their murders elsewhere. Colonel James Sleeman, grandson of Sir William, described Feringheea as "the Beau Nash of Thuggee". Like the Assassins, most convicted Thugs met their deaths with remarkable bravery, which impressed their British executioners. It is this Jekyll and Hyde character that makes the Thugs so baffling. One old Thug was the nurse of a family of British children, and obviously regarded his charges with great tenderness; for precisely one month of every year he obtained leave to visit his "sick mother"; the family found it unbelievable when he was arrested as a Thug. For the Thugs were capable of murdering children as casually as adults. A Thug leader described how his gang decoyed a group of twenty-seven, including five women and two children, away from a larger group of travellers (arguing that they could travel more cheaply). At midnight they stopped to rest in a grove, already chosen in advance as the murder place. There the Thugs strangled the adults; the children were given to two Thugs; but one of them kept crying for his mother, whom he had just seen murdered. The Thug picked him up by his feet and dashed out his brains against a rock. This was one of the few occasions when retribution followed. The adults were buried, but the Thugs overlooked the boy's body. It was discovered the next morning by the local landowner, who set out to hunt the Thugs with armed men. After a chase, the Thugs were located; when the armed men opened fire, they scattered, leaving behind much of their booty. Four thugs were arrested, and kept in captivity for a few years. (Sleeman points out that the landowner's motive was not a sense of justice, but to seize the spoils.) The other boy was brought up as a Thug.

The male children of Thugs were automatically initiated into the sect. They were first placed in the care of a Thug tutor, who insisted upon absolute obedience, and acted as their religious instructor. (It must be emphasized that the killing was only a part of the ritual of the Thugs, as Communion is of Christians.) At the age of nine or ten, the boys were allowed to act as scouts, and later to watch the killing At eighteen they were allowed to take part in the killing and eat the *goor*.

By the year 1850, Thuggee had virtually ceased to exist in India. Over 4,000 Thugs had been brought to trial; some were hanged, others sentenced to transportation or life imprisonment. Sleeman came to know many of them, even to establish a kind of friendship; for example, he was instrumental in getting the notorious Feringheea a pardon (in the face of some opposition, for when the Thug leader was caught, he admitted that he had just returned from an expedition in which 105 men and women had died).

The mystery of the origin of Thuggee is still unsolved. Feringheea told Sleeman that all the Thug rituals were portrayed in the eighth-century carvings in the caves of Ellora. (Ellora is a village in north-east Bombay province, and its Hindu, Buddhist and Jain temples extend for over a mile, with some of India's greatest sculptural treasures, whose dates range from the third to the thirteenth century.) If this is true, then the Thugs pre-dated the Assassins by three hundred years. In his book *The Assassins*, Bernard Lewis suggests that the Thugs may have been connected with the stranglers of Iraq – the heretical sect that sprang up after the death of the Prophet. But these stranglers flourished in the first half of the eighth century, and four more centuries were to elapse before the Moslems made deep inroads into India. (The greatest of the early Moslem invaders of India, Mahmud of Ghazni – Khayyam's "mighty Mahmud" – confined himself to the Punjab, in north-western India: Delhi fell to Mohammed of Ghur in 1192.) So it is altogether more likely that Ismailis, fleeing from persecution after the fall of Alamut, discovered that India already possessed its own Order of Assassins, and formed an alliance with the Thugs. Other Ismailis formed their own sects in India, and continued to regard the Persian Imam as their head. In 1811, the French consul Rousseau observed that

Ismailis flourished in India, and that they regarded their Imam almost as a god. In 1850, a sect of Ismailis known as the Khojas decided to settle a religious dispute by their old methods, and four dissenting brethren were assassinated in broad daylight. The four killers were hanged. The quarrel centred around the question of whether the Khojas of Bombay province still owned allegiance to the Persian Imam. This Imam was known as the Aga Khan; and a few years later, he was forced to flee to India after an unsuccessful attempt to overthrow the Shah of Persia. He became the spiritual head of the Ismailis not only in India, but also in Persia, Syria and central Asia. And so the homeland of the Thugs became eventually the homeland of the descendants of the Assassins.

All the chroniclers of the Thugs have talked about the "mystery" of their psychology. And what exactly is this mystery? Not that criminals may appear to be law-abiding citizens; this is a commonplace of criminal investigation; Deacon Brodie and Charlie Peace are the rule, not the exception. But the Thugs were not criminals in the ordinary sense. What emerges on every page of Sleeman's book is that they were driven by a *compulsion* to kill. This exciting game of stalking and strangling human beings became an addiction. This is what troubled the British investigators, who were ordinary soldiers and civil servants, men of the Dr Watson type. They sensed that the Thug murders were an inverted creative act, which brought its own peculiar, deep satisfaction, and the thought made them shudder.

The Thugs, on the other hand, took the obsessional nature of their vocation for granted. It was the result of entering the service of the dark goddess, and eating her *goor*. Feringheea told Sleeman: "My mother's family were opulent, her relations high in office. I have been high in office myself, and become so great a favourite. . .that I was sure of promotion; yet I was always miserable when absent from the gang, and obliged to return to Thuggee. My father made me taste of that fatal *goor* when I was a mere boy, and if I were to live to a thousand years, I should never be able to follow any other trade." They were the chosen of Kali; the first Thugs had been created by Kali to help her destroy a horde of demons. (These had to be strangled, for their blood, once shed, turned into more demons.) No Thug entertained the slightest doubt that the goddess accompanied them on their expeditions. She made the sacred pickaxe fly out of the well, where it was sometimes thrown overnight, into the hand of its carrier. (Many Thugs assured Sleeman that they had seen this happen.) And if they buried the pickaxe, she turned it in the night, so it pointed in the direction where the richest booty lay. Since she was a goddess of destruction, it was natural enough that her slaves should be possessed by the urge to destroy.

A modern psychologist would probably explain this obsession in terms of sex; for a man with a compulsion to kill is in the grip of sadism: and sadism is surely sexual in origin. This is an assumption that will be questioned in a later chapter; for the moment, it is enough to note that a Thug would have rejected this view with indignation. They were puritanical about sex, because their goddess was a woman. Sleeman says: "No Thug was ever known to offer insult, either in speech or act, to a woman they were about to murder." A Thug theologian, if such a thing existed, would have explained the "mystery" of Thug psychology in terms of the nature of Kali herself. She is the goddess of Time and Saviour of the Universe. (Her husband, Shiva, upon whom she stands, is the god of Space.) She represents the ultimate reconciliation of opposites: terror and motherly tenderness, death and creation. The ancient Greeks might have regarded her as an incarnation of Dionysus, the god of wine, who also induces divine frenzy in his worshippers. The Hindu saint Ramakrishna saw in her the ultimate vital force of creation, with all its contradictions, an infinite power that transcends merely human notions of good and evil.

The western mind finds this difficult to grasp, for Christianity has no counterpart of Kali. It is like asserting that God and the Devil are halves of the same godhead, both equally powerful, equally necessary to the scheme of things. The Church persecuted the heresy known as Dualism, which asserted something very similar. In *A Glastonbury Romance*, the novelist John Cowper Powys explained sadism as a consequence of this fundamental split in the godhead: "Its primordial goodness warring forever against its primordial evil holds life up only by vast excess of energy and oceans of lavish waste. Even though the cry of a particular creature may reach the First Cause, there is always a danger of its being intercepted by the evil will of this vast Janus-faced Force. . ." Powys's sadist, an antiquary named Evans, is obsessed by a certain passage in a book describing a killing blow with an iron bar. "The nature of his temptation was such that it had nothing to redeem it. Such abominable wickedness came straight out of the evil in the heart of the First Cause, travelled through the Interlunar spaces, and entered the particular nerve in the erotic organism of Mr Evans which was predestined to respond to it." Mr Evans is tortured by his obsession with killing. "He saw his soul in the form of an unspeakable worm, writhing in pursuit of new, and ever new mental victims, drinking new and innocent blood." The Thugs accepted their own murderous obsession, because killing was ordained by their goddess.

Whether we can accept Powys's form of Dualism as literally true is beside the point. What is important is that we recognise the *autonomous* nature of this urge to destroy, which seems to be as basic as the sexual or territorial drive. For whatever reason, man *is* capable of experiencing a morbid involvement in the act of destruction, as if some deep erotic nerve had been touched by a craving for violence. And, like the sexual impulse, this destructive impulse has the power to blind him to everything but its own satisfaction. The future becomes unimportant or non-existent; all that counts is fulfilment of the need for violence.

And it is the presence of this impulse, this "worm of destruction", that distinguishes "assassination" from the ordinary murder case. It can always be sensed underneath the apparent motive for the killing, whether it is sexual, or political, or simply a general resentment against society. The obvious motive is only the excuse that allows the "erotic nerve" to be touched by the energy of destruction. In some cases, the two are so intermingled that they can hardly be separated. In Peter Kürten, the Düsseldorf sadist, the sexual impulse and the urge to violence had become interdependent: violence provoked a sexual orgasm; sexual excitement released a desire for violence. When Kürten returned to Düsseldorf after a long prison sentence there was a red sunset, and he saw it as an auspicious sign for the reign of terror he was about to inaugurate. When he walked around the streets of Düsseldorf, he had dreams of blowing up the city with dynamite. A Thug would have recognized in him a fellow devotee of Kali.

Again, in the case of the unknown sadist known as Jack the Ripper, one recognizes again the autonomous nature of the destructive impulse. Indeed, it is difficult to form any kind of mental picture of the Ripper without assuming that he was in the power of Mr Evans's "worm". The "mystery" one senses in this case is the mystery Sleeman sensed about the Thugs. The incredible violence of the murders – the disembowelling of the victims, the hacking of the features, the removal of vital organs – all indicate a man giving expression to an urge that has become a torment. When he woke up the next morning, he probably found it unbelievable that it had actually happened, that it was not a nightmare.

The New Orleans Axeman murders, which took place in 1918 and 1919, provide an interesting parallel with the Ripper case. Jack the Ripper, writing to a member of the Whitechapel Vigilance Committee (and enclosing part of the kidney of his latest victim), begins his letter: "From Hell. Mr Lusk, sir, I send you half the kidney I took from one woman. . ." The Axeman wrote a letter to the editor of the *Times Picayune* in which he declared: "I am not a human being, but a spirit and fell demon from the hottest hell." It would seem that both murderers felt themselves to be demonic emissaries, agents of a dark force, sent to scourge mankind. The parallel with the Thugs needs no underlining.

The "demonic" element is again clearly displayed in the Ratcliffe Highway murders of 1811 – described in the appendix to De Quincey's essay on "Murder Considered as One of the Fine Arts". Towards midnight on 7 December, Timothy Marr, who kept a hosier's shop in the East End of London, sent out the servant girl to buy oysters; when she returned, it was to find everyone in the house dead: Timothy Marr, his wife Celia, their baby, and the apprentice boy, James Gowen. It looked as if a giant with a sledgehammer had been at work. The force of the blows had been so great that the apprentice's brains were spattered over the ceiling. The hood of the baby's cradle had been smashed, as if in a frenzy of violence; the child's head was battered, and its throat cut. The murder weapon was found in the bedroom: a type of sledge-hammer called a "penmaul", which, in a poster about the murders, can be seen to bear a striking resemblance to the sacred pickaxe of the Thugs.

There was still no clue to the killer's identity or motive when, two weeks later, a second family was slaughtered in the same area. A publican named Williamson, his wife and their maidservant, were slaughtered with an iron bar, and their throats cut. A lodger named John Turner came downstairs while the murders were taking place, and saw a man bending over Mrs Williamson's body: he tiptoed back upstairs, made a rope of his bedsheets, and escaped from the bedroom window. A crowd, attracted by his yells, broke into the house but the killer escaped through a rear window. (He seems to have been on the point of killing a fourteen-year-old girl in her bed when the noise disturbed him.) A certain amount of money had been taken.

The pen-maul was traced to a sailor's lodging house, and a young Irishman named John Williams arrested. He had access to the tool chest that contained the maul. On the morning of the murder, he had returned to a room he shared with other lodgers, and shouted at someone to put out a candle that was burning. The next morning, it was noticed that his shoes were muddy (the murderer had escaped by scrambling up a muddy bank); so were his socks, which he thereupon washed. A shirt was found to be bloodstained. Later on, bloodstained trousers were found in the bottom of the privy in the house. A coat belonging to Williams had heavy bloodstains in the pocket, as if it had held a knife; the bloodstained knife was later found in a mousehole. (De Quincey states, mistakenly, that it was found in the pocket.) Williams hanged himself before he could be brought to trial; his body was buried at the crossroads near the scene of the murders, with a stake driven through the heart.

In *The Maul and the Pear Tree* (1971), T. A. Critchley and P.D. James argue that Williams was probably "framed". The actual killer, they suggest, was a man named Ablass, a shipmate of Williams with a history of violence. The motive was robbery, and Ablass was probably aided by a man named Hart. The authors even suggest that Williams was actually murdered in jail, with the connivance of the jailer. The theory is well-argued, but the basic objections remain. If the motive was burglary, why kill the baby? If two men were concerned, why did the lodger, Turner, see only one? But the basic objection is that the murders were committed with the ferocity of a maniac; talk about "motive" is irrelevant. It is true that Williams had no history of violence, but on examination, it turns out that Ablass's "violence" amounted to fomenting a mutiny on board ship. Ablass had reason to dislike Williams, who had escaped punishment after the mutiny; but again, what has this to do with the violence of the murders? The Ratcliffe Highway murders fascinated De Quincey's generation for the same reason that the Ripper murders fascinated the late Victorians: because of their "demonic" quality, because the killer was a man obsessed by violence for its own sake.

In reading accounts of assassinations, one is struck by the assassin's indifference to his own death. In the "golden age" of political assassination, towards the end of the last century, assassins often went to the scaffold or guillotine crying "*Vive l'anarchie!*" We have already noted the indifference to death shown by the Assassins of Persia and the Thugs of India. In some cases, this was due to genuine idealism. Kaliayev, who blew up the Grand Duke Sergius in 1904, declined an offer by the widow to plead for his life, saying that his death would do more for the cause of revolution in Russia. Sometimes, it was bravado, as when the train robber and murderer Charrier told the jury: "I am a desperate enemy of society, and my hatred will only finish with my life. I defy you, gentlemen of the jury, to take my head." (They obliged.) But the indifference is so general that it is tempting to conclude that the assassin hopes to destroy himself as well as his victim. It is almost as though "Mr Evans's worm", like the monkey in Le Fanu's *Green Tea*, were a demon tempting man to self-destruction. This, again, may serve as a criterion to distinguish "assassination" from murder.

Two examples will serve to illustrate my point. On 8 February, 1872, Lord Mayo, the Viceroy of India, spent the day inspecting the prison settlements on the four Andaman Islands in the Bay of Bengal. Towards dusk, as he was about the leave the fourth of them, Hopetown, he suddenly decided to climb a hill called Mount Harriet. As his party moved towards the summit, they were shadowed by a man carrying a long knife. The killer's opportunity came as Lord Mayo walked along the jetty, on his way to the boat; he leapt on his back, crooked an arm round his neck, and stabbed him twice in the shoulder blades. Lord Mayo died shortly afterwards. The killer, an Indian named Shere Ali, was captured, and violently beaten by the soldiers.

Five years before, Shere Ali had been sentenced to death by the British authorities for killing a relative in a blood feud; the sentence was later commuted to life imprisonment. It was his feeling that the British had no right to interfere in a hereditary feud, so although he was a model prisoner, he kept the carving knife hidden in his cell, and prayed for the day when he might murder some distinguished European. After the assassination of Lord Mayo, Shere Ali was asked why he had done it. "By the order of God." During the month when he awaited hanging, he remained defiant and boastful; he seemed to regard his own death as a good exchange for the murder of a British Lord. On one occasion, he succeeded in overpowering a guard and stabbing him twice with his own bayonet: on another, he showed a British officer a sharp stone which he had levered out of the floor; he said it was a good thing the officer had been civil, because he had intended to kill him.

In the early hours of 20 July 1948, a car pulled up in front of the house of the Superintendent of the Ohio State Reformatory Farm. Two ex-convicts, Robert Daniels and John West, burst into the house, where John Niebel, his wife and twenty-year-old daughter had been sleeping. While John West pistol-whipped Niebel and his wife, Daniels beat the girl in another room, then raped her. Then all three were made to strip, and marched into a nearby field. They were made to kneel, and then shot. Mrs Niebel was shot in the stomach, and allowed to writhe on the ground for a while before she was despatched with a bullet in the head.

The killers were at large for another twenty-four hours, but escape was impossible. As soon as the bodies were found early next morning road blocks were thrown up around the whole county. During their flight, Daniels and West committed two more murders: one of a car driver, one of a truck driver asleep in his cab. Stopped by the police at a road block, West tried to shoot his way out and was killed; Daniels was arrested and later executed.

At first sight, there seems an abyss of difference between this case and Shere Ali's. West and Daniels hoped to escape, and nearly succeeded. But on closer scrutiny, it becomes more problematic. West was a near-moron; but Daniels was described by the prison psychiatrist as "brainy". Yet a few hours before the murder of the Niebels, they committed two tavern robberies in Columbus, Ohio, in the second of which they murdered the owner. Daniels was driving his own car, and its make and number were noted by customers as the bandits fled. Knowing there was a state alert out for them, they drove to the Niebels', and parked the car in front of the house, where it was observed by a neighbour. If Daniels had really been determined to escape, he would have taken elementary precautions such as wearing a mask in the two hold-ups, using a stolen car instead of one registered in his own name, and parking some distance away from the Niebels' house. Every stage of the operation was conducted in a manner that made their capture inevitable, and the two extra murders in the course of flight – both completely gratuitous – strengthen this view. Like Shere Ali, Daniels and West thought only of the supreme satisfaction of revenge; they took no interest in what lay beyond it, because their planning of the operation made it certain that only death lay beyond it. In the sense already defined, Daniels and West were assassins rather than murderers.

It is clear that what drives a killer like Shere Ali is a curious mixture of self-esteem and emotional self-deception. In fact, this applies to a surprising number of political assassins. Luigi Lucheni, who stabbed to death the Empress Elizabeth of Austria in 1898 had written in his diary: "How I would like to kill someone – but it must be someone important so it gets into the papers." (And in 1966, a young student named Robert Smith walked into a beauty parlour in Mesa, Arizona, made five women and two children lie on the floor, then shot them all in the back of the head: he explained, "I wanted to become known, to get myself a name.") Another example is Charles Guiteau, the assassin of President Garfield, of whom Robert J. Donovan remarks (in his book *The Assassins*):

> Guiteau, as a young recruit unskilled in any manual craft, was given menial chores in the fields, the workshops and the kitchen [of the Oneida Community]. Under this drudgery, he took to sulking, daydreaming of future glory and tacking up on the walls of his room signs like this:

CHARLES J. GUITEAU

PREMIER OF ENGLAND
WILL DELIVER A LECTURE IN
ST JAMES HALL, LONDON.

It sounds like insanity; but Guiteau was not insane in the ordinary sense – only permanently tormented by a desire for "recognition", to *be* somebody. Neither was he, in the strict sense of the word, a religious crank, although he wrote to his father: "I claim that I am in the employ of *Jesus Christ and Co*, the very ablest and strongest firm in the universe. . ."; for Guiteau, religion was just another means of self-assertion. When religion failed to pay off, he went in for confidence swindling. After six years of this hand-to-mouth existence, he discovered the possibilities of politics as a stepping stone to eminence; he devoted a great deal of 1872 to campaigning for Horace Greeley, the Democratic candidate for the presidency. He had visions of being appointed Minister to Chile. But Greeley was defeated, then died, and Guiteau was temporarily plunged into total depression. During Grant's two terms of office, he went back to religious oratory, billing himself as "the Little Giant from the West", and managing to scrape a poor living by charging fifty cents for admission to his sermons on the existence of Hell. In 1880 he decided to switch back to politics, and this time to support Grant, who seemed the likely winner. Garfield was nominated as candidate instead, so Guiteau simply changed "Grant" to "Garfield" in the speech he had written, and hung around Republican headquarters, making a nuisance of himself and unaware that he was regarded as a joke. He had no opportunity to actually deliver his speech; but when Garfield became president, Guiteau felt nevertheless that he was due for some reward such as a post as foreign ambassador. His first choice fell on Vienna, but he later decided that Paris would be preferable. For months he haunted the White House, becoming such a pest that the staff were finally instructed not to admit him on any account. Finally he decided that a man who could behave in this heartless way "to the men that made him" (i.e. himself) was a "danger to the American people and should be eliminated". "Besides," he added (in a note about his decision) "it will create a demand for my book *The Truth*". So he bought a revolver with borrowed money, and on 2 July 1881, walked up behind the President at the railway station and shot him in the back. Garfield died two months later, on 19 September. At his trial, Guiteau's defence of insanity failed perhaps because he went to such lengths to explain that he was neither a fool nor a lunatic; it was also obvious that he was enjoying every minute of his notoriety. He was executed in June 1882.

The prosecution argued that Guiteau was completely sane in the normal sense of the term, and even the defence neurologist admitted that the chief trouble was "the exaggerated self-feeling of the morbid egotist." After reading a detailed account of Guiteau's life with its endless miscalculations and humiliations the reader comes away with the feeling that Guiteau was rebelling against fate, against life: that is to say, the murder was a "magical" act of self-assertion directed, like all magical acts, at the wrong person.

It should not be assumed that only males are capable of self-esteem murders. In the course of revising this book, I mentioned its theme to Clive Gunnell, a reporter for Westward Television. He surprised me by saying that my theory of the self-esteem killer was confirmed by his own observation of Ruth Ellis, who was executed in 1955 for the murder of her lover, David Blakely. Clive Gunnell was the friend with whom David Blakely left the Magdala public house in Hampstead. As they left the pub, Ruth Ellis, a pretty twenty-eight-year-old divorcée, stepped forward and emptied a revolver at Blakely; Clive Gunnell was bending over him on the pavement while she continued to shoot over his shoulder.

Most writers on the case have assumed that this was a passion killing, a case of violent jealousy. Clive Gunnell denied this. Although Ruth Ellis and David Blakely had been lovers for two years, both had had other affairs; in fact, at the time of the murder, Ruth Ellis was living with one man, having an affair with another, and was married to a third. "She just had a craving for recognition," said Clive Gunnell. "In these days of television, she'd have probably got on to some quiz team or panel and become a public figure – which is what she really wanted. She was quite a strong personality." In France or Italy, her shooting of David Blakely might have achieved precisely this; as a distraught and jealous woman – moreover, one who had suffered a miscarriage only a few days before the murder – she would probably have received a year in jail for second degree murder, and thereafter featured in books and articles about *crimes passionels*. The English, unfortunately, lack this kind of romanticism. In spite of a public outcry, she was executed.

In 1943, the American psychologist Abraham Maslow produced a theory that sheds an interesting light on "self-esteem killers", like Charles Guiteau and Ruth Ellis. What he suggested is that human motivation can be described in terms of a "hierarchy of needs" or values. Expressed very simply, what the theory states is as follows. The most basic of our human needs is the need for food; when a man is starving, he is incapable of thinking about anything else. And he imagines that if only he could have three good meals a day, he would be ideally happy. But if, in fact, he achieves his three good meals, he tends to become obsessed by the next "level" of need: for security, a roof over his head. Every tramp dreams of retiring to a country cottage with roses round the door. And if he satisfies this craving and becomes a householder, the next level emerges: the desire to be loved and wanted, the desire for a person of the opposite sex. If *this* level is satisfied, the next emerges: the need to be liked and admired, the craving for self-esteem. This is the level at which men join rotary clubs and women give coffee mornings. They want to be "recognised" – if possible, to be famous. And if *this* level is also satisfied, the next level is what Maslow calls "self-actualisation" – the desire to do something more or less creative. It may only be something like putting model ships in bottles, but it satisfies the desire to do something constructive and to do it well.

It is interesting to note that each level except the last has its own type of crime. A starving man will steal or even kill for food. And a man whose domestic security is threatened may turn to crime to remove the threat. (In the Victorian age there were many such cases. Madeleine Smith poisoned a lover who threatened to send her love letters to her father. Professor Webster murdered his fellow academic Dr Parkman because the latter threatened to sue him for debt.) A sexually frustrated man may commit rape or sexual murder. And a man like Charles Guiteau, with an unsatisfied craving for "recognition", may kill simply to become "known."

Equally interesting is the fact that we can see these "levels" in the crimes of the past two centuries. In the late eighteenth and early nineteenth centuries, most crime was at the most basic level; it sprang out of the need to keep alive. As society became more prosperous through the industrial revolution there was an increasing amount of "domestic" crime. (In December 1902, an unemployed clerk named Edgar Edwards even murdered a whole family – a grocer named Darby, together with his wife and baby – simply to sell their business and rent himself a home.) Towards the end of the century the "age of sex crime" began. This has lasted down to the present day. But the 1960s saw the emergence of a new type of crime, the crime of self-esteem. In an increasing number of killers, like Robert Smith, or the moors murderer Ian Brady, we see a smouldering resentment at being "unknown", and the desire to become famous by doing something spectacular. This is the level of the "assassin."

The assassin's main problem, of course, is that in the process of "becoming known" he is also likely to forfeit his life, or at least, his liberty. And if he manages to avoid being caught, he fails to achieve his object of becoming known. So the "self-esteem" criminal finds himself trapped in an absurd dilemma – a dilemma typified by the case of San Francisco's "Zodiac" murders.

Between 20 December 1968 and 11 October 1969, an unknown killer committed five murders, and seriously wounded two more victims. On 20 December, two teenagers, David Farraday and Bettilou Jensen, were attacked as they sat in a station wagon in a lovers' lane near Vallejo, California. Both were shot dead; but the youth's wallet was untouched, and the girl had not been sexually assaulted. On 5 July 1969, a caller with a gruff voice phoned the Vallejo police station, and said that he had just committed a double murder on the Columbia Parkway; he added that he had "killed those kids last year". In the car park of a golf course, not far from the spot where the other victims had been found, police discovered another couple who had been shot. Darlene Ferrin, a waitress, was dead; Michael Mageau was still alive. He was able to tell police that a man had stepped out of a parked car, fired several shots at them, then turned and walked away. A month later, three San Francisco newspapers received letters, signed with a cross superimposed on a circle (the astrological sign of the zodiac). The letters stated that the writer was the man who had shot both couples, and gave details that made it clear that he was telling the truth. Apart from the block-letter text, these letters also contained passages in cipher – a different cipher for each. A schoolteacher who cracked the code discovered that the cipher read: "I like killing people because it is so much fun; it is more fun than killing wild game in the forest because man is the most dangerous animal. . .when I die I will be reborn in Paradise and all I have killed will be my slaves. . ."

On 27 September 1969, the same caller rang the Napa police department to report a double murder. Rushing to the scene on the shores of Lake Berryessa, police discovered a man and a woman had been stabbed. Again, the man, Brian Hartnell, was alive; the girl, Cecilia Shepard, died soon after. Hartnell described how they had just finished a picnic when they were approached by a paunchy figure in a hood-mask; on the lower part of the hood was the sign of the Zodiac, marked in white. The man asked for money, tied them both up, then stabbed them repeatedly. On the door of Hartnell's white sports car the police found a drawing of the Zodiac sign, and the dates of the previous murders.

Two weeks later, on 11 October 1969, the killer shot a taxi driver, Paul Stine, in the back of the head in San Francisco, then walked off, taking the driver's wallet, and a fragment torn from his shirt. The bullet was found to have come from the same gun that killed Darlene Ferrin. The next day, the San Francisco *Chronicle* received another Zodiac letter, enclosing a bloody fragment of shirt. The writer declared he was the murderer of Paul Stine; he complained of the inefficiency of the police, and went on: "Schoolchildren make nice targets. I think I shall wipe out a school bus some morning. Just shoot out the tyres, then pick off the kiddies as they come bouncing out."

Zodiac did not carry out his threat; the murder of the taxi driver has proved to be the last to date. But on 21 October, a caller claiming to be Zodiac rang the Oakland police station, and declared that he would be willing to give himself up if he could be represented by a famous lawyer – F. Lee Bailey and Melvin Belli were his first choices. He also asked that time should be reserved for him on an early morning talk show on television. This was accordingly done. The call had come in after midnight; the show went out at 6.45 a.m. The event was announced on television; listeners were asked not to phone in with their usual questions, but to leave the line free for Zodiac. By the time the Jim Dunbar show came on, an enormous audience was watching the show. At 7.41, a call came on the line; a caller with a soft, boyish voice identified himself as Zodiac. He called back fifteen times, and talked to the lawyer Melvin Belli about his murders and the headaches he suffered from. He ended by agreeing to meet Belli in front of a store in Daly City, but failed to turn up.

Whether or not this caller (who asked to be addressed as Sam) was the genuine Zodiac, the actual killer did not disown him; two months later, he sent a Christmas greetings letter to Belli, enclosing another fragment of Stine's bloodstained shirt as identification. The letter said he needed help: "I am afraid I will lose control and take my ninth and possibly tenth victim." The figure alarmed the police, but a careful check of unsolved homicides failed to substantiate Zodiac's claim. In March 1971, the Los Angeles *Times* received a Zodiac letter, this time boasting of seventeen murders; but again, this claim would appear to be unfounded.

Zodiac letters have continued to be received at intervals, some of which are regarded as genuine by handwriting experts. In some of them the writer threatens to torture future victims, and one of them contained a parody of Koko's song in *The Mikado*, describing all the people he would like to kill "who never would be missed".

It is possible, of course, that "Zodiac" may be a sadist of the Kürten type, who experiences orgasm at the moment of stabbing or shooting his victims, but there is no indication of this. Kürten never used a gun; his own peculiar obsession was blood, so he preferred to stab his victims. A man who walks up to a car, empties his revolver through the window, then walks away, does not sound as if his aim is sexual enjoyment. Two youths who heard the shot that killed the taxi driver Paul Stine described how the killer emerged from the cab a moment later, reached in through the window to tear the driver's shirt, then hurried off; again, there is no indication of a sexual motive. On the other hand, the evidence *does* suggest a man who kills out of the desire for self-assertion. The killings cause shock waves throughout California; this is what he wants. He writes letters in cryptogram, and threatens that if they are not published, he will go on a murder rampage. They *are* published, and he has the satisfaction of knowing that thousands of people are trying to puzzle out his message; it is like being an author; in a sense, he is famous. And the taste for publicity is the most marked trait of his character, the desire to shock and to intrigue. It is tempting to assume, on the basis of the attacks on courting couples, that he enjoys killing women, and that some kind of sexual jealousy is involved; but the murder of the taxi driver fails to bear this out. This is committed for the publicity, and is followed by the threat to attack a school bus – a threat which, it seems fairly certain, he had no intention of carrying out. For a week or two, he is the most talked-about man in America. He follows this up with a television "appearance", and has the satisfaction of knowing that the show is watched by the largest audience ever to see the same show in the Bay area. Was the caller with the boyish voice Zodiac? It seems probable. If Zodiac had changed his mind about calling the programme, and some hoaxer had taken his place, Zodiac would quickly have denounced the phoney; his highly developed sense of publicity guarantees that.

But all this exercise in anonymous publicity must have been peculiarly frustrating. He wants to be a public figure, and in a sense he achieves this; he enters into friendly discussion with a famous lawyer on television, and later drops him a Christmas letter beginning "Dear Melvin". But he can advance no further into this world of celebrity – at least, not without being caught. He tries to keep the excitement alive with more letters, mentioning more murders; but as no more murders follow, the interest wanes. The logical next step would be more killings; but his ambiguous celebrity has released some of the frustration that made him into a killer. We observe again the same "vicious circle" mechanism that we have noted in the case of sadistic pornography, and of sex crime. The killing is a response to a powerful desire whose non-satisfaction forms an evolutionary blockage. But the correct way to deal with this blockage is to find a socially acceptable way of satisfying the desire. It is true, for example, that Casanova was a sexual criminal; he admits in his memoirs that he and a crowd of friends kidnapped a girl, and all raped her. But although sexual desire dominated his life, he did not make a habit of rape;

he usually found that a certain amount of effort and charm was enough to persuade a girl to give him what he wanted. A certain amount of confidence swindling was involved; he often promised marriage, with no intention of honouring his word; still, this was socially acceptable, and there was nothing to stop him from turning his attention to other fields: to cutting a figure in society, or writing philosophical essays.

For each step we take up the "hierarchy of values" involves an *increased integration into society*. When a man thinks only of survival or security, he is thinking solely in terms of himself. When he thinks about sex, he is thinking in terms of one other person, and perhaps of a family. When the self-esteem needs become paramount, he begins to think in terms of other people and their opinion of him. And if he rises to the self-actualizing level – as a scientist or artist or philosopher – then he is thinking in terms of society, of the human race. At any level beyond the very lowest, anti-social activity is self-defeating. *This* is the paradoxical absurdity that lies at the root of the assassin's violence.

Dr Laurence Freedman remarked of "Zodiac": "He kills senselessly because he is deeply frustrated. And he hates himself because he is an anonymous nonentity. When he is caught, he will turn out to be a mouse, a murderous mouse." This may be true as far as it goes, but it overlooks one of the central points about the self-esteem killer: the "absurd" reasoning, the "magical" non-logic. In his letters, Zodiac attacks the police for their inefficiency, as though he is an indignant member of the public, not the man they are hunting. He implies that it takes considerable courage to kill "that most dangerous of all animals", man, when all he has done is to shoot defenceless courting couples in their cars.

This magical non-logic is characteristic of a type that A. E. van Vogt has called "the violent man" or "the right man". Van Vogt's theory of "the right man" is one of the most important contributions to the psychology of violence; unfortunately, it was cast in fictional form, and so never achieved the serious attention it deserved. A pamphlet describing the theory was printed for private circulation; the following is a summary of its contents.

In the pamphlet, "A Report on the Violent Male", van Vogt explains that he has been collecting stories of a certain type of violent man for more than a decade. A psychologist told him of a typical case. The man was divorced, and had set up his ex-wife in a surburban home, on condition that she did not re-marry, and should spend the rest of her life being a perfect mother to their son. The man apparently thought this was a fair arrangement.

The story of their marriage was as follows. She had been a nurse, and had had two affairs with doctors. Before marrying, she thought she ought to tell her future husband about this. He went into an insane frenzy of jealousy, and the next day, brought her a legal document in triplicate to sign. He refused to let her read it. She felt so guilty that she finally signed. Van Vogt says: "My years of observation of other males of this type tempts me to speculate that in [the document] she agreed that she was a prostitute, and that in marrying her he was raising her from the status of a fallen woman; but she must agree that she had no rights as a wife, except what he bestowed on her." After the marriage, the husband treated the wife as a chattel. He expected complete freedom. "He was always driving his secretaries to and from work, and taking an unconscionable long time to do it, or visiting one or another of his women employees in their apartments. Any questioning by his wife of this activity put him into a rage that often included violence." He roamed the country, reporting home when he felt like it. He was subject to sudden violent rages. After an evening listening to music with friends he might fly into a temper as he was preparing to leave the house for a cross-country flight, and knock his wife down. The next day he would ring up from some distant part of the country and beg forgiveness.

Van Vogt describes several other relationships with the same basic features – men who treat their wives and families in a violently despotic manner, and expect total, unquestioned obedience, becoming violent at the least sign of resistance. Such a man, says van Vogt, has an absolute obsession about being "in the right". He totally lacks self-criticism, and can storm and rage about some triviality with no glimmer of recognition that he is simply indulging himself and wasting everybody's time. If he has power – for example, like a Russian landowner of the last century, cited by van Vogt – he may use it with horrifying ruthlessness, having men flogged to death for minor offences. If actually proved wrong, he is likely to evade the issue by flying into an even greater rage at some invented affront or reflection upon his dignity, his attitude being that a wife who truly respected her husband would not tell him he was wrong. If she does so, it is because she wants to insult him.

Van Vogt calls this man "the right man" because of his obsessional need to be right. And he makes the interesting observation that if he is left by his wife, he goes to pieces; he may become an alcoholic, or a drifter, or even kill himself. Her submission forms the basis of his self-respect: her desertion pulls away his psychological foundations.

A point to bear in mind about the "right man" is that he belongs to the "dominant five per cent": but in our highly competitive world, many of these men may not possess the qualities necessary for gaining recognition from the rest of society. His immediate circle – his wife and children – has to provide the urgently needed psychological vitamin. Because they are unsatisfactory substitutes for the real thing, they also have to bear a certain amount of resentment, which may take the form of outrageous bullying. But since this bullying constitutes the last bulwark of his self-esteem, he needs the victims more than they need him. Children may leave home (in which case, they are never forgiven); but the desertion of the victim-in-chief, his wife, causes the total disintegration of his ego. Van Vogt argues that dictators – Hitler, Stalin, Mao – are often violent men. (Hitler's treatment of Geli Raubal, and his shock at her suicide, seems to confirm this: close friends thought he would kill himself; an earlier woman friend had also attempted suicide because of his unending supervision.)

Van Vogt's explanation of this attitude is that men have always dominated society, and that slightly unstable males show an exaggerated form of the normal male characteristic. He mentions that in China in 1950, the communists introduced laws designed to increase the rights of women, and that in one district alone, in 1954, 10,000 wives were murdered by their husbands for attempting to take advantage of the new law. In Italy in 1916, two women were sentenced to a year in gaol for adultery. Their defence was that their husbands were also unfaithful. The court overruled this plea on the ground that there is a legally established double standard.

I am inclined to suspect that the male attitude to women is based on something deeper than social usage, no matter how ancient. The compulsion that drives some men to rape is, oddly enough, a kind of worship of women. This probably develops in childhood – many male children think of their mother as a kind of goddess. They may be deeply shocked when they learn the facts of sex; it seems unutterably indecent that these goddesses should allow the coarse male to strip away their veils and use their bodies to satisfy his lowest appetite. A goddess ought to consort with a god. It could be argued that this sexual idealism is the result of immaturity, inexperience; but in that case, experience would be enough to dissipate it; and it doesn't. In Agnar Mykle's autobiographical novel *Lasso Round the Moon*, there is an episode that catches the essence of this male vision. He describes falling in love with a pretty girl at a party. "He had felt as though he held an elf in his arms; the night became magical, the air was full of delicate crystal; he hardly dared touch her. . ." The next morning he overhears a conversation: ". . .two boys, who had been in the car with the girl, told how on their way home they had decided to take her to one of their homes. The girl had shown no reluctance, not to either of them. The boy's parents were away and it had taken place in the parents' room, in the double bed. She had been so hot that both the boys had to have a shower afterwards. . ." This strikes at something deeper than male possessiveness: at some vision of the eternal feminine. The same feeling emerges in Gorki's story *Twenty-Six Men and a Girl*, where the twenty-six bakers, in their damp cellar, idealize the girl Tanya, until she gives herself to a soldier, when they turn on her and call her names. Conversely, when the male finally succeeds in possessing the goddess, he may experience a sense of power, non-contingency:

> What were all the world's alarms
> To mighty Paris when he found
> Sleep upon a golden bed
> That first dawn, in Helen's arms?

If it were not for this "magical" vision of woman, wives would have less to complain about; once the male curiosity had been satisfied, a man would lose all interest in other women. Very young men, possessed by unsatisfied desire, find it difficult to understand how a married man could commit rape or a sex crime; surely he could simply undress his wife? But this is to forget the romantic craving for the "eternal womanly" that can turn sour and violent. The fact that these infinitely desirable creatures can offer themselves like tarts touches some nerve of morbid, masochistic pleasure which incubates jealousy and violence.

The violent man may not be particularly interested in sexual intercourse; it is the self-esteem needs that obsess him. He may care for nothing but his work. (On the other hand, there would be nothing contradictory in a violent man being obsessed by sex: by the *conquest* involved.) His violence arises from insecurity; he is like a tyrant in perpetual fear of being dethroned. His only chance of outgrowing the violence lies in success, in being accepted at his own valuation. Van Vogt summarises: "[Realise] that most 'right' men deserve some sympathy, for they are struggling with an almost unbelievable inner horror; however, if they give in to the impulse to hit or choke, they are losing the battle and are on their way to the ultimate disaster. . ." Perhaps inner hunger or craving would be a better term than inner horror, bearing in mind that the need for self-esteem is, at its own evolutionary level, as much a hunger as the need for food.

A couple of centuries ago, most murders sprang out of frustration of the lowest level of the need-hierarchy: the need for food and security; the motive was economic. In an increasingly "affluent" civilization, the next level of need has emerged: the sexual. It began to emerge about a century ago; Freud's psychology was an intuitive recognition of the emergence of this new level. The pornography boom shows it becoming accepted as a norm; so do Britain's new abortion laws, which accept that twelve-year-old girls may need advice on contraception. To be afraid of this new development is irrational. In all ages, men (and women) of talent have accepted a certain promiscuity as a norm, because it is a part of their need for self-expression. (And the greatest of them have later outgrown it.) If the whole society is slowly evolving, then a certain level of promiscuity – casualness about sex – is bound to become a norm. Sex crime is bound to increase, because there will be vast numbers of "sexually underprivileged" males who are capable of "stealing" their sex gratification as a burglar steals money. Logically, strictly economic crimes should decrease, while sex crimes and crimes of violence should increase. This, in fact, is what the figures show. While the number of cases of rape and violence against the person increase steeply, cases of larceny and breaking and entering show only a small increase, and occasionally even a decrease.

There *should* come a time when sex crimes show a continuous tendency to decrease. In that case, what kind of crime would replace them? With luck, none. The self-esteem level is a social level. It does produce crime, but this is a rarity. A man with an acute self-esteem hunger may be a boaster, a bully, an appalling husband; but his involvement with other people and his desire for their good opinion will usually prevent him from developing into a criminal.

It should now be apparent that van Vogt's theory, if correct, may be as important to our own time as Freud's sexual theories were to the world of 1900. The violent man becomes one of the main problems of our time. The increasing number of revolutionary movements throughout the world is a sign of the increasing number of "violent men" rather than of political consciousness.

Van Vogt's account of the violent man could be criticised as too restricted. The "right man" is only a particular kind of violent man – one might call him the "opinionated type". The hunger for self-esteem affects different character structures in different ways. In the remainder of this chapter I will try to suggest some of these.

One of the most sensational murder trials of the 1960s received no publicity in the British or American press: the trial of Hans van Zon, the Dutch mass murderer. As in so many cases discussed in this book, the puzzling thing about the van Zon case is the motive. After his trial, his ex-headmaster remarked: "About some boys you can, as a teacher, almost predict with certainty that they will become criminals, but I cannot say that about Hans, although I always did think that there was something mysterious about him."

Born on 20 April, 1942 in Utrecht, Hans van Zon was something of a mother's boy – descriptions by psychiatrists of his relationship with his mother bring to mind D. H. Lawrence's self-portrait in *Sons and Lovers*. His father was a workman and the mother resented this, and dreamed of her son making a successful career. Hans was apparently a quiet and rather lethargic child, noted for his politeness to adults. He preferred to play with younger children at school. One of the psychiatrists later described him as a case of infantile autism, an odd, subjective frame of mind, total lack of interest in the outside world and other people. When he left school, he went through a succession of jobs. He seemed to live in a world of fantasy, and here the literary parallel seems to be with Keith Waterhouse's *Billy Liar*, who lies gratuitously, simply for the fun of it. Petty dishonesty led to his dismissal from most of these jobs.

In 1958, at the age of sixteen, van Zon went to Amsterdam, bought himself some expensive clothes, and began passing himself off as a young student. Apparently the very word "student" had a romantic ring for him. He became a kind of con man, but without real interest in money. At one point he borrowed money from a Catholic priest, who made it a condition of the loan that he went to a Catholic institute in Doorn. He went – and ran away almost immediately.

Being a good-looking and plausible young man, he had a number of love affairs, and not always with girls. There was a distinct homosexual streak in him.

In July 1964, when he was twenty-two, he committed what was probably his first murder. Van Zon later admitted the murder, then withdrew his confession. According to the confession, he had taken out a girl named Elly Hager-Segov on the evening of 22 July, and during the course of the evening, suddenly felt the urge to kill her. He took her home, then went off to a café, where he stayed until closing time. He then returned to Elly's lodging and told her he had missed the train. She allowed him to come in to stay the night. They made love. When he tried to make love a second time, she refused. He strangled her into unconsciousness, undressed her, then cut her throat with a bread-knife.

Later, after withdrawing his confession, he made the curious statement that he knew about the murder by a kind of second-sight, through "visions". This is just wild enough to be possibly true. We should bear in mind that there are two well-known Dutch clairvoyants, Peter Hurkos and Gerard Croiset, who often help the police to solve crimes, and that their method is to touch some object connected with the crime; this sometimes leads to a clear picture of the scene of the crime and of the criminal. Croiset and Hurkos both declared that one of the chief problems is that they may "pick up" images from the minds of the police officers. Again, the English psychiatrist Arthur Guirdham has argued convincingly in a number of books that many "mentally sick" people actually possess second sight, or other "mediumistic" powers, and that their strange visions or dreams may be due to the operation of these powers rather than incipient psychosis. Van Zon described in detail how he had two types of vision: two dimensional and three dimensional, and claimed that his knowledge of the murdered girl's room came from such a vision. Van Zon also claimed to have been responsible for the murder of a homosexual film director called Claude Berkeley in Amsterdam in 1965, and later offered the same explanation about his knowledge of the Berkeley case.

After the death of Elly Hager-Segov, van Zon met an Italian girl named Caroline Gigli, and married her. She supported him by working as a chambermaid in hotels. In 1967, she accused her husband of planning to kill her. He was still on probation for some minor offence against morality, and the police decided to allow him to cool off in goal for a month. After that, he returned to live with his wife.

In April 1967, van Zon murdered another girl, Coby van der Voort, thirty-seven, whom he had known for some time. They spent weekends together periodically. On 29 April, van Zon joined her in Amsterdam; they spent a pleasant afternoon, and made love. Then he placed a pink powder on his tongue and swallowed it. When she asked him what it was, he told her it was a sexual stimulant. Naturally, she asked to try some. In fact, the powder he had taken was pink icing sugar; the powder he offered her was Soneryl, a sleeping drug. When she became dizzy, he took a lead pipe from his bag – he had made it himself from melted lead – and struck her several times on the head, killing her. He undressed her and washed the body, stabbed it several times with a bread-knife, and tried to make love to the body.

What happened next sounds like an episode from a Dickens novel. One day, when in a drunk and boastful mood, Hans van Zon described the murder of Coby van der Voort to an "old lag" named "Old Nol" (Oude Nol), who proceeded to blackmail him into committing more crimes. On 31 May 1967, van Zon went to the shop of an eighty-year-old maker of fireworks, Jan Donse, known as Opa Cupido (Grandad Cupido). He seems to have taken a long time to make up his mind to go through with it, visiting the shop twice, but in the late afternoon he struck Donse with the lead pipe, and left him dead. Presumably he then robbed him.

In August, again inspired by "Old Nol" (according to Zon and other witnesses) he murdered a forty-seven-year-old farmer, Reyer de Bruin, who lived alone at Heeswijk. Claiming to be a journalist who wanted to write about the life of a bachelor farmer, he gained de Bruin's confidence, then struck him down with the lead pipe. He also cut his throat with a bread-knife – he explained later that this was because he thought de Bruin's face changed into that of Old Nol as he lay dead.

His relationship with Old Nol seems to have been ambivalent. At the trial, the psychiatrist, Dr Schnitzler, told the court that van Zon was fascinated by the old man, with his flamboyant manners and Dylan-Thomas-like voice. Old Nol also apparently admired Hans, or was clever enough to make him think so. He seems to have given Hans the idea of becoming a professional criminal.

It was Old Nol who suggested that van Zon kill a widow named Mrs Woortmeyer, whom he (Old Nol) had courted. Van Zon made a mess of it – or rather (he claimed) was suddenly unable to put enough force into the blow to kill her. Pretending to be a revenue official, he got into her house and knocked her unconscious, after which he took a large sum of money from her. When she recovered consciousness she called the police. It was the end of van Zon's career of crime. He implicated Old Nol, who was sentenced to seven years. Van Zon was sentenced to "life", a minimum of twenty years.

The most interesting thing to emerge at the trial was the curious fantasy world in which van Zon lived. He had enormous charm, and an air of being different from other men; "he was able to get as many girlfriends as he wanted", said a witness. He was kind and attentive to his girlfriends, and there was a touch of something Byronic, darkly tragic, in his manner. When he became interested in a girl, he began to spin elaborate fantasies: he was an orphan, and now intended to establish an import business in Iceland; he was a psychology student, and undercover detective, a CIA spy hunting war criminals, a young fashion designer who would one day dominate the Parisian scene. The latter suggests the homosexual aspect of his character. Since he was fourteen he had made money by selling himself to men; but he also maintained a number of homosexual relations without expecting payment. Back in Utrecht, after a short period in gaol for petty theft, he mixed with students, and could talk upon a wide range of subjects with a confidence and apparent erudition that made his claims to be a student plausible. But his understanding of the subjects was often superficial; he was interested in effect rather than in ideas.

One of the most interesting comments on him was made by a psychiatrist, Professor Kloek, who talked about van Zon's "autism". "Victims of this disability are unable to see a human being *in his totality*. When he sees a baby, it is a hand or a leg he singles out. It doesn't satisfy his need to see or hear something; he wants to touch it as well. For example, when such a person is part of an audience at a piano recital, he is not satisfied to hear the music; he has a strong urge to put his hands on the piano and feel it as well. During the examinations by two psychiatrists, Hans van Zon showed an often irresistible urge to touch the clothes of the interrogators." The same psychiatrist also mentioned that van Zon "tried desperately to explain that he couldn't explain his feelings and share them with other people".

All this will be of considerable importance in considering other cases besides this one. He is unable to see things *as a whole*; the world strikes him as a collection of bits and pieces. But when you respond to something – to a piece of music, or scenery – your response is a kind of electric shock that comes as you suddenly grasp its overall *meaning*. Van Zon is like a man wearing gloves, and who consequently can never really feel anything with his fingertips. And this is a description of schizophrenia which, contrary to the usual notion, does not mean a "split personality", but a permanent *detachment* from one's experience, as if surrounded by cotton wool. It is a lack of involvement. Van Zon's endless affairs, with men as well as women, are an attempt to remedy this. When he seduces a strange girl, he is for a moment a real *actor* in the affair, not a spectator. Emotionally, he lives in a desert; he feels that life is meaningless, and it is this that leads him to spoil chance after chance with petty crime.

But why the violence? Van Vogt's description of the "right man" does not fit him. He is not "opinionated" in the obsessive sense. But his psychological mainspring is the craving to be regarded with respect and admiration, and this dominates everything he does. When he reads a book on popular science, he is thinking about quoting it in a students' café. When he meets a young girl, he puts on his mysterious, Byronic air, and is not sure whether he is a secret service man or a dress designer, or some hero out of a romantic novel. And periodically, his frustration boils over into violence. Whether the violence is an attempt to assert that he *is* capable of action, or whether it is some strange, sadistic compulsion that creeps over him with certain people, it is difficult to say. The only thing that seems clear is that the violence is connected with the need to be something more than he is.

This same pattern of boastfulness and self-assertion can be discerned in some of the most widely publicised English murder cases of recent years. The Kray brothers, whose underworld empire extended from Whitechapel to Chelsea, took great delight in the celebrities they knew; their "opening nights" of new clubs were crowded with film stars and politicians. The two murders with which they (and eight other men) were charged seem oddly motiveless. Jack McVitie had called Ronald Kray "a great poove", and George Cornell told him to bugger off in front of other people. Kray subsequently walked up to Cornell in a crowded pub – the Blind Beggar in Stepney – and shot him through the head in front of a crowd of people. The killing seems to have been in the nature of a "dare". Later, Reginald, the other brother, shot Jack McVitie to prove (to his brother) that he was also tough enough to commit murder.

This same motivation is again apparent in the case of the Richardson brothers (Charles and Eddie), the Krays' chief rivals in the protection business. Accounts of the events that led to their arrest make it clear that it was an orgy of motiveless violence. The brothers instituted "underground courts", at which Charles Richardson wore mock judge's robes. But the tortures that were practised were out of all proportion to the offences that their underworld employees were supposed to have committed. One man who told them that he wanted to withdraw from the "business" was beaten with a knuckle-duster, then held down while deep razor cuts were made. The "trials" opened with the victim being struck with an iron bar or a golf club and whipped with barbed wire. Teeth were pulled out with pliers, and electric wires attached to the genitals of the victim. This kind of torture might last for hours, with the victim being revived with cold water whenever he fainted. This can only be called sadism if sadism is understood to mean an insane, frenzied self-assertion that would explode into violence at the slightest resistance. Both the Richardsons and the Krays were sentenced to life imprisonment. To compare their careers with those of gangsters of an earlier era – Al Capone or Lucky Luciano – is to recognize that they were more interested in sheer self-assertion than in making a fortune illegally. "The Krays' success in the East End swelled their heads", said Mr Barry Hudson, a defence counsel at their trial. "They moved into the West End and began to get hold of gentlemen with high titles, peers of the realm, baronets; and gradually they tried to get into this world." A belted earl was actually employed in one of their clubs.

Arthur Hosein, convicted in 1970 of the kidnapping and murder of Mrs Muriel McKay (whose body was never found), is altogether closer to van Vogt's picture of the violent man. His German wife (ten years his senior) described how he "came and went as he pleased", and said that she was not allowed to ask where he had been, although she was fairly certain that he was having affairs with other women. In local pubs, Hosein was known as a boaster who talked about his plans for becoming a millionaire. In a BBC television programme about the case, a relative in Trinidad (which Hosein left in 1954) said that his family expected him to become highly successful, and that on a return visit home a few years later he gave the impression that he was already rich. In fact, he was an excellent tailor, and his business in the East End of London prospered to such an extent that he was able to buy a £6,000 house in Chipping Ongar. This was not enough; in 1968 he sold it, and moved into Rooks Farm at Stocking Pelham, for which he paid £16,000. The picture he now set out to create was of the gentleman farmer, always immaculately manicured and barbered (his hair was dressed weekly by a private hairdresser), strolling around his estate or drinking in pubs with local businessmen. In fact, the money he earned as a tailor and farmer was inadequate; the result seems to have been the decision to kidnap the wife of a newspaper owner, Rupert Murdoch. The wrong woman was accidently kidnapped – Mrs McKay's husband had borrowed Murdoch's car while the latter was out of the country – and a huge ransom was demanded. Police hiding near the scene where the ransom money was left managed to get the number of a Volvo car, belonging to Hosein. Although no trace of Mrs McKay was found, other evidence pointed conclusively to the guilt of Arthur Hosein and his younger brother Nizam, and both were found guilty of murder. It is typical of the "right man" that there was no breakdown, no confession. And pub acquaintances who saw Hosein on the night of the murder found it hard to believe that he had anything on his mind. Relatives in Trinidad also said that it was hard to believe that Hosein could plot a murder; he was not the criminal type. This is undoubtedly true. Crime was only the means to an end: becoming a millionaire, achieving the success he felt to be his right. The "right man" is seldom a "criminal type"; on the contrary, he is usually above average intelligence, and strikes people as charming and sensitive.

Raymond Morris, who was sentenced to life imprisonment for the murder of seven-year-old Christine Darby, also fits the pattern described by van Vogt. Morris was also the chief suspect in the murder of Diana Tift, five, and Margaret Reynolds, six, who disappeared separately in 1965, but whose bodies were found together near Cannock Chase, Staffordshire. In November 1968, Morris tried to drag a ten-year-old girl into his car, and his licence number was taken by a woman who observed the attempt. He had already been among those questioned about the murder of Christine Darby in August 1967 (because his car was of the same type as the car in which the child had taken a lift), but his wife supported his false alibi. When police searched Morris's home, they found a number of blue films and pornographic photographs. Two of these showed a man's hand fondling the genitals of a five-year-old girl: the child turned out to belong to a cousin of Morris's wife, and a wristwatch in the picture identified the man as Morris. He had been photographing the child for a soap advertisement competition, and she had thought that it was all a game.

The picture that emerged after Morris's conviction was of a man of considerable charm and intelligence (I.Q. 120) whose fantasy life seems to have been as elaborate as van Zon's. He was a foreman engineer who could earn high wages, and his employers all described him as completely satisfactory. On the other hand, his workmates said that he was cold, without emotion, and that no one ever had a sense of getting to know him.

In 1951, Morris had married "the girl next door", two years his junior, a slim, slightly built girl. She spoke of his gaiety and charm, and of his sudden moods of violence. "Life with Ray was ferocious, and often frightening. I always had the feeling that if I didn't submit to him immediately the way he wanted me to, he'd kill me. Often when we were watching television together he'd suddenly say 'Strip!' And if I didn't obey at once, his eyes would go cold and expressionless, and his cheeks would go very white." Morris had the curious habit of play-acting his favourite characters: pop stars, Humphrey Bogart, the "Saint", Winifred Atwell, and this apparently triggered some craving for instant satisfaction of the urge to dominate. "Sex wasn't a thing he could take or leave. It was an overpowering maniacal urge which took complete control of his mind and body. One minute I'd be laughing at his attempt to impersonate the latest pop singer, the next I'd be in a cold sweat as he quietly commanded me to strip." His self-esteem fantasies were obviously closely connected to his sex life.

After eight years of marriage, Morris decided he had had enough of his wife. He told her he intended to start his own business, and there would be no room for her in his new life. "It was his calmness that hit me. There was just no emotion at all. He said: 'You must go to your mother tomorrow. Leave the key in the dustbin for me to get in.' I sent our two little boys to my mother but I waited for him." She tried hard to persuade him to change his mind but he refused and ordered her to leave. (Notice there was no question of his leaving *her* in the house.) "A week later I had a letter from him asking me to go to the house to see him. I thought he wanted me back. That day I went to town, bought myself a new skirt and blouse, and had my hair done. . . But when I walked into the house. . .the first thing he said to me was: 'I've asked you to come round because I've decided to kill you'. I started to sweat with fear. . . Suddenly he changed his tune. 'I'll give you five minutes to get undressed', he said, 'or I'll kill you'. I was so frightened I could hardly get my clothes off. Ray, icily calm, went into the kitchen and made coffee. That night he took me over the table. Then he said: 'I don't want to live with you but I'll see you twice a week, Tuesday and Thursday evenings. If you visit me on those two evenings I'll pay you £5 a week maintenance'. This may sound incredible, but for the next few weeks, I visited him on those two evenings. . . Each evening he'd make coffee first, then order me to make love. Then he'd turn me out." When she stopped going, he stopped paying her, and she had to go on national assistance. Later, when she had someone else's child, he divorced her on grounds of adultery. He then married a girl fourteen years his junior.

At the same time, this highly intelligent man, described by his second wife as "so debonair, so much the perfect gentleman", lacked the kind of drive that would have satisfied his dreams of fame and power. He lived in the same working-class area of Walsall all his life, a few streets away from his parents. He made up for the lack of excitement by leading a violent fantasy life, hiring blue films, and reading horror literature and pornography. He had cards printed that described him as "Midland Representative of Regent Studios, Birmingham". The need to express violent sexual dominance, which emerges clearly from the statements of his first wife, went underground during his second marriage, and erupted in the form of child murder, in which the dominance fantasy could be carried to a new extreme. His first wife found it hard to believe that he had killed a child. "He always seemed so good and gentle with children." But this gentleness did not prevent him from walking out on his own children, and later refusing to contribute to their support. Frustration had produced a permanent state of inner tension that blocked all normal feeling.

It would be an over-simplification to say that his frustration was the result of an unsatisfied power-urge. Morris was basically an artistic type. As a photographer, he was close to professional standard. One reporter spoke of his "fanatical attention to detail", which was apparent, for example, in the dolls' houses he made in his spare time. Blake said: "When thought is closed in caves/ Then love shall show its root in deepest hell"; that is, when creation is blocked, the outcome is likely to be cruelty and violence. "It is only too obvious what she suffered before she died," said the prosecuting counsel of Christine Darby. Frustration had soured into murderous savagery.

It may also be noted, in passing, that although the case was solved by accident, Morris was already on a short list of police suspects. An Identikit picture of the killer, put together from accounts of witnesses who saw him on the day of the murder, and comments by a doctor on the temperament of the killer, led a relative of Morris's to tell the police that the description fitted him closely. Only his wife's false alibi saved him from arrest.

In a footnote to *A Casebook of Murder* (1969), I spoke of a rape murder that had been committed in the Ypsilanti area of Michigan, USA, and added: "It is typical of this area – which has figured in spectacular murder trials since 1931, when three men killed four teenagers in a car and set it on fire – that a second body was found on the same day. This was identified as Mary Fleszar, aged nineteen, who had vanished a week before. . . She was naked, and her hands and feet had been removed. At the time this book goes to press, it is clear the murder of Mary Fleszar was the first in the series of a new Ann Arbor Jack the Ripper, who sometimes mutilates, stabs and shoots his victims, as well as sexually assaulting them. There have been five other cases since then. . ."

In fact, by the time the book went to press, this murder case had "broken", and the man who was subsequently convicted was already under arrest.

The body of Mary Fleszar was found on 7 August 1967 on a farm two miles north of Ypsilanti; she was a student at Eastern Michigan University. Clearly, she had been tortured and raped. It was almost a year later when another body, that of Joan Schell, also a student of Eastern Michigan University, was found not far from the previous site. She had been stabbed twelve times, and the body apparently kept in an earthen cellar for several days.

When, on 21 March 1969, the fully clothed body of Jane Mixer, twenty-three, a University of Michigan Law School student, was found in the Denton Cemetery, police at first assumed that the three murders were probably unconnected. Jane Mixer had been shot twice through the head with .22 bullets.

Murders then followed fast. The next victim was a sixteen-year-old girl, Maralynn Skelton. The pattern was here closer to the Mary Fleszar murder; she had been strangled, raped, and also tortured with a knife. Her body was found only four days after Jane Mixer's. Three weeks later, on 16 April, a thirteen-year-old schoolgirl, Dawn Basom, was found; she had been killed in the same manner as Maralynn Skelton.

The sixth murder led police to revise their assumption that the Schell murder was unconnected with the others. On 9 June 1969, boys crossing a field connected to an abandoned farm discovered a half-nude body: the purple blouse was ripped and cut, and the white mini skirt had been pulled below the knees. Her underclothes lay under the body. She had been shot through the top of the head – with a .22 bullet, it was later revealed – stabbed twice in the heart, several times in the throat, and the throat was also cut. The body had been slashed and cut, "like someone in a frenzy", said a policeman. She had been raped. Now it became possible that all six killings so far were connected. With the exception of Jane Mixer, the connection was the sadism and rape; in the Mixer case, it was the .22 bullet. Twenty-four hours later, the body was identified as Alice Elizabeth Kalom, a twenty-three-year-old graduate of the University of Michigan. Two days later, the *Ann Arbor News* reported that the murder investigation had "begun to stall"; police admitted they had no lead.

On 26 July, the seventh – and last – body was discovered in a wooded ravine. It was naked except for a pair of sandals on the feet.

Police decided this might be their opportunity to trap the killer. The body was removed, and replaced with a tailor's dummy. (They had wanted to try this same plan in the case of Alice Kalom, but a local radio station had leaked the story.) In two of the earlier murders, police had found evidence that indicated that the killer had returned to the scene of the murder – perhaps to see if the body had been discovered. The trap was laid; the police waited near the "body". It began to rain. Shortly after midnight, the police were startled to see that a man had quietly approached the manikin on the other side from where they were hiding. When the police jumped up, the man ran away; in the rain and darkness, they lost him.

The body was identified as that of Karen Sue Beineman, another co-ed of Eastern Michigan University. The post mortem revealed that she had been stunned with a heavy blow on the side of the head that caused serious brain damage, then strangled. Her wrists and ankles had been tied, and a piece of cloth rammed to the back of her throat to prevent her from screaming – an indication that she was not killed immediately after being knocked unconscious. One breast showed an area of "burning" as if with a caustic fluid, possibly ammonia. Her torn panties had been jammed into her vagina, where male semen was also discovered.

She had last been seen on 23 July, three days before the body was discovered. At about 12.30, she had entered a shop called "Wigs by Joan", to be fitted for a wig. She had remarked jokingly that she had only done two foolish things in her life: one was to buy herself a wig, the other to accept a lift from a stranger. The proprietor of the shop, Mrs Joan Goshe, and her assistant, both looked out of the window, and saw a good-looking, heavily-built young man sitting on a motor-cycle. The girl left the shop and rode off on the pillion seat.

On 18 July, five days before the murder, State Police Corporal David Leik took his family on holiday, and asked his nephew, Norman John Collins, twenty-two, to feed the dog while they were away. Collins was a student at Eastern Michigan University. They returned from the holiday on 29 July, and Leik called at a police post; there he was told that his nephew fitted the description of the man wanted for Karen Beineman's murder. The man on the motor cycle had been wearing an orange, green and yellow polo shirt and dark trousers, a distinctive costume. Leik went home and discovered, in the laundry room in the basement, signs of black paint that seemed to have been recently sprayed. Black paint could be used to hide something. Leik scraped some of it up, and discovered on the wood underneath a brown stain that could have been blood. In fact, tests showed that it was blood, of the same group as Karen Beineman's. There were no fingerprints in the basement. But there were some clipped hairs, which came from the heads of Corporal Leik's children: he used it as a barber shop. Similar clipped hairs had been found in the panties inside Karen Beineman.

At first it seemed possible that two men might be charged with the Beineman murder. In June, Norman Collins had taken a trip to California with his room mate, Andrew Manuel, twenty-five, in a rented caravan. Manuel had moved out of their room the day after the murder; it seemed possible that he might be an accomplice, particularly since they had stayed near Salinas, California, where the naked, mutilated body of Roxie Ann Phillips, seventeen, had been found in mid-July. When last seen alive, she had told a friend that she was going off to date a Michigan University student. However, when Manuel was located, it was decided that he had played no part in the murders. Collins was also charged with the murder of Roxie Ann Phillips.

Collins, it was revealed, possessed two motor cycles, as well as a car. Girls had seen no objection to accepting lifts from the good-looking boy, who did not remotely resemble a sex killer. Apart from a brooding, morose sort of temperament (which became apparent in court, where he sat silent and impassive throughout an exhausting trial), there seemed to be nothing abnormal about him. He even had a regular girlfriend, with whom he went motor-cycling. My friend Roger Staples, an assistant professor at Eastern Michigan, taught Collins, and never noticed the slightest abnormality, although he mentions that he once suspected Collins of some fairly ambitious cheating.

The trial lasted a month, beginning 20 July 1970. It had been due to start in June; but the defence tried to have its location changed, on the grounds that the case had inflamed public opinion too much in Ann Arbor; when this was overruled, the defence took full advantage of its privilege of challenging jurymen who might be prejudiced. Most of them – apparently – were, and it took a month to select the eighteen-member jury. The evidence was largely circumstantial: the bloodstains in the basement (although there were no fingerprints), the ends of hair found in the panties. Various people, including the two women from the wig shop, identified Collins as the man with whom Karen Beineman had left that day. He was found guilty and sentenced to life, a minimum of twenty years. He did not speak throughout the trial, except at the end, to state that he was not guilty.

It may seem that Collins should be classified with straightforward sex killers, like Christie and "Jack the Stripper", rather than with killers in whom the self-esteem motivation can be traced. But when we compare him with Christie or the Thames nude murderer, an immediate difference can be sensed. Collins is colder, more self-sufficient. There was no attempt by the defence to suggest mental unbalance, neither was it suggested in any of the reports devoted to the case in Ann Arbor and Detroit newspapers. Collins gave the impression of knowing exactly what he was about. In the *Ann Arbor News* for 4 August 1969, there appeared the following item:

> *Collins is known to have been acquainted with Richard C. Robison Jnr, eldest son of the Lathrup Village family of six found slain one year ago in their summer home near Good Hart, north of Petoskey. The two young men met at Eastern Michigan University in 1966 when they were going through orientation for new students. . . The Robisons were all shot with .22 caliber slugs in a grisly "execution style" series of killings. These murders have never been solved.*

There has been no evidence to link Collins with these killings, but they would be typical of the image he presented: controlled, precise, vengeful, capable of incredible violence. I have remarked earlier that most sex killers are of low I.Q., and seldom noted for a high level of self-esteem. Many of them are petty criminals; confidence swindlers (like Neville Heath), burglars (like Kürten); some are simply mentally deranged, like Ed Gein. By comparison, Collins seems as cool and deadly as a Murder Incorporated executioner. Even the sadism is puzzling, giving the impression of savage but controlled violence. This is a case that would seem out of place in an earlier decade; the only comparison that comes to mind is with the Leopold and Loeb case of 1924. The two Chicago University students, sons of wealthy parents, kidnapped and murdered fourteen-year-old Bobby Franks because they wanted to prove themselves capable of an act of calculated lawlessness. They were fascinated by the Nietzschean concept of the superman. (And, in fact, Nathan Leopold had the I.Q.

of a man of genius, 210. His parole lawyer, Elmer Gertz, said "All knowledge seemed to be his sphere – whether of languages, of which he knew 27, of medical research in leprosy and malaria, of bird lore.") But the students were trying to prove their courage and nerve *to one another*. Collins was alone; his crimes have the air of a one-man war against society; this is why he seems to demand classification with "Zodiac" and van Zon as a "violent man".

5.
Murder –
Elizabethan Style

WHY IS it that certain murders come to fascinate the general public? In 1823, a cheat and gambler named William Weare made the mistake of accepting an invitation to a weekend cottage in the country; his hosts were three villains named John Thurtell, Joseph Hunt and William Probert. As they were approaching the cottage near Elstree in a gig, Thurtell produced a pistol and shot Weare in the face, then he pursued him and cut his throat with a penknife, then jammed his pistol against his head so violently that it went through his skull and into his brain. The bloody knife, and the pistol with its barrel full of brains, got mislaid in the dark, and were found the next day by some labourers, who raised the alarm. Weare's body was found in a pond, and Probert turned King's evidence. Thurtell and Hunt were hanged in January 1824. A pointless, featureless murder, and yet it caused more sensation than almost any other murder of the nineteenth century. Why? It is difficult to guess. Five years later, a farmer named William Corder murdered a mole catcher's daughter named Maria Marten, who had got herself pregnant by him and was pressing him for marriage, and buried her in a barn. The girl's stepmother had a dream in which she saw Corder shoot Maria and bury her in a corner of the red barn; her father went to the spot and dug up the body. Corder, who had fled to London, was arrested and subsequently hanged. *Murder in the Red Barn* went on to become the most popular melodrama of the nineteenth century, and a book about the case remained a bestseller for a hundred years.

What have two such cases in common? Only one thing: that you or I can read them with a certain horror that springs from identification with the murderer. In the ordinary adventure story we identify with the hero as he swims a crocodile-infested river or plods across the waterless desert in search of King Solomon's mines. We don't really envy him, but we enjoy putting ourselves into his shoes. And as we read of William Corder going to such desperate lengths to untangle himself from Maria Marten, we experience the same horrified fascination, glad not to be in his shoes, but willing to put ourselves into them temporarily, just to see what a bad end he comes to. And at the end, it is almost as pleasant as wakening from a nightmare and finding yourself in your own bedroom. It is enjoyable putting yourself into somebody's shoes when you can take yourself out of them at a moment's notice.

This seems to be the only explanation of why certain crimes fascinated the Elizabethans so much that dramatised versions of them played to packed houses. J.A. Symonds says of the *Yorkshire Tragedy*: "Like the asp, it is short, ash-coloured, poison-fanged, blunt-headed, abrupt in movement, hissing and wriggling through the sands of human misery." What happened was that a man called Walter Calverley, of Calverley in Yorkshire, had a fit of temporary insanity in which he killed his two young children with a knife, and also stabbed his wife; he was on his way out of the house to kill his third child – who was with a nurse – when he was caught. Nowadays he would have been committed to Broadmoor, for the thing was clearly unpremeditated. *Stow's Chronicle* (1580), which tells the story in a few lines, does not explain why Calverley committed the crime, whether he was an alcoholic or had suffered previous fits of insanity. The unknown author – some scholars attribute the play to Shakespeare – had to provide a motive, so he set out to draw the kind of moral lesson the Elizabethans loved. Calverley has got himself into trouble by gambling and loose living, mortgaged his lands, and is thinking of bigamy. His brother, a university student, has been thrown into prison since he stood guarantee for his brother's debts. The husband is portrayed as a snarling villain, growling: "Bastards, bastards . . . begot in tricks, begot in tricks. . . ." The scene in which he kills both children, one of them while the mother is trying to protect it, would be too strong on stage for modern stomachs. His wife recovered from the attack, and the play concludes with a scene in which the husband, on his way to execution, sees her and expresses repentance. Calverley was, in fact, pressed to death: that is, stretched under a board upon which heavy weights were played until he was crushed or suffocated – a curious and inhuman punishment.

After the *Yorkshire Tragedy*, the best known Elizabethan "domestic tragedy" is *Arden of Faversham*, an altogether more expert piece of work. Again, it has been attributed to Shakespeare, and in this case, the attribution seems more likely. The story on which it is based was told by Holinshed, on whom Shakespeare drew heavily for material for his histories. Like the *Yorkshire Tragedy*, it is, by modern standards, a singularly straightforward murder case, with none of those interesting "angles" that would excite a Fleet Street crime reporter. Thomas Arden was a Kentish gentleman, the Mayor of Faversham, who married Alice North, the sister of the North who translated Plutarch. Arden was more interested in money than sex, and Holinshed suggests that he married Alice for her powerful family connections rather than because he was in love with her. Probably her dowry was generous. And having secured her, he went back to his main business of accumulating money and land – he managed to defraud a man named Greene of some abbey lands by using his influence to get a Chancery grant of them. Alice now met a tailor called Thomas Morsby (or Mosbie, as it is spelt in the play) and became his mistress; Morsby was in the service of her father, Sir Edward North. Arden was perfectly happy about handing over his marital duties to Morsby. He invited Morsby to come and live in his house, and left him there to console Alice when he had to go on business trips. He certainly knew what was going on; there was an occasion when he saw Alice with her arms around Morsby's neck, and heard them referring to him as a cuckold. What pleased him less was the discovery that the couple were thinking of murdering him; however, he didn't take this too seriously, and continued to encourage Morsby to keep up the good work. Presumably this left Morsby too tired to do the murder himself; for he approached Greene – the man who has been defrauded – and Greene, in turn, hired two assassins with the beautiful names of Black Will and Shagbag. These proved to be a pair of incompetents, and Charlie Chaplin could have made a superb comedy out of their attempts to kill Arden. Even Shakespeare – or whoever dramatised the case – has a preposterously funny scene in which two murderers wait for Arden by a market stall, and the stall-keeper swings his shutter into place and cracks the skull of Black Will.

Morsby tried various sophisticated and over-subtle methods of killing Arden – a poisoned crucifix, poisoned pictures, etc – but finally, they were forced to summon Black Will and Shagbag to the house to kill Arden as he sat at table. Morsby finished him off with a blow on the head from a flat iron, after he had been stabbed and throttled. They then dragged the body to a nearby field. It was snowing, so the footprints were obvious, and one of the accomplices forgot to throw the blood-stained knife and towel into the well. The law took violent retribution. Murder of a husband by his wife was regarded as a form of treason, and the penalty was to be burned alive. The servants who had helped in disposing of the body were also tried. Shagbag, Greene and the painter who had supplied poisons managed to escape; the last lines of the play mention that Shagbag was murdered in Southwark. The law was so anxious to make an example of everyone concerned in the murder that an innocent servant named Bradshaw was tried with the others, and sentenced to death, although the rest of the conspirators all asserted that he was not concerned. "These condemned persons were diversely executed in sundry places," says Holinshed; the servant Michael hung in chains at Faversham; a maid servant who had been an accessory was burnt alive, "crying out on hir mistresse that had brought hir to this ende". Mosbie and his sister were hanged at Smithfield in London; Alice Arden was burnt at Canterbury on 14th March, and Black Will was also burnt on a scaffold at "Flishing in Zeland". Greene – the man who had procured the murderers – returned some years later, and was promptly executed and hung in chains. Even a man named Adam Foule, who had merely acted as Alice's messenger to Mosbie, was sent to London with his legs tied under the horse's belly and imprisoned in the Marshalsea. Holinshed adds the legend that the imprint of Arden's body could be see in the grass for many years afterwards; he also notes that Arden had stolen the field in which his corpse was found from a poor widow. The archives of Canterbury contain the entry: "For the charges of brenning Mistress Arden and execution of George Bradshaw [the innocent servant], 43 shillings."

The play itself is remarkably successful as drama; but it can hardly be called a realistic presentation of the case. Arden, who was obviously a vicious miser, is portrayed as a doting husband who loves his wife so much that he closes his eyes to her infidelities. Alice is made to repent fulsomely when she sees her husband's body; in fact, it was Alice who accused the innocent Bradshaw – hardly the act of a repentant woman.

We also learn something of the Elizabethans from the fate of the maid, who had been merely an accessory after the fact. She was burned alive, while Mosbie, the instigator, was only hanged. Why such severity over the murder of a highly unpleasant miser? It is surely a reasonable inference that it was the sexual aspect of the case that aroused this universal morbid interest. The Elizabethan public was very like the public of today, except that it was far less sophisticated, since there were no sensational newspapers to spread the details of every divorce case. There is an immense reservoir of sexual frustration under the surface of working class life, and this case offered it an outlet. Alice Arden was one of these upper class women who spend their days in the arms of lovers; probably every woman in the case was somebody or other's mistress. So when the story was made into a play, Arden had to be whitewashed – otherwise the sexual motive was made less important, and nobody wanted that. . .

Those who followed the Max Garvie murder case in England in 1968 will note that human nature has changed very little in four hundred years. Garvie, a wealthy farmer, was murdered by his wife, Sheila (33), and her lover, Brian Tevendale (22); like Arden, he had connived at the affair. There was also some titillating evidence about wife swopping and nude parties, and the sensational press gave the story the fullest treatment for week after week – the story of Garvie's wife's lover, the story of Garvie's mistress, the story of Garvie's mistress's husband, the story of Garvie's mistress's brother's mistress. . .There is only one major difference between the England of 1968 and the England of 1568. If anyone turns the Garvie case into a play or a novel, everybody in it will be represented as sex-mad; there will be no innocent parties and no final repentance. Whether this is an advance on Elizabethan morality is difficult to say; but there can be no doubt that the punishments meted out in the Garvie case – life imprisonment – represent a moral advance on the part of society.

The pamphlet called *A Brief Discourse of the late Murther of Master George Sanders* was published in 1573, and an anonymous author used it as the basis of another popular play, *A Warning for Fair Women*. The case again concerns the murder of a husband by a wife and her lover; but it has one touch that, if true, gives it a certain psychological interest. A young Irish captain named Browne was introduced to Sanders, who was a merchant of Shooters Hill, London, and to his wife Anne. Browne conceived a violent passion for Anne; but she was a virtuous girl, and it was not returned. Browne therefore approached a friend of hers, a certain Widow Drury, whose side-line was fortune-telling, and persuaded her to help. The widow seized an opportunity to read Anne Sanders' hand, and told her with amazement that it indicated that she would soon become a widow, and marry a handsome man who would become wealthy and powerful. The widow claimed to be able to read what the man would look like – and, of course, her description bore a remarkable resemblance to Browne. Mrs Sanders was told that the stars would bring about her marriage to Browne in due course, and all she had to do in the meantime was treat him with common courtesy. This was enough. Obviously, if a woman is convinced that a certain man is destined to be her future husband, common courtesy will soon give way to warmer feelings.

Probably Browne meant only to seduce her; the chronicle suggests he was a roué. But having persuaded her to allow him into her bed, he made up his mind that he was in love with her. They decided to kill Sanders, and Browne and a manservant fell on him in a wood near Shooters Hill and killed him; they also attacked his servant, John Beane, and left him for dead. But Beane was alive; he crawled away, badly injured, and identified the murderer. He later gave evidence at the trial. Browne, his mistress, and the accomplice, were all hanged. Browne showed himself to have more spirit than Mosbie; he denied her complicity to the end, and she might well have escaped the penalty if she had not suddenly decided to confess in prison. Widow Drury was also hanged.

One more case that became the subject of a drama deserves mention here: the case of the wife-murderer Francis Thorney, executed in 1621. The drama is *The Witch of Edmonton* by Ford, Rowley and Dekker, and the murder scenes are almost certainly by Ford. Frank Thorney was a rather weak young man who seduced a fellow-servant, Winnifrede, who had already been seduced by their master, a certain Sir Arthur Clarington. The latter was pleased about the match and helped them with money. Thorney's father, described as "a poor gentleman", had other plans for his son; he wanted to marry him to a pretty farmer's daughter named Susan, who was perfectly willing. Thorney was weak enough to allow himself to be swept into a bigamous marriage with the latter, although he was in love with Winnifrede. Both women were so gentle and sweet that he began to experience agonies of guilt. One day, he set out on a journey with Winnifrede, who was disguised as a page, and the innocent and infatuated Susan insisted on accompanying him part of the way, until his overburdened emotions found relief in stabbing her. He then tied himself to a tree, and made several cuts on his body to support his story of being attacked by two former suitors of Susan's. Everything went well until Susan's sister discovered the bloodstained knife in his pocket, upon which Thorney confessed.

This theme is united to the story of a "witch", Mother Sawyer, who was burned at the same time Thorney was executed. The authors did this by suggesting that Mother Sawyer had bewitched Thorney into murdering his wife, for which there is no evidence whatever. But it might be mentioned that the authors showed a rare insight into the psychology of witchcraft, in showing Mother Sawyer as an ugly poverty-stricken old woman who is generally regarded as a witch because her ugliness excited so much repulsion; the harmless old creature is finally driven to seeking a compact with the devil out of sheer desperation at the injustice. This is the kind of insight that we tend to flatter ourselves is uniquely "modern".

I cannot resist a few words on the most fascinating of unsolved Elizabethan murder cases: the murder of Christopher Marlowe. It is true that, from the point of view of literary history, it was neither unsolved nor a murder. But there are too many unanswered questions about Marlowe's death to allow us to accept the story told to the Queen's Coroner. This story was as follows. On Wednesday, 30 May 1593, the twenty-nine year-old poet and dramatist – one of Shakespeare's most powerful rivals – was supping in a room of Eleanor Bull's tavern in Deptford, which is now a London suburb. There were three others present: Ingram Frizer, a servant of Sir Thomas Walsingham, Nicholas Skeres, his friend, a definitely crooked character, and Robert Poley, a spy. They had spent the day together, and drunk a great deal. At about nine in the evening, there was a scuffle, and the hostess was informed that she had a corpse on her premises. Marlowe had been stabbed above the right eye. The story the other three told is that Marlowe had been lying on the bed, and had suddenly seized Frizer's dagger and attacked him with it, giving him a couple of cuts on the head. Frizer wrested the dagger from him and killed him in self-defence. It was said that the scuffle was due to a dispute over the bill; but for some odd reason neither Poley nor Skeres was involved in this dispute, although they were also presumably paying their share. All that is certain is that Marlowe was killed with one clean stab above eye, and that all three men who were present had the same story to tell.

The first questions we are tempted to ask concern the nature of the struggle and the wounds. Marlowe was lying on the bed; Ingram was a few feet away, between Poley and Skeres, so that he could not escape when Marlowe grabbed his dagger and attacked him. It seems odd that Marlowe should have failed to kill Frizer if he stood behind him with a dagger. One blow driven downwards through the top of the skull would have done it. But would a man attacking another man from behind stab him in such a way as to inflict two cuts (each two inches long) on his scalp? Surely he would go for his back, or the back of his neck? And supposing that Ingram then wrestled with Marlowe and got the dagger, while Skeres and Poley looked on without attempting to interfere; would he be likely to stab him above the eye? Two men wrestling for a dagger are more likely to inflict body wounds on one another. Whereas a deep wound above the eye might be consistent with a man being attacked suddenly as he lay on his back on a bed, with his eyes closed.

The wound was described as being two inches wide and one inch deep, and Dr S.A. Tannenbaum in his book *The Assassination of Christopher Marlowe* reaches the conclusion that such a wound would almost certainly not kill instantaneously; the victim might linger for hours, or even days.

Dr Tannenbaum believes that Marlowe's death was premeditated assassination, and he may well be right. The three men in the room with him were all unsavoury characters. Frizer was a confidence trickster; Skeres was a robber and cutpurse; Poley was a spy, and had served prison sentences for various minor crimes. Frizer was in the employ of Sir Thomas Walsingham, and Skeres and Poley had both been associated with Walsingham in uncovering the Babington Catholic conspiracy against the Queen.

But Walsingham was an old friend and patron of Marlowe's, and all the evidence indicates that he and Marlowe were lovers. The knowledge that Marlowe was homosexual raises another interesting possibility – that he was murdered in the course of making amorous advances to Frizer. But this would not explain why Frizer was taken back into the employ of Walsingham after killing Walsingham's lover. Perhaps Walsingham and Marlowe had quarrelled? This seems the only theory that is consistent with the facts (which were unearthed as recently as 1925, when the coroner's report was found in the public archives). Or perhaps, as Francis Meres wrote five years after the murder, Marlowe was killed by "a rival of his in his own lewd love". Perhaps Frizer had replaced Marlowe as Walsingham's favourite pathic. It is even possible, as some later writers suggested, that Meres meant the quarrel was over a woman.

Two weeks before Marlowe's death, constables searched the room of his friend Thomas Kyd, author of the sensational and sanguinary *Spanish Tragedy*, and found certain theological arguments denying the divinity of Jesus. Kyd protested that these papers were not his, but Marlowe's. Atheism was a very serious matter in those days; Marlowe's schoolfriend Francis Kett was burned for it at Norwich in 1589. (Kyd's betrayal of Marlowe did him no good; after a period in Bridewell prison, he died in the following year, aged thirty-six. He had been "put to the torture" in prison.) Marlowe was arrested at Sir Thomas Walsingham's and appeared before the Privy Council on 20th May; he was released on bail, perhaps through the offices of powerful friends. But he was in trouble; friends or no friends, he would probably end in Bridewell or the Tower, like his friend and fellow rationalist, Sir Walter Raleigh. Did Walsingham feel that Marlowe would seriously compromise him at court, and that it was time the connection between them was severed, before Marlowe dragged him down with him?

Perhaps the most interesting, and unprovable, theory about Marlowe is the one put forward by Calvin Hoffmann in *The Murder of the Man Who Was Shakespeare*. He believes, very reasonably, that Walsingham was determined to save his friend, and contrived a fake murder to get him out of England. He argues convincingly that the jury who acquitted Frizer was "rigged", and that the body they saw was not that of Marlowe but of some other man who had been killed earlier. This supposition is supported by Dr Tannenbaum's argument that Marlowe would not have died instantaneously of the inch-deep wound over his eye.

The remainder of Dr Hoffmann's theory is even more startling. He believes that Marlowe went to the Continent, under Walsingham's protection, and continued to write. What happened to his later plays? They were published under the name of Shakespeare. It is interesting that Shakespeare's first publication, *Venus and Adonis*, appeared in the September after Marlowe's death. And no Shakepearean scholar has ever tried to deny that *Henry VI*, *Richard III* and *Titus Andronicus* are so like Marlowe that it is generally supposed that Marlowe had a hand in the writing of them (the assumption being that they were written before May 1593, of course). Seven years after Marlowe's death the publisher Thomas Thorpe "brought to light" a translation of the first book of Lucan by Marlowe; Thorpe later published Shakespeare's sonnets, dedicated to "Mr W H". (Hoffmann speculates that this was Walsing-Ham – Elizabethan names were often hyphenated like this.)

Dr Hoffmann has only one really weighty argument on his side. He speaks of Dr Thomas Corwin Meadenhall, who believed that every writer's work has certain stylistic characteristics that are as ineradicable as a thumb print. Chief among these "constants" is the number of times he employs words of a certain number of letters. Meadenhall set out to count the number of letters in every word in several works by various writers, and apparently proved his theory. The writer's vocabulary is his thumb print, and each writer's print was absolutely consistent throughout his work. No two authors were alike.

According to Dr Hoffmann, a wealthy Baconian (an advocate of the theory that the plays of Shakespeare were written by Bacon) asked Dr Meadenhall to compare Bacon's "thumb print" with Shakespeare's. Shakespeare's average word was four letters long. The words Shakespeare used with most frequency were also four letters long. Bacon tended to use much longer words, and his letter average was also well above four.

Meadenhall tested various other writers besides Bacon and Shakespeare. One was Marlowe. And Marlowe's thumb print was identical with Shakespeare's.

I accept that Dr Hoffmann is writing in good faith. But if he is correct, then he has proved his case, and no further argument is needed. His book should have been devoted to Meadenhall, and to demonstrations that no two "thumb prints" *are* alike; and finally, that Marlowe's and Shakespeare's are. In these days of electronic computers, it should be possible to prove this beyond all possible doubt. If Dr Hoffmann can prove his thesis, he has accomplished the most remarkable piece of literary detective work in European history.

It might be mentioned in passing that Clemence Dane's play *Will Shakespeare*, written in 1921, four years before the Inquest

Report turned up, argues that Marlowe was murdered by Shakespeare in a quarrel over a girl.

For readers who are unfamiliar with the various theories about the authorship of Shakespeare's plays, it might be worthwhile to point out that the basic problem is this: that there is no evidence whatever connecting an actor called William Shakespeare of Stratford with the plays published under his name. Shakespeare was not known in Stratford as a writer but as a businessman. The bust of Shakespeare that was put up in the Stratford church about 1630 does not show him holding a pen, but with both hands resting on a sack, a symbol of trade. There exist no manuscripts of Shakespeare, although there are of plenty of the other Elizabethans. He left no manuscripts in his will, or copies of his plays, which seems odd – surely he had enough pride to keep copies of his various works in his house? His father was illiterate; so were his children; the few signatures of Shakespeare that exist support the notion that he was little better. Whether Shakespeare was Marlowe or Bacon or anybody else – that is to say, whether the actor was bribed to allow the use of his name on the little page of somebody else's work – is a matter that may never be proved; but let us acknowledge at least that it is very strange that there exists no evidence whatever to link the actor-businessman of Stratford with the playwright.

And incidentally, if Hoffmann's theory is correct, Shakespeare may well have been a murderer; *somebody* killed the man whose body was passed off as Marlowe's.

If this cross-section of Elizabethan murder is representative – and there is every reason to believe it is – then the Elizabethans belonged to the age of innocence. Murder was generally committed for such straightforward motives as money or passion. No one thought of dismembering bodies or burning them in furnaces. And the attitude of the Elizabethans towards murder was also very simple. It must be borne in mind that England was still united in matters of religion, and that religion was still the supremely important subject, the cause of all the major disputes and national crises. Even a century and a half later, in the time of Dr Johnson, this was still so. That was an age when volumes of sermons became best-sellers, and Johnson could discourse with Boswell about the relative merits of the sermons of a dozen different divines. We can look back upon such an age with a certain nostalgia. But then, we are not required to live in it. Religion was absolute, in a way that it has ceased to be in Britain except, perhaps, in some remote community in the far reaches of Scotland or Wales. Everybody went to church every Sunday, and listened to sermons on the seven deadly sins. What horrified and fascinated them about murder was not primarily that Thomas Morsby killed his mistress's husband with a flat iron, but that he had committed a mortal sin for which he would fry in hell. It was his *wickedness*, his defiance of the standards they were told about every Sunday of their lives, that shocked them. If Frank Thorney killed his bigamously married wife, it must have been the Devil operating through Mother Sawyer who was responsible. The forces of evil were very real to them; not one of them doubted that the Devil really existed, and that he probably had horns on his head and a long tail. The gibes for which Marlowe was arrested were not directed against God or the Devil – he no doubt believed in them like everybody else – but against Adam, Jesus, Moses, and so on. ("He affirmeth that Moses was but a Jugler and that one Harriot, being Sir Walter Raleigh's man, can do more than he.")

But for all this religious streak that made the Elizabethans so interested in murder and violence, it was still an age of cruelty. Lytton Strachey describes the death of the Queen's physician, Dr Lopez, a Portuguese Jew, accused of plotting with Spain against the Queen and the Portuguese Pretender, together with two others, Ferreira and Tinoco (the latter had been lured to England by a safe-conduct, which carefully forgot to mention whether he would be allowed out again):

A vast crowd was assembled to enjoy the spectacle. The Doctor, standing on the scaffold, attempted in vain to make a dying speech: the mob was too angry and too delighted to be quiet. . .He was strung up and – such was the routine of the law – cut down while life was still in him. Then the rest of the time-honoured punishment – castration, disembowelling and quartering – was carried out. Ferreira was the next to suffer. After that, it was the turn of Tinoco. He had seen what was to be his fate, twice repeated, and from close enough. His ears were filled with the shrieks and moans of his companions, and his eyes with every detail of the contortions and the blood. And so his adventures had ended thus at last. And yet, they had not quite ended; for Tinoco, cut down too soon, recovered his feet after the hanging. He was lusty and desperate, and he fell upon his executioner. The crowd, wild with excitement, and cheering on the plucky foreigner, broke through the guards, and made a ring to watch the fight. But, before long, the instincts of law and order reasserted themselves. Two stalwart fellows, seeing that the executioner was giving ground, rushed forward to his rescue. Tinoco was felled by a blow on the head; he was held down firmly on the scaffold, and, like the others, castrated, disembowelled and quartered.

It was later discovered that Dr Lopez was innocent.

The Queen herself was almost certainly accessory to a murder. Her lover, Sir Robert Dudley, had married a girl named Amy Robsart eight years before the Queen's accession to the throne, and the Queen was interested in making Dudley Prince Consort. In September 1560, the Queen told a foreign envoy that Lady Dudley was dying, when there was certainly nothing wrong with her. Four days later, Amy Robsart was found at the bottom of a great staircase in her Oxfordshire house; her skull was fractured. She was twenty-eight years old, her husband a year older. Elizabeth seems to have changed her mind about marrying her lover, or perhaps political necessity made it impossible. There seems to be little ground for doubt that Dudley (later the Earl of Leicester), whom the Spanish envoy had described as "heartless, spiritless, treacherous and violent", had his wife killed, and that the Queen knew about it in advance. Perhaps she disliked the violence of the method; the Simancas archives indicate that there was a plot to poison Amy Robsart. No doubt this was what the Queen had in mind when she said that Lady Dudley was dying.

So how can we begin to understand this strange Elizabethan age, in which the chief objection to murder was that it was a mortal sin, and yet in which the Queen could be privy to a murder? Obviously, it differed from ours in respects that are so fundamental that the Elizabethans are as alien to us as a tribe of aborigines. They were driven by their passions to an extent that is incomprehensible in our self-divided age, and passion was the stuff of their literature; they could understand *Macbeth* and *Othello* in a way that is impossible to a modern scholar, no matter how closely he studies the period. When we read Hoffmann's theory of Marlowe's escape, our main thought is for the innocent man who was murdered to provide the coroner with a body; the Elizabethans would have thought this irrelevant. If Marlowe really escaped, he probably never lost a single night's sleep over the murdered man. Neither would the Elizabethans have agreed with the modern notion that genius and crime are inconsistent. As recently as 1926, it was discovered that Sir Thomas Malory, author of *Le Morte D'Arthur* (which Caxton printed in 1485) was a rapist and an outlaw, who led a band of robbers that sacked monasteries and stole herds of cattle; he wrote *Le Morte D'Arthur* in jail. (The indictment against him mentions that on 23 May 1450, Malory "broke into the house of Hugh Smyth and feloniously raped Joan, the wife of the said Hugh", and on 6 August of the same year, he broke into Hugh Smyth's house and "feloniously raped Joan" again as well as stealing forty pounds' worth of Smyth's property.)

One of the greatest musicians of the Elizabethan period, Carlo Gesualdo, Prince of Venosa, discovered his wife in bed with her lover, the Duke of Andria, and killed her himself, while his retainers killed the Duke. (Anatole France, who based his account on earlier records, does not spare the barbarous details of Gesualdo hacking at his wife's naked body with his sword even after her death.) Gesualdo then hastened off to one of his castles and murdered his second child, in case the Duke of Andria was the father. His strange, neurotic madrigals, with their modern-sounding harmonies, were regarded as evidence of his insanity for centuries after his death; but in recent years it has been recognised that they are as important as Monteverdi's.

Records of crime between the Elizabethan age and the age of Dr Johnson are scanty; only some of the most famous have survived in historical records. The most notable murder during the reign of Elizabeth's successor James I was that of Sir Thomas Overbury by James's favourite, Robert Carr, Duke of Somerset.

Carr was a tall, blond young lout, completely illiterate. When he was eleven years old and a page boy, he met Thomas Overbury, a brilliant young homosexual. Carr came heavily under the influence of Overbury, and was presumably seduced by him. Five years later, Carr broke his leg at a tournament when the King was present. James was also a homosexual, a strange, feeble man, given to bursting into tears; he slobbered as he talked and his legs were so weak that he often leaned on the shoulders of the people he was talking to. James was soon infatuated with the tall, blond illiterate, and even took his advice on dissolving Parliament.

Overbury now became Carr's secretary, a reversal of positions that he did not particularly relish; however, it was a gain in power. And Overbury was interested in power. This was about the only thing he had in common with Carr; otherwise they were opposites: Carr, tall, pink-cheeked, open-faced and not particularly bright; Overbury, swarthy, brilliant (his *Characters* is a classic of English literature), brooding, inclined to resentment.

Carr soon fell in love with a teenage beauty, Frances Howard, who was already married to the Earl of Essex. The marriage had not been consummated – Essex was abroad – and it never was. Frances Howard returned the feeling, and she and Carr became lovers. Overbury – now Sir Thomas – wrote Carr's love letters for him. But he never liked the girl. She had the face of a juvenile delinquent and the temperament of a younger Lady Macbeth. When he realised that Carr was serious about her and intended marrying her, if she could get a divorce, he began to resent her very openly. This was his mistake. The Countess of Essex was a very strong character, and basically as neurotic and unbalanced as Overbury. When her husband returned from abroad she refused to grant him marital rights, even though they slept naked in the same bed. She approached a certain Mrs Turner, a "witch" who had concocted love potions to ensnare Carr, and obtained more powders to kill her husband. (Mrs Turner also wove spells aiming to make the Earl of Essex impotent.) Although these failed to work, Essex finally agreed to a divorce. Carr, now the Duke of Somerset, was displeased when Overbury told him he would be a fool to marry Frances Howard; the lady herself was furious. She tried to bribe a knight to murder Overbury, but he declined. So she persuaded Carr to plot against her enemy. Carr went to the King and suggested that Overbury should be made ambassador to France or Russia, and the King agreed. Carr then went to Overbury, and advised him to refuse. Overbury allowed himself to be persuaded. The King was infuriated by the refusal, and ordered Overbury to be committed to the Tower, which was what Carr and his mistress had counted on. Overbury was now at their mercy. Mother Turner was again called upon for poison; Overbury's keeper Weston was in charge of administering it. Sir Gervase Elwes, a friend of Frances Howard, was made Governor of the Tower; at first, he was ignorant of the poisoning; but when he learnt about it, he kept quiet. Overbury died on 15th September 1613, and no one was curious.

Frances Howard obtained her divorce and married Carr, who remained in royal favour. But without Overbury, Carr's stupidity became steadily more obvious. He began to cause scenes with the King, failing to recognise that what James needed most was someone on whom he could lavish affection. James found a new favourite, a Cambridge student called Villiers. And then, two years after Overbury's death, Carr's edifice collapsed. The chemist's assistant who had prepared the poisons died, and confessed before he died. The King was told, and he asked Sir Edward Coke to investigate. As a result of that investigation, Mrs Turner, Sir Gervase Elwes, Weston (the jailer) and Dr Franklin (supplier of the poison) were all sentenced, and hanged at Tyburn. Carr and his wife were tried in Westminster Hall, since they were of the peerage. Carr tried hard to put pressure on the King. Apparently he threatened to blurt out details of their relationship in court, and two men stood behind him with a cloak, ready to put it over his head if he made any such attempt. But the King assured him he would not be executed. Although they were both sentenced to death, husband and wife were only confined in the Tower. By now, they hated one another, and never spoke. Both probably blamed the other for the murder. They were there for six years, then allowed to retire quietly to their country home, where Lady Somerset died of a cancer of the womb at the age of thirty-nine.

The new favourite, George Villiers, was the victim of another famous murder. He became the Duke of Buckingham under

James and was made Lord High Admiral of the Navy. He made love to the Queen of France at one point, and as a consequence, appears in Dumas' *Three Musketeers* and various other novels. But after James's death, he became involved in the quarrels between the new King, Charles I, and his parliament. Charles dissolved two parliaments which wanted to impeach Buckingham. But on 23 August 1628, a soldier called John Felton, who thought he had various causes for complaint against the Duke, waited outside the door of the room in which Buckingham was breakfasting, and stabbed him in the heart as he came out. Felton, a Puritan fanatic, hoped for immunity, since Parliament had declared Buckingham a public enemy; but he reckoned without the King. Felton was hanged at Tyburn. Buckingham's rival, Robert Carr, outlived him by seventeen years. After Buckingham's death, Charles I's career began the slow downward curve that ended under the axe of Richard Brandon in 1649.

No account of murder in the seventeenth century would be complete without at least a mention of the unsolved murder of Sir Edmund Berry Godfrey, the effect of which was to cause a persecution of Catholics as brutal as any under Henry VIII. Godfrey was a man of good reputation, and had displayed a rare public spirit in his efforts of help to sufferers in the Great Plague of 1665.

Three weeks before his murder, Godfrey, who was a magistrate, had been approached by Titus Oates – a kind of seventeenth-century Senator Joe McCarthy – who talked about Catholic plots. The Gunpowder Plot of 1605 had not been forgotten, and a great many people thought a new one all too likely. On the afternoon of 12 October 1678, Godfrey left his house at Charing Cross to make a call near St Clement Danes, and did not return home. Five days later, his corpse was found in a ditch at Primrose Hill, a few miles to the north. His sword was driven into his body, so that suicide was a possibility. But, in the climate of opinion created by Titus Oates (who alleged a Popish Plot by Don John of Austria and Père la Chaise to murder Charles II and establish Catholicism in England), everyone was certain he was murdered by Catholics. Charles was tolerant towards Catholics (in fact, he *was* a Catholic, secretly), and the Queen's residence, Somerset House in the Strand, was a hive of them. Godfrey had passed Somerset House after dark on the day of his disappearance, so an investigation was conducted there. Soon a man named Praunce "confessed" – under torture, it was later claimed. He declared that a group of conspirators knew that Godfrey intended to spend the night at the house near St Clement Danes, perhaps a brothel. He left at seven in the morning, and as he was passing Somerset House was lured into the courtyard with some story of a fight between two of the Queen's servants. There he was strangled, and his neck broken. Praunce alleged that the body was moved from room to room in Somerset House for several days, then taken to Primrose Hill and stabbed with the sword.

Three men – Green, Berry and Hill – were arrested; three more (two of whom were priests) escaped. These three were placed on trial before Lord Chief Justice Scroggs, whose reputation is as vile as that of his associate Jeffreys. Praunce gave evidence against them. They had no chance of escape; the whole country was up in arms about the Popish Plot. Titus Oates appeared against them. (He was a turncoat Catholic who had been expelled from the Jesuits for misconduct.) As far as justice goes, this must rank as one of the worst trials in English history, although, of course, that does not prove the conspirators were innocent. Green, Berry and Hill were executed for Godfrey's murder; but it is generally acknowledged that the murder remains unsolved. Why should Catholics have murdered Godfrey, who was merely the magistrate who took Oates' deposition? They must have had the sense to know it would lead to a persecution. On the other hand, Titus Oates and some of the Protestants behind him had an excellent motive for the murder. Part of Godfrey's job as a magistrate was to investigate their allegations; Godfrey may well have recognised from an early stage that the Popish Plot was basically nonsense.

It is satisfying to record that Titus Oates, like Senator McCarthy, eventually overdid it. His revelations led to massive reprisals against Catholics; five Catholic peers were sent to the Tower, and two thousand Catholics thrown into prison. All Catholics were ordered to leave London, and a bill was passed excluding them from Parliament. Another imaginative villain named Bedloe tried to top the revelations of Titus Oates, and Oates invented more freely than ever – plots for the landing of Catholic armies and the massacre of all Protestants. Finally, he charged the Queen with knowledge of a plot to murder Charles II. The King gave his brother James, later James II, permission to do something about it, and Oates was tried for perjury and libel, and sentenced to life imprisonment, with periodic whippings at a cart-tail.

The murder of Godfrey was one of those minor events that changed the course of English history. Without it, the Popish Plot furore would have died down much sooner, or perhaps never have started, and the violent measures against Catholics, including large-scale judicial murder, would never have been taken. The clashes between the Catholic James II and his parliament would have been avoided, and the revolution that brought William of Orange to the English throne would not have taken place. The full consequences of that will become clear in the next chapter.

6.
The Age of Gin

ELIZABETHAN ENGLAND drank beer, wine, sherry (Falstaff's "sack"), mead and cider; they drank a lot because the water was not fit to drink unboiled. But although Thomas Dekker wrote in 1632 of a street that was almost a continuous ale-house (or tavern, as they were starting to be called), it is doubtful whether these beverages were responsible for much of the crime rate in the first half of the seventeenth century. To begin with, James I took measures to raise the price of wine from the fourpence a quart it had cost under Elizabeth, and the ordinary labourer could now afford to drink only beer; and even that had increased in price.

Somewhere around 1650 or 1660, a Dutch professor of chemistry called Sylvius discovered that a powerful spirit could be made by distilling the fermentation of juniper berries; this drink was called "*geneva*" (the French for juniper). It became popular in Holland, and when William of Orange became King in 1689, *geneva* began to flow into England in large quantities, and the name was shortened to "gin". Gin was cheap and easy to make. The English quickly realised that an even cheaper and stronger spirit could be distilled from low-grade corn; and an Act of Parliament in 1690 allowed anyone to brew and sell spirits without a licence, with the consequence that every town in England was suddenly full of gin shops, many of which carried the famous advertisement: "Drunk for a penny, dead drunk for twopence, clean straw provided." Beer, wine and sherry had been too expensive for most labourers, but gin was within the reach of anybody who could earn or beg a penny. Inevitably, the crime rate rose; people in the slums had a great deal they wanted to forget, and twopence assured forgetfulness for at least twelve hours. In 1734, a dipsomaniac named Judith Dufour was executed for the murder of her baby. She had collected it from a workhouse, where it had been newly clothed, and strangled it, throwing the body into a ditch. The clothes sold for 1s 4d, which she spent on gin. On 6 July 1750, one Elizabeth Banks was hanged at Tyburn for "stripping a child" – no doubt with the same motive. Eight million gallons of gin a year were consumed in England at this time, the consumption in London alone being fourteen gallons per head.

Within ten years of the accession of William and Mary, the crime rate had risen so alarmingly, and crimes of violence "carried to a degree of outrageous passion" were becoming so common, that a new law of exceptional savagery was placed on the Statute books: the 1699 Act that made any theft of goods valued at more than 5s a capital crime. Any kind of shoplifting was a crime; and since the majority of these offenders were women and children, the execution of women and children became a commonplace. As the number of gin shops increased – at one point, one house in every six sold gin – so did the neglect and ill-treatment of children, and John Fielding, a Justice of the Peace and half-brother of Henry, spoke of children of twelve "half eaten up with the foul distemper" of the pox. Children were trained to pick pockets, and many of them were hanged for as little as the theft of a handkerchief. The authorities were becoming desperate at this "crime wave" (which would last more than a century), and they reacted in the manner with which we are becoming familiar: by trying to stamp out crime with cruelty.

No doubt the Elizabethan mob was as unfeeling as the mob of the eighteenth century. But the gin made it all the more obvious. Christopher Hibbert says of the period in *The Roots of Evil*:

"Pity was still a strange and valuable emotion. Unwanted babies were left out in the streets to die or were thrown into dung heaps or open drains; the torture of animals was a popular sport. Cat-dropping, bear-baiting and bull-baiting were as universally enjoyed as throwing at cocks. . .

"The Mohocks, a society whose members were dedicated to the ambition of 'doing all possible hurt to their fellow creatures', were mostly gentlemen. They employed their ample leisure in forcing prostitutes and old women to stand on their heads in tar barrels so that they could prick their legs with their swords; or in making them jump up and down to avoid the swinging blades; in disfiguring their victims by boring out their eyes or flattening their noses; in waylaying servants and, as in the case of Lady Winchilsea's maid, beating them and slashing their faces. To work themselves up to the necessary pitch of enthusiasm for their ferocious games, they first drank so much that they were 'quite beyond the possibility of attending to any notions of reason or humanity'. Some of the Mohocks also seem to have been members of the Bold Bucks who, apparently, had formally to deny the existence of God and eat every Sunday a dish known as Holy Ghost Pie. The ravages of the Bold Bucks were more specifically sexual than those of the Mohocks and consequently, as it was practically impossible to obtain a conviction for rape and as the age of consent was twelve, they were more openly conducted."

The age had its ideal chronicler in William Hogarth, born in 1697, for he delighted in the portrayal of the sordid and horrible. Anyone who wants to understand the spirit of the first half of the eighteenth century should study Plate 7 of his "Industry and Idleness" series, showing the idle apprentice in bed with a prostitute. The walls are bare bricks with a few decaying fragments of plaster; some of the floor is missing; the "bed" is simply a sloping plank; there seems to be no window; the room is as cold and dark as a prison cell. The prostitute is an ugly, snub-nosed girl with small firm breasts – she is probably sixteen or seventeen. To stare at such a picture for five minutes is to gain all kinds of insights that the literature of the period cannot convey, because we read it with our own age in mind.

One can begin to understand, for example, why the highwaymen of the period became popular heroes; they were hitting back at the system. Modern writers on Dick Turpin take care to point out that he was a brutal scoundrel, whose chief distinction was the manner of his death: he bought new clothes to die in, and hired five poor men to walk behind the cart as mourners; he also gave hatbands and gloves to others who would attend his execution, to give it a fashionable touch; he joked with the crowd on his way to the scaffold, chatted amiably with the executioner for half an hour, then threw himself off the ladder. He died with style; it was a gesture of defiance at the forces of money and rank that kept the poor in their places, as if to say: "You hold all the cards, but we have more spirit than you." It is true that Turpin's career was not marked by any spectacular bravery, or even elegance. When forced to become an outlaw for stealing his neighbours' cattle, he led a gang that simply burst into isolated houses and carried off all the money. If necessary, they tortured the inhabitants, and an occasional servant girl was raped. On the run again, Turpin met a highwayman named King, and they became partners. Turpin committed his only murder during this partnership – he shot a man who tried to arrest him. Later still, he shot and killed King, but this seems to have been an accident; he intended to shoot the man who was trying to arrest King. Turpin was now not badly off, and he moved to Lincolnshire and set up as a gentleman under the name of John Palmer; but horse-stealing got him into trouble, and he moved to Weston in Yorkshire. Here he often joined the local gentry in hunting and shooting. One day, he shot a cock, and when his companion remonstrated, threatened to shoot him too. This led to his arrest, and since he did not have the money to put up surety for good behaviour, he was committed to prison. He remained there for some time, under suspicion of horse-stealing. A letter written to his brother finally led to the discovery of his identity; the schoolmaster who had taught him to write recognised the handwriting on the envelope, and informed on him. John Palmer the suspected horse-thief was discovered to be Dick Turpin, England's Public Enemy Number One. He was executed on 7 April 1739.

It is true that there is nothing in this record that would distinguish a modern criminal, but for the poor of his time – that is, for ninety-five per cent of Englishmen – he was a man who had done what they all dreamed of doing: taking what society would not give him.

Dick Turpin never became the subject of one of Hogarth's engravings, perhaps because his trial and execution took place at York; but he engraved the portrait of an equally celebrated criminal, Sarah Malcolm, accused of a treble murder committed in the course of robbery. She was a middle-class girl whose father wasted the family's goods, so that she was eventually obliged to become a laundress. She decided to rob one of her customers, an old lady of eighty called Duncomb. When friends of Mrs Duncomb came to tea on the afternoon of Sunday, 4 February 1733, they found that Mrs Duncomb and a female servant named Harrison had been strangled, while a servant girl of seventeen was in bed with her throat cut. As Mrs Duncomb's char, Sarah Malcolm came under suspicion, and money was found in her room, as well as a silver tankard stained with blood. She claimed that the actual murderers were two brothers called Alexander and a woman named Tracy. When the brothers heard of the charge, they presented themselves to the magistrate, and declared they were innocent. No doubt they were, for they were not tried with Sarah Malcolm, and this was in a period when the law preferred to hang a dozen innocent people rather than let one guilty one escape. After her execution, her corpse was dissected, and the skeleton presented to the Botanic Gardens at Cambridge, "where", said a writer at the end of the century, "it remains to this day". Hogarth was so interested in the attractive murderess, who was only twenty-two when she was executed, that he made two portraits of her.

The custom of handing over criminals for dissection to a barber-surgeon became law in 1752. For some odd reason, this seemed to worry criminals more than the thought of being hanged. It was one of many measures the government considered to try to reduce crime, upon the false hypothesis that a sufficiently cruel punishment would act as a deterrent. Another suggestion was to torture criminals before hanging them, breaking them on the wheel or burning them with hot irons, but this was rejected; there would be too many criminals to do this efficiently. But there were other ideas that seemed more practicable. For example, to leave bodies rotting on the gibbet until they became skeletons; to hang them "in irons" – that is, in a kind of iron cage, that would prevent the corpse from disintegrating too quickly (someone suggested that it would be a good idea to hang living malefactors in irons, and allow them to starve to death; this idea was rejected because the cries might upset people); there was even a custom of dumping the body on the doorstep of the person he had wronged, to demonstrate that the law had carried out the sentence. If one had travelled around England after 1752, one would have found many good views spoilt by the gibbet with its corpse in irons. Hilltops that could be seen from afar were selected as suitable spots, to deter the maximum number of criminals. Hanging in irons went out of fashion mainly because it was too expensive, as the suit might cost seventy-five pounds, and the gibbet had to be coated with lead to prevent relatives of the dead man from burning it down.

The most famous of English gallows was the one at Tyburn. It was a few yards to the west of Marble Arch, on the banks of a stream, the Tyburn, that flowed from Hampstead down to the Thames (it now runs underground for most of its length). In the time of Henry VIII, the gallows were simply a cross-beam supported on two trees; Queen Elizabeth had it changed to a triangle of beams supported on three uprights. As many as ten offenders at a time could be hanged on each beam, and the sight of thirty bodies swaying in the wind must have been an impressive sight. The phrase "gala day" is derived from "gallows day", gala being the Anglo-Saxon for a gallows; the hanging of notorious criminals was often the occasion for a public holiday, with a great deal of drunken merrymaking. England adopted hanging mainly because beheading large numbers of criminals was impracticable; before the time of Alfred the Great (about AD 850) criminals were often boiled alive; women were drowned in a special pit. This was given up because it was too much trouble, and an attempt to introduce the guillotine in Halifax in the first half of the seventeenth century never caught on in the rest of the country.

Beheading continued to be a fate reserved for those convicted of high treason. The most famous of English hangmen, Jack Ketch, who operated under Charles II, was a bungler as a headsman. When he executed Lord William Russell in 1683 for his part in the Rye House plot to kidnap the King, he took several strokes to do it, and the crowd became angry. Before the Duke of Monmouth was executed after his unsuccessful rebellion, he handed Ketch six guineas, and told him there would be another purse-full if he made a clean job of it. Then he felt the axe and commented: "I fear it is not sharp enough." Perhaps his coolness unnerved Ketch, who botched the job completely. After an unsuccessful blow that only partly severed the neck, he dropped the axe and shouted, "I cannot do it." Stern persuasions were brought to bear, but he was now so weak with nervousness that the head was still unsevered after four more blows, and he had to finish it with a knife. The crowd was so angry that he had to be taken away under escort.

He was hardly more efficient as a hangman, but fortunately, this hardly mattered, for his clients strangled to death if he left them long enough and pulled on their legs. (This is the origin of the phrase "to pull someone's leg", according to J.D. Potter's history of hanging, *The Fatal Gallows Tree*.) It was not until the latter part of the nineteenth century, when William Marwood became public hangman, that prisoners were given a drop long enough to dislocate the neck and bring instantaneous death.

When Hogarth produced his etching of the idle apprentice being hanged at Tyburn, the public executioner was Jack Hooper, the "Laughing Hangman", a good-natured soul of phenomenal ugliness, who did his best to make the last hours of his clients pleasant with jests and stories. Since prisoners of means usually rewarded the hangman, he probably found it a lucrative occupation. It is recorded that one of the few occasions when Laughing Jack's high spirits failed him was when he had to execute a particularly barbarous sentence on the forger Japhet Crook, alias Sir Peter Stranger, who had swindled a man out of two hundred acres of land. The sentence was to stand in the pillory, have his ears cut off, his nostrils slit open and seared with a red-hot iron, and to be imprisoned for life. The pillory could be the worst part of such an ordeal, for if the prisoner was unpopular, the crowd would pelt him with bottles and stones, often killing him. Crook survived this part of his ordeal – the crowd liked him – but neither he nor the executioner enjoyed the next part. Hooper sliced off his ears from behind with a sharp knife, and held each one up for the crowd to see, then slit his nostrils open with scissors. When he applied the red-hot iron to his nose, Crook leapt out of his chair, and the hangman decided to leave that part of the sentence uncompleted. Later in the day, Crook was well enough to drink himself insensible in a nearby tavern, no doubt on gin, after which he was taken off to jail.

The Hogarth etching conveys a clear notion of the scene at a hanging: the sellers of apples and muffins, the mothers holding babies, the "last confessions" of the prisoner being sold to the crowd, and the prisoner himself, seated in an open cart, of the type used during the French Revolution, with lattice-work sides, reading his Bible, leaning against his own coffin, and wearing his shroud. In the background are the grassy hills of Maida Vale, all open country.

Hogarth's two pictures, "Beer Street" and "Gin Lane", leave no room for doubt that he attributed the rising crime rate to gin. In "Beer Street", jolly-looking men and women drink cheerfully outside a tavern, a copy of the King's speech on a table indicates that they have been engaged in a serious discussion of politics, and an artist, ragged but cheerful, paints the inn sign. The only sign of poverty is the dilapidation of the pawnbroker's shop; a post-boy hands him a half pint through a hole in the door. "Gin Lane" is one of Hogarth's exercises in the gruesome. A drunken mother is allowing her baby to fall out of her arms into the area below; a madman has impaled another baby on a spit; a woman is being lifted into her coffin, and a hanged man is visible in a garret. The only prosperous person is the pawnbroker, with whom a carpenter is depositing his tools to buy gin. An interesting touch here is the "gin palace", which seems to be an open barn, full of barrels of gin, in front of which a mother is pouring gin down her baby's throat.

If a modern artist had engraved these pictures, or the even more horrifying "Four Stages of Cruelty", he would be accused of sadism; but in the age of Hogarth, stomachs were strong, and less violent protests would have made no impression at all. This was an age when people were used to violence. In 1731, an informer named John Waller was placed in the pillory at Seven Dials for some minor offence. He was the target for stones, bottles and cabbage stalks. Then, an hour later, a man dragged him down – he was standing upright, with his head and his hands held in the pillory – and tore off his clothes, after which the mob trampled him to death. A procuress named Mother Needham escaped alive, but died of her injuries two days later.

It was "Laughing Jack" Hooper who hanged Sarah Malcolm, and who was saddened by it because he thought her probably innocent – that the actual killings had been done by males. (Hogarth said that her face "showed that she was capable of any wickedness".) But it was not the hangman's job to be sensitive about his task. Hooper's successor, John Thrift, was so timid and good natured that he suffered agonies in the execution of his task. He was visibly close to vomiting when he had to hang, then decapitate and disembowel nine of the Jacobite rebels in 1746. Later the same year, he almost came to grief over the beheading of two more of the rebels, Lord Kilmarnock and Lord Balmerino. Thrift fainted on the scaffold and had to be revived with wine, then when Lord Kilmarnock arrived, he fell on his knees and burst into tears; Kilmarnock had to comfort him and pat him on the shoulder. But he did a better job of the beheading than Jack Ketch had with the Duke of Monmouth, severing the neck with one clean blow. Lord Balmerino was less fortunate; by now, Thrift's tears blinded him, and he only lacerated the neck with the first blow, it took two more to finish the job. The tender-hearted Thrift was one of those hangmen who was also a murderer: when being booed and stoned by a crowd, he drew his sword and ran one of them through. Sentenced to death, he was reprieved, and restored to his post of hangman. But his years of hanging and whipping had been too much for his sensibilities; he was subject to fits of delusion in which past victims came and made faces at him, and he died soon after his reprieve.

Another of Hogarth's contemporaries, John Price, has the dubious distinction of being the only hangman who was hanged and gibbeted. One night when drunk, he tried to rape an old apple-seller, who resisted. Price beat her to death, knocking out one of her eyes and breaking her arm. He was hanged in 1718. Price's type was far more usual among hangmen than Thrift's. This is hardly surprising, since the job involved tasks that must have been a sadist's delight. A receipted bill by Thomas Turlis, the hangman who succeeded Thrift, mentions "For whipping of Elizabeth Fletcher, five shillings, For whipping of Sarah Johnson, five shillings, For whipping of Anne Eaton, five shillings, For whipping of Jane Hodgson, five shillings", while for whipping Mary Dolley from Cavendish Squate to Duke Street (tied to a cart-tail) he received ten shillings. His successor, Edward Dennis, had the disagreeable task of hanging a pretty young girl named Mary Jones, who had stolen four pieces of muslin. Her husband had been kidnapped by a press-gang, and she stole the muslin to feed her two babies, one of whom was at her breast as she was driven to Tyburn. But she has her place in history for a more interesting reason. In 1776, Sir William Meredith told her story in the House of Commons during a debate, and moved some of his audience to tears. It was a sign that the era of brutality and callousness was coming to an end, and that a new age of reform was beginning. The "age of gin" lasted approximately one century.

But the age of crime is also the age in which we have the first adequate records of crime. In 1735, when Dick Turpin was still engaged in his gleeful depredations, a bookseller called John Osborn, of the Golden Ball in Paternoster Row, thought that it might be a profitable idea to gather together some of the lives and exploits of remarkable criminals from the pamphlets that were hawked at Tyburn, and he issued three volumes of *Lives of the Most Remarkable Criminals* in that year. Forty years later, in 1774, a gentleman named George Theodore Wilkinson brought the records up to date in the famous *Newgate Calendar*.

The high moral tone of both these works makes them tiresome to read. Their authors were recording the lives of criminals in order to make money, and they felt they had to disguise this by making their accounts sound like sermons. "There cannot, perhaps, be a greater misfortune to a man than his having a woman ill-principled about him, whether as a wife or otherwise," says Osborn severely, in writing of a highwayman named Picken. One is struck by the commonplace nature of most of the crimes, the lack of the kind of features that would have interested Sherlock Holmes. The first case in the volume is typical. Jane Griffin, a forty-year-old housewife with a hot temper, lost the cellar key, and went to the maid's room to upbraid her. She and the maid had already had several disagreements, and the maid returned the bad language with interest. Jane Griffin, was holding a kitchen knife with which she had been cutting a chicken for the children's supper, and she suddenly saw red and stabbed at the maid. Unfortunately, it was a good blow that went straight to the heart. Today, Jane Griffin would get two years for manslaughter, and possibly psychiatric treatment. In 1720, she was hanged.

Osborn's book contains a lengthy account of the eighteenth-century equivalent of the Arden of Faversham case. Catherine Hayes was born Catherine Hall, in Birmingham, the daughter of poor parents. In 1705, when she was fifteen, she was noticed by some army officers, who persuaded her to return to their quarters; there she became their collective mistress for a while, until they moved on. She then found a job as a servant with a Warwickshire farmer named Hayes. The son of the house, a carpenter, fell in love with her; one morning, they went secretly into Worcester, and were married. John Hayes was then twenty-one. After six years in the country, his young bride began to dream of London, and persuaded her husband to move there. She was so excitable and quarrelsome that her in-laws raised no objection. In London, John Hayes became a successful coal merchant, pawnbroker and moneylender. His success in this latter occupation lends colour to his wife's assertion that he was unbearably mean. At all events, Hayes was successful in business, and in a little over ten years, made enough money to sell his shop in the Tyburn Road and take lodgings nearby. His relations with his wife had deteriorated badly. This may have been due to his meanness and her desire for luxury, or there may have been deeper causes. She later told one of her accomplices in the murder that Hayes had murdered two of his children in the country, presumably when they were newborn. *If* Hayes was pathologically mean, there might just possibly be some truth in this story.

Early in 1725, a young man named Thomas Billings, a tailor, came to their house, and Catherine Hayes declared him to be an old friend or relative. He stayed with them, and when Hayes went to the country on business, Billings took his place in Catherine's bed. The two lovers made the most of their freedom, throwing parties and spending a great deal of the money that Hayes had taken so long to accumulate. When Hayes returned, he was furious, and gave his wife a beating. But for some reason, he did not turn Billings out of the house.

Another friend from Warwickshire now arrived, a Thomas Wood. It was to him that she told the story of her husband killing her two children, and she mentioned that Hayes had also killed a man. Wood also became her lover, and her promise that her husband's estate – some fifteen hundred pounds, a fortune for those days – would be put at his disposal when she became a widow, finally made him agree to help her kill her husband.

On 1 March 1725, Wood came back from a visit to the country, and found Billings, Catherine and John Hayes in the midst of a drinking session. Wood, who was young and boastful, declared that he had just drunk a guinea's worth of wine and was still sober, and Billings challenged Hayes to drink the same amount – six bottles. If Hayes could do it without getting drunk, Billings would buy the wine; if not, Hayes should pay for it. Hayes accepted the offer; perhaps the prospect of six bottles of free wine was too much for his miserly soul. Billings, Wood and Catherine Hayes set off for a tavern in New Bond Street, and on the way, she pointed out that this would be a good opportunity to kill her husband.

In the Brawn's Head the three of them drank a pint of "best mountain wine", and asked for six pints to be sent up to their lodgings. Catherine Hayes paid 10s 6d for it – perhaps its quality was only half as good as the stuff Wood claimed he had been drinking.

Hayes downed the six pints of wine without much trouble, while the other three drank beer. His wife quietly sent out for another pint which Hayes, now too fuddled to count the bottles, also drank. He then fell down on the floor, woke up after a few minutes, and staggered off to bed in the next room. The bed was probably the kind that Hogarth portrayed, with its lower end actually on the floor. Hayes fell asleep on his face. Billings came in with a coal hatchet and hit him on the back of the head with it. The blow fractured his skull, and Hayes began to kick his feet in agony, making such a noise that the woman in the room overhead came down to investigate. By this time, Wood had seized the hatchet and given Hayes two more blows, which completed the work of killing him. When Mrs Springate complained that the thudding noise had awakened them, Catherine Hayes explained that her husband had some noisy guests, but that they were about to leave.

It must have been a tense moment, and both Wood and Billings were badly unnerved.

The next problem was what to do with the body. They had to get it down two flights of stairs to the street. Then suppose they bumped into a member of the watch? As soon as Hayes was recognised, they were done for. But Catherine Hayes refused to be panicked. She pointed out that if they cut off her husband's head, and disposed of that first, the body would not be identifiable, even if they had to flee from the watch and leave it in the street.

The two men were already nauseated. The bed was drenched with blood; blood had even shot up to the ceiling with the hatchet blows. Catherine Hayes suggested that they decapitate her husband with his neck over a bucket to catch the blood. The two men must have been wishing that this business had never started, but there was obviously no way out except to dispose of the body. So they placed the body on the bed so the head hung over. Catherine Hayes held the bucket underneath the neck, Billings twisted his fingers in the blood-soaked hair, and Woods sawed away at the neck with a carving knife – hatchet blows would have brought Mrs Springate down again. When the head was off, they dropped it in the pail, and left the headless body to bleed into it.

Catherine Hayes recognised that there was still danger. If the head was identified, it would be traced back to her. She proposed boiling it in a pot until the flesh came away, a revolting but sensible idea, but the others were too nervous. They became even more nervous when Mrs Springate shouted down irritably to know what was going on. Here Catherine Hayes showed a presence of mind that entitles her to be ranked with Alice Arden and Lady Macbeth. She called back that her husband had been suddenly called away on a journey, and was getting ready to go. Now the two Thomases could hardly wait to get out of the house. They poured the blood from the bucket down the sink, then had to tiptoe up and down the stairs half a dozen times to get water from the well to wash it down. When that was done, the men crept downstairs, one of them holding the bucket under his coat, while Catherine Hayes walked down behind them, talking in her normal voice, saying goodbye to her husband, in case any of the neighbours was listening. According to the sharp-eared Mrs Springate, she put up an excellent and convincing performance. Then the two men made off as fast as they could, and Catherine Hayes hurried upstairs to clean up the blood before it clotted. It was a long task, because the unpolished floorboards had soaked up the blood like a sponge; even when she had washed it and scraped it with a knife, the marks were still visible.

Meanwhile, Billings and Wood hastened towards the river, a long walk, from the present day Oxford Street down to Whitehall. It was nearly midnight. People of that time tended to go to bed early, and the watch were likely to challenge people who were out after midnight. Billings must have looked as if he was pregnant, with the pail under his greatcoat. They reached Whitehall, but the dock gates had already been closed. The tide was out, and the foreshore of the river was mostly mud; wading across that would attract attention. They walked on along the river, past Westminster, to the Horseferry wharf, at the end of the present Horseferry Road, under Lambeth Bridge. They went to the end of the dock, and threw the head over. Instead of a splash, there was a thud as it landed on mud. But they were too frightened to worry. They threw the bucket after it, and hurried away. The nightwatchman on the wharf heard the thud, and a man on board a boat saw them throw the bucket, but it was a dark night and no one was very curious. Billings and Wood hastened back home, now feeling slightly better. They found Catherine Hayes still scraping at the floor-boards, trying not to make too much noise. The headless body still lay across the bed. The two men made up a makeshift bed in the other room, and tried to sleep. Catherine Hayes sat by them, brooding. She must have been wishing that they had disfigured the face with a knife to prevent recognition. But with luck, the head was already on its way out to sea. . . She was still sitting there when the two men woke up at dawn.

And also at dawn, the nightwatchman, a Mr Robinson, walked to the edge of the dock to stretch his legs, and saw the bucket and the head lying in the mud. A small crowd soon gathered, and the lighterman from the boat mentioned seeing a man throwing the bucket into the river.

Back in the lodgings, the murderers were discussing what to do with the body. The first and most obvious thing was to conceal it in case someone came into the room. Mrs Hayes went out and got a large box, but it was not big enough. They cut off the arms, and the legs at the knees, but the body was still too long. They hacked off the thighs, and finally managed to pack most of the pieces into the box, leaving some of the smaller items in an old blanket. That evening, at nine o'clock, Wood and Billings crept downstairs with the trunk in a blanket. It was early and there were too many people about, but they were not going to risk being stopped by the watch. This time they went north – fortunately there was not far to go before they were in the fields of Marylebone. They tossed the trunk into a pond that Wood had located during the day, then went back and collected the rest of the body. It was Mrs Springate who let them in at midnight. Fortunately, she had no reason to be suspicious, even though her husband had found clots of blood in the drain that morning. Blood was common enough.

The next day, Wood made off to the country to soothe his shattered nerves. Billings resumed his place in his mistress's bed.

The parish officers of Westminster had not been idle. They ordered the blood and dirt to be washed from the head and – a macabre touch – the hair to be combed. Then the head was set on a stake at St Margaret's churchyard in Westminster. It drew a fascinated crowd, but no one recognised it. But the next day, a young apprentice named Bennett saw it, and flew to tell Catherine Hayes that he thought it looked like her husband. She told him angrily that he could get himself into serious trouble if he spread such reports – her husband was alive and well. Bennett apologised and promised to say nothing about it. And a Mr Patrick also thought he recognised the head, and went along to a pub called the "Dog and Dial" in Monmouth Street, at which Hayes and his wife used to drink, to mention his suspicion. Billings happened to be working there at the time, and someone replied that the head couldn't belong to John Hayes, because Billings was his lodger, and he would know if anything had happened to Hayes. Billings immediately confirmed this, saying that he had left Hayes in bed that morning.

Mrs Hayes must have been feeling nervous, but she recognised that flight would be a mistake. When a neighbour asked after her husband, she said he was out taking a walk. The visitor mentioned the head in the churchyard, and Mrs Hayes expressed horror at the wickedness of the age. "Why, they even say they've found bits of a woman's body in a pond at Marylebone," she declared, and the neighbour said she hadn't heard about that.

Wood came back to town on the fifth, two days after he had fled. Catherine Hayes gave him some of her husband's clothes and five shillings. She told him that the head had been found, but that no one had yet identified it.

The head was beginning to stink; worse still, the features were already beginning to turn black. The parish officers had it placed in a large jar full of spirit, perhaps gin, and continued to exhibit it to anyone who was interested. For a short period it looked as if the mystery was solved when a woman said she thought it was her husband. But after a long look at it, she said she couldn't swear to it.

Catherine Hayes remained remarkably cool. Less than a week after the murder, she left her lodgings and moved to another in the neighbourhood, taking Billings, Wood, and Mrs Springate. No doubt she was afraid that the latter might gossip; she even paid a quarter's rent for the lady. She then proceeded to collect as many of her husband's debts as possible, even threatening to sue her husband's brother-in-law for money he owed. She wrote various letters in her husband's name to other debtors.

Inevitably, Hayes' friends began to wonder what had become of him. A man called Ashby called on her to enquire. She then told him, in strict confidence, that her husband had killed a man in a quarrel and had fled to Portugal. Mr Ashby asked if the head found in the river belonged to the murdered man, but Mrs Hayes said no, they had buried the body entire.

All this was bound to arouse suspicion. Ashby communicated with the neighbour who had already enquired; they talked with another neighbour. And finally, a Justice of the Peace was informed. They hurried to Catherine Hayes' lodgings and knocked on the door. She was in bed with Billings; she dressed and went to the door. Billings was sitting on the edge of the bed without shoes or stockings when the officers came in. When asked if he had been sleeping with her, she said no, he was mending his stockings. The Justice remarked that he must have been doing it in the dark, since there was no candle or fire.

Wood was not present, but they arrested Catherine Hayes, Billings and Mrs Springate, and took them off to different prisons, to prevent them concocting a story. Catherine Hayes continued to assert her innoncence, and asked if she might see the head from the churchyard. The Justice agreed, and they took her to the barber-surgeon, a Mr Westbrook, who was keeping the head. Here, Catherine Hayes called upon all her histrionic powers, and shouted: "Oh, it is my dear husband's head!" and proceeded to kiss the jar. Mr Westbrook came in and said he would take the head out of the jar – it was generally believed in those days that murderers would reveal their guilt if forced to touch the corpse. But Catherine Hayes was equal to anything. She seized the head and kissed it, then asked if she could have a lock of its hair. Her performance must have been a little too dramatic. The barber-surgeon replied sardonically that she had already had too much of his blood; at which Catherine Hayes fainted, or pretended to. She had already run through the emotional spectrum; it was the only thing left for her to do.

While all this was taking place, someone saw the blanket floating in the Marylebone pond and pulled it out. The rest of the body was soon recovered. But Catherine Hayes and Thomas Billings continued to assert their total innocence.

Wood was the weak link in the chain. On the following Sunday, he came back to London from Harrow, and went along to Catherine Hayes' old lodgings. They told him she had moved to a house nearby, and someone offered to show him. His informant took him to the wrong place, to the house of Mr Longmore, one of the neighbours who had caused the arrest. There the terrified Wood was dragged off his horse and taken to the Justice who had been questioning the others. At first, Wood declared himself innocent, but in Newgate, his nerve broke, and he made a full confession. He explained that Mrs Hayes had told him that her husband was an atheist and free-thinker, and that "it would be no more sin to kill him than to kill a dog". When the other two were told of the confession, they decided that there was no further point in keeping silent, especially as it might lead to torture, and also confessed. Mrs Springate was released.

It was after this that Catherine Hayes suddenly realised that the charge against her was not of murder, but petty treason – the killing of her lord and master – and that the penalty for this was to be burned alive. But she still hoped that her crime might be regarded simply as murder, since she had not struck any of the blows that killed her husband. At her trial, with the fear of a painful death hanging over her, she denied that she had any hand in the actual killing of her husband, and said that she had kept silent only because she was afraid that Wood and Billings would kill her too. When it was clear that all three would be sentenced to death, Wood and Billings begged that they might not be hanged in chains, and she again repeated her plea to be hanged rather than burned. But the judge sentenced her to be burned, and she screamed all the way back to Newgate.

She revealed a better side to her nature before her execution: she sent messages to her two ex-lovers, regretting that she had involved them in all this. When she saw Billings in chapel, she sat holding his hand and leaned her head on his shoulder. She was obviously in love with Billings.

A few days before her execution, she somehow managed to get a bottle of acid into her cell. Unfortunately, a fellow prisoner saw it and tasted it. A little spilt on a handkerchief burnt it. So the prisoner smashed the bottle on the floor.

Wood caught a fever in prison and died before he could be executed. He is the only person in the case who seems to deserve much sympathy. His age is not recorded, but it seems fairly certain that he was still in his teens. He seems to have been a good-natured, easy-going young man who was too easily influenced.

Billings was also young. Osborn records that when he first came to stay at the Hayes' lodgings, there was a rumour that he was Catherine Hayes' son by a previous "connection". He was executed before Catherine Hayes, and when the executioner, Richard Arnet, Laughing Jack's predecessor, came to fetch her, she asked him if he had killed her "dear child" yet.

Her last moments give the case a final touch of horror. It was customary to strangle a woman condemned for petty treason before burning her. Arnet lit the brushwood around her, then started to pull the strangling rope from behind, but the fire reached his hands too quickly and he had to let go. The spectators watched her trying to push the burning faggots away while she screamed. More faggots were thrown on, to try to put her out of her misery soon, "but", says Wilkinson, "she survived amidst the flames for a considerable time, and her body was not perfectly reduced to ashes in less than three hours".

I have discussed this case at length, not merely because its details are dramatic in themselves, but because it illustrates what it was about murder that so interested the people of the eighteenth century. If the author of *Arden of Faversham* had been alive, he could have made a classic play of the Hayes murder. Osborn tells it with as much detail as Holinshed related the Arden murder, no doubt because he was in London at the time, and probably went to view the head. But the kind of thing that would interest a modern reporter struck him as irrelevant. Why did Catherine Hayes want to murder her husband? She mentioned in her confession that John Hayes had been a bad husband to her, and kept her half starved; this seems consistent with his meanness. Did she find in Billings an important emotional experience after years of living with a husband who thought of little besides money?

Again, why did Hayes allow Billings to remain in the house after he had beaten his wife for throwing parties while he was away? He must have had some suspicion. He was forty-one years old, and at that time, this was the beginning of old age. Had he gone past the point of feeling sexual jealousy? There may be another reason why he wanted Billings to remain. In those days, most farmers kept their money in an old sock, or hidden somewhere in the house, as Dick Turpin discovered. Hayes was a farmer's son; he was also a money-lender, therefore it is almost certain that he kept his money – fifteen hundred pounds of it – on the premises. (It could not have been in a bank, or there would be records of Catherine's attempts to get it after his death, as well as of her collecting his debts.) They lived in two rooms, in a house in which some of the tenants were poor – Mrs Springate was a quarter of a year behind with her rent. One of them must have stayed at home all the time in case of thieves. And since John Hayes must have been out on business, his wife was confined to the premises. A lodger who could be trusted was a valuable addition to the household, even if he did assume some of the husband's rights.

How did Billings feel about Wood? We may assume that Wood became her lover, for two reasons: that he was otherwise unlikely to join in the murder plot, and because Osborn speaks of her "taking every opportunity to caress him". She even slept with the two of them on the night after the disposal of the body. Although frightened, he continued to return from Harrow to see her, when he would have been more sensible to stay away for six months. The emotional complications of this triangle – a healthy, sex-starved woman of thirty-four and two virile teenagers – are enough to excite the interest of any dramatist. Billings was the one who stuck by her after the murder, which may explain why she transferred her affections completely to him before the end.

A final touch of mystery to the whole story: what about Mary Springate? On the night of the murder, she complained that they had wakened her husband. What became of the husband when Mrs Springate moved out with Catherine Hayes? Why was it Mrs Springate who complained about the noise, rather than her husband? Could he, perhaps, have been a market porter who had to rise very early? But if so, why were they a quarter of a year behind with the rent? No, it seems more probable that he had been ill for some time. Perhaps he died in the week after the murder. And Mrs Hayes took care to become more closely acquainted with the neighbour who had opened the door to Wood and Billings after the disposal of the body. Of course, it is just as likely that the husband was simply lazy, and that he left his wife sometime during the week after the murder. John Osborn was not interested in such commonplace details, and so we shall never know.

Catherine Hayes was by no means the only woman who was burnt for the murder of her husband in the eighteenth century. There was Ann Williams, burnt in 1753 for poisoning her husband with arsenic (the dying man gave her away). Amy Hutchinson, who also used arsenic – she married her husband to spite a former lover, but decided she preferred the lover after all – was strangled before being burnt in 1750. Ann Beddingfield, a farmer's wife who persuaded her lover to strangle her husband: unfortunately, the lover decided to do it on the spur of the moment one night, without telling his mistress, who was alarmed by the noise and woke up a servant girl; although the coroner failed to notice that the farmer had been strangled, the servant girl gave it away, waiting until she had received her quarter's wages. Ann Beddingfield was burnt in 1763, and her lover hanged at the same time. The last woman to be burnt alive in England was Phoebe Harris, who was executed for husband murder in 1788, which was, after all, the time of Blake, Wordsworth and Goethe.

The main impression one receives from the *Newgate Calendar*, apart from the savagery of the sentences, is of the savagery of so many of the crimes. The Brownrigg family – mother, father and son – were sadists who enjoyed beating their female apprentices, girls from the workhouse or Foundling Hospital who were taken on as servants in exchange for their keep. The girls were frequently stripped and hung from a hook in the ceiling while they were whipped. Brownrigg, a plumber, was supposed to supply clothes, but he bought them only one lot of clothes each, of poor quality. If they tore these, Mrs Brownrigg was likely to force them to strip and to do their work naked for several days. One of the girls who wet her bed was made to sleep in an icy coal-cellar on straw, without blankets. Even after one of these apprentices escaped and was examined by parish officials, who saw that she was a mass of cuts and bruises, nothing was done about it except to threaten Mrs Brownrigg. Even so, Mrs Brownrigg had no difficulty in replacing the runaway with another apprentice. This was a girl called Mary Clifford, who was eventually flogged so mercilessly that the wounds, never allowed to heal, began to gangrene. The next-door neighbours, hearing groans and cries issuing from the Brownriggs' house every other day, managed to peep in through the attic skylight, and saw a girl so badly beaten that she could not reply to them. The parish officers were called again. Brownrigg tried to brazen it out, but they searched his house and found one of the girls, Mary Mitchell. When a doctor attempted to remove her leather bodice, it stuck to the open sores. The officers returned, by which time Brownrigg had called a lawyer to threaten them with serious legal action if they didn't leave his premises. They used their legal authority, and Brownrigg was finally forced to produce the other girl, Mary Clifford, who had been ordered to hide in a sideboard cupboard. She died shortly after being taken to a hospital. The Brownriggs fled but were arrested. At the trial, Mrs Brownrigg was found guilty of murder, for she was officially the employer of the girls. The father and son received six months each. When Mrs Brownrigg was taken to Tyburn in September 1767, the mob howled and threw things. The records do not mention what became of the father and son, but the *Newgate Calendar* account leaves no room for doubt that they were equally responsible, possibly more so.

Less than a year later, another couple, a mother and daughter, were hanged for the same crime, and this case has some more interesting features. Sarah Metyard was a milliner, who had several girls from the parish as her apprentices, and she treated these as badly as the Brownriggs treated their girls. After an attempt to run away, one of the girls was starved for three days and kept tied in a position that would not allow her to sit down or stand up. At the end of this time, she died, and the mother and her teenage daughter, also called Sarah, moved the body up to the attic and told the other apprentices that she had had a fit and was recovering. Then they announced that the girl had run away. The girl's sister doubted this story and mentioned her doubts to a lodger in the house. Mrs Metyard killed her too and put the body in the attic with her sister's. After two months, the stench was so great that the old woman cut up the bodies and dumped them in a sewer. The coroner who was shown the pieces of the bodies, observed the state of decay and declared that they were corpses stolen from a churchyard and dissected by a surgeon.

Two years later, a man named Rooker came to lodge with the Metyards and was shocked by the old woman's cruelty. By this time, mother and daughter were constantly quarrelling, so when Rooker offered the daughter a place in his house, she accepted eagerly. She soon became his mistress, and they moved out to Ealing. The old lady was wildly resentful, and spent a great deal of time making disturbances. One day, after a quarrel in which hints of the murders were dropped, Rooker asked his mistress what she meant. Sarah confessed to the murders, and Rooker thought he now had the ideal way of getting rid of the mother – he assumed that the daughter would not be indicted, since she was under age at the time and had acted on her mother's orders. He was mistaken; mother and daughter both died at Tyburn.

A great number of murders in the eighteenth century were committed by smugglers, or in the course of smuggling. The case known as the "trial of the smugglers" will serve as a typical, and particularly violent, example. Seven smugglers were tried in 1749 for the murder of a customs man named Galley and a shoemaker named Chater, when the latter was on his way to give evidence against the smugglers. The names of the smugglers were Benjamin Tapner, John Cobby, John Hammond, William Jackson, William Carter, and a father and son named Mills. The customs officer and his witness were on their way from Southampton to Stanstead, in Sussex, where Chater would be examined by a Justice of the Peace.

Smuggling in those days was not merely a family affair; it might involve the whole village or district, and to do anything about it was as difficult as breaking up the Mafia in Sicily. So when the pair stopped briefly at an inn at Rowlands Castle, in Hampshire, they had walked into the lion's den. The widow who kept the inn confided to a customer that she was afraid the two men "were come to hurt the smugglers". A gang of smugglers soon gathered, and one of them asked Chater what had happened to a man called Diamond. Chater replied truthfully that Diamond was under arrest and that he was being taken to give evidence against him, although he didn't want to. At this, one of the smugglers, Jackson, knocked him down with a blow in the mouth. The two men must have realised the extent of their mistake and asked for their horses. The smugglers apologised for Jackson and asked them to stay and drink. They saw they had no alternative and stayed. The smugglers got them drunk and the took the letter to the Justice of the Peace. Its contents enraged them so much that they immediately proposed to hang the two men, egged on by two of their wives who said, "Hang the dogs, they are here to hang you".

Now the episodes of incredible cruelty began. Galley and Chater were asleep. Jackson jumped on the bed with a pair of spurs and slashed their foreheads with them to wake them. The men were then both whipped. After this, they were both tied on horses and whipped along the road by the whole gang. When they fell off and hung upside down under the horse's belly, their ankles being tied, they were quickly pulled upright and whipped again. One of the smugglers seized Galley's testicles and squeezed them until he fainted; Galley was then whipped to death.

Chater must have been wishing that they would kill him too, but first they wanted to find out what happened to Diamond, so Chater was chained up in a coal house with a man to watch him. The smugglers then buried the customs man, and went on a drinking spree for three days, the beverages being gin and rum. At intervals the guard was changed and several smugglers visited Chater to beat him. Then they decided that he had to be killed and someone suggested putting a loaded gun to his head, and attaching a long string to the trigger, which would be pulled by all of them at once – there were now fourteen – so that no one of them could be blamed.

Finally, the smugglers went to kill Chater. One of them slashed him across the eyes with a heavy knife, blinding him and cutting through the bridge of his nose. Then Chater was whipped again. After this, they took him to a well near a wood. There a rope was tied around his neck and the other end was tied to some railings; he was then pushed into the well. Unfortunately, the rope was too short and he was still alive after a quarter of an hour, the weight of his body being supported by the side of the well. Eventually, they tossed him in, head-first. When he still continued to groan after half an hour, they threw in stones until he stopped.

All this cruelty had not sickened them; they stopped to drink on the way home and boasted about the murders openly. When officials started searching for the two missing men, it was not too difficult to find someone to drop a hint about the murderers. Seven of the fourteen were arrested; the trial was short, and six of them were executed the next day. The exception was Jackson, the ringleader, who died in prison the evening before his execution was due. No doubt the story of the spurs had got about, and the police had taken the opportunity to get some of their own back.

There is a curious postscript to this story that again illustrates the barbarity of which country people were capable. Another son of the elder Mills was a member of a gang who, only a few weeks later, whipped and kicked to death another man who was suspected of stealing two of the smugglers' bags of tea. They dumped the body in a pond and Mills moved to Beckenham in Kent, where he became a highway robber. Another smuggler gave him away and he was executed six months after his father and brother. Mills seems to have been the only one of the gang who was hanged for the murder. The leader, a man named Curtis, told the man they were whipping that "he would whip him till he died, for he had whipped many a rogue and washed his hands in the blood". Clearly, this kind of cruelty was not uncommon among smugglers.

Gin can hardly be blamed for the barbarity of the eighteenth century, for tales of equal barbarity can be told of earlier centuries. But it certainly played its part in releasing those impulses that civilisation aims to control. Reading the *Newgate Calendar*, it is impossible not to note that a large proportion of the crimes are due simply to loss of temper, like Jane Griffin's stabbing of the servant girl. In fact, apart from murders committed in the course of robbery, the most familiar type of murder was the "crime of passion", in the most straightforward sense. The last nobleman to be publicly executed in England was Lord Ferrars, who flew into a fury with his bailiff and shot him. Ferrars was undoubtedly mentally unbalanced, but the sentence was carried out nevertheless. The hangman was the famous Thomas Turlis. The old triangular gallows erected in the time of Queen Elizabeth had been removed in 1759, and a new one had to be built for Ferrars in the following year. (A movable gallows was used for ordinary miscreants, but a Lord obviously deserved something better.) A picture of the execution, made at the time, shows the prisoner faced by a huge grandstand, of the kind now used in football grounds, and a huge and impressive gallows nearly the size of Marble Arch. The gallows is surrounded by mounted soldiers. This impressive occasion was marred by a sordid squabble: as Turlis was reaching out his hand to take the five guineas his lordship was offering, one of his assistants leapt forward and snatched it. The dignified Turlis, who had just begged his lordship's forgiveness, turned round in a rage and unleashed a string of violent oaths. The execution was delayed until the money was restored.

The case of Captain John Porteous illustrates that the mob was still capable of taking justice into its own hands. Porteous was a tailor who married an ex-mistress of the Provost of Edinburgh, and often received favours from his wife's ex-lover, one of which was a post as captain of a band of men employed to keep the peace. Porteous was a brutal man, disliked by everybody. One day, when he was presiding over the execution of a smuggler, the crowd started to throw stones, one of which hit Porteous on the nose. He immediately fired his pistol at the nearest man, killing him, and ordered his men to fire on the mob. The soldiers fired over the heads of the crowd, but some of the shots hit people watching from windows, while Porteous continued to fire his own pistol. Nine people were killed, and many more injured. For the sake of appearances, and to avoid riots, Porteous was tried and sentenced to death, but the execution was delayed until the King could return from Hanover to review the case. The mob recognised the aim of these delaying tactics, and stormed the jail. Porteous was dragged along to the grass-market, where the previous outrage had taken place, and hanged from a pole outside a shop. This was in 1736.

Before we cease to speak of Tyburn, it might be mentioned that there were a number of cases in which hanged people were revived. The most famous was of a sixteen-year-old youth, William Duell, who in 1740 raped and murdered a girl in a barn. After he had been cut down and taken to the surgeons' hall for dissection, he began to move. The surgeon bled him, and half an hour later Duell sat up. Since the sentence of hanging had been carried out, he could not be hanged again; instead, he was transported for life.

Ann Greene was a servant girl who was found guilty of killing her newly born baby. Her friends hung on her legs to try to put her out of her misery more quickly – one can only presume the rope was badly tied – and when she was cut down, and still twitched, one of them jumped on her stomach, and a soldier hit her on the head with his musket. In the surgeons' hall, a rattling was heard in her throat and she was put into a warm bed; the next day, she was almost fully recovered. She died in 1659, nine years after her hanging, during which time she had married and had three children.

In 1728, a girl named Margaret Dickson established the basis of a lifelong reputation by hanging for an hour, and then being taken away in her coffin. Knocking noises were heard from inside the coffin, at which everyone fled, but someone had the courage to return and take her out. She not only recovered, but had to marry her husband a second time, since she was legally dead, and her marriage therefore dissolved. Her murder of her baby had also been the result of the kidnapping of her husband by a press-gang. Under the name of Half Hanged Meg, she was still a notable public figure in Edinburgh twenty-five years later.

"Half Hanged Smith" was a housebreaker who was hanged at Tyburn. After five minutes, some merrymakers in the crowd began to shout "A reprieve", as if a man had arrived waving a document. The executioner cut him down, and he revived at a nearby house. Later, he described his sensations: "I felt a very great pain caused by the weight of my body, and my spirits felt in a strange commotion violently pressing upwards. They forced their way into my head, and then I saw a great blaze of glaring light which seemed to go out of my eyes with a flash. After that I lost all sense of pain until I was cut down, when I experienced an intolerable pricking or shooting" – the latter obviously the "pins and needles" that comes when blood returns to a part of the body from which it has been cut off. This was in 1705.

Towards the last part of the century, there was a gradual change in public opinion towards violence. Tyburn gallows was removed because it hindered traffic, but also because these spectacles were beginning to offend people. This should not be taken to mean the ordinary people, who semed to feel no sympathy for the criminal and enjoyed the hangings in the way that schoolboys enjoy seeing other schoolboys being caned. The crowds who threw things at Elizabeth Brownrigg in 1767 were not horrified by her cruelty; it was simply a demonstration by the underdog against the "middle classes" who could beat and starve them.

No, the change in sensibility was taking place in the educated classes, and it was the result of increased national prosperity and the gradual relaxation of religious bigotry. The *Newgate Calendar* contains an interesting example of this change of sensibility in the chapter on Thomas Colley, hanged in 1751 for drowning a woman believed to be a witch. Colley was the ringleader of a mob who seized an old couple called Osborne from the workhouse – they were believed to be a witch and a wizard. Both were stripped and ducked in a pond; Colley kept pushing them under with a long stick. The woman died with her mouth and nose choked with mud. Wilkinson's account declares indignantly: "It is astonishing to believe that any persons could be so stupid as to believe in the ridiculous doctrine of witchcraft," and goes on to offer several pages of cases from the past of witches being forced to confess by torture. One realises, with mild amazement, that Wilkinson felt he was living in a rational and enlightened age, and that all this barbarity was behind him.

In fact, it would be more than fifty more years before there was an attempt to introduce even such simple reforms as preventing children from working down mines or being forced to climb chimneys as sweeps, or preventing landowners from setting mantraps and spring guns, and passing safety regulations to prevent ships from being grossly overloaded. But at least the age of Dr Johnson, who supported public hanging because he thought it deterred criminals, was giving way to the age of William Blake and Wordsworth. Blake's early poems, full of pity for children forced to sweep chimneys and girls forced into prostitution, date from the same time as the *Newgate Calendar*.

The man who was chiefly responsible for a new attitude towards crime in London was the novelist Henry Fielding, who became a magistrate in 1748, after he had failed to make a living as a playwright. Before Fielding, the law attempted to repress crime by the savagery of the sentences and by gibbets and dissection. Fielding was the first to make a simple and obvious suggestion: why not try to prevent crime in advance by having an efficient police force? This struck the government as a wildly illogical proposal; after all, each parish employed its constables and watchmen. Fielding's predecessor at Bow Street had been Sir Thomas de Veil, a good magistrate by all ordinary standards, although he boasted of making a thousand pounds a year by "trading justice"; he was also a satyr who shamelessly used his office to procure himself "a great variety of young ladies". Fielding's kind of honesty and dedication was regarded as slightly insane, and after six years of struggling against the government, he died. But he had created the core of a small army of efficient policemen in Bow Street. His blind half-brother John carried on his work, and the Bow Street Runners became famous for their efficiency. In 1785, the new Prime Minister, Mr Pitt, introduced a police bill that represented the final triumph of Henry Fielding's proposals. By the year 1800, there were nine "police offices" in London, and the century-long crime wave was at last over.

7.
Cannibals and Rapists

FROM THE criminal point of view, I find the nineteenth century far more interesting than the eighteenth. Why? Because murders that spring out of poverty and misery do not really involve much human choice, much good or evil. Bernard Shaw asked the explorer Stanley – the man who found Livingstone – what proportion of his men could lead the expedition if necessary. Stanley replied promptly: "Five per cent." Shaw asked if this was an exact or an approximate figure. "Exact," said Stanley.

Modern biology has made the same discovery, although at the time I am writing, it is not widely known. In *all* animal groups, including human, there are five per cent who possess enterprise, leader-qualities. But, of course, there are wide extremes in the range of the dominant five per cent, from sadistic wife-beaters to Beethovens, from champion boxers to great mathematicians. In an experiment performed with rats, John Calhoun (at the Bethesda Institute of Mental Health in Maryland) showed that when rats are overcrowded, the dominant five per cent become criminals. This is obviously also true for human beings. Place them in squalor and misery, and the dominant five per cent will tend to become a criminal five per cent. The more intelligent ones will use their intelligence to escape the squalor, recognising that to become a criminal is, in a way, to surrender to the squalor as much as becoming a drunk or a drug-addict. But these will only be a tiny minority.

The criminality of about five per cent of slum dwellers is scientifically predictable, and therefore of no particular interest to a writer like myself who is more interested in questions of human freedom. Crime becomes psychologically interesting only when people are sufficiently well-off to satisfy their basic needs for food, drink, sex, security. With a few interesting exceptions, all the "great" murder cases of the nineteenth century – Lizzie Borden, Charles Bravo, Dr Pritchard, Professor Webster – concerned the socially comfortable classes. Not the extremely rich or the aristocracy – they were seldom involved in murders, except occasionally as victims – but the middle classes. And in well over fifty per cent of these cases, the means used was poison.

In an introduction to the Folio Society edition of selections from the *New Newgate Calendar* (1960), Lord Birkett remarked that the trials of the nineteenth century do not differ very greatly from those of the eighteenth. This may be true as far as the trials are concerned, but anyone who has the original two-volume edition of Camden Pelham's *New Newgate Calendar* (1886) will immediately note a difference in the crimes themselves. Pelham's Volume One is largely a rehash of the original *Newgate Calendar* (in many cases using the original text of Wilkinson). Volume Two deals with the nineteenth century, and we are immediately in a different world. In fact, the opening case might have taken place in New York almost a century later. Three Irishmen, named Quinn, Riorton and Conolly, were standing in Cheapside and hoping for employment when a man named Barry approached them and offered them a job on condition they took an oath of secrecy. They took the oath and, being Irish Catholics, were convinced that their souls would be damned if they broke it. Barry then took them to a room where there was brass and various tools for shaping it into counterfeit shillings. Before they had been at work long, the Bow Street Runners came and arrested them. They were tried and condemned, but luckily a priest told them that they need not be bound by an oath that was unlawful, and they then told the true story. Their accusers and the police officers were now arrested, and it suddenly became clear that a number of police had been supplementing their incomes for a long time by "framing" out-of-work labourers. The three false witnesses were sentenced to transportation. Three police officers were tried soon afterwards for conspiring to persuade five youths, one of them only thirteen, to commit a burglary; their aim was to arrest them and claim the reward for the conviction of housebreakers.

The Irishmen who avoided the gallows excited general sympathy, and a Lord Mayor's fund opened for them raised enough money to enable them to buy a farm in Ireland.

Even this more or less happy ending to the story distinguishes it from cases of the eighteenth century. Fifty years earlier, the Irishmen would have been hanged, and then, possibly, the false witnesses might have been hanged too.

The habit of transporting prisoners to Australia or America aroused a great deal of indignation among respectable colonists in those countries; Benjamin Franklin asked how the English would feel if America transported her rattlesnakes to England. In both countries, the crime rate was enormous; there were more highway robberies in New South Wales every year than there were robberies of all kinds in England. Conditions were appalling. The first colony, at Port Jackson, was founded among fever swamps, and half the prisoners had died on the long journey out. Discipline was ferocious, and the work was long and hard, so that men escaped into the bush as often as possible and became outlaws – bushrangers. Several of these were simply homicidal maniacs. Major Arthur Griffiths mentions one called "Jeffries the Monster" who had been hangman in Edinburgh before his transportation, and who became the official flogger in the penal colony. His murders were apparently prompted simply by the pleasure of killing, for he later admitted that in a large number of them, he had not stolen anything (probably because the wretches he killed had nothing to steal). Like many of the bushrangers, he became a cannibal at one point. The crime that finally roused the community was the kidnapping of a mother and baby, presumably with the motive of sexual assault. He killed the baby with a blow on the head. Even convicts were allowed to help in hunting him down. He was eventually captured and executed.

Cannibalism was not unfamiliar. A convict named Alexander Pierce escaped in a stolen boat from one of the island prisons, together with five other men. Hiding out in the hills, they began to starve, and one of them remarked that he could eat a man. The idea took root, and that night one of the men was killed; his heart was fried and eaten. A few days later, two more were killed, and their liver and hearts eaten. When one of the remaining three collapsed with exhaustion, he was killed with a blow from a hatchet, and partly eaten. The man who did the killing strapped the hatchet to his body in case Pierce attacked him with it in the night. Pierce decided to anticipate attack, and killed his companion, carrying off an arm and a thigh. Recaptured, he escaped again a year later with a man named Cox; Cox's dismembered body was found a few days later. When Pierce was captured, the meat and fish he had taken when he escaped were still intact – he admitted to preferring the taste of human flesh.

These early bushrangers were noted for their incredible barbarity. A man named Dignum who flourished in the area of Port Phillip in 1837 decided to murder his eight companions when food ran short. One of them, a young man named Cornerford, woke up as he was about to start, and had to be taken into his confidence. The two of them killed the other seven, by shooting them, and then became companions in a number of robberies in the area of Adelaide. Neither trusted the other, and when Dignum tried to shoot Cornerford in the back one day, the latter rode into Melbourne and gave him away. Cornerford managed to escape before their trial, and made such a nuisance of himself that he was quickly hanged when they captured him. Dignum escaped with life imprisonment on Norfolk Island, since the chief witness against him was dead.

One more story of the bushrangers before this narrative returns to England: when I was about ten years old I remember reading in *The Saturday Evening Post* of a particularly ferocious bushranger named Morgan who seems to have been a homicidal maniac – I suspect it may have been the "Morgan" whom Major Arthur Griffiths mentions briefly. His robberies usually ended in the death of the victim. One day, he and a companion called at the home of a woman whose husband was at work, and asked for food. While she was cutting the bread, the baby started to cry in the next room, and Morgan said: "Don't worry, I'll go and see." A moment later, the crying stopped and the mother congratulated him on his skill with babies. When the men had left, she went into the next room, to find that the baby's throat had been cut.

The crime made the district too hot to hold the outlaws, and they had to flee. Some time later, they were rowing a stolen boat down a river when they saw a reward notice on a tree that declared there was a large sum on Morgan's head. His companion waited his opportunity, and knocked Morgan unconscious. He then severed the head, and took it into the nearest large town to claim the reward. Unfortunately, he was seized too: the woman whose baby had been killed identified him, and he was immediately executed. Major Arthur Griffiths says of Morgan: "he was afflicted with blood madness, and pitilessly slew all his victims." But according to Griffiths' account, Morgan was found one day riddled with bullets, so my memory may be faulty in attributing the child-murder to Morgan.

This kind of thing explains why the settlers in Australia and Virginia objected to having convicts dumped on them. When the colonial government of Tasmania was on the point of bankruptcy in 1852, it refused to take any more convicts. Queensland was asked if it had room for convicts, and countered by asking if there was not some part of Britain to which they could send Queensland's criminals. The last convict ship sailed for Western Australia in 1867. After that, England had to think of a more convenient way of dealing with criminals than sweeping them under the carpet.

This digression may have conveyed some notion of what was in store for the various criminals whom the *Newgate Calendar* mentions as having been sentenced to transportation. As the climate of public opinion caused some slight relaxation in the severity of the law, an increasing number of criminals were sentenced to transportation; in the second volume of the *New Newgate Calendar*, headings like "executed for robbery" and "executed for body stealing" become steadily more rare.

Another reason for the change of climate can be seen in this second volume: the increasing number of men who were convicted for provoking riots or making seditious speeches. The workers had found a voice. Men like Tom Paine, William Cobbett, John Wilkes, Henry Hunt, raised their voices against oppression. The Calthorpe Street riot of 1833, in which a policeman was stabbed to death, began as a meeting of working men to form a union. In 1834, six men led by a labourer called James Lovelace were tried at Dorchester for attempting to start an agricultural union to raise farm wages from seven shillings to ten shillings a week. The actual charge was that they had unlawfully administered oaths to prospective members of the union. These men, who became known as the Tolpuddle Martyrs, were sentenced to transportation to Australia. What all this meant was that *some* of the "dominant five per cent" among working men preferred protest to crime. The most sensational case of 1820 combined the two. A man named Arthur Thistlewood hatched a plot to murder the whole Cabinet while they sat at dinner at the house of Lord Harrowby in Grosvenor Square, and then to blow up the Bank of England, set fire to London, and take over the Mansion House. Thistlewood was a hater of authority; he had been imprisoned briefly after the Spa Fields riots, which he organised. He then challenged Lord Sidmouth to a duel and received another year. The thirty or so Cato Street Conspirators, as they became known, made the mistake of admitting a police informer to their ranks, and they were set upon by the police as they waited in a barn for the signal to murder the Cabinet. Most of them escaped, but a dozen of them were later arrested. One of them turned King's evidence. Thistlewood and four others were sentenced to death, the remaining six escaped execution on a technicality and were hanged and then beheaded outside Newgate prison. When the first man was beheaded there was a gasp of horror from the crowd, but by the time the fifth head fell, the crowd was laughing.

Apart from this new element of revolutionary unrest, the reader of the *New Newgate Calendar* observes another element that was far less common in its predecessor: the increase in crimes connected with sex. There was still not a great deal of "sex crime" in the modern sense: that is, men who could be labelled "sexual criminals". But sex certainly began to play an increasingly important part in the records of the nineteenth century. In Ireland, the abduction and raping of heiresses became something of a hobby. A girl of seventeen named Elizabeth Crockatt was an heiress with some two thousand six hundred pounds; there were two attempts to seize her, apparently by different men. After the first – she was kidnapped after church – her brother and uncle managed to rescue her. The second was carried out by a young man named Samuel Dick, with the help of his sister Jane, who invited Elizabeth Crockatt to stay with them. The girl agreed, and for the first day, everything seemed normal. Then, when she went outdoors in the evening, she was seized and bundled into a chaise. Jane Dick and her brother took her to another house, where she spent the day crying and refusing to eat. Finally, utterly exhausted, she agreed to sleep in the same bed with Jane. Halfway through the night, she discovered that her sleeping partner had been changed: it was now the brother, who proceeded to commit upon her offences over which Pelham decently draws a veil. The next morning, Dick rushed off to get a marriage licence; the others were now presumably confident that Miss Crockatt was anxious to become Mrs Dick, and they relaxed their vigilance, with the result that Miss Crockatt escaped, and Dick ended on the gallows.

Four years later, in 1822, a young man named Brown was so anxious to secure the hand of an heiress named Honoria Goold that he hired a gang of men to storm her house. They dragged her off, and Brown was waiting outside to sweep her on to the saddle of his horse and gallop away. When they arrived at the house of a farmer named Leahy, he proposed to her, and she refused him. Brown then locked himself in a room with her and "in spite of her entreaties and screams, proceeded to undress her". Pelham adds indignantly: "The reader need not be told the rest – the purity of female innocence was grossly violated in the person of this young and lovely creature, and her destroyer arose from his bed of lust, the polluter of one whose peace of mind neither the world's sympathy nor the world's wealth could restore." (This is typical of Pelham's style in recounting rapes.) After three weeks of refusing to marry Brown, the girl was finally set at liberty, and the abductors fled. Brown had the money to escape abroad, the others didn't. They were tried at Limerick and all sentenced to death, although four of the eight escaped on a point of law.

Now the subject of rape has arisen, we may as well pause to examine it more fully. Of the two hundred or so cases in the original *Newgate Calendar*, only four concern rape, and one of those is an assault on a youth by a homosexual. (Wilkinson is so shocked he can barely bring himself to splutter out the basic details.) Only one of these cases excited much attention: the abduction of a demure little Quakeress named Sarah Woodcock by Lord Baltimore in 1768. For three nights she wailed and protested so violently that he left her alone; on the fourth night, she undressed for bed – a four poster with curtains – then discovered Lord Baltimore waiting in it, who then "effected his horrid purpose" twice. During the next two days she was apparently menstruating, but later in the week his lordship "sent for her to go to bed" and she complied. And "What passed this night is too horrible for relation". Lord Baltimore had already sent her father a two-hundred-pound note, and now her relations managed to trace her, and got her out of Lord Baltimore's clutches with the help of a warrant from Sir John Fielding. At his trial he alleged her consent, and was acquitted. He died four years later, at the age of thirty-nine, apparently worn out by his libidinous excesses.

Fifty years later, his chances of acquittal would have been slim, lord or no lord. Juries had begun to feel more strongly about virtue in danger; the Victorian cult of the distressed damsel was established long before Queen Victoria came to the throne in 1837. In fact, a man accused of almost anything by a girl was likely to be found guilty, just to be on the safe side. In 1831, a young Irishman called Luke Dillon was sentenced to death for rape. The complainant was a Miss Frizell, who admitted that she and Dillon had met several times at parties, and that "he professed to be her warm admirer". She agreed to meet him one day, and they spent three hours sheltering from the rain in an empty cottage, during which time he proposed to her and she accepted. They then drove off in a carriage, and he persuaded her to stop for "refreshment", which included fish and a glass of punch. She claimed she then lost consciousness until she woke up and found herself naked in bed. She jumped up screaming, and ran into the wall, upon which Dillon threw her on the bed and "completed an outrage which, there was no doubt, was a repetition only of an act of violence of which he had before been guilty". He promised to marry her again, and in the morning, she went back to the house of relations, and told them she was married. Dillon took care not to see her again, and did not answer a letter she wrote him beginning: "My dearest Dillon" and asking him to recollect his solemn promise. When he failed to keep it, he was arrested and charged with rape.

Even this brief account of the facts makes it apparent that her story has several weak points. She had known Dillon for two years and admitted that their acquaintance "soon ripened into an intimacy". She agreed to marry him, and accompanied him to a private room, with a bed, for supper. She implies that Dillon gave her some powerful drug in a glass of punch. In those days, most people believed that villains could procure drugs that would render a girl immediately unconscious, but this seems unlikely. What is more probable is that she drank more whisky punch than she would admit. We can assume that Dillon then removed her clothes and raped her. But is it likely that, when she woke up screaming and tried to rush out of the room, he hurled her on the bed and raped her again? His first reaction would be to soothe her and assure her that they were already man and wife in the sight of heaven, etc. Even in a house of ill-repute (and no one suggested this one was), a screaming girl would have aroused attention. Besides, a noisy and excited girl is not likely to arouse lust, especially in a man who has already accomplished his purpose once. And even supposing that Dillon was the type of man whose desires were aroused by a struggle, he would not find the task of raping a frightened virgin, or near-virgin, easy.

No, it is surely obvious that he soothed her and persuaded her to get back into bed, so that the second "outrage" was by her consent. And since she had agreed to marry him, and eaten supper with him in a room with a bed, it is arguable that the first time was not strictly a rape either. In short, Dillon's crime was not rape; he had only done what a great many other libertines did: promised marriage and then changed his mind after receiving an advance payment of conjugal favours. This is a censurable activity, but not a crime.

Dillon's sentence was later commuted to transportation to Australia. Pelham ends his account by adding that "the unhappy object of Dillon's machinations and brutal crime died in the month of June 1831, a victim to her own sensitive feelings. She had gone to Bangor, in Wales, in hope that a change of scene might relieve her of the melancholy which appeared to have settled upon her mind, but she died there of a broken heart." No doubt Pelham's late Victorian readers found this perfectly understandable; the modern reader finds himself reflecting that people do not literally die of a broken heart. What did she die of? Perhaps the "consumption" to which languishing young ladies of that day were prone? If so, she probably had it before the offence took place. But the main point is that a chronicler who can record that the girl died "a victim to her own sensitive feelings" may be regarded as biased, and the whole account becomes suspect.

This is even clearer in the case of a publican, George Cant, who was transported for rape in 1840. The woman, Jane Bolland, went to work as a barmaid at the Windsor public house in Holborn, and claims that the landlord immediately began to make advances to her, and to ask her to leave her door open at night so he could come in. "She told him she was not the sort of person he imagined her to be." Later in the day, "she became unwell", and went to bed; she could not recall who went up with her. She woke in the night to find the prisoner at her bedside, and he put one hand on her mouth; a struggle took place and she fainted. When she woke at six in the morning she found her clothes (which had not been taken off) in disorder and the bone of her stay broken. The landlord came to her door, and she called him a villain; he retaliated by calling her a drunkard. The landlord's wife also called her a drunken hussy when she accused her husband of rape. Jane Bolland left the Windsor public house, and returned to the house of her brother, with whom she usually lived. On Saturday, she was examined by a doctor, who verified that she had been raped.

The defence did not deny the rape, but declared that it had been committed by another man called Edwards, who was also living in the house. When the landlord was arrested, Edwards went voluntarily to Cant's solicitor and confessed that it was he who raped the girl, going into her room in the dark and finding her unconscious.

Edwards was cross-examined, and said that Jane Bolland had gone off to bed between nine and ten (when a public house would be very busy), apparently drunk. He had gone into her room at eleven, and had intercourse with her. She seemed quite willing. The next morning, he walked home with her to the East End, and she said that Cant had called her a drunkard and she would "fix" him. He said she seemed quite happy.

In spite of all this, Cant was sentenced to death, although the interest aroused by the case finally led to his being transported for life.

On this evidence, there seems to be hardly any doubt that Cant was wrongly convicted. As to what really happened, there seem to be two possibilities. Jane Bolland got drunk on her first day as a barmaid. Later that evening, Edwards went to her room, which was in darkness, and had intercourse, with or without her consent. In the morning, the landlord called her a drunkard; she retaliated by accusing him to his wife, who also refused to listen. (Why? Did she know perfectly well that her husband had not left the room all night? Their bedroom was directly below the girl's.) Jane Bolland then left, swearing revenge, and accompanied by the man who had been in bed with her. It was not until the next day that she was examined by a doctor, who pronounced that she had been raped.

The second possibility is that Jane Bolland was not drunk. Her brother declared that she had suffered from a severe attack of erysipelas in the head, and that from that time she had been insane. Erysipelas is a disease that causes severe inflammation of the skin, accompanied by fever. And so it may well be true that Jane Bolland was overcome by an attack of giddiness that made her seem drunk. It could also be that she remained passive during intercourse, giving the impression that she had no objection.

In either case, it is unlikely that Cant was the man in bed with her. If he was, he would have been unlikely to stir up her indignation by accusing her of drunkenness the next morning. Assuming, then, that Edwards was the man in her bed, how far can we accept his account? Rape was a hanging offence. If he had really committed it, he would be unlikely to have made a confession: it would merely put his neck in the noose. His action in declaring that he was the one who climbed into her bed is the action of a man with nothing on his conscience.

If Jane Bolland reached home on Friday morning and told her brother she had been raped, why did she wait until the following day to see a doctor? And what could such a medical examination, thirty-six hours after the event, demonstrate anyway? If the hymen had been recently ruptured, it would prove recent intercourse, but not rape. If she was not a virgin, it could have proved nothing at all. Doctors in those days had no method of detecting male sperm, even if any remained so long after. The only fairly certain proof of rape is the presence of bruises or scratches in the area of the genitals, but Jane Bolland admitted she was passive at the time of the assault.

Pelham's account suggests one more possibility, that Jane Bolland's whole story was a fabrication to get revenge on Cant. It is true that the defence was exceptionally generous about her: "[Mr Phillips] disclaimed all intention of impeaching the young woman's character, and was happy that he had no reason for making even an insinuation against her in regard to her conduct previous to this occasion." That was because his line of defence was completely different, and he might only have damaged his client's chances by making the prosecution angry. (As it was, the prosecution "rejoiced that Mr Phillips had not attempted to cast any aspersion" on Jane Bolland's character.) If the conclusive medical proof of sexual intercourse was a torn hymen, she might have acquired it after leaving the public house. (Her brother visited her at the Windsor with a man named Balfour who is not heard of again. Her lover?) She got drunk on her first day at the pub (the pot boy gave evidence that she struck him as drunk, and he must have known what a drunken woman looked like). She was thrown out, and told Edwards she intended to "fix" Cant. That same night, she finally admitted Balfour into her bed, and in the morning, went to see a doctor with her story of rape. Cant saw that his only chance lay in bribing Edwards to claim that it was he who had intercourse with Jane Bolland, with her consent. This version fits the facts. At all events, it is perfectly clear that George Cant was wrongfully convicted, as far as the evidence against him was concerned.

Compare this with a modern case cited by C.R.M. Cuthbert in *Science and Detection of Crime*, Superintendent of the Metropolitan Police Lab. A married woman and her friend went to a village dance while the husband stayed at home baby-sitting. The wife flirted with a soldier, who walked home with them. At the corner of her lane, the married woman asked her friend to walk on. Ten minutes later, she came home and declared she had been raped. She was not injured in any way, but there was mud on her coat, and stains of sperm in the fork of her panties. The soldier was easily traced, and admitted frankly to having had intercourse with the woman, but he declared it was with her consent. What must have happened is fairly clear. The married woman obviously had something in mind in asking her friend to walk on. After allowing the soldier intercourse, it strikes her that her husband will be extremely suspicious and that the mud on her coat will be difficult to explain. So she invents the story of the rape. Presumably the soldier was not charged (there was clearly no evidence against him). In 1850, he would have been executed or sentenced to transportation on the word of the housewife, even though the ultra-violet and microscopic methods of detecting seminal stains had not then been invented.

I have often wondered whether this cult of the distressed damsel explains one of the most baffling features of the "crime of the century", the Red Barn murder. When William Corder became Maria Marten's lover, she already had an illegitimate child and had lost another. Even Pelham has some difficulty making her sound innocent and virtuous: "An unfortunate slip ruined the character of the young woman, and a second mishap with a gentleman of fortune left her a child." She quickly became pregnant by Corder, but the baby died soon after birth. But why did he now murder her, instead of taking the obvious course of vanishing which, in fact, he did after the murder? There was nothing to stop him from simply walking out. After the murder, he went to London, advertised for a wife (and received fifty-three replies), and married a young lady with whom he set up a school. Maria's mother's dreams of murder in the red barn led to the discovery of the body, which had been shot and stabbed. (Corder's confession denied stabbing her.)

There are two possibilities as to why Corder murdered her rather than absconding. The first is that Maria might have taken legal action, not only against William Corder, but against his brother Thomas, who was her first seducer (and the father of the child that died). In the climate of opinion in 1827, she had a strong case: the poor wronged girl, doing her best to be virtuous, but with an unfortunate predisposition to "slips" and "mishaps", each one of which left her pregnant.

The other possibility, a remote one, is that she was in a position to blackmail Corder about the death of her baby. Even Pelham and the anonymous author of *Murder in the Red Barn* admit that there is no reason to attribute the baby's death to anything but natural causes. Admittedly, Corder and Maria vanished for two days with the body, and Corder later told people that the baby had been buried at Sudbury, which proved to be untrue. In his confession, he says that he murdered Maria as a result of a quarrel about the place where they buried the baby. It is not clear why they didn't have it buried in the normal way, since there was no suspicion of murder.

Maria Marten played to crowded houses for another seventy-five years. And almost as famous was the victim of a similar murder. Ellen Hanley's story was novelised by Gerald Griffin as *The Collegians* (1829), dramatised by Dion Boucicault as *The Colleen Bawn* (1860), and finally turned into an opera *The Lily of Killarney* by Sir Julius Benedict (1863). She was the pretty niece of a ropemaker named Connery, who lived in Ballycahane, near Limerick. The squire of Ballycahane Castle – actually a group of farm buildings – was a twenty-six-year-old ex-officer who had fought against Napoleon, and was now retired on half pay; his name was John Scanlan. Scanlan's batman in the army had been Stephen Sullivan, six years his senior, and he continued to be Scanlan's manservant in Ballycahane. The relation between the two was very close.

Everyone seems to agree that Ellie Hanley *was* an extremely pretty schoolgirl – she was only fifteen when she was murdered – although her incisor teeth were rather prominent and fang-like, making her look like one of Dracula's wives. Scanlan was familiar with the brothels of Europe, and the response provoked in him by the farmer's daughter was quite impersonal – he wanted her maidenhead. Ellie was impressed by the sporting squire but, being a Catholic, she was determined to remain virtuous. Scanlan persuaded her to elope with him and they were married, in late June 1819, by a defrocked priest. Almost immediately afterwards, Scanlan discovered that the marriage was legal, Ellie was his wife. He began to feel that he had paid an exceptionally high price for his maidenhead. Ellie was socially naïve and sexually inexperienced. Her attitude towards her husband was one of uncritical admiration; after a few days of soft words and caresses, Scanlan began to think longingly about horses and hounds. They spent the first days of their honeymoon at Glin, on the Shannon, then moved to an island in the river. Glin is a very small and very dull village. After two weeks, Scanlan was impatient to return home. But there was a problem. When Ellie left home, she took the life-savings of her uncle, one hundred and twenty pounds in notes and twelve guineas in silver. She promptly spent a great deal of this on silk dresses. It began to dawn slowly on the sporting squire that his guardian angel had been off duty on the day he asked Ellie to marry him. He was the spoilt son of the family – his father had died when he was a child – and his impetuosity was a local legend. And now he was tied hand and foot.

Stephen Sullivan understood his employer's feelings; in fact, he shared them. He had thought it an excellent idea for the squire to add one more maidenhead to his list, and had entered into the spirit of the thing. But Ellie was very definitely not a lady, and it was easy to guess how Scanlan's mother would feel when her son introduced the future mistress of Ballycahane Castle. He was also aware that a relationship like the one between himself and Scanlan would not survive marriage. And when Scanlan's thoughts began to run on getting rid of Ellie, Sullivan was inclined to agree that it was the only solution. So one moonlit night, Scanlan suggested an excursion to an island in the river, to look at the ancient shrine of some saint. The boat was a fairly large one, Scanlan sat behind Ellie, Sullivan in front. It was agreed that when they reached mid-channel, Scanlan would give the signal, and Sullivan would seize a club and beat

Ellie's brains out, while Scanlan would, if necessary, hold her arms.

This came to nothing. Scanlan gave the signal, Sullivan raised the club. Ellie thought he was joking, and laughed. Sullivan was already unnerved, he dropped the club and ignore his master's impatient signals. The excursion went off as planned, except that Ellie wondered why the two men looked so gloomy.

A few days later, Scanlan prevailed on Sullivan to try again. By this time, they had lost the large stone with a chain attached with which they had intended to sink the body; it had fallen overboard on a fishing expedition, and Scanlan bought some rope from a man in Glin. Then Ellie was persuaded to take a moonlight row with Sullivan. Scanlan provided his servant with a bottle of whisky this time, and Sullivan drank most of it rather quickly. Four miles out from land, Ellie had fallen asleep. Sullivan picked up his gun and swung it down with all his strength, but his drunkenness spoiled his aim, and he hit her arm at the shoulder, breaking it. Ellie woke up, but the next blow shattered her skull. Sullivan went on raining drunken blows on the body, until he was certain she was dead. Then he removed her clothes, with the exception of the bodice, which would take too long to unlace, tied her knees against her chin, and weighted the body with a heavy stone from the boat's ballast.

When he returned to Carrig Island, where Ellie and Scanlan had spent most of their honeymoon, the two men cleaned out the boat. Then they rowed back to Glin. Sullivan's sister Maureen was given some of Ellie's clothes and her pocket book. A friend of Ellie's called Ellen Walsh saw the men and asked after Mrs Scanlan. Scanlan told her that she had "misbehaved" and that they had put her on board a boat bound for America.

Ellie was murdered on 14 July, less than three weeks after her marriage. The Reverend Richard Fitzgerald, who was staying with the Knight of Glin at the time of the murder (and who wrote his account of the case in 1869) states that by the time of her death, Ellie was already a living skeleton from moving from place to place with her husband and not eating enough food. This sounds like a typical Victorian attempt to throw in some extra pathos.

Scanlan and Sullivan decided to separate for the time being, there was already gossip about Ellie in Glin. And on 6 September the body of Ellie Hanley was cast up on the sand at Money Point, near Glin. The knees were still tied to the neck. One arm was missing, the one that Sullivan broke with his first blow, and one of the legs was found to be broken in several places. The head was devoid of flesh, and the teeth were also missing, although the large sockets of the incisors could be identified. The stench was so appalling that they had to keep burning gunpowder to lessen it.

It took a hastily empanelled jury no time at all to decide that this was the body of Ellen Hanley, and that she had been murdered by John Scanlan and Stephen Sullivan (alias Humphreys). But the accused men were nowhere to be found. Gossip had it that Sullivan had gone to Galway and Scanlan to Cork, and the Knight of Glin suggested publishing a description of them in the *Hue and Cry*, the Irish "police gazette". Scanlan's family was horrified by the accusation, and took a great deal of trouble to stop the news from spreading. Since they were very influential in Limerick, they succeeded to a large extent. And the Limerick police decided to ask the help of the police of neighbouring County Clare for help, to overcome this problem of family influence. One day in November, Major Warburton of the Clare police was told that Scanlan had been seen at his family home in Ballycahane. He moved quickly, surrounding the house with troops. A lengthy search of the farm failed to uncover the suspect. Two dragoons glanced into an outhouse with straw inside and decided Scanlan was not there either. To make sure, one of them drove his bayonet into the straw. There was a yell, and Scanlan leapt to his feet – the dragoons were probably as startled as he was.

The great Daniel O'Connell was engaged for the defence. His account of the murder cast the blame entirely on the missing Sullivan. According to O'Connell, Sullivan realised that his master was ruined by the marriage, that his wife would never be acceptable to the social circle of Ballycahane. He offered to put Ellie on a ship bound for America. And until the discovery of the body, Scanlan went on believing that his unwanted bride was on the Atlantic.

It was no good. The jury found Scanlan guilty of murder, and the judge ordered his immediate execution, afraid that his family might engineer a reprieve. On 10 March 1820, he was publicly hanged at Gallows Green, Limerick. At the last moment, public sympathy swung in his favour. As the horses pulling the carriage approached Ball Bridge over the Shannon, they stopped and refused to go forward. People murmured: "It's the hand of God. He's innocent." Scanlan continued to protest his innocence until he was hanged.

No one seemed to have a clue to Sullivan's whereabouts; it was generally believed that he had escaped abroad. Scanlan had rejoined the army after the murder, and then deserted a month later. But Sullivan had not been with him.

In fact, Sullivan had moved a mere thirty miles south, to Scartaglen, and changed his name to Clifford. At about the time Scanlan was hanged, Sullivan was being married to a local heiress. But in May, his luck gave out: he was accused of passing forged money and committed to Tralee jail. He was undoubtedly innocent of the forgery charge, but someone in the jail recognised him and passed on the information to the Knight of Glin. On 25 July 1820, Sullivan stood trial in the same dock as Scanlan. He was found guilty, and hanged on Gallows Green on 27 July 1820. On the gallows he made the following speech: "I declare before Almighty God that I am guilty of the murder. But it was Mr Scanlan who put me up to it."

For the modern reader, the case of the Colleen Bawn ("white girl") is altogether less interesting than it was to the Victorians. They saw it as a moral tale of a wicked seducer, an innocent country girl, and so on, forgetting that Ellie Hanley stole the life savings of the man who had brought her up, and then spent most of it on clothes. She may have been injured, but she was not innocent. Scanlan himself certainly provides material for moralising: spoilt, selfish and cowardly, without even the courage to commit his own murder. The most interesting person in the case is Sullivan. His attitude to Ellie was thoroughly ambivalent. His first attempt to kill her failed because she smiled at him; after this, he apparently tried to persuade Scanlan to let her return home, and even offered to take the blame for seducing her. And then, when it comes to the actual killing, he falls into a sadistic frenzy and continues beating the body long after she is dead.

He then undresses her. Why? It is true that her clothes might identify her, but the clothes will have to be disposed of anyway. It sounds as if his attitude to Ellie is strangely self-divided. He has participated actively in her seduction; probably it is not the first time he has played Leporello. She is a girl of his own class. (In Ireland there were no middle classes, only the peasantry and gentlemen.) And if Scanlan had agreed to allow Sullivan to take the blame, no doubt Sullivan would have ended by marrying her – such arrangements were common in those days. (Fitzgerald is of the opinion that Scanlan's marriage to Ellie was invalid anyway.) Scanlan has her but does not want her; Sullivan wants her but cannot have her. But the act of murder itself has sexual implications, and when it comes to killing her, the frustrations and repressions explode.

And then, why should the body rise to the surface? Rope that is wholly immersed in water does not rot, and seaman's rope is tarred – it should have been as durable as a chain. If the stone had been placed inside Ellen Hanley's clothes, and the body bound with rope, it would not have risen to the surface. Perhaps Sullivan was too drunk to tie the body efficiently? Or does his attempt at disposal of the body display the same ambiguity as the murder itself? If Sullivan was killing someone he would have preferred to caress, then the act of murder had overtones of suicide.

8.
Into the
Age of Violence

THE GERMANS invented the useful term *lustmörd*. This does not mean, as one might suppose, lust-murder, but "murder for pleasure", joy-murder. Unfortunately, the Germans have no corresponding term for what might be called "business-murder", murder carried out in a purely practical spirit. For these are the two chief types of murder. I think that Oscar Wilde must probably be given the credit for founding that school of writers who are chiefly interested in "murder-with-an-eye-to-business". He was delighted by the remark of the forger and poisoner, Thomas Griffiths Wainewright, that he had killed his sister-in-law because he didn't like her thick ankles. His essay on Wainewright, published in *Intentions* in 1891, is one of the first to treat murder as if it were an elaborate joke; Roughead, Pearson and William Bolitho adopted the manner. Writers of this type feel no interest in "joy-murder" because such cases lack clear-cut motives. But it is "joy-murder" that raises some of the profounder questions of human psychology. In the present chapter, I intend to examine some typical examples of both types.

The Germans can perhaps claim not only to have invented the word for joy-murder, but the thing itself. The earliest cases I have come across are to be found in the Journal of Master Franz Schmidt, the Nuremberg hangman in the sixteenth century. Of one murderer, Nicklaus Stüller, who was torn with red-hot tongs and broken on the wheel in 1577, he writes: "First he shot a horse-soldier; secondly he cut open a pregnant woman alive in which was a dead child; thirdly he again cut open a pregnant woman in whom was a female child; fourthly he once more cut open a pregnant woman in whom were two male children. Görgla von Sunberg [an accomplice] said that they had committed a great sin and that he would take the infants to a priest to be baptised, but Phila [another accomplice] said he would himself be priest and baptise them, so he took them by the legs and dashed them to the ground." Another murderer mentioned by Schmidt, Kloss Renckhart, broke into a mill and shot the miller, raped the wife and a maid, then made the wife fry eggs and eat them off the body of her husband.

For some reason, German murder cases often seem to have this touch of brutality; it must be something in the German temperament. (I remember an old military man assuring me that the German temperament is naturally violent and brutal, and that all German men of genius have been Bavarians.)

Major Griffiths offers an account of a German Jack the Ripper named Andrew Bichel, who lived at Regensdorf in Bavaria. In 1808, a girl named Seidel happened to recognise a piece of dimity from which a tailor was making up a waistcoat; she thought it was the same material as a petticoat worn by her sister Catherine, who had vanished earlier the same year. On enquiry, she discovered the waistcoat was being made for a fortune-teller named Bichel. This confirmed one of her worst suspicions. Her sister had last been seen shortly before a visit to this same fortune-teller. He had told her to come in her best clothes, and to bring three changes of clothes – this being part of his method of foretelling the future. Bichel declared that the girl had eloped with a man she met at his house.

Bichel's house was searched, and a chest of women's clothes was discovered. A police dog got excited in the wood shed, and rushed to a corner where there was a heap of straw. Buried under this were the dismembered bodies of Catherine Seidel and another girl who had vanished the previous year, Barbara Reisinger. Bichel finally confessed. He had been tempted by Barbara Reisinger's clothes when she applied for a post as a servant girl. He persuaded her to have her eyes bound and her hands tied behind her, promising to show her her future in a magic mirror. He then stabbed her three times in the neck. This was all so easy – reminiscent of the method later employed by Christie – that he decided to do it again. But perhaps his manner made girls suspicious, or his request that they bring their wardrobe. His only other success seems to have been Catherine Seidel; at least, this was the only other murder brought home to him. Several other girls made appointments, and thought better of them. Bichel was sentenced to be broken on the wheel, but his sentence was commuted to beheading. The judge who tried him remarked that he would commit crimes that only required no courage. He might administer poison or murder a man in his sleep, but he would never commit highway robbery or burglary. All of which would seem to indicate that Bichel was an example of the "furtive criminal" – not a man who needed to express an aggression against society, but who was attracted by the idea of secret crime. The American murderer Ed Gein, of whom I shall speak later, is a typical example. The motive of such men is always sexual (a fact that Major Griffiths did not seem to recognise). Bichel may have been a homosexual who was fascinated by women's clothes, or he may have been simply a transvestite.

Major Griffiths classifies with Bichel the crimes of the Dumollards in L'Ain (near Lyons) in the late 1850s, but here the motive was obviously peasant avarice. Madame Dumollard, the wife of a peasant, or her husband, would visit an employment agency in Lyons and ask for a servant girl. The girl would arrive at their cottage near Mollard, and never be seen again. In 1855, the body of a girl was found in a wood, with several stab wounds, and Martin Dumollard was suspected. She was a servant girl from Lyons. Several girls actually escaped from Dumollard, but for some reason, he was still not arrested. Finally, in May 1861, Dumollard accosted a girl named Marie Pichon in Lyons, and told her he was the gardener at the château at Montluel and had been sent to find a servant girl. Marie Pichon accompanied him to Montluel, but began to worry as he led her across fields. Finally, when she refused to go any farther, he tried to slip a noose over her head. She managed to escape, and found her way to a farm, where she stayed overnight. The police investigated, and eventually Marie

Pichon identified Martin Dumollard as her attacker – he was a distinctive looking man with a tumour on his face and a scar on his upper lip. Clothes of several girls were found in the cottage, and Mme Dumollard led the way to a female skeleton – the girl had died of a blow on the head. Her confession, made in prison, stated that she had nothing to do with the murders; her husband would simply come and say: "I've killed a girl in the woods of Montmain. I must go and bury her." Some writers on the case are inclined to believe that Dumollard was a homicidal maniac and that his wife accepted his murders with peasant indifference. But it is worth noting that he tried to kill Marie Pichon by slipping a noose over her head, which would not have damaged her clothes. The corpse in the forest of Montaverne had been stabbed in the head. The other skeleton had a shattered skull. Dumollard killed in such a way as not to damage the clothes, and his wife confessed that she would wash out any bloodstains and then wear the clothes. Whether the girls were sexually attacked is not known. Dumollard's last words on the scaffold were to remind his wife that a neighbour owed him money. It is estimated that he killed ten girls, and that nine more escaped. (It was discovered that one of his victims had been alive when buried.)

There are only two English cases of the nineteenth century, if we except Jack the Ripper, that deserve classification with Bichel and Dumollard: the Ratcliffe Highway murders of 1811, and the murders of the body snatchers, Burke and Hare.

The Ratcliffe Highway murders are the subject of a classic piece by de Quincey, an appendix to his essay "On Murder Considered as one of the Fine Arts". On Saturday 7 December 1811, a servant girl named Margaret Jewell was sent out sometime before midnight to buy oysters. She returned home to the hosier's shop in the Ratcliffe Highway (in London's East End) at 1 a.m. to find it locked up. She thought she heard footsteps inside, but when no one answered her knock, she summoned a neighbour, who forced his way into the house, and found four corpses: Timothy Marr, his wife Cecilia, their baby, and an apprentice boy of thirteen. The violence of the murders was incredible: all had their skulls smashed and their throats cut. There had been no robbery – perhaps the girl interrupted the killer. Twelve days later, a man broke into an East

End public house just off the Ratcliffe Highway, the King's Arms, and killed the servant, a woman named Harrington, as she was cleaning the grate, with a blow from a crowbar; then proceeded to kill the owner, a Mr Williamson, and his wife. A twenty-six-year-old apprentice, aroused by the noise, crept downstairs and saw the murderer cutting the throats of the three victims, then searching for keys. The lodger hurried upstairs and climbed out of his bedroom window by means of knotted sheets. He quickly spread the alarm, and the murderer leapt out of the back window, ignoring a sleeping child in the same room.

A few days later, an Irish labourer named John Williams was arrested. The evidence against him was circumstantial. A mallet had been found at the scene of the Marr murders with the initials "J.P". This was identified as belonging to a Swede named John Petersen who was at present at sea. When Petersen was ashore, he lived at the Pear Tree Inn, close to the Ratcliffe Highway, in a room where several other sailors lodged, including Williams. On the night of the second series of murders, he had returned to the room late and shouted at some German sailors to extinguish the candle. De Quincey asserts that a bloodstained knife was found in the lining of Williams' coat, but his account is perhaps not as reliable as it might be. Williams knew both Marr and the publican Williamson; in fact, he had sailed on the same ship as Marr, and been dismissed for general misbehaviour. He was also a customer at the King's Arms, and it seems fairly certain that the publican opened his door to a customer he recognised, and had gone to the cellar to get beer when his caller slammed the front door and proceeded to wield his crowbar.

Williams committed suicide before coming to trial, by hanging himself in his cell. He was buried at the crossroads with a stake through his heart.

There is one point upon which de Quincey is obviously reliable – his account of the terror that spread all over the Home Counties as a result of the murders. There was nothing like it again until Jack the Ripper. It emphasises the point that although murder was common enough, crimes of real atrocity were rare.

This is the reason that the crimes of Burke and Hare were the sensation of their day. In retrospect, they are interesting largely because of the light they throw on social conditions in a large town at about the time Maria Marten was murdered at Polstead. Both were Irishmen, in their mid-thirties at the time of the murders. Burke had been in the army as a "substitute", then worked on the Union Canal in Scotland. He met William Hare – a tall, thin wolf of a man with a cast in one eye – in 1826, and the two men moved to a "beggar's hotel", Log's Boarding House in Tanners Close, Edinburgh. Both had common law wives: Burke's was called Helen McDougal, a prostitute, and Hare's, Maggie Laird. When Log died, Hare took over the house. One day, a tenant called Old Donald died, owing three pounds ten shillings in rent. Hare had an idea of selling the body to the medical school – at this time, body snatchers (also known as Resurrection Men) made an excellent living. Old Donald's corpse was sold to Dr Knox, of 10 Surgeon's Square, for seven pounds ten shillings, and Old Donald's coffin filled with a sack of bark. Dr Knox asked no questions; corpses were hard to come by, and the medical students had to learn most of their anatomy from books. The medical school would pay from eight to ten pounds for a body and ask no questions.

It naturally struck Hare that there was a lucrative trade here, if one could only find corpses. The simple solution would be to make them. It was far less dangerous than digging up a newly buried body in a graveyard, for the victim could be quietly killed in the rooms of Burke or Hare, and conveyed to Dr Knox in a barrel. When a tenant called Joe the Mumper (or Miller) was ill, Burke and Hare hastened his exit with a pillow pressed over his face, and sold his body for ten pounds.

In February 1828, they decided that this was a business worth pursuing, but they almost lost their nerve over the first planned murder. A female hawker named Abigail Simpson was lured into their house and persuaded to get drunk. Burke and Hare also got drunk, and Abigail was still alive the next day. Then they got her drunk again, and Hare suffocated her while Burke held her legs. Dr Knox paid ten pounds. The method was now established, and the turnover was quick. An old vagrant named Mary Haldane; an attractive young prostitute named Mary Paterson – this almost became a double murder, but her friend, Janey Brown, could hold more whisky, and left hastily when Helen McDougal started to quarrel; an unnamed female vagrant (killed by Hare and his "wife"); yet another unnamed woman; an Englishman weakened with jaundice; Mary Haldane's idiot daughter (who asked after her mother, and was taken to "join her" by Hare); and old Irish beggarwoman and her grandson – Hare broke the boy's back over his knee after strangling the woman; and old cinder woman (killed by Hare alone); a cousin of Helen McDougal's from Falkirk; an idiot named Daft Jamie, and a widow woman named Docherty. It was after this last murder, in October 1828, that two of Hare's lodgers, a beggar couple named Grey, stumbled upon the body, and had to be plied heavily with whisky to keep them silent. No doubt Burke and Hare considered more lasting methods of establishing their silence, but the couple talked to the police before anything could be done. Mrs Docherty had been killed carelessly, and there were bloodstains on the bed. Hare quickly turned King's Evidence, and so was not tried, neither was Maggie Laird. Burke and Helen McDougal were tried; she was acquitted for lack of evidence, but Burke was hanged on 28 January 1829. Hare apparently gave his evidence at the trial with such gloating delight that the crowd struggled to reach him. He vanished after the trial and is said to have died in London as an old beggar man, blinded by quicklime that had been thrown in his eyes by some workmates who discovered his identity.

Quite clearly, the murders of Burke and Hare, like those of John Williams, were "economic" murders. If they were carried out with a certain brutality, it was the brutality of "criminal rats", of men who had been rendered brutal by the slums and the hardness of their lives. And if we look back over the murder cases of the past three chapters, it will be seen that they are all, to some extent, "economic" murders, or "business-murders" (Bichel being the only possible exception). Murders of unwanted mistresses, of unwanted husbands, murder in the course of robbery, very occasionally of rape – these have been the common motives. But it is during this nineteenth century that there is a slow but perceptible change in the style of murder. The industrial revolution has brought a higher degree of prosperity, and where it has not brought prosperity, it has brought a new class-consciousness, and eventually, a new self-consciousness. Most of the murders in the *Newgate Calendar* might have been committed by cunning animals;

now a new note enters. It is the note of rebellion, and there are times when the rebellion becomes a psychotic explosion.

Paris during this period was as full of poverty and crime as Edinburgh. We catch glimpses of it in the memoirs of the detective Vidocq, the convict who turned police-spy and became the founder of the Sûreté, and also in the novels of Balzac, who made Vidocq the basis of his great criminal Vautrin. There were about two hundred murders a year, most of them committed in the course of theft. In France, a thief could be executed, or sent to the galleys, which was in many respects worse than the guillotine. It was common sense to murder their victim if there was any chance that he might identify them.

It was after Vidocq's retirement in 1827 that France's most notorious criminal appeared upon the scene – Pierre-François Lacenaire, the "Manfred of the gutter", as Gautier called him, referring to Byron's rebel-hero. Lacenaire's actual crimes were unspectacular enough; in fact, he was a consistently unlucky criminal. Before his first known murder, he attempted to kill his mistress, a girl named Javotte (who was also a receiver of stolen goods), but a locket around her neck deflected the dagger, and after a quarter of an hour of wrestling, the neighbours came to investigate. Lacenaire told them it was merely a marital quarrel, and Javotte did not contradict him.

After some petty and not very remunerative thieving, Lacenaire decided that robbing bank messengers would be a good idea. In those days, the messenger would call at a house to collect money to save the depositor the trouble of going to the bank. Lacenaire requested a messenger to call at a certain address, giving a false name, and then he and an accomplice waited with knives. . . The porter told the messenger that no one of that name lived there, and the messenger went away. Lacenaire tried again, borrowing a well-appointed flat. This time, the messenger forgot to call; Lacenaire stole the curtains and sold them.

At 271 Rue St Martin lived a homosexual begging-letter-writer named Chardon, whom Lacenaire had met in jail. He supported his bed-ridden mother and was said to have money saved. Lacenaire and an accomplice named Avril called on him on 14 December 1834, and met him in the street. Chardon told them to come up to his room. As soon as they got into Chardon's apartment, Avril seized him by the throat and Lacenaire stabbed him in the back. Then Avril finished him off with a hatchet, while Lacenaire went into the bedroom and quickly killed the old woman with a shoemaker's awl. Their profit on this venture was about seven hundred francs. The bodies of the Chardons were not found for two days.

Two weeks later, Lacenaire decided to have another try at the bank messenger idea. Under the name of Mahossier, he hired an apartment at 66 Rue Montorgueil. Avril was temporarily in jail so this time he used an accomplice named François. They slammed the door behind the bank messenger, and Lacenaire stabbed him in the back with the shoemaker's awl as François grabbed him by the throat. However, François was over-excited and got his fingers into the man's mouth. As the man struggled, François panicked and ran away, slamming the door behind him. Lacenaire, hearing approaching footsteps, also ran away.

Vidocq's successor Allard put his best man, Chief Inspector Canler, in charge of both cases, although there was no reason to connect them. It is interesting to study the way in which the detective went about his task in those days before fingerprints or comparison microscopes. He did not use strict logic so much as a knowledge of the working of the criminal mind. Obviously, Mahossier was not the man's name. But criminals sometimes became fond of an alias and used it many times over. So Canler plodded from lodging house to lodging house, asking to look through the registers. It was tedious work, but after several days, he came across the name "Mahossier" in the register of a cheap doss-house. Underneath it was the name "Fizellier". The lodging-house keeper couldn't remember Mahossier, but he was able to describe "Fizellier". His wife was able to supply the information that Mahossier had stayed there before under the name of Bâton. And Bâton sounded like the man who had stabbed the bank messenger – a distinctive man whose manner was courteous and polished, who had a high forehead and silky moustache. (Lacenaire's pictures make him look a little like Edgar Allen Poe, except for the curved, beaklike nose.) Canler seemed to recall a prisoner at the Préfecture who resembled the description of Fizellier. Canler went to the jail, engaged the man in conversation, then asked casually: "By the way, what made you call yourself Fizellier when you stayed at Pageot's?" The man made no attempt to deny it. "Because I don't believe in using my real name when I can avoid it."

Next, Canler traced a homosexual thief named Bâton and placed him under arrest. But Bâton was totally unlike the descriptions of Mahossier. However, Canler again used his knowledge of criminal psychology. Why should Mahossier call himself Bâton? It might be chance. More likely, he knew Bâton. So Canler questioned people who knew Bâton, asking about his friends. And the description of a man named Gaillard sounded promising. Canler ordered Bâton's release, and talked amicably with him as they strolled towards the doors of the Préfecture. Bâton agreed that he knew a man called Gaillard, and gave a description of him: high forehead, silky moustache, a fastidious dresser. . .

But where was Gaillard to be found? With incredible patience, Canler went back to checking doss-house registers. Eventually, he found the signature "Gaillard". The keeper remembered him because he had left some papers behind – a packet of Republican songs and some poems. The stabbed bank messenger had noticed that "Mahossier" had a copy of Rousseau's *Social Contract* sticking out of his pocket.

Avril, Lacenaire's accomplice in the Chardon murder, happened to be in jail. Now, with the usual lack of honour among thieves, he came forward and offered to help the police find "Gaillard". After a week of wandering around low cafés he had still not succeeded, so he was put back in jail; but he added another useful piece of information: Gaillard had a rich aunt who lived in the Rue Bar-du-Bec. The indefatigable Canler went off to see her. She admitted that she had a disreputable nephew, and said that she had had a grille installed in her door because she was afraid that he might decide to murder her one day. She added the information that his name was not Gaillard, but Lacenaire.

Now, at last, the police knew the name of the man they wanted. A general alert went out. And on 2 February the police at Beaune notified the Sûreté that they had arrested a man matching the description; he had been trying to negotiate a forged bill of exchange.

Lacenaire arrived back at the Préfecture in irons, and he greeted Canler politely. When accused of the attempted robbery of the bank messenger, he agreed. Obviously, the messenger would identify him anyway. He refused to name his accomplice, but the police told him it was François, alias Fizellier. Then they told him that François had volunteered the information that Lacenaire had been the killer of Chardon. He refused to believe them. When they added that his accomplice in the Chardon killing, Avril, had tried to get him arrested, Lacenaire was thoroughly disturbed. He soon discovered that the police were not lying, that each of his accomplices had volunteered to betray him, and he decided that he would drag them down with him. He gave a full confession, implicating them both.

In prison before his execution, Lacenaire wrote the famous *Memoirs* (which Dostoievsky later published to increase the circulation of one of his magazines). He was a considerable celebrity and many people came to see him. One man offered him an expensive coat. Lacenaire refused it on the grounds that he would not have time to wear it out. The execution was carried out quietly and unannounced, on a cold and foggy morning in January 1836, just over a year after the murder of the Chardons. Lacenaire remained calm and polite and watched Avril's execution without flinching. The two men had made it up at the end. The night before the execution, Lacenaire called to his old accomplice: "The earth will be pretty cold tomorrow." "Ask to be buried in a fur coat," shouted Avril.

When Lacenaire's head was on the block, there was an accident that would have broken another man's nerve. The blade of the guillotine dropped, then stuck halfway. As it was hauled up again, Lacenaire twisted his head to look up at the triangular blade. A moment later, it fell again. Lacenaire was thirty-six years old when he died.

The *Memoirs* is an interesting book, but not because it contains any detailed descriptions of crimes. He is more concerned to explain how he became a criminal, how his parents greatly preferred his elder brother, and he reacted in the classic way by stealing, to gain attention. The story reeks of self-pity, although Lacenaire's lucid Gallic style keeps this under control. It becomes clear that Lacenaire was driven by self-pity into a suicidal state, that finally became an obsession. Rather than commit suicide, he decided to "have the blood of society". He experienced the same trouble as Vidocq; that once a man had served a prison sentence, he was unable to escape crime. Too many criminals knew him; he knew too many criminals. He could always reckon on being accosted by someone he had known in prison. (There were reckoned to be eight thousand criminals in Paris alone.) The population of Paris in 1836 was about 800,000, so that one person in every hundred was a criminal. Modern crime figures are not far behind this.

Before he made the mistake of trusting Avril and François, Lacenaire had always worked alone, and he prided himself on it. His *Memoirs* tell how, in Lyons, he met a man with a gold watch-chain staggering home late at night. Lacenaire throttled him, robbed him, then threw the unconscious man into the Rhône. When the body was found, it was assumed that he had fallen in when drunk. On another occasion, Lacenaire lost heavily at the gaming tables, and followed a more fortunate player home. As he was about to stab the man in the back, a police patrol approached and he took to his heels. In his own eyes, Lacenaire was a single man against "Society".

Lacenaire was a highly intelligent man, driven by self-pity. His intellectual perception of the social injustice around him did not lead him to plan to overthrow the social order; it led to an ironic and embittered defeatism. He was a true romantic: looking at the world in which he found himself, he decided that his situation was tragic, and that this was inevitably so. So there was an odd fatalism about his crimes. In his own eyes, they were always justified. When an acquaintance in Italy opened one of his letters by mistake and notified the authorities, Lacenaire took him out for dinner, drove to a secluded spot, and then offered the man one of two pistols – one loaded, the other empty. When the man refused to play this odd game of Russian roulette, Lacenaire shot him through the head. But he would have been equally willing to have died himself. On another occasion, he asked the driver of a cab to deliver a letter at a house they were passing; when the man was inside, he drove away the cab and sold it. But he made no attempt to hide, and was sitting outside his usual café when the driver approached with the buyer of the cab. Lacenaire admitted his guilt with grave politeness – the cab-driver was unsure of his identity – and served thirteen months in prison for a theft that brought him only fifty francs.

The *Memoirs* make clear why he took the idea of execution so calmly. To begin with, he had convinced himself at sixteen that he would die on the guillotine, and this idea of being dedicated to the "triangular blade" gave his life a quality of obsession. He sometimes referred to the guillotine as his "mistress". (He was too fastidious to gain any great pleasure from ordinary sexual activity.) If he had been a better poet, he might have written *Les Fleurs du Mal* a quarter of a century before Baudelaire. Once he had decided that he was living in a world that could never understand him, he decided that his life would be "a prolonged suicide". "I belonged no longer to myself but to cold steel." He was the true predecessor of Raskolnikov in *Crime and Punishment*. He wanted to "cancel his relations with society".

And this is the distinctive element in so much crime of the nineteenth century. Men like Burke and Hare had not cancelled their relations with society; they were only attempting to live in it, to keep their heads above water. They had nothing against society or the human race as such. If they had accidentally stumbled on a fortune, they would have given up their trade of murder with pleasure. Dick Turpin did not want to revenge himself on society, only to live like a gentleman. As soon as a murderer begins to enjoy killing for its own sake, he has taken up a conscious attitude of alienation from society, like a disguised wolf in a flock of sheep. Even Thomas Griffiths Wainewright eventually crossed the border-line between murder-for-business and murder-for-pleasure. He started with forgery, then poisoned his grandfather for the sake of the inheritance. The motive here was to keep up his social position – he was a friend of Lamb and Hazlitt, and William Blake admired one of his paintings – and to live "in a manner befitting an artist", a motive with which Wilde sympathised deeply. Then he poisoned his mother-in-law, whom he was supporting, and his sister-in-law (the one with the thick ankles) after insuring her life. The insurance company refused to pay up and Wainewright vanished to Boulogne, where he dropped strychnine in the drink of the father of a girl he wanted to seduce. It is true that he had insured him for three thousand pounds, but the money would go to his next of kin, not to his poisoner. Wilde suggests that Wainewright was out for revenge on the insurance companies. It seems more likely that he had become an habitual poisoner. Wainewright was eventually tried for forgery, not murder, and sentenced to transportation.

The earliest example of "joy-murder" I have come across is the case of Gesina Gottfried, who was executed in Bremen in 1828. Details of the case are unfortunately sparse. Gesina was born in a small town in North Germany. She seems to have had the temperament of Flaubert's Emma Bovary – desire for excitement, wealth, travel. She was attractive and had several suitors. From these, she chose a businessman named Miltenberg. By the age of twenty she had two children. But her husband was a drunkard, and his business was on the verge of bankruptcy. And, like many working-class husbands of the period, he beat his wife. One day, Gesina saw her mother using a white powder to mix bait for mice and rats. She took some of it, and dropped it into a glass of her husband's beer. He was dead by the next morning. She now pursued a young friend of her husband's called Gottfried, who had displayed signs of being interested in her before Miltenberg's death. But Gottfried was shy and cautious. Her patience soon wore out, and she began to slip small quantities of the white powder, arsenic, into his drink. As he became more ill, he became more reliant on her, and her chances of administering minute doses of poison increased. When her parents got wind of the intimacy with Gottfried, they opposed it. Gesina did not hesitate for a moment; she got herself invited to supper, and dropped arsenic in their beer. Then, carried away with her new-found power, she went on to poison her own two children. Gottfried, now permanently weakened, was persuaded to marry her; a day later, he was dead. His wife succeeded to his property, which had been her central motive all along.

A merchant she met at Gottfried's funeral began to court her. She did not like him, but he had more money than her former lover. She poisoned him with the same patient deliberation that she had already shown in the case of Gottfried. When her brother turned up one day, on leave from the army and drunk, she disposed of him quickly with a glass of poisoned beer – she was not prepared to risk having him around while she poisoned her current lover. The latter was persuaded to make a will in her favour, then he died. It is not known exactly how many more she poisoned. Charles Kingston mentions *In Remarkable Rogues*, another lover, a woman to whom she owed five pounds, and an old female acquaintance who tried to borrow money. She moved from place to place during the course of these murders, and ended in Bremen, where she poisoned the wife of her employer, a master wheelwright named Rumf. The wife died shortly after giving birth to a baby, so Gesina was not suspected; it was assumed to be puerperal fever. Rumf's five children died one by one after Gesina took charge of the family. Rumf himself began to feel rather ill after Gesina's meals. One day, when she was away, he tried a meal of pork, and was delighted that it seemed to agree with him. He was so pleased with his pork that he went to look at the joint in the larder when he came home from work the next day. Gesina had sprinkled it with white powder in the meantime, and Rumf knew it had not been there that morning. So he took the leg along to the police, who quickly identified the powder as arsenic. When arrested, Gesina made no attempt to deny her guilt; on the contrary, she confessed to her various crimes with relish. Her execution followed as a matter of course.

This account of Gesina Gottfried's career sounds so fantastic that one is inclined to believe that it must be exaggerated. But a glance at Major Griffiths' chapter on female poisoners reveals that Gesina is by no means an uncommon type. Hélène Jegado, who was tried at Rennes, in Brittany, in 1851, was an habitual poisoner as some people are habitual rapists. She simply could not resist introducing poisons into food, and since she was a cook, her opportunities were unlimited. Seven people died in one house where she was a servant, including her sister. She moved on, but she was never in a house for long before somebody died. "Wherever I go, people die," she commented mournfully. She was a kleptomaniac, and whenever thefts were brought home to her, someone in the house died with stomach pains, or was seriously ill. When she retired to a convent for a while, the nuns began to be sick after meals. She had been poisoning for more than twenty years, and was over fifty years of age, when she poisoned a fellow-servant in the house of a M Bidard, at Rennes, and was arrested. Her past was investigated as thoroughly as her extensive travels would allow: during the period 1833 to 1841, she was discovered to have poisoned twenty-three people, an average of three a year. Other periods were impossible to check on, but if the average was maintained, her total number of victims exceeded sixty. A Dutch nurse named van den Linden passed the hundred mark. It could be said of all these women, as it was said of another German poisoner, Anna Maria Zwanziger, that they regarded arsenic as "their truest friend". Griffiths quotes the jurist Feuerbach on Mrs Zwanziger as saying that "she trembled with pleasure and gazed upon the white powder with eyes beaming with rapture". All this makes it sound as if poisoning can become a sexual obsession with women, as more violent types of *lustmörd* can become with male sex-maniacs. There are no cases of male poisoners who became addicted to the practice for its own sake. Dr William Palmer, the Rugely poisoner who was executed at the age of thirty-two (in 1856), poisoned at least fifteen people in the course of his brief career, but in every case, there was clearly a motive. (The only exception was the death of a poor shoemaker named Abley, apparently Palmer's first murder. But in his book on Palmer, *They Hanged My Saintly Billy*, Robert Graves has pointed out that Palmer was believed to be having an affair with Abley's wife. This is not improbable, next to horse-racing, the fathering of bastards was the doctor's chief delight: he was responsible for fourteen of them in the five years before his marriage.) The story of Palmer's murders is a sordid tale of a man plunging into debt and killing to try to get out of it. The same is true of most of the other noted poisoners of the nineteenth century, which is the reason that I do not propose to devote a great deal of space to them. It might be mentioned in passing that Palmer holds the record for medical poisoners. It is true that Dr Marcel Petiot, who was executed in 1946, killed sixty-three people by poison, but he injected it with a hypodermic syringe. His victims were mostly Jews who wanted to escape from occupied France and who believed they were being inoculated against smallpox.

It is worth studying two exceptions to the rule about the male poisoner, for the crimes of Neill Cream and George Chapman were so motiveless that they must be classified with the poisonings of Gesina Gottfried and Hélène Jegado. These cases took place towards the end of the century, when the sadistic murder was already becoming common.

Dr Thomas Neill Cream is one of the oddest figures of the nineteenth century, a kind of criminal Leopold Bloom. Like

Joyce's hero, he was an introvert with feelings of sexual inadequacy, given to writing strange letters to women, and sometimes to men. He was also cross-eyed, bald-headed, and covered with black hair like a troll. He undoubtedly suffered from a mild but permanent form of insanity. Cream confined his activities to Lambeth, the slum area south of the Thames, much as the Ripper had confined himself to Whitechapel. Like the Ripper, his victims were all prostitutes.

On the morning of 13 October 1891, a nineteen-year-old prostitute named Ellen Donworth, who lived with her pimp at 8 Duke Street, Lambeth, received a strange letter in the post:

> *Miss Ellen Linnell [the surname of her pimp],*
>
> *I wrote and warned you once before that Frederick Smith, of W. H. Smith and Son, was going to poison you, and I am writing now to say that if you take any of the medicine he gave you, you will die. I saw Frederick Smith prepare the medicine he gave you, and I saw him put enough strychnine in it to kill a horse. If you take any of it, you will die.*
>
> *HMB*

A second letter arrived by the same post, asking her to meet the writer at the York Hotel and to bring the two letters with her. Presumably this was "HMB". The girl mentioned the letters to an Inspector Harvey. That evening, she set out to meet the writer, taking the letters. She mentioned to a friend that she was going to meet a tall, (he was 5 ft. 9 in.) cross-eyed man. An hour later, she fell writhing on to the pavement of the Waterloo Road. She was helped home, and told her landlady that the tall, cross-eyed man – who also had bushy whiskers and a silk hat – gave her two drinks of "white stuff" out of a bottle. She died on her way to hospital. Analysis of the contents of her stomach revealed that she had died of strychnine poisoning.

A few days before the death of Ellen Donworth, a young prostitute named Elizabeth Masters had received a letter from a client she had met a few days before, a cross-eyed man, saying that he would call on her that afternoon. The girl and a friend waited by the window, until they saw the cross-eyed man in the street. But he was following another prostitute, a girl named Matilda Clover, who was turning round and smiling at him. The two women went out and watched Cream speak to Matilda Clover and go into her house, where she lived with her two-year-old child. Obviously, the man liked variety. Ten days later, and only a week after the death of Ellen Donworth, Matilda Clover received a letter making an appointment, and also asking her to return the letter. It was signed "Fred". She met Fred that evening, and at three in the morning woke up another girl in the house with her screams. She died a few hours later, and a doctor's assistant diagnosed the cause of death as *delirium tremens*.

Cream was now living at 103 Lambeth Palace Road. He was so curious about the results of his pills that he asked his landlady's daughter to go to a house in Lambeth Road and enquire whether a certain young lady who had been poisoned was dead yet! The girl refused. Cream (who was known as "Dr Neill") told her that he knew the name of the poisoner; it was Lord Russell, who was at present involved in a matrimonial case. A few days after the murder, the Countess Russell received a letter telling her that her husband had poisoned Matilda Clover. Frederick Smith, of W. H. Smith and Son, also received a letter that accused him of poisoning Ellen Donworth. The writer, who signed himself H. Bayne, asked that his services as "counsellor and legal adviser" be retained, and enclosed a copy of the letter that Ellen Donworth had received on the morning of her death. "H. Bayne" said that if Smith agreed, a note should be exhibited in W. H. Smith's shop window in the Strand. The police advised that the note should be exhibited, but "H. Bayne" did not appear.

The Lambeth Coroner received a letter signed "A. O'Brien, detective", offering to find the murderer of Ellen Donworth for £300,000. Finally, Sir William Broadbent, a well-known doctor, received a letter signed "M. Malone" that asserted that he was the poisoner of Matilda Clover. "The evidence is in the hands of one of our detectives, who will give the evidence either to you or to the police authorities for the sum of £2,500." It pointed out that an accusation of this sort could ruin him for ever.

The pattern is fairly clear. Cream meets a prostitute, takes her out and buys her presents (he bought Matilda Clover some boots), then makes an appointment by letter, asking her to return the letter. He gives her medicine or capsules (he obtained empty capsules after the poisoning of Ellen Donworth, and filled them with *nux vomica*, which contains brucine and strychnine). Then he becomes immensely curious about the result of the poison, and also experiences a desire to make as much of a stir as possible. He wants to disturb people. He is obviously a man who feels totally insignificant, and who wants to prove to himself that he really does exist. Although the motive of the letters would appear to be to obtain money, he fails to show up for either of the appointments he makes.

After these murders, Cream went to Canada for a few months, having first got himself engaged to a girl named Laura Sabbatini in Berkhamsted. He returned to England on 2 April 1892. And on 11 April two more prostitutes, Alice Marsh and Emma Shrivell, died of strychnine poisoning. And Cream, with the curious dislike of the medical profession he had already shown, told his landlady's daughter that another lodger, a Dr Harper, was the murderer of the two girls. Dr Harper himself later received a letter accusing him of the deaths of Alice Marsh, Emma Shrivell and Ellen Donworth, and demanding £1,500 to suppress the evidence. Cream also told a young photographer named Haynes that he had definite proof not only that Harper had killed the three named above, but also Matilda Clover and another prostitute named Lou Harvey. (It later transpired that Cream had spent the night with this girl, and later persuaded her to take capsules; she pretended to swallow them, but kept them in her hand. Later, she threw them away.) Cream insisted that Haynes call at the house of Matilda Clover, to verify that she had died of poison. Finally, Haynes went to Scotland Yard to lay information against Dr Harper, but without mentioning Cream's name (Cream had made him give a promise to this effect).

Cream's letter to Dr Harper demanding £1,500 was passed on to the police. Ellen Donworth and Matilda Clover were exhumed and found to have died of strychnine poisoning.

Meanwhile, Cream was recognised by the young constable who had seen him leaving the house of Emma Shrivell and Alice Marsh. Constable Comley followed Cream back to his address and thereafter kept a watch on him. Cream noticed he was being watched and indignantly approached Scotland Yard, asking one

Inspector McIntyre (who was the man Haynes had already seen about the murderous misdeeds of Dr Harper) to investigate the matter and save him from further nuisance.

Obviously, it did not take McIntyre and Constable Comley long to get together and exchange information. On 3 June, Cream was arrested in his rooms. The result of the trial was a foregone conclusion: he himself had supplied most of the evidence. He was sentenced to death and hanged on 15 November 1892.

Quite obviously, the verdict should have been "guilty but insane". It is difficult to find a single action connected with the murders that could be described as remotely normal. Cream was living in some kind of strange dream world; nothing was real. When Leopold Bloom writes letters to upper-class housewives containing lewd suggestions and the request that they should "soil his letter unspeakably", the act may be abnormal, but its motivations are clear enough. But how can one explain what motivated Cream to have the following circular printed in Canada and shipped back to England?

> *"Ellen Donworth's death. To the guests of the Metropole Hotel. I hereby certify you that the person who poisoned Ellen Donworth on the 13th day of last October is today in the employ of the Metropole Hotel, and your lives are in danger as long as you remain in this hotel.*
>
> *W.H. MURRAY"*

To Laura Sabbatini he wrote shortly after his arrest:

> *"Was at Bow Street yesterday, and heard such good news that I have not been able to sleep since. A member of Parliament sent me word that he had over two hundred witnesses to clear me if I wanted them."*

Cream was obsessed by sex, in a perfectly ordinary sense. He told one prostitute that he lived only to indulge in women. In reading the account of the case, one is reminded of the anonymous author of that immense Victorian compendium of erotic experience *My Secret Life*, who apparently never had a thought that was not connected with sex. The evidence of various women makes it clear that Cream aimed to sleep with a prostitute more or less every day of his life. It is more than likely that his softening of the brain was due to syphilis. After he saw, or thought he saw, the prostitute Lou Harvey take two capsules full of strychnine, he was convinced she was dead. Some time later, he saw her in Piccadilly Circus and she spoke to him. They went into the Regent Hotel for a drink, and it was only then that she asked if he did not recognise her. He said no. She then identified herself, and Cream leapt to his feet and hurried out. Yet it was after this that he included her in the list of Dr Harper's "victims".

The poisoning of Ellen Donworth was not Cream's first murder. In 1878, when Cream was twenty-eight, a chamber-maid named Kate Gardener died of chloroform poisoning behind Cream's house, in circumstances that pointed to murder rather than suicide. (Cream had written a paper on chloroform during his days as a medical student.) In 1880, a girl named Julia Faulkner died in Chicago as a result of an illegal operation performed by Cream. The death may have been due to an accident of the kind that is likely to occur in the course of an abortion but, knowing Cream's strange obsession, the abortifacient may have been strychnine. In 1881, a Miss Stack died of medicine prescribed by Cream, and he wrote a blackmailing letter to a chemist, accusing him of her death. Later in the same year, he poisoned the epileptic husband of his mistress, Julia Stott. No suspicion was directed at Cream – the death was attributed to natural causes – until he contacted the coroner and accused a chemist of poisoning Stott. Cream even insisted on an exhumation. As a result, he was tried for murder, and spent ten years in jail. (He was in jail from 1881 to 1891, which disposes of a theory that he was Jack the Ripper. Cream's last words on the gallows were, "I am Jack the. . .") During that time, his father died, leaving Cream $16,000. And on leaving jail, he hastened to the city that obsessed him, London. And within a few days, Ellen Donworth died.

Cream was obviously fascinated by London, where he studied medicine at the age of twenty-six at St Thomas' Hospital, Lambeth; it was then that he discovered the delights of the Waterloo Road and its prostitutes. Oddly enough, his first wife – who died suddenly in 1877 – lived in a town called Waterloo, Canada. On returning to Canada with his medical degree, Cream chose to practise in a town called London, Ontario.

It has also been suggested that George Chapman was Jack the Ripper, and this is at least a possibility, since Chapman was actually living in Whitechapel at the time of the Ripper murders in 1888. The chief argument against it is that a man who has been killing prostitutes with a knife is not likely to change his method to poisoning with arsenic. Chapman – whose real name was Severin Klossovski, and who was born in Poland – came under suspicion in 1902 when a glass of brandy he had prepared for his sick wife was drunk by his mother and the nurse. Both became violently ill. Mrs Marsh, mother of his wife Maud, thereupon called in a doctor, who decided that Maud was being poisoned with arsenic. Chapman, who was thirty-six at the time, finished Maud off with a large dose, but his doctor refused to sign the death certificate and discovered arsenic in Maud Chapman's stomach. When the police reviewed Chapman's career, they became fairly certain that he had killed two earlier wives in the same way. Chapman's trouble, like Cream's, was women. But unlike Cream, Chapman married them. After a bigamous second marriage to a Polish lady in London, his first wife turned up, and the three of them lived together for a while. Finally, both women left him. After a trip to America, he lived with a woman named Annie Chapman, whos surname he later adopted, and then met Mary Spinks, an alcoholic, who became his first known victim. She died after living with Chapman for two years. By this time, Chapman had become a tavern keeper (with his wife's money). A year later, he married his barmaid, Bessie Taylor, and in due course, Bessie Taylor died in agony. Maud Marsh was also Chapman's barmaid before she became his wife, and died of arsenic poisoning.

Why Chapman poisoned his wives will never be known. Obviously, the motive was not sexual, as in Cream's case. What seems most likely is that Chapman was simply insane, perhaps suffering from a brain tumour or some venereal disease that caused outbursts of violent rage. He treated his women very badly; he beat Bessie Taylor even when she was weak after a spell in hospital. (This was after he had started to poison her.) Chapman was suspected of being Jack the Ripper at the actual time of the murders. He had a barber shop in the basement of George Yard Buildings, where the Ripper's first victim died. Chief Inspector Abberline remarked in 1902, when he heard of

Chapman's arrest: "You've caught the Ripper then?" But I doubt whether he really believed it himself. By 1902, the police were fairly certain the Ripper had been dead for more than a decade. Chapman was hanged in April 1903.

In the seventeenth century, poison was known as "succession powder". The Marquise de Brinvilliers, a nymphomaniac who was beheaded in 1676, poisoned her father and her two brothers simply to gain possession of the family wealth. Two centuries later, a young barrister named Charles Bravo died of antimony poisoning at the Priory, Balham. His beautiful but alcoholic wife Florence was suspected of administering tartar emetic, but never accused, and the case has been the subject of endless discussion ever since. John Williams in *Suddenly at the Priory*, is of the opinion that Florence Bravo did it. Yseult Bridges believes that Bravo himself accidentally took the poison with which he had been slowly poisoning his wife. Agatha Christie has suggested that Florence Bravo's former lover, Dr Gully, did it. Many writers on the case suspect Mrs Cox, Florence Bravo's companion.

The point to observe here is that the case is as baffling today as it was in 1876. Murder has lost its old simplicity. It is no longer a simple question of inheritances or the removal of a husband by a lover. Motives are more complex, and in some cases unfathomable. A sociologist of the seventeenth century, if such things had existed, might have predicted that when social poverty and misery disappear, the crime of murder would disappear too. Nothing of the sort has happened. As civilisation gradually eradicates the poverty that made the crimes of Burke and Hare possible, the murder rate rises. It begins to look as if man will never outgrow the practice of murder. If he lacks a motive, he will murder without one.

9.
The "Ripper"
Mystery

THE REAL significance of Lacenaire was that he was the first great "loner" in the history of nineteenth-century crime. Perhaps this is why Major Griffiths applies to him the description "one of the most cold-blooded destroyers of life the world has ever known".

Half a century after the death of Lacenaire, occurs the case that has become the symbol of the "man on his own", the criminal loner: the unknown who killed several women in Whitechapel in 1888. At least five women died between 31 August and 8 November: all were killed by a sadistic maniac with a knife, who (except in one case, where he was interrupted) opened the bodies and took out some of the inner organs. Two unsolved murders of women earlier the same year may also have been the work of the Ripper, although in these cases the women were stabbed, not mutilated. The first victim, a prostitute named Mary Anne Nicholls, picked up her murderer sometime after 2.30 am on Friday 31 August. In a street known as Bucks Row he clamped a hand over her mouth and drove a knife into her throat, severing the windpipe, then, when the woman lay on the ground, cut the throat with one powerful sweep. He turned his attention to her abdomen and made several slashing stabs in a normal downward direction on the right side of her stomach. (This, of course, indicates that the killer was left-handed; the throat wound, running from left to right, confirms this.) The killer was apparently not interested in her genitals. In most rape cases, the victim is left with her legs spread apart; Mary Nicholls' killer placed hers tightly together, and pulled down her skirt. He then cleaned his hands and knife on her clothes, and walked away. She was found twenty minutes or so later, at 3.45 am, by a carter on his way to work.

Annie Chapman was forty-seven years old, five years older than Mary Anne Nicholls, and looked sixty. She was dying of consumption and malnutrition, and the skin under her eyes was permanently blue. She was turned out of a cheap lodging house at two in the morning, when the keeper discovered she lacked the few pence necessary to pay for a bed. It is not known how long she wandered around looking for a pick-up, but probably she walked around for three hours or so before meeting Jack the Ripper. She met him in Hanbury Street, not far from the place where Mary Nicholls was murdered. They made their way down a passageway between two houses, into the backyard of No. 29 – a yard into which prostitutes often took their customers. There, against the fence, the man pressed his hand violently over her mouth, and drove the knife into her throat. It is unlikely that she struggled; she was undernourished, and weak from hours of walking the streets. It had been only a week since the man had killed Mary Nicholls, but sadistic frenzy was more powerful than ever. He was reasonably certain he would not be disturbed this time, so he took his time.

At some point, the murderer seems to have decided to remove the head completely, and proceeded to saw away at the neck; but when it was almost removed, he changed his mind, and tied a handkerchief round her neck to hold it together. The obsessive tidiness that he had manifested in the "laying out" of Mary Nicholls now appeared again. He removed two brass rings from her fingers and placed them neatly at her feet, together with a few coins. But for some reason he decided to leave this body in the normal rape position, with the knees bent and the legs wide open. And he left her dress pulled up over her breasts. Twenty minutes later, he went quietly down the passage again. While he had been killing Annie Chapman, a man had come into the yard next door to go to the lavatory, and had actually heard her say, "No, no", and the sound of a struggle. The neighbour was incurious, and the murderer was too obsessed by his strange need to care about interruption. He was like a male dog copulating with a bitch on heat: he had to finish before he became interested in anything else.

Certain things about the Ripper can be inferred from what has already been said. The neat laying out of Mary Nicholls' corpse, the trinkets placed round the feet of Annie Chapman, the handkerchief tied round the throat to hold the head on – all these bring to mind Neill Cream's weirdly irrational activities already discussed. This man was probably a full-blown psychotic, the kind who believes that voices speak to him from the air. Secondly, he was a sex-pervert of many years' experience. He had worked up morbid fantasies that included disembowelling women. In cases of violent sex crime, it is not uncommon for the genitals themselves to be attacked with a knife, and Paul de River (in *The Sexual Criminal*) cites a case in which the victim's intestines were torn out through her vagina. The Ripper was not interested in the genitals, his fantasies were all about cutting bellies. It was the womb itself that fascinated him. Freudians will draw a great many inferences from this, about hatred of the mother, perhaps of younger brothers and sisters stealing the parents' affection, etc. I would draw only one inference: that this destruction of the womb indicated a suicidal tendency in the Ripper – it was the place that bore him about which he felt ambivalent.

What did the Ripper wish to do with the organs he took away? In a letter written to a member of the Vigilance Committee a man who claimed to be the murderer said that he had fried and eaten half a kidney removed from a later victim, and he enclosed the other half. This letter is generally agreed to be genuine, since the half enclosed *was* a human kidney, and was "ginny" – affected by the large quantities of gin its former owner had drunk. The victim (Catherine Eddowes) had been a heavy gin drinker. At that time, it was common for the poorer classes to buy the intestines of animals, the part normally thrown away, and to eat them fried into a crisp state.

This desire to eat the body of a victim is rare, even among sex murderers. One of the few examples I can call to mind is Albert Fish, executed in 1935 for the murder of ten-year-old Grace Budd in New York. He cooked and ate parts of the body with carrots and onions. But by this time, Fish was a pervert of long experience, who began with a taste for being spanked, and graduated to such curious activities as driving needles into his scrotum, and inserting cotton wool soaked with methylated spirit into his anus, then lighting it. He preyed on boys as well as girls, and sometimes castrated them. He was fifty-eight years old when he murdered Grace Budd, so the eating of parts of her body might be regarded as the culmination of a lifetime of sexual perversion. On the other hand, the parallel does not necessarily indicate that the Ripper was middle-aged or old. The Birmingham YWCA murderer, Patrick Byrne, who decapitated the girl he assaulted just before Christmas 1959, and cut off one of her breasts and tried to eat it with sugar, was only twenty-eight. But he later admitted that he had been fantasising for years about torturing girls, and particularly about cutting one to pieces with a circular saw. Melvin Reinhardt has pointed out, in *Sex Perversions and Sex Crimes*, that most sadistic sexual murders are preceded by years of this kind of violent fantasising.

The Ripper's next attempt at murder was a failure as far as the satisfaction of his tensions was concerned. A man driving into the back yard of a working men's club in Berners Street at about 1 am saw a woman's body lying against the wall, and rushed into the club. The Ripper was either in the yard at that moment, or had only just left it as he heard the approach of the horse and cart. The victim's name was Elizabeth Stride, a Swede who was also known as Long Liz. She was an alcoholic and a pathological liar, one of her favourite stories being of how she had been on the Thames steamer *Princess Alice* that sank with seven hundred passengers in 1878, and that her husband and two children had been drowned. She added that she had escaped by climbing the mast, and that a man above her had kicked her in the mouth and knocked out her bottom row of teeth. (Like most of the Ripper's victims, she had many teeth missing; women of her class never visited a dentist.) But she never had any children, nor was she on the *Princess Alice*. The Ripper had only just managed to sever her windpipe when the appearance of the horse and cart interrupted him.

He hastened along Commercial Road – this murder had been farther afield than the others – and in the area of Houndsditch, was in time to meet a prostitute who had only just been released from Bishopsgate police station, where she had spent a few hours for being drunk and disorderly. He had no difficulty persuading her to accompany him to Mitre Square, a small square surrounded by warehouses, only a few hundred yards away. A police constable patrolled the square every fifteen minutes, and at 1.30 am he saw nothing unusual. Possibly the Ripper pressed Catherine Eddowes into a doorway in Church Passage, which connects Mitre Square with Duke Street. He then worked as quickly and silently as ever: the hand over the mouth and the knife thrust upwards, perhaps with the thumb on the blade, into the windpipe. And now, bending over her in the corner of the square, the killer went almost insane with the delight of having another victim under his knife. At some point, he allowed himself a few delicate cuts at the face, slashing upwards across the right cheek, removing the lobe of the right ear, underlining both the eyes, and cutting through the upper lip. All this took him about a quarter of an hour. He now strolled off through the passage to the north of the square, pausing to wash his hands in a sink (which was still there when I looked at the scene of the murder in 1961). The policeman discovered the body a few seconds after the Ripper left it, and sounded the alarm at 1.45 am. A watchman who had been only a few yards away, in the warehouse of Kearley and Tonge, was dispatched to find more policemen. The Ripper, strolling along Creechurch Lane and across Houndsditch, heard the police whistles, and no doubt smiled with satisfaction. He stopped in Goulston Street to wipe the blade of his knife on a piece of his victim's apron, which he had cut off, and then chalked on a wall: "The Jewes are not the men to be blamed for nothing". Then, chuckling to himself, he went on. The East End of London was full of Jews, and whenever there was a case of violent murder, someone was bound to bring up the "blood accusation", the notion that part of the Jewish religious ceremonies was the ritual slaughter of Christians. He felt like stirring things up a little. Like Neill Cream.

It was a few days after this that Mr Lusk, Chairman of the Whitechapel Vigilance Committee (which aimed at patrolling the streets) received the half-kidney, with the inch of renal artery still attached, which the Ripper had removed from his last victim. The kidney was in an advanced stage of Bright's disease, a kidney disease, which seems to rule out all possibility that it was a hoax. Catherine Eddowes was suffering from Bright's disease. It was accompanied by a letter. (It was an earlier letter to the Central News Agency, signed "Jack the Ripper", that gave the killer his nickname.)

What is generally agreed to be the last of the Ripper murders took place six weeks later, on 9 November. Possibly the intensive activity of police and vigilantes made the streets too dangerous for the killer.

With his usual sense of dramatic timing, which Neill Cream would have envied, the Ripper chose the evening of the Lord Mayor's Show, which would pass through Houndsditch. Outside a narrow passageway called Miller's Court, off Dorset Street, he picked up a twenty-five-year-old Irish prostitute named Mary Jeanette Kelly. She was a stoutish, heavily-built young woman, with long black hair, a great deal better looking than any of the previous victims. But like the others, she was a heavy drinker of gin, and like them, she was a down-and-out. She was several weeks behind with her rent, and a few hours before her death, tried to borrow half-a-crown from an equally broke acquaintance.

She took a customer back to her room about midnight, but perhaps he had no money. At all events, she was out again a couple of hours later, and spoke briefly to an ex-night watchman named Hutchinson. After she left him, he saw her picked up by a swarthy-looking man in Commercial Street. He thought the man looked too well-dressed to be hanging around the East End at such an hour, but had no suspicion that it was the Ripper. He had a gold watch chain and a heavy moustache that curled up at the ends. Hutchinson followed the couple, and saw them go into Miller's Court. Mary Kelly lived in a small room that used to be the back parlour of 10 Dorset Street. This was shortly after 2 am. Two witnesses later testified to hearing a cry of "Murder" at sometime between 3 and 4 am. Perhaps the Ripper had intercourse with Mary Kelly and then let her fall asleep. She was a powerful young woman, and her cries would have brought police within minutes. He killed her by clamping his right hand over her mouth and driving his knife into the carotid artery on the right hand side of her throat using his left hand. Blood spurted up the walls and over the killer, but he was almost certainly naked. He spent two more hours in the room. Mary Kelly was his most attractive victim so far; he could drink the cup of his strange obsession to the dregs. He could leave Mary Kelly unrecognisable as a human being.

He discovered the three-month-old foetus of a child in her womb. Was this, perhaps, an ultimate thrill? His psychosis had something to do with a horror of birth. Now he had destroyed a baby as well as the mother.

He was very thorough, he even removed the nose and ears. It is not clear how the Ripper managed to see well enough to do all this. He took care not to light the candle, the muslin curtains were thin and there were two panes missing from the window. But at some point he lit a fire in the grate, burning all the clothes he could find, and it flared up so strongly that it melted the handle of a kettle that stood nearby.

At about six o'clock, Jack the Ripper left 13 Miller's Court and walked out of history. There were no more murders. It is true that parts of the body of a prostitute named Elizabeth Jackson were found in the Thames in June 1889, that a woman called Alice Mackenzie was found with her throat cut and gashes on her abdomen in July 1889, and that a woman named Frances Coles was found dying of injuries to her throat and stomach in 1891. The Ripper did not confine himself to cuts on the abdomen; his pleasure came from plunging his hands into the victim and pulling out the intestines. He probably performed most of the mutilations by the sense of touch alone. He did not bother to dispose of the bodies, he left them where they were. And he would not have left a woman dying; his hand was as skilful as a butcher's.

Understandably, the case has continued to excite morbid curiosity ever since. For many years after the crimes, the most widespread theory was that the killer was an insane doctor, perhaps suffering from "religious mania". This story was given its definitive form in 1929 in *The Mystery of Jack the Ripper* by a Member of Parliament, Leonard Matters. The Ripper, he said, was a certain Dr Stanley, whose only son had contracted venereal disease from a prostitute. Mad with grief, Dr Stanley set out to track her down. Every woman he questioned about her he murdered, in case they warned his intended victim. The latter was, of course, Mary Kelly. Years later, Matters claims, Dr Stanley died in Buenos Aires, where he confessed his crimes to a former student, who was present at his deathbed.

But then, the medical report on Mary Kelly says nothing about venereal disease. What it *does* say is that she was three months' pregnant. And it was this that led another Ripperologist, William Stewart, to the odd conclusion that Jack the Ripper was actually a woman, a sadistic midwife, who had gone to Miller's Court to perform an abortion.

Another story that is almost certainly pure fiction is recounted by the novelist William Le Queux. In a book called *Things I Know* (1923), he claims that after the murder of Rasputin in St Petersburg, the Kerensky government handed him a manuscipt written in French. It had been found in the basment of Rasputin's house and was called *Great Russian Criminals*. This, says Le Queux, revealed that Jack the Ripper was a mad Russian doctor named Alexander Pedachenko, who had been sent to London by the Russian secret police to embarrass their British colleagues. He committed his murders with the aid of two accomplices. In an appendix to my own biography of Rasputin, I have disposed of Le Queux's story by pointing out that Rasputin spoke no French, and that his house had no basement – he lived in a flat on the fourth floor. In 1959, the Pedachenko theory was revived by a journalist named Donald McCormick, buttressed by "new evidence", the manuscript of a book called *Chronicles of Crime* by a Dr Thomas Dutton. McCormick had seen this book, and taken extensive notes, in 1932, while the doctor was still alive. Dutton believed that Pedachenko was also called Konovalov, and that he made a living as a barber surgeon, like another Ripper suspect, George Chapman, the sadistic poisoner. But then, anyone who has read Le Queux's two books on Rasputin will have no difficulty in concluding that the man was an unscrupulous inventor of "facts", and that therefore, the "French manuscript" story is certainly invention. And since Dutton's manuscript, *Chronicles of Crime*, has also vanished, there is no way of knowing how he came to be convinced that the Pedachenko story has some basis in fact.

Another expert on the case, Robin Odell, has suggested that Jack the Ripper was a *shochet*, a ritual Jewish slaughterman. This is possible, but it strikes me as psychologically improbable – as improbable as the notion of a gynaecologist becoming a sex maniac. The essence of sadistic sex crime is the *fantasy* beforehand, and fantasy flourishes in a vacuum. The only case of a butcher committing sadistic murder that I can call to mind is of the French murderer Eusebius Pieydagnelle, on whom Zola based *La Bête Humaine* (according to Arthur Koestler, who compiled the volume called *Sexual Anomalies and Perversions* which purports to be a summary of the work of Magnus Hirschfeld). He became a butcher because he was fascinated by blood. But, significantly, Pieydagnelle did not start murdering until his family insisted he become a lawyer. It was after this that he became depressed and experienced the compulsion to kill; otherwise, the slaughter of cattle completely satisfied his sadistic compulsions. This seems to me the chief argument against Mr Odell's theory.

In 1959, a new Ripper suspect suddenly emerged. He was Montague John Druitt, a briefless barrister who committed suicide soon after the murder of Mary Kelly. The first teasing reference to such a person appeared in *Mysteries of Police and Crime* (1899) by Major Arthur Griffiths. He mentions three men whom the police had suspected of being the Ripper. One was an insane Polish Jew, one an insane Russian doctor (the origin of "Pedachenko"), and the third, who was the chief suspect, "was also a doctor", in November 1888. Griffiths had his information from Sir Melville Macnaghten, chief of Scotland Yard's C.I.D., who became a policeman six months after the Kelly murder. Macnaghten had made notes on these three men, and they had been published in his autobiography *Days of My Years* in 1915, but without the names of the suspects.

The first to pick up the scent of Montague Druitt was the writer and television interviewer Dan Farson. In 1959, he made a television documentary about Jack the Ripper, in the course of which he visited Lady Rose McLaren in North Wales. Her mother-in-law was the Dowager Lady Christabel Aberconway, the daughter of Sir Melville Macnaghten. And Lady Aberconway was able to give Farson the original notes made by her father. These identified the chief suspect as "M.J. Druitt, said to be a doctor and of good family, who disappeared at the time of the Miller's Court murder, and whose body (which was said to have been upwards of a month in the water) was found in the Thames on 31 December – or about seven weeks after that murder. He was sexually insane and from private info I have little doubt that his own family believed him to be the murderer".

In the television programme, Farson referred to Druitt, at the request of Lady Aberconway, only by his initials, but began to write a book about it. Meanwhile, the same clues were being followed up by a journalist named Tom Cullen, and his book *Autumn of Terror* (1965) was the first to name Druitt as a Ripper suspect. Farson's own *Jack the Ripper* finally appeared in 1972.

We know, then, that Macnaghten believed Montague Druitt to be the Ripper. What we do not know is why he thought so. And the researches of Dan Farson and Tom Cullen provide us with no clue. On the contrary, they leave us baffled how such an apparently "normal" person, a cricket-playing schoolmaster, could have been suspected of being the Ripper. Druitt had been born in August 1857 at Wimborne, in Dorset. His father was a surgeon and Justice of the Peace. The family lived in one of the largest houses in the town. Druitt went to Winchester public school and distinguished himself academically: he was also the secretary of the school debating society, and played Sir Toby Belch in *Twelfth Night*. He was a good footballer and an excellent cricketer, playing for the school's eleven at Lords in 1876. He was one of nineteen candidates to be successful for the university exams, and was awarded a scholarship to Oxford. His academic career there was less brilliant – he only managed a third in Greats – but was elected Steward for the junior common room, which indicates his popularity with his fellow students.

Farson states that it was after Winchester that Druitt's life seems to have gone into decline. He was called to the Bar in 1885, at the age of twenty-seven, but seems to have had few, if any, clients. He had to borrow money from his father to keep going.

But Farson's statement that he went into decline does not seem wholly accurate. Irving Rosenwater, a cricket enthusiast, conducted an investigation into Druitt's cricketing career, which appeared in *The Cricketer* for December 1972. He discovered that Druitt was a member of the Kingston Park and Dorset County Cricket Club, the principal club side in Dorset, and played regularly for them through the 1880s until the time of his death. He seems to have been an excellent player, taking eleven wickets in one match in 1883. He became a member of the MCC in the following year. Rosenwater also discovered that he accepted the teaching post at a Blackheath "crammers" as early as 1884, and this no doubt explains how he was able to survive three years at the Bar without a case. Rosenwater notes that Druitt played for many sides, in dozens of matches, throughout the 1880s. It is conceivable that he made no attempt to practise as a barrister, preferring teaching and cricket. He played for the Blackheath Cricket Club, and was one of its principal bowlers, playing more matches in 1886 than anyone else. Blackheath was a fine team, and many of its members were county cricketers. So the picture that emerges of Druitt during the 1880s is of an upper-class young man who has been popular at school and university, and who prefers to continue to live the life of a kind of permanent public schoolboy. It is extremely difficult to perceive in this career any hint of the obsessive mania of Jack the Ripper.

The blow that seems to have made Druitt doubt his sanity fell in July 1888, when his mother became insane – she was to die of disease of the brain in 1890. But he continued to play cricket: on 21 July he played against Beckenham, on 3 and 4 August he played for the Gentlemen of Bournemouth. On 1 September he was playing in Canford in Dorset, three days after the murder of Mary Ann Nichols in Bucks Row, which Macnaghten regarded as the first of the Ripper murders. And on the morning of Saturday 8 September, six hours after the murder of Annie Chapman, Druitt was playing cricket on the Rectory Field at Blackheath.

When the Michaelmas term ended on 1 December 1888, Druit was dismissed from the Blackheath school, but it is not clear why. The obvious suspicion is that he may have been guilty of a homosexual offence. But if, as he believed, he was going insane, then he may simply have become unpunctual and unreliable. That Sunday he went to see his mother and seems to have been acutely depressed, for on his return to his chambers he wrote a note to his brother William, a Bournemouth solicitor, saying: "Since Friday I felt I was going to be like mother and the best thing for me was to die". On Monday 3 December he went for a walk by the river and threw himself in, his pockets weighted with stones.

What is immediately clear is that Druitt did not commit suicide because, as Griffiths and Macnaghten imply, his mind had snapped after the final murder of 9 November. He committed suicide because he was in a state of acute depression about his mother's breakdown and his own mental condition. Macnaghten also implies that "the Ripper" committed suicide soon after the final murder; in fact, we know that it was nearly a month later. Albert Backert, a member of the Whitechapel Vigilance Committee, complained to the police in March 1889 that they were being too complacent because there had been no new Ripper murders in five months, and was told that the Vigilance Committee could be disbanded because the Ripper was known to be dead: "He was fished out of the Thames two months ago".

It seems perfectly clear that there is not a shred of real evidence that Montague Druitt was Jack the Ripper. All that we know is that Macnaghten, who joined the Yard after the murders, chose to believe he was. The real question that remains to be answered, then, is had Macnaghten any reason for believing that Druitt was the Ripper, or was it merely a kind of wishful thinking? Bear in mind that the murders took place over a very brief period indeed, between August and the beginning of November 1888. We are told by Macnaghten: "No one who was living in London that autumn will forget the terror created by these murders. Even now I can recall the foggy evenings, and hear again the raucous cry of the newspaper boys: 'Another horrible murder, murder, mutilation, Whitechapel'. Such was the burden of their ghastly song, and when the double murder of 30 September took place, the exasperation of the public at the non-discovery of the perpetrator knew no bounds. . ." This exasperation became so great that the Commissioner of Police, Sir Charles Warren, was forced to resign on the eve of Mary Kelly's murder. And then, after this particularly horrific crime, the murders ceased. Why? What had happened? The natural assumption was that the murderer had committed suicide, or been confined in a mental home – Griffiths mentions both these possibilities, so it is clear that he does not take it for granted that Druitt was the Ripper. Yet his wording is close enough to that of Macnaghten's notes, made in 1894, to make it relatively certain that he was quoting Macnaghten. He also repeats Macnaghten's assertion that the body of the suspect was taken from the Thames seven weeks after the murder of Mary Kelly. So we can see that although Griffiths is aware of the Druitt theory, he does not wholly accept it.

But then Macaghten, who apparently did accept it, reveals that he knows very little about Druitt. In is memoirs he says: "I do not think there was anything of religious mania about the real Simon Pure (i.e. Jack the Ripper) . . . I incline to the belief that the individual who held up London in terror resided with his own people; that he absented himself from home at certain times, and that he committed suicide on or about the *10* of November 1888".

This is completely incomprehensible. It would surely be reasonable to assume that if Druitt was one of three chief suspects after the last murder, the police would have checked on his background. They would have visited the Blackheath school to find out why he was dismissed, and would have known that he lived in chambers at 9 King's Bench Walk in the Temple. They would certainly have known that he was taken out of the water on 2 January, and that he had vanished almost exactly a month before that. Yet Macnaghten makes the mistake of asserting that Druitt was a doctor, that his mind collapsed as a result of his "awful glut" in Miller's Court, that he committed suicide on the day after the final murder, and that he lived with his family. It suddenly becomes very clear that Macnaghten actually knew very little about Montague Druitt and about his suicide. We must assume that there was no police file about Druitt, and that Macnaghten was operating largely upon hearsay. This also throws doubt on his statement: "From private information, I have little doubt that his own family suspected this man of being the Whitechapel murderer; and it was alleged that he was sexually insane". If, in fact, the police suspected Druitt *because* some member of his family had reported their suspicion, surely Macnaghten would say so, not "I have little doubt. . ." And again, if there was some kind of evidence that Druitt was "sexually insane" it seems reasonably certain that Macnaghten would say so. Phrases like "it was alleged" and "I have little doubt" reveal that there was no real evidence against Druitt.

To summarize: the case against Druitt rests solely on the word of Macnaghten, and as soon as we examine Macnaghten's statements critically, it becomes obvious that he knew little or nothing about Druitt. Certainly our own knowledge of Druitt makes him as unlikely a suspect as J.K. Stephen or the Duke of Clarence. Young men of this type – men who have enjoyed a successful public school and university career, men who are popular, articulate and good at sport – lack the peculiarly morbid and obsessive temperament of the sadistic maniac.

Then why did Macnaghten come to suspect him in the first place? It may be supposed that when the Ripper crimes suddenly came to an end, the police made the natural assumption that the criminal was either dead or confined in an asylum. They were already predisposed to believe that the man they were looking for was a doctor, and that he either lived in Whitechapel or within easy walking distance. When Druitt's body was taken from the Thames, they felt that this could easily be the man they were looking for. The belief that they had finally located a likely suspect led them to overlook the fact that he was not a doctor, then to forget it, and then to create the myth that Druitt had been, in fact, a medical man. What we are seeing here is the perfectly normal human tendency to believe what we want to believe.

I have mentioned these various theories because it is as well to dispose of them before we turn to the most startling theory of all – the scandalous suggestion that Jack the Ripper was a member of the royal family. There are, in fact, now no less than three theories, all involving the same man: Edward, the Duke of Clarence, grandson of Queen Victoria, and heir to the throne of England. The simplest way of introducing these theories is to speak of my own involvement.

In 1960, I wrote a series of articles for the London *Evening Standard* under the title "My Search for Jack the Ripper". I had been interested in the case ever since, as a child, I had heard my grandmother describe how she had been a child in East London at the time of the murders, and how the children were always made to come home before dark for fear of the Ripper. In the early

1950s, I began to write a novel based loosely on the murders – it was called *Ritual in the Dark*. When I married and came to live in London, I began to study the case, wandering around the murder sites in Whitechapel – most of them looking exactly as they had in 1888 – and reading accounts of the murders in the *Times* for 1888. (This is available in the Reading Room of the British Museum.)

As a result of these articles, I received many letters. One of them came from a doctor named T.E.A. Stowell, who told me that it was clear that I knew the identity of the Ripper, even if I had been careful to conceal it. I replied that I had no idea of his identity, and saying that I would be glad to hear Doctor Stowell's own theory. The result was that he invited me to lunch at the Athenaeum.

Stowell proved to be a charming old gentleman who was obviously close on retirement. From something he said, I vaguely gathered that he was a brain surgeon – an idea I later found to be erroneous – and I remember observing with a certain fascination the shaking of his hand as he cut his steak.

Stowell had a strange story to tell me, and one that, I must confess, I found hard to follow. (My knowledge of the royal family was minimal, and I was too embarrassed to admit that the only Duke of Clarence I'd heard about was the one who was drowned in a butt of Malmsey.) In essence, it was as follows.

In the 1930s, Stowell was acquainted with Caroline Acland, the daughter of Sir William Gull, Physician in Ordinary to Queen Victoria. At some point, she asked Stowell's advice about certain of her father's papers, which contained some curious matters pertaining to the Duke of Clarence. Their most interesting revelation, he said, was that the Duke (who was known as Eddie) did *not* die in the flu epidemic of 1892, as stated in the history books, but in a mental home near Sandringham, of a softening of the brain due to syphilis. There was also some mysterious hint about Jack the Ripper, and about a scandal in Cleveland Street, Soho (concerning a homosexual brothel) in which the Duke had been concerned.

At all events, Stowell had apparently advised Caroline Acland to destroy the papers, or perhaps this was a decision she had taken anyway. Then Stowell began brooding on the strange documents and on the secrets they concealed. And he soon came upon some interesting clues. There was, for example, the odd story of the medium R.J. Lees, who is often mentioned in spiritualist circles as the man who caught Jack the Ripper. The story goes that Lees dreamed of some of the murders before they happened, and clearly saw the face of the killer. One day, on a London bus, he suddenly recognised the "Ripper" sitting opposite him. He followed him home, to a large house near Park Lane, then went to the police. They checked, and told him that the house belonged to a well known doctor who was connected with the royal family. They were so impressed by Lee's sincerity that they watched the house, and one night caught the doctor as he was setting out to prowl the East End, his knife concealed in a black bag. His wife admitted that her husband had been overworking, and had been behaving oddly recently. The doctor was incarcerated in a mental home in Islington, and Lees was rewarded with a pension from the Privy Purse.

There is, in fact, no evidence of a pension from the Privy Purse. But Queen Victoria *had* invited him to the palace on two occasions. It could have been because she was hoping to receive messages from Prince Albert. It could, said Stowell, have been because there was some grain of truth in the story about Lees and Jack the Ripper. In fact, Caroline Acland had told him that a detective, accompanied by a medium, *had* visited their house at 74 Grosvenor Square (near Park Lane) and asked Lady Gull some impertinent questions that had infuriated her.

This made it sound as if Gull was Jack the Ripper. But that was impossible. Gull had had a stroke in 1887, the year before the murders, and had died three years later of a second stroke. He was in no condition to stalk around the East End. But there was an odd story in Gull's papers to the effect that Gull suffered from lapses of memory, and one day awoke with blood on his shirt. Somehow, Stowell inferred that Gull knew that Eddie, Duke of Clarence, was Jack the Ripper, and set out to shield him. He had probably got the blood on his shirt from examining Eddie after one of the murders.

It was all bewildering stuff and I found it hard to take in. Stowell's own attitude puzzled me. He told me solemnly that he wanted the story kept secret in case it "upset her majesty" – he told me this later, when I suggested writing about it – yet he gave me the impression that his "secret" filled him with mischievous schoolboyish delight, and that he would not have been too worried if I had ignored his prohibition and published it.

I never met him again, but we corresponded, and some time later had a long talk on the telephone – by then he had retired to the south coast – during which he repeated much of what he had told me; I made notes as he talked. In retrospect, I get the feeling that he actually wanted me to publish the story, but against his express wishes, so to speak, so that he could feel completely absolved. But although I talked about his theory to various friends with an interest in "Ripperology" (a word I coined in a *Books and Bookmen* review), I stuck to my promise not to write about it. One of these friends was Nigel Morland, editor of *The Criminologist*. And, in 1970, Nigel persuaded Dr Stowell to tell his astonishing story for the benefit of his readers. The article, "Jack the Ripper – A Solution", appeared in the issue for December 1970. The good doctor was still being coy. He declined to actually name his suspect, but dropped some very broad, and titillating, hints. The *Sunday Times* got wind of the revelation in November 1970, and rang up Donald McCormick (who worked for the newspaper) to ask if he had any idea of the identity of Stowell's suspect. He did, since I had told him. The result was an article by Magnus Linklater stating that, according to Stowell, the Duke of Clarence was Jack the Ripper. The following evening, Kenneth Allsop questioned Stowell on the "Twenty Four Hours" programme on TV, and although Stowell declined to name his suspect, he made no objection when Allsop tacitly assumed it was Clarence. (Allsop was, in fact, another close friend whom I'd told about the theory years before.)

Having let the cat out of the bag, I think Stowell was startled at the publicity he received. It was a piquant news item, and it went round the world within hours. A correspondent to the *Sunday Times* pointed out that Clarence had been on a world tour in 1889 – to which Stowell might have replied, had he been inclined, that he had already discussed that very point in his article. But an article in the *Times* was more to the point: someone had checked on the Court Circular for 1888, and discovered that Eddie was at Balmoral, in Scotland, on the day after the murders. Yet even this discovery was less conclusive than it looked, since the murders had taken place not long after midnight on Sunday, and the Duke was not in Scotland until Monday. Even in those days,

British Rail was efficient enough to convey an heir to the throne from London to Scotland in twenty-four hours. (In fact, train times in those days were incredibly swift – only modern high speed trains have surpassed them.)

The sudden burst of publicity, and indignant criticism from royalists, was too much for Stowell, who died a few weeks after the article was published. His son seems to have become so bored with enquiries about his father's papers that he burnt – or claimed that he had burnt – everything that related to the Ripper case.

It made no difference, of course, since Stowell had already told me everything. By way of preserving it while it was still fairly fresh in my mind, I wrote it all down in an article for my home town newspaper, the *Leicester Chronicle*, and the bulk of this article was subsequently published as an appendix to my book *Order of Assassins*.

About a year after Stowell's death, I received a letter from an old friend, Michael Harrison, asking if he could quote my *Leicester Chronicle* article in a book he was writing – a biography of Eddie, the Duke of Clarence. In a postscript, he mentioned casually that he had now definitely established the Ripper's identity, and that he at present had a letter written by the Ripper lying on his desk . . . It was about six months later that I was allowed to see a proof copy, and finally learned the identity of Michael Harrison's suspect. Again, it was a man of whom I'd never heard. But in this case, at least, I was able to follow the chain of reasoning that had led to the identification.

From the beginning, Michael Harrison was convinced that Stowell's theory was absurd; Eddie was simply not the type of person to become a mass murderer. Let me, at this point, summarise the essence of Stowell's theory, based, let us recall, on what he had seen of the papers of Sir William Gull. According to Stowell, his suspect, whom he calls "S", was an "heir to power and wealth". At the age of sixteen he went on a round the world cruise, and in the course of a "gay party" in the West Indies, contracted syphilis. Stowell believed, although he does not say so in his article, that "S" was homosexual, and that the syphilis was contracted from another man. It was the syphilis, according to Stowell, that gradually led to a softening of the brain, and to the Whitechapel murders. Immediately after the double murder,

"S" experienced total collapse, and was confined at a mental home near Sandringham. By this time, the royal family were aware that he was Jack the Ripper, and had placed him under the care of Sir William Gull. In November, Eddie escaped and committed the final murder of Mary Kelly, after which he was again locked up. He recovered enough in the following year to go on a five-month cruise, and to undertake a few public engagements. He even made short speeches. But he was now "on the downward path from the manic stage of syphilis to the depression and dementia which in time must inevitably overtake him". And when the final collapse came, his death was blamed on the flu epidemic.

As Michael Harrison read this account of the life of the Duke of Clarence (Stowell mentions in his article that "S" was nicknamed "Collar and Cuffs" – a name first applied to Eddie by the journalist Henry Labouchere, on account of "the extravagance of his dress"), he was puzzled by certain inconsistencies. For example, Stowell says that "S" resigned his army commission at the age of twenty-four. But Eddy never resigned his commission. Stowell says that, according to Gull's papers, "S" had another relapse towards the end of 1889, and then slid into the final stages of syphilis. But Eddie was in India in 1889, returning in March 1890, after which he appeared in public three times, making speeches on each occasion.

There was another interesting minor puzzle. Why on earth did Stowell choose to disguise Eddie under the initial "S"? Could it have been because Gull himself referred to some mysterious person as "S", and that Stowell *mistook* this for a reference to the Duke of Clarence?

In short, was there a real person, a friend of the Duke of Clarence, a patient of Sir William Gull, who *did* fit Stowell's description?

Indeed, there was. His name was James Kenneth Stephen. He became Eddie's tutor and friend in the summer of 1883 – he had been selected to "look after" Eddie at Cambridge. Jim Stephen was ambitious, he saw himself as a future power behind the throne. But it was not to be. Eddie was not noted for brilliance; he didn't really enjoy mixing with Stephen's decadent literary friends, like the homosexual Oscar Browning, a fellow of King's. Eddie spent only two years at Cambridge. During that time, theorises Mr Harrison, he and Jim Stephen became lovers. Then Eddie plunged into public life, and he and Stephen met only occasionally. In 1886, Stephen made the mistake of reining his horse under a windmill, and was knocked unconscious by a descending vane. This blow on the head produced an abcess on the brain which would finally undermine his sanity. He became a patient of Sir William Gull.

Michael Harrison believes that Jim Stephen was Jack the Ripper. He argues his case convincingly. In the summer of 1888, Stephen was appointed a Clerk of Assize for the South Wales Circuit, but he was in London on all the dates of the Ripper murders. Mr Harrison quotes two poems by Stephen that reveal a capacity for pathological hatred. He points out that both Stephen's father and his grandfather died insane. Stephen *was* confined for two years in a mental home, at Northampton, where he died in 1892.

If Michael Harrison is correct, then Sir William Gull knew that Stephen was Jack the Ripper, and said so in his papers, referring to him by his initial "S". He also knew that, to some extent at least, Stephen's illness was brought on by his frustrated attachment to Eddie, who now avoided all contact with his former tutor. His mysterious references to "S", Eddie and Jack the Ripper were misconstrued by Stowell, who thought that "S" referred to Eddie, and that Eddie was therefore the Ripper.

I have to admit that I am far from convinced. To begin with, I find it hard to swallow Harrison's theory that Stephen and Eddie had a homosexual affair, and that Stephen's insanity was triggered, to some extent, by sexual jealousy. In his book *The Cleveland Street Scandal*, H. Montgomery Hyde comments: "There is no evidence that [Eddie] was homosexual, or even bisexual. On the contrary, he formed several romantic attachments to women, of which the first was to Princess Alix of Hesse who turned him down for the future Tsar Nicholas II of Russia". Neither is there any evidence that Stephen was homosexual, apart from his friendship with decadents like Oscar Browning. Michael Holroyd states in his biography of Lytton Strachey that not long before his death, Stephen made "violent advances" to Virginia Woolf's half-sister Stella Duckworth. This, admittedly, proves nothing – Stephen could have been bisexual – but in the absence of any definite evidence of Stephen's homosexuality, it would surely be reasonable to regard it as unproven.

It remains true that Stephen became insane in the late 1880s, and that he *could* have committed the Ripper murders. If I remain unconvinced, it is largely because I find it hard to imagine a brilliant, languid young man-about-town becoming a mutilator of women. My own mental picture of the Ripper, compounded from a number of descriptions given by women who saw the victims in conversation with a man, is of someone with dark hair and complexion, more powerfully built than either Eddie or Stephen, and of a distinctly lower social class. He is good looking in a coarse, brutal way, rather like Severin Klosowski, alias George Chapman, the sadistic poisoner who was executed in 1903. (Readers who are curious will find photographs of him in the Notable British Trials volume.) And he has never, at any time, had the slightest inclination to homosexuality.

In 1978, an American, Frank Spiering, produced a book called *Prince Jack, The True Story of Jack the Ripper*. It is an excellent summary of the murders, and of Stowell's theory, but in the last analysis, it is basically as unconvincing as Stowell's original article in *The Criminologist*. But in a letter to me (13 March 1980), Spiering mentioned at least one interesting piece of evidence. He told me that in November 1977 he visited the archives of the New York Academy of Medicine, where he was able to study Gull's medical papers. There was a printed volume of Gull's writings, and a brown leather volume with nothing on the spine; this, he said, contained Gull's handwritten notes. And thirty or so pages into these notes, he came upon the comment: "On 3 October I informed the Prince of Wales that his son was dying of syphilis of the brain. Under suggestion, using the Nancy method, my patient admitted to the details". So it would seem that at least some of Gull's original material still survives. But it is not quite clear why Gull should have been obliged to use the "Nancy method" – a kind of waking hypnosis – to lead the Duke of Clarence to admit to syphilis; presumably an ordinary physical examination would be all that was required.

In 1973, the year after the publication of Michael Harrison's biography of the duke, *Clarence*, I received a letter from a BBC producer, Paul Bonner, asking me if I would be willing to act as consultant on a series of programmes on Jack the Ripper. Apparently these would be semi-fictionalized, and would star two popular television policemen, Barlow and Watt of *Z Cars*. Donald Rumbelow, the policeman who had rediscovered the original morgue photographs of the Ripper's victims, had also been consulted.

A few days later I happened to be delivering a lecture at Scotland Yard, so I arranged to meet Paul Bonner in the pub next door. He explained that what he now intended to tell me must be treated as a secret. The BBC research team had apparently uncovered a completely new theory of the murders. Its origin, it seemed, was Joseph Sickert, known as "Hobo", son of the famous Victorian painter Walter Sickert.

Sickert's story was as follows. In the mid-1880s, Walter Sickert, who was then a Bohemian young painter living in Cleveland Street, Soho, became acquainted with Eddie, the Duke of Clarence, a young man who loved wine, women and song (Sickert apparently rejected the notion that Eddie was homosexual). In Sickert's studio, Eddie met a young shop girl who modelled for him; her name was Annie Elizabeth Crook. Annie was a Catholic. She became Eddie's mistress, and on 18 April 1885 she gave birth to Eddie's child, a girl who was named Alice Margaret. Soon after this, Eddie and Annie Crook went through a ceremony of marriage at a private chapel, with Sickert as a witness. The other witness was an Irish Catholic girl named Marie Jeannette Kelly, who was the child's nanny.

Inevitably, the secret leaked back to the palace. The Prime Minister, Lord Salisbury, was horrified. What was to be done? Eddie had married a woman who was not only a commoner but a Catholic. One day, early in 1888, a carriage drove up to the house at 6 Cleveland Street where Annie lived, and she and Eddie were hustled away. Annie was certified insane, and confined in a mental home. Eddie was presumably given a good talking to by his grandmother and had to promise never to see Annie again.

The child, Alice Margaret, was taken away to the East End to live with Mary Kelly. She found her way back to Sickert, who took her to Dieppe. When she grew up she became his mistress, and Joseph Sickert was born to them.

Mary Kelly made the mistake of telling the story to some gin-sodden prostitutes, and decided to blackmail the royal family. This was her downfall and, according to Joseph Sickert, Sir William Gull was given the task of eliminating Kelly and her friends. He did this with the aid of a coach driver named Netley, who took him to and from Whitechapel. Sir William Gull was the Ripper, and Mary Kelly's fellow blackmailers – Mary Nichols, Annie Chapman and Elizabeth Stride – were his victims. (Catherine Eddowes was killed by mistake because she was also known as Mary Ann Kelly.) So, finally, was Marie Jeanette Kelly.

This was the story on which Bonner wanted my opinion. I said it was obvious nonsense. I was not aware then that Gull had had a stroke in 1887, and was almost totally incapacitated (or if I was, I had forgotten about it). But surely it was obvious that if a group of blackmailers are murdered one by one, they would begin to suspect an organized plot long before the Ripper completed his task, and would hasten to the nearest police station to tell their story. Besides, no theory of the Ripper's identity makes sense that fails to recognize that he was a sadistic maniac; no other motivation could account for the disembowelling of the victims and for the final dismemberment of Mary Kelly. There is no evidence whatever that Gull was a sadist. And the notion of driving around the East End at 4 am in a carriage looking for prostitutes is grotesque.

Nevertheless, said Paul Bonner, there *was* a certain amount of evidence for the story. They had checked at the Cleveland Street address, number 6, and a woman called Elizabeth Cook – obviously a careless misprint for Crook – had lived in the basement in 1888, as the rate book showed. They had located the birth certificate of Alice Margaret Crook, and no father's name was given. They had even discovered that there had been a "driver" named John Netley who had been born in May 1860 and had died in 1903 when thrown from his van as it went over a stone. Bonner also mentioned Stowell's story about the police inspector who called on Lady Gull, together with a medium, and quoted Stowell's comment that Gull had been seen in the Whitechapel area around the times of the murders, and his admission that he had been suffering from lapses of memory and had once found blood on his shirt.

The story still sounded absurd to me. Nevertheless, it was duly told in a BBC television serial in six parts, *The Ripper File*, in July and August 1973, and Joseph Sickert took part in the final episode and repeated his rather unlikely story.

A young north London journalist named Stephen Knight, who had been conducting his own investigation into the Ripper case, decided to write a book about Sickert's theory. This appeared in

1976 with the optimistic title *Jack the Ripper, The Final Solution*. I reviewed it in *Books and Bookmen*, and the central paragraph of the review ran as follows:-

"What we are being asked to believe is, basically, a far taller story than any of the earlier theories about the Ripper – the mad surgeon, the sadistic midwife, and so on. We are asked to believe, first of all, that Eddie, the Duke of Clarence, became a close friend of Walter Sickert. This is unsupported. We are asked to believe that he became sufficiently involved with a shop assistant to actually marry her although, like everyone in the family, he was terrified of Queen Victoria, and knew that he might – almost certainly would – be king of England one day. We are asked to believe that the queen's physician, Sir William Gull, was a party to the kidnapping of the shop assistant, and that he probably performed some gruesome operation on her to make her lose her memory. And then that Gull, with the approval of the Prime Minister, went around Whitechapel killing prostitutes with appalling sadism (when, after all, a single stab would have done the trick). Moreover, that Gull was a Freemason, and committed the murders according to Masonic ritual. (The Prime Minister and Commissioner of Police were also Masons.) Mr Knight admits that Gull had a stroke in the year before the murders, but insists that he was still spry enough to wield the knife".

The question is then asked why was Annie Crook not also murdered, if the aim was to eliminate everyone who knew about the morganatic marriage? And why not Sickert too, since he was virtually to blame? Stephen Knight answers this by saying that Sickert himself was *also* the Ripper – that he had accompanied Gull on his murder expeditions and may have killed some of the victims himself. In his Afterword to the book, Joseph Sickert concedes reluctantly that this may be true, but suggests that his father may have been blackmailed into it by threats on his life.

Stephen Knight's book was a considerable success, so much so that he decided to give up his job as a journalist and become a full-time writer. Regrettably, soon after a paperback edition of the book came out in 1977, a story by David May appeared in the *Sunday Times* that stated that Sickert had now admitted that his whole story was a hoax. Stephen Knight, understandably, declined to accept his view, and in his best-selling book about the Freemasons, *The Brotherhood* (1984), he reiterated the whole story. By that time, sadly, he had discovered that he was still suffering from a brain tumour, of which he had believed himself cured, and he died in 1985.

In the *Sunday Times* piece, Sickert insisted that only the Jack the Ripper part of his story was a hoax, and that he was, in fact, the grandson of the Duke of Clarence, as a result of the affair between Clarence and Annie Crook. This is, of course, the only part of his story for which there is some sort of documentary evidence: viz. the rate book for 6 Cleveland Street, and Alice Margaret's birth certificate in which the name of the father and his occupation are left blank. We may also recall that Stowell spoke of Eddie in connection with Cleveland Street – not the basement flat of "Elizabeth Cook", but the homosexual scandal at the brothel at 19 Cleveland Street. In fact, there is no evidence that Eddie was homosexual, but in his book *The Cleveland Street Scandal* (1976), H. Montgomery Hyde reveals that the Assistant Public Prosecutor mentioned "PAV" (Prince Albert Victor – Eddie's real name) in connection with the case. Hyde points out that the man who ran the brothel, Charles Hammond, also advertised *Poses plastiques*, the Victorian equivalent of striptease (although the nude lady had to remain as still as a statue), and that if Clarence visited the house, it may well have been under the impression that it provided "female entertainment". But we might also speculate that if Gull referred to some scandal involving Eddie and Cleveland Street in his diary, he might well have been referring to the duke's affair with a common shop girl named Annie Crook.

Hyde mentions one more piece of evidence that adds credibility to Stowell's story. A young doctor named Alfred Fripp was called in on one occasion when Prince Eddie was ill at Scarborough; among Fripp's papers after his death (he became a famous surgeon) Fripp's biographer discovered a prescription for Eddie indicating that he suffered from gonorrhoea.

Yet this still leaves us with an interesting question. We have dismissed Joseph Sickert's statement that Sir William Gull was Jack the Ripper, and it seems fairly clear that the Duke of Clarence was, according to the Court Circular, "otherwise engaged" at the time of the murders. Yet Stowell undoubtedly saw *something* in Gull's papers that suggested that Clarence was Jack the Ripper. Michael Harrison's identification of "S" as Jim Stephen is plausible, until we look more closely at Stephen's personality: the young Cambridge aesthete, a member of what Harrison describes as the "epicene literati", who wrote poetry and mixed with homosexuals. Even when he was going insane, his madness does not sound like the kind that drives a man to prowl Whitechapel looking for women to disembowel. In his biography of Virginia Woolf (Jim Stephen's cousin), Quentin Bell writes: "One day he rushed upstairs to the nursery at 22 Hyde Park Gate, drew the blade from a sword stick and plunged it into the bread. On another occasion he carried Virginia and her mother off to his room in De Vere Gardens; Virginia was to pose for him. He had decided that he was a painter, a painter of genius. He was in a state of high euphoria and painted away like a man possessed, as indeed he was. He would drive up in a hansom cab to Hyde Park Gate, a hansom cab in which he had been driving all day in a state of insane excitement. On another occasion he appeared at breakfast and announced, as though it were an amusing incident, that the doctors had told him that he would either die or go completely mad . . ". None of this sounds in the least like the cunning and sadistic maniac of Whitechapel.

But if we dismiss Stephen, then who was "S"? There is one more obvious candidate – Sickert. In fact, Stephen Knight's chapter on Sickert is one of the most convincing in his book. Sickert *was* undoubtedly obsessed by Jack the Ripper. Sickert's friend Marjorie Lilly told Knight: "After the stroke Sickert would have 'Ripper periods' in which he would dress up like the murderer and walk about like that for weeks on end". And Knight points out how many of Sickert's paintings contain gruesome-looking heads of women or similar puzzling items. Sickert painted several pictures of the Camden Town murder, in which a young artist named Robert Wood was accused of cutting the throat of a prostitute. According to Joseph Sickert (whose word, admittedly, seems to be less than reliable) these paintings were really about the Ripper murders.

Another curious and enigmatic painting shows a young woman in a large room standing underneath a bust on the wall. It is the title that is so baffling: Amphytrion, or X's Affiliation Order. Knight points out that an affiliation order fixes the paternity of an illegitimate child, and that the legend of Amphytrion tells how Jupiter disguised himself as a lesser being to seduce an ordinary woman, who becomes pregnant by him. Knight speculates that the bust on the wall is a death's head, but this seems to me an obvious misinterpretation. The ordinary-looking young woman in a blouse and long skirt is obviously the woman who was seduced by Jupiter, so the bust on the wall above her must be her seducer, the father of her illegitimate child. The picture may be regarded as strong supporting evidence for Joseph Sickert's claim that the Duke of Clarence was the father of Annie Crook's baby. This in turn suggests that the story of the friendship between Clarence and Sickert is true. If Gull knew about Annie Crook and her illegitimate child, then he also knew about Sickert's role in the story. If Sickert was obsessed by the murders – and he was known to be obsessed – then it *is* conceivable that he was the "S" Gull referred to in connection with the Duke of Clarence and Jack the Ripper.

Does this mean that Sickert was Jack the Ripper? Almost certainly not. Artists and writers may become morbidly obsessed by certain murders, but, no artist has ever been known to commit a premeditated murder. Sickert may have been Gull's suspect, and therefore the man who inadvertently caused suspicion to fall on the Duke of Clarence. But there is no evidence that he was capable of harming a fly. We must look for Jack the Ripper elsewhere.

And that may sound like the last word on a fascinating if unlikely theory. But in March 1987, a new magazine called *The Bloodhound* added an interesting postscript. Its editor, Simon D. Wood, had decided to make his own investigation into the evidence on which Stephen Knight based his book. He began by writing to Mr Alan Neate, the Record Keeper of the Greater London Record Office, to ask for any information he could furnish on the life of the unfortunate Annie Elizabeth Crook. And in fact, this information was to undermine Knight's theory even more effectively than "Hobo" Sickert's confession.

Knight's investigation had shown that the address given on the birth certificate of Annie's daughter Alice Margaret (who was born in 1885) was 6 Cleveland Street. And the rate book for the same address in 1888 listed one "Elizabeth Cook" as occupying the basement. "The address", says Knight, "shows that the Elizabeth

Cook of the Rate Book and Annie Elizabeth Crook were one and the same."

Unfortunately, it shows nothing of the kind. For between 1886 and early 1888, numbers 4 to 14 Cleveland Street were pulled down, and replaced by the block of flats that still stands there today. That means that Annie Elizabeth Crook must have left 6 Cleveland Street, at the latest, in 1886. It was after the completion of the flats that Annie *Cook* moved into the basement of number 6. And the rate book shows that she lived there until 1893, long after, according to Knight, Annie Crook was dragged off by the wicked Sir William Gull and forced to undergo brain surgery to destroy her memory.

Moreover, the same records show that there is no truth in the story that Annie Crook was incarcerated in a mental home for the rest of her days. In 1889 she was admitted briefly to the Endell Street Workhouse, together with her daughter Alice Margaret. She was destitute, but quite obviously free. In 1894 the records show that Annie was in prison. Her daughter, aged nine, was sent to a kind of holiday camp for two weeks, so presumably Annie received fourteen days.

In 1902 Alice Margaret was admitted to St Pancras Infirmary suffering from measles, and the records show that she and her mother were living at 5 Pancras Street, where they paid two shillings a week in rent. But in 1903 Annie Crook was admitted to the St Pancras Workhouse suffering from epilepsy. Her occupation was given as "Casual hand – Crosse and Blackwells". And so the sad record continues. In 1906 Annie was living, together with her mother and daughter, at the Poland Street Workhouse. In 1913 Annie and her mother were admitted to the Endell Street Workhouse. In 1920 Annie Elizabeth Crook finally died in the Lunacy Ward of the Fulham Road Workhouse. But the records show that this breakdown in her mental health occurred only at the very end of her life. There is certainly no evidence that she was imprisoned in lunatic asylums from 1888 until 1920 by a "Freemasons' conspiracy".

Finally, the report of her death lists her religion as Church of England. So Knight's story that she was a Roman Catholic – and that this was what caused so much consternation at Windsor – is without foundation.

Simon Wood ends his article by revealing that he placed his evidence before Stephen Knight, and that Knight remained "smilingly unrepentant". But, in a postscript to the paperback edition, Knight admits that "other evidence" has now come to light, which he is in the process of examining. Sadly, says Mr Wood, he never took up the challenge.

But Wood's article makes it clear that Stephen Knight must have known, even while he was writing his book, that his theory was untrue: that Annie Crook and Elizabeth Cook were two different persons, and that Annie lived out a perfectly normal, if miserable, life until her death in 1920. I am forced to the reluctant conclusion – for Stephen Knight was an old friend and I was fond of him – that he wrote the book with his tongue in his cheek, then found himself caught up in a success that prevented him from retracting or quietly disowning it.

In 1988, the centenary of the Ripper murders, an interesting crop of new books and theories about the case appeared, including one by myself and Robin Odell, *Jack the Ripper, Summing Up and Verdict*. Robin Odell continued to defend his view that the Ripper was a Jewish slaughterman, while admitting that the records that might have supported his theory had been destroyed during the blitz. Otherwise, we confined ourselves to a summary of the facts about the case, and an outline of the theories.

Martin Fido's *Crimes, Detection and Death of Jack the Ripper* took its starting point from some remarks made by Sir Robert Anderson, Assistant Commissioner of Police, to the effect that the identity of Jack the Ripper was known to the police, and that he was a Polish Jew. Sir Melville Macnaghten had named his suspect number two as "Kosminski, a Polish Jew and resident in Whitechapel. This man became insane owing to many years indulgence in solitary vices. He had a great hatred of women, especially of the prostitute class, and had strong homicidal tendencies: he was removed to a lunatic asylum about 1889. There were many crimes connected with this man which made him a strong suspect".

Martin Fido looked through records of asylums and tracked down a man called Aaron Kozminski, who was committed to Colney Hatch asylum on 6 February 1891. By 1894 he was transferred to Leavesden asylum as an incurable imbecile. Doctors ascribed his illness to self-abuse (masturbation), which in those days was believed to lead to insanity, blindness, deafness and various other problems. But the asylum records made it clear that this man was regarded as harmless; he was suffering from paranoid delusions, and would certainly not have possessed the kind of cunning that enabled Jack the Ripper to run the gauntlet of so many policemen and vigilantes. But after a further search, Fido came upon a suspect called Nathan Kaminsky, a twenty-three-year-old bootmaker, a Polish Jew who was treated for syphilis at public expense. He lived in Black Lion Yard, at the centre of the Ripper murders. But apart from the record of his treatment for syphilis in March 1888, Fido could find nothing more about him. But he *did* discover that a Polish Jew was arrested in December 1888, wandering the streets of Whitechapel and rambling incoherently. He spoke only Yiddish. In the workhouse infirmary he became violent, and he was registered under the name of David Cohen. He was too violent to associate with fellow patients, and died in Colney Hatch of "exhaustion of mania", in the late summer of 1889. Fido argues that a lunatic who mutters that his name is "Nathan Kamin" could easily be registered as the easier-to-spell David Cohen. It is an interesting and ingenious theory, but open to the objection that it contains too many "ifs". Paul Begg, another writer who produced a book for the centenary, *Jack the Ripper: Uncensored Facts*, also points out that another close associate of Anderson, Inspector D.S. Swanson, wrote in the margin of Anderson's autobiography (*The Lighter Side of My Official Life*) that Anderson's "suspect" "had been identified at the Seaside Home". David Cohen was found wandering the streets of Whitechapel, babbling incoherently, so it would seem that he could not have been Anderson's suspect.

Perhaps the most impressive piece of research to emerge during the Ripper centenary was conducted by two authors, Martin Howells and Keith Skinner, and published in their book *The Ripper Legacy*. Their starting point was Dan Farson's book of 1972. Farson had mentioned that Montague Druitt had a cousin called Lionel Druitt, who had immigrated to Australia in 1886, two years before the murders. And a certain Mr Knowles had written to Farson from Australia after his programme, mentioning that he had seen a pamphlet called "Jack The Ripper – I Knew Him" by one Lionel Druitt, privately printed in 1890 by a Mr Fell of Dandenong. I myself had been so intrigued by this reference that I had asked a researcher to see if the pamphlet could be found in the Melbourne Public Library – she had no success. Farson himself had actually visited Dandenong in search of the pamphlet, and failed to find it. Howell and Skinner were more successful. They finally tracked down Lionel Druitt's address when he lived in Australia. It was in Dandenong Road in a suburb of Melbourne called Oakleigh. So Farson had simply been looking in the wrong place.

With incredible persistence, the authors went on to track down a man called Maurice Gould, who had been in Australia in the 1920s, and who had also been told that the identity of Jack the Ripper was known to a certain W.G. Fell. Fell had talked to a journalist called Edward MacNamara, and told him that Druitt had lived in his house, and left papers that proved the Ripper's identity. Mr Gould was able to tell them that he had talked to MacNamara in a Melbourne pub about another mass murderer, Frederick Bailey Deeming, executed in 1892 for the murder of six people, including his wife. MacNamara had then shown him some handwritten pages which, he seemed to remember (after a lapse of sixty years) had been a confession by Jack the Ripper himself. Deeming had apparently confessed to two London murders that bore some resemblance to the Ripper crimes, giving rise at the time to a theory that he was the Ripper. And when Deeming had arrived in Melbourne from London, he had assumed the alias Drewen, not dissimilar to Druitt. What Farson's correspondent, Mr Knowles, had remembered was a story that related to Deeming, not Druitt.

It sounds as if this was the end of the trail. But Howells and Skinner still had some interesting ideas. They had looked more closely into Montague Druitt's background, and discovered that when Druitt was at Cambridge, he knew various people who were members of a society called the Apostles, most of whom were homosexuals. (In later years, the spies Guy Burgess and Anthony Blunt, both homosexuals, were members of the Apostles.) Moreover, the Duke of Clarence, Dr Stowell's suspect, was also at Cambridge at this time, and on friendly terms with many of them. Druitt, of course, was dismissed from a school in Blackheath shortly before his suicide, and this may have been for homosexuality.

The theory put forward by Howells and Skinner, based on their researches into the Apostles, is that Montague Druitt was indeed Jack the Ripper. And friends who had been Apostles learned this disturbing fact. To have Druitt arrested and tried as Jack the Ripper would have brought disgrace to his former friends, and even to the Duke of Clarence himself. So he was murdered, and his murder made to look like a suicide by drowning. What followed then was a "cover-up" to prevent scandal – a cover-up that filtered through to Sir Melville Macnaghten and others who investigated the case.

Again, a remarkable and fascinating theory, but one that is difficult to take seriously. There is no real evidence that Druitt was closely associated with the Apostles. But even if it could have been proved that he was a member of the group, it would still remain to be proved that he was Jack the Ripper. And if this in turn could be proved, it would still leave the greatest improbability of all, that a group of Cambridge homosexuals would succeed in learning his secret, and that they would decide that he had to be murdered. The same objection applies here as to Fido's Kosminski theory – that there are simply too many "ifs".

Perhaps the most intriguing theory to be advanced, or rather, revived, on the Ripper centenary was the notion that he was a black magician named D'Onston. It was first advanced by the notorious Aleister Crowley, who was known as "the wickedest man in the world". Crowley speaks of his suspicions in his autobiography, *The Confessions*, and wrote an article in his journal *The Equinox*. This article was tracked down by another Ripper expert, Richard Whittington-Egan. Crowley's story, briefly, is this.

In 1912 he met a tough lesbian named Baroness Vittoria Cremers, who told him that she knew the identity of Jack the Ripper. It was a doctor named Roslyn D'Onston Stevenson, who prefered to be known as D'Onston. Baroness Cremers had been a lover of a beautiful woman called Mabel Collins, a disciple of Madame Blavatsky, but Mabel had shared her favours with D'Onston, who claimed to be a black magician. The murders, seven in all, according to Baroness Cremers, had been committed as part of a magical ritual to obtain Supreme Black Magical power, and the victims had been in places that, connected together, made a Calvary cross. D'Onston had told the ladies that the murderer had eaten parts of the bodies at the scene of the crime. And one day, the baroness had gone into D'Onston's room – he was living with Mabel Collins – when he was not there, and looked in a tin box under the bed. She found some books, and some old fashioned black ties stained with something that could have been blood. (Crowley declared they were white ties.)

What finally convinced the baroness that D'Onston was Jack the Ripper was a statement he made to the effect that there would be no more murders, and that he himself had known Jack the Ripper. This is interesting, but if D'Onston *was* Jack the Ripper, why should he claim merely to have known him?

The D'Onston-Ripper connection becomes yet more complicated. A journalist named Bernard O'Donnell had investigated the story, and discovered that D'Onston had gone to Scotland Yard with a five-page document identifying Jack the Ripper as a Dr Morgan Davies of Houndsditch, East London. His reason was as follows. When he (D'Onston) had been a patient at the London Hospital he had seen Davies discussing the Ripper murders with five fellow doctors. Davies had startled them by arguing that the Ripper had cut his victims' throats from behind as he sodomised them. And as he put forward this interesting theory, he acted it out with such blood-curdling realism that D'Onston was instantly convinced that he was the killer. D'Onston then discovered that one of the women had indeed been sodomised.

The document remained in police files – I have a copy – until it was stolen. But it seems to indicate very clearly that D'Onston thought Dr Morgan Davies was the Ripper. If D'Onston himself was the Ripper, why should he draw attention to himself in this way?

D'Onston was a friend of the editor W.T. Stead, and Stead published some of his articles on magic. Stead himself once stated in print that he had once believed that the author of the articles (who used the odd pseudonym Tautriadelta) was Jack the Ripper. This seems to suggest that D'Onston himself liked to drop hints to this effect, and that he was something of an exhibitionist.

Richard Whittington-Egan, who first published this astonishing story in *A Casebook on Jack the Ripper* (1976), suggested to his friend Melvin Harris that it might be a good idea to write a book on D'Onston for the Ripper Centenary, while at the same time admitting that he did not believe the theory himself. (The story of the bloodstained ties and the bodies "in the form of a cross" are equally preposterous.) Harris took him up on the suggestion, and the result was *Jack the Ripper: The Bloody Truth*. In fact, Harris did some interesting research into D'Onston's background, obtaining some of his most important results after his book was published. Richard Whittington-Egan had stated that D'Onston was actually Robert Donston Stephenson, and that he was something of a liar and a con-man. He claimed to have come of a wealthy family. In fact, he was the son of a mill worker at Sculcoates, in the East Riding of Yorkshire.

Harris's researches revealed that this, at least, is untrue. Donston's father was a mill owner and the City Treasurer of Hull. Donston's story of service under Garibaldi also turns out to be true, as does his tales of travels in India. He had some sort of medical diploma, so the title "Dr" was not wishful thinking. In short, D'Onston Stephenson is by no means the fake that Whittington-Egan assumed. But does this come any closer to proving that he was Jack the Ripper? Clearly, it does not. So while, like Fido, Howells and Skinner, Harris deserves high marks for research, his interesting theory has to be discounted.

Since I had been writing about Jack the Ripper and since I wrote a series called "My Search for Jack the Ripper" (which appeared in the London *Evening Standard* in August 1960), I have become something of a clearing-house for new theories, and my file of letters about the Ripper's identity is enormous. The four that strike me as the most outstanding are as follows.

Thomas Toughill of Glasgow (now of Australia) became convinced that the Ripper was a homosexual artist named Frank Miles, who once shared rooms with Oscar Wilde in Tite Street. He became a considerable success as an artist, but Wilde eventually threw him out, and Miles began to suffer a decline. He died in an asylum of general paralysis of the insane in July 1891. Toughill's still unpublished book on Jack the Ripper is full of fascinating sidelights on the 1890s, and throws some interesting light on Wilde. Yet in the last analysis, he has no real evidence that Miles actually killed five women in Whitechapel in 1888. The person who emerges is a young "aesthete" of the type W.S. Gilbert satirised as Bunthorne in *Patience*, and it is impossible to imagine him killing anybody, even in a fit of insanity. Yet Toughill's book is so well written and researched that it certainly deserves to take its place with the many other studies by "Ripperologists".

Another suggestion, put forward by John Morrison of Leytonstone, in a pamphlet called *Jimmy Kelly's Year of Ripper Murders*, is that the Ripper was the "husband" of the final victim, Mary Kelly. James Kelly died in Broadmoor in 1929, at the age of sixty-nine. Morrison discovered that in the early 1880s, Kelly met an Irish girl named Mary, and made her pregnant. His wife learned of this, and Kelly killed her in the course of a quarrel, as a result of which he was imprisoned in Liverpool – significantly, in the hospital wing. Meanwhile, Mary had gone to London and become a prostitute. Kelly escaped from Broadmoor on 28 January 1888, and went to London in search of her. He tracked her down as, according to Leonard Matters, "Dr Stanley" tracked down Mary Kelly, by questioning prostitutes and then murdering them. Finally, he killed Mary herself. Then he fled to America, where there were more "Ripper-style" murders. And in 1927, he finally returned to Broadmoor and surrendered, confessing that he had escaped thirty-nine years earlier. As already noted, he died there two years later. Morrison, who succeeded in unearthing documents relating to Kelly's original incarceration and escape, points out that he is an obvious suspect, and suggests some kind of conspiracy among the authorities at the time to prevent the public from becoming aware that a madman was at large. The weak link in the story is obviously the connection between Mary Kelly and John Kelly – there is no evidence that he ever knew her. And so one more interesting theory has to be dismissed as inadequately documented.

More convincing in many ways was the theory put forward by Bruce Paley and published in *True Crime* magazine for April 1982. Paley believed that the Ripper was Joseph Barnett, the man who had lived with Mary Kelly until a week before her death. He was a thirty-year-old Irishman who worked as a fish porter, and he had a bad stutter. He told Inspector Abberline that he and Mary had separated because he did not have enough money to give her, and she kept returning to prostitution. The trouble, he felt, was that she had so many friends who were prostitutes – she knew most of the Ripper victims – that it was a continual temptation to return to the streets.

Paley's belief that Barnett was the Ripper is based upon what might be called "the mystery of the missing key". The police had to break into the room in Miller's Court – it had been locked with a key. But the key had been missing for some time. Barnett explained that the door had to be bolted from the inside, by reaching in through the broken windowpane. So apparently the Ripper had a key, which argues that he was Joseph Barnett.

And why should Barnett kill five prostitutes? Paley's theory is that he was deeply in love with Mary, which may well be true, and wanted to scare her out of prostitution. The killing of Martha Turner in George Yard Buildings on 7 August (probably by a drunken soldier) may have given him the idea. Besides, the women who died were friends of Mary, and he probably blamed them for tempting her back on to the streets. On that last night, he may have watched Mary vanish into her room with her last customer, the man with the gold watch chain, and waited outside, mad with jealousy. And when the customer had gone, he went into the room and killed Mary with a ferocity that had been building up for many months.

An ingenious theory that deserves to be taken seriously. Yet it has one fatal flaw. From all accounts, Barnett was a mild little man, of what would now be called relatively low "dominance". Is it likely that such a man would murder and disembowel four women, merely in order to frighten the woman he loves into giving up prostitution? I personally find it hard to believe. Although if some new evidence should turn up proving that Barnett was a sadistic pervert, or a man given to fits of blind rage, I would certainly be ready to place Barnett at the head of my list of suspects.

In the year of the Ripper centenary, I was more than half convinced that the mystery had finally been solved by a Norwich accountant named Steward Hicks. Mr Hicks had first written to me some time in December 1985, telling me that he was at that time unwilling even to hint at the identity of his suspect. We kept in touch, and in June of the following year, he intimated that he had now written enough of his book to look for a publisher. He suggested coming down to see me, and was obviously not put off by the considerable distance between East Anglia and Cornwall.

The story he had to tell me was remarkable. He had become interested in the identity of Jack the Ripper after reading about Stowell's Duke of Clarence theory, which he at first found convincing. And after reading every available book on the subject, he decided to go to London and see if previous researchers had overlooked anything in the Public Record Office. One of the favourite theories was that the Ripper was interned in a lunatic asylum after the final murder, so Mr Hicks went to look at the Minutes of the Lunacy Commissioners in Chancery Lane. And almost immediately he stumbled upon an interesting clue. A man named J. Hewitt had written the Commissioners a letter from the Coton Hill Asylum in Staffordshire about 17 December 1888 (the date of the minute is 18 December), and the minute noted that he was a doctor. But a second look revealed that this doctor was, in fact, a patient in the asylum. Most early "Ripperologists" had assumed that the killer was a doctor. Moreover, the name Hewitt rang a bell. Mr Hicks's exhaustive reading had included Donald McCormick's *Identity of Jack the Ripper* (1959), which noted that Sir Osbert Sitwell had an interesting Ripper story to tell in a book called *Noble Essences*. Sitwell was a close friend of the painter Walter Sickert, and he told how, some time in 1889, Sickert took a room in Mornington Crescent, Camden Town. His landlady there was convinced that the previous occupant of the room had been Jack the Ripper. He had been a young veterinary surgeon, and in spite of poor health he had often stayed out all night. He had then paced his room, and rushed out to buy an early newspaper. On one occasion his landlady noted that he had burned his clothes in the grate. Although all London was talking about the Ripper murders, this young man had never even mentioned them. His health finally broke down in November 1888, and his widowed mother took him back to Bournemouth, where he died of consumption three months later. The name of this young man was John Hewitt.

Another author, Mr Hicks had forgotten which, had also told a story about Lady Anderson, wife of Sir Robert, who had stated at some point that Jack the Ripper was interned in an asylum near Stone. There is a Stone in Staffordshire, not far from the Coton Hill Asylum.

Could it be, wondered Mr Hicks, that Hewitt's mother, knowing her son's terrible secret, had committed him to the Coton Hill Asylum, and told his former landlady that he was dead? The first thing Mr Hicks did was to check with the Wellcome Foundation for the History of Medicine in Euston Square. If the "J" stood for James or Jeremy, then the doctor in the Coton Hill Asylum could not be Sickert's suspect. But the records showed that Hewitt's Christian name *was* John. Mr Hicks also learned that John Hewitt practised in Manchester, but that by 1892 he was living in Bournemouth, apparently in retirement – another link with the vet. Further research revealed that Hewitt had died at Kings Norton, in Staffordshire, on 27 February 1892, at the age of forty-two. Cause of death was General Paralysis of the Insane.

If it could be proved that Hewitt had been admitted to the asylum after 8 November 1888 – the date of the last murder – the notion that he was Jack the Ripper would begin to look rather plausible. From his local reference library, Mr Hicks learned more about the Coton Hill Asylum. Now, apparently, it was closed down. Further enquiry revealed that its records were now in the Stafford Public Asylum. In October 1983, Mr Hicks decided that he would pay the asylum a visit and see whether he might be allowed to see the records relating to Hewitt. In fact, a friendly nursing sister told him that there should be no problem. But in due course, he received a letter from the Mid-Staffordshire Management Committee telling him that patients' records were strictly confidential, and that since he was not a relative of the late Mr Hewitt, it would be impossible to allow him access to the file.

Yet the more he studied the case, the more he became convinced that Hewitt could be the Ripper. Some "Ripper letters", generally thought to be spurious, had been sent from Manchester. Hewitt had given up his practise in Manchester some time in 1888. He could have moved to London, to the Mornington Crescent address (where he told his landlady he was a veterinary student), and committed the murders, then been committed to the Coton Hill Asylum. Mr Hicks even discovered that Hewitt had married a nurse from the asylum, and moved with her to Bournemouth. She had died quite recently. What he now needed to know was simply whether Hewitt had been in the asylum before November 1888, in which case he was certainly not Jack the Ripper. This is the story that Steward Hicks told me on his visit to me in June 1986.

It seemed a pity that he should not be able to obtain such a simple item of information. I agreed to see what I could do to help. My first step was to write a letter to Sir Robert Mark, the ex-Commissioner of Police, whom I had known for some years, asking his advice. Mark's advice was to make a direct approach to the Staffordshire Health Authority and tell them the full story. Steward Hicks had been unwilling to do this unless he slammed the door on any further information, but when I told him about Mark's advice, he agreed that I should try it. I learned that the head of the Health Authority was Mr David Elliott, and I telephoned him on 7 August 1986 and explained the problem. He was kindly and helpful. It would be impossible, he explained, for him to hand over the information, since the Management Committee had already refused. But since Hewitt had been in the asylum as long ago as 1888, there seemed to be no good reason why the documents about him could not be released, under the Hundred Year Rule, in November 1988. I pointed out that that would be too late for the Ripper centenary – could he not possibly tell me whether Hewitt had been admitted to the hospital before or after November 1888? He pointed out that this would amount to revealing confidential information, but agreed to take a look at the records, and tell me if they indicated that Steward Hicks would be wasting his time by continuing to pursue his investigation.

A few days later I rang him again. I must admit that I felt a slight sinking of the heart as he told me that John Hewitt *had* been committed to the asylum before November 1888. "In other words, he couldn't possibly be Jack the Ripper?" There was a long pause, then Mr Elliott replied: "I wouldn't go that far". I was baffled. "But surely . . ." Then it dawned on me. "Are you saying that he was able to leave the asylum periodically?" There was another pause. "I am unable to confirm that. Let me just say this. Hewitt was a very badly disturbed man. And when you get access to the records, I think you will find something that will greatly interest you".

That was all he would say. But it was enough. If Hewitt had committed himself voluntarily, then there was no reason why he should not take trips to London whenever he felt inclined. And if the records indicated that the dates of his absences corresponded to the dates of Ripper murders, it would be virtually a proof that Hewitt was Jack the Ripper. I wrote and told Steward Hicks what I had discovered, and we agreed that there was nothing for it but patience.

It was two years later that I learned that all Steward Hicks's work had been wasted. When the papers were finally placed in the Public Records Office, they showed conclusively that the dates when Hewitt was absent from the asylum were not the dates of Ripper murders. It was totally impossible that John Hewitt could have been Jack the Ripper.

It was disappointing for me almost as much as for Mr Hicks. Yet in retrospect, I could see that we had both been unduly optimistic. The landlady in Mornington Crescent had said that her tenant was young – Hewitt would have been thirty-eight in 1888 – and that he was suffering from tuberculosis. Admittedly, anybody would have been unwilling to admit that he was actually suffering from syphilis, but the symptoms of tuberculosis can hardly be mistaken. If this discrepancy had struck Steward Hicks in 1983, he would have been spared a great deal of work. In spite of which, I am fairly certain that he has no regrets about his five years search for the identity of Jack the Ripper.

What are my own final conclusions about the Ripper's identity? They are mostly negative – I am more certain of who the Ripper was *not* than about who he was – but may nevertheless be worth stating.

The killer left no clues. But there is one piece of evidence that is less ambiguous than the rest: the letters sent to the Central News Agency, and to the head of the Whitechapel Vigilance Committee, George Lusk. The first letter, dated 25 September 1888 (seventeen days after the murder of the second victim, Annie Chapman), was signed "Jack the Ripper". The name caught the imagination of journalists, and from then on, this is how they referred to the Whitechapel killer. (Before that he was often referred to as Leather Apron, a man reputed to be a homicidal cobbler.)

The letter read:-

25 Sept. 1888

Dear Boss

I keep on hearing the police have caught me but they won't fix me just yet. I have laughed when they look so clever and talk about being on the right track. That joke about Leather apron gave me real fits. I am down on whores and I shant quit ripping them till I do get buckled. Grand work the last job was. I gave the lady no time to squeal. How can they catch me now. I love my work and want to start again. You will soon hear of me with my funny little games. I saved some of the proper red stuff in a ginger beer bottle over the last job to write with but it went thick like glue and I cant use it. Red ink is fit enough I hope ha. ha. The next job I do I shall clip the ladys ears off and send to the

police officers just for jolly wouldnt you. Keep this letter back till I do a bit more work, then give it out straight My knifes so nice and sharp I want to get to work right away if I get a chance. Good luck

yours truly
Jack the Ripper

Dont mind me giving the trade name

wasnt good enough to post this before I got all the red ink off my hands curse it No luck yet. They say I'm a doctor now. ha ha

The postcard sent on 30 September gave details of the double event before they were generally known.

The most convincingly genuine of the letters purportedly from the Ripper was sent with part of a human kidney to George Lusk, head of the Whitechapel Vigilance Committee.

A jeering letter, signed 'Jack the Ripper' and postmarked 29 October, was sent to Dr Openshaw, who had examined the kidney.

HANDWRITING SAMPLES

Jack the Ripper

25 September, the first 'Ripper' signature.

Jack the Ripper

30 September, details of the double event.

Catch me when you can Mishter Lusk

6 October, 'From hell' to Mr Lusk.

jack the ripper

29 October, 'Old boss' to Dr Openshaw.

> *Dear Boss,*
>
> *I keep on hearing the police have caught me but they won't fix me just yet. I have laughed when they look so clever and talk about being on the right track. That joke about Leather Apron gave me real fits. I am down on whores and I shan't quit ripping them till I do get buckled. Grand work the last job was. I gave the lady no time to squeal. How can they catch me now? I love my work and want to start again. You will soon hear of me with my funny little games. I saved some of the proper red stuff in a ginger beer bottle over the last job to write with but it went thick like glue and I can't use it. Red ink is fit enough I hope* ha ha. *The next job I do I shall clip the lady's ears off and send them to the police officers just for a jolly. Wouldn't you? Keep this letter till I do a bit more work, then give it out straight. My knife is nice and sharp I want to get to work right away if I get a chance. Good luck!*
>
> Yours truly
>
> JACK THE RIPPER
>
> *Don't mind me giving the trade name.*
> *Wasn't good enough to post this before I got all the red stuff off my hands curse it.*
> *No luck yet they say I am a doctor now* ha ha.

This letter may or may not be genuine; there *was* apparently an attempt to cut off the right ear of Elizabeth Stride and Catherine Eddowes; yet it should have been easy enough to do so, even though he was interrupted in the first case, and in a hurry to escape in the second.

The next letter is more convincing. It was posted to the Central News Agency early in the morning after the double murder, and read:

> *I was not codding dear old Boss when I gave you the tip. You'll hear about Saucy Jack's work tomorrow. Double event this time. Number one squealed a bit. Couldn't finish straight off. Had not time to get ears for police. Thanks for keeping last letter till I got to work again.*
>
> JACK THE RIPPER

It is arguable that the second letter is genuine, since the writer knew about the double murder almost immediately after it had taken place. (On the other hand, the news had probably spread all over Whitechapel within half an hour.) And since he knows about the first letter to the Central News Agency (which *had* been kept back) it looks as the same person wrote both letters.

The next letter was sent to George Lusk, head of the Vigilance Committee, on 16 October. It read:

> *Mr Lusk*
> *Sir I send you half the Kidne I took from one woman prasarved it for you tother piece I fried and ate it was very nise I may send you the bloody knif that took it out if you only wate a whil longer signed Catch me when you can Mr Lusk.*

A kidney *had* been taken from the body of Catherine Eddowes. And an examination of the half a kidney sent to Mr Lusk revealed that it was a "ginny" kidney, of the kind found in alcoholics, that it belonged to a woman of about forty-five, about the right age, and that it had been removed in the last three weeks.

In August 1968, there appeared in a magazine called *The Criminologist* an article called "A 'Ripper' Handwriting Analysis" by C.M. MacLeod. Charlotte MacLeod is a Canadian handwriting expert who had read an article containing reproductions of two Ripper letters in a previous issue. Her verdict on the Lusk letter is that it is almost certainly genuine. She draws attention to the "knife-edged or dagger-like strokes", evidence of nervous tension and aggression.

The second letter she analyses is one sent to Dr Openshaw of the London Hospital, who had analysed the "ginny" kidney. This read:

> *Old boss you was rite it was the left kidny I was going to hoperate agin close to your ospittle just as i was going to dror mi nife along of er bloomin throte them cusses of coppers spoilt the game but i guess i will be on the game soon and will send you another bit of innerds*
>
> *Jack the ripper*
> *O have you seen the devle with his mikerscope and scalpul a-lookin at a kidney with a slide cocked up.*

Charlotte MacLeod is of the opinion that the two letters were not written by the same person. She speaks of the "huge ornate capitals" of the first letter and the lack of capitals in the second.

The "J" of Jack is smaller than the "K". In the second letter "I" is written "i"; in the first it is a huge flourishing capital. This seems to mark a sense of inferiority; yet the small "r's" are enormous, sprawling things, and Ms MacLeod quotes a colleague as believing that this type of "r" invariably indicates a craving for attention. She summarises:-

"If there was only one real Jack the Ripper, I should cast my vote for the writer of sample 1. He shows tremendous drive in the vicious forward thrust of his overall writing, and great cunning in his covering up of strokes; that is, the retracing of one stroke of a letter over another, rendering it illegible while appearing to clarify . . . Whereas, although sample 1 appears to be written better than sample 2, it is in fact extremely difficult to decipher; whereas sample 2 except for the atrocious spelling, is fairly readable.

"I would say that this writer was capable of any atrocity, and of carrying it out in an organised way. I would say he had enough brains and control to hold down some steady job which would give him a cover up for his crimes. He has imagination, as revealed in the upper-zone flourishes. Those hooks on the t-bars, among other signs, indicate tenacity to achieve a goal.

"I would have looked for this killer among men such as cab-drivers, who had a legitimate excuse to be anywhere at any time. I should have sought a hail-fellow-well-met who liked to eat and drink; who might attract women of the class he preyed on by an overwhelming animal charm. I would say he was in fact a latent homosexual (suggested by the lower zone strokes of the 'y's' returning on the wrong side of the letter) and passed as a 'man's man', the roistering blade who made himself the life and soul of the pub and sneered at women as objects to be used and discarded.

"The writer of sample 2 may or may not have done any of the killings, but I would tend to think not. He certainly had the sadistic urge, but I question whether he had the drive and organisation to carry them through. I would rather believe that his extreme self-contempt coupled with his strong desire to be noticed would turn him into the sort of person who enters a police station demanding to be arrested for a crime he obviously cannot have committed. He could be the sort of toady who hangs around the flashy type". She goes on to suggest that the second writer could be a thief or pickpocket.

Unfortunately, Charlotte MacLeod says nothing of the first two Ripper letters sent to the Central News Agency, but it needs only a glance to see that their handwriting is far neater than in the "From Hell" letter. If Charlotte MacLeod is right in believing the writer of the Lusk letter to be Jack the Ripper, then we must probably dismiss the earlier ones as hoaxes.

But whether or not she is correct, she is at least examining evidence and drawing scientific deductions based upon her experience as a graphologist, not advancing "plausible" theories, like so many Ripperologists.

When, in 1988, I began to study serial killers for a history of forensic medicine called *Written in Blood*, I was struck by the fact that all serial killers so far have been working class. Further study of serial killers, for a book on them written with Donald Seaman, confirmed that observation. The serial killer is a man with an irrational grudge against society. He has often had a difficult or traumatic childhood, and is inclined to self-pity and resentment. If that analysis applies to Jack the Ripper – the first modern serial killer – then it rules out most of the candidates we have considered in this chapter, including Dr Stanley, the Duke of Clarence, J.K. Stephen, Frank Miles, Donston Stephenson, Dr Morgan Davies, Montague Druitt and John Hewitt. The Ripper could not have been an insane member of the upper or middle classes. He must be sought among the working class.

One of the letters received by Dan Farson after his television programme on the Ripper came from a seventy-seven-year-old man in Melbourne, Australia, and was signed G.W.B.

"When I was a nipper about 1889 I was playing in the streets about 9 pm when my mother called, 'Come in Georgie or JTR will get you'. That night a man patted me on the head and said, 'Don't worry Georgie. You would be the last person JTR would touch'." (This man was apparently the writer's own father.) "I could not remember the incident but it was brought to my mind many years later. My father was a terrible drunkard and night after night he would come home and kick my mother and us kids about something cruelly. About the year 1902 I was taught boxing and after feeling proficient to hold my own I threatened my father that if he laid a hand on my mother or brothers I would thrash him. He never did after that, but we lived in the same house and never spoke to each other. Later, I emigrated to Australia. I was booked to depart with three days' notice and my mother asked me to say goodbye to my father. It was then he told me his history and why he did these terrible murders, and advised me to change my name because he would confess before he died. Once settled in Melbourne I assumed another name. However my father died in 1912 and I was watching the papers carefully expecting a sensational announcement". But this never came; his father died without confessing.

In Melbourne, "Georgie" changed his name, but after the death of his father, changed it back again.

"Now to explain the cause of it all. He was born 1850 and married 1876 and his greatest wish was his first-born to be a girl, which came to pass. She turned out to be an imbecile. This made my father take to drink more heavily, and in the following years all boys arrived. During the confession of those awful murders, he explained he did not know what he was doing but his ambition was to get drunk and an urge to kill every prostitute that accosted him."

Georgie's father seems to have been a collector of horse manure. On one occasion, after killing a woman, he was wearing two pairs of trousers. He removed the bloodstained outer pair and buried them in the manure. Later, when he and his mate stopped at the Elephant and Castle, where they usually ate sausage and mash, his father told his mate he was not hungry, and would bury himself in the manure to keep warm. While he was hidden there he heard a policeman asking questions about Jack the Ripper, and was "scared to death".

This letter certainly sounds authentic, and it is hard to imagine why a seventy-seven-year-old man in Melbourne should take the trouble to write a long anonymous letter if it was not true—it could hardly be a craving for attention. (Presumably, in spite of the anonymity, it should not be too difficult to discover G.W.B's name by studying sailing lists of ships to Melbourne in 1902.) Assuming, then, that "Georgie" believed every word he wrote, is it not conceivable that his father invented the story about being Jack the Ripper simply to get a kind of revenge on his son after years of ignoring one another? This is obviously a possibility. Yet in all other ways, Georgie's father sounds like the kind of suspect who *could* be Jack the Ripper – a highly dominant type, a heavy drinker, a bully where his family was concerned (one of van Vogt's

"Right Men?"), and capable (as Charlotte MacLeod suggested) of holding down a job. Many serial killers and sadists have been heavy drinkers and have committed their acts of violence when drunk. If Georgie's father was not Jack the Ripper, then it is at least possible to state that he was the type of person who easily *could* have been. That is probably as far as we shall ever be able to go in solving the problem of the identity of the most notorious killer of all time.

10.
The Age
of Detection

WHAT SHOULD be quite clear by now is that up to 1800 or so, crime was purely a social problem, the outcome of poverty and man's animal nature. Throughout the Anglo-Saxon period, it was not a serious problem, no doubt because communities were smaller, and the death penalty was rare. Under King Ethelbert, in the seventh century, most crimes from fornication to murder were punished by fines. With the increase of cities, crime increased, and the punishment became more and more savage; that is to say, the authorities held the naïve idea that the answer to crime was punishment. This attitude had already begun to change by the time of Burke and Hare, otherwise Hare would not have escaped. (The police had a watertight case against the two of them without Hare's evidence, since they had the body). There was not a jury in England or Scotland that would not have been happy to hang Hare as well as Burke, Hunt as well as Thurtell.

I have cited the Lacenaire case to show how the new police of London and Paris began to recognise that the answer to crime was *organised* crime-fighting. And, very slowly, the methods became more sophisticated. In 1802, Thomas Wedgewood attempted to take the first photographs, utilising a discovery made in 1725, that silver salts darken when exposed to light. He succeeded in taking photographs, but as soon as they were exposed to daylight, they went dark. Nicéphore Niépce discovered that this could be prevented if the photograph was washed in nitric acid or ammonia immediately after it was taken, then the unaffected silver chloride was dissolved away, leaving only that which retained the photograph. He took his first successful picture from nature in 1826, the view out of his workshop window. The view shows sunlight on both sides of the courtyard because the plate had to be left exposed all day. It was a long time before photographs could be taken quickly enough to make it worth while for criminal investigation. In the early days of "mug shots", the criminal had to be held still by two or three brawny detectives while he was exposed to the camera for five minutes.

No doubt the preservation of the head of Catherine Hayes' husband deserves to rank as one of the first successful collaborations between the forces of science and the law. A century and a half later, photography made such gruesome experiments unnecessary. For example, on 8 November 1876, two children playing on the banks of the Seine noticed a bundle caught against some piles, and called passers-by to drag it to land. It contained the head and parts of the body of a woman. The head was photographed, and the photographs sold cheaply in the streets of Paris. One day, a man in a café recognised it as the wife of a soldier named Billoir. Billoir at first declared that his wife had left him, but a search of his room revealed bloodstains and some human hair. He now changed his story and asserted that his wife had died when he kicked her during a quarrel, and that he had decided to get rid of the body when he discovered she was dead. The doctors replied that was impossible. A corpse bleeds far less than a living body because the heart has stopped; the amount of blood proved that Mme Billoir had been stabbed to death. Moreover, there was no bruise on her. Billoir was guillotined. Here is a case that parallels that of Catherine Hayes in many respects, except that it cost the police far less trouble to bring home the crime to Billoir.

The man who took the first great step in scientific crime detection was Alphonse Bertillon, who took up his duties in 1879. But before speaking of Bertillon, let us examine a classical case of the pre-scientific era, a case that sounds as if it had been invented by Georges Simenon.

On 26 January 1869, a restaurant owner in the Rue Princesse, off the Boulevard St Germain in Paris, decided to investigate his well, the water of which tasted foul. He went into his basement and looked through a narrow window halfway down the well and a few feet above the surface of the water. There was a parcel floating in the water, and after some difficulty, the restaurateur fished it out. It contained the lower part of a leg. A young detective, Gustave Macé, was called, and he peered into the well. He saw another parcel floating below the surface. It proved to contain another leg, encased in part of a stocking. There was a laundry mark on the stocking, but this played less part in the investigation than it would in a modern case.

The legs were declared to be those of a woman and Macé went about his task in the same painstaking way that Canler had traced Lacenaire looking through the file of women missing during the past six months (eighty-four of them) and trying to trace them all. Weeks of work gradually eliminated them all. But Macé had discovered more clues. A human thighbone had been found in the nearby Rue Jacob. On 17 December another thigh, wrapped in an old shawl, was pulled out of the river. Two days later, a laundry proprietor had seen a man in a long coat scattering pieces of meat from a basket into the river. When questioned, the man explained that he was baiting the river for fish, because he intended to spend all the next day fishing. But after this, chunks of flesh were fished out of the river and from St Martin Canal, some of them fairly large. On 22 December a police officer had met a man wandering up the Rue de Seine with a parcel in one hand and a hamper in the other. They questioned him, in case he was a robber, but he explained that he had just arrived by train from Nantes, and had been unable to find a cab; he pointed to railway labels on the parcel to prove his story. The police thought he looked so honest they allowed him to go. But his description sounded very like that of the enthusiastic fisherman.

Macé had another clue. One of the parcels fished out of the well was sewn up in black glazed calico, and the stitches had a professional look. Macé was beginning to get a picture of the suspect – short plump, round-faced, with a black moustache, and a cheerful, confident manner – and almost certainly a tailor.

Meanwhile, the great Alexandre Tardieu, one of the first police pathologists, now near retirement, had examined the legs, and pronounced that they were a man's, not a woman's. All Macé's early weeks of labour had been wasted.

Why had the killer dumped the legs in a well, rather than in the Seine? Obviously, it must be someone who knew the house. Macé investigated the building that contained the restaurant. The concierge was old and inefficient, practically anybody could wander in and out. Macé got her to talk about former tenants, and asked if there had ever been a tailor in the house. No, she said, but there had been a tailoress. It sounded an unlikely lead, but the indefatigable Macé followed it up. For whom did the girl work? Various people, said the old lady. Other tailors used to pass on work to her. There was one in particular who caused her endless work; he used to spill water on the stairs. What water? asked Macé. Water from the well.

So there had been a tailor who knew about the well. Macé managed to trace the seamstress, who was now a café *chanteuse*. She obviously had nothing to hide. She told Macé that the man he was asking about was Pierre Voirbo. He had once been her lover, but now he was married and living in the Rue Mazarin.

Macé asked if Voirbo had any special friends. The girl named a certain Désiré Bodasse, an old man who often drank with Voirbo. She had no idea of his address, but she knew that his aunt lived in the Rue de Nesles.

Macé traced Mme Bodasse, and she told him that her nephew lived in the Rue Dauphine. He had not been seen for a month but that was not strange. He was like that. He had been a craftsman who manufactured tapestry; now he was retired. He was pathologically mean: on one occasion, he had vanished for six weeks, and it turned out that he had been ill in hospital, masquerading under another name so the hospital authorities could not trace him to get him to pay for his treatment.

They went to look at Bodasse's apartment. The concierge said she was certain he was in, she had seen a light behind the curtains the night before, but he would not answer the door. He liked to be left undisturbed, he was an eccentric kind of recluse.

Mme Bodasse came to look at the legs in the morgue, and declared that she recognised the stockings, as well as a scar on one of the legs. It was her nephew Désiré, beyond all doubt.

The more Macé heard of Pierre Voirbo, the less Macé liked the sound of him. He was a man of dissolute habits, and he was a police spy. He pretended to be a rabid anarchist, and made speeches at Left Wing meetings, while all the time he was reporting the activities of the comrades to the secret police.

Macé decided to break into Bodasse's apartment. Everything looked in order, although there was dust on the furniture. Someone had been in recently, for an eight-day clock was still ticking. But Bodasse's strong box was empty. In the back of a watch, Macé found a piece of paper with the numbers of various securities on it. The securities were nowhere to be found.

It seemed fairly certain that Voirbo returned periodically to the flat, to give the impression that Bodasse was still alive. Macé borrowed a couple of men from the secret police to watch the flat. This was a bad move. They knew Voirbo, and when he came to the flat, they accosted him openly and asked him what was going on. Macé's quarry was alerted.

Meanwhile, Macé discovered that Voirbo had changed his lodgings since he married. The landlord of his old lodging said that he had paid his rent before he left. How? With a five-hundred-franc share of Italian stock, which the proprietor had changed for him at the corner. It was the kind of security that could be cashed by the bearer. Macé hastened to the money-changer. He had kept the counterfoil of the share, and the number was one of those in the watch.

The cleaner of Voirbo's old room also had an interesting story. Voirbo was normally the untidiest and laziest man on earth. But on the morning of 17 December she had found his room not only tidied but scrubbed. He explained he had dropped a bottle of cleaning fluid on the floor, which made such a smell that he had cleaned out the whole place.

Macé knew he had no evidence. Even the matter of the stock could be easily accounted for – Voirbo would say it was a loan, or the payment of an account. Macé decided to see Voirbo himself. He was a plump young man of thirty, but the face and eyes revealed that he was a man of some resource and character. He acknowledged frankly that he had been rather worried about Bodasse's non-appearance, although he was aware that his old friend had peculiar habits. He behaved as if he was Macé's colleague rather than a suspect which, in a sense, was true enough. Macé had no alternative than to accept his offers of assistance, and hope that evidence would finally appear. He even attended a revolutionary meeting with Voirbo and heard the police spy make an inflammatory speech to his Republican colleagues.

Voirbo told Macé that he was fairly certain of the identity of the killer of Bodasse – it was an alcoholic butcher named Rifer. He was probably assisted by three criminal acquaintances, whom Voirbo also pointed out. Macé checked on them. Two of them had perfect alibis, in that they were in jail in the second part of December.

And Voirbo, with the calculation that was typical of him, now began encouraging Rifer to drink heavily, very heavily. There was nothing Macé could do about it. One night, Rifer had a fit of DTs, and smashed all his furniture, which he threw into the street. He was arrested, not over-gently, and taken to an asylum, where he died in the night.

The next morning, Macé arrived early at his office and found Voirbo already there. Macé decided to arrest him. But it was so early that he was there alone, and Voirbo was a formidable man. Macé excused himself, and said he had to answer a letter immediately. Then he sat down at his desk, and while Voirbo read a newspaper, wrote careful instructions to his subordinates to surround Voirbo and arrest him. He placed the letter in the outer office, then engaged Voirbo in conversation until his men came in and made the arrest.

Voirbo was calm and sardonic, he was sure Macé had no evidence. And of course he was right. He was thoroughly searched, and Macé realised he had made a wise decision; Voirbo had a ticket to Havre, and had intended to flee to America. The ticket was in the name of Saba. Was Voirbo's choice of the name of the great assassin accidental?

Voirbo would admit nothing. Macé went to his apartment and talked to his wife, a quiet girl, who had brought a dowry of 15,000 francs (about £600 at that time). She obviously knew nothing about her husband's activities. She allowed Macé to open the box which, she said, contained her dowry (in securities) and the 10,000 francs-worth of shares he had brought to the marriage. (This was the exact value of Bodasse's securities.) The box was empty. Macé proceeded to search the house, from attic to cellar. And it was in the cellar that he found what he was looking for – Bodasse's securities, soldered into a tin box, and suspended on a string inside a cask of wine.

Macé needed only one more proof to make his case watertight – that Voirbo had dismembered the old man in his old lodging at Rue Mazarin. A young couple had moved into the room, and Macé asked them to describe the arrangement of the furniture when they moved in. They did and it became clear that the only place in which the old man could have been struck down on the floor was a certain spot in the centre of the room, where a table had stood. If Bodasse had been killed there, then he had probably been dismembered on the table. The floor revealed no marks of blood; but Macé observed that it sloped slightly, and that the tiles under the bed had cracks between them. He decided to stage a grand denouement scene. Voirbo was brought to the room, perfectly calm. Macé took up a jug of water and said: "I am assuming that Bodasse was killed where I am standing. I shall now pour water on the floor, and try to get an idea of how the blood ran". Voirbo became noticeably nervous. He watched the water that flowed under the bed and formed a pool. A mason was called in to take up the tiles. He did so, and the undersides were found coated with a dark brown substance that was clearly blood. Voirbo's nerve broke, and he made a confession on the spot, which is worth quoting at length:

"Tell me who you really are" [said Macé].

"My real name is not Voirbo, but for the present I shall not tell you what it is; later on we will see. I am an illegitimate child, however, I know my father and must acknowledge that I am not proud of him. Everybody, including my wife, believes me to be an orphan, but my parents are still in existence. I see my mother occasionally; I help her more or less, for she is poor and old in years and, besides, the unfortunate woman worships me in spite of all my shortcomings. I likewise love her! My father is a bad man. When I was quite a child he was in the habit of beating me frequently and as I grew up he continued to do so brutally, and occasionally in his fits of anger he would shake his clenched fist at me saying: '*You – you shall perish by my hand!*' I trust you may never know the precise meaning of those terrible words. In the main my father was right enough, I was indeed a good-for-nothing fellow. Not wishing to die by his hand, I tried to kill him but, doubtless guessing my thoughts, he kept on his guard. I left the house, anger in my mind, hatred in my heart. Even now I still hate my father, as much as, and even more than, formerly, because of the suffering he subjected my poor mother to, and the harsh treatment he inflicted on me in my childhood. Perhaps he is the cause of my misfortunes."

"Does he bear the same name as yourself?"

"He does not. I told you I was a *bastard* – my father never acknowledged me. His only way of testifying to his paternity was by means of blows."

"Then tell me his name, since it is different from yours."

"I cannot do so, for you know him. You must have had something to do with him under very painful circumstances. I will recall him to your memory, but not now."

"What did you do when you left your parents' home?"

"I battled for life, in which everything is either chance or trickery – I did my best, and that unsuccessfully, to make up for bad luck by more or less fair means. I was an obscure personage, and I longed to shine; I was poor, and I worshipped wealth. My marriage with Mademoiselle Rémondé would have given me a modest competency, and perhaps, with such a good woman as she is, I might have taken to work again and atoned for my faults."

"Say rather your crimes."

"*Crimes*, you are right. Yet, I sometimes forget that I am a criminal, and like a great many scoundrels I was anxious to settle down and become an honest man. Some manage to succeed; I am acquainted with such men – as for me, I have failed. If that selfish old man, Désiré, had lent me the ten thousand francs I begged him to advance me I would never have killed him. I had told the Rémondés that I possessed that amount, so I had to produce it – my marriage was at that price. I begged and implored Bodasse, but nothing could move him; on the contrary he laughed at me, laughed at my matrimonial projects, and at every argument I brought forward. Then, well, I murdered him."

"At your own lodging!"

"As you have proved."

"How did you manage to entice him to your room?"

"On Monday 14 December, after leaving the baths and dining together at the restaurant in the Rue Grégoire-de-Tours, I invited him to take a cup of tea at my place. He followed me without the least mistrust. Besides, he was often in the habit of coming to my room, not, let me tell you, because he wanted to see me, but in the hope of meeting some of my work-girls. On the night in question, I told him that my betrothed was going to spend the evening there, with a relative and, in order to make him believe all the more that I had company, I left him for a few minutes while at the restaurant, and went and lit some candles in my room. I had also thrown open the shutters so that he might see the light from the street. My determination had been taken. No sooner was he in the room, when he asked me, as he sat down by the side of the table, why I had hoaxed him, since there was nobody there. I replied that my betrothed was coming. Then, passing behind him, and without his noticing it, I seized one of the flat irons standing on my work-table – that's the one, there – and without any argument, without saying a word, I dealt him, unawares, a terrific blow on the skull. Not a sound escaped him. His head sank on to the table, his arms hung down inert. I was astonished, and satisfied with my strength and skill.

"Then, blowing out the light, I opened the window and pulled the shutters to. In silence and darkness I listened to discover if he stirred. But I heard nothing, except his blood which fell on the floor, drop by drop! This monotonous drop, drop, drop, made my flesh creep. Still I kept on listening, listening. All of a sudden I heard a deep sigh, and something like a creaking of the chair. Désiré was moving, he was not dead! Suppose he were to cry out. This thought restored all my presence of mind to me. Lighting a small lamp, I saw that the body had moved sideways, he was then still living. He was certainly no longer in a condition to make himself heard, to call for help, but his death-agony might be spun out and I did not want to see him suffer a long while. I therefore took a razor, approached him from behind and placed my hand

under the chin of my ex-friend. Yielding to my pressure, the head
rose up and then fell backwards. The lamp was shining full on his
blood-smeared face. His round eyes were not yet lifeless – for a
moment they fastened on the blade of the razor I was holding
above him, and suddenly assumed such an expression of terror,
that my heart beat violently. It was necessary to put an end to
it. The same as a barber does when about to shave a customer,
I pressed the blade just below the Adam's apple, where the beard
commences, and with a vigorous sweep I drew the blade from left
to right. It entirely disappeared in the flesh, the head fell lifeless
on the back of the chair. My first gash had severed the carotid
artery and the larynx. A death rattle, and his last breath issued
from the wound I had made. A rush of blood spurted out, and
fell in part on a sugar-basin, which had been left uncovered on
the table.

"I now let the body slide gently to the floor and, fearing lest I
might be seen through the openings in the shutters and the muslin
curtains, I fastened a thick blanket before the window, which,
in my hurry to draw the shutters to, I had forgotten to close.
Returning to Bodasse's body, I examined it for a moment, and
saw that death had done its work! So as not to stain my clothes, I
took everything off with the exception of a pair of drawers and my
socks. Then, taking a sponge and wash-hand basin, I commenced
by wiping up the blood which had fallen in almost every direction.
I threw the discoloured sugar in the stove. Then, laying the corpse
on a board, I wholly undressed the upper part, cutting the clothes
away with my scissors. The lower portion of the trousers, which I
had separated some little distance above the knee, I threw back
over the legs. They were in my way, those two legs which became
the starting-point of your inquiry. I therefore detached them from
the thighs, hacking them off by means of that butcher's chopper
you found at my residence. But I did not chop like a butcher
would when cutting up a quarter of beef – I pressed the sharp
edge on the flesh, and then struck the back of the chopper with the
metal bobbin you have there – it does not make the least noise.

"The legs now being off, I put them in the trunk I kept in the
little closet. Oh, how heavy they were! Although the man was but
small in stature, and in spite of the absence of the legs, Désiré
struck me as still being much too big. I commenced cutting up

the body altogether, but the head, already half severed from the trunk, would not keep still. Every time the least motion was given to the bust it moved, swaying either to the right or to the left, and splashed my face with drops of blood.

"It was horrible! So I severed it completely from the body, and contemplated it for a moment as I held it in both hands. I can see it still. What a terrible *tête-à-tête*! On ceasing my inspection I placed it in a pan, with the face downwards, so that I might no longer see it.

"I then cut off the arms and completely flayed the bust. I thought that, once freed from the outer skin, the flesh, after a longer or shorter stay in the water, would be sure to be taken for the remains of some animal. And, in truth, it certainly did look like so much butcher's meat. After having opened the belly with a knife, the handle of which broke off during the operation, I removed the entrails, liver, lungs and heart to the water-closet close to the door of my room. In order to dispose of the body more easily I cut it up into small pieces, which I then packed in the same trunk as the legs. There being no door-keeper to the house I was enabled, without disturbing anyone, to get an unlimited supply of water, at the foot of the stairs, to scrub the room out with. What a quantity of blood there is in a human body! I thought I should never see the end of it. Oh! What a terrible winter's night I passed! I was red with perspiration yet I shivered with cold, my weary fingers were no longer able to handle the scissors I used for cutting."

"What did you do with Bodasse's clothes?"

"I burnt them in the stove, with my own, as well as the chair and board which were wet with blood. During the remainder of that night, as well as the whole of Tuesday, I never stirred from my room, but on the following night I carried the pieces of flesh out of the house and scattered them everywhere. I had soon only the legs left. Fearing lest they might be recognised, I had decided to drop them down the well of the house in the Rue Princesse. Having formerly visited a girl, named Gaupe, there, I was aware of the existence of the well, and knew also the secret of gaining admission to the premises. On the night of 21 December, after having tied these two limbs in wrappers that I was in the habit of using, and having pasted railway labels on them with the intention of showing, if I were surprised, that I had just come back from a journey, I went out, towards one in the morning, bearing my funeral burden which was carefully tied up.

"By way of extra precaution, and to make anyone I might meet believe that I was a belated traveller, I threw a rug over my shoulder and carried a basket, in which I placed various articles which I had shortly before received from Langres. I was going along full of anxiety, when all of a sudden police constables Ringué and Champy barred my way at the Carrefour de Buci. Knowing the rotation of their duty and the usual rounds of the force, I was certain that, at such an hour, I ought not to meet a single policeman on my way. Therefore I stood speechless on finding myself face to face with them. Never in the whole course of my life have I experienced such fear. But recovering, fortunately, my self-possession I was able to deceive them, and continue on my road.

"The very first time I called here I recognised those two officers and, as you rightly guessed, I did my best to avoid meeting them again. This encounter in the Carrefour de Buci had perplexed me and, whilst going in the direction of the Rue Princesse, I asked myself whether it would not be better to alter my plans and to throw the remains I was carrying into the Seine. Before entering the street, I again hesitated, but my evil genius urged me onward. I entered my former work-girl's dwelling without making the least noise, and once in the yard I was careful to see that no lights were burning in the windows. I removed the cover from the well and slipped my lugubrious bundle down it by means of a string I had rolled round it, and which gradually unwound. It disappeared in the water without the least noise. After having again made sure that nobody was watching me, I regained the street, and quietly returned to the Rue Mazarine, by way of the Carrefour de Buci, feeling sure I should not meet the same constables there. On getting back to my room, I looked in my glass and grew frightened at my own pallor. My interview with those two constables had curdled the blood in my veins. I was trembling with cold and yet in a perspiration, as at the time when I was cutting up Désiré's body. But the thought of the old man's ten thousand francs and of my betrothed gave me fresh courage. I went to bed and fell asleep as

I thought of them. That, Mr Commissary, is the true account of my crime."

"But what became of the head? You have not told me that."

"The head is safe enough. You will probably never find it, even if I tell you what I did with it. Had I only done the same with those confounded legs, I should now be quietly seated at the fireside, with my wife."

"Tell me, though, what did you do with the head?"

"As it was the part which could most easily be recognised, I poured lead into it by the ears and mouth. At two o'clock in the morning, I threw it into the middle of the Seine, from the top of the Pont de la Concorde. You may be quite sure that it will never rise to the surface. I melted the lead by means of that zinc worker's mould you have in your possession, and which a customer forgot at my place one day."

"That customer was probably a criminal of some kind or other?"

"If you like."

"An accomplice, maybe?"

"No, I alone conceived, prepared and executed the project of Bodasse's murder."

"But was your victim's death an absolute necessity?"

"Yes, since I was in want of ten thousand francs, and Désiré happened to possess that amount."

"You might have stolen it from him, that would have been bad enough; but after all, it would not have been a murder."

"No matter who might have stolen his hoard, he would always have suspected me."

"You are scarcely thirty years of age, and your life is already terribly burdened with crime."

"True enough, but I was determined to make myself a position at all costs. To effect this, I played against society at large, a bold game, of which my head was the stake. I have made every effort to save it and in spite of all my energy the game is lost, and quite lost this time."

Macé strongly suspected Voirbo of being involved in other murders. One of Voirbo's aliases was Saba, an agriculturalist of Aubervilliers, and he had all the necessary papers. There had been a murder at Aubervilliers, and Voirbo had the press cuttings about it. There was also a cutting about the murder of a servant girl in the Rue Placide in Aubervilliers. But before Macé could investigate these crimes, Voirbo succeeded in cutting his throat with a razor smuggled into jail in a loaf of bread. Before this, he had made a determined attempt to escape, but had been caught.

He had made only one mistake in a perfect murder – to sew the legs into the calico bags, which had given Macé his first clue. But for this, Macé would have been confronted with an insoluble crime. Voirbo would also have stood a fair chance of escape if he had continued to deny the murder after Macé's little "demonstration" in the Rue Mazarin; for in those days, there was no conclusive test for human blood. In his room, Voirbo had another press cutting about a double murderer called Avinain, a butcher, whose advice to posterity, delivered from the steps of the guillotine, was "Never confess". Voirbo should have remembered this.

In the 1870s, France was in ferment, and political turmoil always brings crime. If one considers the patient months that Macé spent solving the Voirbo case, and then remembers that Voirbo's murder was one of the two hundred or so in 1868, it can be seen that the old detective methods were becoming inadequate. Vidocq and Canler relied on their memory for criminal faces; in Macé's time, there were far too many faces. Even photography was inadequate for, obviously, an archive of one hundred thousand photographs is completely useless unless they are classified in a way that will enable the police to compare the description of a criminal with photographs that might match it. And how does one go about describing someone? Just as an experiment, try describing the face of someone sitting opposite you on a bus, as if you had to describe it for the police. Unless it is a fairly distinctive face, with a broken nose or completely bald head, there is very little to say. This was the Sûreté's problem.

When the twenty-five-year-old Alphonse Bertillon became a clerk at the Sûreté in 1879, most of the old identification procedures were practically useless. Bertillon was a dreary, pedantic young man whom most people found rather repellent, but he came from a cultured and scientific family, and the chaos irritated him. He was certain there *ought* to be some simple way of arranging the hundred thousand photographs and descriptions.

Bertillon's story would be ideal for Hollywood. He compared photographs of criminals to see if there was some way of classifying noses and faces. Then he thought it might be a good idea to take measurements of criminals when they were arrested – height, reach, circumference of head, height sitting down, length of left hand, left foot, left leg – Bertillon chose the left-hand side because it was unlikely to be affected by work. He was subject to constipation, stomach upsets, headaches and nose-bleeds, but he had a certain stubbornness that made him ignore the knowing smiles of colleagues. A doctor named Adolphe Quetelet had asserted that the chances of two people being exactly the same height are four-to-one. If that was so, and the same thing applied to the other statistics, then you needed only two or three measurements of each criminal to raise the odds to a hundred-to-one. When the prefect of police ignored Bertillon's letter about this method, Bertillon bought himself a set of filing cards, and started to work on his own, staying in the office until late at night. Macé revealed a lack of insight when he read Bertillon's report and said it was too theoretical. The prefect, Andrieux, told Bertillon to stop making a nuisance of himself. And three years went by before Bertillon could persuade a new prefect, Jean Camecasse, to give him an interview. Camecasse was as sceptical as his predecessor, but he was impressed by the clerk's persistence. He told Bertillon that they would introduce his method experimentally for three months. This was obviously absurd; it would take more than three months to build up a file, and a method like Bertillon's depended on accumulation. But with the great Macé himself opposed to the whole idea, he knew his only chance lay in working on and praying for luck. His card index swelled at the rate of a few hundred a month. But with more than twenty thousand criminals in Paris alone, the chances of identifying one of them was low. Towards the end of the third month, Bertillon had towards two thousand cards. Theoretically, his chance of identification was one-in-ten – fairly high. But it must be remembered that a large number of his criminals were sent to jail, often for years, so most of his file was lying fallow, so to speak.

On 20 February 1883, luck was with him. His system led him to identify a petty criminal who had been measured three months earlier. It was a very small triumph, but it was enough to make Camecasse decide to allow the experiment to continue. This was not far-sightedness. The post of prefect was a political appointment, Camecasse was hoping for fame. Unfortunately, a new prefect had been appointed by the time Bertillon became a celebrity, but history allows Camecasse the credit. As the file swelled, identification became more frequent. Before long, it averaged one a day. But what Bertillon needed was a really sensational case, something as newsworthy as Macé's pursuit of Voirbo. He had to wait until 1892 for it, but when it came, it spread his name all over the world. And the reason for the notoriety of the case was more or less accidental.

Since the early 1880s, a terrifying group of people known as the Anarchists became steadily more well known. People were not all that interested in their idealistic doctrine of the inherent goodness of human nature, which means that man does not need Authority to keep him virtuous. In 1881, Russian anarchists, they called themselves Narodniki, blew up Tsar Alexander II with a bomb. In Chicago, in May 1884, someone hurled a home-made bomb into a crowd of policemen who were about to break up a meeting of strikers, killing seven of them. Eight anarchists were condemned to death, one of them blew himself up with a bomb, and wrote in his own blood: "Long live Anarchy!" Four of the anarchists were eventually hanged. In France, anarchists like Malatesta, Grave and Reclus spoke darkly of the "propaganda of the deed", and the bourgeoisie shuddered. On May Day 1891, three anarchists were arrested for taking part in demonstrations at Clichy, and badly beaten up by the police. At their trial, the prosecuting attorney Bulot demanded the death penalty for all three, although no one had been killed in the riots. The judge, Benoist, acquitted one of them and gave the other two prison sentences of three and five years. In March the following year, 1892, a tremendous explosion shook the house in which Judge Benoist lived, destroying the stairway. Two weeks later, another explosion blew up Bulot's house in the Rue de Clichy. Luckily, no one was killed in either explosion. But the panic was tremendous. Large quantities of dynamite had been stolen from quarries at

Soiry, and the Parisians wondered where the next explosion would occur. A Left-Wing professor was arrested for the first explosion, and he agreed that he had planned it, however, a man named Ravachol had carried it out. Ravachol was known to the police, not as an anarchist, but as a burglar who was suspected of murder. He had killed an old miser and his housekeeper, two women who kept a hardware store, and an old miser who lived in a forest hut. He was also believed to have robbed the tomb of a countess to steal her jewellery. The alias of this forty-year-old criminal seemed to be Konigstein.

On the day of the Rue de Clichy dynamiting, Ravachol dined in the Restaurant Véry in the Boulevard Magenta, and tried to convert a waiter named Lhérot to anarchism. Two days later, he returned, and Lhérot noticed a scar on his thumb, which had been mentioned in descriptions of Ravachol. He notified the police, and the man was arrested.

Here was Bertillon's chance to prove his system to the world. Luckily, "Konigstein" had been briefly under arrest at St Etienne as a suspect in the murder of the old man, and the police there had taken his measurements before he managed to escape. Bertillon himself measured Ravachol, and the measurements corresponded exactly. The idealistic anarchist Ravachol was the murderous criminal Konigstein, and for the time being, at least, the anarchist movement was discredited. On the evening before Ravachol's trial, the Restaurant Véry was blown up by a bomb, which killed the proprietor and a customer – it was obviously retaliation for the arrest of Ravachol, and an attempt to intimidate the judges. It succeeded: Ravachol was only condemned to prison. But the judges of St Etienne were less scared of anarchist bombs. With Bertillon's proof in their hands, they were able to bring home the five murders to Ravachol, and he was executed on 10 July 1892. For the next few years Paris rocked with bombs – there was even one in the Chamber of Deputies – and President Carnot himself was assassinated. Bertillon luckily escaped the wrath of the anarchists.

But, absurdly enough, the method known as "Bertillonage", which had revolutionised almost every police force in the world, was already out of date by this time. In India in the 1860s, a civil servant named William Herschel had observed that no two fingerprints are ever alike. He put it to use in his job of paying off pensioned Indian soldiers. These men could seldom write, and they all looked alike to English eyes. And when they realised this, the pensioners began collecting their pensions twice, or returned and collected other people's pensions. When Herschel noticed that fingerprints were always different, he made them sign for their pensions by placing the index finger on an inked pad, and pressing it gently at the side of his name on the list. The swindling ceased. Some years later, a Scot named Henry Faulds made the same discovery, and wrote a letter to *Nature*, declaring that this might be a means of identifying criminals. The year was 1880, two years before Bertillon was allowed to start making his experiments in measurement. Faulds and Herschel were later to be involved in bitter disputes about priority, but these do not concern us here.

A disciple of Darwin, Sir Francis Galton, became interested in Bertillonage because he thought it would help in the study of problems of heredity. He became friendly with Bertillon, and this interest in police work led him to write to Herschel about his methods of fingerprinting; he had read the exchange of letters between Herschel and Faulds in *Nature*. Galton settled down to the study of fingerprints, and soon decided that there were only four basic classifications – the core of his method was the triangle, or "delta", in the centre of a fingerprint. In 1892, Galton's book *Fingerprints* came out. So in the year of his greatest triumph, Bertillon had become redundant. He refused to acknowledge it, for years he fought grimly for his system, betraying an unfortunate lack of the truly scientific spirit. But fingerprinting was bound to prevail in the end, it was so much simpler than Bertillonage.

The first murder ever to be solved by a fingerprint took place in Necochea, Argentina. A twenty-six-year-old woman named Francesca Rojas ran into the hut of a neighbour saying that her children had been murdered. The two children, aged four and six, lay dead in bed, their heads beaten in. She accused a man named Velasquez, who was in love with her. She wanted to marry another man, and she claimed that Velasquez had threatened to kill "what she loved most". She had returned from work to find the children dead.

Velasquez was arrested and badly beaten, but he denied the murders, while agreeing to the threat. The police methods in Necochea were primitive: they tortured Velasquez for a week, without result, then the police chief tried making moaning noises outside the woman's hut, hoping to frighten her into confession by pretending to be a ghost.

A police inspector named Alvarez went out to investigate from La Plata. And he knew something about the work of a Dalmatian named Juan Vucetich, head of the Statistical Bureau of Police in Buenos Aires, who had developed his own fingerprint system after reading an article by Galton. Alvarez went into the woman's hut and searched for clues. All he could find was a bloody thumb-print on a door. Alvarez sawed off the portion of the door and took it back to headquarters. Then he sent for Francesca Rojas, and made her give her thumb-print. Alvarez knew very little about classification, but it was quite obvious that the two prints were identical. When he showed the woman the two prints through a magnifying glass, she broke down and confessed – she had murdered her own two children because she wanted to marry a young lover who objected to them. This Argentine Lady Macbeth, who tried to rid herself of illegitimate children and an unwanted lover with one blow, obviously deserves to stand very high on a list of the world's worst women.

In England, Major Arthur Griffiths and Sir Melville Macnaghten were both on a panel whose task was to consider the comparative merits of fingerprinting and Bertillonage. Sir Francis Galton had still not completed his system of classification, and the British had made a typical compromise involving both systems. And then another British civil servant, Edward Richard Henry, solved the problem that was baffling Galton. Henry had some experience of Herschel's old system in India. Henry worked in Bengal, and became increasingly dissatisfied with the system of Bertillonage, even though the file cards also contained fingerprints. Bertillon's system depended upon a fanatical accuracy in taking the various measurements, and the Indian police lacked the fanaticism. Henry visited Galton's laboratory in 1899 and examined his findings. And it was Henry who finally invented the classification that Galton had been seeking for so many years. A straight line drawn across the delta would cross various ridges, which could be counted. He also distinguished five types of arches or whorls, and assigned them letters. A combination of these numbers and letters gave a formula through which a fingerprint could be quickly located from thousands of others.

Henry's methods were triumphant in India. When his book *Classification and Uses of Fingerprints* came out in England in 1900, he was appointed to sit on a committee in London to decide whether Bertillonage should be dropped altogether. It was. The British police were the first in the world to adopt the new system completely. He was also made Assistant Commissioner of the CID. His enthusiasm soon had a fingerprint department at Scotland Yard working as smoothly as it had at Calcutta. The method first proved its value on Derby Day, 1902. Criminals arrested for various offences at the Derby – picking pockets and so on – were dealt with quickly in court the next morning, and since there was no time to investigate their records, they got off with minimum penalties. Sir Melville Macnaghten decided it was time to stop this. He had the fingerprints of fifty-six men arrested on Derby Day sent to the Yard. Let him tell the rest of the story in his own words:

"The first prisoner on this occasion gave his name as Green of Gloucester, and assured the interrogating magistrate that he had never been in trouble before, and that a racecourse was, up to this time, an unknown world to him. But up jumped the Chief Inspector, in answer to a question as to whether 'anything was known', and begged their worships to look at the papers and photographs, which proved the innocent to be Benjamin Brown of Birmingham, with some ten convictions to his discredit. 'Bless the fingerprints', said Benjamin with an oath, 'I knew they'd do me in'!"

Twenty-nine of the fifty-four were found to be old offenders, and received sentences twice as long as would otherwise have been awarded.

The first Englishman whose murderer was brought to justice by a fingerprint was the manager of a tea plantation at Jalpaiguri, in Bengal. In August 1897, he was found dead in bed, his throat cut. All the servants had fled, so had the man's Indian mistress. In the dead man's wallet there was a calendar with a right-hand thumb-print in blood. Police enquiries revealed that, two years before, the manager had had his servant, a man named Charan, arrested for some theft, and Charan had sworn vengeance. Charan's prints were, of course, in the file, and it was found that the bloody thumb-print was his. But the court did not feel like imposing a death sentence on the evidence of a thumb-print – Charan was sentenced for the robbery, but not the murder.

The first English murder case involving fingerprints took place in Deptford in 1905. At 7.15 am on 27 March of that year, a passing milkman saw two men emerge from a shop at 34 High Street, Deptford, and slam the door behind them. It was a paint shop, and the manager, an elderly man called Farrow, ran the shop with his wife.

At half past eight, the shop boy arrived and found the place closed up; he went to fetch the shop's owner, and they forced a kitchen window. Farrow was found dead on the ground floor, his head battered in; his wife was found dead in bed. What had happened was clear enough. The two men had broken into the shop and Mr Farrow had heard the noise and hurried downstairs, where he was beaten over the head with jemmies and left for dead. The men went upstairs and killed his wife in the same way. They found the cash box under her husband's pillow and emptied it. Farrow was not dead. After the men left the shop he staggered to the door and looked outside, where he was seen by a little girl who thought nothing of a bloodstained man. Then he locked the shop door and died.

The police were on the scene by 9.30, and soon found a thumb-print inside the cash box. It was photographed and enlarged. The police now checked on local criminals, and discovered that two brothers named Stratton were missing from their usual haunts. They were known as a violent and brutal pair, who had been in the hands of the police several times. They were picked up later in the week and fingerprinted. The thumb-print in the cash box was identical with that of the elder brother, Alfred. The police had no other evidence against them, since the milkman had been unable to identify them. Sergeant Collins, the fingerprint expert, would be the most important prosecution witness.

It was obviously an important case, and the future of finger-printing might stand or fall by it, for a few years at least. Neither the judge, an elderly gentleman named Channell, nor the jury knew anything about fingerprints. The defence decided to take no chances, and called two of their own fingerprint experts. One of these was none other than Henry Faulds, the Scot who had discovered fingerprinting and declared that it should be used for police work. Through an unfortunate accident, he had never received the credit that was his due. When Sir Francis Galton had written to ask *Nature* for the addresses of the two men who had been conducting a correspondence about fingerprinting, the editor accidentally sent him only the address of Herschel. Herschel, like Galton, was a generous and disinterested sort of person, who immediately handed Galton all his results, with the consequence that Galton never had reason to consult Faulds. But Faulds, unfortunately, was an obsessive egoist who wanted credit for his discovery. (It will be remembered that Herschel actually discovered fingerprinting first, but Faulds was the first to publish the discovery.) For years, Faulds fought a violent battle to gain recognition. The British felt this was rather unsporting and ignored him. So now Faulds decided to make himself felt by opposing the Crown case. The other "expert" was yet another disappointed egoist, Dr Garson, who had first sneered at fingerprinting (he was a champion of Bertillonage), then decided to change horses, and invented his own system. And it was Garson's appetite for recognition that swung the case against the Strattons. Sergeant Collins gave a lecture on fingerprints and drew sketches on a blackboard. Garson and Faulds made no attempt to deny that no two fingerprints are ever alike, but they *did* assert that the print on the cash box was not identical with the print of Alfred Stratton's thumb. To the judge and jury, all fingerprints looked alike, and they were inclined to credit the assertion that the two prints were not really identical. Collins replied that the discrepancies were the kind that are bound to occur when fingerprints are taken, because lines will look thicker or thinner according to the pressure applied and the angle at which the finger is pressed on to the paper. He demonstrated this convincingly by taking fingerprints of the jury on the spot, and showing exactly the same discrepancies. But the seeds of doubt had been sown. The prosecutor now played his trump card. Garson was called back to the stand, and was asked whether it was not true that he had written a letter offering to testify for the prosecution? Yet he was now testifying for the defence. Clearly, this was a man who would change his opinions for the sake of being an important witness in an important trial. The judge remarked that he was obviously untrustworthy. And the last hope of the Stratton brothers vanished. They were found guilty, and both of them proceeded to shout abuse at the court, dissipating the impression of wronged innocence they had been aiming for. The judge sentenced them to death. England's first fingerprint murder had established that a fingerprint alone is enough to hang a man.

Sir Melville Macnaghten has a gruesome little story to tell of another fingerprint case. In 1911, a policeman in Clerkenwell noticed a finger stuck on a spike on top of a gate to a warehouse yard. A man had obviously been climbing over the gate when he had slipped and fallen backwards into the yard. A ring on his finger caught on a spike, and its top drove into the finger, so the man was left hanging, until his struggles tore the finger off his hand. The finger was taken to the Yard and identified as belonging to a thief who proved to be missing from his haunts. A few weeks later, a policeman who arrested a suspected pickpocket observed the bandage on his right hand. The man's finger proved to be missing, and the constable recalled the story of the finger from Clerkenwell. The man was accused of attempted robbery, and convicted on the purely circumstantial but very damning evidence. He received a year in prison.

It was fingerprinting that revolutionised crime-fighting, but other discoveries were of equal importance. I have already mentioned the case of the sex murderer Tessnov, who was convicted when stains on his clothes were proved to be of human blood. The story of how this came about is almost as interesting as the story of fingerprints, although it will have to be dealt with more briefly. When blood is left exposed to the air, it slowly separates into two parts: a colourless liquid known as serum, and a thick, brown substance, which consists of blood cells. The serum part of the blood has amazing properties. If, for example, a human being is bitten by a snake, the serum immediately proceeds to develop the chemicals necessary to neutralise the poison, and if the dose of poison is not too great, it will be destroyed by this defence system of the body. In the 1890s, a doctor named von Behring took one of the greatest strides forward in the history of medicine when he discovered that if horses are injected with dead diphtheria germs, their serum can be injected into children suffering from diphtheria, and will destroy the germs. Snake-bite serum obviously works on the same principle.

Blood serum can be made to develop defensive properties against many other substances besides diphtheria germs and snake venom: against quite harmless substances like milk, egg-white and other kinds of blood. In these cases, the serum of the blood attacks the protein in the alien substance and causes it to turn into a harmless, insoluble substance. In 1900, Paul Uhlenhuth obtained serum from rabbits that had been injected with egg-white. If he then took a tiny drop of egg-white, and introduced it into a test tube of the clear serum, the serum immediately turned milky. So obviously, if a murder case ever hinged on whether a certain stain on a man's clothes was egg-white or sperm, it could be tested easily and quickly. For it did not seem to matter how old a stain was, the serum would react just as definitely. Moreover, serum made by injecting goat's milk would not turn cloudy if cow's milk was introduced into it, and conversely, serum made from cow's milk would not react to goat's milk.

The next step was obvious. If serum was made by injecting rabbits with human blood, it would react by precipitating the protein of human blood, but not of animal blood. So testing a bloodstain became very simple. The bloodstain was left in salty water to dissolve the blood, then a drop of this salty water was poured into serum that reacted to human blood. If the bloodstain was animal blood, the serum remained clear, if it was human, it immediately darkened.

The case that gave wide publicity to the new method of detecting human bloodstains took place in Berlin in 1904. On 11 June of that year, a boatman on the River Spree fished a paper parcel out of the river, and found in it the headless torso of a

young girl, still clad in petticoat and child's bloomers. Medical
examination quickly revealed that the child had been raped. She
was soon identified as nine-year-old Lucie Berlin, who lived at
130 Ackerstrasse, a gloomy lodging house for slum families.
Lucie had last been seen at about 1 o'clock on 9 June, when
she had asked for the key to the lavatory, which was up two
flights of stairs – it was kept locked for the use of tenants only.
But it seemed she had never reached the lavatory. By evening,
her parents decided to notify the police. The problem was that
Lucie had been repeatedly warned never to go off with strange
men – child rape was fairly frequent. This made the police suspect
that she had never left the house, even though neighbours spoke
of seeing her walk off with a man wearing a straw hat. A prostitute
who lived on the floor above Lucie's parents was among those
questioned, but it was obvious that she knew nothing of the
murder, for she had just returned from three days in jail for
insulting a client. Her name was Johanna Liebetruth. The man
in the room with her identified himself as Theodore Berger, of
another address. But the police began to wonder about Berger
when it was discovered that he actually lived with Johanna as her
pimp. He had been avoiding marrying her for eighteen years, but
now proposed to do so very shortly. Why? And on the morning
the body was discovered in the river, a man fitting Berger's
description was seen near the river with a rectangular parcel.

Lucie Berlin's head and arms had now been found in the river,
and Berger was taken to see them. But he persisted in denying
that he knew anything about her death. Johanna was questioned
for hours until she finally told an interesting story. She had
returned from jail on the morning of the 11th and heard about
Lucie's disappearance. She noticed that a certain wicker suitcase
was missing, and became convinced that Berger had slept with
another woman. Berger finally admitted that he had, and that
he had given her the suitcase because he had no money to pay
her. This story struck Johanna as likely enough. When Berger
wanted sex, "he was like a bull". He might well have taken a
woman back to his room, driven by the need for sex, and then
admitted that he had no money afterwards. Johanna was furious
nevertheless, and it was at this point that Berger placated her with
the promise of marriage.

When Berger was asked if he knew the suitcase, he quickly denied it. This was odd, he had been with Johanna for eighteen years, he *must* have seen it. It looked as if the suitcase was the clue that they were still seeking. If there had been blood in the apartment, it had been scrubbed away immediately after the murder.

An alert was put out for the wicker suitcase. And on 27 June, it turned up: a bargeman who never read newspapers had found it, and he knew nothing of its value until his aunt mentioned it in a conversation about the murder.

The suitcase was the evidence they needed. Johanna definitely identified it as hers. And stains inside it were proved to be of human blood. What had happened was pieced together at the trial. Lucie Berlin knew Theodore Berger well and called him "uncle". Berger was occasionally in the apartment of Lucie's parents, and Lucie sometimes came into Johanna's. Johanna mentioned in the course of conversation that on the day before she went into jail, Lucie had been playing with Berger's dog on the floor of the kitchen, and at one point had lain on her back with her legs up in the air. Johanna had noticed that they were very full and shapely legs for a girl of nine. Berger had no doubt made the same observation. Two days later, deprived of the sex that he needed very frequently, he noticed Lucie on her way upstairs to the lavatory. There was also an old lady, who was walking downstairs, and she recollected Berger standing and staring at her until she went out of sight. Berger invited Lucie into the room; she knew him and trusted him. But when he began to caress her, she became alarmed and struggled. Berger seized her by the throat, choking off her scream, and assaulted her. Later, he carefully dismembered the body on newspapers, and wrapped up the parts, which he took down to the river in the early morning.

Berger was still protesting his innocence when he was sentenced to life imprisonment.

The ability to distinguish human from animal blood was a great advance. Another followed almost immediately. Not only would the serum distinguish between the blood of a man and the blood of a sheep, it would also distinguish between various types of human blood. Something of the sort had been guessed by Dr

Theodor Billroth thirty years before, when he tried giving blood transfusions: 146 people out of 263 died, and Billroth reasoned that this must be because all human blood is not exactly alike. A great deal of investigation finally revealed that blood seems to have three distinct types or groups, which were labelled A, B and O, and that there is a "typeless" group, called AB.

One of the first important criminal investigations to make use of this new discovery took place in the north German industrial town of Gladbeck in 1928, and it concerned a strange sex crime. In the early hours of 23 March, cries were heard from in front of 11 Schultenstrasse, and a few hours later a nineteen-year-old youth, Helmuth Daube, was found dying in his own blood. His throat had been cut, and for a few hours, a theory of suicide was held, until a detective pointed out that the razor or knife was missing, and that the youth's genitals had been cut off. Daube lived in the house near which he was found, and the police had little difficulty finding the youth with whom he had spent the previous evening, Karl Hussmann, a year older than Daube. Hussmann was hurried to the scene of the crime, and a police officer noticed that his shoes were soaked, as if they had been washed, and were also bloodstained. Certain of Hussmann's clothes were also found to be bloodstained. His story to account for the stains on the shoes was that he had trapped a cat that had been chasing birds, and had killed it. Later, he also insisted that he had come across a frog on his way home, after saying goodnight to Daube in front of the latter's house, and had torn it to pieces.

Research into his background revealed that he was a homosexual with strong sadistic tendencies. He had met Daube two years before. Daube was passive, feminine, rather dreamy; Hussmann was dominant and given to violence. It seems likely that he first forced his homosexual attentions on Daube on a school hiking expedition. When Daube fell in love with a girl, Hussmann was furiously jealous, but the affair broke up, and the old relation between Daube and Hussmann was resumed. But Daube wanted to break away. Schoolfriends testified to seeing Hussmann hurting Daube, once by bending back his finger to force Daube to sit on his knee. The night before the murder, a group of students had met to discuss another hiking party, and Daube had indicated that he did not mean to go. What had then happened was fairly clear. Hussmann had tried to force his will on Daube; the thought that the youth whom he regarded as his property was about to break with him excited a murderous jealousy. As Daube turned away from saying goodnight, Hussmann seized him from behind and cut his throat. He then emasculated him. The back of Daube's head had struck Hussmann's nose, causing a nosebleed, but this did not become apparent until later.

Preliminary tests revealed that the blood on the shoes and coat was human blood, not from a frog or cat. Hussmann was unconcerned; he said he had had a nosebleed, and that they could not prove otherwise. The detective in charge of the case was inclined to be overawed by Hussmann, whom he regarded as being socially superior to himself.

A week after the murder, the clothes were sent to Viktor Müller-Hesse, in charge of the Forensic Laboratory at Bonn University. Although the earlier examination had destroyed many of the bloodstains, Müller-Hesse had no difficulty in proving that the bloodstains on Hussmann's jacket were Type O, Hussmann's own type, while those on the shoes were of Type A, Daube's group.

The evidence was complete; it should have hanged Hussmann. But the jury were not quite convinced by all this talk of blood groups. They ended by deciding that although they were by no means convinced of Hussmann's innocence, they were not absolutely certain of his guilt. Hussmann was acquitted. Even so, the case drew universal attention to the importance of blood groups in criminal investigation.

It is true that if Hussmann and Daube had belonged to the same blood group, the case would never have reached court. It is only as recently as 1966 that two young biologists in England, Margaret Pereira and Brian Culliford, have discovered what might be termed "the blood fingerprint" – that every individual's blood is as unique in character as their fingertips. The protein in blood has characteristics that are never the same in any two individuals. In the future, a spot of blood at the scene of a crime will be as important as a fingerprint. This work was a development of work done on blood groups by Robin Coomb of Cambridge and Barbara Dodd of London University, whose methods of finding the blood group of an old bloodstain were successful on the vest worn by King Charles I at his execution. In the future, a spot of blood the size of a pinhead will be able to prove innocence or guilt.

It is tempting to speculate how many of the great mysteries of the past might have been solved if the police had been able to use modern methods. The Ripper murders would fairly certainly remain unsolved; in the few parallel modern cases I can think of (I shall speak of them in a later chapter) the murderer has either remained uncaught, or was caught by chance. But some of the domestic mysteries, the Bravo case, for example, would almost certainly not remain mysteries – a fingerprint on a bottle would have been enough. One of the great Victorian *causes célèbres*, the Pook case, would have been solved within hours if there had been tests for human blood in 1871. The victim, a servant girl named Jane Clouson, was found lying in a lovers' lane at Eltham, south London, her face and head horribly lacerated. She died shortly afterwards without speaking. The constable found a lathing hammer near the scene of the crime – a cross between a hammer and a chopper. This had made more than a dozen wounds, through one of which the girl's brain was protruding. It was discovered that she was two months pregnant. The young man who was believed to be responsible was Edmund Pook, the son of a Greenwich printer, in whose house Jane Clouson had been a servant for two years. Shortly before her seventeenth birthday, the girl had been dismissed through the agency of Pook's mother, who felt the girl was too familiar with her son.

Edmund Pook proved to be a spoiled, swaggering, altogether unpleasant young man. He flatly denied any intimacy with Jane Clouson, and said she was dirty. But he was unable to explain bloodstains on the cuff of his shirt, or on his clothes.

Fifty years later, it would have been a simple matter to test his later assertion that the blood was his own – he was subject to epileptic fits and nosebleeds. It is possible, of course, that his blood and Jane Clouson's were of the same group, but then, he certainly left fingerprints on the hammer. As it was, all the evidence was against Pook. The shopkeeper from whom he bought the hammer identified him. He had no alibi for the evening of the crime. Jane Clouson had told her landlady that she was going out to meet "her Edmund" shortly before the murder, and she told a cousin at length of how Edmund wanted her to run away with him and marry him secretly, and then promise not to communicate with relatives or friends for several months. The same cousin also stated that Jane had received a letter, which she immediately burnt, after telling her cousin that she meant to meet Edmund shortly. It seems fairly plain that the letter contained instructions to burn it. This also explains why, when the police inspector asked him if he had written Jane a letter, Edmund told him arrogantly that if he thought so, he had better produce the letter and prove it was in his handwriting. He knew it had been burned, and it was no doubt the first question he asked the girl when he met her.

Pook was acquitted, largely because so much confusion surrounded the case, and his solicitor, Henry Pook (no relative), managed to throw up even more dust. Every possible contradiction of witnesses was endlessly pursued, and evidence of police incompetency was made to sound at least as shocking as the crime itself. When the prosecution pointed out that a hair that matched Jane Clouson's was found on Edmund Pook's trousers, his solicitor leapt to his feet to say that if that was all the evidence they could present, then the case against Edmund was hanging by a single hair. Today, it would be possible to state definitely whether the hair belonged to Jane Clouson or not. And there are few writers on the case who feel any doubt about it.

I am inclined to doubt whether modern forensic methods would throw any light on the classic American murder mystery, the Lizzie Borden case. However, modern research has now thrown so much light on the case that it may be regarded as solved.

At 11.15, on the morning of 4 August 1892, the hottest day of the year, Lizzie Borden called the maid Bridget Sullivan and told her that someone had killed her father. The seventy-year-old banker was found on the divan in the parlour, his face unrecognisable; someone had struck him several blows with a hatchet. Borden's second wife, Abby, was believed to be out visiting a sick friend, according to Lizzie, but she was later found upstairs in the guest room, lying face downwards. She had also been killed with blows from a hatchet, much heavier, more savage blows than those that had killed Andrew Borden. Lizzie's story was that she had been out in the barn, and had heard a cry from the house. She rushed back to find her father dead.

It soon became clear that Lizzie had much to hide. Her mother had died when she was two; two years later her father remarried. Abby Gray was six years his junior, twenty-two years older than Lizzie's sister Emma. Two days before the murder, Lizzie had tried to buy prussic acid. Lizzie's father and stepmother had been experiencing stomach pains for some time before the murder. Lizzie hated her stepmother.

Moreover, medical evidence proved that Abby Borden had died shortly after 9 am, while her husband was not killed until about two hours later. It was just within the bounds of possibility that an unknown assassin had entered the house and murdered the couple, but not that he had remained concealed for two hours, in a small house in which there were two women. (Lizzie's sister was away staying with friends.)

Lizzie was arrested and tried. The evidence against her was purely circumstantial; the prosecution merely attempted to demonstrate that she was the likeliest person to have committed the murders. But she was a respectable girl of unblemished reputation, and the jury found her not guilty. She lived on until 1927. During her lifetime it was impossible for writers to speculate about whether she killed her father and stepmother. But after her death, Edmund Pearson lost no time in publishing his opinion that she was the killer. (Even during her lifetime, the local newspaper in Fall River, Massachusetts, printed sarcastic articles on the anniversary of the murder, one of which concluded that the Bordens had not been murdered at all, but had died of the heat.) His *Trial of Lizzie Borden* in the Great American Trial series came out in 1937, and the book is dedicated to the district attorney who built up the case against Lizzie Borden. In 1959, a new piece of evidence turned up. In a book called *Murder and Mutiny*, published in 1959, E.R. Snow tells how he received a letter from an elderly gentleman named Thomas Owens, who had listened to a broadcast about the Borden case by Snow. Owens had a strange story to tell. In 1896, four years after the murder, Lizzie Borden went into the art gallery and shop of Tilden-Thurber in Providence, Rhode Island, and when she left, the assistant found that two expensive paintings on porcelain were missing. The following February, a lady went into the shop with one of the two paintings, and asked if a crack could be repaired. The manager was told, and he asked the lady where she had obtained the painting. "From Miss Lizzie Borden of Fall River." As a result of this, a headline "Lizzie Again" appeared in the *Providence Journal*, which stated that a warrant for her arrest had been issued for the theft of two paintings. What had happened, said Owens, was that the owners of the gallery had put a proposition to Lizzie: sign a confession to the murders, or we prosecute. Lizzie refused, and the item was published in the newspaper. This caused Lizzie to change her mind. After promises that the confession would not be used, Lizzie typed on a sheet of paper: "Unfair means force my signature here admitting the act of August 4, 1892, as mine alone, Lizbeth A. Borden". The store decided to have the document photographed in case of accident, and Owens was asked to do it. He did, but he also made a second copy, or, he said, decided that the first copy was indistinct, and made another one for the store, without mentioning that he had the other. As the four principals in the episode died – there were two other men besides the store owners – he expected it to be publicised. And now, Owens was willing to sell the photograph of Lizzie's confessions for one hundred dollars. Snow persuaded him to take fifty and printed the story in his book.

Another crime writer, Edward Radin, decided to look into the matter, and he soon established that Snow had been the victim of a swindler. It was Lizzie's signature, and the type face was that of a machine of the period, but the signature had been traced from Lizzie's will. It would be interesting to know whether Mr Snow demanded his fifty dollars back.

But obviously, the first part of the story was true. Lizzie *had* stolen the paintings, and the item really appeared in the *Providence Journal* in February 1897. Lizzie was a kleptomaniac. Although she had plenty of money (she left over a million dollars), she was a compulsive stealer. Oddly enough, she was also capable of great generosity.

Radin's book *Lizzie Borden, The Untold Story* asserts that Lizzie was innocent. The killer was Bridget Sullivan, the servant girl. It is known that Bridget was feeling ill on the morning of 4 August; yet Mrs Borden had her cleaning all the outside windows at 7.30 in the morning. Later that morning, Bridget vomited. Certainly, she had a motive of sorts – sheer resentment at her employer. Radin tells how he was completely convinced by Pearson's view of the case until he read the actual trial reports for himself and discovered that Pearson had suppressed many pieces of evidence in Lizzie's favour.

In 1964, Gerald Gross edited a volume of selections from Edmund Pearson's articles on murder, and wrote a postscript to Pearson's "final word" on the Borden case. Gross says, very fairly, that Radin has distorted the evidence for Lizzie's innocence as carefully as Pearson distorted that for her guilt, and he points out that Pearson had to do a great deal of omitting anyway, to pack the trial into one fair-sized volume. But Gross's theory is that Lizzie killed her parents aided and abetted by Bridget. There is a persistent story that Bridget returned to Ireland after the trial, with a great deal of money given to her by Lizzie. Radin points out, quite correctly, that Bridget could certainly not be said to have testified in Lizzie's favour at the trial; on the contrary, most of her evidence told against her employer. If, however, she was an accomplice, or an accessory after the fact, perhaps to helping Lizzie conceal the murder weapon or the bloodstained dress (which Lizzie burnt), then Lizzie would certainly have a motive for giving her money.

In 1967 there appeared in America Victoria Lincoln's *A Private Disgrace*. When Foster Damon, another expert on the Borden case, sent me a copy, he enclosed a card which said: "I think this is the final word on Lizzie". I am inclined to think he is right.

Victoria Lincoln was born in Fall River, so her insight into the town is obviously authentic. She was able to uncover some facts that suddenly make the whole case quite clear. There is only one point in Miss Lincoln's account that might be described as "speculation": from accounts of the periodic fainting illness that Lizzie suffered from, she arrives at the conclusion that Lizzie suffered from epilepsy of the temporal lobe of the brain. Psychomotor epilepsy is distinguished by seizures of automatic activity. Miss Lincoln cites a case from a medical textbook in which a man woke from a seizure, to find that the boss had raised his salary, impressed by the lucid and forceful way in which the man had asked for a raise. Lizzie undoubtedly had strange attacks about four times a year, always at the time of her menstrual period. The evidence about these attacks points to psychomotor epilepsy. And Lizzie was menstruating at the time of the murders.

But Miss Lincoln's theory is not an attempt to prove that Lizzie committed the murders in a trance-like state. She intended to kill her stepmother, but by poison. She hated her and was violently jealous of her. A year before the murders, her stepmother's room had been broken into and robbed when Lizzie was in the house. The thief was supposed to have flitted in silently, without alerting Lizzie, Emma and the maid Bridget, broken into the room taken money and jewellery, and flitted out via the cellar door. Andrew Borden soon asked the police to drop the investigation. He had a fairly shrewd idea of the identity of the thief.

Lizzie felt she had reason for hating her stepmother. First of all, it was a quarrel about a house. Mrs Borden's sister had not married so well, and she lived in half a house, the other half of which belonged to her mother. Her mother wanted to sell, but could hardly turn her own daughter out. So Andrew Borden came to the rescue, and quietly bought the whole house, giving half to the sister, and half to his own wife Abby. He did this with great secrecy, knowing the feelings of his children about their stepmother and her family, but the news leaked. Lizzie was furious. She told her father that charity should begin at home. She ceased to call Abby "mother", and from then on, addressed her, when she had to, as Mrs Borden. Andrew Borden tried to restore peace in the home by giving Lizzie and her sister another house, which had belonged to their grandfather. Lizzie was placated, but she never forgave her stepmother, and continued to address her as "Mrs Borden" after twenty-three years of calling her "mother".

The trouble that led directly to the murder was an identical situation which took place five years later, just before the murder. Uncle John Vinnicum Morse was a mid-westerner, and he decided that he would like to move closer to his brother-in-law's home (he was the brother of Borden's first wife). Borden owned a farm at nearby Swansea, and Morse asked if he could rent it. Borden said yes and decided to do again what he had already done over the business of his sister-in-law's house – to transfer the farm to his wife's name. Miss Lincoln dug up this curious transaction, the immediate motive of the murder; Pearson and the other writers on the case were unaware of it. Lizzie already disliked Uncle John because he had aided and abetted her father in the previous house transaction. So now he moved into their house again as a guest, she felt distinctly edgy. Miss Lincoln does not produce a convincing explanation why Borden decided to transfer the farm to Abby – perhaps he wanted to give her a present – he had recently bought back the other house from his daughters for two thousand more than its value, thus making them a present of a thousand dollars each. But Borden was seventy. No doubt he wanted to leave his wife well provided for in the event of his death. This was also why Lizzie was so bitterly opposed to these property deals. And it did not take long for the news about the Swansea property to leak back to her. This is when she started trying to buy poison. And although she was unsuccessful in her attempts to buy prussic acid ("for cleaning a fur"), she presumably bought *something*, for that evening Mr and Mrs Borden were very sick indeed. Lizzie said she had been sick too, but we have only her word for this.

There was another factor that has been largely ignored by Pearson and Radin. Lizzie had a deep love of animals, and she owned some pigeons, which lived in the barn roost. Borden kept everything locked up – he was capable of obsessive meanness – and when the barn was broken into twice by youths who wanted pigeon pie for supper, he chopped off the heads of all the pigeons with a hatchet. It was not exactly unkindness; in those days, America was still close to the pioneers, and most people killed their own chickens and butchered their own hogs. But he failed to calculate the effect on Lizzie.

This, in summary, is the new evidence dug up by Victoria Lincoln, and it certainly makes the case in every way more straightforward. The transfer of the deeds on the Swansea property was to take place on the day of the murder. Borden had thought up a stratagem to do this without arousing Lizzie's suspicions. A carriage would be sent to the door, and a note requesting that Mrs Borden visit a sick neighbour. The note arrived, or so Miss Lincoln believes, but by then Mrs Borden was already dead, or about to die. She was working in the guest room, on all fours, when Lizzie came in behind her with the hatchet, and sliced into her skull with blow after blow. At this point, Miss Lincoln embarks on a speculation that I find difficult to accept. John Morse had left the house much earlier. He had no alibi for the time of the first murder, but an extremely detailed one for the second. Miss Lincoln believes that Morse went along to the house just to make sure that all went according to plan – after all, the affair of the farm was of immediate interest to him. He watched the boy deliver the note, and observed Lizzie's very abrupt manner as she took it, followed by her slamming of the door. Obviously, she was having one of her queer spells. Ever since Morse had been in the Bordens' house, there had been a brooding tension, and Mrs Borden probably suspected Lizzie of wanting to poison her. So Morse listened with more than usual attention to what followed, and rightly interpreted the heavy thud from the upstairs room – its window was wide open on the hot August morning – followed by a succession of squelching noises. Probably Mrs Borden groaned the first time. Bridget was out at the other side of the house cleaning windows, so she would not hear. And Morse, realising what had happened, knew that an uncle from the mid-west would be a far more likely suspect for a murder than the respectable daughter of the house. So he hurried away and started establishing an alibi.

This *could* have happened, but there is no evidence that it did. All that seems moderately certain is that, with the stifling heat of the August morning, and the irritation of her menstrual period, Lizzie had one of her queer spells, and decided that she could not stand her stepmother a moment longer. Miss Lincoln may well be right; it may have been committed in a dream-like state, and the dream may have involved the headless pigeons. Miss Lincoln could be wrong in her diagnosis of psychomotor epilepsy, but it is hard to doubt that all kinds of factors – the knowledge of another property deal, her hatred of her stepmother and determination to kill her, the heat, menstrual irritation – suddenly decided her to use violence. Earlier writers on the case were not aware of just *how much* violence and tension there was in the air in the

Borden house in the weeks before the murder; it was a storm that had to break. Borden broke his usual habit of reticence to tell a business associate that he was having a lot of trouble at home at the moment.

What Lizzie did about her bloodstained dress after this first murder is rather a mystery. Presumably she took it off. At 10.45, Andrew Borden arrived home unexpectedly, no doubt puzzled by his wife's non-appearance at the bank. His daughter was on the point of leaving the house, to establish an alibi. The doors were locked, as usual, and Bridget had to let him in. Lizzie was heard to give a strange laugh as her father came in. She told her father that Mrs Borden had been called away to see a sick neighbour. Possibly Andrew Borden accepted this story, possibly he supposed Mrs Borden and Uncle John were now signing papers that he had already signed. At all events, he went into the sitting room and fell asleep. Bridget Sullivan testified that he was carrying "something like a book". Miss Lincoln is inclined to believe that this "something" wrapped in white paper was the deeds to the Swansea property, and the agreement to transfer it. Lizzie was later seen burning something in the kitchen stove.

What happened next? Miss Lincoln believes that Lizzie genuinely loved her father, but that seeing him asleep was tempted to spare him the horror of seeing his wife's body, and knowing that Lizzie was the killer. (For he *would* have known, just as he knew that Lizzie was the invisible thief of a year earlier.) Undoubtedly, he loved her, and he would cease to do so when the body was discovered. And so, according to Miss Lincoln, she regretfully raised the hatchet.

I find this hard to accept. Andrew Borden was killed with nine blows, one of which sliced down through his eye. Lizzie must have gone back upstairs to change her dress before the murder, unless she disposed of two bloodstained dresses, and then gone to get the hatchet from the basement. (It is true that she may have kept the dress in the basement too.) Two days before, her father had suffered from the same serious stomach complaint as her stepmother. She had made up her mind to kill him too. She did it less violently than in the case of her stepmother, nine blows instead of seventeen, but unflinchingly. Then she went to the barn and washed the hatchet, smashed off its bloodstained handle in a vice, which she burnt, and rubbed the blade in ashes. She removed the dress and folded it into a bundle. Or she may have simply hung it in her closet among her other dresses, as Miss Lincoln suggests, simply putting it inside another. By the time Bridget came in from cleaning the windows, and went to her room to lie down for a moment, Lizzie had changed and was ready to give the alarm.

There is some evidence for the epilepsy theory. Lizzie's mother suffered from severe migraines and sudden violent seizures of unmotivated rage. The evening before the murder, Lizzie called on a friend, Alice Russell, and said: "I'm afraid someone will do something. I don't know but what someone will do something." The heat wave had started the day before. She was experiencing the sense of brooding depression that Dostoievsky has described as preceding epileptic fits. "I feel depressed," she told Miss Russell. "I feel as if something was hanging over me that I can't shake off." Only that morning there had been a strange scene: her stepmother had approached a Doctor Bowen who lived opposite, and told him that her husband had received a letter threatening to poison him, and that they had been sick all the previous night. Doctor Bowen finally agreed to come to the house and was met by a furious Andrew Borden, who told him to mind his own business and go away. And meanwhile the heat was tremendous, oppressive – it was one of the hottest days recorded in Fall River in living memory – and Lizzie's abdomen was aching in a way that indicated the approach of a menstrual period. She may well have foreboding.

No, forensic medicine would have made no difference to the Borden case. It might have established blood on the blade of the ash-coated hatchet, and drawn the net of circumstantial evidence a little tighter. And if someone had had Miss Lincoln's shrewdness, the forensic laboratories might have examined the *inside* of all Lizzie Borden's dresses for bloodstains that proved that a bloodstained dress had been hung up inside one of them. For what Lizzie did with the bloodstained dress between the day of the murder, Thursday, and Sunday morning, when she burnt it, is the chief unsolved mystery of the case. Emma and Alice Russell walked into the kitchen, and interrupted Lizzie, who was holding the Bedford cord dress. "I'm going to burn this old thing," said Lizzie. "It's all covered up with paint." Alice and Emma must have exchanged a horrified glance. It was their moment of decision. If they snatched it from Lizzie, or casually asked to look at it, it would undoubtedly send Lizzie to the scaffold. But what was the point? The Bordens were dead, and both Emma and her friend Alice knew about Lizzie's "queer spells". Alice merely said: "I wouldn't let anyone see you doing that if I were you," and then conveniently forgot the incident for four months. When Alice was questioned about Lizzie's dresses the next day, she went in to Lizzie and told her she really ought not to have burnt the dress. Lizzie simulated concern and said: "Why did you let me do it?" Quite.

Perhaps I might be forgiven for dwelling on the Borden case with a certain nostalgia. I have never visited Fall River, but I have spent some time in nearby Providence, with its clapboard houses, which look exactly like the photograph of the Borden house, and its streets ankle-deep in leaves in the autumn. The old part of the town, around Brown University, is full of memories of H.P. Lovecraft and his horror stories, and there is something timeless about it. There may be television aerials, but apart from that, you feel that the place is exactly as it was in the 1890s. You can still find parts of the sea-front that are straight out of *The Shadow Over Innmouth*. But I think it is safe to say that crimes like the Borden mystery are a thing of the past, not because emotional stepdaughters will cease to take choppers to their parents, but because when they do, the crime will be solved within hours. Fall River was a sleepy, quiet community, in which everyone knew everyone else. Uncle John Morse did not come home and say reproachfully: "Lizzie, why did you do it?" – as he obviously knew she had. Emma and Alice did not say: "Could I see that dress a moment?" Murder or no murder, one's upbringing made such an approach impossible. It would simply not have been tactful. Nowadays, the police would be grilling Lizzie at the station within hours, while a squad of detectives went over the house with the "murder bag", examining the soles of Lizzie's shoes for samples of dust from the barn, wondering about the burnt papers in the kitchen stove, noting the minute splinter of bloodstained wood clinging to the inside of the vice

. . . Lizzie would not go to the gas chamber, of course. A good psychiatrist would soon get the secret of the "queer spells" from her, or from Emma; the charge would be reduced to one of second degree murder; or the case might not even come to trial. Lizzie would vanish into the violent ward of the Providence mental institution.

11.
The Age
of Gaslight

NOW WE have reached the threshold of the twentieth century, let us pause to take a final backward look at the age of gaslight – the century of Charles Dickens and Sherlock Holmes.

One cold, foggy evening in the late 1860s, Sir Frederick Treves, a surgeon at the Mile End Infirmary in East London, was walking home along the Whitechapel Road. Hansom cabs clattered by on the wet cobbles, and Sir Frederick had to walk cautiously to avoid cracks in the pavement. Perhaps this was why he noticed a strip of canvas flapping in the cold wind. By the dim gaslight he could just make out the words: "Elephant Man – admission twopence". He pushed aside a greasy canvas flap and found himself in a narrow space between two buildings. In Victorian times, these were known as "holes in the wall" – space was so valuable in the overcrowded slums that the gaps between houses were covered with a canvas roof and let out at low rents. There was a single dim light, and the surgeon could see a huddled figure, covered in tarpaulin, and sitting on a packing case. The surgeon gently pulled back the tarpaulin, and the man looked up at him. What he saw made him gasp and shrink back. The "Elephant man's" face was hardly human: the nose was a swollen, trunk-like mass of flesh, and everything else about him was distorted.

The surgeon drew up a packing case and sat talking to this human creature who looked like a beast from a fairy tale. The elephant man proved to be a man of mystery. His body was as distorted as his face, so it was not even clear to which sex "he" belonged. He knew that his name was John Merrick and that he was about twenty. But he could only speak in an incomprehensible mumble, and could apparently remember nothing of his origins, or where he had grown up. When his "keepers" came back from the pub where they had been drinking to keep out the cold, they told Treves that they had simply found the elephant man wandering in the street, and had decided that he might bring them in a few pence as a freak show. But he was so horrible that women fainted at the sight of him and children had fits. When the surgeon offered them five pounds for the monster, they could scarcely believe their luck. The next day, Treves took the elephant man to the hospital, and gave him a private suite of rooms, cut off from the rest of the hospital. Few nurses could bear to see him, and before a nurse was asked to bring him food or help him to dress, she was given a preliminary look at him to see if she could bear it without fainting.

Yet the elephant man proved to be gentle and charming. His gratitude touched everybody. Obviously, his life had been hard and miserable; no one had ever been kind to him. Now, at last, he had warmth and comfort, and he found it almost impossible to believe that fate had finally relented towards him.

One of his favourite occupations was cutting pictures out of illustrated magazines. One of these, his most treasured, was of Princess Alexandra, who would later be queen of England when her husband, later Edward VII, came to the throne. The princess was the patroness of the hospital, and she was deeply interested in the elephant man. One day, she told Treves she wanted to see him. Treves tried hard to dissuade her, but it was impossible. She was shown into the elephant man's presence. She did not flinch as the twisted, monstrous creature dragged himself towards her, or as he took her hand in his own distorted claw, and bent over to kiss it. Then she was shown out. As the door closed behind her, she slumped down in a faint.

This strange story of the pathetic human monstrosity involves no crime, yet it is thoroughly typical of that foggy, gaslit London that was drawn so powerfully by Gustave Doré. It was a grim city, in which mothers with babies at their breast slept out on the freezing pavements, a city of disease, violence and corruption. It comes to life in the pages of that curious work called *My Secret Life* by an unknown Victorian whom we know only as Walter. Walter often wandered around the slum streets, seeking satisfaction of his peculiar desires. He might have a sudden impulse to have sex with a pregnant woman, or with a young virgin, or even a child. On one occasion he picked up a woman and a ten-year-old girl, went back to a cold, dismal room with them, and spent the night possessing them both. Moreover, it was not the first time the child had been made to give herself to a man for money. Again and again, Walter describes possessing young girls for a shilling.

It was a city of unsolved mysteries. The Jack the Ripper murders are undoubtedly the most famous of these, but there are many others that are equally strange. For example, there was the case of the disappearing German baker. His name was Urban Napoleon Stanger, and he and his wife were natives of Kreuznach, in Germany. They bought a house at 136 Lever Street, behind Gray's Inn Road. It was a rough area, which had been the scene of many crimes, and Pentonville Prison was not far away. However, it was densely populated, and Stanger's grocery business prospered. There were many Germans living in the area, mostly of Jewish extraction. Stanger became friendly with another baker called Felix Strumm. Strumm had a dark beard, a hooked nose, dark, deep-set eyes and a powerful body. He gave an impression of cunning and malice, but Stanger seemed to like him. So did Mrs Stanger, a hard-faced, coarse-looking woman.

On the evening of 12 November 1881, Stanger's journeyman baker walked past the shop around midnight, and saw Stanger, Strumm and two other men talking outside the shop; then Stanger went inside. He was never seen again. When the journeyman got to the shop the next day, Mrs Stanger immediately sent him to get Strumm, who lived nearby. He came, and stayed all day. Two people who came to see Stanger were told he had been called away suddenly to Germany on business.

Elizabeth Stanger and Strumm began to be seen in public together, usually arm in arm. And a few weeks later, residents of Lever Street were amazed when they saw Strumm painting out the name of Stanger from above the shop and substituting his own. Rumour went around that Mrs Stanger had found an interesting way of disposing of her husband: converting him into meat pies. The sale of their meat pies dropped, but otherwise business prospered. And the police decided there were no grounds for taking action, even though several neighbours had talked to them about Stanger's disappearance.

In April 1882, six months after the disappearance, an advertisement appeared in the press offering a £50 reward for anyone who could give information leading to the discovery of the whereabouts of Stanger. It seems to have been inserted by a relative of Stanger's who was not satisfied with Mrs Stanger's story about the sudden visit to Germany.

Finally, Stanger's solicitors brought a charge against Strumm, accusing him of forging a cheque in Stanger's name. Strumm and Mrs Stanger were both arrested. In court, Mrs Stanger was shrill and defiant. Strumm was sullen and defiant. Their story was that Stanger had been a spendthrift and was heavily in debt. The virtuous Strumm often lent him money. One day, after Mrs Stanger had taxed her husband with his feckless ways, Stanger announced he was going to leave her. Mrs Stanger went to bed in tears, and when she came down the next morning, her husband had gone. Ever since then, she said, Strumm had helped her run the business.

It was all manifestly untrue. Stanger had nearly £500 in the bank, and Strumm had been out of work and in debt before he moved in to the bakery in Lever Street.

Stanger's will deepened the suspicion that he had been murdered. He left his money to his wife, on condition she did not marry or live with another man. This suggested he suspected her of being involved with Strumm – something the whole neighbourhood knew in any case.

Mrs Stanger was questioned as a witness and made a bad impression; she was hooted and hissed as she left court. When the jury announced a verdict of guilty, Strumm stood up and bellowed with rage. The judge, perhaps irritated by this display of contempt of court, sentenced him to the maximum for forgery, ten years. Strumm proved to be a bad prisoner, violent and resentful, and he served the whole term. Mrs Stanger, surrounded by hostile neighbours, returned to Germany, in the company of Mr Strumm, it is said.

It seems fairly certain that Mrs Stanger murdered her husband that night in November, and that she sent for Strumm to help her dispose of the body. But how she killed him, and what became of the body, will never be known. Strumm's rage was undoubtedly due to a sense of the sheer unfairness of it. He had not killed Stanger, his mistress had. He had only forged a cheque. Yet it would have done him no good to denounce her to the court; the result would only be that she would probably hang, and he would get another ten years added to his sentence as an accessory. Hence, one presumes, his baffled rage.

Two other unsolved murders created a great deal of public excitement. One of these became known as the Euston Square Mystery. One day in 1879, a man named Severin Bastendorf brought in some workmen to help him clear rubbish out of his cellar at 4 Euston Square, so that he could use it for storing coal. Under a pile of old refuse, they found the skeleton of a woman, with a piece of rope around the neck. Bloodstains on the floor suggested she had been stabbed as well as strangled. The woman had suffered from curvature of the spine, and this made it easy to identify her. She had been a lodger of the Bastendorfs, and her name was Matilda Hacker. She was a strange, eccentric woman with golden curls, who dressed like a teenage beauty, although she was approaching middle age. She apparently came from a wealthy Canterbury family, but one of her eccentricities was to skip from lodging to lodging to avoid her creditors. She had vanished eighteen months before, and a maidservant named Hannah Dobbs had announced that the eccentric lady had done another moonlight flit. Shortly thereafter, Hannah Dobbs herself had left.

Hannah Dobbs was the obvious suspect. And this view was confirmed when the police traced a gold watch belonging to Miss Hacker to a pawnbroker, and learned that it had been pawned by a woman answering to Hannah's description.

She was located in prison, where she was serving six months for theft, and put on trial. But since there was no definite evidence against her, she was acquitted. Some time afterwards, a pamphlet was published, apparently written by Hannah Dobbs. She claimed that the murder of Miss Hacker had been committed by her lover, the younger brother of Severin Bastendorf. She said that she had only helped conceal the body. This is probably the solution of the "Euston Square Mystery", although it is not clear why Hannah Dobbs should want to denounce her lover, and implicate herself as an accessory, after she had been acquitted.

Equally baffling, was the murder of Mrs Sarah Millsom. On Wednesday 11 April 1866, Mrs Millsom, a housekeeper who lived at 3 Cannon Street in the City of London, was sitting in her room reading, while the cook, Elizabeth Lowes, sat sewing opposite. Just after nine in the evening, there was a ring at the doorbell. Mrs Millsom jumped up. "That's for me." She went downstairs. After a while, the cook wondered what had happened to her. She lit a candle and went downstairs. Mrs Millsom lay dead at the bottom of the stairs, her face and head a mass of blood. Someone had battered her to death. There had been no robbery – her keys were untouched – and the motive was not sexual, for her clothes were undisturbed. It was found that she had borrowed money from a moneylender to pass on to a man called George Terry. But Terry had been in the poorhouse at the time of the murder. A friend of Terry's with a bad reputation, a man named Smith, was charged with the murder, but was able to establish a perfect alibi. And the police were never able to discover why a highly respectable housekeeper should rush downstairs obviously expecting a man, and then meet a violent death.

But perhaps the strangest of all the insoluble mysteries of Victorian London was the series of disappearances that have become known simply as "the Vanishings". They began in 1881, and centred around the areas of East Ham and West Ham. Because these disappearances were unsolved, there is no complete account of them. An eleven-year-old girl named Eliza Carter left home one day wearing a blue dress with buttons down the front. A few hours later, she was seen by a friend, and seemed to be in a state of terror. For some odd reason, she said she didn't dare to go home. Then she simply vanished. The blue dress was found on the East Ham football ground, minus all its buttons. Eliza was never seen again. Charles Wagner, the son of an West Ham butcher, vanished one day, and his body was later found at the foot of cliffs at Ramsgate, seventy-five miles away. The odd thing was that it was not a fall that had caused death, neither was he drowned. The body bore no signs of injury, and there was no obvious cause of death. In January 1890, three girls vanished together from West Ham. Only one of them, fifteen-year-old Amelia Jeffs, was found in West Ham Park; she had been strangled after a violent struggle. But the "vanishings", a dozen or more, had finished. A woman had been seen talking to the three girls just before their disappearance. Seven years earlier, an old woman had been speaking to Eliza Carter just before she vanished. The coroner who examined Amelia Jeffs made the curious remark that "women are susceptible to the lowest forms of mania as men". Presumably he was hinting at sadistic sexual perversion, probably with the Ripper in mind. (The Ripper murders had all taken place in the second half of 1888, and had ceased after the disembowelling of Mary Kelly on 8 November.) But the bodies of the Ripper's victims were always left lying where he killed them. What was the coroner hinting at? That the vanished children had been kidnapped, and perhaps maltreated until they died? If so, why was Charles Wagner's body free of injury? No doubt there are modern speculators in the "occult" who would favour the theory that the children were snatched up by flying saucers. It has to be admitted that that explanation is just about as likely as any other. The vanishings remain one of the most disturbing mysteries of the age of gaslight.

But it would be a mistake the convey the impression that the most famous crimes of the age were all confined to London. Charlie Peace pursued his burglarious profession in Sheffield; Dr Pritchard poisoned his wife and mother-in-law in Glasgow; Constance Kent almost decapitated her four-year-old brother at Road, in Somerset; and America's classic "crime of the century" – Professor Webster's murder of his colleague Dr Parkman – took place in the Boston Medical College. And in the 1870s, it was enough to mention the name "Sheward" to make Victorian ladies grow pale and reach for their smelling salts. The case, which has now been almost forgotten, caused something like hysteria at the time.

It began, as far as the general public was concerned, on a Saturday evening, 21 June 1851, when a dwarf named Charles Johnson took his dog for a walk in the countryside near Norwich. The dog vanished behind a hedge, and reappeared with a disgusting lump of flesh in its teeth. It was only when they got home, and the dog presented its find to its master, that Johnson realised it was a human hand. The police were called, and more pieces of flesh were found in the field. The following day, a female pelvis was found nearby. Doctors announced that the remains were those of a teenage girl, who had been dead about a fortnight. And since Victorian newspaper readers were just as prone to jump to conclusions as those of today, the case immediately excited a universal morbid excitement. It seemed horribly probable there was a sex maniac loose in the Norwich area.

More pieces of the body continued to turn up: in ditches, sewers, fields. It was as if the murderer had embarked on some gruesome cross-country chase, scattering clues behind him. When a left foot was discovered in a churchyard, and the left hand was found nearby – with the ring finger missing – the whole of East Anglia talked of nothing but the mystery. Relatives of a missing servant girl named Ann Bailey were certain that she had been murdered by a man named Gouch, with whom she had eloped. When Ann Bailey turned up safe and sound, the police seemed to become discouraged. It seemed incredible that no one had observed the disappearance of a young girl from the area. But as the months drifted by, it seemed clear that no one had. And finally, the Norwich mystery went into the "unsolved" file. A part of the body was preserved in spirits of wine at the local Guildhall – its appearance suggested that it had been boiled.

Seventeen years passed. On New Years Day, 1869, a bearded, haggard-looking man walked into the police station at Walworth, south London, and said he wanted to confess to a murder. He gave his name as William Sheward, and said that for the past two days, he had been trying to work up the nerve to commit suicide. Unable to do it, he had decided to give himself up. The murder, he said, had taken place in Norwich in 1851, the victim had been his fifty-six-year-old wife.

Now, at last, it was clear how Sheward had got away with it for so long. Although many relatives had enquired after Mrs Sheward, and been suspicious of her disappearance, no one thought of connecting it with the remains of a "teenage" girl.

The story that emerged in Sheward's confession was of a thoroughly unhappy marriage. He was an unsuccessful tailor. At the age of twenty-four in 1836, he had married his thirty-nine-year-old housekeeper, Martha Francis. They quarrelled a great deal. Sheward began to drink as his business failed. He and his wife had never been sexually compatible – he was highly sexed and she was not. On 15 June 1851, they quarrelled about money. Sheward lost his temper, seized a razor and "ran it into her throat". This took place in the bedroom. The next day, the corpse began to smell, so Sheward began to hack it up. He took some pieces in a bag, and threw them away on a country walk. The next day, he continued the mutilation, boiling the head in a saucepan to stop it from smelling. It took him all week, during which time, anyone walking into the house while he was at work, could have solved the mystery of the hands and feet that were now being picked up around Norwich. He ended, the following weekend, by burning the sheets and blankets. From then on, he told relatives that Mrs Sheward had gone to New Zealand. Not long after, he met a younger woman, who lived with him and bore him several children. But the memory of his gruesome deed haunted him, giving him no peace, until he suddenly decided to end it all by killing himself.

The jury found him guilty, with no extenuating circumstances, no doubt influenced by the horror of the crime. Sheward was executed in April 1869.

It would be a pity to leave the nineteenth century without some account of a case that continues to baffle students of crime. It is true that the Adelaide Bartlett poisoning does not qualify as one of the great mysteries. Yet conoisseurs of Victorian crime agree that it is one of the most *peculiar* cases of all time.

Theodore Edwin Bartlett was a hard-working and highly ambitious grocer. By the time he was twenty-nine, he and his business partner owned a chain of small shops in south London. This explains why, although he was a good-looking man, fond of the open air, he had never married; life was too busy for romance. Then, one day in the early 1870s, he went to call on his brother Charles, who lived in Kingston, and was introduced to a dazzlingly attractive eighteen-year-old girl named Adelaide Blanche de la Tremoile. She had dark curly hair, large appealing eyes, and a sensual mouth. Edwin found her fascinating. But it seems likely that, at this stage, marriage did not enter his head. Adelaide was definitely a "lady", and therefore far above him socially. Then he learned that there was some odd secret in her background. Adelaide's mother had borne her out of wedlock. Her father was a wealthy Englishman who preferred to keep his identity secret – it has been suggested that he was a member of Queen Victoria's entourage when she visited France in 1855, and was therefore probably titled. Now Adelaide lived with a guardian in a house in Richmond – she was staying in the Kingston house as a guest of Charles's sixteen-year-old daughter. So it seemed that, although she was a "lady", her chances of being accepted into English society were minimal. Edwin saw his chance, and pursued it with single-minded vigour. He called on her when she returned to Richmond, and seems to have persuaded her guardian, or her father, that a virtuous and successful grocer would make a desirable husband. To Adelaide he explained solemnly that his intentions were more than pure – there was no element of carnal desire in his feeling for her, and when they were married, their relationship would be wholly platonic. And by way of proving his good faith, Edwin Bartlett packed off his newly-wedded bride to a ladies' finishing school in Stoke Newington. She came to stay with her husband during the school holidays but, according to Adelaide, their relationship was like that of father and daughter. And when she had finished at the Stoke Newington school, Edwin sent her off to a convent in Brussels. She stayed there until 1877, two years after their marriage, when she returned home to a newly furnished flat above Edwin's largest shop in Herne Hill. And for just one month, life was pleasant and peaceful, and Adelaide no doubt enjoyed being a young married woman in charge of her first home. Then Edwin's mother died, and the dutiful son invited his father to come and live with them.

It was a mistake. The old man was a bad-tempered old sponger, and he had never liked Adelaide. He made himself so unpleasant that Adelaide ran away from home – there is evidence that she went to stay in the house in Kingston where Edwin had first met her. And this seems to have led to further trouble. Edwin's younger brother Frederick also lived in the house, and the old man suspected a love affair. One writer on the case states that she became Frederick's mistress, but there is no evidence whatsoever for this assertion. All we know is that the old man accused Adelaide of having an affair with Frederick, and that Edwin was so incensed that he made his father sign an apology, which was drawn up by a solicitor. Then an uneasy peace reigned in the household.

Four years later, in 1881, two things broke the monotony of their lower middle class lives: Edwin had a nervous breakdown (brought on, according to his father, by laying a floor), and Adelaide had a stillborn baby. The latter accident was Edwin's fault; the nurse he engaged to look after his wife had sensed that this might be a difficult birth, and begged Edwin to call in a doctor. But the Victorian Edwin was rather shocked at the idea of another man "interfering with her", and refused. By the time a doctor was finally called in, the baby was dead.

Soon after this, perhaps to distract her, they moved to the village of Merton, near Wimbledon. Edwin's motive may also have been to get rid of his father – he selected a house that had no spare bedroom. So the old man was forced to find a home elsewhere.

Early in 1885 – the Bartletts had now been married ten years – the couple decided to try another place of worship one Sunday morning. They attended the Wesleyan chapel in Merton. The preacher that day was a young man named George Dyson. He had a black moustache, a receding hairline, and was of slight build. Dyson made a pastoral call soon after that. And when he told Edwin Bartlett that he was about to go to Trinity College, Dublin, to take his degree, Bartlett was deeply impressed. He had an almost pathetic admiration for anyone with education – he himself was an avid but disorganised reader. He cross-questioned Dyson about his studies, and pressed the young man to come and visit them again as soon as he returned from Dublin. Slightly overwhelmed – for he was modest and not very clever – Dyson agreed. And a warm, if rather peculiar friendship, began between these three rather lonely people.

Dyson found Edwin Bartlett "exceedingly odd". He seemed to have eccentric ideas on all kinds of subjects. For example, he was a devotee of a work called *Esoteric Anthropology* by Thomas Low Nichols, whose long sub-title declared it to be a "confidential" treatise on the passionate attractions and perversions of the most intimate relations between men and women. It was not, as the judge later assumed, disguised pornography, but an early "women's lib" discourse on the unfairness of using women as sexual objects. It recommended birth control, and suggested that sexual intercourse should only be practised for the purpose of begetting children. Another of Edwin's rather peculiar beliefs was that men should have two wives, one for "use" and one for intellectual companionship. He was also, like many Victorians, interested in hypnotism, and in the doctrines of Anton Mesmer, according to which human beings possess a "vital magnetic fluid" that can be passed from one to another.

Soon, Edwin Bartlett was professing the warmest affection for the Rev. Dyson. In fact, he proposed that Dyson should continue Adelaide's education, teaching her geography, history, Latin and mathematics. Dyson, who was making a mere hundred pounds a year, agreed. He would arrive in the morning while Edwin was out at business, and often stay all day. During most of this time, he was alone with Adelaide. Whether she became his mistress depends on one's final view of her guilt or innocence, but certainly she often sat at his feet, with her head on his knee, and he often kissed her, alone and in her husband's presence. And, oddly enough, Edwin seemed delighted with the whole arrangement. His wife was lonely – she had only one close female friend, a Mrs Alice Matthews – and now he had found her a male friend and teacher who could be trusted implicitly. Edwin had unlimited faith in clergymen. If he found Edwin still in the house when he came in for supper, he warmly pressed him to stay for the evening. When the Bartletts went to Dover for a month, Edwin tried to persuade Dyson to come too, and offered him a first class season ticket so he could rush down every time he was free. Dyson refused, but Edwin still found time to travel to Putney (where Dyson lived) and whisk him off to Dover as an overnight guest. And he asked Dyson to be an executor of his will, in which, naturally, he left everything to Adelaide.

That September, the Bartletts moved into a new lodging – it was to be their last – in Victoria. Edwin told their new landlady, Mrs Doggett, that they would be having a regular visitor, a clergyman, as a dinner guest. And George Dyson continued to call as regularly as ever, travelling from Putney, where he was now in charge of his own church, on a season ticket presented by Edwin Bartlett. They even kept a special jacket and slippers for him to change into. Dyson was finding this close friendship with a young married woman disturbing, and he confessed openly to Edwin that he was growing attracted to Adelaide and that it was upsetting his work; he felt he ought to stop seeing them. Edwin dismissed the idea, assuring Dyson that Adelaide had become a better and nobler woman since she had known him. He seemed to be trying to throw them into one another's arms. And Mrs Doggett noticed one day, after Dyson had left, that the window curtains were not merely drawn, but pinned together. It is hard to imagine why they should do this unless, at the very least, they had been engaging in some heavy petting.

And now, suddenly, Edwin became ill. One day he felt so exhausted at work that he hurried home. The next morning, he and Adelaide and Dyson went to a dog show – dogs were one of Edwin's main interests – but he felt so ill that they had to return home. Adelaide went out to fetch a doctor. She found a young man called Alfred Leach, whom she had never met before, but who immediately accompanied her back home. Edwin was suffering from sickness, diarrhoea and bleeding of the bowels; he had also had toothache. When Dr Leach looked into his mouth, he observed a blue line round the gums, a symptom of mercury poisoning. When he asked Edwin if he had taken mercury, Edwin denied it, but admitted that he had swallowed a pill he had found in a drawer – he had no idea what it was for. Leach arrived at another explanation. Edwin's teeth were in an appalling condition and his breath smelt foul. Apparently the dentist who made his false teeth had failed to draw the stumps; for some reason, he had sawed off the teeth at the gums. When these had rotted, the dentist merely made more false teeth, and the condition of his mouth made it impossible for Edwin to clean his remaining teeth. Leach's theory was that Edwin had, at some time, got a dose of mercury into his system, and that the sulphides produced by his rotting teeth had combined with it to form mercuric sulphide, hence the blue line. A dentist who was called in verified that Edwin was suffering from mercury poisoning, and extracted fifteen roots and stumps.

So throughout December the patient remained in bed. On Christmas Day, 1885, he received an unpleasant shock when he went to the lavatory and passed a round worm. He was naturally something of a hypochondriac, and this gave him "the horrors". He swore that he could feel worms wriggling in his throat, and became deeply depressed.

On the last day of December, and the last day of Edwin's life, he went to the dentist for yet another tooth extraction. Young Dr Leach, who had become a devotee of Adelaide, went with them. On the way, Adelaide remarked that they had just been saying that they sometimes wished they were unmarried, so they could have the pleasure of getting married again. Later, when Edwin got home, his appetite had improved, and he ate a large meal of oysters, jugged hare and cake, with a helping of chutney. He told Mrs Doggett that he would have a haddock for his breakfast, Obviously, he was at last on the road to recovery.

Just before 4 am on New Year's Day, Adelaide knocked on the Doggett's bedroom door. "Go and fetch Dr Leach. I think Mr Bartlett is dead." She explained that she had fallen asleep, holding Edwin's foot, which apparently soothed him, as she sat beside his bed. She had awakened and felt that he was cold. She had tried to revive him with brandy, but without success. Dr Leach observed a glass of brandy on the shelf, with a smell of chloroform.

The moment old Mr Bartlett heard of his son's death, he concluded he had been murdered. He sniffed his son's lips, then turned to Dr Leach and said, "We must have a post mortem".

The post mortem revealed a baffling and astonishing fact: that Edwin Bartlett had died of chloroform poisoning. This was so astonishing because chloroform is an unpleasant-tasting substance that would be almost impossible to swallow; moreover, it causes vomiting. If chloroform was poured down someone's throat when he was unconscious, for example, from the fumes of chloroform, it would get into the lungs. And there was no chloroform in Edwin Bartlett's lungs. Which seemed to point to the completely mystifying conclusion that Edwin Bartlett had drunk the chloroform voluntarily. Yet his cheerfulness before he went to sleep, and the fact that he had even ordered his breakfast, made it unlikely that he intended suicide.

And where had the chloroform come from? This was soon revealed. The Rev. Dyson had bought it, at Adelaide's request. He had even gone to three separate chemists to get a fairly large quantity, claiming that he wanted to use it as cleaning fluid. Adelaide had told him she wanted it to make her husband sleep. And now, when he heard that chloroform had been found in Edwin's stomach, Dyson was panic stricken. He saw it as the end of his career. He rushed along to see Adelaide, and when Mrs Matthews came unexpectedly into the room, she heard Dyston saying: "You did tell me Edwin was going to die soon." And when Adelaide denied it, he bowed his head on the piano and groaned: "Oh, my God!" Later that day, he saw Adelaide alone, and she asked him to say nothing about the chloroform. Dyson refused, and said he was going to make a clean breast of it.

And so he did. And the result was that Adelaide Bartlett found herself on trial for murder. When, in the spring of 1886, it became known that she was to be tried for poisoning her husband, and that the Rev. George Dyson would probably stand in the dock beside her, public excitement was intense. It had all the signs of being a thoroughly scandalous murder case, complete with revelations of secret adultery and a plot by the lovers to kill the husband. And when it was known that the great advocate Edward Clarke would defend Adelaide, people nodded significantly. Clarke was not one of those barristers who depended on verbal fireworks and bullying to win his cases; he was known for a certain quiet sincerity. Yet for all that, he had a formidable reputation. It was obvious that no suburban grocer's wife could afford his services, which could only mean that her mysterious father had intervened.

In the event, Adelaide finally stood alone in the dock; Dyson had managed to clear his own name by shamelessly doing his best to hand her over to the hangman. Edward Clarke had an apparently impossible task: to convince a Victorian jury that this pretty Frenchwoman, quite probably an adulteress, was innocent of her husband's murder. He had only one thing on his side: the total mystery of how even the most cunning murderess could have got the chloroform into Edwin Bartlett's stomach.

Clarke's defence was brilliant. His line of argument was that Edwin was a highly eccentric man who had almost thrown his wife into the arms of the clergyman, and who had actually told them that he expected them to get married when he was dead. He had insisted that his marriage to Adelaide should be purely platonic, and they had only had sexual intercourse once, as a result of which a baby had been born. But in the last days of his illness, Edwin had suddenly shown a desire for sexual intercourse. Adelaide felt this was wrong, since she now regarded herself as affianced to Dyson. So she asked Dyson to get her chloroform, so she might wave it in his face if he made sexual demands. However, she had been unable to go through with it. She had never been able to keep a secret from Edwin, and on that last evening of his life, had confessed her intention and showed him the bottle of chloroform. Edwin had been rather sulky about it, and had placed the bottle on the mantelpiece. And somehow, while Adelaide dozed by his side, holding his foot to comfort him, some of that chloroform had got into Edwin's stomach. (She admitted she had disposed of the rest by throwing it from the window of a train.) The main point of the defence was that Edwin was eccentric to the point of insanity, and that such an unpredictable man might easily have swallowed chloroform, perhaps simply to upset his wife and gain attention.

Amazingly enough, the jury swallowed this unlikely story of a wife too virtuous even to permit her own husband sexual intercourse, even when it was revealed that Edwin had rubber contraceptives in his pocket and undoubtedly used them in making love to Adelaide. But the central point of the defence, of course, was that baffling mystery of the chloroform: if Adelaide poisoned her husband, how did she get it into his stomach? To that question the prosecution had no answer. After that, there could only be one verdict. "Although we think there is the gravest suspicion attaching to the prisoner, we do not think there is sufficient evidence to show how or by whom the chloroform was administered." So the verdict had to be Not

Guilty. The judge had to reprove the court sternly as it burst into cheers.

The question of Adelaide's guilt or innocence has been argued by criminologists ever since. Some, like Nigel Morland, have no doubt that she was innocent, and that Edwin took the chloroform himself in a spirit of resentment or mischief. The majority are inclined to believe that Adelaide was poisoning Edwin from the beginning with some mercury compound, and only decided on the dangerous expedient of ether when he looked like recovering. And one, Yseult Bridges, believes that Adelaide somehow used hypnosis to induce Edwin to swallow the chloroform. None, as far as I know, have hit upon what seems to be the simplest and most obvious solution.

Let us try to reconstruct a hypothetical scenario. When Edwin Bartlett meets the beautiful Adelaide, he is too shy to hope that she will become his mistress as well as his wife, and so he assures her that their relationship will be a purely platonic one. But after two years of marriage, he is less humble and self-effacing, and insists on his marital rights. As a result, Adelaide becomes pregnant, but due to her husband's peculiar ideas about doctors, she loses the baby.

Edwin's curious attitude, his feeling that a doctor who examined his wife would be "interfering with her", indicates a powerful physical jealousy. It is surely the attitude of a man who has the utmost difficulty in persuading his wife to permit him the use of her body, so the idea of another man examining her intimately arouses intense jealousy. Adelaide, for her part, finds sex with her husband rather unpleasant, perhaps because his rotten teeth cause permanent halitosis, and she does her best to persuade him to abide by their "platonic" contract by petting him, fussing over him, showing him a great deal of affection, in fact, everything but allowing him into her bed. (At the trial, it was emphasised that they seemed to be an extremely happily married couple.) She makes use of the standard excuse, that she is afraid of becoming pregnant again, but Edwin counters that by buying contraceptives.

For Edwin, life becomes a permanent siege on his wife's virtue, with very infrequent successes. In his efforts to soften her, he deliberately introduces the Rev. George Dyson into their household, and encourages a flirtation. In effect, he is asking the clergyman, whom he trusts implicitly, to "warm her up". While she is feeling kindly and grateful to her husband, she can hardly refuse him the occasional embrace.

Edwin falls ill; we do not know whether, as Yseult Bridges believes, she has been administering small doses of lead acetate or some mercuric poison. But it gives her a flash of hope, she sees the end of her martyrdom in sight. Then he begins to recover and to indicate that his sexual appetites are returning to normal. Perhaps she finds the contraceptives in his pocket.

And it is at this point that she asks Dyson to buy the chloroform. Presumably the idea of killing Edwin is at the back of her mind – it is hard to believe that she intends to soak a hankerchief in the drug and try and press it over his nose whenever he becomes amorous. But she also knows Edwin well enough to know that, as a hypochondriacal invalid, he quite enjoys taking "medicines". He is in a state of neurotic depression about his "worms". Dr Leach has given him all kinds of medicines for them, without effect – Edwin is convinced he is still swarming with worms. All Adelaide needs to do is to produce the chloroform, and tell Edwin that Dr Leach has recommended this to get rid of worms. Perhaps only the lightest of hints is needed. Perhaps she offers him a little chloroform mixed with brandy, but he finds it unpleasant. Then, as she sits beside him, holding his foot and breathing deeply, he decides that he will win her approval by taking his medicine, and he cautiously reaches out for the bottle.

Sir James Paget, a well-known doctor, made the famous comment: "Now the case is over, she should tell us in the interests of science how she did it". The answer is surely that she did not do it, Edwin did. Whether it was at Adelaide's suggestion we shall never know.

12.
The Century
of Espionage

ALL CRIME is a form of betrayal. But in the twentieth century, one form of betrayal, espionage, has been recognised as a political necessity, and given a kind of dubious respectability. The moral dilemma involved has fascinated writers like Graham Greene and John Le Carré, one result being the immense popularity of the spy novel in the second half of the twentieth century. If, as seems likely, the downfall of Russian Communism puts an end to the need for "cold war" politics, our grandchildren may look back with nostalgia on the "age of espionage" that came to an end about 1990.

For all practical purposes, the age of modern espionage began on a day in September 1914, when a corpse was dragged out of the icy waters of the Baltic clutching two hefty books in its arms. The Russian captain of the vessel that found him was puzzled. Why on earth should a sailor want to leap into the sea holding heavy books, and why hadn't he let go of them when he was drowning? The Russian was a novice in modern warfare; it was only September, 1914, and most naval and military men were still naïve enough to believe that wars were fought only with soldiers. They knew little about spies and secret codes. His superiors in the

Russian Admiralty were not much wiser. They recognised that they had captured German code books, handed by the captain of the sinking *Magdeburg* to one of his men, with orders to drop them into the sea. But it did not strike them as a particularly exciting discovery. A few days later, the Russian attaché in London called on Winston Churchill, and told him that they had found the German naval code books. If the English would care to send a ship, they were welcome to have them.

Churchill appreciated their value. He sent the ship, and rushed the books to Admiral Oliver, head of Intelligence. Oliver handed them to one of his best men, an ex-teacher named Alfred Ewing. Ewing knew all about codes: he had been trying to crack the German naval code for months. And here it was being handed to him as a gift. It seemed too good to be true. Either it must be some kind of a trick, or the Germans must have already discovered their loss and changed the code. He grabbed the latest batch of coded messages, picked up from radio signals sent out from the German naval base at Wilhelmshaven. And within a few minutes, he knew that fortune had presented him with a prize. It was possible for him to read the secret orders of Grand Admiral Tirpitz and other senior commanders.

Two months later, in November 1914, Ewing was given a new boss, Captain William Reginald Hall, known as "Blinker" (because of a twitching eyelid). The new head of Naval Intelligence did not look in the least like a spy: he was short, rotund and cheerful. In fact, he was one of the most brilliant spymasters in the history of espionage.

The first thing Hall wanted to know was whether the codes could tell them something useful. On 14 December 1914, Ewing decoded a report that announced that the German Fleet intended to sail. Quietly, Hall moved his own ships into position in the North Sea. Two days later, Britain suffered its first naval bombardment, as ships of the German navy pounded Scarborough and Hartlepool with their heavy guns. Hall signalled his own battle cruisers, lying nearby, and told them to move in for the kill. All day, Churchill and Hall waited tensely for news. When it came, it was disappointing. Fog and rain had swept down over the North Sea as the British navy moved in. There had been a few shots exchanged, and the Germans had vanished into the mist.

Churchill was disappointed. To his surprise, Hall was looking jubilant. "There'll be a next time . . ." But that stoical reaction hardly explained his delight. He had been struck by a kind of vision. Modern warfare depended on *surprise*. The Germans had gained the element of surprise when they invaded Belgium. But ever since Marconi's discovery of radio in the 1890s, the surprise depended on a man with a transmitter and a code book. *If* he could get hold of the code books, it would be possible to anticipate every important move of the enemy. But how did one get hold of the code books? The two he had were important, but they were not the only ones.

For example, there were the strange signals coming from a transmitter in Brussels. Ewing had been working on the code for months, without success. Hall had a feeling it concealed important secrets. He ordered his spies to find out everything they could about the Brussels transmitter. This was not difficult: it had been there, in an office in the Rue de Loi, before the war. More enquiries revealed that it was operated by a young man called Alexander Szek. "That name doesn't sound German," said Hall thoughtfully. He made more enquiries, and suddenly knew that he was getting close to a solution. Alexander Szek, he discovered, was an Austro-Hungarian subject who had been born in Croydon, in south London, and members of his family were still living in England. Hall persuaded one of them to write Szek a letter, begging him to work for the British. A British agent in Holland smuggled it to Brussels and soon discovered that Szek was not particularly pro-German. The Germans had persuaded him to work for them because he was a good radio engineer. But he was not a born spy – the idea of stealing the German secret code terrified him. The British hinted that his family in England might be put in prison if he refused. Finally, Szek agreed.

He was not actually in possession of the code; a German Intelligence officer worked with him, and showed it to him when he needed it. But he could memorise it, a few figures at a time, and write it out. In the early months of 1915, Szek began stealing the code. Every time he completed a page, he handed it over to the British agent. But his nerve was beginning to crack. He told the agent that he wanted to be smuggled to England as soon as he had finished copying out the code. The agent pointed out that if he did that, the Germans would immediately change the code. But Szek was insistent. And then, one day, Szek was found dead in his room in Brussels. He appeared to have been killed by a burglar. The British later said he had been killed by the Germans. The truth, almost certainly, is that he was murdered by the British. But the Germans suddenly discovered that their "surprise" moves were no longer surprises; their European armies found they were being outgeneralled because the enemy seemed to be able to anticipate their moves. And the day of modern espionage, the espionage of the "cold war", had arrived.

In fact, this story, which sounds like an episode from *The Spy Who Came in From the Cold*, is grimly typical of the methods of twentieth-century spying. Blinker Hall was not a ruthless man; everyone who knew him agreed that he was cheerful, sympathetic and kindly. But he knew that if he wanted the secret codes, Szek had to be prevented from giving himself away. And since Szek was inclined to panic, there was only one answer – an "accident". Obviously, Hall justified the murder by saying that it saved thousands of British lives, which is true. The fact remains that it is typical of the underhand, stab-in-the-back morality of modern espionage, that appalling ruthlessness that Ian Fleming caught so well in the James Bond novels.

The First World War was a watershed in the history of espionage. Before that, spying had been an altogether more gentlemanly business. In fact, in the last great European spy case before the war, the traitor had been allowed to borrow a revolver and shoot himself through the head, to avoid scandal. Colonel Alfred Redl's treason probably cost his country a quarter of a million lives.

Redl was a highly intelligent man who came from a poor family. He was also a homosexual. In the Austria of the nineteenth century, the army offered a certain mode of advancement to one of Redl's character. In the early years of the century, his rise was rapid. His intelligence brought him to the attention of Baron von Giesl, head of the Austro-Hungarian intelligence service. He placed the young officer in charge of espionage, hardly an important activity in that rather old fashioned, militaristic nation. But Redl proved to be brilliant. He had the kind of imagination that would have taken him far in the CIA. He learned to use hidden cameras to photograph unsuspecting visitors; he coated objects with a fine dust, to get their fingerprints; he made recordings of their conversations (on old Edison cylinders). For the first decade of the twentieth century, he was a high-powered spy.

Unfortunately, he lived in a country where homosexuality was regarded as pure, deliberate wickedness. In the drawing rooms where the elegant and witty Colonel Redl was a welcome guest, any suspicion of his sexual tastes would have been enough to ruin him. It was necessary for him to be discreet. And since his sexual appetite was strong, this meant that, like Oscar Wilde, he had to be prepared to pay male prostitutes. It was an expensive business.

A Russian secret agent got wind of Redl's secret. And sometime around the year 1903, he informed Redl that if he wanted his secret to be kept, it would be necessary to aid the Russian secret service in certain minor matters. No one knows the details. All that is certain is that a combination of blackmail and bribery turned Redl into a traitor.

Von Giesl moved to Prague, and Redl went with him. His place in Vienna was taken by an adoring disciple, Captain Maximilian Ronge. Ronge was not a brilliant innovator, like Redl, but he was painstaking and precise. One of Redl's ideas was the institution of strict postal censorship; Ronge made sure it was carried out thoroughly. And in 1913, in the course of routine inspection, one of his agents came across two *post restante* letters, addressed simply to "Opera Ball 13". Both envelopes contained fairly large sums of money. Ronge ordered his agents to watch the post office and see who came for the envelopes. They waited for weeks in the police station next door, waiting for the ringing of a bell that would tell them that the letters were being collected. One day, it rang. They rushed next door in time to see a taxi vanishing. They managed to trace the cab to a hotel; there they were told their quarry had taken a cab to another hotel, the Klomser. And on the cab seat, one of the agents picked up a small suede sheath, of the sort that contained nail clippers. He asked the clerk at the Klomser if he knew the owner of the sheath. The clerk took it and approached a good-looking man of military bearing. The man nodded and slipped the sheath into his pocket. It was Colonel Redl.

One agent shadowed Redl, the other telephoned Ronge. Ronge was shattered. It was surely impossible that the ex-head of the Secret Service could be a traitor! He got hold of the receipts that Redl had signed to get the letters, and compared them with some of Redl's own handwriting in the files. They were identical. By this time, Redl had noticed that he was being followed. He did a stupid thing. He had some incriminating receipts in his pocket, for money from Russia. He tore these into small pieces, and cautiously scattered them as he walked. But Ronge's agents had been trained in Redl's own counter-espionage methods; they collected every tiny fragment and took them to Ronge's office.

Ronge went to the Commander-in-Chief of the army. He was stunned by the possibility that Redl might have been an enemy agent for years. For Austria had plans for attacking Russia and the Balkans, particularly Serbia. Redl had access to these papers, known collectively as Plan Three.

The Austrians behaved like gentlemen, which was their mistake. They called on Redl at his hotel and laid the facts before him. Redl looked pale and composed. He told them that they would find all the evidence they needed at his flat in Prague, and asked to be excused a moment. There was a shot from the next room; he had done what was expected of an officer and gentleman. Probably he didn't think too badly of himself in his last moments. He had no way of knowing that an Austrian archduke was about to be assassinated in Serbia, and that Europe would soon be at war. And it was only when that war began that the Austrian general staff found out just how far Redl had betrayed his country, and that the Serbians and Russians knew every detail of Austria's plans in advance. Redl was more than a traitor: he was the executioner of the Austro-Hungarian empire.

At the time of Redl's death, a fifteen-year-old German boy was beginning to read revolutionary pamphlets by Karl Liebknecht and Rosa Luxembourg, leaders of the embryonic German Communist Party. His name was Ernst Wollweber, and as the son of a Ruhr miner, he knew the meaning of poverty and misery. In 1917, Wollweber joined the German navy. The Russian Revolution inspired him: he preached socialism below decks, and when the war ended, he was recognised as one of the most promising members of the German revolutionary movement. Wollweber played his own part in the defeat of Germany: his propaganda helped to stir the Fleet to mutiny in November 1918, and it was Wollweber who hauled up the Red Flag on the cruiser *Heligoland* at the entrance to the Kiel canal – the signal for the revolt. Shortly afterwards, the Kaiser abdicated. For a while, it looked as if communism was going to triumph in Germany as it had in Russia. But Germany was not ready; in 1919, the Weimar Republic was formed. Wollweber went to Moscow to train as a spy, convinced that one day Germany would be communist. He was mistaken. To the astonishment and dismay of international communism, Hitler and his Nazis smashed the German Communist Party with remarkable ease. But by that time, Wollweber had learned the value of secrecy; he had become one of the Kremlin's most powerful and successful undercover agents, and saboteurs, in Germany.

Was Wollweber a traitor to his country? The question is almost academic. He was a convinced communist; he regarded Russia as his country. He was the first of the great ideological spies, and the first of a long line of traitors that includes names like Klaus Fuchs, the Rosenbergs, Alger Hiss, Alan Nunn May and Kim Philby. Wollweber became on of the great spymasters of all time. He liked to work in dock areas, and recruit his saboteurs from international seamen's clubs. A whole series of fires and explosions on ships, from the French *Georges Phillipar* in 1932 to the *Queen Elizabeth* in 1953, were almost certainly the work of Wollweber. Again and again he was almost arrested by the Gestapo; again and again, his agents were seized and executed, but Wollweber's luck held. When Hitler's Secret Service discovered his existence, he moved to Denmark and directed operations from there. When the Germans invaded Denmark, he moved to Sweden, and was promptly arrested and thrown into jail. The Swedes kept him in prison through most of the war, and they might have handed him over to the Gestapo if it looked as if Germany was going to win the war. But by 1944, it was clear that Russia had a stronger claim on Wollweber. The Swedes were told that he was wanted for misappropriation of party funds. In fact, when he got back to

Moscow, Wollweber was treated as a Soviet hero. He entered Berlin not far behind Marshall Zhukov. After the war, he again organised a spy network in East Germany, and British and French ships again began to suffer from mysterious fires and explosions. In 1953, he was appointed Minister of State Security in East Germany. He did his job brilliantly, but there was friction with Walter Ulbricht, Secretary of the East German Communist Party. Ulbricht may have felt that Wollweber was more vulnerable after Kruschev had Beria, the Soviet spy chief, arrested and shot, and one historian declares that an order for Wollweber's arrest was issued by Ulbricht in 1961. Wollweber took refuge in the Soviet headquarters in East Berlin, and Ulbricht's fury was suddenly punctured by a telegram from Moscow, ordering him to let Wollweber alone. It was signed Kruschev . . . Wollweber died the following year, aged sixty-four.

In retrospect, it seems strange that it took the western powers so long to recognise that most communists regarded Russia as their mother country, and were therefore capable of treason. In 1941, the British Security Services committed an almost unpardonable error when they allowed a German scientist named Klaus Fuchs to sign the Official Secrets Act and gain access to secret information. Fuchs had left Germany in 1933, at the age of twenty-two. He was not a Jew, but a Quaker, another minority persecuted by the Nazis. He was allowed to become a British citizen and work on the atomic bomb because British Security reasoned that he was more likely to give information to Russia than Germany, and in 1941, Russia was an ally anyway. From the beginning, Fuchs had no intention of observing his pledge of secrecy. He promptly contacted the Russian military attaché in London and offered to pass on nuclear secrets to Moscow, for Stalin had authorized full scale research on the atomic bomb. He collaborated closely with Russian spies in England until 1943, then he was sent to America, to work on the bomb project at Los Alamos, New Mexico. For a while, he failed to contact the American branch of the Russian espionage network, and there was a frantic effort to find him. Fuchs was enjoying the sunshine of New Mexico, and a temporary sense of freedom from anxiety. Then the Russians located him when he called on his sister in Cambridge, Mass, and once again he began passing the secrets of the atomic bomb to

Russia. By this time, the English and Americans had recognised that Russia would be a rival for world power after the war, and took the most elaborate precautions to prevent Soviet scientists finding out about progress on the bomb. One single man, Klaus Fuchs, completely negated the immense security precautions of the Allies. The odd thing is that he was beginning to have pangs of conscience. Perhaps he was beginning to grow up politically. He declined to meet his contact for six months, but it made no difference; the Russians kept up a firm and gentle pressure, and eventually, Fuchs handed them the secret of the enormous advances that were being made on the atomic bomb.

In 1946, he returned to England, as the head of the theoretical division of the atomic Energy Centre at Harwell. The Russians wanted to know about the secrets of the hydrogen bomb now, but Fuchs was unable to help. He seems to have been sick of being a spy, but there was now nothing much he could do. He went on handing over information, less valuable now, until the arrest of other spies, notably Nunn May, brought him under suspicion, and a British security agent set about the task of talking him into confessing. By this time, Fuchs was no longer at Harwell – the appointment of his father as a professor in East Germany provided an excuse for removing him. And on 30 January 1950, over a quiet lunch with the British agent, William Skardon, at an Abingdon hotel, Fuchs suddenly poured out the story of his years as a Russian catspaw. He had had enough of being a traitor. Without this confession, it is almost certain that he would never have been charged with spying. The technical charge at his trial was not treason, but spying; it lasted only ninety minutes, and Fuchs went to jail for nine years. Released in 1959, he went to East Germany and became head of the Nuclear Research Institute at Karlsruhe.

And how did Fuchs come to be suspected? Ironically through the revelations of another traitor, this time a Russian. Igor Gouzenko was not a spy; in 1945 he was simply a clerk at the Soviet Embassy in Ottawa. Gouzenko had been brought up as a good communist, that is to believe that the capitalist countries enslaved their people, and hated all members of the "free" communist world. In Canada, he was amazed to discover that the worker fared better under capitalism than he had been led to expect, and that Canadians were friendly and open. Gouzenko shrank from the prospect of a return to Moscow and he decided to defect. So he opened the safe of the Soviet Military Attaché and removed a large file. Then began a comedy of errors. The Canadians didn't seem to *want* a Soviet defector. An Ottawa newspaper declined to accept the secret documents and the Canadian police also felt this was none of their business. The Canadian Prime Minister was contacted, and told the police to hand Gouzenko back to the Russian Embassy. Gouzenko fled back to his flat. The Russians now made their mistake – they broke his door down and tried to drag him away. In a democratic society, that is strictly against the rules. So Gouzenko was once again taken into police custody, and the Canadians slowly began to realise that they were holding the key to Russian spy rings all over the world. And spies and traitors suddenly began to pop up like worms after a shower.

There was Alan Nunn May, a British physicist who was also a communist. He had worked in nuclear research in Ottawa, and given the Russians samples of uranium isotopes (in exchange for which he was given $200 and two bottles of whisky). The Gouzenko papers included notes about contacting May on his return to England in 1945. And when May was arrested in 1946, the prosecution had no difficulty in proving that he had spied for the Russians; he was sentenced to ten years. His defence was that he felt it was his job as a scientist to make sure that the nuclear discoveries went to the world, not just to America – a plausible argument and one that convinced many liberal intellectuals. No one seemed to question whether Stalin would have taken the same generous attitude if Russian scientists had been the first to discover the bomb. May was basically guilty of political naîvety. The Americans took a sterner view of this character defect. Gouzenko's revelations led them to Klaus Fuchs's American contact, Harry Gold, who was sentenced to thirty years in jail without a trial. Gold led them to David Greenglass, an American soldier who worked at Los Alamos and who had also spied for the Russians. Greenglass saved his neck by claiming that he had been dragged into spying by pressure from his sister, Ethel Rosenberg, who together with her husband Julius, was a devoted communist. The Rosenbergs were sentenced to death, and, in spite of a violent campaign for clemency – or perhaps because of it – the Rosenbergs went to the electric chair on 19 June 1953.

But even the atom spies were amateurs compared to the British super-traitor who is regarded as "the most important spy the Russians ever had in the West" – Kim Philby. Philby's name first came to the notice of the British public soon after the defection of the spies Burgess and Maclean in 1951. A British Member of Parliament asserted that Burgess and Maclean had been alerted a few hours before their imminent arrest by a "third man", and had made their escape to Moscow. He named this third man later – Harold Philby, known as Kim, son of the respected Arab scholar, St John Philby, and friend of many literary men, including W.H.Auden, Cyril Connolly and Philip Toynbee. The Prime Minister, Harold Macmillan, defended Philby's character. The M.P. withdrew his allegation. But Philby left his job in the foreign office and became Middle East correspondent for *The Observer* and *The Economist*. Then, in January 1963, Philby vanished and turned up again a few weeks later in Moscow, where his American born wife later joined him. There was frantic investigation into his career. And it soon became evident that the British diplomat, and member of the British Secret Service, had been a Russian agent since the early 1930s.

Philby became a Communist at Cambridge, when he was a young man, and it was the fashionable thing to do. In Berlin and Vienna in the early thirties, he saw Nazism at first hand, and began actively working for communism. As a cover, Philby apparently became a fascist sympathiser, working for an "Anglo-German Friendship" group, and later going to Spain as a press-man during the Civil War and working at Franco's headquarters. The disguise was perfect. And when the Hitler war came, Philby had little trouble becoming a member of the British Secret Service. Starting in a very minor capacity, he soon demonstrated his value by putting British Intelligence in touch with a Russian spy network in Switzlerland which had infiltrated the German High Command. From then on, Philby's rise was steady, until he ended as MI5's chief liaison officer with the CIA, with access to just about every military secret possessed by the British and Americans. No one will ever know how many secrets – atomic and otherwise – Philby passed to the Russians, but the number was certainly enormous. With his old Cambridge friend, the homosexual Guy Burgess, Philby blackmailed another Foreign Office man, Donald Maclean, to join their spy network. But by 1950, both Burgess and Maclean were beginning to crack under the strain of being Russian spies, and were drinking too much and causing public scenes. MI5 became suspicious; Philby warned them, and Burgess and Maclean vanished to Moscow.

Oddly enough, this was not the end of Philby's career as a spy, even though he had been publicly named as a suspect. He went back to the Middle East as a newspaperman, and worked there for another twelve years, until 1963, before he also felt that the hounds were getting too close, and he slipped on a Russian ship. The British Secret Service will remember him, ruefully, as one of the great arch-traitors of all time.

Spying was not always such a dirty business. When King Edward IV introduced the "King's espials" in the 1460s, it was regarded as an honourable branch of international diplomacy. In the reign of Queen Elizabeth I, her Lord Treasurer Burghley controlled one of the most powerful intelligence networks in Europe. Oddly enough, one of his spies was the Elizabethan playwright Christopher Marlowe, who died mysteriously in a tavern brawl in May 1593, near the beginning of a career that might have made him as great as Shakespeare. One Elizabethan historian, Calvin Hoffmann, is even convinced that Marlowe *was* Shakespeare. Marlowe died just as Shakespeare's career was beginning, and the style of the early Shakespeare plays is certainly very much like Marlowe's. In *The Murder of the Man called Shakespeare* Hoffmann advances the astonishing theory that Marlowe "died" with the aid of his espionage boss, Sir Francis Walshinghame, then continued his existence under another name – Shakespeare. The theory has never been widely accepted by scholars, but Hoffmann has produced some convincing evidence in its favour.

During the American War of Independence, there were some notable spying exploits. Nathan Hale, spying for the Americans, was captured and executed in the first year of the war. He died saying, "I only regret that I have but one life to lose for my country" – the kind of sentiment that would make a modern spy snort cynically. Hale became a martyr; so did the British spy, Major John André, carrying messages to the infamous traitor Benedict Arnold. Women spies also came into their own during the War of Independence, since no one could tell *which* side a woman belonged to, and the officers of both sides were far too gallant to search a woman. Belle Boyd, a "rebel" spy, had Northern officers quartered in her house in Martinsburg, Virginia, so was able to gather all kinds of information about troop movements, which she promptly relayed to Stonewall Jackson. (On one famous occasion, she got through the Northern lines and delivered a message that enabled Stonewall Jackson to win an important battle.) The most amusing thing about her career is that the Northern officers were soon convinced she was a spy, but were forbidden by chivalry to take any action. She *was* finally arrested, when one of her despatches fell into the hands of a Union agent, but she was exchanged for a Northern prisoner, and became a heroine in the South. The careers of "Rebel Rose" Greenhow and Pauline Cushman (a spy for the North) were equally remarkable, and have become a part of American folklore.

The German Kaiser Wilhelm I was another of the old school who thought spying was "*infra dig*". When he became Kaiser, he had in his service one of the most brilliant spymasters in Europe, Wilhelm Stieber. Stieber was put on trial in 1858, and had to defend his profession of spying in open court; he was acquitted, but was out of work for five years. Then Bismarck decided to employ him, and it was due to Stieber's work that the conquest of Austria in 1866 took only forty-five days: Bismarck knew all the enemy's military plans in advance. Stieber went on to make the German spy service one of the finest in Europe.

But it was under the Soviet regime that spying became the industry we know today. The Russians had always had their tradition of secret police. Under the last of the Tsars, it was called the Ochrana, and its chief business was to root out revolutionary activity. Lenin's secret police, the "Cheka", soon became the dreaded "Gay Pay Oo", G.P.U. But after Lenin's death, the congenitally suspicious Stalin felt uneasy about the increasing power of the secret police. Its head, Yagoda, was executed in the purges of 1937. It was fortunate for the Russian Intelligence

Service that two of its greatest spies – Ernst Wollweber and Richard Sorge – were working abroad.

It is generally agreed that Sorge was probably the greatest spy of all time. Born in Russia in 1895, Sorge's family moved to Germany when he was a child. As a student he became passionately left-wing; he joined the German Communist Party, and eventually became its intelligence chief. He trained in Russia, then moved around Europe, building up spy-rings in Scandivania and England. (The British Secret Service spotted him fairly quickly; after that, Sorge always maintained that it was one of the best in the world.) In Russia in the late twenties, he was involved in clashes between the Army Secret Service and the Secret Police (K.G.B.), and his fate might well have been the same as that of Yagoda; fortunately, the Communists decided that he would be useful in the Far East. And this was the sphere of the sensational operations that have made him the most famous name in espionage. His instructions were simple. The Soviets were already convinced that the great threats of the future would come from Germany and Japan; Sorge's job was to set up a spy network in Japan.

He was well qualified for the job. A highly intelligent man, who spoke several languages, he also had the perfect cover. He was an ardent womaniser. His success with beautiful women was phenomenal. (It is interesting that many of the great spies have been womanisers – Wollweber was another – as if spying and love affairs were complementary activities.) With so many shreds of scandal attached to his name, and a reputation for being an incorrigible philanderer, who could believe that Sorge was also a spy and a top level communist official? He didn't seem to be serious enough.

In Japan, Sorge began to recruit colleagues: Agnes Smedley, a well-known author of books on China, and a friend of Mao Tse Tung; Ozaki, a Japanese correspondent; a Yugoslav pressman, Voukelitch. Slowly, Sorge built up an intelligence network in China. Then, when Hitler came to power in 1933, he was given another task: to spy on the Germans in Japan. There was one important preliminary: Sorge applied for membership of the Nazi Party. And Hitler's Intelligence system was so poor that Sorge was given a party card. Back in Japan, Sorge completed his own Japanese spy network with the addition of an American-Japanese, Miyagi Yotuka. Miyagi and Ozaki were ordered to form their own network of Japanese spies.

Sorge's charm soon made him a favoured guest at the German Embassy. He became friendly with an assistant military attaché, Lieutenant Colonel Eugen Ott. No one ever suspected that the philandering correspondent of the *Frankfurt Times* was a Russian spy. Ozaki became a leading member of a "breakfast club" of Japanese intellectuals, with close connections with the cabinet. It was he who told Sorge in advance of Japan's projected attack on China: information that delighted the Kremlin, because while Japan was fighting China, it was unlikely to invade Russia. And when Colonel Ott was appointed German ambassador, Sorge then had sources of information about German and Japanese policies that made him the most important secret agent in the world. Sorge knew about the Japanese attack on Pearl Harbour weeks before it happened. He knew the exact date when the Germans intended to invade Russia, and if it had not been for Stalin's stupidity in ignoring his information – convinced that Hitler was a man of his word – Operation Barbarossa would have been defeated within days.

The head of Japanese Intelligence, Colonel Osaki (not to be confused with the spy Ozaki) knew there was a major spy network in Japan: his radio receivers picked up their coded messages, but he could not read them. Finally, he became convinced that Sorge was his man. He knew Sorge's great weakness – women. (At one point, Sorge had even risked breaking up the network by having an affair with Voukelitch's mistress.) He asked a German attaché to arrange a meeting with Sorge at a nightclub. Over a bottle of *saké*, he told Sorge about the beautiful girl who danced in the cabaret – about how many men were in love with her. Sorge was curious and his curiosity was increased by the mask the girl wore. He began to spend every evening at the cabaret, until finally the girl became his mistress. But she was an agent of Colonel Osaki – an aristocratic Japanese girl who had been asked to sacrifice herself for her country.

One night Sorge stopped his car and started to make love to the girl; he wanted her to come back and spend the night with him, because he felt his work in Japan was completed at last.

He took out his cigarette case and a tiny roll of paper fell out. Sorge carefully tore it up and threw it out of the car window. The girl made an excuse to get to a telephone and rang Japanese Intelligence; almost as soon as the car drove away, Japanese agents were collecting the torn fragments of paper. The next morning, as Sorge lay asleep beside the girl, Colonel Osaki walked into the bedroom. He handed Sorge a piece of paper – the message he thought he had destroyed. Sorge stood up and bowed. He knew he was defeated.

According to one account, Sorge faced his executioners, in November 1944, with complete nonchalance, smoking a cigarette. But there is no definite evidence that Sorge *was* executed. We know that he claimed a reprieve on the grounds that he was a Soviet citizen, and that Russia was not at war with Japan. A British diplomat who knew Sorge claimed that he saw him in Shanghai in 1947. And it was at about this time that the girl who had betrayed Sorge was murdered. It seems possible that he ended his days behind a desk in the G.R.U. headquarters in Moscow.

After the war, Soviet Intelligence suffered a heavy blow when the attaché Gouzenko defected to the West and took with him a complete list of Russian spies and their contacts. The result was that Russia decided to reorganise her spy system in America. The man who was chosen for the job was Colonel Rudolph Abel, who ranks with Sorge and Wollweber as one of the most successful spies Russia has produced. Abel was in fact already in New York when Gouzenko's defection led to the arrest of the Rosenbergs and the rest of their network. He had been a veteran of the secret service ever since Trotsky had founded it after the revolution. Now, in 1948, after the collapse of the Soviet spy network in America, Abel patiently set about rebuilding it. The master spy established himself in an artist's studio in Fulton Street, Brooklyn. On the door was a notice: Emil Goldfus, Photographer. The place was also full of radio equipment – Abel explained that he was a radio enthusiast, and supplemented his income with radio repairs, which was true. His cover, like Sorge's, was almost perfect. A good-looking, intelligent, middle aged man, he liked girls, played the guitar well, and painted very passably indeed. The artists who attended parties in his studio regarded him as a typical Bohemian.

In fact, his job was to contact the remnants of Russia's spy ring in America, and reorganise them. It was also to re-contact various American Embassy officials who had been blackmailed into aiding Russian Intelligence when they were stationed in Moscow. By 1953, the Russian spy ring in America was stronger than ever. And the secrets that flowed back into Russia via his transmitter included details of the American hydrogen bomb, atomic submarines and rockets.

His downfall was a new assistant, Reino Hayhanen, a Russian Finn. Like many Finns, he was a heavy drinker. He was also unhappy about this spying job in a foreign country. Abel managed to get Hayhanen's wife sent out to join him, but this proved to be a mistake; they quarrelled all the time, and Hayhanen became less efficient than ever. He resented his lack of contact with Abel – their meetings were often in public parks or casually in the New York underground. In 1955, Abel went to Russia; when he returned, he discovered that Hayhanen had been drunk for weeks. He told his demoralised assistant that it was time he returned to Russia for a holiday. Hayhanen was terrified; with his reputation as a drunk, it was a 50:50 chance that he would have to be eliminated. He travelled as far as Paris, then went to the American Embassy and explained that he wanted to defect. And one more Russian spy network collapsed. Abel was sentenced to thirty years in jail, but he spent only five there. In 1962, he was exchanged for the American pilot, Gary Powers. And Russia's greatest spy since Sorge returned to end his days in peaceful retirement in Moscow.

But perhaps to talk of a "great spy" is something of an absurdity, like talking about a great pickpocket or handbag-snatcher. On the whole, the story of espionage in the twentieth century reflects no credit on any of the nations concerned. If the end of the cold war means the end of espionage, only the writers of spy thrillers will have any cause for regret.

13.
British Murder
1900–35

IN ENGLAND, the twentieth century was late in arriving. Most of the murder cases of its first decade have an oddly Victorian flavour. We can survey them quickly by glancing through a fascinating compilation called *The Hangman's Record*, a list of all the major executions since 1600. In the entries for the year 1900 we do not find a single famous, or infamous, name. Instead we learn that on 9 January Louisa Masset was hanged for the murder of her son in the lavatory of Dalston Railway Station; that on 14 August William Irwin was hanged for the murder of his wife; and on 27 December James Bargin was hanged for the murder of his sweetheart. We have to skip on to 21 March 1901, before we encounter an even moderately well-known name. This was a man called Herbert John Bennett, and the case was a classic eternal triangle. On Sunday morning, 22 September 1900, a boy walking on Yarmouth beach came upon the body of a young woman whose disarranged clothing suggested sexual assault. She had been strangled with a bootlace and apparently raped. No one seemed to know who she was, until a local landlady identified her as a woman called "Mrs Hood", who had been staying with her recently. Finally, through a laundry mark on her clothes, she was identified as a married woman called Mary Bennett, aged twenty-one, who had last been seen drinking in a pub a few hours before her death with a man who had a large moustache and an abundance of hair. The police sought her husband, but it took them seven weeks to find him – he was arrested in Woolwich on 6 November 1900. Among his possessions were found a wig and moustache, and a long gold chain with a silver watch which "Mrs Hood" had been wearing on the evening she was last seen alive.

It emerged that Mr and Mrs Bennett were basically crooks. He had met her three years earlier, when she was eighteen and he was only seventeen; she was his music teacher, and they had married in the same year. Their first attempt at establishing themselves in the world was a minor swindle; he bought old violins in junk shops, then she went round from door to door, telling a hard luck story about her husband's tragic death, and trying to sell his "last possession" to avoid starvation. In this way they made the considerable sum of £400, which they invested in a grocery business; their shop was burnt down when they were absent, and the insurance paid. They stocked another shop on credit, then decamped leaving the creditors unpaid. In South Africa, Bennett probably enrolled as a Boer spy and was deported back to England; he then took a job at Woolwich Arsenal, and probably continued his spying activities – at all events, he always seemed to have plenty of money. It was at this time that he began an affair with a pretty chambermaid named Alice Meadows. On 15 September 1900, Mrs Bennett was somehow persuaded to go to Yarmouth for a holiday, where she posed as a widow and told her landlady various lies for the sheer joy of lying. She went out on her first night there and got mildly tipsy. And on the following Saturday she went for a drink with the man with a moustache, and ended up dead on the beach. When the pub landlord identified Bennett as the man with the moustache, and a railway booking clerk recognised him as a man who had travelled back to London on the early train a few hours after the murder, it was obvious that the evidence against him was overwhelming.

The motive, it seemed clear, was pretty Alice Meadows. Bennett's spying activities – or whatever dubious occupation he was engaged in – were bringing him in fairly large sums of money, and he longed to be rid of his less-than-innocent wife and marry the child-like chambermaid. The eminent Marshall Hall, who defended Bennett, believed totally in his innocence: he agreed he was a scoundrel, but did not believe he was stupid enough to murder his wife in such a bungling manner. And even after his client had been hanged, Marshall Hall continued to believe, in the face of all the evidence, that the murder had been committed by a "sex maniac".

Like so many other murders of the period, it seemed doomed to failure from the beginning. One of the few killers who made a better show of it was Samuel Herbert Dougal, a cockney scoundrel with an Irish brogue whose two wives had died, by an odd coincidence, of oyster poisoning. He was an incorrigible seducer, with the charm of an accomplished con-man. In 1898 he met a cultivated spinster named Camille Holland, who at fifty-five felt the need for a male in her life. Dougal soon persuaded her to move with him into a remote farmhouse, but when she caught him trying to seduce the chambermaid, she ordered him to leave. In fact, it was she who left, according to Dougal, on a yachting trip, while he lived on at Moat Farm and seduced a series of chambermaids. It was not until four years later that the police became suspicious, and investigated his bank transactions. It was soon clear that he had been forging cheques in the name of the missing Camille Holland. After his arrest for forgery, they began digging up the grounds of Moat Farm, reasonably certain that they would find the body. It was not easy – Dougal had planted a hedge over the drainage ditch where it was buried. But when it was finally located, the pathologist discovered that she had been shot in the head. Dougal continued to protest his innocence until he was on the scaffold, but admitted the murder to the chaplain moments before the trap fell.

In America, the style was more gruesomely ambitious. In 1905, a middle-aged man named Johann Hoch was arrested in a New York boarding house; he was wanted for absconding with his wife's money. Police investigation revealed that Hoch was a "bluebeard" who had married twenty-four women over the past decade, and killed half them by poison after getting his hands on their savings. The others he simply abandoned. He had previously been married to the sister of his present wife, Julia Walker, but she had died suddenly after handing over her savings; he had then married sister Amelia, who was to be his downfall. Arsenic was found in Julia Walker's body, and Hoch was hanged in February 1906, his international notoriety earning him an entry in *The Hangman's Record*.

In France, meanwhile, a swindler named Henri Desire Landru had already commenced the career that would earn him the nickname of Bluebeard and lead him to the guillotine (for eleven murders) in 1922. In Germany, the horrific case of Ludwig Tessnow, the child-murderer who tore his victims to pieces, had ended with his execution in 1904. Also in Germany, a young man named Peter Kürten, in his early twenties, had already killed two school friends and made it look like drowning accident. In the late 1920s he would subject Dusseldorf to a reign of terror comparable to London's Ripper murders. In England, the only case to achieve comparable notoriety was that of George Chapman, alias Severin Klossowski, described in an earlier chapter. There is something pathetically incompetent about most British murderers of this period; they seem doomed to failure from the start.

The Crippen Case

The first British murder of the twentieth century to achieve international notoriety occurred in 1910, and the killer was an American, Hawley Harvey Crippen. It is a puzzling case, and even eighty years after his execution, no one has been able to solve the problem of why Crippen decided to murder his wife, when he might just as easily have walked out of her life and gone to live with his mistress Ethel LeNeve.

Crippen was born in Coldwater, Michigan. His parents were intensely religious and hardworking, and they imbued him with the American Dream. Until he was twenty-five he worked like a slave to achieve his medical degree; then he immediately made the mistake of marrying a dim-witted Irish nurse who bore him a son and died of apoplexy. He moved to New York, became a locum, and soon fell in love with a Polish nymphomaniac bearing the charming and Voltairean name of Cunegonde. This plump and excitable young lady – she was nineteen when Crippen met her and he was thirty – was already the mistress of a rich manufacturer, and was convinced that it was her destiny to be a great singer. Cunegonde, who preferred to be called Belle, played on Crippen's jealousy, and told him that her rich patron wanted her to run away with him; the guileless Crippen, who was short-sighted in more ways than one, immediately proposed marriage. It soon dawned on him that doctors made less money than quacks who sold patent medicines, and he needed very little persuasion to forget the Hippocratic oath. The little doctor was soon selling baby-teething medicines that consisted of almost pure opium, and a cure for piles that was advertised under the symbol of a hand with an upraised finger. He was so successful that his employer moved him to London. There Belle tried to become a music hall singer, failed to achieve the success she felt she deserved, and began to give way to outbursts of screaming temper. (To do her justice, she was much admired by her colleagues for her sheer vitality, and became a close friend of Marie Lloyd.) She also began to take lovers. Crippen bore up under blow after blow. When sacked from his patent medicine company, because his boss felt it was *infra dig* for a "doctor" to be the manager of a music hall singer, he immediately found himself another job with an equally disreputable firm of ear specialists.

There he became fond of the shorthand typist, Ethel Neave, who preferred to call herself LeNeve. She fell in love with him when she realised that he was being bullied by his wife, and that Belle spent all his money. They began meeting secretly, although Ethel withheld the final favour for no less than seven years, finally yielding her virginity in a hotel room hired by the hour. Belle knew her husband was in love with another woman, yet was apparently indifferent – she was happy to overlook his peccadilloes if he would overlook hers.

Why, then, did he decide to kill his wife on the first day of February 1910? Why did the forty-eight-year-old doctor not simply leave her and go off with Ethel?

There have been many theories. One is that he killed her by accident. The poison he administered to her was called hyoscine, which is used in small doses to calm the violently insane. One view holds that he gave her small doses to lessen her sexual demands, but it seems unlikely that she made any demands on him during their last years together. In a novel called *Dr Crippen's Diary*, the writer Emlyn Williams suggested that Crippen simply got the "tranquiliser" mixed up with the sleeping tablets in their badly-lit bathroom. But in that case, why not simply go the the police and tell them what had happened? He would undoubtedly have been acquitted.

What, in fact, happened was that Belle said goodnight to friends who had come to dinner, and was never again seen alive. The following night, Ethel slept in the house at 39 Hilldrop Crescent, Camden Town. The following day, the Secretary of the Music Hall Guild received a letter signed Belle Elmore, explaining that she was leaving for America and resigning her membership. A few weeks later, Crippen told friends that she was dangerously ill in Los Angeles, then that she had died.

Her friends were suspicious. They checked with shipping lines, and discovered that no one of that name had sailed for America in early February. One music hall performer named Lil Hawthorne even made enquiries in New York, but could find no trace of Belle. Towards the end of June 1910, Lil Hawthorne and her husband called at Scotland Yard, and communicated their suspicions to their friend Superintendent Frank Forest, who in turn sent for Inspector Walter Dew. Instead of turning it over to a subordinate, Dew decided to go and see Crippen himself. He went to Hilldrop Crescent and talked to Ethel LeNeve – "she was not pretty, but there was something oddly attractive about her" – then went on to Crippen's dental office. Here Miss LeNeve introduced him to a mild, short-sighted little man with an American accent. When Dew explained his business, Crippen sighed and said: "I had better tell you the truth." "Yes," said Dew, "that would be much the best thing." The truth, it seemed, is that Belle had run away with a lover, and Crippen had decided to announce her death to avoid scandal.

Dew was more than half-convinced. And when a search of 39 Hilldrop Crescent revealed nothing suspicious, he decided that Crippen was probably telling the truth.

That was on Friday evening. On Monday morning Dew went to see Crippen again, and found that his birds had flown. Crippen had made the mistake that cost him his life. If he had stayed quietly in Hilldrop Crescent, Dew would almost certainly have dropped the enquiry. Crippen's flight was a proclamation of guilt. Dew and his assistant, Sergeant Mitchell, searched the house from top to bottom. Finally, they went to the cellar, and levered at the bricks on the floor with a poker. The first brick came out. Soon they had cleared an area of several square feet. Mitchell went to the garden and fetched a spade. And after the first few shovelfulls of earth, a nauseating stench told them that they had found Belle Elmore. They had to keep rushing outside to gulp breaths of clean air.

Sir Melville Macnaghten arrived – the man who thought he knew the identity of Jack the Ripper – and he brought the local police surgeon. What lay on the cellar floor were fragments of a human body, part of a torso wrapped in a man's pyjama top, together with various organs – heart, lungs, windpipe, gullet, kidneys, spleen, liver, stomach, pancreas and intestines. It was impossiuble to establish the sex of these remains, since the sexual organs had been removed. The arms, legs and head were missing, and the bones had all been carefully filetted from the flesh that remained.

As newspaper headlines screamed MURDER AND MUTILA-TION, Crippen and Ethel were in Brussels. They sailed on the *S.S.Montrose*, from Antwerp to Quebec, on 20 July. But the captain of the *Montrose*, Henry Kendall, had bought the continental edition of the *Daily Mail* before sailing, and saw a photograph of the wanted man. That first day, he invited his passenger John Robinson, and his son, introduced simply as "Master Robinson", to lunch at his table; he realised within minutes that Master Robinson was a woman. He made an excuse and slipped down to their cabin; they had very little luggage, but Master Robinson's hat was packed with tissue paper to make it fit his head. He looked at the photographs of Crippen and Miss LeNeve in the *Daily Mail*; there could be no doubt that they were his passengers. The next day he sent a cable, on Marconi's newly-invented wireless telegraph, to the ship's owners: "HAVE STRONG SUSPICION THAT CRIPPEN LONDON CELLAR MURDERER AND ACCOMPLICE ARE AMONG SALOON PASSENGERS . . ."

Inspector Dew booked a passage to Quebec on a fast liner, the *Laurentic*, and as Crippen paced the deck in Quebec harbour, a man dressed in a pilot's uniform approached him and said: "Good morning, Dr Crippen." And after staring at him in shock, Crippen replied quietly: "Good morning, Mr Dew."

For his defence, Crippen took the line that he had no idea whose remains had been found in his cellar. He was fairly certain that he had left nothing that could positively identify his wife, and that the police could not prove him a murderer. But he had not been as careful as he thought. He had wrapped the torso in one of his own pyjama tops. And he had left a part of the skin of the stomach that contained an old operation scar, which Belle's women friends were able to describe. The prosecution medical team consisted of several of England's most eminent forensic experts, including Drs Pepper, Willcox and Luff, and an unknown young man called Bernard Spilsbury.

The prosecution had a powerful case: hyoscine had been found in the body, and Crippen had bought seventeen grains of the drug not long before his wife's death. The defence medical team argued that the scarred piece of skin was from a thigh, and that the scar was actually a fold; but Spilsbury asserted with quiet confidence that it *was* a scar. And a part of the rectus muscle attached to the skin proved his point beyond all doubt.

In fact, it was the pyjama jacket that was Crippen's downfall. The police had found some pyjama trousers without a jacket, but Crippen insisted that these had been purchased three or four years earlier. The prosecutor, Richard Muir, was able to tell the court that the cloth of which they were made was not manufactured until 1908. Crippen had been caught out in a direct lie. And on 27 October 1910, the jury foreman announced their verdict: Crippen was guilty. He was hanged on 23 November 1910, less than ten months after killing his wife. Ethel NeNeve was tried separately, but a jury composed largely of men found her large eyes and slim figure too appealing to believe her an accessory to murder; she was acquitted.

Although public opinion would have been outraged if Crippen had been found not guilty, or guilty on a lesser charge, it swung in his favour after his execution. Because he had done everything he could to protect Ethel, he was clearly a "gentleman". After being described as a ghoul and a monster, Crippen soon became a kind of folk hero: the mild little doctor with the bullying, unfaithful wife, who killed her by accident, or possibly in an uncontrollable outburst of emotion when she was sneering at his mistress. This is the Crippen of Ernest Raymond's novel *We the*

Accused and of Wolf Mankowitz's musical *Belle*. In Raymond's book, Crippen becomes the symbol of mildness and patience, Belle of coarseness and nymphomania, Ethel of sweet feminity. The shade of Crippen also seems to lurk behind James Hilton's novel, *We Are Not Alone*, about a mild little man whose wife is poisoned by accident, but who is found guilty of murder largely because he is having an innocent affair.

The book that probably came closest to telling the truth about Crippen appeared in 1977: *Crippen, the Mild Murderer*, was written by Tom Cullen, best known for his book identifying Druitt as Jack the Ripper. What his research uncovered was that none of the characters concerned were much like their fictional counterparts. Belle was not an alcoholic virago, she was a gay, generous person with sparkling black eyes and a kind heart. She was not a great music hall artiste, but her colleagues adored her. She was an indefatigable fund-raiser, and a loyal friend. It was true that her kitchen was always filthy, and she slept with her male lodgers; but that could be excused as part of her Bohemian temperament.

This "bird of bright plumage" was married to a thoroughly dull little man who was simply not in her class. But before we feel sorry for Crippen, we should also try to see him in a more realistic perspective. The flat truth is that he was, from the beginning of his marriage, a confidence man; he knew that his patent medicines were fakes. When fired by his American employer, he became a consultant physician to a firm of quack ear specialists who sold worthless remedies. In fact, he was not even a genuine doctor; his medical degree came from a college of homoeopathy. A magazine editor who called to see Crippen about his hearing was shocked when Crippen examined his ears with a filthy speculum which he made no attempt to disinfect, either before or after the examination. He was also startled by Crippen's flamboyant dress – the loud shirt and yellow bow tie, the enormous diamond stick pin. For a quiet, unassuming little man, Crippen had an odd taste in clothes. He also had a reputation for meanness – in this respect he was the opposite of his wife – and made a habit of offering to buy a drink, then discovering that he had left his wallet behind, and borrowing half a crown. The editor commented on his "flabby gills and shifty eyes". In fact, the ear specialist went bankrupt after being convicted of gross neglect in the death of a locksmith, and other examples of what amounted to medical homicide. We should not lose sight of the fact that Crippen was something of a crook.

And what of sweet and womanly Ethel LeNeve? We have already seen that she changed her name from Neave, because LeNeve sounded grander. Cullen's discoveries led him to write of her: "Ethel . . . lied from sheer perversity . . . in fact, she appeared incapable of telling the truth". When Crippen first came to work at Drovet's – the ear specialist – Ethel was a moaning hypochondriac, whose endless complaints of headache and catahrr had earned her the nickname of "Not very well, thank you". She had been a miserable child, painfully conscious of a deformed foot, and hating her father because he refused to let her have an operation; he insisted it would cure itself if she walked properly, and proved to be right. She was jealous of her younger sister, who was cleverer and more vivacious than she was. Yet underneath these unpleasant traits she had a strong and assertive character. She was undoubtedly more dominant than Crippen. There is a scene in James Joyce's *Ulysses* where its mild little hero Leopold Bloom fantasises about being a horse, and his wife riding him with whip and spurs. If we substitute Crippen and Belle for Bloom and Molly, we probably have an accurate picture of the basic element in their relationship. Crippen *liked* dominant women. This was why he fell in love with Ethel – not because she was sweet and feminine (although she was probably both when she felt like it), but because she was strong-minded. And, like himself, she had a touch of dishonesty. The relationship seems to bear some resemblance to that between Herbert John Bennett and his wife, whom we discussed in the opening paragraph.

They became lovers in 1906, after Crippen had caught Belle in bed with the German lodger. By 1910, Ethel was utterly sick of being "the other woman". At one point, in an effort to force Crippen's hand, she became pregnant, but she had a miscarriage. Towards the end of January 1910 she had a particularly violent fit of hysterics that went on for days. This is probably what made Crippen decide to get rid of Belle. Ethel probably planned the murder with him, she was certainly an accessory in disposing of the parts of Belle's body that were never found. She wanted her man and was willing to kill, or help her lover to kill, to achieve her ambition.

Then why did he decide to kill Belle instead of simply running away with Ethel? The answer is probably too obvious to have occurred to any of the subtle-minded writers on the case. He was a dull, unimaginative little man, lacking in all enterprise. If he abandoned Belle, it would also mean abandoning his career as a dentist and setting up in some other town. The thought of the inconvenience must have appalled him. On the other hand, he had a comfortable home and a comfortable job. Left to himself, he would have gone on living with Belle and sleeping with Ethel in hotel rooms, always hoping that Belle would solve the problem by leaving him. But Ethel wanted to rouse him from his sloth: she brought things to a head by having hysterics until he probably felt he was going mad. An honest man would have looked for an honest solution, but Cripen was a crook through and through, and could only think in terms of convenient short-cuts. Ethel got her way and got her man. She lost no time in moving in and wearing Belle's jewellery and furs. But within months he was no longer her man but Inspector Dew's. The gamble failed to pay off because Crippen lost his nerve (or, more likely, Ethel lost hers). Her lover went to the gallows, and Ethel married a man who looked oddly like Crippen, and lived to a ripe old age. No doubt she read books like *We the Accused* and *We Are Not Alone* with approval; they presented the case in a tragic light. But it was not a tragedy: just a rather sordid farce with touches of melodrama.

"You can't beat a British crime" sings the chorus in Wolf Mankowitz's *Belle*. In fact, few British crimes in the first half of the twentieth century have the status of "classics". In the year after Crippen's execution, a Russian-Jewish immigrant and convicted burglar named Steinie Morrison was tried for the murder of a miserly slum-landlord named Leon Beron on Clapham Common; the motive was robbery. The main evidence against Morrison was a cab driver who claimed that he had taken two men resembling Morrison and Beron from the East End to Clapham Common, and another cab driver who thought he had driven Morrison back from the common. Morrison was found guilty and sentenced to death, later commuted to life imprisonment. The evidence suggests that he may have been innocent: while Morrison was still under sentence of death, an Englishwoman named Maude Rider overheard a strange conversation between two Frenchmen in a Paris omnibus, and it seemed clear that they knew that Morrison was innocent, and also knew the identity of the real murderer. It seems possible that Beron's death was part of some political conspiracy – the East End of London was full of foreign Anarchists – two of them died in the famous "Siege of Sidney Street" only two days after the murder of Leon Beron. But Mrs Rider's evidence was ignored and Morrison spent the next ten years in Parkhurt Prison; he was consumed with bitterness and always maintained his innocence. He starved himself to death in 1921.

The Seddon poisoning case (1912) and the Brides in the Bath case certainly deserve a place in any collection of twentieth-century crime. Seddon was a miser, who killed his lodger – another miser named Eliza Barrow – with arsenic for the sake some India stock. Seddon's defence argued that he was already well-off and did not need the money, but Seddon's performance in the witness box made it obvious that he was an obsessional miser who would probably have killed for a five pound note. When, after his appeal against the death sentence had been dismissed, he heard the poor price that his property had fetched, he exploded: "Well, that finishes it".

George Joseph Smith was a confidence man who married lonely spinsters, relieved them of their cash, then deserted them. When one lady, Bessie Munday, refused to part with her money, he persuaded her to make a will in his favour, and drowned her in a zinc bath tub in July 1912. In December 1912, his next wife, a nurse named Alice Burnham, was also found drowned in her bath. In December 1914, the third and last victim, Margaret Lofty, was found drowned. And when a relative of Alice Burnham read the report, she went to the police. Spilsbury and Inspector Arthur Neil decided to experiment to see how a woman could be drowned in her bath; they found that it was remarkably simple – the killer simply had to grab her knees and raise them. The experiment almost cost the life of a "volunteer" in a bathing suit. But the jury were convinced; in any case, it was impossible to believe that the deaths of three wives in zinc bathtubs could be coincidence, and Smith was hanged, still tearfully protesting his innocence.

The Harold Greenwood case of 1920 is of interest largely because the obviously guilty man, who had poisoned his wife with arsenic so he could marry a younger woman, was acquitted on the grounds that there was no proof he had done it. But his solicitor's practice was ruined by the case, and he died eight years later.

Another poisoner, and solicitor, Herbert Rouse Armstrong, was less lucky. After the death of his wife, he began to make attempts on the life of a rival solicitor in the Welsh town of Hay by sending him poisoned chocolates, then (when these only made dinner guests ill), by inviting him to tea and sprinkling a scone with arsenic (Armstrong handed it to him personally saying "Excuse fingers".) The rival became violently ill but survived, whereupon Armstrong bombarded him with more invitations to meals. Eventually, Mrs Armstrong was exhumed, and found to be full of arsenic. He was hanged in May 1922.

In the same year, twenty-eight-year-old Edith Thompson was executed, together with her lover Frederick Bywaters, for her part in the murder of her husband by stabbing. Bywaters, a P&O liner steward, who was eight years her junior, had been her lover for some time, and the two engaged in a curious correspondence fantasising about killing her husband. Edith claimed that she had put a ground-up light bulb in his porridge, but at her trial Spilsbury discounted this as impossible. Bywaters finally stabbed Percy Thompson to death as he and Edith were walking home from the theatre. There was no evidence that Edith was in any way to blame, but the judge was shocked at the letters, and the suggestion of adultery, that she was sentenced to death.

1923 was an unusual year, it had no famous murder trial. But 1924 made up for it with the bizarre case of Jean Pierre Vacquier, a dandyish, vain little Frenchman who looked rather like Agatha Christie's Hercule Poirot, and who, like Frederick Bywaters, murdered his paramour's husband. In January 1924, Mrs Mabel Jones, the wife of a publican of Byfleet, Surrey, went to Biarritz for a holiday, and in the hotel met the voluble little Frenchman – who, at forty-five, was some ten years her senior – who was maintaining the radio there. They quickly became lovers, although he could speak no English and she no French; they exchanged endearments by means of a dictionary. When she returned to England, he followed her, and she went to London to see him. On 14 February he arrived at the Blue Anchor, the pub run by Mrs Jones's hard-drinking husband Alfred. Vacquier explained that he was in England to sell rights to one of his inventions, a sausage machine. He was still there six weeks later, when Mr Jones staggered into the bar parlour after a late night party and swigged down a glass of bromo-seltzer, exclaiming after he had drained it: "My God, they're bitter!" He died soon afterwards, and the post mortem disclosed strychnine poisoning. The bromo bottle proved to be empty – Vacquier had washed it out – but the water left in it showed traces of strychnine. When it was proved that Vacquier had been to London four weeks earlier to purchase strychnine, his protestations of innocence were futile. He was hanged in August 1924.

There followed another three years without a sensational murder trial. But in 1927, an unprepossessing youth of eighteen, named John Donald Merrett, stood trial in Edinburgh accused of the murder of his mother. In March 1926, Bertha Merrett had been found lying on the floor with a bullet in her head, and she had died two weeks later, denying that she had fired the shot herself. Yet it was not until months later that Merrett's guardian realised he had been forging cheques on his mother's account for some time, and that he therefore had a motive for murder. The trial was made memorable by the appearance of Spilsbury for the defence, and the equally eminent pathologist Sydney Smith for the prosecution. Unfortunately, Spilbury's view that Mrs Merrett could have shot herself without producing powder burns impressed the jury, and Merrett was acquitted of the murder charge on a Scottish verdict of "Not Proven". The ballistics expert Robert Churchill, who also appeared for the defence, lived to realise his error when, in February 1954, Merrett – now calling himself Ronald Chesney – murdered his wife and mother-in-law in Ealing, and subsequently committed suicide while on the run in Germany. By that time, Sir Bernard Spilsbury was dead; he had committed suicide in 1947.

The sensation of 1928 was the trial of two *desperadoes* named Browne and Kennedy, who had been stopped by a policeman while driving a stolen car, and shot him through both eyes. The police made no progress until an old lag told them that he believed Frederick Browne to be the murderer of P.C. Gutteridge. The murder weapon was found in Browne's garage, and his accomplice William Kennedy confessed, insisting that Browne was the murderer. But since Kennedy had tried to shoot the policeman who arrested him – only the jamming of the gun saved the man's life – the jury felt no misgiving about finding him guilty. Both were hanged.

In 1929, another matricide, Sidney Fox, came close to avoiding detection. His mother had apparently died of suffocation as a result of a fire in her hotel room. Fox had insured her life for £6,000. But the suspicions of the insurance company led to her exhumation, and Sir Bernard Spilsbury discovered that death was actually due to manual strangulation. She had been dead before Fox scattered petrol on the carpet and set it alight. He was hanged in April 1930.

Perhaps the most brutal crime of the decade was the carefully planned murder committed by a philandering garter salesman named Alfred Arthur Rouse. Since he received a skull injury during the First World War, Rouse had changed from a quiet teetotaller to a liar with an obsessive Casanova complex. After seducing more than eighty women and fathering a flock of illegitimate children, several of whom he had to maintain, Rouse evolved an ingenious scheme for ridding himself of all his problems in a single night. On the evening of 6 November 1930, he picked up a stranger in his Morris Minor, and on a lonely road close to Northampton, asked the man to refill the petrol tank from a can while he went into a field to urinate. He knocked the man unconscious with a mallet, dragged his body into the driver's seat, and then set the car on fire with petrol. It had been his intention to quietly "disappear" and start life with a new identity, assuming that the body would be mistaken for his own. But it was Guy Fawkes night, and before he could escape, he was seen by two young men returning from a bonfire party. He made some jocular remark and hurried away. When Rouse's wife identified some partly burnt clothing as her husband's, it looked as if his scheme had succeeded. But a newspaper photograph of the burnt-out car, and a description of the man seen nearby, made

Rouse realise that his scheme had gone wrong. He had gone to see a pregnant nurse, whom he was promising to marry, but now hurried back to London, where he was arrested as he climbed off the bus. Once again it was Spilsbury's evidence that convinced the jury: he was able to say that the man had been alive when the fire started, and that a fragment of petrol-soaked rag trapped between his legs proved that the blaze had been started deliberately. The jury took only an hour to find Rouse guilty of murder, and he was hanged in March 1931.

The Wallace Case

It should by now be plain that British murder cases during the first three decades of the twentieth century lack the element of mystery – there is not a single one in which the motive is not crudely obvious. The Wallace case, which took place in Liverpool in 1931, is the exception; it might have been devised by Agatha Christie. And in spite of recent evidence that seems to point towards a solution, it retains that tantalising quality of a classic unsolved mystery.

William Herbert Wallace seemed to be a completely ordinary little man. The critic James Agate once said of him: "That man was born middle-aged". But the appearance of ordinariness concealed a certain sadness and unfulfilment. Wallace was born in Keswick, in the Lake District, in 1878, the child of lower middle class parents. But he had an intellectual turn of mind, and when he discovered the *Meditations* of the Roman emperor Marcus Aurelius, decided that he was by nature a stoic – that is, one who doesn't expect much out of life, but who thinks it can be improved by hard work and discipline. Like H.G. Wells's Kipps or Mr Polly – of whom he constantly reminds us – he became a draper's assistant, and found the life just as boring as they did. His quest for adventure took him to India – but still as a draper's assistant – then to Shanghai; he found both places a great disappointment, and inevitably caught a bad dose of dysentery, which further undermined his already delicate constitution. So with his Marcus Aurelius in his pocket, he returned to England. He became a Liberal election agent in Yorkshire, and on a holiday in Harrogate, met a mild-looking, dark haired young lady named Julia Thorp. She was undoubtedly cleverer than Wallace; she was well-read, spoke French, played the piano and made excellent sketches. They talked about Marcus Aurelius and other intellectual matters and, in a rather leisurely manner, decided they liked one another enough to get married. They married in 1913 and lived in Harrogate. But in the following year, the outbreak of war cost Wallace his job – political agents were not needed during a war. Fortunately, it also caused many job vacancies, and Wallace soon found employment as an insurance agent in Liverpool, working for the Prudential. They moved into a rather dreary little terrace house in a cul-de-sac called Wolverton Crescent, in the Anfield district. And for the next seventeen years, they lived a life of peaceful and rather penurious dullness. Wallace pottered about in a chemical laboratory in his home, and even gave occasional lectures on it at the technical college. He also joined a chess club that met regularly in the City Café in North John Street. Julia read library books and sang at the piano. They had no children and, apparently, no real friends. And although life on less than £4 a week was hardly idyllic, they seemed happy enough.

The evening of 19 January 1931, was chilly and damp, but by seven o'clock, a few members had already arrived at the chess club in the City Café. Shortly after 7.15, the telephone rang. Samuel Beattie, captain of the club, answered it. A man's voice asked for Wallace. Beattie said that Wallace would be in later to play a match, and suggested he ring back. "No, I'm too busy – I have my girl's twenty-first birthday on". The man said his name was Qualtrough, and asked if Beattie could give him a message. Beattie wrote it down. It asked Wallace to go to Qualtrough's home at 25 Menlove Gardens East the following evening at seven-thirty. It was, said Qualtrough, a matter of business.

Wallace slipped quietly into the club some time before eight. Beattie gave him the message, and Wallace made a note of the address in his diary.

The following evening, Wallace arrived home shortly after six, had "high tea" – a substantial meal – and left the house at a quarter-to-seven. He instructed his wife to bolt the back door after him – that was their usual practice. Julia Wallace, who was suffering from a heavy cold, nevertheless went with him to the back gate and watched him leave. Wallace walked to a tramcar, asked the conductor if it went to Menlove Gardens East, and climbed aboard. The conductor advised him to change trams at Penny Lane, and told Wallace where to get off. The conductor of the second tram advised him to get off at Menlove Gardens West.

Wallace now spent a frustrating half hour or so trying to find Menlove Gardens East. Apparently it did not exist; although there *was* a Menlove Gardens North and a Menlove Gardens West. Wallace decided to call at 25 Menlove Gardens West, just in case Beattie had taken down the address wrongly; but the householder there said he had never heard of a Mr Qualtrough. Wallace tried calling at the house of his superintendent at the Prudential, a Mr Joseph Crew, who lived in nearby Green Lane, but found no one at home. He asked a policeman the way, and remarked on the time: "It's not eight o'clock yet". The policeman said: "It's a quarter to". He called in a general shop, then in a newsagents, where he borrowed a city directory, which seemed to prove beyond all doubt that Menlove Gardens East did not exist. He even asked the proprietress to look in her account book to make sure that there was no such place as Menlove Gardens East. People were to remark later that Wallace seemed determined to make people remember him. Finally, even the pertinacious Wallace gave up, and returned home.

He arrived back at 8.45, and inserted his key into the front door. To his surprise, it seemed to be locked on the inside. He tried the back door; that was also locked. Receiving no reply to his knock, he called on his next-door-neighbours, the Johnstons, looking deeply concerned, and asked them if they had heard anything unusual – only a thin partition wall separated them from the Wallaces. They said no. John Johnston suggested that perhaps Wallace should try his own back door key, but advised him to try the front door again. And this time, to Wallace's apparent surprise, it opened. Wallace entered the house, and the Johnstons waited politely. A few moments later, Wallace rushed out, looking shocked. "Come and see – she's been killed." They followed him through to the sitting room or parlour, which was at the back of the house. Julia Wallace was lying on the floor, face downward, and the gash in the back of her head made it clear that she had been the victim of an attack. The floor was spattered with blood. Wallace seemed curiously calm as he lit a gas mantle, walking around the body to do so, then suggested that they should look in the kitchen to see if anything had been taken. There was a lid on the kitchen floor, which Wallace said had been wrenched from a cabinet. He took down the cash box from a shelf, looked inside, and told the Johnston's that he thought about four pounds had been taken. Then, at Johnston's suggestion, Wallace went upstairs to see if anything was missing, and came down almost immediately saying: "There's five pounds in a jar they haven't taken". At this point, Johnston left to fetch the police. Wallace had a momentary breakdown, putting his hands to his head and sobbing, but quickly recovered himself. Mrs Johnston and Wallace then returned to the sitting room, where Wallace commented: "They've finished her – look at the brains". And indeed, Julia Wallace's brains were oozing on to the floor. Then Wallace said with surprise: "Why, whatever was she doing with her mackintosh and my mackintosh?" There was, in fact, a mackintosh under the body, which Wallace shortly identified as his own.

There was a knock at the door; it proved to be a policeman. Wallace told him about his fruitless search for Qualtrough, then accompanied him upstairs. Constable Williams felt that Wallace seemed "extraordinarily cool and calm". The bedroom seemed to have been disturbed, with pillows lying near the fireplace, but the drawers of the dressing table were closed.

Another policeman arrived; then, just before ten o'clock, Professor J.E.W. MacFall, the professor of forensic medicine at Liverpool University. MacFall concluded that Mrs Wallace had died of a violent blow, or blows, to the back left hand side of the skull, and deduced that she had been sitting in an armchair, leaning forward as if talking to somebody, when the blow had been struck. She had fallen to the floor, and the attacker had rained about eleven more blows on her. He also reached the interesting conclusion that Mrs Wallace had died about four hours earlier – that is, at six o'clock.

This, it later proved, was impossible, for the fourteen-year-old milk boy, Alan Close, was to testify that he had delivered a can of milk at 6.25, and that it had been taken in by Mrs Wallace, who advised him to hurry home because he had a cough.

But MacFall had planted suspicion of Wallace in the minds of the police. Two weeks later, on 2 February 1931, Wallace was charged with his wife's murder. He became very pale and replied: "What can I say to this charge, of which I am absolutely innocent?"

His trial began on 22 April, before Mr Justice Wright. The prosecution case was that Wallace had concocted an elaborate plan to murder his wife, and had phoned the café to make the appointment with Qualtrough on the evening before the murder. The endless and elaborate enquiries about Menlove Gardens East were intended to provide him with a perfect alibi; but Mrs Wallace was already lying dead in her sitting room when William Herbert Wallace left the house. In the closing speech for the crown, Mr E.G. Hemmerde made much of the "inherent improbabilities" in Wallace's story: that surely an insurance agent would not spend his evening on such a wild goose chase, that he would have hurried back home the moment he knew that a Menlove Gardens East did not exist. He also made much of Wallace's apparent calmness immediately after the discovery of the body, and mentioned in pssing the possibility that Wallace had stripped naked and then put on his mackintosh, and battered his wife to death, before leaving the house to look for Qualtrough.

The judge's summing up was favourable to Wallace, and there was some surprise when, after only an hour, the jury returned a verdict of guilty. Wallace was shattered, he had been confident of acquittal. But he appealed against the verdict, and in the following month, the Court of Criminal Appeal quashed it, and Wallace was freed.

He was taken back at his old job. But most of his colleagues had doubts about his innocence. He was given a job in the office. He moved house, to Meadowside Road in Bromsborough, a Liverpool suburb. And on 26 February 1933 – less than two years after his ordeal – he died in hospital of cancer of the liver. Ever since that date, writers on crime have disputed his guilt or innocence.

The main problem, of course, is that of motive. Wallace was a lifelong keeper of diaries, and his diaries make it clear that his married life was peaceful and serene. There was no suggestion of another woman, or that he was tired of his wife. His diaries after his trial continue to protest his innocence, with entries like: "Julia, Julia my dear, why were you taken from me?" The crime writer Nigel Morland, who examined the case at length in *Background to Murder* and who was convinced of Wallace's guilt, has to fall back on generalisations like: "The human heart is always a vast mystery".

Yseult Bridges, who also wrote about the case, became convinced of Wallace's guilt when she read a series of "ghosted" articles about his life which appeared in *John Bull* in 1932. There Wallace remarks that he had matched his brains against some of the greatest chess players in the world. Yseult Bridges comments that "he was never more than a third rate player in an obscure little club", and concludes that Wallace was a pathological liar. But another writer, Jonathan Goodman, looked more closely into the matter, and concludes (in *The Killing of Julia Wallace*) that Wallace was telling the truth after all; in the 1920s he *had* played in "simultaneous exhibition matches" against world-famous players like Capablanca – and been thoroughly beaten.

Kenneth Gunnell, a parliamentary candidate from Redruth, Cornwall, independently discovered that Wallace was telling the truth about his chess opponents, and so began to study the case in detail. He made one odd discovery. Amy Wallace, the wife of Wallace's elder brother Joseph, was a tough and dominant lady, and Gunnell found out that in Malaya – where she had lived in the 1920s – Amy had been a member of a flagellation sect, and indulged in beating black boys. He noted that after his acquittal, Wallace sometimes acted like a man with something on his mind – not murder, perhaps, but some guilty secret. Could it be that Amy Wallace was Herbert Wallace's mistress, and that *she* murdered Julia? Mr Gunnell even speculated that the murder weapon was the metal handle of a riding whip. Unfortunately, Mr Gunnell's stimulating theory remained unpublished. Yet when I read the typescript of his book, I found myself ultimately unconvinced. Although my view of Wallace was rather negative – he seemed to me a cold-hearted egoist who had married Julia for her money (which he used to pay his debts), then treated her purely as a piece of domestic furniture – it seemed clear that he was simply not the type to engage in affairs with highly dominant women; Amy Wallace probably terrified him.

In 1960, I collaborated with Patricia Pitman on *An Encyclopaedia of Murder*. Mrs Pitman was convinced of Wallace's guilt, I – in spite of misgivings about his character – of his innocence. He simply had no reason to kill Julia. Two or three years later, she surprised me by telling me that she was now convinced of Wallace's innocence. It seemed that she had been talking to one of Britain's leading crime experts, J.H.H. Gaute, a director of Harraps publishers, and he had told her the real identity of the murderer. I hastened to contact Joe Gaute, with whom I had had much friendly correspondence about murder. It was from him that I first heard the name of the man he was certain was the killer of Julia Wallace: Gordon Parry. Wallace himself, it seemed, had believed that Parry murdered his wife, and after his retirement had made a public statement to the effect that he had had an alarm button installed inside his front door.

After the murder, Wallace had been asked by the police what callers might have been admitted to the house by his wife; he named fifteen people (including his sister-in-law Amy). Asked if he suspected any of them Wallace hesitated, then admitted that he was suspicious of a young man named Gordon Parry. This man had called at his house on business, and was trusted by Julia. But he had a criminal record. And he knew where Wallace kept his collection money. At the time of the murder, Parry was heavily in debt. Questioned by the police, Parry alleged that he had been with "friends" on the evening of the murder, and the friends corroborated this; however, two years later, Parry admitted that it had been "a mistake".

Joe Gaute had been curious about Parry's present whereabouts, and had casually looked him up in the London Telephone Directory. It was a long shot, but it paid off. Parry was listed at an address in south London. The author Jonathan Goodman, who was writing his book on the Wallace case, and another crime expert, Richard Whittington-Egan, went to call on him.

Parry, a powerfully built little man with sleeked-back grey hair and a military moustache, received them with the "bogus bonhomie of a car salesman", and talked to them on his doorstep. They decided that "his manner masks . . . considerable firmness, even ruthlessness. He would be a nasty man to cross". Parry hinted that he could reveal much about Wallace, and described him as "a very strange man" and "sexually odd". He seemed to know what had become of everybody involved in the case, as if he had been carefully following its aftermath over the years. And when he finally dismissed Goodman and Whittington-Egan, they both had the feeling that he was thinking that he had fooled better people than they were . . . In his book *The Killing of Julia Wallace*, Goodman refers to Parry as "Mr X", and it is fairly clear that he regards him as the chief suspect.

In 1980, a news editor in Liverpool's Radio City, Roger Dilkes, became interested in the Wallace case, and started researching it for a programme. He contacted Jonathan Goodman, who at first was understandably cagey about revealing Parry's identity, in case he found himself involved in a libel suit. But through Wallace's solicitor, Hector Munro, Dilkes tracked down Parry's identity. At the time of the murder, Parry was twenty-two. The son of well-to-do parents, he had worked for the Prudential for a while, but had failed to pay in various premiums he had received—his parents had paid the money. Parry had been charged at various times with theft, embezzlement and indecent assault—at his trial a medical expert had described him as "a sexual pervert".

Dilkes persisted, but when he finally tracked down Parry to North Wales, he discovered that he had died a few weeks before, in April 1980. Nevertheless, he continued with his investigation. Who were the "friends" who had given Parry his alibi for the night of the murder? The answer that emerged was that it was not friends but *a* friend – a Miss Lily Lloyd, to whom Parry was engaged. And from Jonathan Goodman he learned that when Parry had jilted her two years later, Miss Lloyd had gone to Wallace's solicitor and offered to swear an *affidavit* saying that the alibi she had given Parry for the night of the crime was untrue. Dilkes then managed to track down Miss Lloyd, who had played a piano in a cinema in the 1930s. If the police had taken the trouble to check *her* alibi, they would have learned that she could not have been with Parry at the time of the murder – she was working in the cinema.

Finally, Dilkes uncovered the clinching piece of evidence. At the time of the murder, a young garage mechanic named John Parkes had been working near Parry's home. He knew Parry as a "wide boy"—in fact, had been to school with him. On the night of the murder, Parry had called at the garage in an agitated state, and washed down his car with a high pressure hose. Parkes saw a glove in the car, and pulled it out to prevent it getting wet. It was soaked with wet blood.

Dilkes had finally tracked down the murderer of Julia Wallace, but half a century too late.

In England, the Wallace trial was the last notable English murder trial for four years, although in Scotland, the 1934 trial of Jeannie Donald was rendered memorable by the brilliant forensic detective work that convicted her. The murder, of an eight-year-old girl named Helen Priestly, took place in a working class tenement in Aberdeen. On 20 April 1934, Helen failed to return from an errand; her body was found a few hours later in a sack under the stairs. The missing knickers and blood trickling from the vagina suggested a sex crime. But forensic examination revealed no traces of semen, and suggested that the injuries had been inflicted with some instrument like the handle of a pudding spoon. The body had been found close to the flat of a woman called Jeannie Donald, who was known to have a violent temper and to dislike Helen Priestly—the child liked to chant the nickname "Coconut" in her hearing. Jeannie Donald seemed to have a perfect alibi—she said she had been out shopping at the time of the murder – but when she named the prices she had paid for various items, it was noted that they were the prices charged the *previous* Friday.

Sydney Smith, Professor of Forensic Medicine at Edinburgh, was called in to see what he could make of the clues. A magnifying glass showed human and animal hairs in the sack in which the body had been found, and some washed cinders. Many people in the block re-used partly burnt cinders, but Jeannie Donald was the only one who washed them first to remove the ash. The human hair proved to be virtually identical to Jeannie Donald's, and the potato sack resembled others found in her flat (her brother was a farm worker who supplied the Donalds with vegetables). Blood spots found on a newspaper in Jeannie Donald's flat were type "O", the same as Helen Priestly's. But they could, of course, have been Jeannie Donald's. She refused to have a blood sample taken, but Smith was able to obtain one of her used sanitary towels from the prison; it proved to be of a different blood type. Finally, bloodstains found on a floorcloth in the flat were found to contain a rare type of bacterium, which was also found in Helen Priestly's intestines. It became clear that Helen had run past the Donald's flat chanting "Coconut", and that Jeannie Donald had grabbed her on the way back and dragged her inside. Her intention was probably to shake her violently by the throat, but Helen may have fainted. Then, assuming she had killed her, Jeannie Donald attempted to make it look like a sex crime, and placed the body in a sack.

The defence underestimated the strength of the scientific evidence, and decided to plead "Not Guilty". But Smith's performance in the witness box convinced the jury, who took only eighteen minutes to find Jeannie Donald guilty of murder. She was sentenced to death, but it was later commuted to life imprisonment, of which she served ten years.

The Ruxton Case

The following year was to see another sensational murder case in which forensic science played the leading role. The "medical detective" whose work was so vital to the prosecution was Dr John Glaister, Regius Professor of Forensic Medicine at the University of Glasgow. And he became involved because the murderer had made the mistake of disposing of the remains in Scotland.

September 29th 1935 was a cool autumn day. A young lady from Edinburgh had paused in her afternoon walk to lean on the parapet of a bridge across a pretty stream called the Gardenholme Linn. It was an attractive spot: the stream, shaded by trees and ferns, ran in a narrow rocky bed, forming small pools and waterfalls. But as she stared at this delightful scene, she noticed something that made her stomach turn over. Below the bridge, resting on the boulders, there was some kind of a bundle wrapped in a piece of cloth. It had burst open and something that looked like a human arm was sticking out.

The girl hurried back to her hotel in Moffat, two miles away, and told her brother what she had seen. He went back with her, clambered down under the bridge, and quickly realised that she was correct. It was a part of a human arm and the parcel it was sticking out from looked as if it contained several more pieces. They hurried back to the police station.

The police soon located four bundles. And it immediately became clear that they were dealing with a case of double murder. For one of the bundles contained a human head, and a few feet away, under the bridge, there was another head. The other parcels contained severed pieces of arms and legs, and chunks of flesh.

The next morning, the remains were examined by two local doctors in the morgue; then Professor Glaister arrived, together with a colleague, Dr Gilbert Millar. They were confronted by a problem that would have made Sherlock Holmes rub his hands. This killing was not the work of some frightened amateur. It had been carefully thought out and executed by a man who knew exactly what he was doing. He had made only one major miscalculation. He had dropped the parcels into a swollen, flooded stream, and assumed that they would be carried away into the River Annan, a few hundred yards downstream. Once in the Annan, they might have ended up in the Solway Firth. But the Linn was full of boulders, and some of the parcels had caught against them. Then the rain stopped, and there were a few days of Indian Summer; the stream dwindled to a trickle among the rocks, and the incriminating parcels were left high and dry.

Even so, the murderer had taken care in covering his tracks. He had not only dismembered the bodies, he had also removed skin from the heads, to make the faces unrecognisable and had cut off the fingertips from some of the hands, to prevent fingerprint identification. Glaister and Millar found themselves confronted by a gruesome pile of decomposing flesh, a few stray pieces of two bodies of unknown age, unknown sex, unknown identity. It was difficult to know where to begin.

The first step was to make sure that no further decomposition took place. The remains were sent to the Anatomy Department at the University of Edinburgh. There they were treated with ether, to destroy the maggots, then left in a weak formalin solution, to "pickle" them. This also had the advantage of removing the worst of the smell. As the weeks went by, a few other pieces of body turned up from the Linn area—one even found by the side of the road. Glaister and Millar found themselves confronted with a human jigsaw puzzle with seventy pieces. But the puzzle was far from complete: one "body" consisted only of head and limbs.

Now it is true that there have been plenty of examples of dismembered bodies in British criminal history. But in most of the famous cases, there was no problem of identification. In 1875, Henry Wainwright, a London businessman, murdered his mistress, Harriet Lane, and buried her dismembered body in his warehouse in East London. But he was caught when he tried to remove the remains to another hiding place. In 1910, the notorious Doctor Crippen murdered his wife Belle Elmore, and buried her body in the basement of his house. Sir Bernard Spilsbury's examination and reconstruction of the body was another masterpiece of medical detection; but there was never the slightest doubt about the identity of the body—Crippen was caught running away to America. In 1924, Patrick Mahon murdered his mistress, who was pregnant, and scattered bits of her dismembered body from the windows of trains; but his wife's suspicions led the police to a bungalow in Sussex, where they found the remaining parts of the unwanted mistress. And in the following year, a poultry farmer named Norman Thorne killed his mistress and buried her pieces under a chicken run; but he ended by showing the police where to look for them.

Of course, there *had* been the occasional case where the body was difficult to identify. In March 1725, a nightwatchman found a severed head on the Thames mud, near Lambeth Bridge. The parish officers ordered the head to be set on a stake in a churchyard at Westminster, and it was finally recognised as the husband of a woman called Catherine Hayes. She was convicted, together with two of her lovers, of her husband's murder, and burned alive. The preservation of a head also caused the downfall of James Greenacre, who in 1836 murdered and dismembered a woman he had promised to marry. The head was found in the Regent Canal in Stepney, and was kept in spirits; it was identified by her brother. (The motive here seems to have been robbery.) And in 1917, a torso found wrapped in a sheet in Regent Square, Bloomsbury, was quickly identified by means of a laundry mark, and a Frenchman named Louis Voisin was hanged for the murder of his mistress. (This was probably a miscarriage of justice—it is almost certain that she was murdered by another mistress, in a jealous fit, and Voisin merely helped dispose of the body.)

In all these cases, the problem of identification was fairly simple. But Glaister and his colleagues were confronted by a case in which there had been a systematic attempt to destroy all means of identification.

The first step was certainly the easiest – to sort out the pieces into two separate bodies. Fortunately, one of the victims was more than six inches shorter than the other. So it was not difficult to separate the smaller from the larger body. When this was done, Glaister and his team found they had one almost complete body, the taller one, and one body without a trunk. They also found one relic that at first caused them much bafflement: an enormous single eye, a "Cyclops eye", which certainly did not belong to either of the bodies. A Cyclops eye is a physical malformation that occurs in some human beings and animals—the two eyes have run together into one, like Siamese twins. The doctors dissected it, but they never found out where it came from, or even what animal it belonged to. It remains one of those minor mysteries connected with the case.

And what could Glaister say about the remains of the two bodies? His first guess was that one of them was a man, the smaller of the two. The other was certainly a woman, for the remains included a pelvis. This looked like a crime of passion. A jealous husband who found his wife in bed with her lover, who killed them both in a fit of rage, then set out to cover up all trace of the crime.

And what could they deduce about the murderer? Well, it was almost certain that he was a medical man, or had had some medical training. For there was one feature that distinguished this case from nearly all other cases of dismemberment. The killer had used a knife, not a saw. Unless you have some knowledge of anatomy, a human body is a difficult thing to dismember with a knife. It is easier to use a saw. This man had separated the limbs neatly at the joints, which argued that he was either a butcher or a doctor.

He had carefully removed most of the skin from both the heads. But he seemed to have been interrupted in the case of the smaller of the two, for he had left some of the hair, although it had been cut short. Teeth had been removed from both heads, obviously to prevent a dentist from identifying them by means of his dental records. For some strange reason, the killer had even removed part of the foot of the taller body. He had obviously spent a lot of time making sure it should not be identified. It looked hopeless. Even if the police could find a case of a missing man and woman, they would find it difficult to prove that these were their remains.

But Glaister was in luck. The hands that were found under the bridge had no fingertips, and therefore no fingerprints. But in later bundles, the police found the hands of the other body, plus fingertips. After being soaked in hot water, it was possible to get fingerprints from them. It seemed incredible, but the murderer had made an elementary error, and made it possible to identify one of his victims beyond all doubt.

Glaister and his team, which included Dr James Brash, another brilliant anatomist, now settled down to the gruesome work of examining the small pieces of flesh that had been found in the bundles. Many of these were unrecognisable. There were two breasts present, which is what had been expected. Then the team made a discovery that cast an entirely new light on the case. Another piece of flesh also looked like a female breast. Under a microscope, there could be no doubt whatever: this was mammary tissue. So the bodies were those of two women, not a man and a woman. A closer examination of other pieces of flesh revealed that this was undoubtely so, for there were also parts of the external genital organs of two women.

The next major question was the age of the two bodies. There are several methods of determining this. Our skulls have "joining lines" which are called sutures. While we are still growing, these remain unclosed. When we cease to grow, they very gradually seal themselves up; this is usually around the age of forty. One of the two skulls – the smaller of the two – had unclosed sutures. On the other, the sutures were almost fully closed. This indicated clearly that one of the victims was around forty, and the other was certainly under thirty. X-rays of the jawbone of the younger woman showed that the wisdom teeth had still not pushed their way through. This meant that she was probably in her early twenties. The joints of the bones also gave a reliable indication of age. The cartillage – the soft material of which bones are originally made – gradually changes into "caps", called "epiphyses", and age can be estimated from how far this change has taken place. The epiphyses of the two bodies confirmed that one was of a girl of twenty or so, the other of a woman approaching middle age.

As to the cause of death, this was fairly clear, in spite of the condition of the two bodies. The taller woman had five stab wounds in the chest, several broken bones, and many bruises. The hyoid bone was fractured, suggesting that she had been throttled into unconsciousness before the other injuries were inflicted. The swollen and bruised tongue confirmed this inference. A murderer who strangled his victim, then beat and stabbed her, was obviously in the grip of violent rage—the kind of rage often inspired by jealousy. Since the trunk of the other body was missing, there was no way of telling whether she had also been stabbed, but the evidence was against it. Glaister concluded she had been battered to death with a blunt instrument. It hardly needed a Sherlock Holmes to infer that she had been killed as an afterthought, probably to keep her silent. The fact that the murderer had taken less trouble to conceal her identity pointed to the same conclusion.

But if he was really anxious to conceal the identity of the bodies, there was one major point he had overlooked. The older woman had an unusually long face; in life, her appearance must have been distinctly "horsey". He would have done well to make sure it was never found.

And so even if there had been no other clues, the facts uncovered by Glaister's team would have provided the police with all the necessary leads. In fact, the police were already working on another set of clues. The head of the younger woman had been wrapped in a pair of child's rompers. One of the bundles had been wrapped in a blouse with a patch under the arm. Some of the remains had been wrapped in newspaper before being tied in sheets. Some of these newspapers had dates in August, but the most recent was a *Sunday Graphic* of 15 September 1935, which indicated clearly that the murder had taken place on or after that date. Moreover, this *Sunday Graphic* was a special local edition, printed especially for the Morecambe and Lancaster area.

In Lancaster at this time, the police were investigating the murder of a woman called Mrs Smalley, and in the course of their investigations, they questioned the servant of a Persian doctor named Ruxton. Ruxton's real name was Bukhtyar Hakim, and he was born in Bombay; he had been practising medicine in Lancaster since 1930. Ruxton was upset by the questions about Mrs Smalley, a lady from Morecambe whose body had been found a year earlier. On 24 September, five days before the bodies were found in the Linn, Ruxton went to the Lancaster police to complain about the questioning of his servant. The doctor was a short, rather good-looking man of thirty-six, with a wildly excitable manner; he talked volubly and waved his hands. It was not the first time the Lancaster police had met this excitable foreigner. Two years before, Mrs Ruxton had come to the police station to complain of her husband's brutality. Ruxton was brought to the police station, where he waved his arms, foamed at the mouth, and screamed that his wife had been unfaithful and he would kill her if it continued. Then, quite abruptly, he calmed down, and gave his wife money to go to see her sister in Edinburgh. Later that day, after she had packed her bag, she changed her mind and decided to stay. Obviously, the relations between this couple were somewhat stormy.

So when Ruxton came to complain about the questioning of his servant, the police were not surprised when he added that his wife had left him again—the second time in a year. He said she had gone off to Scotland a fortnight before. She had apparently taken the maid, a twenty-year-old girl named Mary Rogerson, with her.

Mary Rogerson was a Morecambe girl, and her parents were not at all happy about her disappearance. She was strongly attached to her family; every time she had a day off, she spent it with them. She once spent a fortnight's holiday on a farm with Ruxton's three young children, but then she wrote every day. Now they had heard nothing from her for nearly two weeks, and they were worried. They were even more worried when Ruxton called on them, the day after he had been to see the police, and told them that Mary had got herself pregnant with the laundry boy, and that his wife had taken her away for an abortion. The Rogersons were flabbergasted. Mary just wasn't that type. She was rather a quiet girl, not particularly pretty – she had a cast in one eye – who was strongly attached to the three Ruxton children. (Their ages ranged from four to seven). She was as unlikely to get herself pregnant by a laundry boy as to rob a bank. Yet Ruxton assured them that Mary *was* pregnant; he implied he had examined her himself. The father, upset and suspicious, told Ruxton that he was going to the police. Ruxton looked alarmed. "Don't do that," he told them, "I'll bring her over on Sunday". They agreed to wait that long.

But Ruxton didn't bring her over on Sunday. Three days later, in spite of Ruxton's pleas, Mary Rogerson's stepmother reported to the police that Mary was missing. One week later, she gave the police a description of her stepdaughter, which was circulated to the newspapers and to other police forces. That evening, 9 October, Ruxton again appeared at the Lancaster police station, in his usual state of feverish excitement. The police would have to help him find his wife, he said. It was being suggested that she had been murdered and thrown in the Linn, and it was ruining his practice. He burst into tears. "Can't you have it published in the papers that there is no connection between the two?" The Chief Constable made soothing noises, and drew up some kind of non-commital statement to be issued to the press. This seemed to satisfy Ruxton, who went away.

But in fact, he had been the chief suspect in the Linn case since earlier that day. The Chief Constable of Dumfriesshire had seen an article in the Glasgow *Daily Record* describing the disappearance of Mary Rogerson. He immediately decided to contact the Lancaster police and Mary's parents. The Scottish police arrived in Morecambe, bringing with them the blouse and the children's rompers. As soon as Mrs Rogerson saw the blouse, she knew her stepdaughter was dead. She recognised it as one she had bought in a jumble sale and patched under the arm; she had given it to Mary the previous Christmas. She was unable to identify the rompers, but she suggested someone who might know – a woman with whom Mary and the Ruxton children had spent a holiday earlier that year, a Mrs Holme. Mrs Holme dispelled the last vestiges of doubt about the bodies; she identified the rompers as a pair she had given to Mary for the children. She was able to be positive because she recognised the knot which she herself had tied in the elastic.

The Lancaster police were now certain they had their man, but they acted with caution. Ruxton had no less than three charladies who worked at the house: Mrs Smith, Mrs Oxley and Mrs Curwen. The police talked to Mrs Oxley, who usually arrived at the Ruxton house, 2 Dalton Square, at seven in the morning. On the morning of Sunday, 15 September – the day Mrs Ruxton and her maid had disappeared – Ruxton had arrived at her house at 6.30, and told her husband that she needn't go to the house that day, because Mrs Ruxton had gone to Edinburgh, and he intended to take the children to Morecambe. She went to the house the following day, and found it in a state of chaos. The stair carpets had been removed, and the bath was full of yellow stains. In the backyard there was a pile of some material that seemed to have been burned with petrol.

But the clinching evidence came from one of Ruxton's patients, a Mrs Hampshire. She told how Ruxton had called on her on Sunday afternoon. He had apparently taken his three children over to Morecambe, five miles away, to stay at the house of a dentist called Anderson, Ruxton's closest friend. His wife had gone to Blackpool, Ruxton explained, and Mary Rogerson had gone for a holiday. The decorators were coming to his house the next day, and he had to remove the carpets. Unfortunately, he had cut his hand badly on a tin of peaches, and he needed some help . . . Mrs Hampshire and her husband obligingly returned with him to 2 Dalton Square, and helped "prepare" the place for the decorators. There was an untouched meal, for two people, in the lounge, and an uncooked Sunday joint. The carpets had been taken up from the stairs and the landings, and one of them was stained with blood. The bath was stained yellow. Mrs Hampshire scrubbed at it with scouring powder, but there was still a great deal of stain left in it. Her husband scrubbed the stairs. Ruxton left them there while he went off to Morecambe again. Here he suggested that his children should stay the night with the dentist and his wife. The Anderson's agreed, and Mrs Anderson and the children returned with Ruxton to collect their nightclothes. On the way, they stopped at the home of Mary Rogerson's parents, where Ruxton left a message that Mary had gone to Scotland for a

few weeks. Back at Dalton Square, Ruxton told the Hampshires –
who were still busily scrubbing – that they could have the carpets,
and also a blue suit which he had been wearing at the time he
cut his hand; it was badly bloodstained. Once again, he went off,
leaving the Hampshires to their cleaning. They stayed until 9.30,
and then locked up and went home. They noticed that the doors of
Ruxton's bedroom and Isabella Ruxton's bedroom were locked.

What would the Hampshires have seen if they could have found
the keys and looked into the locked rooms? In all probability, they
would have found Isabella Ruxton's body already hacked into
pieces, and perhaps already parcelled up. They would probably
have found Mary Rogerson, naked but so far untouched. Her
body would be dismembered in the bath that night, for when
Mrs Oxley came the next morning, the bath was again stained
yellow.

So Ruxton had actually given the bloodstained carpets to the
Hampshires. These carpets were outside in the yard. Ruxton's
original intention had probably been to burn them but it had
rained heavily. The carpets were so wet that the Hampshires
decided to take them home later. But they took the suit.
And early the next morning, Ruxton called on Mrs Hampshire
again, and told her he wanted to send the suit to be cleaned.
Ruxton looked ill and unshaven, and he was wearing an old
raincoat, although he was normally careful of his appearance.
Mrs Hampshire promised she would send the suit to be cleaned.
Ruxton insisted that she cut out the tag with his name on it, and
burn it in his presence. When this was done, he seemed satisfied
and went away.

Mrs Oxley, the charlady, further added that when the newspapers published the story of the finding of the remains in the
Linn, Ruxton seemed very pleased with himself. He read the
account to her, and said: "So you see, Mrs Oxley, it is a man
and a woman. It is not our two".

All this made it fairly clear that Ruxton was the man the police
were looking for. And Ruxton himself realised how close the
chase was getting. On the day Mrs Rogerson identified the blouse
as Mary's, Ruxton went off the Edinburgh to see his wife's sister.
He asked her if Isabella was staying with her. The sister, Mrs
Nelson, countered by asking him if he had done anything to her.

(She had read of the finding of the bodies in the Linn.) Ruxton said of course not, he loved her too much.

When he got back to Lancaster in the early hours of the morning, 10 October, he was met by a detective. Ruxton must have thought for a moment that he was about to be arrested, but the detective only wanted to ask him a few questions. Ruxton told him that he had been to Edinburgh, looking for his wife. And he added that a man called Bobbie Edmondson probably knew where she was. Edmondson, said Ruxton, was having an affair with his wife. A few weeks earlier, Bobbie Edmondson and Isabella Ruxton had gone to a hotel in Edinburgh, and stayed there together.

Oddly enough, this was true, but not in the way Ruxton suggested. Robert Edmondson was an assistant solicitor in the Town Hall, opposite the Ruxton's house. His whole family, including his parents and sister, were friendly with the Ruxtons, and he had often been a guest in their home. A week before Mrs Ruxton's disappearance, the whole Edmondson family went to Edinburgh with Mrs Ruxton. They all stayed in a hotel, in four separate rooms. Ruxton did not tell the detective that the whole Edmondson family had gone to Edinburgh; and he told a lie when he added that Edmondson and Mrs Ruxton had booked into the hotel under the name of Mr and Mrs Ruxton.

Later that day, Ruxton called on Mrs Hampshire, ans asked what had happened to the blue suit; she said it was upstairs. "Then burn it," said Ruxton. He asked about the carpets, and was told that one of them was too badly stained to be cleaned. "Then burn that too". He went off saying he intended to make a statement to the police. In fact, he called at the police station and complained about the gossip; he also gave a description of his wife, which was written down. The following day he spent writing out a long account of his movements for the police, and paid more visits to the police station; it was on this occasion that he asked the Chief Constable, Captain Vann, to issue a statement to the press saying there was no connection between Mrs Ruxton and the bodies in the Linn.

The next day, Saturday 12 October, was his last day of freedom. He called on several people, asking them to support his account of various facts. But most of the "facts" he wanted them to confirm were false. He asked Mrs Oxley to say that she had spent a couple of hours cleaning his house on the Sunday morning of Mrs Ruxton's disappearance; Mrs Oxley replied that she couldn't say it, since it was not true. He also asked an odd job man to swear that he had come to the house on the Saturday evening before the disappearance, and that Mary Rogerson had opened the door to him; the odd job man pointed out that this was untrue. (The exact point of this request is not clear, for there can be no doubt that Mary Rogerson died in the early hours of Sunday morning but Ruxton was becoming confused by this time.)

That evening, 12 October, Ruxton was asked to call at the police office. Both the Scottish and the English police were present. Ruxton was questioned all night, and at 7.20 the next morning, he was charged with the murder of Mary Rogerson. He indignantly denied it. In the face of overwhelming circumstantial evidence, Ruxton continued to deny that he was guilty of either of the murders. His story, and that of the defence, was that the bodies found in the Linn were not those of Isabella Ruxton and Mary Rogerson. They had disappeared, and it was not the business of the defence to say where they were now. But Ruxton was innocent of their deaths. This meant, of course, that the whole weight of the prosecution depended on the medical evidence. If the jury could be convinced that the bodies in the Linn were Mrs Ruxton and Mary Rogerson, then Ruxton was condemned; if not, he was free.

Judges are normally unhappy about sentencing a man to death on purely circumstantial evidence, but in this case, it must be admitted that the evidence was overwhelming and irrefutable. No murderer has ever taken more trouble than Ruxton to spin the net around himself. At the trial, ninety-nine per cent of the evidence was for the prosecution; Ruxton himself was the only witness for the defence. It is the kind of case that makes the layman feel that our legal system is an elaborate game. Ruxton's counsel, Norman Birkett, must have known that his client didn't stand the remotest chance. Every witness who appeared drove another nail into his coffin. The opening speech for the crown by J.C. Jackson made Ruxton's guilt so obvious that the jury could have filed out there and then. He pointed out that two years before the murders, Ruxton had threatened to murder his wife in front of policemen. He was convinced his wife had been unfaithful. Again, in 1935, he "behaved like a madman", accusing his wife of infidelity – again to a policeman – and threatening to kill her. The week before the murder, Mrs Ruxton went to Edinburgh with the Edmondson family, and Ruxton hired a car (his wife had taken his car) and followed them. He was convinced his wife had spent the night in Bobbie Edmondson's bed. The following Saturday, Mrs Ruxton drove to Blackpool to visit her two sisters; she spent the evening with them and drove back to Lancaster around midnight. It did not take much imagination to guess what happened next. Ruxton had worked himself into a frenzy of jealousy; throughout the evening he was probably conjuring up visions of his wife being possessed on the sands at Blackpool or in the back of his own car . . . The fact that there was a meal set out in the dining room implies that he had expected her back in time for supper. When she came back after midnight, he was half insane with rage and jealousy. He probably beat her in an attempt to make her confess her infidelity, then throttled and stabbed her. Mary Rogerson probably heard the screams and came to the bedroom, or perhaps Ruxton went to her room and killed her. In the previous year he had told a policeman that there were *two* people in the house he felt like killing. Why two? Because he believed that Mary Rogerson was Mrs Ruxton's confidant and accomplice, who knew exactly what was going on?

At 6.30 the next morning he was at the house of the charlady, telling her that she needn't come that day. At ten-to-nine, the woman who delivered newspapers rang the doorbell of Ruxton's house but got no reply; she went back at nine, and this time Ruxton opened the door. He told her his wife had gone to Scotland with the maid. When the girl with the milk came, Ruxton let her in; his hand was bandaged and he told her he had "jammed" it – presumably in a door. Later he told other people he'd cut it while opening a tin of peaches. At 10.30, Ruxton was at a local garage, not his usual one, and bought two large cans of petrol; then he went to his own garage and had another four gallons put in the tank of his car. Why use two garages, unless to cover up his tracks? The petrol in the cans was used to burn something in his yard that day – bloodstained clothing and carpets. When he had taken up the carpets from the stairs, he asked Mrs Hampshire, one of his patients, to help him get the house ready "for the decorators". (Two days later, he called on a decorator, and tried to persuade him that he had promised to come and start work the previous day; the decorator flatly denied this.) Mrs Hampshire noticed the bloodstained bath, bloodstained carpets, and fragments of straw – the bodies were partly packed in straw. He took the children to his friends the Andersons, and asked them to look after them overnight. And that night, he made his first trip to dispose of the bodies. He certainly went *somewhere*, for the charlady who called at 7.10 the next morning could get no reply to her knocks. At 9.00, he was again at Mrs Hampshire's house, looking tired and dissheveled, asking her about the bloodstained suit and carpets. Later that day, he told Mrs Hampshire that his wife had left him with another man and gone to London. The next day, Tuesday, he put his own car in the garage for a service, although it didn't need one, and hired a larger car. He had evidently decided that if he was not to make several more journeys, he needed a larger boot. Later the same day, this hired car knocked down a cyclist in Kendal and drove on without stopping. The cyclist got the car's number and reported it. Ruxton was stopped half an hour later; he had one of his children with him. He made an incoherent statement about having been to Carlisle, and afterwards changed it and said he had been to Seattle, the place where his family had spent their holiday. It seems that Ruxton had dumped more parts of the body somewhere, but it could not have been in the Linn this time, Moffat was at least three hours from Lancaster. But Lake Windermere was well within his range. (No parts of bodies were ever found in Windermere but then, there is no reason why a well-weighted parcel should ever come to the surface.)

And so the evidence went on piling up. On the morning of Wednesday the 18th, Ruxton made several trips up and down to his bedroom, telling the charlady he was going to see a specialist about his hand. (But why a specialist for a flesh wound?) When he left, the charlady entered the bedroom, now at last open, and noticed the foul smell – later Ruxton told her to spray it with *eau de Cologne*. And later that day, with the last part of the body disposed of, he turned his attention to other problems – pacifying the Rogersons about Mary's disappearance, scraping the wall in his backyard with an axe. (He even told the charlady he was doing it to remove bloodstains.) Never, at any point during the trial, was there the faintest hope of convincing the jury of Ruxton's innocence. But when the doctors entered the box – Professor Glaister, Dr Millar, Professor Sydney Smith (who returned from abroad in time to add his own comments to the case for the prosecution) – all hope of a recommendation to mercy vanished: those gruesome photographs of severered feet (neatly fitted into the shoes of the dead women) hands without fingertips, heads without eyes or ears, were enough to convince the most humane jury that they were dealing with a monster. And Ruxton's own performance in the witness box was pathetic. Whenever possible, he simply contradicted the statements of witnesses – witnesses who had no reason to lie, unless the whole town of Lancaster was in a conspiracy against him. Where he had explanations, they were feeble: it was his children who had scattered straw over the house that Sunday morning . . . The defending counsel summarised the matter when he said: ". . . if you are satisfied that the identity of those remains in the ravine at Moffat had been satisfactorily proved to be the remains of Mrs Ruxton and Mary Rogerson, then your task is well nigh completed. Members of the jury, with all the powers I have, I deny it . . ." But there was not a person there who didn't realise that he was whistling in the dark. The jury took only one hour to decide unanimously that Ruxton was guilty. Three months later an appeal was dismissed, and Ruxton was hanged at Strangeways Jail, Manchester, on 12 May 1936.

The question remains: should Ruxton have been hanged? He was guilty, but guilty of what? Of an unpremeditated murder, committed in a state of mindless, frenzied jealousy? If he had walked into the Lancaster Police Station in the early hours of that Sunday morning, and said: "I have just murdered my wife and I think I may have killed the maid as well . . ." there would have been a 50:50 chance of a life sentence, or perhaps of confinement in Broadmoor. It may be argued that his subsequent actions show cunning but they also show a kind of insanity – the kind of insanity of Lady Macbeth trying to wash imaginary bloodstains off her hands. A psychiatrist examining Ruxton's activities after the murders would say that he showed no sense of reality. The house was full of bloodstains, so that even if he could have made the bodies vanish into thin air, his chances of escaping were still a hundred-to-one. He showed apparent cunning in mutilating the bodies – pulling out teeth, even amputating a bunion from his wife's foot – yet forgot that the length of his wife's face was unmistakable identification, as Glaister showed when he superimposed a photograph of Mrs Ruxton on to the skull. He might have convinced the police that one of the bodies was that of a man, or at least left some doubt in their minds, if he had not included three breasts and two lots of female genitals in the parcels – items that could have been burnt in his stove in ten minutes.

If Ruxton had had any sense, he would have pleaded guilty; then his defence might have stood a chance of saving him from the gallows. For the only real chance of saving Ruxton would have been to tell the whole story of his "marriage". This can be read between the lines of the account of his trial, but it is overwhelmed by the other evidence. Now that Ruxton has been dead for fifty-four years, we can afford to examine his side of the story dispassionately.

Ruxton was born in 1899 in Bombay. He qualified in 1922 and served in the Indian Medical Corps. When he came to England in the mid-1920s, he was a Captain. He spoke French better than English. He was good-looking, clever, extravagantly affectionate and extravagantly emotional. As a human being, he certainly lacked self-discipline. We should also bear in mind that he grew up in India at the time of the Raj, that is, at the height of the British empire's power there. The British gave the native Indians a strong inferiority complex – anyone who has read E.M. Forster's *Passage to India* will understand this.

Isabella Kerr was a Scot, two years Ruxton's junior. She was not pretty, but she had a great deal of vivacity and charm. She was also intelligent and efficient enough to have held several jobs as manageress in restaurants. She had married at the age of nineteen, a Dutchman called Van Ess, but the marriage broke up. Not long after, she met the handsome Captain Hakim, who was studying at Edinburgh to become a surgeon. The attraction that sprang up between them was deep and powerful. For her, he was the mysterious and romantic foreigner – this was the era of Rudolph Valentino – totally unlike the phlegmatic Dutchman from whom she was separated. He was also a qualified doctor. For him, she was the cool, detached Englishwoman, balanced, level-headed, but very sexually desirable. She represented a kind of dream. There can be no doubt that she was far from sexually cold. They hurled themselves into a passionate physical relation, intoxicated with each other. When Ruxton went to study in London, she gave up her job as a manageress and followed him. Possibly there was some masochistic element in her; they had violent quarrels, followed by violent love-making sessions. "We were the kind of people who could not live with each other and could not live without each other", Ruxton said in court. She tried living without him, leaving him to return to Edinburgh; but she returned to London after a few months. They never married, although she told relatives they were married. Her previous marriage had been dissolved. This again suggests a masochistic element in her makeup: at that time, to "live in sin" meant a great deal more than nowadays, particularly to a respectably brought-up Scotswoman.

Ruxton found her infinitely desirable physically. The list of exhibits at the trial includes a great many silk garments: a silk nightdress, silk corsets, silk underskirt, silk blouses, fawn silk stockings. There are also a pair of silver evening shoes and a green silk coatee. Ruxton liked to see her beautifully dressed, and undressed; and, as a Persian, he wanted his lady dressed in silk.

Was she actually unfaithful to him? There is no evidence of it. In a small town like Lancaster in the mid-thirties, it would have been all over the town if the doctor's wife had been misbehaving herself. But she was lively and vivacious, and she may have flirted with men like Robert Edmondson. And Ruxton, with his eastern ideas of a woman's position in the home, would find it hard to realise that in England there may be an abyss of difference between flirting with a man and going to bed with him. He found his wife so maddeningly desirable that he could believe that every man in Lancaster wanted to undress her. Hence the violent quarrels that sometimes ended with her being beaten black and blue, and which led her to leave him on at least two occasions. After one of these quarrels, she tried to gas herself.

Yet they remained together, and she continued to produce babies – three who lived, and one stillborn. Ruxton adored his children, and seems to have been an excellent father. Their colour would have made it clear to him that he was the father. Yet, with his inferiority complex, he would still find it difficult to believe that she would not prefer an English lover. He was convinced that Edmondson was her lover, and the night in the Edinburgh hotel certainly gave them the opportunity to sleep together, yet he continued to be polite, even friendly, towards him. Again, the inferiority complex.

After that trip to Edinburgh, he was convinced that she was unfaithful to him. She was stupid enough to lie to him about it, claiming she had spent the night at her sister's house. So when she went to Blackpool, he was almost certainly convinced that she was with her lover. And who knows what happened when she finally returned home after midnight? In their quarrels, she was certainly not tongue-tied. (Ruxton said that she sometimes came into his surgery smiling, and asked "I'm wondering how I can pick a quarrel with you?") Perhaps she admitted that she had been unfaithful. Or perhaps Ruxton simply drove himself to a new height of screaming, manic fury. He hit her, he choked her, he stabbed her, he went on battering the body with some heavy instrument. It was the final transport of his strange, sadomasochistic love for her. The maid interrupted, and he struck her with the blunt instrument too, although the original fury had probably by now evaporated, he was killing her to prevent her rushing out and giving the alarm.

The children were still asleep, in spite of the shrieks and groans. (They slept in Mrs Ruxton's bedroom – the murder probably took place in his bedroom). Now Ruxton was left alone with the bodies, and it must have seemed to him as if he was waking up. The woman he had loved for ten years was dead. The pattern of his rages involved a swing from one extreme to another – hysterical anger, followed by tearful contrition. And usually he could undo any damage he'd done. Now there was no way back. He probably thought of suicide, then decided against it because of the children. Finally, he made the decision to hack up the bodies and dispose of them piecemeal. No doubt he at first considered the possibility of weighting the bodies and dropping them in the sea or in a lake, but that would require a boat. Since the place was already covered with blood, he might as well go ahead with the dismemberment scheme. But he was not a cool, level-headed man; he was accustomed to indulging his violent fits of emotion. How did he feel when he hacked off his wife's head, then pulled out the teeth with pliers, then levered out the eyes? Dismembering Mary Rogerson was probably just an unpleasant job; but Isabella was the mother of his children, the woman he adored. To mutilate her body must have seemed like a form of self-destruction.

By daylight, he must have been physically and emotionally exhausted. But the charlady was due at seven o'clock, and the house was still covered in bloodstains. He had to rush out and tell her not to come. Then he went back and started to tear up the carpets. He kept discovering new bloodstains on the walls and on the floor; obviously, the wallpaper would have to be stripped and the place redecorated. And all the time he worked, he thought of the children: what would happen to them now? By this time, he must have wished a thousand times that he could bring Isabella back to life and ask her forgiveness; it must have seemed like a nightmare, that her dismembered body now lay in his locked bedroom, while her blood had flowed down the drain. The doorbell rang; for a moment he panics, then he realises it is the girl with the newspapers. His hands and arms are bloodstained; there is no time to wash before he goes downstairs; he decides not to answer it. Then he hears voices in the children's bedroom; in a few minutes, they'll be coming out and asking where their mother is. Will they notice the bloodstains on the carpet? No, they're too innocent. They'll believe whatever he tells them . . . And the thought of their innocence wrenches his heart and makes him want to burst into tears of self-pity. But this is no time for self-pity. Someone is ringing the doorbell again . . .

Everything was against Ruxton; all his lies found him out. Even his assertion that Mary Rogerson had been pregnant was disproved when the charlady found some used sanitary towels in her bedroom. Fate was against Ruxton. After the murder, every decision he took went wrong, from the dismembering of the bodies to the decision to plead "Not Guilty", which meant that the prosecution had the easy task of proving that he was a murderer, a liar and a monster. If he had pleaded "Guilty", it would have given the defence a chance to play for sympathy, to plead that he had already suffered torments as a result of that burst of jealous frenzy.

It seems, in fact, as if Ruxton had *wanted* to be sentenced to death: everything he did after the murder of his wife shows a powerful subconscious desire to join her. "We were the kind of people who could not live with each other and could not live without each other". It sounds enough like Shakespeare's "one that loved not wisely but too well" to make us wonder if he had read *Othello*.

14.
An American Classic – The Lindbergh Kidnapping

FROM THE forensic point of view, the Ruxton case is undoubtedly the British "classic" of the 1930s. In America, that distinction undoubtedly belongs to the Lindbergh kidnapping case.

On 21 May 1927, Charles Lindbergh became the most famous young man in the world. For thirty-three hours, the whole of Europe and America had held its breath as his tiny plane, *The Spirit of St Louis*, made the first solo flight across the Atlantic. As one biographer remarked, he had single-handedly christened and launched the air age.

Less than five years later, Lindbergh had become one of the most deeply pitied men in the world. On the evening of 1 March 1932, his nineteen-month-old son, Charles, was kidnapped from his cot. It was the beginning of a ten-week ordeal that left Lindbergh an embittered man whose only desire was to escape from America.

The Lindberghs were all suffering from colds on that rainy and windy day in March, which is why they had decided to delay their departure to the home of Lindbergh's in-laws at Englewood, New Jersey, by twenty-four hours. At 7.30 that Tuesday evening, Anne Lindbergh and the nurse Betty Gow put the baby to bed in his cot, and closed and bolted all the shutters, except one which was warped and refused to close. Fifty minutes later, Charles Lindbergh arrived back from New York – only half an hour's drive away from their new home in Hopewell, South Jersey. Supper was waiting, and they ate in front of a blazing fire. At about 9.10, Lindbergh looked up sharply. "What was that?" He had heard a sound, he said, like an orange crate smashing. But there was no further noise, and he forgot about it.

Just after 10.00, Betty Gow knocked on the door of the Lindbergh's bedroom and asked: "Mrs Lindbergh, do you have the baby?"

"Why, no."

They went down to the library to see if Lindbergh had taken the child – he was fond of practical jokes. Then all three rushed back to the baby's bedroom. They could see the imprint of young Charle's head on the pillow, and it would obviously have been impossible for him to have climbed out on his own. Lindbergh said: "Anne, they've stolen our baby."

Then he saw the envelope on the radiator under the window. He told them not to touch it. When the police opened it an hour later, it was found to contain a ransom demand for $50,000.

There were few clues. Under the window, the police found a few smudged footprints; nearby there was a ladder in three sections and a chisel. The ladder – a crude home-made one – was broken where the top section joined the middle one. This was almost certainly the noise Lindbergh had heard earlier. There were no fingerprints; the kidnapper had apparently worn gloves.

The kidnapping caused a nationwide sensation. But at this stage the Lindberghs were not too worried. Anne wrote to her mother in law: ". . .the detectives are very optimistic though they think it will take time and patience. In fact they think the kidnappers have gotten themselves into a terrible jam – so much pressure, such a close net over the country . . ." And the pressure was indeed tremendous. Crooks all over the East Coast had reason to curse the kidnappers as the police turned on the heat. Sympathetic letters arrived literally in sackloads – two hundred thousand of them in a few days. Carloads of police, F.B.I agents and secret servicemen arrived in Hopewell; so did carloads of reporters and photographers. The Lindberghs were given no privacy. The great American public continued to love "Lindy", but Lindy's love affair with the American way of life was at an end.

The note offered a few clues. It had various spelling mistakes: "anyding" for anything, and "gut" for good. A handwriting expert said it had been written by a German with low educational qualifications. It was signed with two interlocking circles, one red and one blue.

The kidnapper was obviously scared off by the hullaballoo. He made no attempt to contact the Lindberghs. From his prison cell, Al Capone, America's most famous gangster, offered to recover the baby if he was allowed out; the authorities declined. Mrs Lindbergh broadcast an appeal, and newspapers printed a diet sheet of the baby's meals. This drew a letter from the kidnapper – signed with the two coloured circles – explaining "We can note (sic) make any appointments just now", and promising to adhere to the diet. It had the typical German spelling errors: "gut" for good and "aus" for "out".

A week after the kidnapping, a well-wisher named Dr John F. Condon sent a letter to his local newspaper in the Bronx, offering a thousand dollars of his own money for the return of the child. The result was a letter addressed to Condon signed with the two circles. It began: "Dear Sir: if you are willing to act as go-between in the Lindbergh cace pleace follow stricly instruction". It asked him to collect the money from Lindbergh and then place an advertisement in the *New York American*: MONY IS REDY. Then further "instruction" would be forthcoming. When Condon succeeded in speaking to Lindbergh, the famous flyer sounded exhausted and indifferent – until Condon mentioned the signature of interlocking circles; then his voice became excited, and he offered to see Condon immediately. The advertisement duly appeared in the *New York American*: "Money is ready, Jafsie". That same evening, a man's deep voice spoke to Condon on the telephone – Condon could hear another man in the room speaking in Italian – and told Condon that the gang would shortly be in touch. The next day he was handed a letter that instructed him where to find yet another message. The second message told Condon to meet the writer at a cemetery at 233rd Street. At the cemetery gates, a young man wearing a handkerchief over his face asked Condon if he had brought the money – the demand had now been increased to $70,000. Condon explained that the notice had been too short. Suddenly the man took fright. "Have you brought the police?" "No! You can trust me." But the man ran away. Condon chased after him, and caught up with him in a nearby park. Here the young man – who identified himself as "John" – asked a peculiar thing: "Would I burn if the baby is dead?" Appalled, Condon asked: "Is the baby dead?" But "John" assured him it was alive. It was on a boat, about six hours away (he pronounced it "boad"). Finally, "John" offered a token of his good faith – he would send Condon the baby's sleeping suit. And, in fact, it arrived by post. The Lindbergh's identified it as that of their son.

On 2 April, a second rendezvous at a cemetery was made. This time, Lindbergh himself accompanied Condon. He was carrying $70,000 in a cardboard box. Unknown to Lindbergh, the treasury had listed the number of every bill. Condon spoke to the kidnapper, and managed to persuade him to accept only $50,000. As he returned to Lindbergh's car, the kidnapper shouted: "Hey, doctor", and Lindbergh heard the voice clearly. A moment later Condon handed over the money, and "John" promised to send details of the whereabouts of the missing baby by the next morning's post.

The letter, when it arrived, claimed that the child was on a boat called the Nelly, near Elizabeth Island. Condon accompanied Lindbergh on the flight to look for the boat at the specified location. It was not there. Bitterly, they realised they had been tricked.

Five weeks later, on 12 May 1932, the last hope vanished when a negro teamster, walking in the woods near the Lindbergh home, found a shallow, leaf-covered grave. It contained the decomposing body of a child. The shirt in which the body was dressed had been made by Betty Gow from a flannel petticoat. Charles Lindbergh junior – "Buster" – had been dead since the night on which he was taken from his cot. He had died of a blow on the head.

The trail seemed to be cold, yet the hunt for the kidnapper – and killer – was intensified. Betty Gow was widely suspected by the public, but the Lindberghs were convinced she was innocent. Another person suspected of complicity – Violet Sharpe, a maid at the home of Lindberghs' in-laws – committed suicide with poison.

Meanwhile, a wood technologist named Arthur Koehler was continuing his own investigations into the ladder. He had written to Lindbergh offering to try to trace its wood, using the laboratory of the Forest Service. It took him eighteen months, and dozens of visits to lumber yards, but eventually he found the place where the wood had been bought: The National Lumber and Millwork Company in the Bronx. It confirmed what the police had already come to accept: that the kidnapper of the Lindbergh baby lived somewhere in the Bronx – that was why he had seen Condon's original advertisement so quickly . . .

In May 1934, President Roosevelt abandoned the gold standard. This was bad luck for the kidnappers, for $35,000 of the ransom money had been in gold certificates. These were now called in, so the gold certificates had ceased to be legal tender.

The break finally came on 15 September 1934. A dark blue Dodge sedan drove into a garage in upper Manhattan. The man who drove asked for petrol with a German accent, and paid with a ten dollar gold certificate. The gas attendant hesitated, but the man said: "They're all right – any bank will take them". So the attendant gave him his change, but made a note of the number of the car. Other gold certificates had been exchanged in New York, and had proved to be part of the Lindbergh ransom money, but no one had ever noticed the person who had changed them. The certificate was taken to the local bank.

Four days later, a bank teller realised that this was yet another gold certificate from the Lindbergh ransom money. He turned it over. On the back there was a car registration number: 4U – 13–41- N.Y. He tracked the gold certificate back to the service station in Manhattan, and the attendant verified that he had written the number on the back. The police now checked with the New York State Motor License vehicle bureau. Who owned a car of that number? The answer soon came back: Richard Hauptmann, 1279 East 222nd Street, the Bronx.

Police surrounded the small frame house all that night, and when a man finally stepped out of the front door, they still waited, watching him climb into the blue Dodge sedan and drive off. A few minutes later, they forced him over to the kerb – perhaps working on the theory that a man with a steering wheel in both hands would not be able to pull out a gun and start shooting. But Hauptmann was unarmed. In his wallet, they found a $20 bill that proved to be from the Lindbergh ransom. Back at Hauptmann's home, in the garage, a further $14,600 in ransom bills were found, carefully concealed. On a strip of wood in a dark closet they found Condon's telephone number. Asked to write down a passage containing words in the various notes from the kidnapper, Hauptmann misspelled them exactly as in the notes.

How did he come to be in possession of the money? Hauptmann said it had been left in his care by a friend, Isidor Fisch, who had since died.

Hauptmann was a carpenter by trade, and he was 35-years-old. He also had a criminal record in Germany – burglary and highway robbery – and had been sentenced to five years. Paroled, he had been arrested for more burglaries, and had escaped and fled the country. He had entered the United States illegally, married a waitress, and set up in business as a carpenter, in which trade he was extremely successful, earning $50 a week. He had not worked for the past two years, and his account books – which he kept meticulously – showed that his fortunes had improved considerably since 1932.

Hauptmann's own story was that he and Fisch had gone into business in 1932, and that Fisch owed him $7,500. In 1933 Fisch had gone to Germany, but had died in Leipzig in 1934. Later in 1934, heavy rain had seeped into a closet in which he had left a shoe box that Fisch had consigned to his care, and only then had Hauptmann discovered it was full of money, which he dried out. But he failed to tell his wife, or Fisch's family, about his find. He had started using occasional bills from the shoebox because, after all, Fisch owed him money . . .

But perhaps the most damning piece of evidence at Hauptmann's trial – which opened in Flemington, New Jersey on 2 January 1935 – was the ladder. In Hauptmann's attic, claimed the prosecution, the police had discovered that a floorboard was missing. Sawdust showed that it had been sawn off. And the left hand board of the kidnap ladder – known as "Rail 16" – was of the same type of wood as the missing board. When placed in position in the attic floor, four nail holes in Rail 16 matched exactly four nail holes in the joist below. That seemed to prove once and for all that Hauptmann had made the ladder. Hauptmann replied scornfully that he was a carpenter, and that the ladder had been made by an incompetent amateur, not a man who took pride in his work, as he did. But the jury discounted this protest. On 13 February 1935, the jury found Hauptmann guilty of murder. By October, the Court of Appeals had denied Hauptmann's appeal. The prison governor Harold Hoffmann interviewed Hauptmann in his cell in December, and emerged a badly puzzle man. Hauptmann again pointed out that he would never make such a ladder, and begged to be given a truth drug or lie detector test. Hoffmann felt that his pleas rang true, and began an investigation into the case. A few days after Hauptmann's arrest, Mrs Hauptmann had left home, unable to stand the continual commotion; the police had "found" the missing board after that. Could they have removed it themselves? They could certainly have planted Condon's phone number in the dark closet. Condon had at first been uncertain that Hauptmann was "John". It was only later that he changed his mind. The prosecution had insisted that Hauptmann was alone in planning and carrying out the kidnapping, but what about the Italian voice Condon had heard on the telephone?

Governor Hoffmann's intervention was interpreted by most of the American press as an attempt to get publicity, and others felt he was politically motivated – he was attempting to sack the attorney general, David Wilentz, who had prosecuted Hauptmann. For Lindbergh this was the last straw. Totally convinced that Hauptmann was the man who had killed his son – and that American justice could be influenced by politicians – he sailed for England. He would remain in Europe for nearly five years, and would become an admirer – and frequent guest – of the Nazis. During the Second World War, he would try hard to prevent America entering the war on the side of the Allies – an attitude that led the British to change their minds about the American they had regarded as a hero . . .

Hoffmann's efforts were of no avail, and on 3 April 1936, Richard Hauptmann was finally electrocuted, still protesting his innocence.

Is it conceivable that Hauptmann was innocent? According to one investigator, Ludovic Kennedy, it is almost a certainty. In the early 1980s, Kennedy took the trouble to interview all witnesses who were still available, and to look closely into the evidence – that which was presented in court and that which was not. His book *The Airman and the Carpenter* (1985) makes one thing very clear; that if all this evidence *had* been presented in court, Hauptmann would have been acquitted. Hauptmann came to America as a stowaway in 1924; he had a minor police record for burglary during the black days of inflation. But in America he prospered; he and his wife worked hard, and by 1926 he was in a position to lend money and to buy a lunchroom; the day after the Wall Street crash he withdrew $2,800 from his account and began buying stocks and shares at rock bottom prices. Hauptmann had no need to kidnap the Lindbergh baby, for by modern standards, he was very comfortably off in 1932.

Kennedy's investigations revealed that Hauptmann's story about his friend Isidor Fisch was true. Fisch *was* a confidence swindler. He and Hauptmann were in the fur business together, and Fisch *did* owe Hauptmann over $7,000. His swindles were uncovered only after his death in Leipzig in 1934.

Then how did Hauptmann – or Fisch – come to be in possession of so much ransom money? The probable answer, Kennedy discovered, is that the Lindbergh ransom money was selling at a discount in New York's underworld – one convict bought some at 40 cents in the dollar. Nothing is more likely than that Fisch, with his underworld connections, bought a large quantity, and left it with Hauptmann when he sailed for Germany. Forensic examination of the money showed that it *had* been soaked and dried out, confirming Hauptmann's story that he had left it on a top shelf in a closet and forgotten about it.

But Kennedy's major discovery was that so much of the evidence against Hauptmann was fabricated. When arrested, he was asked to write out various sentences; the court was later told that Hauptmann's misspelling of various words had been exactly as in the ransom note. This was untrue. He had spelled correctly the first time, then been *told* to misspell various words – "singature" for signature, "were" for where, "gut" for good. The court was also assured that handwriting experts had identified Hauptmann's writing as that of the ransom notes. Kennedy submitted the samples to two modern experts, who both said they were *not* written by the same man. Kennedy's investigation revealed that Millard Whited, the farmhand who identified Hauptmann as a man he had seen hanging around the Lindbergh property, had earlier flatly denied seeing anyone suspicious. He was later offered generous "expenses", and changed his story. As to Lindbergh himself, he had been invited to sit quietly in a corner of the room in disguise when Hauptmann was brought in for questioning. He therefore knew him well when he identified him in court as "John". As to the writing in the closet, Kennedy established that it was made by a reporter, Tom Cassidy, who did it as a "joke". Hauptmann had no reason to write Condon's telephone number on the back of a door; he had no telephone, and in any case the number was listed in the directory. The numbers of bills written on the door were not, in fact, those of Lindbergh ransom bills.

The most serious piece of evidence against Hauptmann was, of course, the ladder. This constituted the "greatest feat of scientific detection of all time". Examined closely, it is seen to be highly questionable. Koehler's efforts established that some of the yellow pine was sent to the Bronx timber yard, and it may have been from this consignment that the rungs of the ladder were made. But this was only one of thirty timber yards to which the same wood was sent; the man who made the ladder could have bought the wood at any of them. Hauptmann rightly pointed out in court that he was a skilled carpenter, and that the ladder was made by an amateur. If the jury registered this point, they may have felt that he had deliberately botched it to mislead investigators – for, after all, was there not the conclusive evidence of the sixteenth rung, whose wood was found in Hauptmann's attic? As Kennedy points out, this plank was "found" when Mrs Hauptmann had abandoned the house to the investigators. Was it likely that Hauptmann would go to the trouble of tearing up his attic floor, sawing out a piece of wood from the plank, then planing it down to size, when it would have been simpler to get another piece of wood? He was, after all, a professional carpenter. Kennedy quite clearly believes that rung 16 was concocted by Detective Bornmann or one of the other investigators – he refers to the whole story as "Bornmann-in-Wonderland".

So in retrospect, it seems clear that the "greatest feat of scientific detection of all time" was based on false or suppressed evidence. The police firmly believed that Hauptmann was guilty, and they strengthened their case where necessary. Hauptmann may well have been guilty, but all the latest evidence points clearly to his innocence.

Another book, *In Search of the Lindbergh Baby*, by Theon Wright – a reporter at the trial – raises an even more startling possibility: that "Buster" Lindbergh was not murdered at all. A Connecticut businessman named Harold Olson had been told as a child that he belonged to a family of gangsters, who had placed him with Roy and Sarah Olson when he was a baby. His real father, he was told, may have been Al Capone. But when he was an adult, his mother's cousins had told him that he might be the son of Charles Lindbergh. And a woman who had been his nurse as a baby told him authoritatively that he *was* the Lindbergh child. Olson was certainly the right age for the Lindbergh baby, and photographs of him as a child show the same eyes as "Buster" Lindbergh's, and the same scar on the chin. Olson spent years trying to track down his origins, and finally came to believe that the Lindbergh kidnapping was a plot organised by Capone lieutenants to get Capone out of jail. It may be recalled that Capone offered to locate the Lindbergh baby in exchange for his freedom.

But what about the child's body? A photograph in Wright's book shows that it was little more than a skeleton. The shirt in which it was wrapped was rotten, so little faith can be placed in Betty Gow's identification of it as the one she made. And in *The Trial of Richard Hauptmann* there is one rather odd piece of evidence, given by William J. Allen, the truck driver who found the body: that the land on the other side of the road belonged to "a Catholic home – a kind of hospital for children that ain't got no home". Could the skeleton, which even Lindbergh was doubtful about identifying, have come from there?

This may seem a far-fetched theory, but one thing is certain: that Richard Bruno Hauptmann should never have been found guilty on the evidence offered by the prosecution.

15.
The Rise
of Sex Crime

UNTIL HALFWAY through the nineteenth century, as already noted, most murders were "economic" – committed for money. The majority of people were living below subsistence level, and for a hungry man, sex is a secondary consideration.

One of the first recorded sex murders occurred in England in July 1867. Three children were playing in a meadow near the town of Alton, in Hampshire, when they were approached by a young man named Frederick Baker. He was known to be subject to "depressive fits", and was the son of a man who had attacks of "acute mania". He worked as a clerk and was regarded as "a young man of great respectability". He gave the children a ha'penny each, and persuaded eight-year-old Fanny Adams to go with him for a walk. A few hours later, Fanny's mother accosted Baker and asked what had become of her daughter. Baker, looking calm and self-possessed, told her the child had gone off to buy sweets. Many hours later, Fanny's remains were found in a nearby hop garden; she had been hacked to pieces and scattered over a wide area; the head was the first part to be found. The child's genitals had also been cut out. Baker protested his innocence, but his diary contained the entry: "Killed a young girl today. It was fine and hot." He later tried to persuade the jury that it meant: "Killed – a young girl today. It (the day) was fine and hot". But they disbelieved him and he was executed.

Four years later, in 1871, a French youth named Eusebius Pieydagnelle was tried for four murders. He told the jury that he came of a respectable family and had had a good education. Opposite their house in Vinuville there was a butcher's shop run by a M. Cristobal, and he was fascinated by the smell of fresh blood and the lumps of meat. "I began to envy the butcher's assistant, because he could work at the block, with rolled up sleeves and bloody hands." With some difficulty, he persuaded his parents to apprentice him to Cristobal. In the butcher's slaughter house he secretly wounded the cattle and drank the blood. What caused him the greatest excitement was being allowed to kill an animal himself. "But the sweetest sensation is when you feel an animal trembling under your knife. The animal's departing life creeps along the blade right into your hand. The mighty blow that felled the bullock sounded like sweet music to my ears."

The boy's father was ashamed of his son's profession and decided to remove him, apprenticing him to a lawyer instead. Pieydagnelle was seized with deep depression, which eventually led him to commit murder. His first victim was a girl of fifteen – he had crept into her bedroom. "As I looked at the lovely creature, my first thought was to kiss her. I bent down . . . But I paused – a stolen kiss was no use. I could not bear to wake her up. I looked at her lovely neck, and at that moment the gleam of the kitchen knife that lay beside her struck my eyes. Something drew me irresistably to that knife." After the murder he was horrified. He fought the craving to repeat the experience, and even went to live in a cave in the woods. It was no use. Driven by an irresistible compulsion he went on killing – his last victim being his employer, M. Cristobal. After that, he gave himself up. He begged the jury to sentence him to death, saying that he would have killed himself, but was afraid that it would be a mortal sin that would damn him further. Hirschfeld, who records the case, makes no mention of the sentence.

In the same year, an Italian youth named Vincent Verzeni, was charged with attempted strangulation of several women, and suspicion of three murders. A fourteen-year-old girl named

Johanna Motta had been murdered in the fields; she had died through suffocation, her mouth being filled with earth. The body was naked, and the genitals had been torn out. On 28 August 1871, a married woman, Signora Frigeni, was found by her husband lying naked in a field, her stomach slit open and the intestines hanging out; she had been strangled with a cord. The following day, a nineteen-year-old girl named Maria Previtali was followed into the fields by her cousin, Vincent Verzeni, aged twenty-two; he threw her to the ground and began to choke her. But she begged for her life and he finally let her go. It was after this that he was arrested.

Verzeni confessed to the murders, explaining that as soon as he grasped a woman by the throat, he experienced intense sexual excitement, "an indescribably pleasant feeling". Four years earlier, he had choked his nurse as she lay in bed, but on achieving orgasm, had let her go. He had done the same with two other women, and in both cases achieved orgasm. But in the three murder cases, he had gone on strangling until the victim was dead.

Verzeni had first realised that he enjoyed throttling when he was twelve, when he killed chickens. He began strangling chickens, telling his family that a weasel had got into the chicken coop. Then, at the age of eighteen, he began throttling women. "I had an unspeakable delight in strangling women, experiencing erections during the acts and real pleasure. It was even a pleasure to smell female clothing . . . I took the greatest delight in drinking Motta's blood. I took the clothing and intestines because of the pleasure it gave me to touch and smell them . . . It never occurred to me to look at the genitals or such things. It satisfied me to seize the women by the neck and suck their blood." Verzeni was sentenced to life imprisonment.

In Boston in 1873, a young bellringer named Thomas W. Piper, experienced a sudden change of character, and began to leer at girls and make indecent suggestions. That December, he attacked a servant girl named Bridget Landregan, knocking her unconscious with a club. He dragged her into some bushes and stripped her, but when a passer-by came to investigate the noises, he ran away. Hours later he knocked unconscious a girl named Sullivan and raped her; she died later in hospital. A prostitute named Mary Tynam was also battered unconscious and raped while she slept; she also died in hospital.

On Sunday 23 May 1875, in the Warren Avenue Baptist Church, Piper invited a five-year-old girl named Mabel Young to come to see the pigeons in the belfry, and battered her unconscious with a cricket bat. But her absence had been noted, and as a search party came up the stairs, Piper scrambled out of a window and dropped to the ground. However, he had been observed and was arrested. Meanwhile, the unconscious child had been taken to hospital, where she died. Piper was found guilty of her murder and sentenced to hang. A few days before his execution he confessed to five sex murders, as well as several rapes of children. He also admitted that he usually felt the compulsion to commit rape after heavy drinking.

Also in Boston, in April 1874, a fourteen-year-old boy named Jesse Pomeroy was questioned about the murder of a four-year-old named Horace Mullen, whose mutilated body had been found in a marsh near Dorchester. Two years earlier, Pomeroy had been sentenced to reform school for enticing seven young boys to lonely places, where they were stripped and beaten, or sadistically injured with a knife. Pomeroy was a tall, gangling boy with a hare lip and a "white eye". When he was taken into custody, a knife with bloodstains was found on him; mud on his shoes was similar to that of the marsh where the child's body had been discovered. Plaster casts of footprints were taken, and they proved to be Jesse Pomeroy's.

Pomeroy lived with his mother, a poor dressmaker. She had moved from a house on Broadway Street, south Boston. When the landlord sold the property in July 1874, labourers digging in the cellar found the remains of a girl of about ten. She proved to be a neighbour of the Pomeroys called Patricia Curran, and she had vanished in the previous March. Pomeroy finally confessed to her murder, and to that of Horace Mullen. He admitted that he was driven by an overwhelming desire to inflict pain, and that he chose children because they were easy to overpower.

Pomeroy was sentenced to death, but on appeal this was reduced to a life sentence. He spent most of his imprisonment in solitary confinement, and "became a highly educated man" through reading. But he made several attempts to escape. The most ambitious involved gaining access to a gas pipe behind a granite block in the wall of his cell, and filling his cell with gas, after which he struck a match. He was hoping that the explosion would blow open the door; it did, but it also blew Jesse Pomeroy out of it. He was badly injured, but recovered. One newspaper report stated that other prisoners were burnt to death in their cells, but this seems unlikely. Pomeroy was finally transferred from the Charleston prison to the Bridgewater State mental hospital. He died there in 1932, after fifty-two years in prison.

In Paris on 15 April 1880, a four-year-old girl named Louise Dreux vanished from her home in the Grenelle quarter. The following day, neighbours complained of the black smoke pouring from the chimney of a retarded twenty-year-old youth named Louis Menesclou, who lived on the top floor of the same building as the Dreux family. When police entered his room they found a child's head and entrails burning in the stove. A forearm was in Menesclou's pocket, and other parts of the body were found in the toilet. In Menesclou's room the police found a poem that contained the lines "I saw her, I took her". Menesclou admitted to strangling the child and sleeping with her corpse under his bed. He indignantly denied raping her, but became embarrassed when asked why the child's genitals were missing. Menesclou had been suffering from convulsions from the age of nine months, and came of a family with a history of insanity and alcoholism; his mother had periods of "mania" when menstruating. He had spent some time in a reformatory, and also in the marines, but proved "lazy and intractable". After his execution, his brain was examined, and found to have various "morbid" abnormalities.

France's own Jack the Ripper, who became known as the "disemboweller" (*l'eventreur*) operated during the 1890s. Between 1894 and 1897 he committed at least eleven murders, mostly in the south-western region. His first victim, a twenty-one-year-old mill girl named Eugenie Delhomme, was strangled, raped and disembowelled behind a hedge outside Beaurepaire, near Lyon. Two more victims were teenage girls, and then a fifty-eight-year-old widow was strangled in her home. In September

1895, the unknown "ripper" began sodomising and castrating boys.

On 4 August 1897, a heavily-built peasant woman named Marie-Eugenie Plantier was gathering pine cones in a forest near Tournon when a man crept up and attacked her. As he clamped a hand over her mouth from behind, she struggled violently and screamed. Her husband and sons came running, and after a fierce struggle, the man was overpowered, and taken off to a nearby inn. There he played his accordion until the police arrived. He proved to be a twenty-eight-year-old ex-soldier named Joseph Vacher, and he had a black beard and a suppurating right eye. Doctors who examined him discovered that he had always been given to fits of self-pity and resentment. In the army, during his national service, he became so angry when his promotion to corporal failed to materialise that he tried to cut his throat, and was discharged. He had tried to shoot a girl who had turned down his proposal of marriage, then shot himself; the bullet entered his right ear, making him deaf and paralysing the facial muscles on that side. Committed to an asylum, he was discharged as cured in April 1894, and embarked on his career of sex murder. In spite of attempts to convince doctors that he was insane, Vacher was found guilty and executed.

While Vacher was on trial, two schoolgirls disappeared in the village of Lechtingen, near Osnabruck; their corpses were found in nearby woods. The murderer had hacked them to pieces and scattered the fragments as if in a frenzy. A carpenter named Ludwig Tessnow came under suspicion because he had been seen near the woods. Stains on his clothes looked like blood, but he insisted that they were wood dye. The police finally had to let him go for lack of evidence, and the fact that he went on living in the village convinced many residents that he was innocent. In the following year, he left.

On 1 July 1901, two brothers, aged six and eight, failed to return to their homes in the village of Gohren, on the island of Rugen, off the Baltic coast. Their mutilated bodies were found in the woods – the heart of one of them was missing and was never found.

Tessnow, who lived in Gohren, again came under suspicion: a stained pair of boots was found in his home, and his clothing, recently washed, were also coverd with dark stains. He again insisted that this was wood stain. A farmer whose sheep had been mutilated identified Tessnow as the man he had seen running away; again, Tessnow denied it. The examining magistrate happened to recall the earlier case in Lechtingen, and when he learned that the suspect was Tessnow, had no doubt that this was the killer. By this time – as described in Chapter Ten – Paul Eulenhuth had devised a method of testing whether stains were of animal or human blood. The clothes were sent to him, and he was able to identify over a hundred spots of both human blood and the blood of sheep. Tessnow was found guilty, and executed.

It can be seen that these gruesome cases, from Baker to Tessnow, have certain factors in common. Again and again, we encounter the strange passion for throttling, and for tearing bodies to pieces. And in most of the cases, psychiatric examination revealed insanity and alcoholism in the family. (This suggests that the same would almost certainly be true for Jack the Ripper.) In short, Baker, Pieydagnelle, Piper, Verzeni, Pomeroy, Menesclou, Vacher and Tessnow were all mentally unbalanced. Dr Magnus Hirschfeld, the expert on sexual deviation, who was widely known, and hated, for his liberal views, was indignant that someone as obviously deranged as Tessnow should have been executed. It was the general opinion that sex killers like these could only be understood in terms of insanity.

Yet even in the 1880s, it was becoming clear that a man did not have to be insane to commit murder for sex. In San Francisco in 1885, a young Sunday school teacher named Theodore Durrant lured a girl named Blanche Lamont into the belfry of the Emanual Baptist church and strangled her, then raped her. The body remained undiscovered, and a week later, Durrant lured Blanche's friend Minnie Williams into the church library. He left the room, and when he returned naked, she screamed. Durrant pulled up her skirt, rammed it into her mouth, then raped and stabbed her to death. After that he raped her a second time. Later that evening, after a church meeting, he returned to the library and probably raped her again.

When it was established that Durrant was the last person to be seen with Minnie Williams, he was arrested; meanwhile, the body of Blanche Lamont had been found in the belfry. Psychiatric examination seemed to indicate that Durrant was perfectly sane, and his lengthy trial caused a sensation that reached the newspapers of Europe. But in spite of many appeals, he was finally hanged. The evidence suggests that both murders had been planned in advance, and were not sudden impulsive acts. And the repeated rapes of Minnie Williams make the motive clear – a high sex-drive combined with intense sexual frustration.

In 1902, a fifteen-year-old girl called Norah Fuller was lured to a house in San Francisco by means of an advertisement for a nanny. Her naked body was found there a month later, and it was established that she had been strangled and raped, then mutilated. A clerk named Charles B. Hadley was sought by the police – it was established that he had placed the advertisement – but he was never caught.

Australia's first recorded sex murder took place at Gatton, west of Brisbane, on 26 December 1898. Gatton was a farming community, and on Boxing Day, a dance had been arranged in a hall. Two brothers and two sisters set out to go to it. Patrick Murphy went on a horse; his elder brother Michael, twenty-nine, set out with his two sisters Norah, twenty-seven, and Ellen, eighteen, in a sulky or buggy. But so few people turned up that the dance was abandoned, and the sulky turned back for home, six miles away. It never arrived. The following morning, their brother-in-law set out to look for them, and found them apparently sleeping in a nearby paddock. The clothing of the girls had been torn and disarranged, and medical examination revealed that both had been raped. Ellen's hands were tied behind her with a handkerchief, and she had been killed with a violent blow to the head with "a heavy blunt instrument". Norah's hands were also tied, and a strap had been pulled tight around her neck. Michael had also been killed by a violent blow. The horse had been shot. It seemed likely that at least two men must have been involved, and that they had held up the sulky and forced it into the paddock where it was found. Then Michael Murphy had been knocked unconscious, and the girls had been tied up and raped, then battered to death. Although a number of men were suspected, no one was ever charged with the murders.

And so "sex crime", in the modern sense of the word, had finally arrived. Yet it was still rare enough to cause a sensation.

In April 1914, a fourteen-year-old girl named Mary Phagan went to collect her wages from a pencil factory in Atlanta, Georgia, and was found strangled in the basement the next day; the motive was obviously sexual, but rape had not been completed. The manager of the pencil factory, a Jew named Leo Frank, came under suspicion, and in spite of evidence pointing clearly to the guilt of the negro caretaker, Jim Conley, Frank was tried and convicted of the murder. He was sentenced to life imprisonment, but shortly afterwards, an angry mob stormed the jail, took him to a town 125 miles away, and there lynched him. More than sixty years later, the testimony of a man who had seen Jim Conley moving the girl's body, made it clear that Frank was innocent, and he was granted a posthumous pardon. The case received unprecedented publicity and sold hundreds of thousands of newspapers – in retrospect it is clear that Frank was virtually hanged by unscrupulous reporters who invented "scandal" stories about him to sell newspapers.

But *why* had sex crime arrived at this point in history? The reason has already been touched upon in an earlier chapter. But it had been anticipated by Tolstoy as long ago as 1889 in a short novel called *The Kreutzer Sonata*. A wife murderer named Podsnichev explains why he killed her: his jealousy began when she played Beethoven's Kreutzer sonata for violin and piano with a young aristocrat. And this, says Podsnichev, is the trouble with modern society. Not so long ago, most people had to work from morning till night just to stay alive, and even aristocrats had plenty to do running their estates. Now there is too much leisure, and the result is that society has plunged into a kind of sexual insanity. When people have nothing else to occupy their empty heads, they allow their thoughts to turn to "romance" which, in practice, means sex.

The average peasant, says Podsnichev, has no time for such nonsense: he gets up at dawn and staggers into bed, exhausted, at dusk. He keeps sex in its proper place, which is as a means of reproducing the human race, just as the Catholic Church has always taught. *This* is the only time the sexual act is justified, when it is aimed at reproduction. Otherwise it is mere self-indulgence, a kind of masturbation.

Considering that this was written in the year after the Ripper murders, it is an amazingly perceptive analysis. The Industrial Revolution had brought leisure to vast numbers of people, and sex suddenly assumed an importance that would have struck our ancestors as absurdly exaggerated. This new attitude was reflected in the prudery of the Victorians, and the embarrassment with which they began to approach our natural functions. Even table legs were covered up with a long tablecloth in case the thought of legs made a lady blush. The undergarment known as "drawers" (because they were drawn on), also became a source of embarrassment, because the word seemed to imply they could also be drawn off. The name of the female undergarment was changed to knickers, short for knickerbockers, or short trousers. (In the garment industry, boys' trousers are still called knickers.) In due course, knickers also became a rather "naughty" word, and in the mid-twentieth century, "panties" was substituted. In America, that still had too many sexual associations, so that the female undergarment is now usually referred to as "underpants". It remains to be seen how long this will remain unchanged.

The battles about censorship in the late nineteenth and early twentieth centuries were another indication of this new attitude to sex. Fielding and Smollett and Sterne wrote about sex with a cheerful lack of inhibition, just as Rabelais wrote about the excretive functions; they felt that it was a natural part of human existence. Zola, Strindberg, H.G. Wells and D.H. Lawrence had to fight a battle against censorship in order to be allowed to treat it with some degree of realism. Yet it is important to recognise that, to some extent, the defenders of "purity" were right. Sex cannot be treated as "naturally" as, say, cookery, because merely to describe it is to cause sexual arousal. The "puritans" argued that if writers were free to write about sex without restraint, society would become increasingly "sex conscious", and the result would be a rise in immorality and sex crime. They were perfectly right. The age of sex crime begins at the same time as the battle against censorship.

In 1890, Emile Zola cashed in on the sensation caused by the Ripper murders in a novel called *The Human Beast* (*La Bête Humaine*), about a man who had a sadistic compulsion to hurt women; it is actually based on the case of Eusebius Pieydagnelle.

Zola was the first to describe a man in the grip of an abnormal sexual compulsion. Eighteen years later, Henri Barbusse created a sensation with a novel called *Hell* (*L'Enfer*), about a man who finds a small hole in the wall of his hotel room, and spends his time peeping through at the activities of its transient occupants. This was based on a contemporary case in which a waiter made a hole in the wall of the honeymoon suite and spent a great deal of time spying on its occupants and masturbating. In these two instances, literature was merely reflecting the increasingly "feverish" attitude to sex. But art is always a catalyst, and within a decade, attitudes to sex were being mutually influenced by literature. Scott Fitzgerald felt that he was merely reflecting the "Jazz Age"; in retrospect, we can see that he, and others like him, played an important part in creating it.

The First World War seems to have been a kind of watershed. In 1916, a blacksmith in a village near Budapest became curious about a number of oil drums in the workshop, and forced one of them open. It proved to contain the naked body of a woman, jammed in a crouching position. Six more drums also proved to contain female corpses. The previous tenant of the house, a man named Bela Kiss, was fighting at the front and was never caught. In Paris in 1919, a bald headed man named Landru was arrested and charged with killing ten women and a youth in the course of the previous five years. In 1921, police were called to a flat in Berlin after neighbours heard sounds of a struggle; on the bed they found the trussed-up carcass of a recently killed girl, ready for butchering. Georg Grossmann, a sadist and child molestor, had been killing girls throughout the war and selling their bodies as meat. In 1924, a man named Karl Denke was arrested in Munsterberg when he tried to kill a young travelling journeyman; remains of a dozen more journeymen were found pickled in brine in his house, and a ledger containing detils of thirty victims, including several women. Denke had been living on their flesh. Also in 1924, a butcher named Fritz Haarmann was arrested in Hanover; he was a homosexual who had been killing and raping young men since 1918, and selling their flesh as meat.

It can be seen that in all these cases there was a certain "economic" motive; but all these killers – including Kiss and

Landru – were known to be sexually insatiable, and the economic and sexual motives are inextricably interwined.

By the mid-1920s, sex crime was on the increase in most civilised countries, although this was more obvious in America than in Europe, where the older patterns tended to persist. And even in America, the sex motive and the economic motive tended to get mixed. In the Ypsilanti "car burning" case of 1931 – memorable because the killers only just escaped lynching – the original motive was robbery. Three ex-convicts held up four sixteen-year-olds in a lovers' lane, and robbed them (of $2). One of the girls was then raped, perhaps because the robbers were disappointed with their haul; when the others resisted, all four were battered to death or shot. There is a 1920s atmosphere about the murder, even to the moonshine whiskey the convicts were drinking before they decided to go out and rob somebody.

In England during the thirties, the older patterns remained unchanged: Sidney Fox, William Herbert Wallace, Rouse (the Burning Car murderer), Mancini (the Brighton Trunk killer), Buck Ruxton; any of these murders mights have been used as the basis for a novel – like Ernest Raymond's *We the Accused*, which is based on Crippen. They have an air of belonging to an earlier decade; you could imagine Sherlock Holmes being called in to solve any of them.

In America, on the other hand, the violent and illogical pattern of sex crime becomes increasingly prevalent – although in many cases, the murder was accidental, or for the purposes of avoiding recognition. The Jerry Thompson case may be taken as typical. Thompson, twenty-five, was an engineer of Peoria, Illinois, who was charged in 1935 with the murder of Mildred Hallmark. The girl's half-naked body was found in a cemetery. When police appealed for information, promising anonymity to any woman who came forward, more than twenty-five women admitted they had been raped during the past eighteen months. The rapist, a good-looking, well-spoken young man, usually approached them as they waited at bus stops, and offered them a lift. He would drive to a lonely place, and assault them; if they resisted, he beat them or knocked them unconscious. In several cases, he took photographs of the naked girl in the headlights of the car, and told her he would send them to her relatives if she made any complaint. Mildred Hallmark was the daughter of a man he worked with, and willingly accepted a lift. When she struggled, he knocked her unconscious and raped her. He may have decided to kill her because he was afraid of recognition; his own story is that he realized she was dead after the assault. One of Thompson's victims, a girl he had raped and photographed six months earlier, later met him at a dance and recognized him. When the police appealed for information, she was one of the women who came forward. Thompson's diaries, with details of the rapes, and photographs of naked girls, were found in his room. He told the police he had been committing rape since he was sixteen, and had raped more than fifty women.

The unsolved Cleveland Torso murders also began in 1935. This killer was almost certainly a sadist, of the same type as Jack the Ripper. Between September 1935 and August 1938, the "mad butcher of Kingsbury Run" (as the newspapers called him) killed a dozen men and women. Most of them were derelicts or prostitutes. In most cases, the head was removed (in six cases these were never found); in two cases, he killed two victims at the same time, and dismembered the bodies. Elliot Ness, who became Cleveland's Public Safety Director in 1935 (after "cleaning up" Chicago), reasoned that the killer was large and powerful, probably homosexual, and that he possessed a car and probably had a house of his own (in which he could dismember the bodies undisturbed). Enquiries in Cleveland's social set revealed a man who fitted this description, who was, according to Ness's chronicler, Oscar Fraley. Ness confronted the man and told him he was the chief suspect. But while Ness's men were still trying to build up a case against him, the man had himself confined in a private lunatic asylum and the murders ceased.

In England, there were a number of sex murders during the forties – mostly frustrated soldiers on leave – but nothing to parallel these American cases until the early fifties, the era of Heath and Christie. The case of Alfred Whiteway (1953) recalls the Peoria case in certain details. Whiteway, twenty-two, was also an experienced rapist, and his decision to kill two teenage girls on the tow-path near Teddington may have been made because one of the girls recognized him as he attacked them.

Meanwhile, in America, the trend of sadism and gruesome violence continued. The "moonlight murders" took place in 1946. In 1947, the "Black Dahlia case" shocked the whole country. The body of Elizabeth Short, a would-be film actress, was found on a piece of waste ground. It had been cut in two at the waist, and badly mutilated with a knife. The pathologist established that the killer had suspended her upside down by her feet and inflicted many of the injuries while she was still alive. The body had then been cut in half and carefully washed. In spite of an enormous manhunt, the killer was never found. (And it is probably a safe guess that he committed suicide not long after the murder.) There were dozens of confessions to this murder, all false, and several imitative crimes.

In December, 1953, a courting couple were reported missing near Pamplico, South Carolina. The half-naked body of Betty Cain, sixteen, was found in a newly dug grave, but her head was missing. The head was found later in the grave that contained her fiancé, Henry Allen. An escaped convict, Raymond Carney, thirty-seven, was convicted of the crime. He insisted that his motive was robbery, but examination of the girl's body revealed that she had been raped. It is not clear why the convict decapitated the girl or whether this was before or after the sexual assault, but the motive was probably sadistic.

In 1959, there occurred in Miami, Florida, a murder that in many respects recalls the case of Elizabeth Short, the "Black Dahlia". The victim was a fifty-three-year-old spinster who worked as a secretary. On the night of 14 December, Ethel Ione Little returned home and undressed for bed. Then a man who had been hiding in a closet knocked her to the floor, lifted her onto the bed and tied her wrists and ankles to the four bedposts. The full details of what happened during the next four to six hours have never been published; all that is clear is that she was tortured by a sexual deviant until she died of shock and loss of blood. No male semen was found, but the nature of the injuries, including bite-marks, make it clear that the attack was sexual. In spite of a widespread police search and mass fingerprinting, the killer was never found.

In England, during that same month, there was a case similar in many respects to the double murder in South Carolina. A twenty-eight-year-old Irish labourer, Patrick Byrne, got drunk on Christmas Eve and crept into the grounds of a hostel for women in Edgbaston, Birmingham, hoping to spy on women undressing. As Byrne peered through one door, the girl inside the room came towards him and was immediately attacked by him. He strangled her, raped her, then cut off her head with a breadknife, after which he raped her again. All this excited him so much that he went off looking for another girl to attack, but someone screamed when he struck her on the head and he fled. Byrne was not a suspect in the murder, but when questioned, in a routine investigation, seven weeks later, he immediately confessed. He admitted to indulging in sadistic fantasies about women, and said that he had killed Stephanie Baird as a revenge against all women, "to get my own back on them for causing my nervous tension through sex".

These cases, taken almost at random, show clearly the changing patterns of violent crime in the past thirty or forty years. The Cleveland Torso murders stand out, like Jack the Ripper's murders, as the exception to the rule, the harbinger of things to come. We can see the slow change from murders that are basically economic to murders that are basically sexual, and finally, to the type of murder that seems typical of the second half of the twentieth century: what might be called "resentment murders". All that these murders have in common is that the basic motivation seems to be a rage against society that expresses itself as cruelty. It is difficult to discern a "pattern" because the pattern continues to change so fast.

An increasing number of cases are "first evers". Richard Speck's murder of eight nurses in Chicago in 1966 was obviously a sex killing, and yet only one of the girls was actually raped. Eleven-year-old Mary Bell, of Newcastle-on-Tyne, strangled two small boys (aged three and four) "for fun" in 1968. Because of her influence over a thirteen-year-old girl (accused with her), she is described by the prosecuting cousel as "an evil Svengali". On 14 July 1970, a Californian police patrolman arrested two men who were driving a stolen car. One of them, Dean Baker, a bearded hippy type, told the police: "I have a problem, I'm a cannibal", and then described how he had shot a man who had given him a lift near the Yellowstone Park, cutting out the heart and eating it. In his pockets were found the fingers of the dead man, which he had decided to keep as souvenirs. Dismembered pieces of the body were recovered from the river, but not the heart.

The resentment motif can be seen in crimes of pointless violence, particularly in America. "Sniping" has become an increasing problem – the sniper usually shoots from a slightly opened window or from behind the parapet of a roof, where his chances of being seen are minimal. New York has an increasing problem as snipers from Harlem rooftops fire at passing trains. Twenty years ago, psychologists declared unhesitatingly that the sniper is driven by sexual aggression: the gun is a substitute for the penis. Nowadays, the aggression is more often social. On 3 July 1968, a man climbed onto the roof of the lavatory in the children's playground in Central Park, New York, and began firing at random: an eighty-year-old man and a twenty-four-year-old girl were killed before the sniper was shot by the police. He turned out to be a Bulgarian immigrant "with a deep-seated hatred of communism" that seems to have turned into a deep-seated hatred of American society.

Readers who admire the macabre writings of H. P. Lovecraft may be reminded by the above remarks of a passage in his best known story *The Call of Cthulhu*. Cthulhu is chief of the "ancient old ones", monstrous creatures who once inhabited the earth, but who destroyed their civilization through the practise of black magic. Cthulhu lies in a trance at the bottom of the Atlantic ocean, but the time for his return is approaching, and artists all over the world have horrifying dreams of great alien cities. A professor who suspects what is going on has collected press cuttings that reveal the eruption of strange psychic influences:

Here was a nocturnal suicide in London, where a lone sleeper had leaped from a window after a shocking cry. Here likewise a rambling letter to the editor of a paper in South America, where a fanatic deduces a dire future from visions he has seen. A dispatch from California describes a theosophist colony as donning white robes *en masse* for some "glorious fulfilment" which never arrives, whilst items from India speak guardedly of serious native unrest toward the end of March. Voodoo orgies multiply in Haiti, and African outposts report ominous mutterings. American officers in the Philippines find certain tribes bothersome about this time, and New York policemen are mobbed by hysterical Levantines on the night of March 22–23. The west of Ireland too, is full of wild rumour and legendry, and a fantastic painter named Ardois–Bonnot hangs a blasphemous *Dream Landscape* in the Paris spring salon of 1926. And so numerous are the recorded troubles in insane asylums that only a miracle can have stopped the medical fraternity from noting strange parallelisms . . .

One feels that if this had been written in 1988 instead of 1928, Lovecraft might have added the Manson murders, the killing of the Ohta family, Dean Baker's cannibalism and the Zodiac killer.

The literary parallel is more significant than it appears on the surface. Lovecraft's work is far more than grotesque escapism. When he talks about a "blasphemous" dream landscape, he does not mean that it contains indecent mockery of the Christian religion, but something horrible, frightening, nauseating, something like those odd fungus-like creatures in the paintings of Hieronymus Bosch. His work is romanticism gone sour and bitter: instead of turning away, like Shelley and Keats, to visionary dream-worlds, he creates nightmares that help to relieve his loathing of modern western civilisation. He is fond of the word "loathing", with its suggestion of revulsion from something slimy and slug-like. He writes in one letter of "loathsome Asiatic hordes who trail their dirty carcases over streets where white men once moved", and in another of his "mad physical loathing" of the semitic types who jam the New York subway, and says that he has often felt capable of murdering a few of them. The feeling is reminiscent of certain passages about Jews in *Mein Kampf*. But it would be a mistake to label Lovecraft a cranky racialist. The hatred is curdled romanticism, a frustrated appetite for beauty. (In the case of Hitler, the anti-semitism originated in Vienna in the years when he was an unsuccessful young artist living in doss houses.) It is "love showing its root in deepest hell" again.

Hitler was inspired by a vast, strange work called *Foundations of the Nineteenth Century* by an Englishman, Houston Stewart Chamberlain – the book was published (in German) in Vienna in 1899. It speaks of two "pure" races, the Jews and the Aryans, and the impure mixed breeds of the Mediterranean. It contains a lengthy and nostalgic examination of the legacy of Greece and Rome, and concludes that the Germans are the true heirs to all this glory. (The author says that Jesus was almost certainly an Aryan.) Chamberlain argues, most convincingly, that German culture is the greatest in Europe, that its music, literature and philosophy surpass those of any other European country. The future of the west, says Chamberlain, lies in the hands of this nation that produced Bach, Beethoven, Goethe, Kant, Hegel, Wagner . . .

Hitler was deeply influenced by all this, and also by the music of Wagner and the philosophy of Nietzsche. (He had seen all Wagner's operas many times.) Wagner himself was another idealizer of the German past – The Mastersingers of Nuremberg, The Teutonic Knights – while Nazism must be seen as an idealistic revolt against the aspects of the modern world that Lovecraft also hated: the materialism and cultural debasement. Lovecraft's "loathing" expressed itself in visions of a remote, nightmarish past that can still make incursions into our modern world – Hitler's, in Buchenwald and Belsen. Hitler once remarked (to Hermann Rauschning) that although he did not greatly enjoy Goethe, he had to admire him for his line: "In the beginning was *action*." "To desire and act not breeds a pestilence", said William Blake, expressing the same idea. Hitler desired and acted; Lovecraft desired and acted not. But once we understand the underlying spirit of his writing, with its "blasphemous" horrors and monstrosities, we also understand something important about Norman John Collins and the Zodiac killer, as well as Charles Manson and Ian Brady. The basic spirit of Lovecraft's writing is the basic spirit of de Sade's. There is a desire to shock, to shake his fist in the face of modern civilization. And the use of horror is central to his aim. In fact, many of Lovecraft's stories could be regarded as science fiction rather than horror stories. Great underground cities built a million years ago, creatures from outer space: these themes are not necessarily horrifying. Lovecraft preferred to treat them in a context of horror because the horror story expresses aggressions and science fiction doesn't.

In a story called "The Unnamable", the narrator, a writer of horror stories, mentions that one of his stories had appeared in a magazine in 1922, but that many shops "took the magazine off their stands at the complaints of silly milksops". In fact something of the sort had happened in 1924, but the story that caused the furore was not by Lovecraft, but by C. M. Eddy, and "The Loved Dead" caused *Weird Tales* to be attacked for obscenity rather than frightening the milksops. It is a story about a necrophiliac who becomes a sex murderer. The narrator says of his childhood: "Strictly ascetic, wan, pallid, undersized, and subject to protracted spells of morbid moroseness, I was ostracized by the healthy, normal youngsters of my own age . . . " At the age of sixteen he sees his dead grandfather: "A baleful, malignant influence that seemed to emanate from the corpse itself held me with magnetic fascination". But after two weeks of this morbid excitement, he reverts to his "old time languor" (which sounds like van Zon's "infantile autism"). After the death of his parents he becomes apprenticed to an undertaker, and each corpse brought "a return of that rapturous tumult of the arteries which transformed my grisly task into one of beloved devotion". He adds unambiguously: "But every carnal satisfaction exacted its toll". He becomes a kind of Jack the Ripper, perpetrating (unspecified) "abominable atrocities" – occasionally the corpses of his victims were even sent to him to embalm ("O rare and delicious memory!"). After being caught embracing a corpse, he is dismissed, but luckily the 1914 war begins, and gives him four years of "transcendent satisfaction". Back in America he returns to Jack-the-Ripper-type crimes, until the murder of a family sets the police on his trail. He writes his story as he crouches in a graveyard, listening to the barking of the bloodhounds as they draw closer.

This story catches, more boldly than any by Lovecraft, the basic emotion of the horror story and what lies behind it. The lonely, sickly boy, shunned by healthy, normal boys, who feels a stranger in the world of ordinary people, until he discovers that he belongs to another world, the world of the dead. But on closer examination, this turns out to mean sex crime. He is drawn to the dead for the same reason as Sergeant Bertrand. He is also, he says, a sadistic killer. In fact, necrophilia and cruelty are completely unrelated. The necrophile is interested in the corpse because it is passive; an anaesthetized woman would probably do just as well. With fully conscious women, even willing ones, he has inhibitions; he need have none with a corpse. The sadist's urge has nothing to do with inhibitions, it is a desire to exercise power. In the published annals of sex crime, few necrophiles have been sadists and few sadists have been necrophiles. The narrator of "The Loved Dead", and presumably its author, is ignorant of this. He is thinking vaguely in terms of total sexual gratification. So the story jumps unexpectedly from necrophilia to murder. In fact, it is really a story about a sex maniac who defies every social code, whose whole life is a scream of defiance at society – hence the family murder at the end.

Lovecraft himself was too much of a puritan ever to allow a sexual element to intrude into his stories. Perhaps the nearest he comes to it is a story called "The Picture in the House", which describes an old man who has become increasingly fascinated by a book on cannibalism, full of gruesome pictures. "That feller bein" chopped up gives me a tickle every time I look at 'im – I hev ta keep lookin' at 'im – see whar the butcher cut off his feet?" Lovecraft uses the word perversion to describe the old man's obsession. When drops of blood begin to fall on the book the narrator notices a red stain spreading across the ceiling . . .

More than fifty years after his death (in 1937) Lovecraft's work is enjoying an unexpected revival – like Borges (a writer to whom he is related in spirit) he has become a cult among the young. Paperbacks of his weird tales can be found on every seaside bookstall. There is even a pop group that calls itself "The H.P. Lovecraft" by way of homage. What makes the appeal is not the gothic machinery of the horror tale (otherwise there would be a similar revival of all the authors of *Weird Tales* – William Hope Hodgson, Robert W. Chambers, Zealia Bishop, Clark Ashton Smith). It is the underlying spirit of Lovecraft, the revolt against civilization, the feeling that the material success by which the modern world justifies itself is the shallowest of all standards, that has made him a cult. Lovecraft was not a democrat – like Nietzsche, he felt that democracy is the rise of botchers and bunglers and mediocrities against the superior type of man. He was not a logical philosopher – he did not ask himself what he would like to put in its place – he only knew that he hated the impersonal rush and hurry of the modern city, and all the standards and values of "industrial man".

Things are no worse now than they were in Lovecraft's day, or, for that matter, in the days of the "dark satanic mills" of more than a century ago. On the contrary, they have improved. There is more freedom, more leisure, better education, more public subsidy of the arts. But the increased freedom has also increased the number of rebels and misfits. Blake, Nietzsche and Lovecraft were lone "outsiders" (one of Lovecraft's best stories is called "The Outsider"), solitary rebels in an alien society. As the population increases, and as illiteracy becomes the exception rather than the rule, more and more people come to share their view.

Inevitably, it finds its way into action. Melvin Rees, a jazz musician, told a friend: "You can't say it's wrong to kill. Only individual standards make it right or wrong". One night, under the stimulus of benzedrine, he told another friend that he wanted to experience everything – love, hate, life, death. That was on Saturday 10 January 1959, by which time Rees had already realized his ambition, having killed and sexually assaulted at least one girl, possibly even five. The following day, Rees tried to force a car to drive into the ditch, but as he got out of his own car, holding a gun, the other driver managed to reverse and drive away. Rees's intention was to kill the driver and rape his wife, who was also in the car. Rees's next attempt, later in the day, *was* successful. His old blue Chevrolet forced another car off the road; it contained a family on an afternoon outing. Rees shot the husband, Carrol Jackson, and tossed his body into the ditch, together with their eighteen-month-old girl (who suffocated under her father's body). He then forced the wife and five-year-old daughter to drive off with him. What happened to them during the next few hours is not certain. When the two bodies were found some months later, all that was clear was that Mildred Jackson had been strangled and the child beaten to death with a heavy instrument.

It was not until the following year, 1960, that Rees was arrested in a music shop in Arkansas, where he was working. The friend to whom he had made the comments about murder suspected him of

the Jackson killings, and told the police. A search of his parents'
home revealed the gun that had been used in an earlier murder. A
courting couple in a lonely spot had been held up by a man, who
shot the woman through the head. The killer allowed the man
to run away, and then apparently sexually assaulted the body
of the woman – a thirty-six-year-old nurse. Also in his room
at home were found press cuttings about the Jackson murder
and an account of the crime. Rees was executed. The Dutch
clairvoyant, Peter Hurkos, was called into the case some time
before Rees's arrest. He not only gave an accurate description
of Rees (left-handed, tattooed, ape-like arms) but stated that he
had committed nine murders. Friends of Rees at the University
of Maryland, which he had attended, found it difficult to believe
he was a murderer – one described him as mild-mannered and
intelligent.

Eddy's portrait of a sex killer in "The Loved Dead" is an
imaginative absurdity; Rees is the real thing. It is doubtful
whether he felt any compunction about killing the Jackson
family. They were in every way "bourgeois" and normal: Mildred
Jackson was president of the women's missionary society at the
local Baptist church, her husband was a bank clerk who was a
teetotaller and non-smoker. A man of Rees's views would have
felt that such people were his natural prey. The state of mind is
like that of a spy in an enemy country. He has to pretend to be
something he is not, and to gain the trust of these people. But he is
there in order to work towards their destruction. His loyalty is to
his own people. And if they knew this, they would destroy him.

Why does he feel so alienated? Is it his own fault or the fault of
the society itself? Lovecraft felt that there was something rotten
about the whole trend of modern civilization and that it was this
that forced people like himself into the position of outsiders and
rebels.

Now it must be remembered that this idea was asserted more
than two centuries ago by Jean-Jacques Rousseau. Rousseau's
fundamental doctrine is sometimes summarised by the phrase
"Back to nature", as if he advocated living in the treetops,
but this is to over-simplify. Man has become alienated from his
own basic nature by the artificiality of society, says Rousseau.
The chief enemy is social convention, which encourages pride,

egoism, ruthlessness, at the cost of the natural virtues of kindness, decency, honesty. Culture – by which Matthew Arnold set so much store – is attacked as a product of vanity and pride. Even science and art are really unnecessary to man; their products encourage idleness, artificiality and shallowness. According to Rousseau, civilization has simply taken a wrong turning. Its values are all wrong, and since these values are successful, and success begets success, they will go on getting more wrong. Mankind is happiest, he says, in tribes, or small, quiet rural communities; the city is an abomination.

The romantics were the direct descendants of Rousseau. Wordsworth's sonnet "The world is too much with us" expresses the basic Rousseau sentiment: "Little we see in nature that is ours. We have given our hearts away, a sordid boon . . ." And the complaint echoes down the century. Man is "out of tune" with the universe, trapped in a sordid world of "getting and spending". And the nature of the complaint becomes clearer as industry spreads across Europe. It is *beauty starvation*. According to the romantic poets, beauty is an essential vitamin; without it, the soul shrivels up and becomes dry and brittle. Ruskin tells Yeats's father that as he goes to the British Museum, he sees the faces of the people become daily more corrupt. Yeats himself writes that "the wrong of unshapely things is a wrong too great to be told", and unlike Oscar Wilde, he meant it. The "religion of beauty" of the aesthetes aroused a great deal of mockery, good-natured and otherwise, but the mockery missed the point. The talk of beauty was not "idle chatter of a transcendental kind", it was an instinctive recognition that, in the long run, beauty-deficiency is as serious as calcium-deficiency or exposure to radioactivity. It produces a blight of the will, a sickening of the vital forces. For beauty is, in the last analysis, the same thing as a sense of purpose. When you are hungry and you contemplate a good dinner, the sensation that arises in you is the same as the sense of beauty; it is also a sense of immediate purpose. Likewise, a traveller standing on top of a mountain experiences hunger and a sense of purpose: the wide horizons produce a feeling of an open future, of important things to be done and important meanings to be grasped. It is the feeling of freedom, of *openness*, that constitutes the sense of beauty. Conversely, ugliness is a sense of being trapped, closed-in, suffocated by dirt and triviality. Man is an evolutionary creature who is at his best when possessed by visions of purpose, and who becomes frustrated and soured and embitterd when he is suffocated by the trivial.

But as the nineteenth century drew towards its close, there was no sign of an improvement: everything Wordsworth hated got worse. The romantics wrote sadly about "beauty that has passed away" and dreamed of a return to the courtly days of the middle ages. The 1914 war was the watershed: the sadness changed to anger and hatred. Ezra Pound stopped writing about the troubadors of Provence and turned to denunciation:

> There died a myriad,
> And of the best, among them,
> For an old bitch gone in the teeth,
> For a botched civilization . . .

Pound's *Mauberley* and Eliot's *Waste Land* are direct descendants of Rousseau and Wordsworth. They even use the same method, contrasting the moral ugliness of civilization with the world of nature or of the past: "Sweet Thames run softly till I end my song . . ." There seems to be little enough in common between Proust, D.H. Lawrence, William Faulkner, Ernest Hemingway, Aldous Huxley, Thomas Mann, Robert Musil, Hermann Hesse and Graham Greene. What they share is a feeling of protest, and the protest is about beauty-starvation, the "botched civilization". In *Heartbreak House*, Shotover asks Ellie Dunn how much her soul eats, and she answers: "Oh, a lot. It eats music and pictures and books and mountains and lakes and beautiful things to wear and nice people to be with. In this country you can't have them without lots of money: that is why our souls are so horribly starved." Lawrence or Mann or Huxley would express this in different terms, but they would imply the same thing: that if civilization is to satisfy the evolutionary appetite as well as the material needs, then it must somehow provide *meaning* as well as security. If the sense of meaning is starved, the result is a feeling of futility that will eventually produce violence.

The Russian writer Valery Briussov expressed this in a remarkable fable called "The Republic of the Southern Cross", written about 1910. It describes an ideal city in the South Pole, under a great glass dome. The workers earn good wages and are well fed, they live in identical comfortable houses and wear identical clothes. But one day they begin to develop a curious psychosis called "contradiction mania", a compulsion to do the exact opposite of what they want to do: they say no instead of yes, are rude instead of polite; eventually the natural urge to live becomes an urge to destroy and commit suicide. Finally the whole city is destroyed by mobs of insane rioters. Riot police in every large city of the world understand "*mania contradicens*", the urge of a violent mob to destroy anybody's property, *even their own*. A riot may begin as a protest against a particular injustice, but it ends by becoming a generalized expression of revolt against boredom, the dreary routine of everyday life.

In the Wimbledon "queer bashing" murder case of September 1969, the gang of boys who battered Michael de Gruchy to death were not embittered slum-dwellers, but the children of working-class parents who lived in an "architectural showpiece" called the Alton Estate. One of the mothers of the convicted boys remarked: "We thought we were coming to paradise, and it was sending us to hell". The builders of the Alton Estate had every reason to be proud of their achievement, from the point of view of planning: the huge blocks of glass and concrete flats stood on pillars that raised them above the ground, giving an impression of space and open air; they were surrounded by lawns, and close to the green expanse of Wimbledon Common. But no one had anticipated the psychological effect of transferring families from London slums to this strange, impersonal place in the middle of nowhere, the feeling of boredom and rootlessness. The Common was, and is, a haunt of homosexuals. On 29 September 1969, a dozen boys whose ages ranged between fifteen and eighteen set out to hunt for "queers"; they carried wooden palings. On other occasions they had contented themselves with damaging the cars belonging to the "pooves", but their victims had got wise to this and now parked several streets away. Michael de Gruchy, a twenty-eight-year-old clerk who lived with his mother, parked his Austin 1100 on the Alton Estate and then walked through the underground tunnel leading to the Queensmere – known locally as Queersmere – part of the Common. The twelve boys moved forward, and one hit him with a stick. De Gruchy tried to escape, but he was trapped. There was a shout of "Charge", and de Gruchy received a rain of blows on his back. They were violent blows – the pathologist discovered later that the back of his skull was shattered into fragments like a broken vase. The boys ran away, leaving de Gruchy dying. The next day, Geoffrey Hammond, the ringleader, told his employer what had happened, and his employer took the boys to the police station. Hammond, who was eighteen, received a life sentence; the others received shorter sentences or Borstal training.

But Hammond was not, as might be supposed, an illiterate thug with a chip on his shoulder. He had been a choirboy and had been in the St John's Ambulance and Royal Marine Cadets; he was a Duke of Edinburgh Bronze Medal winner, and had appeared in life-saving demonstrations on the children's television programme "Blue Peter". His father said: "He loves anything to do with nature. He loves children. He's a sentimental boy. He's a sportsman – climbing, swimming, diving". But all this could not outweigh the boredom of a model estate, the slow-burning resentment, the desire for excitement and action.

Melvin Rees and Geoffrey Hammond seem to have little in common, but they share a sense of rootlessness, of meaningless-ness, as well as an above-average I.Q. And although Hammond hardly qualifies as an intellectual, boredom had much the same effect upon him as on Rees, or as on Norman Smith, the sniper who shot Hazel Woodward "for something to do". "Life being what it is, one dreams of revenge", said Gauguin, and the Birmingham YWCA murderer talks of getting his own back on all women for causing his nervous tension through sex – as if the very existence of women is a dangerous provocation of his sexual appetite.

One of the most interesting things about the human mind is its fundamental craving for novelty and its strange tendency to stagnate. It is this appetite for novelty, for strangeness, for adventure and excitement, that distinguishes man from every other animal on earth. Cows seem to possess very little of it, and even lions are content with a few square miles of territory. But human beings devour "newness". You only have to watch the face of a child setting out on a train journey to the seaside to understand the power of this urge. For most human beings, the word "travel" is synonymous with pleasure and relaxation, because the sight of new places, changing scenery, has the power of stimulating delight in all but the most jaded. The more tired we are, the less we notice things; the fresher we feel, the more we notice everything. And "newness", change, adventure, satisfies a basic *hunger* in all of us; there is no human being so dull and cow-like that he would not agree that "a change is as good as a rest". We seem to need change and novelty as much as a growing child needs vitamins. This is why the inhabitants of the Republic of the Southern Cross became murderous. Lack of "newness" produces a kind of sickness which becomes steadily worse.

So why should Melvin Rees become murderous? He had plenty of change – as a jazz musician he was "on the road" all the time. But it is one thing to be on the deck of a luxury liner, watching the shoreline of Alexandria drawing nearer, quite another to move around like a tramp from town to town, staying in cheap lodgings or sleeping rough. Such a life condemns you to endless preoccupation with the trivial, the physical – the mind has no freedom. "Newness" depends upon a certain eagerness and openness of the mind. You would not keep an open mouth in a sandstorm because you would get it full of sand; and you cannot keep the mind "open" when living the life of an itinerant, because triviality is like sawdust. It hands us over to the "robot", because we don't want to waste good attention on something we feel to be dreary and repetitive.

I have said that one of the oddest things about the human mind is not only its craving for novelty, but also its *tendency to stagnate*. A Martian who knew about human beings only from psychological textbooks might well expect us to stagnate when faced with dullness and ugliness, but he would certainly find it very strange that we also stagnate in quite pleasant circumstances, if the pleasantness is *unchanging*. It is the passivity of the human mind that is so baffling. A man who is starving to death struggles frantically to keep alive. But a stockbroker living in the suburbs with an attractive wife and pretty children often becomes so jaded that he has to spend his weekend playing strenuous rounds of golf.

The psychologist John Hughlings Jackson made the discovery that the eye cannot remain focused on an object that does not move. And the same applies, apparently, to human consciousness. No matter how much we have to be grateful for, we stagnate unless change keeps us wide awake. What is more, the effects of stagnation build up from mild boredom to frenzied self-loathing in an amazingly short spell of time. This is why "the black room" – a totally black and silent room – is such a potent instrument for brainwashing. It places people in a boring situation and waits for mental pressure to do the rest. It is as cruel as the torture Tiberius was supposed to have practised: tying catgut around the end of a man's penis, then forcing him to drink large quantities of water.

These are basic facts of human nature. Everybody is vaguely aware of them, but no one has yet seen clearly that they are important because of the danger they represent. A diabetic needs a sugar-free diet, and if he doesn't get it, the results are serious. But this human tendency to passivity and craving for "newness" is a more serious disease than diabetes – as the cases in this book demonstrate repeatedly. We cannot even begin to understand the strange violence of modern society without recognizing that it is not "abnormal", a series of "exceptions to the rule" of peaceful co-existence and non-aggression. If a certain type of aeroplane continues to crash, the experts conclude that there is something basically wrong with its design; it would be blindness to declare that each accident has a different cause. And as irrational, freakish crimes take place with increasing frequency, we should make an attempt to seek the common psychological root of each one, even if this takes us into areas that seem remote from our everyday motivations.

One thing is very clear: that in every type of crime, from terrorism to sex murder, we encounter the same curious type of irrationality, a strange "mirror logic" that refuses to face reality. The criminal somehow manages to blame other people, or "society", for what is basically his own fault. This is the essence of the criminal mind, looking around for somewhere to place the blame. Patrick Byrne's desire to terrorise all women, to get his own back on them for causing his nervous tension through sex, is a textbook example of the mirror logic of the criminal. It can also be seen in some of the strange assertions made by Charles Manson and his disciples at their trial, which amounted to the assertion that, since bourgeois society is full of uncaring "pigs", then they were justified in murdering some of those pigs. But this kind of upside-down logic is not restricted to criminals: the whole philosophy of Karl Marx is based upon this same assumption that the "pigs" are responsible for all the troubles of humanity and, incidentally, for Marx's own misfortunes.

In an early work called *Sketch of a Theory of the Emotions*, Jean-Paul Sartre labelled this tendency "magical thinking". There is an old joke of an Arab in the Sahara asking another Arab why he is carrying an umbrella. "I bought it in London. If you want it to rain you leave it at home." A real life example of magical thinking was given by Malcolm Muggeridge, quoting an item from the *Times* about birth control in Asian countries. The World Health Organisation had issued strings containing twenty-eight beads to illiterate peasant women. It had seven amber beads, seven red beads, seven more amber beads and then seven green ones; the women had to move a bead every day until they had arrived at a "safe period". "Many women thought that merit resided in the beads," said the report, "and moved them around to suit themselves".

Sartre also mentions the tendency of the mythical ostrich to bury its head in the sand as an example of magical thinking: the deliberate attempt to pretend that something does not exist or that it is not what it actually is. This type of magical thinking is typical of the rapist. He is not raping a real woman, but a convenient fantasy object. The case of Leonard Lake is typical: "The perfect woman is totally controlled. A woman who does exactly what she is told and nothing else. There is no sexual problem with a submissive woman. There are no frustrations – only pleasure and contentment".

An even more extreme example is the necrophile, who finds a corpse more satisfactory than a living woman. One of the most remarkable cases on record concerns a French army sergeant named Bertrand. Sergeant Bertrand was by no means a withdrawn or shy personality; on the contrary, he was an efficient

NCO, well liked by his men, and something of a Don Juan with the country girls. His arrest in 1849 came as a shock to his army comrades, for it was alleged, and proved at his trial, that for the past two years he had been in the habit of entering cemeteries at night and seeking out the newly-buried bodies of young girls. These corpses, usually buried without coffins, excited him more than living mistresses. Of the corpse of a sixteen-year-old girl he said: "I did everything to her that a passionate lover does to a mistress", and added, "All my enjoyment with living women is as nothing compared to it". On the first occasion when he saw an unburied corpse in a grave, he was so overcome with frenzy that he leapt into the grave and proceeded to beat it with a spade. Later, he returned, dug it up, and committed acts of necrophia. The compulsion was so powerful that he once swam an icy stream in winter to get into a graveyard. He usually ended by disembowelling the corpse.

It is not surprising to learn that Bertrand's comrades found this unbelievable. Bertrand was not a brutal or violent man, he gave the impression of decency and efficiency. His social personality allowed him no way to express the violent sexual feelings that lay underneath. In courting a girl, he had to play the part of a lover; in possessing a corpse, he could ignore his personality, and hers, and concentrate on the release of pure desire. The more complex personal relationship with a "living" girl did not allow the same release; Bertrand's necrophilia is a perfect example of "magical behaviour" – a violent and unsubtle solution to a subtle problem.

This pattern can be discerned in most of the major sex crimes of the twentieth century. A shy or nervous man, subject to fits of depression, broods on sex until he is obsessed by thoughts of rape. The murders follow, each one succeeded by a still deeper fit of depression. Eventually, he engineers his own arrest or commits suicide. All such cases have a strong element of illogicality, so that the normal, balanced person is inclined to fall back on the explanation of madness. But it is not madness, only "magic" – the confusion of a man who throws a stone at a mirage.

One of the clearest examples of the "head-in-sand" type of magical thinking is the case of another necrophile, John Reginald Halliday Christie, who committed eight sex murders in London's

Notting Hill between 1940 and 1953. The most obvious thing about Christie was his authoritarian character structure. As a special reserve constable during the Second World War, he became notorious for his officiousness – he enjoyed reporting people for minor blackout offences. The first four victims were killed between 1940 and 1950, always when his wife was away on visits to relatives in Sheffield. In 1952, he murdered his wife and buried her under the floorboards. Three more sex crimes followed in quick succession in the following months. The method was to persuade the woman to inhale gas, on the pretext of curing asthma or catarrh with Friar's Balsam, then to rape her while unconscious. The murder, by strangulation, was apparently an afterthought, to protect himself.

The interesting feature of this case is his moral collapse. The first two victims were carefully buried in the tiny back garden, and no suspicion fell on Christie. The third victim was Mrs Beryl Evans, a woman who lived with her husband in the flat upstairs. Christie persuaded her husband that he was a skilled abortionist. The abortion was to take place when the husband, Timothy Evans, was at work. It seems unlikely that Christie intended to kill her – his chances of getting away with it were too small. But the sight of her nakedness was too much for him. He battered her unconscious, strangled her, then raped her. He later murdered the fourteen-month-old daughter, Geraldine. When Evans came home from work, Christie seems to have succeeded in frightening him so much that he ended by confessing to the murder of his wife. (Evans's I.Q. was exceptionally low, but it is still a mystery how he came to confess to Christie's crime.) Evans was hanged in 1950. Many years later, as a result of a public enquiry, he was finally exonerated.

Beryl Evans was murdered in 1949; Mrs Christie in December 1952. After disposing of her body, Christie seems to have lost all caution, as if determined to have any orgy before he was caught. In early January, a prostitute named Rita Nelson entered 10 Rillington Place. She was anaesthetized, strangled and raped, and her body was pushed into the corner of a deep closet in the kitchen. About ten days later, Christie strangled and raped another prostitute, Kathleen Maloney. He left the body in the chair all night and went to bed; the next morning, it was wrapped in a blanket and pushed into the closet. During the next few months, the squalid little flat was allowed to become filthy and untidy. Christie had no job and made no attempt to get one. And in the case of his final victim, he abandoned all attempt to cover his tracks. In early March, he met a girl named Hectorina Mclennan and her lover, a lorry driver called Baker. They spent three nights at his flat, sleeping in chairs or on the floor. On the fourth day, Christie approached Hectorina Mclennan outside the labour exchange, while Baker was signing on, and asked her back to the house. She told Baker where she was going, and went back with Christie. He strangled her, raped her, and put her in the cupboard. Baker called later to ask if Christie knew where she was; Christie said he didn't, and they drank a cup of tea together in the kitchen, after which Christie helped Baker search for her.

A week later, he sub-let the flat to another couple, collected £7–13s for rent in advance, and wandered off, leaving the bodies in the cupboard that was now disguised by a layer of wallpaper. The owner of the house, finding the flat sub-let, told the new tenants to leave, and looked into the cupboard. In spite of the hue and cry that followed, Christie made no attempt to escape from London, even registering at a Rowton House under his own name. He walked around, becoming increasingly dirty and unshaven, until he was recognized by a policeman on Putney Bridge. What happened to him in those last week of freedom? It is tempting to suppose that he ceased to be responsible for his actions. Yet he continued to plan and calculate: even when on the run, he met a pregnant girl in a café, and told her he was a medical man who could perform an operation . . .

What is clear is that beyond a certain point, Christie found himself lost in a kind of maze. His early murders – of Ruth Fuerst and Muriel Eady – were carefully planned: the women were invited back to the house when his wife was on holiday, murdered, then buried in the back garden; no suspicion fell on Christie. In his confession, Christie described his feeling as he looked at the body of Muriel Eady, after raping and strangling her: ". . . once again I experienced that quiet, peaceful thrill. I had no regrets". It was as deliberate as a fox stealing a chicken. The murder of Beryl Evans was less calculated, but in the aftermath, Christie showed his usual skill and calculation.

At the Evans trial, he was a cool and competent witness, and a barrister wrote: "Christie bore the stamp of respectability and truthfulness". But the murders of 1953 were neither calculated nor competent. If Christie had buried his victims in the back garden, and continued to work at his job (with British Road Services), his chances of escaping detection would have been high. None of the three women was likely to be missed. His only problem was to prevent his wife's sister from becoming suspicious, but she lived in Sheffield, and Christie had already explained that Ethel's rheumatism was so bad that she was unable to write letters. The time for calculation had passed: Christie was on the same downhill slope as de Sade, driven by an obsession that turned his life into a desert. His will to destruction was also a will to self-destruction. He was no longer in control; now the "worm" possessed him, hence the curiously aimless, head-in-sand, magical behaviour of those last months of freedom.

The case of the Thames nude murderer, sometimes known as "Jack the Stripper", provides an even more striking example of the build-up of a sexual obsession into aimless destructiveness. The "Stripper's" crimes produced one of the biggest manhunts in British criminal history, which ended, typically, with his suicide.

Between February 1964 and January 1965, the bodies of six women, mostly prostitutes, were found in areas not far from the Thames. The first of the bodies, that of a thirty-year-old prostitute named Hanna Tailford, was found in the water near Hammersmith bridge. She was naked except for her stockings, and her panties had been stuffed into her mouth. Her jaw was bruised, but this could have resulted from a fall. On 18 April, the naked body of Irene Lockwood, a twenty-six-year-old prostitute, was found at Duke's Meadows, near Barnes Bridge, not far from the place where Hanna Tailford had been found. She had been strangled and, like Hanna Tailford, she had been pregnant. A fifty-four-year-old Kensington caretaker, Kenneth Archibald, confessed to her murder, and he seemed to know a great deal about the girl; but at his trial, it was established that his confession was false and he was acquitted. There was another reason for believing in his innocence: while he was still in custody, another naked girl was found in an alleyway at Osterley Park, Brentford. This was only three weeks after the discovery of Irene

Lockwood's body. The dead girl – the only one among the victims who could be described as pretty – was identified as a twenty-two-year-old prostitute and striptease artist, Helen Barthelemy. There were a number of curious features in the case. A line around her waist showed that her panties had been removed after death, and there was no evidence of normal sexual assault. But four of her front teeth were missing. Oddly enough, the teeth had not been knocked out by a blow, but deliberately forced out – a piece of one of them was found lodged in her throat. Medical investigation also revealed the presence of male sperm in her throat. Here, then, was the cause of death: she had been choked by a penis, probably in the course of performing an act of fellatio. The missing teeth suggested that the killer had repeated the assault after death. It was established that she had disappeared some days before her body was found. Where, then, had her body been kept? Flakes of paint found on her skin suggested the answer, for it was the type of paint used in spraying cars. Clearly, the body had been kept somewhere near a car spraying plant, but in some place where it was not likely to be discovered by the workers.

The "nude murders" became a public sensation, for it now seemed likely that they were the work of one man. Enormous numbers of police were deployed in the search for the spray-shop, and in an attempt to keep a closer watch on the areas in which the three victims had been picked up – around Notting Hill and Shepherds Bush. Perhaps for this reason, the killer decided to take no risks for several months.

The body of the fourth victim – Mary Fleming, aged thirty – found on 14 July, confirmed that the same man was probably responsible for all four murders. Her false teeth were missing, there was sperm in her throat, and her skin showed traces of the same spray paint. She had vanished three days earlier.

Her body was found, in a half-crouching position, near a garage in Acton, and the van was actually seen leaving the scene of the crime. A motorist driving past Berrymede Road, a cul-de-sac, at five-thirty in the morning, had to brake violently to avoid a van that shot out in front of him. He was so angry that he contacted the police to report the incident. If he had made a note of the van number, the nude case would have been solved. A squad car that arrived a few minutes later found the body of Mary Fleming in the forecourt of a garage in the cul-de-sac.

The near-miss probably alarmed the killer, for no more murders occured that summer. Then, on 25 November 1964, another naked body was found under some debris in a car park in Hornton Street, Kensington. She was identified as Margaret McGowan, twenty-one, a Scot. Under the name Frances Brown, she had been called as a witness in the trial of Stephen Ward, and Ludovic Kennedy described her (in his book on the trial) as a small, bird-like woman with a pale face and fringe. Margaret McGowan had disappeared more than a month before her body was found, and there were signs of decomposition. Again, there were traces of paint and a missing front tooth indicated that she had died in the same way as the previous two victims.

The last of the Stripper's victims was a prostitute named Bridie O'Hara, twenty-eight. She was found on 16 February 1965, in some undergrowth on the Heron Trading Estate, in Acton. She had last been seen on 11 January in the Shepherds Bush Hotel. The body was partly mummified, which indicated that it had been kept in a cool place. As usual, teeth were missing, and sperm was found in the throat. Fingermarks on the back of her neck revealed that, like the other victims, she had died in a kneeling position, bent over the killer's lap.

Detective Chief Superintendent John du Rose was recalled from his holiday to take charge of the investigation in the Shepherds Bush area. The Heron Trading Estate provided the lead they had been waiting for. Investigation of a paint spray shop revealed that this was definitely the source of the paint found on the bodies – chemical analysis proved it. The proximity of a disused warehouse solved the question of where the bodies had lain before they were dumped. The powerful spray guns caused the paint to carry, with diminishing intensity, for several hundred yards. Analysis of paint on the bodies enabled experts to establish the spot where the women must have been concealed: it was underneath a transformer in the warehouse.

Yet even with this discovery, the case was far from solved. Thousands of men worked on the Heron Trading Estate. (Oddly enough, Christie had been employed there). Mass questioning seemed to bring the police no closer to their suspect. Du Rose decided to throw an immense twenty-mile cordon around the area, to keep a careful check on all cars passing through at night. Drivers who were observed more than once were noted; if they were seen more than twice, they were interviewed. Du Rose conducted what he called "a war of nerves" against the killer, dropping hints in the press or on television that indicated the police were getting closer. They knew he drove a van, they knew he must have right of access to the trading estate by night. The size of the victims, who were all short women, suggested that the killer was under middle height. As the months passed, and no further murders took place, du Rose assumed that he was winning the war of nerves. The killer had ceased to operate. He checked on all men who had been jailed since mid-February, all men with prison records who had been hospitalized, all men who had died or committed suicide. In his book *Murder Was My Business*, du Rose claims that a list of twenty suspects had been reduced to three when one of the three committed suicide. He left a note saying that he could not bear the strain any longer. The man was a security guard who drove a van, and had access to the estate. At the time when the women were murdered, his rounds included the spray shop. He worked by night, from 10 pm to 6 am. He was unmarried.

This is clearly a case of the obsessive mentality – even more so than in the case of Christie. Christie's peculiarity was his inability to have intercourse with a woman who was fully conscious; the Stripper was interested only in fellatio. (This was not revealed at the time of the case, and it is only hinted at in du Rose's book.) If he was the killer of Hanna Tailford and Irene Lockwood, as seems likely, then his obsession had still not reached a climax. Presumably he had been paying prostitutes to satisfy his need. The death of Hanna Tailford could have been, as du Rose says, accidental: at the height of his sexual satisfaction, guiding her head with his hand on her neck, the other probably gripping her hair, he may have lost control, and choked her with the glands of his penis – as if an apple had been jammed in her throat, as du Rose explained in an article written after his retirement. But accident is unlikely, otherwise, why should he have stuffed her panties into her mouth, presumably to make sure she was dead? When he killed Irene Lockwood, he knew in advance what he intended to do. He picked her up on the night of 7 April. The murder almost certainly took place in the back of his van. After this he stripped her and threw her body in the river. One writer on the case has suggested that the victims were stripped to avoid identification, but this would clearly be pointless. Why should the murderer care whether the women were identified, or how soon? The stripping was a part of his sexual need, the desire to feel himself totally dominant. His fantasy involved a naked woman, and it involved treating her mouth as a vagina – hence the removal of teeth. In the later murders, the bodies were kept in the warehouse for several weeks, not because he was waiting for a favourable moment to dispose of them (after all, the longer he waited, the more chance there was that they would be discovered in the warehouse), but in order to repeat his perverse acts. The last corpse was kept longer than any of the others, and was dumped on the Trading Estate. This may have been partly out of fear of being stopped with the corpse in his van, although the police cordon had not been formed at that time. But it is more likely the same indifference that overtook Christie – murder had become a *habit*, and destructiveness involved an element of self-destruction.

Sexual murder is the most extreme form of Sartre's "magical" behaviour. All magical behaviour involves self-delusion, and therefore a certain conflict with reality. But a man suffering from mild delusion of grandeur may be tolerated by his fellow men; they may even humour him, so that there is no head-on clash with reality. A sado-masochist who hires a prostitute to dress up as a nurse, then to allow him to flog her, is paying for the privilege of having a partner to share his fantasies: hence he also avoids the inevitable clash with reality. But the rapist or sex killer forces the "partner" to collaborate, and avoids payment, so the clash with reality is only deferred. In his moment of supreme satisfaction, he is Don Juan and Casanova and Haroun Al Raschid; but ten minutes later, he is only a man on the run, who may spend the rest of his life in gaol if society catches him. The strain is not merely the problem of keeping his secret, it is the problem of living permanently on two levels, like a man trying to walk two tightropes with either foot. This also explains why such a man becomes increasingly careless, or finally commits suicide. He may also develop certain delusions, which help to reconcile him to his Jekyll and Hyde personality. (According to the psychologist Robert Eisler, this is how the belief in werewolves came about – a primitive attempt by the sex maniac to understand his own behaviour.)

The Jersey rapist Edward Paisnel (arrested in 1971) believed that he was possessed by the spirit of Gilles de Rais. Paisnel was charged with fifteen offences, mainly against young children. He would break into the house, carrying the sleeping child out into the garden, and commit the sexual assault. Behind a cupboard in Paisnel's bedroom there was a secret room which contained black magic paraphernalia – masks and strange clothes, an altar, a dish containing toads. Questioned by the police about a raffia cross, Paisnel's face went red and his eyes bulged; he said: "My Master would laugh very long and loud at this". Paisnel had literally developed "magical" behaviour to reconcile himself to his overpowering urges. What is equally typical is that during the eleven years of his reign of terror on Jersey, Paisnel was known as a kind-hearted man who loved children – he played Santa Claus at Christmas and was known to dozens of children as Uncle Ted. There can be no doubt that he *was* a kind-hearted man, except when possessed by his "daemon".

The "demonic" element can be seen in many other cases of sexual murder. Ed Gein, a lonely little bachelor of Plainfield, Wisconsin, was primarily a necrophile who ended by killing women. A deputy sheriff, searching for his mother (who ran a store), called at the Gein farm, since Gein had been her last customer. He found his mother, headless, hanging upside down from the ceiling. Other fragments of women were found in the abominably squalid farmhouse, but these had been obtained from corpses. Gein had lived alone since the death of his highly dominant mother, who had been something of a religious maniac. In spite of his mild appearance and gentle manner, Gein's sexual urges were strong. In 1942, fifteen years before his arrest, he had been fascinated by the bare legs of a female visitor to a neighbouring house – the woman was wearing shorts. The same night, a man broke into the house and asked the woman's small son where she could be found: the boy thought he recognized Gein. But the intruder fled before he was seen by anyone else. Three years later, Gein's mother died. Alone in the house, he brooded on sex. One night, after seeing a newspaper report of the burial of a local woman, he went and dug up her body and reburied the empty coffin. Back at the farm, he was finally able to indulge his sexual desires to the full. "It gave me a lot of satisfaction", Gein remarked, recalling Christie's comment about the death of Muriel Eady. Unlike Christie, Gein *had* regrets every time he gave way to the urge to visit local graveyards. Nevertheless, he ate parts of the corpses, and made waistcoats of the skin, wearing them next to his body. This compulsion occurred about once a year, usually at the time of the full moon. (In this, he resembles Paisnel.) The two women he murdered were both elderly – presumably the murders were intended as some kind of act of revenge against his mother. Gein was sentenced to internment in a mental hospital. Like Paisnel, he was universally liked in the area, and much in demand as a baby-sitter. The incredibly dirty state of the farmhouse indicates that, like Christie, he had retreated into the world of his own nightmare.

On 9 November 1949, the body of a woman was found in False Creek, Vancouver, British Columbia. She had been strangled and beaten before being thrown, alive, into the water – missing panties and suspender belt indicated that the motive was sexual. She was identified as Blanche Fisher, an attractive woman who looked many years younger than her actual age, forty-five. She had failed to return home from a visit to the cinema on the evening before the murder.

A month later, on 5 December, a police patrol car passed a man who wore a raincoat, but whose legs appeared to be bare above rubber boots. He was caught after a chase and found to be wearing only a shirt under the raincoat. He claimed that he had blacked out earlier that evening, and regained his senses to find himself walking along without trousers. Understandably, the police disbelieved him. They went back to the houseboat under Burrard Bridge that thirty-four-year-old Frederick Ducharme gave as his address. On a clothes-line they found six pairs of women's panties, and in the living quarters, Blanche Fisher's shoes and watch. Like Gein's farmhouse, the boat was chaotically untidy. Ducharme (who at first gave his name as Farnsworth) admitted to being with Blanche Fisher on the evening of the murder. He claimed she had entered his car willingly, but had become hysterical when he tried to make love to her and had run away. It was clear that what actually happened was that Ducharme had forced her into his car (perhaps knocking her unconscious), then taken her onto his houseboat, where she was subjected to beating and rape, as well as being cut by a knife. She was then thrown overboard.

It was never established where the panties came from, or other women's trinkets found in the cabin, although Ducharme admitted that he had stolen some of the panties from clothes-lines. The pattern is similar to that of the Gein case: a sex-obsessed man who lives alone, and who periodically wanders the streets at night, exposing himself to women, raiding clothes-lines, perhaps committing the occasional rape. The torture indicates his desire to feel himself complete master of his victim. (And in this respect, the "victimology" deserves comment. Although pretty, Blanche Fisher was unmarried. She was a shy, quiet woman who regularly attended a Christian Science church. To fellow assistants in the store where she worked, she dropped hints of romance and future marriage, but it was later established that these were pure imagination – she had no male friends. She was an enthusiastic cinema-goer and reader of movie fan magazines. For a man like Ducharme, she must have seemed the ideal victim.)

One also notes Ducharme's lack of foresight or caution. If he had thrown away the shoes and watch, there would have been no case against him. And the story he invented failed to explain how, if Blanche Fisher *had* run away, he came to possess her shoes and watch. The evidence suggests that he lived in a dream world, in which sex was the only reality.

The "moonlight murderer" of Texarcana, Texas, was never caught, and almost certainly committed suicide. Between March and May 1946, he committed five murders, two of young couples. The motive was rape. After shooting the male escort, he raped and tortured the girl. This case demonstrates the typical pattern of mounting violence. A young couple who were attacked on 20 February were only knocked unconscious, after which the girl was raped. A month later, the male escort was shot, and the girl tortured and raped for two hours before she was shot. In April, another male escort was shot, and the girl tortured and raped for four hours before she was killed. In the final case, in May (again on the night of a full moon), a farmer was shot as he sat reading his newspaper in front of an open window. The killer undoubtedly intended to assault his wife, but she ran screaming from the house. Tyre tracks outside confirmed that this murder was also the work of the "moonlight murderer". A few days later, a man committed suicide by leaping under a train in Texarcana. At the same time, a burning car was found in a wooded area near the scene of the earlier murders. After this, the murders ceased.

Harvey Glatman, a photographer from San Diego, California, illustrates a different aspect of this "suicidal" tendency. Glatman, another unattractive, bespectacled little man, collected pornography and had a collection of sexy photographs. Finally, he decided to put his fantasies into effect. Three times he advertised for photographic models: on each occasion, he tied up the girl after threatening her with a revolver, took "bondage" pictures, then raped and killed her. The bodies were dumped outside the city, on lonely roads. A fourth girl put up more resistance and Glatman was caught before he could kill her. What is surprising is that he succeeded with three girls. A girl who intends to answer an advertisement for modelling may well mention her destination to a room-mate or friend; Glatman knew this, but he didn't care, the need for sexual satisfaction was more important than the likelihood of being caught. Such a man may be regarded as a suicide-candidate who has decided to have a good time before he goes.

In 1970, a fifty-one-year-old construction worker named Mack Edwards walked into a Los Angeles police station and admitted to a series of child murders stretching over seventeen years. He confessed to six murders – three between 1953 and 1956, and three between 1968 and 1970. His detailed knowledge of the crimes convinced police that the confessions were genuine; they also came to believe that Edwards was responsible too for a series of child murders between 1956 and 1968, bringing the total up to twenty-two. Edwards was sentenced to death, whereupon he requested to be allowed to be the next man executed in California (where there have been no executions for several years, while certain crucial appeals are heard). "My lawyer told me there are a hundred men to die in the chair. I'm asking the judge if I can have the first man's place. He's sitting up there sweating right now. I'll take his place. I'm not sweating. I'm ready for it." He gives the impression of a man who has wakened from a kind of nightmare, whose one anxiety is to make sure it never returns.

This enables us to state the problem of the "assassin" in very clear terms. Man is an evolving creature, with various *levels* of need. Physical survival is the lowest of these; once this is satisfied, he can evolve to the next level: "territorial" security, the need for a home. Beyond this, come the need for sex, family, and so on through Maslow's hierarchy of values. It is also important to recognize that evolution tends to proceed in "leaps". I notice this if I try to master any skill, from learning a foreign language to skiing or walking on my hands: one minute I am doing it clumsily, the next minute, it has "come to me". The same is true of our personal evolution: we quite suddenly "care" about something that was a matter of total indifference a few days before. A child who has always thought nothing of lying or stealing wakes up one morning to find he has outgrown them; a young man who has used his personal charm to seduce girls quite suddenly feels disgust at the dishonesty involved. Bernard Shaw was so fascinated by the abrupt nature of these overnight moral changes that he made them the subject of several of his plays.

The basic law of moral common sense is never to do anything that will block your evolution, just as it is physical common sense not to ruin your health for the sake of some temporary pleasure. This is the real objection to crime: not a religious or moral objection, but a psychological one. For fourteen years, Mack Edwards killed children to satisfy an obsessive sexual need. One morning he woke up and found he had outgrown it, the demon had gone. But how could he evolve into the self-esteem level – which is essentially a social level – with twenty-two dead children on his conscience? He was literally another man, passing judgement on an earlier self. His judgement was a sentence of death.

It should by now be obvious that the problem of "magical thinking" is closely linked to another problem discussed earlier in this book, that of the "Right Man" – the man who will never, under any circumstances, admit that he is in the wrong. He is a compulsive neurotic, whose need for self-belief is so powerful that he cannot permit himself the slightest hint of self-criticism. The need that consumes him is a craving to dominate other people, to feel himself to be "a man of importance". If the circumstances of his life do not allow him to express this dominance in his work or his social relations, then he tries to turn his family into a tiny dictator state. The least sign of resistance makes him violent. And the root cause of this violence is his craving for dominance.

The importance of "dominance", the "pecking order", in animal behaviour has been recognised only in fairly recent times. It was first noticed in flocks of domestic fowl, in which dominant individuals tend to peck subordinate ones. Only then was it slowly recognised that *all* animals, including human beings, have a "pecking order", a kind of chain in which everyone is more dominant or subordinate than someone else. In groups such as lions, gorillas or rats, dominance is usually established by aggressive encounters. But once one of the animals has won the fight, all aggression usually evaporates, and the loser shows submissive behaviour from then on. Once a certain animal, or bird, has established dominance over all the other challengers, he (or she) seems to acquire a sense of social responsibility, and passes beyond the range of quarrels. The same phenomenon can often be seen in politicians who have been promoted to Prime Minister or President: a very mediocre party hack often develops genuine leadership qualities. This helps to explain that fundamental human craving for power, and why those who have acquired power cling to it so tightly. Supreme power places one above the "rat-race".

One of the most exciting observations about "dominance" was made during the Korean war. Attempting to understand why there had been so few escapes of American prisoners, observers discovered that the Chinese had made use of an interesting technique. They had watched the prisoners carefully to establish which of them were "dominant"; then they had taken these dominant prisoners, and placed them under heavy guard. As soon as the "leaders" had been removed, the other prisoners became more or less inert, and could be left almost without guards.

But the most interesting observation was that the number of "dominant" prisoners was always the same: one in twenty, or five per cent. In fact, the explorer, Stanley, had known about this "dominant five per cent" at the turn of the century. Bernard Shaw once asked him how many people in his party could take over the leadership if Stanley himself was ill; Stanley replied: "One in twenty". Shaw asked if that was exact or approximate; Stanley replied: "Exact".

Observations of zoologists like Lorenz and Tinbergen indicated that this applies to all animal species: five per cent are "dominant". But a psychologist named John Calhoun made an equally interesting observation: that when rats are overcrowded, the "dominant five per cent" becomes a criminal five per cent. Overcrowded rats express their dominance in behaviour that is completely uncharacteristic of rats in natural conditions: for example, in rape and cannibalism. Some animals, like Sika deer, simply die of stress when overcrowded. Human beings seem to have a far higher resistance to stress than any other animal – they tend to react to overcrowding, like the rats, by developing criminal behaviour. It is significant that no serial killer has so far emerged from a socially privileged background: the majority were brought up in overcrowded slums. The zoologist Desmond Morris remarked that cities are "human zoos", and added: "Under normal conditions, in their natural habitats, wild animals do not mutilate themselves, masturbate, attack their offspring, develop stomach ulcers, become fetichists, suffer from obesity, form homosexual pair-bonds, or commit murder. Among city dwellers . . . all these things occur". The conclusion to be drawn may be that the "crime explosion" will continue until such time as the population explosion has been brought under control.

But overcrowded slums have always existed. And, of course, crime has always existed in overcrowded slums. Why should they produce sadistic sex killers in the second half of the twentieth century? The answer to this question has already emerged in earlier chapters. In societies with a high level of poverty, theft is the commonest form of crime. In more "successful" societies, sex crime makes its appearance, as overcrowding in slums produces the "criminal rat" syndrome, with the dominant five per cent expressing their dominance through rape. But in "affluent societies", where a higher level of education means that all levels of society begin to glimpse the possibility of wealth and achievement, the craving for "upward mobility" becomes as urgent as the craving for sexual fulfillment, and "self-esteem" crime makes its appearance. (It may or may not be significant that self-esteem murder made its appearance at a time when the pop star had become a well-established phenomenon, so that every under-privileged teenager could begin to glimpse the possibility of wealth and fame.) In the second half of the eighteenth century, thinkers like Rousseau and Tom Paine stated the fundamental principle that all men have a right to freedom. In the second half of the twentieth century, there is a powerful unstated assumption that all men have a right to fame and celebrity.

Abraham Maslow, who was the first to describe the "hierarchy of needs", also made an important observation about "dominance". He had become curious about the subject after observing the behaviour of monkeys in the Bronx zoo. They seemed to engage in almost constant sex – something that has been observed among many animals in captivity. But what puzzled Maslow was that the sex often seemed "abnormal" – males would mount other males, and sometimes females would even mount males. It dawned on him slowly that this was because sex was a form of "dominance behaviour". What was happening was that the more dominant animals were asserting themselves by mounting the less dominant animals. (Robert Ardrey has pointed out that under natural conditions, "sex is a sideshow in the world of animals"; it only assumes exaggerated importance in captivity – another observation that may help to explain the rise in sex crime.)

Maslow also observed that if a new monkey is added to a group of monkeys, the newcomer would often get beaten up, the attack often being led by a previously non-dominant monkey. He noted that the previously non-dominant monkey would often behave with extreme ferocity, as if making up for its previously inferior status. Here again we may glimpse a parallel with the sadistic behaviour of many "self-esteem" criminals.

But perhaps his most interesting observations concerned dominance in women. In 1936, Maslow began a series of Kinsey-type interviews with college women – he preferred women to men as interviewees, because they were capable of greater frankness. Male answers tended to be distorted by self-esteem. His findings, stated in a paper of 1939 (and another, three years later), was that female sexuality is related to dominance. The higher-dominance females went in for more promiscuity, lesbian relations, masturbation and sexual experimentation (fellatio, sodomy, etc).

What surprised him was that he discovered that his subjects tended to fall into three groups: high dominance, medium dominance and low dominance. A medium dominance woman might have a high rating for sex drive, but her sexual experience was usually limited; she tended to be a "one-man woman". A low dominance woman (and these were difficult to get into the study group) was inclined to feel that sex was strictly for child-bearing, and one low dominance woman who was sterile refused her husband sex even though she had a high sex drive. (It is important to note that all three groups could have a high sex drive, but that the *amount* of sex they indulged in depended on how dominant they were.) Medium dominance women had a romantic attitude to sex; they liked to be wooed with candles and flowers and soft music, and they liked the kind of male who would be a "good provider" – someone who was stable rather than exciting. Low dominance women seemed to feel that sex was rather disgusting. Most of them thought that the male sexual organ was ugly, while high dominance women thought it beautiful.

The most significant observation that emerged from the study was that the women tended to prefer males who were slightly more dominant than themselves, *but* within their own dominance group. Low dominance females preferred the kind of man who would admire them from a distance for years without pressing their suit. They found medium and high dominance males rather frightening. Medium dominance women found high dominance males frightening. High dominance women liked the kind of man who would sweep them off their feet, and in love making, hurl them on a bed and take them with a certain amount of force. One highly dominant woman spent years looking for a male who was even more dominant than herself, and failed to find him. When finally she discovered a man of slightly superior dominance, she married him and remained faithful; but she enjoyed picking fights that would make him violent and end in virtual rape – an experience she found immensely exciting. One high dominance woman who could have an orgasm virtually by looking at a man admitted to not having orgasms with two lovers because they were too weak. "I just couldn't give in to them."

When writing a biography of Abraham Maslow in the early seventies, I was struck by the fact that this dominance relation seems to explain many crime partnerships, for example, the Leopold and Loeb murder case in which two Chicago students from wealthy families committed various crimes – ending in murder – for "kicks". Most commentators on the case remain content with the dubious explanation that they wanted to prove that they were "supermen". But the master-slave relationship between Richard Loeb and Nathan Leopold makes us aware of what really happened. Loeb's ego, his self-esteem, was nourished by his "slave"; but it was not enough to express this self-esteem merely by dominating Leopold (who, in any case, wanted to be "used"). Like any juvenile delinquent, Loeb had to express it by "defying society", committing petty crimes for pleasure rather than gain. And it was this craving to *express* his dominance through "defiance" that led to the scheme to kidnap and murder a child. Without his "slave", Loeb would almost certainly never have become a killer.

The most significant observation about this case is that Leopold and Loeb belonged to two different dominance groups: Loeb was high dominance, Leopold medium. This, according to Maslow, seldom happens in ordinary human pair-bondings. To begin with, the high dominance person is seldom sexually interested in people outside his own dominance group. He may cheerfully sleep with medium or low dominance women, but he is incapable of taking any *personal* interest in them. But if, in fact, he consents to a relation with a person outside his dominance group, out of loneliness and frustration, the resultant boost to his ego can amount to a kind of intoxication. In a well-adjusted person, this would usually lead to an increase in self-confidence. In a person whose dominance has been suppressed, as in Maslow's "previously inferior monkeys", the result may be criminal behaviour, which could be interpreted as a kind of chest-beating to demonstrate triumph.

In some cases, the relationship between a high dominance and a medium dominance person may amount to a kind of hypnosis. In November 1899, a scoundrel New York lawyer named Albert T. Patrick knocked on the door of the Madison Avenue apartment of William Rice, a wealthy retired businessman in his eighties. The man who opened the door was Rice's valet, Charles Jones, and Patrick lost no time in trying to persuade Jones to betray his employer, and furnish some evidence that could be used in a lawsuit against Rice. Jones, who was the old man's only friend, refused with horror. But there was something about the beady eyes and dominant gaze of Albert T. Patrick that fascinated him, and when Patrick returned a few days later, he allowed himself to be persuaded, and agreed to forge a letter in which his employer apparently agreed to abandon the lawsuit. When Patrick learned from Jones that Rice had left his fortune of three million dollars to a college in Texas, he persuaded Jones to co-operate in a scheme to forge a new will, leaving the fortune to Patrick. The next step was to poison Rice with indigestion pills laced with mercury. And when these failed to bring about the desired result, Jones was ordered to kill the old man with chloroform.

By now he was so completely under Patrick's domination that he complied. As soon as the old man was dead, Patrick hurried to the bank with a forged cheque for $25,000. But Jones had acidentally made out the cheque to "Abert" T. Patrick, and when the teller noticed this, the scheme began to go wrong. When the bank manager demanded to speak to Mr Rice on the telephone, Jones had to admit that the old man was dead. And soon after this, Jones and Patrick found themselves in adjoining cells. Patrick now handed Jones a sharp knife and said: "The jig's up. It's no use. You go first and I'll follow". Jones was so completely under Patrick's spell that he cut his throat without pausing to reflect that it would be impossible for Patrick to get the knife back . . . In fact, Jones recovered, and turned state's evidence. Patrick was sentenced to death, but was finally pardoned and released.

Almost half a century later, Raymond Fernandez, a petty crook with a *toupée* and gold teeth who specialised in seducing and swindling lonely middle-aged women, met an overweight nurse named Martha Beck, through a lonely hearts club. Fernandez had become a crook after a serious head injury that caused a total personality change. (We have already noted how many serial killers have suffered head injuries.) His first sight of Martha was a shock – she weighed fourteen stone – but she seems to have possessed a certain wistful charm. Once in bed, they discovered that they were soul-mates, and their sex life became a non-stop orgy. When Martha learned how Fernandez made a living, she proposed to join him, posing as his sister, adding only one refinement: that they should murder the women after he had seduced and robbed them. In the course of two years they murdered at least five women, most of whom were contacted through lonely hearts clubs or advertisements, the last being a forty-one-year-old mother and her two-year-old daughter. Suspicious neighbours called the police, who soon discovered two freshly cemented graves in the cellar. Tried in New York, they were both electrocuted on 7 March 1951, Martha having some difficulty squeezing into the electric chair.

Wenzell Brown's book on the case, *The Lonely Hearts Murders*, makes it clear that Martha was the dominant one of the pair, while Fernandez was weak, vain and easy-going. Both had had the unhappy childhood that seems so typical of mass murderers. Martha's obesity made her feel a "freak", and because she was pathetically eager to please, she allowed men to fondle her intimately while still a child. Fernandez was a sickly and puny little boy whose highly dominant father despised him; he spent his childhood wrapped in daydreams. When he and three other teenagers were caught stealing chickens, the fathers of the other boys agreed to act as guarantors and they were released. Raymond Fernandez's father refused to co-operate and he went to prison. Even after the head injury that changed his personality, he never displayed any sadism towards the women he swindled. It was the partnership with Martha that turned him into "America's most hated killer".

Perhaps the clearest example of the influence of the dominance syndrome on criminality is England's Moors Murder case. The bare facts have the quality of a nightmare, like the dreams of a sadistic pornographer: a young man who admires Hitler and de Sade seduces a religious and rather ordinary girl, and persuades her to join him in kidnapping and raping children, then killing them. In spite of the number of books that have been written on the case, the psychology of Ian Brady and Myra Hindley remains something of a mystery. Only one thing is clear: that here once again we have a case of *folie à deux* with obvious parallels to Leopold and Loeb, Patrick and Jones, Fernandez and Beck.

What we know of Brady is this. He was born in a tough slum area, the Clydeside district of Glasgow, in January 1938. He was illegitimate—his mother was a waitress and was only nineteen when she had him. Her name was Stewart, but Ian adopted the name Sloan from the woman who brought him up. Until the age of seven, he continued to live in an overcrowded Glasgow tenement. He lived on Clydeside throughout the heavy bombing. When the war ended, the Sloan family were re-housed on a new estate on the outskirts of Glasgow. He was a diligent student: after passing the qualifying exam at the age of eleven, he was sent to Shawlands Academy—a "posh" school that had come down in the world since the new estate was built. There seems to have been a certain amount of ill-feeling between the re-housed slum boys and the sons of well-to-do tradesmen in their blue blazers, and Brady's reaction to it all was a feeling of resentment. His imagination was active, fed on a diet of Superman comics and gangster films. He was not a mixer; he had few friends. There was something sulky and unfriendly about him—it is still there in the photographs taken after the murder, the look of a delinquent Elvis Presley. Emlyn Williams tells a story—gathered from one of Brady's childhood acquaintances—about a cat which Brady dropped into a deep hole in the graveyard and sealed in with a stone; he wanted to find out how long it would take a cat to starve to death. The acquaintance moved the stone to check on his story and the cat escaped.

His first appearance in court was at the age of thirteen, when he was accused of housebreaking and put on probation for two years. A year later, in July 1952, he was again in a juvenile court on a charge of housebreaking, but got off with a warning. And when the probationary period ended in 1954, he again appeared in court charged with housebreaking, and asked for nine other cases to be taken into consideration. He received another two years' probation. It was in this year, 1954, that he moved to Manchester to live with his mother, who had now married a man called Brady.

If his mother had neglected him in early years, she now tried to make up for it. A next door neighbour remarked that her eyes followed him everywhere. The home life was quiet and dull: films, comedy programmes on the radio, paperback books on gangsters, the *No Orchids for Miss Blandish* type of thing. He found a job as a labourer in a brewery, and a year later was caught stealing lead from the roof. Since he was still on probation, he was sentenced to undergo Borstal training. He spent a year at the Borstal at Hatfield, Yorkshire, and was observed to be moody and unco-operative, but otherwise unremarkable. He told one of the inmates that he had sold himself to homosexuals. After a year in detention, he returned to Manchester, and went on the dole. It was a dull life, alone in the small house with his mother and stepfather out at work, making himself tea, reading the papers. He was twenty-one before he was in regular full-time employment again. He became a stock clerk at Millwards, a chemical firm in Gorton.

It was at Millwards, according to Emlyn Williams in *Beyond Belief* that he became interested in the Nazis and began collecting books about them. It would be interesting to know how it happened, what was the first book on Hitler's Germany that touched his imagination, that convinced him that *here* was something the modern world needed.

It is important to try to see this through Brady's eyes. He was twenty-three years old and reasonably intelligent, and ever since he left school, life had been a succession of trivialities. Yeats said that life is a preparation for something that never happens; but in Brady's case, even the element of preparation was lacking. Life had turned into a succession of wasted days, days and weeks that drifted by, leaving nothing behind except that you got older. Brady was not literary enough to have read *The Waste Land* or *The Hollow Men*, but if he had, he would have recognized his own feelings. He began to read about the Nazis—through anti-Nazi books like *The Scourge of the Swastika*—and it was like a religious conversion. To ask how he could be converted by anti-Nazi books is to miss the point. The idea of violence itself was emotionally satisfying, a reality in a make-believe world. Any strong imaginative experience produces a sense of reality, a feeling of seriousness, of meaning. This is why our Victorian ancestors read Foxe's *Book of Martyrs* on Sundays, and why one of the chief spiritual exercises of saints is to imagine Christ's suffering on the cross. Until it is touched by some serious aim, the mind's powers are diffused, dispersed. In order to experience a sense of its own force, the mind must *clench*, exactly as one might clench one's fists or teeth. And in order to do that, it must *focus* on something that arouses deep interest or strong feelings. Brady found all this in the Nazis: salvation from mediocrity and boredom, a vision of a society in which people like himself would have something more interesting to do than work as a stock clerk.

The field of his interest expanded to books on torture. This could indicate that Brady was a sadist in the technical sense—one for whom the ideas of sex and pain are associated. But not necessarily. De Sade's type of sadism sprang out of a desire for revenge on society, out of a Swiftian detestation of ninety-nine per cent of his fellow human beings. That Brady's sadism was of this nature becomes fairly certain when one considers his attitude to de Sade. Most people who buy de Sade read it for the sex and skip the long discussions. Brady was enthusiastic about the ideas. Society is utterly corrupt. Human life is unimportant, nature gives and takes away with total indifference. We live in a meaningless universe, created by chance. Surrounded by emptiness, we delude ourselves with dreams of a benevolent God, when every earthquake and tidal wave proves that such a Being is pure wishful thinking.

This view is not as irreligious as it sounds. It is, in fact, fairly close to Buddhism and is held by a large proportion of the world's population. To accept it is not the sign of a sick mind, although it is the sign of a pessimistic one. And although Swift went insane, this was not the result of his loathing of his fellow men, but of illness. Shaw also shared Swift's view that man, as he exists at present, is hopelessly inadequate, and Shaw was sane enough. The devil in *Man and Superman* warns Don Juan: "Beware of the pursuit of the Superhuman; it leads to an indiscriminate contempt for the human", and he adds: "To a man, horses and dogs and cats are mere species, outside the moral world. Well, to the Superman, men and women are a mere species too, also outside the moral world". But Shaw agrees with Don Juan, not with the devil. Brady's views about his fellow human beings do not prove him to have been insane or possessed by a spirit of evil. They only prove that he belonged to the "dominant five per cent". And the violence with which he held them proves that he was a particularly frustrated member of the dominant five per cent.

At this point, Myra Hindley enters the story. She was four and a half years younger than Brady, a completely normal, typical working-class girl, not bad-looking, with a blonde hair-do and bright lipstick, interested in boys and dancing, not particularly bright—rather like Gerty MacDowell in *Ulysses*. She had been born a Catholic, brought up Protestant, and decided to become a Catholic again at sixteen. She liked children and animals, and was fond of her family. She had been engaged, but broke it off, finding the boy "immature". This was one of the problems for working-class girls at that time, whose notions of male attractiveness were formed by the cinema and television—hard-bitten heroes with strong jaws—because the youths they met at dance halls were ordinary local boys of no particular ambition.

Brady had been at Millwards for almost two years when Myra Hindley joined the firm as a typist, but he paid her no special attention. If one is to believe her diary, he had still not even spoken to her six months later. By this time, she was a thoroughly infatuated teenager (she was eighteen at the time). By 1 August, her diary records: "Ian taking sly looks at me at work". By the end of the month: "I hope he loves me and will marry me some day". Apparently without any encouragement, she fills her diary with declarations of her love for Ian. She went out with other boys, and on 5 November records that she had finished with Eddie because he is courting another girl. During December, she hates Ian because he is rude, uncouth, uses foul language and loses his temper. "I have seen the other side of him. . ". She called him a big-headed pig and added "he goes out of his way to annoy me". But just before Christmas, he invited her out. On New Year's Eve, 1962, they were drinking German wine and Scotch whisky. Later they went back to Myra's house where Gran was asleep—Myra lived alone with her "gran"—and Myra lost her virginity on the divan bed in the front room.

The next day, Brady was apparently indifferent again. No doubt Myra's soupy bliss bored him. A few days later he took her out on his motor bike and they drank more German wine (Brady was learning German, and wore black shirts). At a fairly early stage, he explained that marriage was bourgeois nonsense and he would have no part of it, but she was willing to wait. He called her Myra Hess, and told her she looked like Irma Grese, the Belsen guard who beat and shot prisoners for fun. He talked to her a great deal about Hitler and the Nazis, and explained that he was a rebel against society. As a love affair, it was never entirely satisfactory; he never told her he loved her—for the simple reason that he didn't. She was a sloppy idiot who didn't mind removing her clothes, and who was good for his ego. She was the slave, he was the master. When he told her that he was planning a series of payroll robberies, she accepted this as another proof of his daring and unpredictable nature.

All this did not happen overnight. She had met him in January 1961, become his mistress in January 1962, persuaded her grandmother to allow him to spend occasional nights at the house by the following autumn. By April 1963 he had persuaded her to buy a gun for him. In England it is against the law to possess a hand gun unless you are a member of a pistol club. Myra accordingly joined the Cheadle Rifle Club, and managed to buy two pistols from members. She also began to take driving lessons—Brady suggested they ought to buy a car. Brady took up photography, and bought a camera with a timing device. He took photographs of Myra in black lace panties and in the nude; she photographed Ian holding his erect penis; then, using the timing device, they photographed themselves in acts of sexual intercourse. In two of the photographs she has whip marks across her buttocks and a whip hangs from the wall.

Exactly when the couple committed their first murder is not known. When police were investigating the case, they started with the file of Pauline Reade, sixteen, who disappeared in the Gorton district of Manchester, where both Brady and Myra Hindley lived, on 12 July 1963. On the evening of that day she set out alone to go to a dance at a railwaymen's club. She never reached the club and was never seen again. An acquaintance saw her turn into the street leading to the club. It seems likely that she was picked up by a car. A sixteen-year-old girl would not get into a car with a strange man, particularly on her way to a dance, nor is it likely that she was dragged into a car on a summer evening in a crowded area. If she got into a car, then it contained someone she knew—either a man or a woman, or both. Myra had bought a car two months before, and she lived only a few hundred yards away from Wiles Street, Pauline

Reade's home. Pauline's body was finally recovered in the summer of 1987, after Myra Hindley had made a detailed confession to Chief Superintendant Peter Topping.

Myra was becoming more like Brady. A neighbour who knew her in her teens described her as "fun-loving", but the manager at Millwards described her as surly and aggressive. A bookmaker who took Brady's bets said of him: "In four years he came into my shop every day. I never saw him smile".

By November, 1963, they had got rid of the second-hand green Morris. On Saturday 23 November, they hired a car and drove out to Ashton-under-Lyne, a small market town not far from Gorton. A twelve-year-old boy, John Kilbride, had spent Saturday afternoon at the cinema, and afterwards hung around the market place, hoping to make a few pence by doing odd jobs for the stall holders. It began to get dark and a fog came down from the Pennines. At that moment, a friendly lady leaned out of a car and asked him if he wanted a lift. It seemed safe enough, so he climbed in. It was the last time he was seen alive.

Nearly two years later, when the body of John Kilbride was dug up on Saddleworth Moor, his trousers and underpants were pulled down around his knees. The body was badly decomposed, but there was no obvious sign of injury: the brain was undamaged and the hyoid bone unbroken; he could have been smothered to death. Only Brady and Myra Hindley know precisely how he died, or what happened before death. The one thing that is certain is that this murder was fully planned, and that they experienced no regret later—Myra Hindley allowed Brady to take a photograph of her kneeling on the grave. It is difficult to believe that this was their first murder. In October 1965, not long after their arrest, Superintendent Arthur Benfield, in charge of the case, told pressmen that the police were considering eight disappearances over the past three or four years (dating back to about 1961–62). But only five names usually mentioned in connection with the case. The names of the other suspected victims have never been published.

Brady had moved into Bannock Street, Myra's home, in June 1963. In early '64, Gran was informed that Bannock Street was due for demolition, and that she had been assigned a house on a new estate out at Hattersley, altogether closer to the moor . . . They eventually moved there the following September. In the meantime, another twelve-year-old boy had vanished. On 16 June 1964, Keith Bennett set out to spend the night at his grandmother's house, in the Longsight district of Manchester. This was where Brady had lived until he moved in with Myra; he still visited his mother regularly. It was eight o'clock when Keith waved goodbye to his mother, who was on her way to a bingo game. The following morning, his mother called at the grandmother's to collect him (and his brother), but he had not arrived. His grandmother had not been worried, she assumed he had stayed at home. There were eight children in the family and some of them stayed at their grandmother's every night. Keith Bennett vanished, like Pauline Reade.

In May, Myra's younger sister Maureen discovered she was pregnant—the father was a sixteen-year-old boy, David Smith, who had been in trouble with the police on a number of occasions. He married Maureen in August. On the eve of the wedding, he called at Bannock Street and met Ian Brady. Brady took to the sixteen-year-old, and talked about Hitler as they drank wine. The following day, Myra and Brady drove the newly weds to the Lake District for the day, and the relationship between the men developed. Brady saw the chance of another admirer. After all, a born leader needs more than one follower. During the next month, the Smiths saw a great deal of Brady and Myra. They had moved into Wiles Street, where Pauline Reade had lived. Brady provided large amounts of cheap red wine—he had discovered that Spanish wine was cheaper than German—and gradually took David Smith into his confidence. He expounded the ideas of de Sade, and found Smith an intelligent pupil. It was not difficult to convince Smith that everyone would commit crimes if they were not afraid, or enslaved by false morality. Smith started to keep a diary, in which he wrote: "Every man and woman is one of two things, a sadist or a masochist. Only a few practise what they feel . . . Rape is not a crime, it is a state of mind. Murder is a hobby, and a supreme pleasure . . . God is a disease, a plague, a weight round a man's neck . . . God is a superstition, a cancer that eats into the brain . . . Sadism is a supreme pleasure . . . People are like maggots, small, blind and worthless". David Smith was an apt pupil. In fact, the excerpts suggest that he had made the philosophy his own.

Later still, Brady talked about robbing banks, of setting up their own small crime syndicate. It is difficult to know whether this was intended seriously or whether Brady was only repeating the tactics he had used to "convert" Myra. He showed Smith his two guns, and they "cased" banks and drew up detailed plans. But all this came to nothing.

In September 1964, Brady, Myra Hindley and "Gran" moved to 16 Wardle Brook Avenue, Hattersley, the end house of a block of four on a raised terrace. It was small, but large enough for the three of them. The Smiths continued to visit, and bank robberies were discussed without real conviction.

On Boxing Day, 1964, Brady and Myra Hindley murdered a ten-year-old girl, Lesley Ann Downey, whom they picked up at a fairground in the Ancoats district of central Manchester. For anyone who had followed the case chronologically and found its motivation baffling, this murder is like a flash of lightning that suddenly makes everything clear. On that day, Myra drove her grandmother to visit an uncle in Dukinfield, as she usually did on a Saturday afternoon. But instead of returning at nine o'clock, she returned two hours late, explaining that a snowstorm was on the way, and that it would be better if the grandmother spent the night where she was. Gran protested, pointed out that she would have to sleep on the floor, but Myra was oddly stubborn, and drove off back to Hattersely at 11.30.

Lesley Ann Downey had gone to the fair in Hulme Hall Lane early in the afternoon; on her way home with a friend, she decided to go back for one more look. Brady and Myra Hindley must have picked her up at about six o'clock. Their intention was to take pornographic photographs of the child, then dispose of her as they had disposed of the others. They recorded what took place, at least, during the first seventeen minutes, on tape. Brady asked her name. For some reason, she gave a false surname. "I have to get home before eight o'clock, honest to God . . ." Against a background of music by the Ray Conniff singers, intended to drown the child's voice, Brady and Myra Hindley keep ordering her to "put it in, put it in tighter . . ." The child screams, cries, and asks to be released. Myra Hindley says: "Hush, shut up or I'll forget myself and hit you one". Presumably what is happening, then, is not actual torture, but something that frightens the child rather than intentionally hurting her. This is the only thing that can be said in favour of the couple. Emlyn Williams remarks: "I purposely emphasize that compared with the rumoured atrocities, the real thing is comparatively mild".

They took nine photographs of the child in various poses, which Emlyn Williams described as looking like ballet exercises. She was naked with a scarf tied round her mouth and she raised her arms or legs at the orders of the photographer. In the ninth photograph she faces the camera with her hands raised in an attitude of prayer. The couple were still amateur pornographers, not yet sadistic maniacs with an urge to torment. But murder *was* a part of the plan, because it was the thought of a body, buried on the moors, that justified the whole thing. It confirmed their feeling that they were not merely two low paid office workers, trapped in working-class lives, but Enemies of Society, dangerous revolutionaries. In order to indulge this feeling, they even went up to the moors in freezing weather and slept out on the graves, covered with a few blankets. To sleep out like that was a kind of ascetic exercise, given meaning by their *own* mythology—by the lives and acts of Brady and Hindley, not of the saints and apostles. The saint sits in his cave and meditates on the crucifixion. They meditated on the gospel of de Sade, and the corpses underneath them. David Smith remarked that after the last murder, they looked exhausted and replete, as if sexually satisfied. But there are other things besides sex that can produce emotional catharsis: art and religion, for example. At the time when the bodies were being dug up on the moors, a BBC commentator remarked that there were rumours that the whole case was mixed up with witchcraft and black magic. And in a certain sense, it was. They were like a black magic cult, performing their own blasphemous ceremony. In effect, they had created their own religion, a religion with something in common with the Hindu sect called Thuggee, which treats murder as a religious duty as well as a pleasure.

The starting point of this religion was sex. This is no doubt why David Smith was so easy to convert. Among the quotations from de Sade in his notebook there are long extracts copied out from novels like *The Carpetbaggers* and *Eternal Fire*. Neither of these novels is pornographic in the technical sense, they simply share the assumption that modern man is sexually frustrated and needs books as aids to masturbation: that no twentieth-century city dweller ever "eats his fill" of sex. How can he when he is perpetually being reminded of it by mini-skirted girls and underwear advertisements? In Shaw's *Major Barbara*, Undershaft says: "I moralized and starved until one day I swore that I would be a full-fed free man at all cost, that nothing should stop me except a bullet . . ." Brady made the same decision about sex, fortified by de Sade. All it needed was the belief that there was nothing wrong in treating other people as objects, as we treated the animals we ate for dinner.

The odd thing is that Myra Hindley remained, in many ways, a quite ordinary girl of normal affections. Her kindness to dogs was exceptional: when, later on, she heard that her own dog had died while in the hands of the police, she burst out: "They're just a lot of bloody murderers". This in itself would seem to indicate that no actual physical cruelty was practised on the children—at least, for its own sake. The children were intended as "props" in a sexual orgy, like the whip and the black lace panties. In *A Casebook of Murder*, I cited two recent cases in which a couple had offered lifts to young girls, and the woman helped to subdue the girl while the man raped her. In another case that took place in Chatham, Kent, in 1968, Mrs Joyce Ballard, thirty, admitted that she had enticed a twelve-year-old girl into their flat so that her husband, Robert Ballard, could assault her. Ballard, who was obsessed by books on torture and witchcraft, tied up the girl, cut open her veins and stabbed her, then committed suicide. The wife was sentenced to three years in prison. In these cases, the woman shared the man's sexual fantasies and derived sexual pleasure from observing the assault. This was the basis of the Brady-Hindley relation.

On 25 September 1965, nine months after the disappearance of Lesley Ann Downey, David Smith called on Brady, and during the course of a drinking session, was taken into Brady's confidence. Brady asked him if he had ever killed anybody, then said: "I have—three or four. The bodies are buried up on the moors". He also told Smith that he had once stopped the car on a deserted street (Myra Hindley must have been driving, since Brady couldn't) and shot a passer-by. Whether Smith believed him is not quite clear. But having committed himself, Brady believed that it was time Smith became involved in the murders. He may have regretted telling Smith; on the other hand, it may have been simply that he wanted to enrol another member in their murder sect, and perhaps involve Maureen Smith too. (By this time, their baby had died, and the Smiths had also moved out to Hattersley.)

Then days later, on 6 October, the plan to involve Smith was put into effect. They had decided that the victim this time was to be a homosexual, who would be picked up in one of the queer bars in the Oxford Street area. Some time between nine and eleven that evening, they became friendly with a seventeen-year-old youth, Edward Evans, a homosexual.

At 11.30 that night, Myra Hindley rang the doorbell of the Smiths' flat. She said she had a message from her mother for Maureen. A few minutes later, she asked David Smith to walk her back home. As they approached the Wardle Brook house, she asked him to come in to collect some miniature wine bottles. Smith went into the kitchen, where Brady handed him some bottles, then went out "to get the rest". A moment later there was a loud scream, and Myra yelled: "Dave, help him". Smith rushed into the sitting room, and found Brady hitting Edward Evans with an axe. It seemed to take a long time for the youth to collapse. When he finally lay, face downward, on the floor, Brady gave him a final blow with the axe—he had been striking with the back of the blade, to avoid blood. There was a noise like gargling—the death rattle. After that, Brady took a cord and strangled the body that still twitched. He was swearing all the time. Myra's two barking dogs were soothed. Brady held out the hatchet to David Smith: "Feel the weight of it". The idea was to get Smith's fingerprints on the handle. Smith took it, then handed it back. The room was covered with spots of blood. And at this moment, Gran called down to ask what all the noise was about. Myra shouted back that she had dropped a tape recorder on her foot. Brady, seeing that Smith looked sick, handed him a glass of wine. Then, while the body lay there, all three of them cleaned the room with a mop and bucket. After this, the corpse was wrapped in a polythene sheet. Smith observed that the flies of the trousers were undone. The body was carried upstairs into Myra's room, Brady joking: "Eddie's a dead weight". Brady was limping, he had been kicked on the ankle as Evans thrashed about on the floor. After this, they all drank tea, and Myra reminisced about a time when a policeman had stopped to talk to her while Brady was burying a body. After this, Smith agreed to return the next day with an old pram, to transport the body to the car. Shortly after three, David Smith left. When he arrived home, he was violently sick, then told Maureen what had happened. It was Maureen who decided they were going to the police. They waited until dawn, Smith was afraid that Brady might be watching the flat, prepared to attack him if he made a move towards a phone. Then, hiding a bread-knife and a screwdriver under his coat, Smith crept downstairs, followed by Maureen.

At 8.40 the next morning, on 7 October, a man dressed as a baker's roundsman knocked at the door of 16 Wardle Brook Avenue. When Myra Hindley, rubbing the sleep out of her eyes, came to the door, the man identified himself as a police officer, and said they had reason to believe there was a body in the house. Brady was on the divan bed in the living room, writing a note to explain why he would not be going to work that day. He was wearing only a vest. Superintendent Talbot—dressed as a roundsman, in case Brady had his guns ready—was joined by a detective sergeant. They demanded to be taken round the house. When they came to the locked bedroom, they asked for the key. Myra said it was at work, and the policemen offered to take her there to collect it. At this, Brady said: "You'd better tell him . . . There was a row here last night. It's in there. . ." Under the window in the bedroom there was a plastic-wrapped bundle, obviously a body. The two loaded revolvers were found in a shoe box in the same room.

Enough evidence was found in the house to charge Brady with the premeditated murder of Edward Evans, including a notebook with plans for the disposal of the body. The book also contained the name "John Kilbride". Myra Hindley was allowed to go free, and she went to stay with her mother. Four days later, she was charged with being an accessory.

In a careful search of the house, the police discovered a cloakroom ticket in the spine of a prayer book. It led them to Manchester Central Station, where they discovered two suitcases. These proved to contain pornographic photos, tapes, books on sex and torture, coshes, wigs, masks and notes on robbing banks. The photographs included the nine of Lesley Ann Downey, and her voice was heard on the tape.

But there was no breakdown or confession. Brady maintained that Lesley had been brought to the house by two men, and had been taken away by them after they had taken the photographs. He knew he stood no chance of escaping a life sentence, but he was determined not to give an inch.

Two doors away, there lived a twelve-year-old girl, Patricia Hodges, who had been friendly with the couple. She told the police that she had been up on the moors with them, and had been given wine to drink. She took the police to the spot where Myra Hindley had parked. It was close to a place called Hollin Brown Knoll. The search began. The method was to look for any patch that might have been dug over, and then to drive a long stick down through the turf and sniff the end for the smell of physical decomposition. Six days later, a policeman noticed a bone sticking up from a bare patch of ground. Three feet down, they found the naked body of Lesley Ann Downey, her clothes at her feet. The spot where John Kilbride was buried was discovered through a photograph that showed Myra Hindley kneeling with a dog; she proved to have been posing on the grave.

The trial provided no surprises. The couple were charged with three murders. The most horrifying moment was when the tape of Lesley Ann Downey was played in court. Myra Hindley hung her head and said: "I am ashamed", but Brady opened a packet of peppermints and popped one into his mouth. Brady showed a disposition to get his own back on Smith by doing his best to drag him into the murder of Lesley Ann Downey and Evans. He also tended to answer questions with a pedantic, schoolmasterly manner, as if insisting on his status as an intellectual. Maurice Richardson in *The Observer* described Myra: "Her hair, naturally brown, has been changing colour from week to week [of the trial]. First silver-lilac, then bright canary blonde. She is a big girl with a striking face: fine straight nose, thinnish curved lips, rather hefty chin, blue eyes. Full face she is almost a beauty. The Victorians would have admired her". Richardson's view was that it was a case of hysteric falling in love with a psychotic and coming to share his delusions.

On 6 May 1966, both were sentenced to life imprisonment. It was more than twenty years before the full story of the murders began to emerge. In 1986, Detective Chief Superintendent Peter Topping, of the Greater Manchester police, went to see Ian Brady in Gartree Prison, and Myra Hindley in Cookham Wood. In the previous year Brady had given a series of interviews to a journalist, Fred Harrison, during which he admitted to the murders of Pauline Reade and Keith Bennett. Now Brady and Hindley agreed to try to help Topping locate the bodies. Pauline Reade was found on 1 July 1987, but the search failed to locate Keith Bennett, and was finally abandoned.

Myra Hindley, who had been hoping for many years to obtain parole, finally decided to "confess" to her part in the murders. According to her story Brady began to talk to her about committing the "perfect crime" in July 1963, and she claimed that he "blackmailed" her into helping him. Brady, she said, had taken pornographic photographs of her after slipping a drug into her wine, and he used these to exert pressure. They set out on their first "murder hunt" on 12 July 1963, with Myra driving the van, and Brady following behind on his motor bike. She passed Pauline Reade, who was on her way to a dance, and offered her a lift. Then she told her that she had lost a glove on Saddleworth Moor, and offered the girl some gramophone records if she would go and help her look for it. Once on the moor, Brady appeared on his motor bike, and was introduced as Myra's boyfriend. Then Brady and Pauline went off to look for the glove, and Myra Hindley claims that she stayed in the car until Brady came to fetch her. Pauline Reade was lying dead, and her disarranged clothing made it clear that Brady had raped her before cutting her throat. They buried her with a spade they had brought with them, then went home.

In her "confession", Myra Hindley continued to insist that she had never been present when Brady had committed the rapes and murders. In the case of Lesley Ann Downey, she claimed she was in the bathroom running a bath, and that when she returned to the bedroom, the child was dead, with blood on her thighs.

Topping makes it clear in his book that he believes that she told him the truth only in so far as it suited her. And in January 1990, in an open letter to the press, Brady declared that she was lying, and that she had played an active part in the murders. The injuries found on Pauline Reade's nose and forehead were, according to Brady, inflicted by Myra Hindley. He claimed that she had insisted on strangling Lesley Ann Downey herself, using a two-foot length of silk cord, and that she later enjoyed toying with the cord in the presence of other people, "in secret knowledge of what it had been used for".

The central mystery of the case remains: how a perfectly normal girl like Myra Hindley could have been persuaded to participate in a series of child murders. In the mid-1970s, I discussed the case with Dr Rachel Pinney, who had been in prison with Myra Hindley. It was her view that Myra had been "framed". She wrote to me: "I still think Myra had no part in the killings, and the end result of my work will be a fuller study of the psychology of being "hooked" – e.g. Rasputin and the Tsarina, Leopold and Loeb, Hitler and his worshippers".

Whether Myra Hindley was telling the whole truth in her "confession" may never be known, but one passage at least has the ring of truth, and supports Rachel Pinney's view. "Within months he had convinced me that there was no God at all: he could have told me the earth was flat, the moon was made of green cheese, and I would have believed him, such was his power of persuasion, his softly convincing means of speech which fascinated me, because I could never fully comprehend, only browse at the odd sentence here and there, believing it to be gospel truth".

In short, Myra Hindley was of medium dominance, and Brady was high. She was undoubtedly the catalyst that turned him into a killer.

16.
The Serial Killer

MOST MASS murderers have been men – or women – who killed because they wanted to achieve a certain goal – usually money – and felt indifferent to the human beings who stood in their way. The Marquise de Brinvilliers, executed in 1676, was a spendthrift who decided that the simplest way of replenishing her coffers was murder by poison – so she poisoned her father and her two brothers. In order to test the poison, she tried it out on her maidservant – who became seriously ill but recovered – and on patients in a charitable hospital to which she took food. The death of her lover caused her downfall; his papers contained incriminating details, and although she fled to a nunnery, Marie was arrested, tortured into confession, and finally beheaded. Martin Dumollard, whose crimes have been described in an earlier chapter, accosted servant girls looking for work, and murdered them on the way to his remote country cottage – merely for the sake of their few belongings.

Other mass murderers are altogether more difficult to explain. Helene Jegado, a Breton peasant woman who worked as a domestic, acquired a large quantity of arsenic at an early stage in her career, and for the next twenty years, used it liberally. In one household where she worked, seven people – including her own sister – died in agony. By 1851 her victims numbered twenty three. The death of a servant of whom she was jealous led an examining magistrate to call on her, and before he had a chance to speak, she declared: "I am innocent!" "Of what?", he asked. "No one has accused you." By that time, forensic tests for arsenic existed, and proved Jegado to be a multiple poisoner. She was executed in 1852. An earlier poisoner, Anna Zwanziger, shared her enthusiasm for arsenic, and administered it to a number of women who stood between her and the employers she hoped to marry. She was also trapped – in 1809 – by a newly discovered test for arsenic, and beheaded two years later. It is reported that she trembled with joy as she looked on the white powder, and declared "Arsenic is my truest friend".

Such crimes obviously have much in common with the murders committed by Countess Elizabeth Bathory, or the random poisonings of Neill Cream. The Germans describe them as "lustmord", or murder for pleasure. In earlier centuries, they were among the rarest types of murder. In the last decades of the twentieth century, they have unfortunately become sufficiently common to deserve their own classification. They have become known as "serial murders".

The term first came into general use in America in the early 1980s. Law enforcement agencies recognised that during the past twenty years, there had been a steep rise in sex crime and so-called "motiveless murder" – murder in which no obvious link can be established between killer and victim. Moreover, the average number of victims in such cases seemed to be increasing. In the 1960s, the Manson "family" had killed at least seven people, all strangers, while Albert DeSalvo, the Boston Strangler, had killed twelve. In the 1970s, Dean Corll had killed twenty-seven boys; John Gacy killed thirty-two; Ted Bundy murdered twenty-three girls; Randall Woodfield, "the I.5 killer", murdered forty-four. In South America, Pedro Lopez, the "monster of the Andes", killed 360 pre-pubescent girls.

The killer who was most responsible for making the American police aware of serial murder was a derelict named Henry Lee Lucas, who claimed that he had killed 360 people in his wanderings around the United States. What was so shocking is that nobody had noticed that there was a mass murderer at large. There had been a similar case in the early 1970s, when a supermarket robbery led to the arrest of middle-aged

Sherman McCrary, together with his son and son-in-law. Police investigating the movements of McCrary's family in the past year realised that they corresponded closely to a series of murders that had become known as "the doughnut-shop slayings". Across the country, from Florida to California, waitresses and shopgirls had been abducted – usually late at night – and left naked and dead. The killers always robbed the till; but they also raped the women. The investigators finally realised that the whole McCrary family – including the wife and daughter – had been involved in these killings.

Once the term "serial killer" had been coined, the American public became avid for information, and journalists were happy to supply it. One police chief was quoted as saying that there could be thirty-five serial killers at large in America, and that the number could be increasing at the rate of one a month. A crime psychiatrist speculated – "authoritatively" – that serial murders could amount to as many as 5,000 a year. And since the American murder rate is about 20,000 a year – roughly forty times higher than that of the United Kingdom – it looked as if serial killers could account for a terrifying 25%.

Subsequent estimates have been a great deal lower. A more realistic figure, suggested by the FBI, is between 300 and 500 a year. Yet even this is highly disturbing. The American murder rate has always been, proportionately, far higher than that of most European countries. It had doubled since the 1960s from 10 to 20,000 a year. But no one seemed to understand what had caused this enormous increase in apparently random murders in the 1970s and 80s.

This question was of special interest to a new law enforcement unit set up in Quantico, Virginia, in the mid-1970s. It was called the Behavioural Science Unit, and its task was to try to construct "psychological profiles" of killers, in order that the police might be able to single out a criminal from a long list of suspects. In 1977, the police in Platte City, Missouri, were confronted with the sex murder of a schoolgirl named Julie Wittmeyer. They telephoned the Behavioural Science Unit, and were told to look for a teenager, probably a schoolfellow of the murdered girl, of low academic achievement and almost certainly suffering from feelings of inferiority. This immediately enabled them to pick out the killer on their list of suspects. In 1983, police in Anchorage, Alaska, were investigating a series of murders of young women, mostly go-go dancers. They were questioning a suspect, but he was a respectable local businessman, and they were inclined to think they might be mistaken. Agent Glenn Flothe telephoned the Behavioural Science Unit, and began to describe their suspect. The man on the other end of the line interupted him. "Never mind that. Just tell me about the crimes." The girls had apparently been forced to strip naked in the snow, then hunted down by a man with a rifle. When Flothe had finished, the FBI agent told him that the killer was probably some respectable member of the community, and that it was likely that he stuttered. He had described their major suspect, a baker named Robert Hansen, who in due course was sentenced for the murders.

As the FBI evolved a psychological profile of the serial killer, certain things stood out very clearly. Most serial murder was sexually motivated. Yet in some odd sense, sex was not the primary aim. The serial killer was a man in whom the craving for self-esteem was the dominant motivation. Serial murder was not about sex so much as about power. One rapist told agent Robert Roy Hazlewood that the rape was the least enjoyable part of the crime. It was the elaborate planning, and the feeling that he was defying the law, that gave him most pleasure. Hazlewood concluded that in such criminals, "sexual assault services non-sexual needs – power needs, anger needs, the need for control".

What has been learned about the serial killer may be briefly summarised. As already stated, his crimes are almost invariably motivated by sex. He is usually a male of high dominance but low self-esteem. His crimes are a gesture of defiance at a society that he feels is not paying him enough attention. There is a sense in which Moors murderer Ian Brady, with his brooding resentment, is the archetypal serial killer. Myra Hindley summarised his basic drive when she said: "He wanted to get rich and become ' somebody' – not just do a nine-to-five job working for somebody else". This is the source of that curious and irrational resentment that seems to typify the "self-esteem" criminal – anger that life has cast him in the role of a nobody, and the conviction that he deserves something better. As we have seen, Brady's resentment began to fester when he was sent to a "posh" school where most of the pupils were far better-off than he was.

Carl Panzram, another typical serial killer, was also driven by a sense of resentment at what he felt to be social injustice. His father, a Minnesota farmer, had deserted the family when Carl was a child, and left them in poverty. At the age of eleven he burgled the house of a well-to-do neighbour because he felt that it was unfair that the neighbour should have money. He was sent to reform school, where his rebelliousness earned him a series of beatings; the beatings only made him determined to "get his own back." Travelling around the country on freight trains, he was violated by four hoboes; this suggested to him another way of "getting his own back", and when he had some "authority figure" – such as a railway guard – at gunpoint he would often sodomise him. Eventually, Panzram began committing random murders. "Then I began to think I would have my revenge", he wrote in his "confession". "If I couldn't injure those who had injured me, then I would injure somebody else." This is the upside-down "looking-glass logic" of the criminal "magical thinking" – that we have considered in an earlier chapter. Panzram liked to describe himself as "the man who goes around doing people good", because he felt that life was so vile that to kill someone was to do him a favour. Yet in another sense, and this is also vital for understanding the serial killer, the twenty murders he committed could be regarded as a form of self-punishment. It was as if he had decided that life was meaningless, and there was no point in trying to achieve something worthwhile. But for a highly dominant male, who is driven by a deep unconscious craving to "be somebody", this is a kind of mental suicide. Panzram's "confession" was written for a young guard named Henry Lesser, who had been kind to him, and may be regarded as an attempt to purge himself, to undo what he had done. In fact, the confession impressed many literary men, including H.L. Mencken. But by then it was too late, and Panzram knew it. Each random murder, and the victims included several children, had killed a part of himself. When he was sentenced to death for murdering a fellow prisoner, it was virtually an act of suicide. He told the hangman: "Hurry it up, you hoosier bastard. I could hang a dozen men while you're fooling around".

A case of the 1980s underlines the point. In June 1983, a serial killer named Gerald Gallego was sentenced to death in California for ten murders. Gallego, with the help of his common-law wife Charlene Williams, daughter of a wealthy Sacramento businessman, had committed the murders because he had an obsessional desire to find "the perfect sex slave". (He had been practising incest with his daughter since she was eight.) Charlene, a spoilt only child, had already been married twice when, at the age of twenty-one, she met the ex-convict Gallego, whose father had been executed in 1954 for three murders. Fascinated by his macho brutality, she finally agreed to help him in his search for the "perfect sex slave". In 1978, she approached two teenage girls in a supermarket and asked them if they would like to smoke some pot. When they got back to the van, Gallego was waiting for them with a gun. He raped them both on a mattress in the back before killing them with bullets in the head. Two years – and six murders – later, they kidnapped a young couple who were leaving a dance in Sacramento. The man was "executed" and the woman raped and subsequently shot. A friend of the kidnapped couple had seen their abduction and taken the license number of the car. The Gallegos fled, but were captured a few weeks later. In exchange for testifying against her "husband", Charlene was allowed to plead guilty to a lesser charge, and received a sixteen-year jail sentence. Gallego was sentenced to die by lethal injection.

Gallego had told a social worker in prison: "My only interest is in killing God". It echoes a comment made by Ian Brady to Chief Superintendent Topping. Although Brady declared that it was nonsense to believe in God, he admitted that after murdering John Kilbride, he had shaken his fist and the sky and shouted: "Take that, you bastard". Nothing could more clearly demonstrate the "magical thinking" of the serial killer.

Gilles de Rais and Countess Bathory could also be classified as as serial killers. Yet it can be seen that they were not driven by "resentment" so much as by sadism. They were also untypical in that they belonged to the upper classes, while all modern serial killers have been either working class or lower middle class. (This, as we have seen, is one reason for rejecting the notion that Jack the Ripper – the first modern serial killer – was a wealthy surgeon or a member of the royal family.)

Not all serial killers have been sadists, and not all were driven by resentment. Earle Nelson, who became known as "The Gorilla Murderer", travelled around the United States and Canada from February 1926 until June 1927, raping and strangling at least twenty-two women. He would knock on the door of houses with a "Room to let" card in the window, and if the landlady was alone, would attack her when she showed him the room. Finally captured near Winnipeg after a nationwide manhunt, he was hanged in January 1928. Although he mutilated one of the victims, a 14-year-old girl, he usually confined himself to strangling followed by rape. Photographs of him show an ape-like face with receding forehead and expressionless eyes, and he seems to be a typical example of the "sex maniac" killer. Yet although he had been suffering from dizzy spells since a serious head injury at the age of ten, he nevertheless possessed considerable intelligence and charm, and impressed some of his fellow tenants as a serious and deeply religious young man. In spite of appearances, he was clearly a member of the "dominant 5%". This seems to be the one invariable common denominator.

When these various factors are taken into account, it is arguable that America's first serial killer was a Chicago "businessman" named Herman Webster Mudgett, and who preferred to use the alias Henry Howard Holmes. When his "castle", a huge house he had built on the corner of 63rd Street in Chicago's Englewood section, was examined, it was found to be a maze of trapdoors and secret rooms. A large number of bones, skulls and teeth were found buried in the basement. Because the crimes that finally led to his arrest were committed for money, he is usually classified with Johann Hoch and Henri Landru as a confidence swindler. But one writer on the case, John Bartlow Martin, shows more insight when he speaks about Holmes's "lifelong preoccupation with cadavers". And, he might have added, his lifelong preoccupation with sex.

Herman Webster Mudgett was born in 1860 in Gilmanton, a small town in New Hampshire, and he came from a lower middle class background – his father was a postmaster. The "preoccupation with cadavers" began as a child, when mischievous schoolfellows dragged him into a doctor's surgery to confront a skeleton. The morbid terror eventually turned to fascination. He graduated at a school in Vermont, became a schoolteacher for a while, then went on to medical school at Ann Arbor, Michigan. It was here that he practised his first swindle, an insurance fraud involving the theft of a body on its way to the dissecting room and the faked death of a patient whom Holmes had insured. He married at eighteen, but deserted his wife and child eight years later, after he had graduated from medical school. He combined the natural temperament of a swindler with a curious interest in hypnotism and the occult. Martin suggests that his later murders were an attempt to put into practice certain "theories about human nature", which he does not specify. It is typical of Holmes that, having deserted his wife, he arranged for her to hear indirectly that he had been in a train wreck and was suffering from amnesia. He had an obsessive need for people to think well of him.

Under his true name – of Mudgett – he practised medicine briefly in Mooers Forks, NY, but when he moved to Chicago in 1886, he had decided to call himself Holmes – presumably so as to be untraceable by his wife, Clara Lovering. In Wilmette, a northern suburb of Chicago, he met a pretty girl named Myrta Belknap, whose family was well-to-do, and married her bigamously in early 1887. The family broke with Holmes after he had forged the signature of her uncle John Belknap on a note, and it is recorded that he invited Uncle John up to the roof of his new house to discuss the matter. Some instinct told Uncle John not to go.

His only venture in legitimate business failing – it was a duplicating company – he discovered an interesting possibility on the south side: a Mrs E.S. Holten, who ran a drugstore on 63rd Street, Englewood, needed an assistant. With his medical knowledge, Holmes was the ideal man. Three years later, in 1890, Holmes had become a partner in the store, and Mrs Holten talked about rigged books and prosecution. Then Mrs Holten vanished, and Holmes owned the store. No one knows what happened to her, and Holmes never told.

Soon he was doing so well in business that he built another house opposite the store – his "murder castle". His method here was to quarrel with the gangs of workmen every few weeks and pay them off – so that no one knew too much about the place. He apparently raised the money for the building by the sale of patent medicines for which he made spectacular claims. It was three storeys high; the ground floor contained shops, the next floor contained Holmes's "chambers", the top floor consisted of apartments. The reason he gave for building the castle was that it was intended as a hotel for visitors to the Chicago World Fair of 1893. But he had gas pipes installed so that he could flood any room with gas – recalling Marcel Petiot – and secret peepholes into every room.

Now, with his second "wife" safely at home in Wilmette, Holmes began to go in for seduction and murder. A jeweller named Conner moved into the drugstore – it was agreed that he should have a corner of the store for his watch-repairing business, while his wife Julia helped Holmes as a clerk. When Conner realised that Holmes and Julia were lovers, he moved out, leaving his wife and her sister Gertie – aged eighteen – behind. Both of them became Holmes's mistresses. Then Gertie became pregnant, and disappeared. Holmes took her in to a business acquaintance to say goodbye, and then told him some weeks later that Gertie had died. The business friend said, "Holmes, you've killed her". Holmes said: "Pooh! what makes you think that?" and nothing more was said.

Holmes was attracted by a sixteen-year-old blonde named Emily van Tassel, who came to the ice-cream parlour, usually with her mother. When Emily disappeared one day, Holmes denied all knowledge of her whereabouts. She was never seen again.

In spite of now owning two drugstores and a "hotel", Holmes preferred to live by various forms of confidence trickery. There was a machine which, he claimed, could make inflammable gas out of water by splitting up its hydrogen and oxygen. Actually, the machine was connected to the gas supply; but it was sold to a Canadian for $2,000. Holmes discovered that the gaseous water was a mild stimulant (alcoholics still use gas bubbled into water when they can get nothing else), and sold it in the shop, claiming he had discovered a medicinal spring. The gas company found out and threatened to sue. He furnished the "castle" on credit. When he failed to pay, the company tried to reclaim its property, but found the house empty. A porter who was bribed with twenty-five dollars told them that the furniture had all been put into a room whose door had been bricked up and then wallpapered; the company recovered its furniture. Huge quantities of crockery were found in a space in the roof, and repossessed. Holmes met a thief named Benjamin Pitezel, who became a partner in his swindles. When Pitezel was arrested in Terre Haute for a dud cheque, Holmes posed as an Indiana congressman and bailed him out with another dud cheque.

Holmes's career as a seducer and murderer was also going forward swiftly. A new blonde secretary, Emily Cigrand, moved into the store. Julia showed signs of jealousy, and would tiptoe from her upstairs apartment to listen outside Holmes's door. Holmes had a buzzer installed under one of the steps to warn him. Finally he got tired of her jealousy. Julia and her eight-year-old daughter disappeared in early autumn, 1892. Miss Cigrand also vanished in December. The reason seems to have been that he had met a girl named Minnie Williams, who had inherited property to the value of $20,000. Minnie, a pretty but brainless girl, lived with Holmes throughout the World Fair, which started on 1 May 1893. The upper apartments were kept permanently filled, and at least two of Holmes's female guests simply vanished; there may have been more. In June, Minnie's sister Annie came to stay with them. Like Minnie, she believed Holmes to be a wealthy businessman. In July, she wrote to the aunt who had brought them up: "Brother Harry says you need never trouble any more about me, financially or otherwise." She was going to Germany to study art. She vanished. Minnie continued to live with Holmes as his wife, and Pitezel often lived with them. (He also had a wife and five children).

It should be clear by now that Holmes was not a successful confidence swindler; something always seemed to go wrong with his plans. But he had now got himself so far into debt that he could see no alternative. When the castle was empty again – the Fair being over – Holmes set fire to it, and tried to collect $60,000 from an insurance company for damage to its upper storeys. They were suspicious, and soon uncovered something of Holmes's past. Holmes was living in a small hotel with Minnie and Pitezel in November, when the insurance company lured him to their office to talk it over. Then a police inspector named Cowrie called on Minnie and sternly told her that the fraud had been discovered. She believed him, and confessed. Cowrie left with the policy, and the insurance company decided not to sue for attempted fraud. But Holmes's other creditors heard about it – no doubt Cowrie took care that they should – and presented Holmes with bills totalling $50,000. On 22 November, Holmes and Minnie fled from Chicago. By this time, she had transferred all her property to Holmes. It was time for her to disappear, and she did. Holmes was later to accuse her of murdering Annie by hitting her with a stool in a jealous rage.

Holmes had met a blonde girl with immense blue eyes during the Exposition; her name was Georgiana Yoke, and she demanded marriage if she was to surrender her virginity. It made no difference to Holmes – he already had two wives, so he married her in Denver in January 1894. Martin adds the astonishing detail that Minnie was a witness, and that she did not "disappear" until some months later, which raises the possibility that Minnie knew more of Holmes's affairs than his previous mistresses had, and was an accomplice – perhaps even in her sister's murder. With Minnie out of the way, Holmes and Pitezel went to Fort Worth to realise her property. They used it to raise a loan of $16,000, and also as collateral for the purchase of a large number of horses. In June, Holmes and Pitezel moved to Saint Louis, where Holmes bought another drugstore, mortgaged the stock, then let Pitezel remove it all. This fraud led to his only period in jail; he was arrested on 19 July 1894, and bailed out by Georgiana on 31st.

It was in jail in St Louis that Holmes met the celebrated train robber, Marion Hedgepeth, of whom the detective Pinkerton said, "He was one of the worst characters I ever heard of. He was bad all through". Hedgepeth dressed like a banker, but was reputed to have the fastest draw in the West. He once killed a man whose gun was already out of its holster when Hedgepeth started to draw. Women fought to get into the courtroom when the good-looking Hedgepeth was tried.

Holmes told Hedgepeth that he had worked out a perfect insurance swindle. It involved insuring a man's life, getting him "killed" in an apparently accidental explosion, and substituting another body for the "victim". (It will be recalled that Holmes started his career with a similar swindle.) He asked Hedgepeth if he knew of a suitable crooked lawyer to deal with the insurance company. Hedgepeth put him on to one Jephta D. Howe. Pitezel was to be the "victim", who would be insured for ten thousand dollars. In the event of a successful swindle, Hedgepeth would get $500, Howe $2,500, and Pitezel and Holmes would share the rest.

What Pitezel did not know was that Holmes had no intention of finding a corpse to substitute for his own. Holmes had a much simpler method. Kill Pitezel, and take his share of the money.

For the purpose of the fraud, Holmes and Pitezel moved to Philadelphia, and rented a house at 1316 Callowhill Street, which backed on to the morgue. No doubt Holmes told Pitezel he intended to get the body from the morgue. Under the name of B.F. Perry, Pitezel moved into the house, and erected a sign that claimed he was a dealer in patents. He moved in on 17 August. A carpenter named Eugene Smith brought him a device for setting saws. Pitezel told him to leave it. On 3 September, Smith called in to find how the sale of his patent was going, and found the place empty, with the door open. After waiting for a while, he looked upstairs – and found Pitezel's swollen and decomposing corpse. The police were called in, and soon decided that Pitezel had been conducting some experiment using chloroform, and had made the mistake of trying to light his pipe too close to it. The inquest found that his death was accidental. Five days later, the Fidelity Mutual Life Insurance Company on Walnut Street received a telegram from their St Louis branch declaring that B.F. Perry was actually Benjamin Fuller Pitezel, and that he was insured by them. A few days later, the company received a letter from the lawyer Jephta D. Howe saying that he represented Pitezel's widow Carrie and would be calling on them. The insurance company tried to trace Pitezel's former address in Chicago, and found their way to Myrta Belknap, the second Mrs Holmes. Holmes apparently kept in touch with her, for she agreed to send him a message – he was on a "business trip" – and in due course, Holmes contacted the insurance company. By this time, Pitezel was buried. Eventually, Holmes arrived in Philadelphia, and offered to identify the body. Jephta D. Howe also arrived with Pitezel's second eldest daughter, Alice, and the body was exhumed and quickly identified. The insurance company paid up without hesitation. But Holmes was less willing to part with the $500 he had promised Hedgepeth, not to mention the $2,500 for Howe. Howe told his elder brother about his grievance, and since the elder brother was Hedgepeth's lawyer, he advised the train robber to make some capital out of it by denouncing "Howard" (Holmes's alias) and trying to get his sentence reduced for his public spiritedness. This did not work – he was still sentenced to twelve years – but the insurance company suddenly realised they had been defrauded. The alarm went out for Holmes. But he had returned to St Louis, and taken away two of the remaining four children – Nellie, aged eleven, and Howard, nine – claiming that they were on their way to rejoin Pitezel. Alice had been left in Indianapolis – no doubt Holmes was afraid that she would reveal that the body *was* that of her father after all – and Holmes then rejoined her.

For the next week or so, Holmes was nowhere to be found. It was later established that he visited his family in New Hampshire, and even his first wife. He defrauded his brother of $300, then went back to Burlington, Vermont, where Pinkerton detectives finally traced him. He was living with Georgiana, and Mrs Pitezel, with two remaining children – a girl of sixteen and a baby – were living nearby. The detectives traced Holmes by following the trail of Mrs Pitezel from St Louis to Detroit and Toronto. When the fugitives moved to Boston, and Holmes began making the round of steamship offices, the police decided it was time to pounce, and Holmes was finally arrested on 17 November 1894. His career of murder had been brief, from 1890 to 1894, but eventful.

On the way back to Philadelphia (with Mrs Pitezel), Holmes lied fluently and involvedly, and offered the guard $500 if he would allow him to hypnotise him. (This raises an interesting possibility about why Minnie Williams and so many other women were so completely in his power.) When he arrived in Philadelphia, it was to find that Pitezel's body had been exhumed again, and that it had now been discovered that he died of chloroform poisoning, not of the explosion. It must have begun to dawn slowly on Mrs Pitezel about now that her husband was dead and the three children had vanished. Holmes had told her he had no idea what Pitezel had done with them, and suggested that the eldest girl Dessie should be sent to join him.

A detective named Geyer did a remarkable piece of work in tracing what had become of the children. Geyer plodded from hotel to hotel in Cincinnati – where Mrs Pitezel thought Holmes had taken the children – until he found one where a man had stayed with three children. Holmes had used an alias, of course. After weeks of checking hotels and houses, he had the photographs of Holmes and the children published in the press, and this led him to a house in Toronto where a man and two girls had arrived in late October. Holmes had borrowed a spade from the old gentleman next door. The bodies of the girls were found in the cellar, buried under a few feet of earth. The boy Howard was more difficult to trace. Evidence showed that he had never even reached Toronto. Accordingly, Geyer returned to Indianapolis, and began patiently checking hotels in every outlying town. At last there was only one left – Irvington. It was in Irvington that Geyer at last discovered that Holmes had arrived at a rented house with a nine-year-old boy and a large stove. The boy had watched two workmen erect the stove. Later in the day, he ended up in it. Geyer found a few charred bones and teeth in the kitchen chimney.

In his *Book of Remarkable Criminals* (1918), H.B. Irving has quoted from the letters the children wrote to their mother on that last trip from town to town, bringing home their misery and home-sickness so sharply that they are almost unbearable to read. And suddenly, it becomes very hard to understand how Holmes can have gone through with it, or why he did it. He was covering up his trail: he had killed Pitezel, now he had to kill the rest of the family to escape detection. All for a few thousand dollars. Mrs Pitezel, Dessie and the baby Wharton were next on the list.

Police now opened Holmes's "castle" and examined it from cellar to roof. There was a large stove in the cellar with charred human bones in it. More bones were buried under the floor. A dissecting table in the corner was heavily stained with blood. Greased chutes ran from the second and third floor down to the cellar. A handyman who had worked for Holmes now gave the information that Holmes had once given him a male skeleton to mount, and on another occasion, asked him to finish removing the flesh from another skeleton. He said he assumed Holmes was engaged in surgical work. The skeletons were then sold to medical schools. Holmes did not believe in wasting anything.

Holmes lied on to the end. He kept a diary in which he recorded his sense of shock at the discovery of the children's bodies, and how he recalls the "innocent child's kiss so timidly given" before they waved him goodbye. He accused Minnie Williams of hiring someone to do the murder to spite him. When condemned to death, as he inevitably was, he wrote a long confession for the newspapers in which he admitted to twenty-seven murders. Then, after selling it for $7,500, he repudiated the whole thing and again declared himself innocent. He conducted his own defence and did it well, but it made no difference. He was hanged on 7 May 1895, at Moyamensing Prison.

Holmes was himself convinced that his career as a mass murderer had turned him into a "monster". He believed that he had undergone certain physical changes – a shortening of one arm and one leg, and the "malevolent distortion" of one side of his face which was so marked that he grew a beard to conceal it. That this was not entirely imagination is proved by photographs of Holmes reproduced in David Franke's book *The Torture Doctor*. In the November 1966 issue of *The Criminologist*, there is an article that discusses the old theory that the left and right sides of the human face reflect two different aspects of the character: that the left side is the "natural" character and the right the "acquired". (If a mirror is placed down the centre of the photograph, so the face becomes two left sides or two right, an interesting difference often emerges.) The difference between the two halves of Holmes's face is marked enough to provide evidence for his assertion that "I have commenced to assume the form and features of the Evil One himself".

Holmes's confession reveals that, as in the case of so many serial killers, murder – and the sense of power over other people – becomes an addictive drug. This is another observation of central importance in understanding the emergence of the modern serial killer. The moral and social inhibitions about inflicting harm on other people gradually crumble away, until nothing is left. When this point is reached, murder has simply become a bad habit, like smoking or nail-biting. In many modern cases, the process of erosion is accelerated by the use of drugs or alcohol, with their power to release inhibitions. The drug cults of the 1960s undoubtedly played their part in the emergence of the serial killer. In that sense, the case of the Charles Manson "family" may be regarded as a kind of watershed.

According to the *Los Angeles Times*, Manson's mother was a teenage prostitute. Manson himself later denied this: "They call her a whore, a prostitute, but that's not true. She was what the flower children were . . ." But he confirmed that his mother became pregnant at fifteen, by a boyfriend of seventeen. His mother went to prison shortly after he was born. Manson moved from home to home, living mostly with an aunt and uncle in Charleston, West Virginia. He was sent to his first reform school at the age of nine – in 1943 – and was there for a year. He was later in the Federal Reformatory at Chillicothe, Ohio. He hated all the schools and ran away repeatedly – twenty-seven times from one of them. An Indianapolis newspaper printed a photograph of Manson in 1949 – looking very young and neatly dressed – and a story saying that he was being taken from a "sinful home" – presumably his mother's – and sent to a local "Boy's Town". He stayed there three days. He later talked bitterly about the bullying that went on in these schools – by the authorities as well as other boys. "You had to be a tough guy. They have to know how tough you are. It's like in here [prison] – *they're* the ones that are scared, the cops." What is abundantly clear, even from the most hostile accounts of Manson's childhood and teens, is that society was treating him the wrong way. He was intelligent, basically affectionate, but also dominant. From the beginning, he had the feeling that he had to fight, to hold his own against a world that had no use for him and no interest in him. A parole officer later said: "Charlie was the most hostile parolee I've ever come across". He was in the reformatory until he was twenty (in 1955). He then married a seventeen-year-old girl named Rosalie, and drove with her in a stolen car to Los Angeles sometime in mid-1955. In March 1956, a son was born;

a month later, Manson was sent to prison for three years for car theft. Rosalie divorced him. He was out of jail in October 1958, but after only twenty months of freedom, was back again on a ten-year sentence – this time for a number of offences including car theft, cheque fraud, stealing credit cards, and transporting girls over a state line for immoral purposes. It was during this period, according to Ed Sanders in his book *The Family*, that Manson began to study magic and hypnotism, and learned to play the guitar from the famous gangster "Creepy" Karpis. He also became enthusiastic about a science fiction novel called *Stranger in a Strange Land* by Robert Heinlein, which is basically a piece of satirical social criticism. Its hero, Valentine Michael Smith, is a man from Mars who finds earth and its weird customs totally alien and frightening. He founds a religious cult whose rituals include cannibalism and free love. One of his disciples explains: "If Mike can show us a better way to run this fouled-up planet, his sex life needs no vindication. Geniuses are justifiably contemptuous of lesser opinion and are always indifferent to the sexual customs of the tribe . . ." Manson apparently found the Messianic Martian so exhilarating that he later named one of his illegitimate children Valentine Michael Manson.

Released from prison again in 1967, at the age of thirty-two, Manson drifted to San Francisco. He later admitted: "I was frightened. I didn't know where to go. I didn't want to leave jail, but they insisted and gave me back my $35 and a suitcase filled with old clothes. For several days I just rode around on buses. I slept on the bus, and drivers woke me when we reached the end of somewhere." He found his way to the Haight-Ashbury district, San Francisco's equivalent of Soho or Greenwich Village.

In 1966, I had walked down Haight Street with the poet Kenneth Rexroth – the father figure of the "beat generation". It struck me as being very much like Soho, except that the flower children were more flamboyant than their London counterparts. Rexroth had been the first critic to describe and analyse the "beat generation" – which came to prominence in 1957, with the publication of Jack Kerouac's book *On the Road*. But it was Kerouac's next book, *The Dharma Bums*, that made clear the affinities of the new type of "bohemian". I gathered from various hippies that my own book *The Outsider* (1956) also played its part in creating the ideology of the beats, particularly the chapter analysing the work of Hermann Hesse. Hesse was, at this time, almost unknown in the English-speaking world, and the few translations of his books had been out of print for a long time. By 1967, reprints of *Steppenwolf, Siddartha, Demian*, had joined *The Dharma Bums* and Ginsberg's *Howl* as basic texts of this generation. The leaning towards Taoism, Zen Buddhism and Hinduism was strong.

This was, in fact, a revival of nineteenth-century romanticism. What lay behind it went deeper than laziness or the desire to opt out of a materialistic society. Hesse's novels are mostly about heroes who become "wanderers", seekers after salvation, and they are full of nostalgic longing for the peace of monasteries and the life of religious communities. One of the most unexpected best-sellers of post-war years was Thomas Merton's *Seven Storey Mountain* (1948), describing Merton's increasing dissatisfaction with modern life until he decided to become a Trappist monk. It was not simply the increasingly exhausting tempo of our society that was being condemned; there was also a feeling that something important was being *missed*. Kerouac found this missing vitamin in jazz rather than in literature, for the basic jazz legend is also tragic and romantic: the great artist who becomes an alcoholic or drug addict because the world is a dreary, murderous place, but who leaves behind a life-affirming perfection on gramophone records. But what they are affirming is their inner life, the soul's innocence and vitality; what they are mourning is their total failure to find any counterpart of this vision in the actual world. Kerouac's heroes were Charlie Parker, Lester Young, Billie Holiday; by the time Manson came along, it would be Bob Dylan, Pete Seegar, the Beatles.

The "beat revolt" might have faded as quickly as its English counterpart, the "Angry Young Man" movement, if it had not been for the discovery of psychedelic drugs. Kerouac had smoked marijuana, and described its effects in *On the Road*, the total relaxation, the feeling that time has stopped. But mescalin and LSD (discovered in Basle in 1948) could produce visions, create strange patterns of colour or intensity perception until every object seemed to *exist more*, to stand out from its background. Aldous Huxley said that the effect of mescalin was to make him aware of the "is-ness" of things, and advocated that it should be sold as openly as tobacco or alcohol. I had reservations about psychedelics, and these were confirmed in 1963 when I took mescalin. What it did was to remove the usual "filters" from perception, as if you were to play a gramophone record at top volume, with all the tone controls turned up to maximum. But the filters are there to aid the mind's work of grasping and ordering reality – the kind of ordering that, at its best, produces great art – or philosophy. Mescalin simultaneously weakens the will, the mind's "ordering power" and strengthens the incoming stimuli. The immediate result is intensified perception of meaning.

But it should also be recognized that our constant relation with the world is a *will*-relation. When something upsets me, I "retreat", I withdraw; when something delights me, I advance. *Everything* that happens to me during my waking life causes small advances and retreats, almost as if my skin were the skin of a balloon, which swells or contracts according to the outer pressure. But there is an important difference; whatever the outer pressure, it is *I* who decides whether to expand or contract. A jazz trumpeter who suddenly begins to play superbly, a boxer who suddenly turns into the perfect fighting machine, even a philosopher who begins to think with magnificent clarity – all these are *in control* to a degree we rarely achieve. And it is this control, this power of expanding and driving forward, that constitutes real greatness in human beings.

Psychedelics weaken this element of control. So, of course, does alcohol. Even music and poetry can have the same effect; (the theme of Mann's *Buddenbrooks*, for example, is the decline of a commercial family once it begins to produce artistic types). It is a question of maintaining a balance, of retaining control. But the psychedelic philosophy propagated by Timothy Leary flatly denied the need for any such control. The ultimate aim was self-abandonment, "to escape the ego shaped by established society". You might say the prize went to whoever could abandon and forget himself most completely. Alan Watts, another powerful influence on the "flower generation", declared that man's basic trouble is his aggressiveness towards his environment, his desire to impose his will on everything; he speaks about space rockets being enormous erect penises pointing at the sky. Man should learn that he is a part of nature, says Watts, like the clouds or trees. He should learn to blend into his universe, stop *willing* so much . . . And perhaps this explains why the whole experiment in love and self-abandonment was petering out by the late 1960s. Kerouac was dead, his talent destroyed by manic drinking sessions. The drug peddlers in Haight-Ashbury became professional racketeers, who ended by throwing out the hippies. Manson and his disciples moved out to Death Valley.

But when Manson came to Haight-Ashbury in 1967, it looked as if the flower culture had come to stay. The hippies had occasional clashes with police, but they had come to a kind of working agreement by which they agreed not to obstruct traffic so long as they were left alone.

It is understandable that all this should have hit Manson as a revelation. He had spent his life being slapped and kicked around – taught that you either joined society as a hard-working, fully paid-up member, or declared yourself a bum and took the consequences. To discover a whole *way of life* that allowed maximum freedom must have seemed an impossible piece of luck, rather like Rousseau discovering that his community of "noble savages" actually existed in some remote Swiss valley. Here was not only immediate acceptance by a community that did not care about his past; it was also a field for the operation of his natural dominance.

It must be borne in mind that although Manson was thirty-three years old, in another sense he was a teenager. He had spent practically all his adult life behind bars or in reformatories. According to Manson, when he came out of jail at the age of twenty-one, "I'd never been with a woman, never made love to one in my life. I'd never had a drink of beer". And his period of freedom was short. In a sense, then, he was learning to live for the first time when he came to Haight-Ashbury.

It must also be recognized that the majority of hippies, like the majority of any other group, do not belong to the dominant five per cent. They are not Nietzschean free spirits, living like characters out of *La Bohème*, roaring with laughter as they burn their manuscripts to keep warm. Most of them are little more than mirrors that reflect their environment; their minds are full of one another's doings, ("Where's Tex today?" "Didn'tcha hear, he got busted . . ."), The Beatles, hippie slang, Vietnam protest, Tom and Jerry Cartoons, *Easy Rider*. Kerouac's later books (*Big Sur, Desolation Angels*) are a free-associating jumble of basic hippie preoccupations. Tom Wolfe's *Electric Kool-Aid Acid Test*, an attempt to catch the hippie life-style in straight reportage, ends by producing a sense of bewilderment and sheer futility. But above all, of the basic mediocrity of most of these drop-outs.

It was inevitable that Manson should soon become an important character among San Francisco's hippies, and also that he should make up for years of lost sexual opportunity. His view of women was definitely Nietzchean. ("Goest thou to woman? Don't forget thy whip . . .") A girl who had hitch-hiked across the country with him described how Manson ordered her to carry both rucksacks, and when she refused, made her walk several paces behind him. After his arrest, this kind of story was cited by newspapers to prove Manson's paranoid tendencies, but this is hardly fair: it is like accusing Casanova of spending his life trying to prove his masculinity. Manson's dominance, like his gentleness and persuasiveness, was a natural part of his personality.

On first moving to San Francisco, Manson stayed with friends in Berkeley. There he met a girl named Mary Brunner, with whom he "shacked up". (She was later described as "his favourite wife".) In Venice, California, he found a girl named Lynn Fromme crying by the kerbside – she had been thrown out of home after a quarrel; she also joined the Manson menage, which now moved to the Haight district. There he continued to collect runaways. The place seemed to be full of girls who were emotionally deprived, obsessed with the need to be loved, looking for a father figure. One of these was Susan Atkins. "Self-confidence, that's what Charlie did for me", she explained. "He gave my faith in myself back to me". The *Life* magazine portrait of Manson as manic messiah, the wild-eyed seducer, seems to have no basis in fact. On the contrary, his extraordinary influence was due to his "Christ-like" appearance and personality. He was small and unformidable, played the guitar and sang protest songs in the manner of Bob Dylan, and had a sympathetic and affectionate manner. He had obviously suffered, and looked as though he had. (Many of the photographs catch this sad-eyed look, the man of sorrows on his way to Calvary.) He was interested in mysticism, scientology and magic. He was full of deep convictions about the rottenness of society and the need for a revolution. If he had not read Marcuse, this is only another proof of the extent to which he had become a vessel for the *zeitgeist*. Marcuse argues that technical civilization *ought* to mean more leisure for everyone. Instead, it has produced "the repressive society". In *Eros and Civilization* (1951) he asserts that our sexuality has become sick. Sex ought to produce "unrepressive sublimation", an unfolding of our higher human possibilities. Instead of that, it has become commercialized, and becomes another instrument of repression by the people who run society. His *One Dimensional Man* (1964) continues the argument, and makes the startling assertion that modern democratic societies – America in particular – are really as totalitarian and repressive as Stalin's Russia or Hitler's Germany. Marcuse has been violently attacked for emotionalism and woolly thinking. But in order to do justice to his thought, he must be seen as a poetic idealist, a kind of twentieth-century Rousseau, with a strong imaginative vision of how delightful society *could* be if it could be cured of its materialism.

Manson instinctively practised the "unrepressive sublimation" advocated in *Eros and Civilization*". He taught a kind of D. H. Lawrentian vision of sex as total release, a religious communion. Susan Atkins's "Confession" describes going to Manson's room for the first time. "I want to make love to you – with you," he said. He then told her to take off her clothes and to look at herself naked in a full-length mirror. "Look how beautiful you are . . . Look, you're perfect." She adds: "And while he was making love with me he told me to imagine I was making love with my father to get me through that particular hangup." (Earlier she mentions that her father wanted to have an affair with her – after her mother's death – and that she would have been perfectly willing.) Manson understood that most girls want a father figure. This explains his remarkable success. "I really felt privileged walking with Charlie because all the girls in the house I was sharing were just in love with him . . ." His peculiar charm and gentleness worked with men as well as with girls – he is quoted as saying that he had 3,000 friends.

By October 1967, Manson had had enough of Haight-Ashbury. Ever since leaving jail, his chief obsession had been the idea of breaking into the field of pop music. He was convinced he could become as famous as the Beatles or Bob Dylan. He traded a grand piano (a present from a friend) for a Volkswagen bus, and later changed this for an old yellow school bus. In October, the "family" moved south. After a trip through Nevada, New Mexico and Alabama, they returned to Los Angeles, and rented a place near Malibu. Manson began to play his guitar in a Topanga Canyon club known as the Spiral Staircase. It was there that Manson met a twenty-year-old musician named Bobby Beausoleil. Beausoleil was a student of magic and an admirer of Aleister Crowley. He had played the role of Lucifer in the film *Lucifer Rising*, made by the "underground" film-maker, Kenneth Anger. Manson and Beausoleil discussed how to break into the field of pop music, and Beausoleil introduced Manson to another musician and music teacher, Gary Hinman, who owned a house in Topanga Canyon. When Manson was evicted from the Malibu place in February 1968, Beausoleil suggested they might move in with him in a small house he shared with a girlfriend in Horseshoe Lane, Topanga. He was shocked when the crowded school bus arrived. "I didn't expect that many people." The family camped on the hillside behind the house. It now included thirteen-year-old Didi Lansbury, daughter of the film actress Angela Lansbury, and a fourteen-year-old named Diana Lake, nicknamed The Snake – according to Ed Sanders, "in tribute to the transverse ophidian wiggles she made during intercourse". They stayed there for six weeks. Bobby Beausoleil had decided to leave before that; he did not see Manson for several months.

In March, the family moved to a house on the other side of the canyon. Mary Brunner's baby, Valentine Michael, was born in April, the family delivering the baby. At this time there were about sixteen girls in the group, and four men. These included Bruce Davis, a disciple Manson had encountered on a trip through Oregon, and Phil Kaufman, a friend from prison days. Sandy Good, the daughter of a wealthy stockbroker, also became one of Manson's mistresses at this time. It was she who told Manson about a ranch owned by a man named George Spahn – eighty years old and almost blind – situated at Chatsworth, thirty miles from the centre of Los Angeles. In May, Manson and the family went to look at the Spahn movie ranch (so called because it had once belonged to the cowboy star William S. Hart and had been used in film sets). It was now a riding stable, and there was some vague suggestion that the family might take it over, in exchange for running the stable. On this occasion, they stayed for only a few days.

It was after this visit that Manson's luck seemed to improve suddenly. He somehow became acquainted with Dennis Wilson, the drummer of an immensely successful pop group, the Beach Boys. Wilson actually allowed the family – now numbering about twenty-five – to move into his luxury home on Sunset Boulevard. Manson was taken to parties and met film stars. (Many were on drugs, and it is possible that Manson did some "pushing".) When Beausoleil returned to Los Angeles, he met Manson in a supermarket, and was invited back to swim in Dennis Wilson's swimming pool.

It was also at the Sunset Boulevard house that Manson met a well-dressed young college dropout named Charles Watson, who owned a wig shop, and seemed set for a respectable middle-class career. It may have been Manson's girls who converted him to the hippie way of life, or it may have been admiration for Manson. At all events, he became another of the regular male disciples.

Manson met Terry Melcher, son the film star Doris Day, who was in the record business, and there was talk of a $20,000 contract. Manson also sold two of his songs to the Beach Boys for $5,000 – at least, according to his own account. (He was angry they changed his title "Cease to Exist" to "Cease to Resist".) Manson also recorded some of his own songs in the studio of Dennis Wilson's brother.

When the family had to move out of the Sunset Boulevard house – leaving it barer than when they arrived – they stayed for a while at the house of Gary Hinman in Topanga Canyon. In August, the family moved back to the Spahn ranch, and persuaded George Spahn to allow them to take care of the stables in exchange for accommodation (in "outlaw shacks" at the back of the ranch). For a few months, it seemed to have been an ideal situation, a realization of the Haight-Ashbury dream of perfect harmony. One girl who lived there for a time said of Manson,

"He was very beautiful in many ways and gave out lots of love". It began to be spoiled by the sheer number of hippies who came to share the fun, and Manson began to get "uptight" about some of these new arrivals. Someone brought venereal disease to the ranch, and it spread so fast that Manson had to call in a doctor to stamp it out. (Manson always accused Susan Atkins of being the carrier.) Much of their spare time was spent "jamming" with drums and guitar – with pot or psychedelics to create a mood – and Manson continued to dream of fame as a singer and composer. (His former prison friend Phil Kaufman arranged three recording sessions during this period, but Manson was becoming increasingly disillusioned about the commercial side of the business.) Manson disliked negro jazz, and Jimi Hendrix records were banned. Books were also banned, although Manson liked to have his girls reading aloud from Hermann Hesse's *Siddartha*.

There were more spectacular successes for Manson at this period. The owner of a ranch behind the Spahn ranch, Richard Kaplan, was persuaded to give it to the family in exchange for a painted tent. (Kaplan was under the influence of a drug at the time). A female schoolteacher who gave a lift to members of the family and returned to the ranch was so enslaved by Manson that she gave him her savings – $11,000.

Not far from the ranch there was the headquarters of a religious cult called *The Fountain of the World*. Its founder, Krishna Venta, had been blown up by dynamite, probably by a disgruntled follower, in 1958. Manson attended many of the Fountain's ceremonies, and it may have been these that inspired him to hold a sort of symbolic crucifixion ceremony in a glade near the ranch. Manson was strapped to a cross, and the crucifixion scene was enacted like a morality play – except that it ended with ritual sex.

There seems to be no doubt that Manson was becoming increasingly obsessive, increasingly embittered, during the three months at the Spahn ranch. He wanted to retreat further away from civilization. One of his followers told him about Death Valley, the national park on the other other side of the Mojave desert, three hundred miles away. In October 1968, the family drove their bus across the desert, abandoned it when the brakes burned out, and finally arrived at the derelict Barker Ranch. Here they established themselves, in the sunbaked solitude. Manson now dreamed of an even remoter retreat from the world. He heard of a legend about a great underground hole from which the Hopi Indians emerged, and he decided that this hole was somewhere under Death Valley. According to Ed Sanders, he actually went looking for this hole, perhaps hoping to use it as a vast air raid shelter when the Bomb dropped. He was convinced that civilization would destroy itself.

In November 1968, Dennis Wilson and a friend drove to Death Valley to collect a jeep Manson had borrowed, and they took Manson back with them to Los Angeles. He returned the following January. But the winter cold made them decide to return to civilization. In February, Manson rented a house in Gresham Street, Canoga Park, in Los Angeles. Manson's next door neighbour told a reporter: "We were on very good terms, but he was very opinionated, and very anti-establishment . . . His whole thing [philosophy] was that sooner or later everyone would kill each other off". It seemed obvious to Manson that in a world with so much hatred, mass killing of blacks by whites would break out sooner or later. He was very fond of quoting the Bible, said his neighbour; (it is, after all, the only book available in many prisons). The Book of Revelation, with its prophecies of doom, appealed particularly. Manson presided over his family of women – ranging in age from thirteen to nineteen – like some Jewish patriarch. "They seemed quite happy. They were not being held against their will. On many occasions they said they would give their lives for Charlie . . ." There were also some children. "Charlie blew up when anyone tried to punish children. He got real mad when the kids in his family tried to spank their kids . . ." The girls stole food from supermarkets. Patricia Krenwinkel, who joined the group at this time, had the job of foraging in waste bins behind stores. (In her court testimony, she also described a "long idyll" with Manson, when they travelled up and down the California coast, living in woods. "We were like wood nymphs . . . we would run through the woods with flowers in our hair, and Charlie would play a little pipe.")

But a fourteen-year-old boy who ran away from home and joined the family for a short period soon left, declaring that all

Manson wanted was servants. There is undoubtedly an element of truth in this; any born leader wants followers. On the other hand, the reporter of the *National Tatler* who declared, "It's obvious that Charlie Manson had an enormous sexual appetite and that this was the chief reason he tempted young girls to enter his cult" was completely missing the point. Manson did not need to be a Rasputin or Svengali-figure to get young girls; the girls came to him because he was a father-figure offering love and protection. The same reporter describes Manson as a "harem keeper [who] treated his women as underlings" out of a neurotic mother-hatred. But Susan Atkins described the attitude of the family towards Manson. "Man is man. He is the king, and I am his queen. And the queen does what the king says. This is the right way. Charlie is man. The king? Look at his name. Manson. "Man's son" . . . And now I have visible proof of God, the proof the church never gave me. There are reflections all around me. Charlie has brought me this truth." But in spite of this adoration, Susan Atkins was the one female member of the family who gave Manson any trouble. She felt impelled to defy him on several occasions, although she usually came to heel when challenged.

Manson was becoming increasingly obsessed with the idea of universal destruction. A new Beatles album contained a song called "Helter Skelter". Manson, apparently unaware that this is a spiral slide down which children swoop on doormats, decided that it should be the code name for the great day of reckoning, when the Pigs would be slaughtered. (There was another Beatles song called "Piggies" on the same album.) It is tempting to believe that Manson began to go insane at this period, although there is no definite evidence to support it. It is possible that psychedelic trips made him unable to distinguish between dream and reality. He began to keep a death list of people who would have to die when the time came. It included various film stars – Warren Beatty and Julie Christie among them – and Terry Melcher. Also on the list – which ran to eleven names – were various disciples who had defected. One of these was Paul Watkins, who had heard about Manson's family in 1968, and called on him in Topanga Canyon. "When I walked in I was knocked off my feet by six naked girls . . . His first words to me were 'Take any of these girls. They're all yours'." Understandably, the sixteen-year-old

Watkins moved in. Watkins also mentioned Manson's love of animals, and said that Manson had some "weird power over animals". They came upon a rattlesnake when walking in the desert. "Charlie told me not to be afraid of it, and to sit in front of it. I did just that. I must have been crazy, but that's the kind of effect he had on me. Anyway the damn thing rattled a few times while I nearly died of fright, then it scuttled away. It was only a coincidence, but at that time I believed Charlie had some weird power . . ." (He seems to have been unaware that snakes, given a chance, will avoid an encounter.) And during this final year – from August 1968 to August 1969 – Manson seems to have cultivated this belief in his magical powers among his followers. Patricia Krenwinkel asserted that she had seen him change a man into a skeleton – obviously a psychedelic hallucination. She also declared that "thirty or forty times Manson made old people regain their youth. But the effect did not last because they did not have faith in the miracle". A legend about the Canoga period mentioned by Sanders declares that a girl named Bo was on her knees sucking Manson's penis when, in a burst of enthusiasm, she bit it in half. Manson miraculously healed himself immediately. Patricia Krenwinkel also seems to suggest that she saw him as a Christ figure: "All he ever does is to give, and if you watched him you could see the love he suggests with everything he does – with his motions, with his infinite gentleness". And this infinitely gentle guru was thinking out a plan for starting the great Revolution: to get his followers to commit a series of murders, which the whites would blame on the Black Panthers – so the slaughter would begin.

According to Sanders, it was during the Canoga Park period that Manson began to cultivate the acquaintance of members of motor cycle gangs, although it is not clear whether he hoped to make use of them when "Helter Skelter" arrived. His method of assuring their loyalty was to order his girls to strip off their clothes and "blow" them – kneel and perform an act of fellatio. One of the motor cyclists, Danny De Carlo, gained the nickname Donkey Dick Dan, due to his unusual endowment.

It is curious that Manson seemed to be colour prejudiced. When a motor cyclist brought a half-Indian male to the house, Manson refused to allow the guest to "make it" with the girls.

The family now began full scale preparations for Helter Skelter. They purchased guns and knives, and began acquiring "dune buggies" – cars or jeeps that would run in the desert. Manson paid for one of these with a forged cheque. Another was bought with money stolen by Linda Kasabian. They bought detailed maps of the Death Valley area.

It is difficult to tell how serious all this way supposed to be. Manson was not a hard-headed realist, brooding on the future. He was a kind of sleepwalker, a fantasist whose wild leaps into the irrational often paid off. The adoration of his family gave him the sensation of being infallible. The pot and LSD kept them all in a semi-dream world. What had happened to Manson resembles, on a smaller scale, what happened to Hitler. He acted according to a kind of inner-inspiration that ought to have brought a head-on clash with reality followed by disaster. Instead, everything he did seemed to come out right. People gave him money and cars and even ranches. His followers trusted him completely and never seemed to come to any serious harm. His success story seemed a proof that what the world needs is inspiration, not calculation. There can be no doubt that, if it had not been for the murders, Manson *would* have ended up as an enormous success in the world of folk music or underground films. The sleepwalking technique would have paid off. The talk about murder and bloody revolution may have been part of a creative fantasy – his own way of writing *The War of the Worlds*, so to speak.

This seems to be borne out by the increasingly wild and confused scene when the family returned to the Spahn ranch, sometime around March or April 1969. The motorcycle gangs were constant visitors. (One was called Satan's Slaves, the name that was later – mistakenly – stuck on the family). Some of these were associated with "black magic" groups in the Los Angeles area. All kinds of people turned up at the ranch and slept on mattresses. Sanders quotes one film starlet as complaining that the moment she arrived, someone dragged her into the bushes and raped her. (Since she continued to come, she presumably had no real objection). Manson continued to negotiate with Terry Melcher and Dennis Wilson about recording contracts, and some songs were actually recorded. Melcher, Wilson and another associate called Gregg Jakobsen seriously considered making a movie about the family. The immense success of low budget films like *Easy Rider* made it a real possibility. Melcher's idea was a film that would capture the gentle, love-pervaded atmosphere of the ranch, with mothers breast feeding their babies, hippies crooning to guitars and Manson sermonizing on universal love. (This *was* the impression most people had of the commune.) Manson wanted something with a more violent impact, conveying some of the ideas of Helter Skelter, with black magic and murder thrown in for good measure. He probably had a keener nose for what the public wanted.

The family income seems to have been large but irregular. Manson was undoubtedly a dope trader. Quantities of stolen goods passed through the ranch, including an NBC Television truck with thousands of dollars' worth of filming equipment. At one point there was a scheme to get the girls to work as topless showgirls in Los Angeles, but this was abandoned when they found they would need silicone injections to enlarge their breasts. Sanders says that Manson was considering turning some of the girls into prostitutes.

There was considerable police harassment at various times. A seventeen-year-old girl who was taken to the ranch complained that Manson raped her in a car, and he spent a few days in jail before being released on bail. Manson apparently provoked the police by deliberately driving at ninety miles an hour when he passed a police car, and spent three days in jail for this. Then there were various questions of auto thefts, forged cheques and stolen credit cards. The police pressed George Spahn to get rid of the hippies, but he apparently liked being surrounded by girls.

As the summer wore on, there is evidence that Manson's fantasies of violence were becoming more frequent. One male follower later declared that Manson asked him if he would be willing to commit a murder in exchange for money; he finally decided against it. Another described how Manson would park outside middle-class homes, and suggest that they went in and slaughtered everyone. But then, Manson was a "manipulator". A small, lightly-built man, surrounded by beefy hippies, many of whom were capable of violence, he may have used the talk of violence and suggestions of murder as a weapon for dominance.

In early July the game began to turn into reality. A negro dope-dealer named Bernard Crowe became violently angry when Tex Watson vanished with $2,400 of his money and failed to deliver pot to that value. He called at the home of another family associate who had been mixed up in the deal – Rosina Kroner – and talked about killing somebody. Miss Kroner rang Manson, who drove to her house, together with a disciple called T.J. the Terrible. Manson was carrying a wild-Western type revolver. Crowe told Manson that he had no quarrel with him, but wanted his money back. Manson – probably high – performed some kind of dance, then pointed the revolver at Crowe's stomach and pulled the trigger. There was a click, and Manson laughed; it looked like another of his dominance games. He pulled the trigger again; this time the gun fired, and Crowe collapsed with a bullet in his torso. Manson told another of the men present that he liked his leather shirt, and the man hastened to remove it and give it to him. Then Manson and T.J. the Terrible drove back to the Spahn ranch. Both were convinced that Crowe was dead. At one point on the drive, Manson told T.J. he did not like the way T.J. was looking at him, because it made him question himself . . . In fact, Crowe was not dead. He was taken to hospital, and there was an unsuccessful operation to remove the bullet. He left hospital – with the bullet still in him – about two weeks later. No one seems to have pressed the matter. Presumably Crowe decided that he would prefer not to be associated with the police.

Why did Manson do this? It brings to mind the two Kray murders – of George Cornell and Jack McVitie – committed as a sort of "dare". Manson was leader. He had to prove it, even though it threw the rest of the family into a panic. It was a question of asserting dominance.

As the days passed, and no police – or Black Panthers – turned up to avenge Crowe, the panic died. No doubt it seemed a further proof that whatever Charlie did came out right.

A few days later, the girl called Gypsy called on an acquaintance, Charles Melton, in Topanga Canyon, and there met a young New Englander, Linda Kasabian, who had a sixteen-month-old baby. Gypsy told Linda about the Spahn ranch, where children were given all the love they needed and everyone shared their possessions. Linda returned to the ranch, and had soon –

according to her own account – made love with just about every male in the place, and a few females too. (She was soon pregnant again, by Bobby Beausoleil.) An orgasm with Tex Watson was so violent that she regarded it as a mystic experience. She also mentioned to Watson that her friend and late host, Charles Melton, had money in his trailer; the next day, they returned for her belongings, and left with $5,000 of Melton's money, which was given to Manson. When Melton arrived in search of his money, Manson got rid of him by a method he had used before. He told Melton that if he had any quarrel with the family, he was welcome to kill him – Charlie; with which he handed Melton a knife. Melton said he didn't want to kill him. In that case, said Manson, perhaps he should kill Melton, to prove that there is no such thing as death . . . Melton decided that argument was useless, and left hastily. More dune buggies were bought with some of the money.

Life at the ranch was never boring. The police came in and out, looking for stolen cars. On 20 July, Manson flew into such a rage that everyone fled. He beat Gypsy, and smashed everything that came to hand. But not long after this, the family held an orgy. A fifteen-year-old girl who helped with the horses was tied down, and ceremonially deflowered by Beausoleil, after which the watching couples plunged into a love-in. Linda Kasabian made up a threesome with Tex Watson and Leslie Van Houten.

A few days later, the slaughter began. On 25 July, Manson sent Bobby Beausoleil to Gary Hinman's house to ask him for $20,000 to finance the move to Death Valley. Relations with Hinman had been deteriorating for some time. Hinman had become a convert to a Japanese sect called Nichiren Shoshu Buddhism and was eager for converts. A friend of Hinman's – who helped him in the manufacture of mescalin – overheard a telephone argument with Manson during which Hinman categorically refused to sell everything he had and join the family. The argument also seemed to be about the question of leadership. Hinman was convinced people needed leading to salvation. Manson – oddly enough – argued that they should be allowed to do what they liked. It was a few days after this that Manson ordered one of the female members of the sect to go and kill Hinman – according to Sanders. But she refused, and left the ranch with her boyfriend.

So Manson persuaded Beausoleil, who was thinking of leaving the ranch, to call on Hinman and try to persuade him to join in the Death Valley exodus. Beausoleil drove over to Hinman's house, together with Susan Atkins and Mary Brunner. They arrived at midnight. Beausoleil explained their scheme, but Hinman was not interested; he was about to leave on a religious pilgrimage to Japan. After a long argument, Beausoleil produced a gun, and told Hinman that he intended to search the house for money – they were convinced that Hinman had $20,000 hidden away. Susan Atkins was left holding the gun. Hinman made a grab for it and it went off, but no one was hurt. Beausoleil came in and grabbed the gun. He gave Hinman a blow on the head with it, which caused bleeding. With Hinman again held at gunpoint, Beausoleil rang Manson at the ranch, and told him that Hinman was being difficult. Whereupon Manson drove over with Bruce Davis. Manson was waving a sword which he seemed to regard as some kind of magical emblem or symbol of power. Manson told Hinman he was determined to have the money. Hinman, in a rage, told him to get out. Whereupon Manson raised the sword and slashed at Hinman's face, cutting deep into the jaw, and half-severing the ear. There was a struggle, in the course of which Manson cut his hand. After this, Manson and Bruce Davis left. Mary Brunner sewed up Hinman's wound, and Beausoleil continued his search.

It was now clear to Beausoleil that Hinman had to be killed – preferably after telling them where he kept the money. (But a police search of the house later revealed that Hinman was telling the truth – there was no money.) Hinman was kept in the house throughout the following day. A couple of people who phoned him were told that his parents had been involved in an accident and he had been called away.

It seems possible that Hinman was tortured, or at least beaten, during the day he spent as a prisoner. Finally Beausoleil rang Manson again, and Manson, according to Beausoleil, told him to kill Hinman. Hinman was forced to sign documents claiming that the ownership of a Volkswagen bus and a Fiat car had passed to Beausoleil. After this, he was stabbed twice in the chest and left. He died of loss of blood. On the wall over his body, Beausoleil wrote, "Political Piggy" in blood, and drew a sign that was supposed to be a panther's paw – the idea being to mislead police into believing that Black Panthers were responsible for the murder.

One of the witnesses, Danny De Carlo, described how Beausoleil came back on the night of the murder, and told him he had tortured Hinman before stabbing him.

With the murder of Hinman, Manson's luck began to turn. Just over a week later, on 6 August, a patrolman saw the Fiat sports car near San Luis Obispo, and checked on the driver. It was Bobby Beausoleil, and he showed the policeman the ownership document signed by Gary Hinman. The decomposing body had been found a week earlier. Beausoleil's story was that he had bought the car from a Negro for $200, which seemed possible – Black Panthers were suspected of the murder. On 7 August, Beausoleil rang the Spahn ranch from the police station. He wanted to talk to Manson. But Manson was in Oceanside, where he was getting a traffic ticket. He came back later to hear the news of Beausoleil's arrest. At the trial, Patricia Krenwinkel asserted that it was at this point that they planned another murder, that of Terry Melcher. It was not clear how this was to be done, but they were all on LSD at the time, so perhaps the connection was not clear to them either.

The bad luck continued. The police made a swoop on the Spahn ranch, looking for drugs and stolen cars. They found Manson seated in a dune buggy. When they asked him what he was doing, Manson explained that he was on guard, looking out for Black Panthers, who were expected to attack the ranch. When the police announced their intention of searching the ranch, Manson solemnly warned them against it. His followers, he said, were armed to the teeth, and might mistake the police for Black Panthers. He should be allowed to go first and prepare the way . . . The police let him go ahead. Assorted hippies fled out of the rear of the ranch, and the raid was a flop.

It was during the next fortnight that Manson took another trip to Death Valley, and also to the Esalen Institute at Big Sur Hot Springs (where weekend courses and group therapy are held). On the trip, Manson picked up another follower, a seventeen-year-old pregnant girl named Stephanie. While Manson was absent,

Beausoleil took the opportunity to leave the ranch. Another young girl, Kitty Lutesinger, also took the opportunity to flee. By this time it was not easy to escape from Manson's ambience. He felt, rightly, that too many of his followers knew too much.

Two days after Beausoleil's arrest, Mary Brunner was arrested for trying to use a stolen credit card. Sandy Good was with her. Their car was found to contain many more credit cards.

When Manson returned to the ranch with Susan Atkins, he heard the various items of bad news, and declared, "Now is the time for Helter Skelter".

This raises the question of whether the murders that took place that night were intended as the beginning of the great war against the "pigs", or were merely part of a plan to get Beausoleil freed. Susan Atkins later testified that they had the idea of committing a "copy-cat" murder, that would appear to be by the same killer as the Hinman stabbing. This latter was probably the immediate motive. But there can be no doubt that everybody at the ranch had an "end of the world" feeling at the time, and Manson's response to being pushed was to erupt into hysterical violence. It is another characteristic in which he resembles Hitler.

The house that had been selected as the murder site was at 10050 Cielo Drive, Benedict Canyon. Terry Melcher had been there until the previous February, then moved out. After this, it was let to the Polish film director Roman Polanski, famous for films like *Repulsion* and *Rosemary's Baby*, and his wife Sharon Tate, the star of *Valley of the Dolls*. Sharon Tate was eight and a half months pregnant.

On the evening of Friday, 8 August 1969, Sharon Tate had three guests to supper: an ex-lover, Jay Sebring, a men's hair stylist; Voityck Frykowski, a Polish writer and friend of her husband, and Abigail Folger, a coffee heiress, Frykowski's mistress. Both Sebring and Frykowski used drugs. Roman Polanski was in London, working on a film.

It has been argued by Manson supporters that he may have been unaware that Tex Watson intended to lead a murder party that night, but this is unlikely. Manson told Stephanie, the seventeen-year-old girl he had picked up, to sleep in a trailer and wait until he came. Then he ordered Susan Atkins to get a change of clothes. Patricia Krenwinkel – who had been on an

LSD trip – was awakened and ordered to get dressed. Some time before midnight, the Ford containing Tex Watson and three girls – Susan Atkins, Patricia Krenwinkel and Linda Kasabian – left the Spahn ranch. About 12.15, it pulled up near the house in Benedict Canyon. It has been suggested that Manson thought Melcher was still in the house, but this is untrue. He had called there in March, looking for Melcher, and was told Melcher had moved. The house was chosen only because Manson knew it.

Tex Watson climbed a telephone pole and cut two wires. Then they all climbed the fence into the garden. At this moment, a car with its headlights on approached them down the drive. A young man named Stephen Parent, who had been visiting the house-boy, William Garretson, was on his way home. He saw the dark figures and called to ask what they were doing. Without hesitation, Watson placed the barrel of a revolver against his head, and shot him five times. Then Watson turned off the car engine, and they went towards the house. They were wearing dark clothes which they had brought with them for the occasion.

Watson cut a screen from a window – a nursery that was being prepared for the expected arrival – and climbed in. He opened the front door, and let in Susan Atkins and Patricia Krenwinkel. Linda Kasabian stayed outside as a lookout.

Frykowski had fallen asleep on the settee, under the influence of a mild psychedelic drug called MDA. Abigail Folger had retired to bed, also under its influence, and was reading. Jay Sebring was in Sharon Tate's bedroom, talking to her as she lay in bed; he was fully dressed.

Frykowski woke up and found Tex Watson standing over him with a revolver. He asked him who he was. Watson said, "The devil", and ordered Susan Atkins to get a towel to tie up Frykowski's hands. After bringing the towel, Susan Atkins looked into a bedroom and saw Abigail Folger. She waved, and Abigail Folger waved back. (Susan Atkins said later that they were all on acid, which explains the casualness on both sides.) She looked into Sharon Tate's bedroom, and saw her sitting up in bed talking to Sebring. They did not see her. She went back to the sitting-room and told Watson that there were people in the bedrooms. Watson ordered her to go and bring them. She walked into each bedroom, waving a knife, and told them to go into the sitting-room. Sebring strode in angrily, asking what was happening. When Watson ordered him to lie on the floor, he made a grab for the gun. Watson shot him in the lung. They demanded money, and Abigail Folger led Susan Atkins to the bedroom, where her money was handed over.

Watson had brought a length of nylon rope with them – it seems to have been part of the scenario, planned in advance. One end was tied around Sebring's neck, and the rope was thrown over a beam. It was then tied around the necks of Abigail Folger and Sharon Tate, who had to stand upright to avoid being choked.

Someone asked, "What are you going to do to us?" and Watson replied, "You are all going to die". Watson told Susan Atkins to stab Frykowski. She tried to, but he managed to jump up. She stabbed him in the back as he ran. Then Watson shot him twice with the revolver; it jammed a third time, and Watson clubbed him with it.

Sharon Tate and Abigail Folger struggled to get free; Abigail managed to run for the door, chased by Patricia Krenwinkel. Sebring now began to struggle, so Watson ran up to him and stabbed him several times. After this, he overtook Abigail Folger, who had been stabbed by Patricia Krenwinkel. He battered her with the butt of the gun, and stabbed her several times.

Meanwhile, Frykowski, badly wounded, had managed to get out on to the lawn and was shouting for help. Linda Kasabian was horrified to realise what was going on, and shouted to Susan Atkins to stop it. Susan replied it was too late. Watson bounded into the garden and stabbed Frykowski again and again. Linda Kasabian fled.

Back in the house, Watson ordered Susan Atkins to stab Sharon Tate. Sharon begged for her life for the sake of the baby. Susan Atkins said: "Look bitch, I don't care . . ." But she couldn't bring herself to stab. Tex Watson stabbed her in the left breast, killing her, and then the other two joined in the stabbing. Susan Atkins said she began to enjoy it at this point, and wanted to gouge out her eyeballs and crush them against the wall – after all, the aim was to excite horror. But it was getting late. Watson said they had to leave. He stabbed Abigail Folger a few more times. Susan Atkins dipped a towel in blood from Sharon Tate, and wrote "Pig" on the hall door – an important point, to link this murder to that of Hinman.

Back in the car, they changed their bloodstained clothing. Linda Kasabian had climbed into the car. The clothes were dumped down a steep embankment (where they were later found by reporters). After this, they found a house with a hose on the lawn, and turned on the water to wash off the blood. The occupants of the house, an old man and woman, heard the noise, and challenged them angrily. The killers drove off, and the irritated householder noted down the number of the Ford.

Back at the ranch, Manson asked why they were back so early, but was pleased when they told him they had left everybody dead. Susan Atkins made love with somebody – she was not sure who – then went to sleep.

What Manson did for the rest of the night is not certain, he did not join Stephanie in the trailer until morning. It seems most likely that he drove over to the Polanski house, either alone or with other family members, to make sure his executioners had done their work efficiently. There were signs that someone came back to the house in the night. There was blood on the front porch, and signs that someone had tried to drag the bodies out there. Sanders's theory is that Manson wanted to arrange a tableau on the porch with suspended bodies, found there was nothing to bear their weight, and rearranged the scene as Watson and the girls had left it.

The bodies were discovered early the next morning by the housekeeper who came in daily. The Manson family watched the television next morning, and for the first time learned the names of their victims. "It really blew my mind," said Susan Atkins, who was delighted that they had murdered such a celebrity as Sharon Tate. Someone commented that The Soul (Manson) had picked a good one this time, and someone else remarked that the aim of the murders was to instil fear in Man himself, Man the Establishment. "That's what it was done for. To instill fear, to cause paranoia. To also show the black how to go about taking over the white man."

It succeeded in its purpose. The murders caused panic in the Los Angeles area, and every gun and guard dog in town was bought before nightfall. The house-boy, Garretson, was arrested, but he claimed he had been playing a record at the time of the murders, and had heard nothing. He was soon released.

That evening, Manson announced they were going to instil further terror into the "pigs". This time, he would lead them himself. He took six helpers with him: Tex Watson, Linda Kasabian, Patricia Krenwinkel, Susan Atkins, Gary Tufts (known as Clem) and Leslie Van Houten. All were high on acid.

To begin with, Manson seemed to have no definite direction. They considered a number of houses and decided against them. When they saw a white sports car ahead, halted at traffic lights, Manson prepared for action. As they drew up alongside the car, Manson started to get out, but the lights changed, and it drove away. The young man at the wheel never knew how lucky he was.

Manson now seemed to have decided where to go. He ordered Susan Atkins to drive to the affluent Los Feliz district of Los Angeles. At some point on the drive, Manson looked into the window of a lighted house, but decided not to break in because there were pictures of children on the wall. The Ford finally pulled up in front of a house belonging to a supermarket owner, Leno LaBianca. Susan Atkins recognized the house next door. She and Manson had taken an acid trip there during the Topanga Canyon period, and Manson had some reason for resenting the owner of the house. But it was the LaBianca's home that Manson chose for their second murder rampage.

Leno LaBianca, forty-four, and his wife Rosemary, thirty-eight, had spent the afternoon water-skiing. They returned to their home at 3301 Waverly Drive at some time after 1 am on Sunday morning 10 August, and removed the water skis from the top of the Thunderbird. They had bought a newspaper that carried the story of the Tate murders, and had been discussing it. They got into their nightclothes and got into bed. And shortly afterwards, Charles Manson walked into their bedroom with a gun. In a calm voice, he ordered them to get up, and said no harm would come to them. Then he tied them up. Next he went back to the car, and told Watson, Patricia Krenwinkel and Leslie Van Houten to go into the house and kill them. After that, they were to hitch-hike back to the ranch. He and the others would find another house and kill somebody else. Manson drove off.

Watson and his two helpers went into the house and found the LaBiancas tied up. Mrs LaBianca was led to the bedroom, where she was tied with an electric light flex, and a pillow case was placed over her head. Then the homicidal Watson pushed Leno LaBianca back on the settee and slashed at his throat four times with his knife. He also stabbed him four times. LaBianca bled to death. His screams caused Rosemary LaBianca to yell, "What are you doing to my husband?" Patricia Krenwinkel began to stab her in the back, severing her spine. Watson joined them in the bedroom, and he helped with the stabbing – forty times in all, mostly in the back. Leslie Van Houten had not joined in, so they asked her to do some stabling. Hesitantly, she started to stab the buttocks, then became more enthusiastic, and stabbed sixteen times.

Watson slashed the word "War" on LaBianca's chest, while Patricia Krenwinkel stabbed both bodies with a carving fork – although both were now probably dead – and left it embedded near the navel of Leno LaBianca. After this, they wrote several words in blood in different rooms: "Death to Pigs", "Rise" and "Healter skelter" (a misprint for Helter Skelter). After this they took a shower and changed their clothes, ate some food and fed the three dogs (who had watched the murders without barking, and even licked the killers' hands). Then they walked out of the house, and hitch-hiked back to the Spahn ranch without any problems. There they found Manson, who had decided not to do any killing after all. He had taken his group to a beach south of Venice, and asked the girls if there was not some "pig" they could kill in a nearby apartment. Linda and Sandy Good had been picked up by an actor some weeks before, and had returned to his apartment near the beach. Linda Kasabian showed Manson the building. They went inside, and she pointed out what she claimed to be the flat of Saladin Nader, a film actor. (It was, she claims, the wrong apartment – she had already decided not to kill him). Manson told his three assassins to knock on the door and overpower Nader when he opened it. Then he left them and went off in the Ford. Linda knocked on a door – the wrong one – and when someone opened it a fraction, apologized, said she had the wrong place, and left. They hitch-hiked back to the Spahn ranch. The bodies of the LaBiancas were found the next morning by their sixteen-year-old son, who had fortunately been elsewhere for the night.

Manson was arrested six days after the LaBianca murder, but not for murder. The local police had decided it was time to clamp down on the hippie commune because of its car-thieving activities. There was a swoop on the ranch, and twenty-five people were arrested. The police seized a number of guns and other weapons, and took down the numbers of the cars – including the Ford that had been used in both murders. Unfortunately, the man who had chased Tex Watson off his lawn after the Sharon Tate murder had not informed the police, otherwise the case might have been solved forthwith. They were all released three days later, when a judge decided that there was insufficient evidence to charge them. Three days later, Manson was again arrested when two policemen walked into a hut where he was lying naked with Stephanie. The police found what they took to be a reefer in Manson's shirt pocket – Susan Atkins had placed it there – but upon laboratory analysis, it turned out not to be pot, and Manson was released.

On 26 August 1969, the family murdered a ranch hand, "Shorty" O'Shea. Manson had various things against him. He had married a negro woman; he knew about the shooting of Bernard Crowe (who was still believed to be dead); and he disliked having the family on the Spahn ranch. Details of his murder are not known. No body was ever found, although his car was discovered in a Canoga parking lot. Sanders says the whole family were involved in the murder, and that he was tortured beforehand. After this, his body was chopped up and partly burned.

In early September, the family once more moved to Death Valley. Little is known of their activities during this final period. Ed Sanders describes the attempted murder of a prospector named Crockett – which came to nothing – and the hi-jacking of a frozen food truck by Susan Atkins and Leslie Van Houten. He also reports a story that there were further murders there – two boys and a girl, but gives no details.

Manson's major mistake seems to have been the wanton burning of a Michigan skip-loader – a kind of bulldozer – which had dug large holes in a dirt road. It belonged to the rangers at the Death Valley National Monument, and they were enraged at this destruction of an expensive piece of equipment. They found tyre tracks leading from the scene, and some miles further along the road, a wrecked Ford car – which the family had driven into a tree – with more identifiable tyre tracks nearby. These tracks belonged to a stolen car, a Toyota, and two days later, rangers saw the Toyota in a canyon near Ballarat. A check on its licence plates revealed that they were false. Eventually, they discovered the stolen Toyota, without licence plates, not far from the hut of the miner Paul Crockett. He talked to the police about the family, and the search for them now began. But the police were still unaware that the hippies were hiding out at the Barker ranch. (In the hundreds of square miles of desert, locating an army would be slow work.) It took them until 9 October to track down the family. Just before dawn, two teams of police officers closed in on the ranch. Manson was not there, but the police arrested a number of his followers, mostly girls, who tried to disconcert the officers by urinating in front of them and taking off their clothes.

Manson returned to Death Valley three days later, on 12 October. A few of the girls who had escaped the raid told him what had happened. A few hours later, they were all eating in the kitchen when more police burst in. Manson dived for a tiny cupboard under the kitchen sink, and was almost overlooked. As the hippies were marched off to jail, police noticed that Manson said something in a a low voice, and the others murmured "Amen, amen".

Kitty Lutesinger – the girl who had earlier run away from the Spahn ranch – was in police custody. She had returned to the family, but decided to desert again in Death Valley. She and another young girl had run away one night, and bumped into the police who were on their way to raid the Barker ranch. Kitty was wanted for questioning in connection with the Hinman murder – since she had been Bobby Beausoleil's girlfriend. She now told the police that she had nothing to do with the murder: it was "Sadie" and Mary. And the police now had Sadie – Susan Atkins – in custody. She was handed over to the Los Angeles police. She soon admitted being present at Hinman's house, but denied having any part in the killing.

Boredom, and perhaps radio news bulletins about the progress of the Tate murder investigation, led her to drop hints to fellow prisoners about her part in the Sharon Tate killing. She told one cell-mate about it, but the woman kept the secret. Later, she told another cell-mate, Virginia Graham, in considerable detail. Virginia Graham let another friend – Ronni Howard – in on the secret. It was Ronni Howard who finally talked to the police about Susan Atkins's detailed confessions. On 1 December, the Chief of Police of Los Angeles told a Press conference that three people had been charged with the Tate-LaBianca murders: Tex Watson, Linda Kasabian and Patricia Krenwinkel. Later, Manson, Susan Atkins and Leslie Van Houten were also charged.

The trial, one of the longest and most expensive in Los Angeles history (by October 1970 it had already passed the quarter million dollar mark, and would continue until late the following March) was noisy and confused. Manson and the four girls were charged with the Tate and LaBianca murders. (Beausoleil was convicted of the Hinman murder.) Predictably, Manson tried to turn it into an indictment of the judges and modern society. "You make your children what they are." "You people put importance on your lives. My life has never been important to anyone . . . The parents kicked them out and I did the best I could and took them up on my garbage dump . . ." "These children – everything they have done, they have done for the love of their brothers . . ."

There was a slightly insane air about the whole trial, as if everyone were talking at cross purposes. Observers in other countries found it difficult to understand – as, no doubt, did many Americans. Manson's general indictment of society could well have some foundation. But if he had really ordered the murder of so many people then he was a mad dog, a paranoiac, and was guilty. But Manson and thousands of young followers did not, apparently, agree. To begin with, this was perhaps understandable. In effect, Manson was condemned from the moment of his arrest. America's middle classes, said one reporter, had gone into convulsions of delight that the hippies had at last got what was coming to them. This was what they had always suspected lay behind the movement. Photographs of Manson made him look insane, a manic Rasputin. When the reporter of the *Los Angeles Free Press* got in to see him shortly after his arrest, he was surprised to find a calm, quiet-spoken little man who talked reasonably and without any sign of paranoia, and who complained that he was not being allowed to see anyone. The newspapers splashed stories about Satan's Slaves, about orgies of sex and drugs, sadism and murder. The "Confession" of Susan Atkins, edited by Lawrence Schiller, was released to the world's newspapers (in full) on 14 December 1969, and the paperback book appeared the following January. (On 9 December, the judge had imposed a "gag" on all media, ordering that the case should not be discussed publicly; ten days later, *Life* carried the full story of the "love and terror cult".) And in August 1970, before the trial was half over, President Nixon referred to Manson's guilt in a speech. All this indicated that justice was not getting done in an ideal manner. But in the long run, it got done.

It was the weird logic of Manson's supporters that created the mad atmosphere. Asked if she thought the killing of eight people was unimportant, Susan Atkins countered by asking if the killing of thousands of people with napalm was important. By the rules of ordinary logic, this is nothing more than an attempt at smart repartee. Had Sharon Tate or the LaBiancas killed anybody with napalm? Or did she mean that eight more people made no difference? But when so many young people made a hero of Manson, the older generation began to wonder if it was not somehow missing the point. Were the murders really their fault, as Manson seemed to imply? And when Manson, Susan Atkins, Leslie Van Houten and Patricia Krenwinkel were found guilty and sentenced to death on 30 March 1970 (Linda Kasabian escaped by turning State's evidence) the question was still unanswered. The murders had caused a certain revulsion among the young, and a "Jesus cult" had sprung up among hippies, old-fashioned Billy Graham-type evangelism, but many still regarded Manson as some kind of a symbol. In a TV programme about the Jesus cult, one girl, asked if she believed in Christianity, said: "No, I believe in black magic and Charles Manson and all that". The interviewer did not bother to ask her to explain herself. Apparently he understood exactly what she meant.

And what is the significance of the Manson case?

As one of the most sensational murder cases of the late 1960s, it certainly has its importance. But this importance has been exaggerated by the social commentators. Kerouac was an archetypal hippie; Manson was not. Manson became a hippie by chance, but fundamentally he was no more a hippie than Netchaev or Hitler or Stalin. The puzzling and paradoxical nature of the case is the result of Manson's own divided personality. To a large extent, he seems to have been a genuinely compassionate and well-meaning person. He was also a Violent Man, in Van Vogt's sense, and this aspect of him developed swiftly after his first acceptance as a kind of messiah in Haight-Ashbury. As he became accustomed to absolute obedience, he also came to feel that people who crossed him – or double-crossed him – were insects who should be stamped out. This tendency must have been encouraged by the slavish admiration he received from his admiring family. Teenaged girls can be hysterical creatures – as anyone who has ever watched a pop concert knows. They are prone to adoration, and a mentally balanced male, while he might take temporary advantage of such adoration, would end by fleeing from it as a spiritual corrosive. Fools are always a bore, whether they are adoring fools or hostile fools. Manson lacked the self-critical faculty to maintain a balanced view of himself. Encouraged by his women, he became increasingly a "right man".

He was also, for the first time in his life, the leader, the tribal chieftain. And the leader is under an obligation to show himself in a good light. To appear, if possible, as the conqueror. But in practical terms, Manson was not a conqueror. He had achieved nothing. No doubt he would assert that he had no desire to achieve anything in a corrupt society, but his attempts to become a record star contradict this.

In another sense, Manson achieved overnight success. He went to Haight-Ashbury an unknown ex-jailbird, a kind of Charlie Chaplin figure, strumming a guitar and singing in a voice as undistinguished as Bob Dylan's. A year later, he had become a sort of Jewish patriarch, surrounded by his tribe, the undisputed leader, the dictator in power. He handed out reefers and acid to his girls. He handed out girls to his male followers. Quite indisputably, he had become Someone.

Success however, brings its obligations. When the dictator is in power, he has to do something to prove that his followers made the right choice. Hitler started a European war for the same reason. And Manson also thought in terms of war, war against the "pigs".

The resentment he felt about society is understandable enough. One of the most interesting features of the case is that, in spite of this hatred, Manson was not a violent type. Netchaev killed the student Ivanov himself. Brady murdered Edward Evans and joked about it afterwards. Manson does not seem to have been personally violent – except in the case of Hinman, when he slashed at his ear with a sword. He directed his followers to commit the violence, at least, in the cases where evidence is available. One suspects that his remarkable capacity for inspiring love was due to his non-violence.

This in turn raises the speculation: how far were his women followers – particularly Susan Atkins – responsible for what happened? Manson may have had natural leader qualities, but to some extent, he was *chosen* by his women. It was they who elevated him into his position, a combination of Elvis Presley and Jesus. But Susan Atkins's attitude towards him seems to have been ambivalent. "He gave my faith in myself back to me." Possibly he gave her too much. "Sadie Mae Glutz" is an ugly name, compared to Susan Denise Atkins, it suggests a prostitute out of a Mickey Spillane novel. But Manson gave her the name while they were still living with Gary Hinman. It was Sadie Mae, according to Beausoleil, who told the ranch hand Shorty O'Shea, that Manson had killed a Black Panther ("and she didn't know who else," added Beausoleil.) It was Sadie Mae who told her cell-mate about the Tate and LaBianca murders, and who implicated Manson. Steve Geller, the American novelist, attended some of the first sessions of the trial, and wrote down his impressions of Susan Atkins:

In the middle stands Susan Atkins . . . wearing a cutesy-pie salmon pink dress with eighteenth-century dollymop puffy sleeves, and ten pink buttons down the front . . . She is wearing an I.D. plastic band, hospital style, on her left wrist. And I notice that she is hairy, her arms and wrists. With a slight trace of a moustache above her lip . . . With her head hanging down slightly, ashamed. The finger girl . . .

I begin to realize why I've such a nasty feeling towards her: because she's too composed; in all this, there seems to be a different kind of effect, a super-star, super-cool self-consciousness. Granted, she's been this way before: she's been arrested eight times in three years . . . Her testimony had been leaked to the press, her story bought for a reported $175,000. In her own way, she's bigger business than her family father, Charles Manson, could ever be . . . It's obvious also that when Judge Keene is addressing the girls collectively, he addresses Miss Atkins as the spokeswoman. He knows the programme. She's one of the stars . . .

Lawrence Schiller describes her as "a sweet-faced young woman with luminous brown eyes", and some reporters described her as pretty. Her photographs contradict this. She is a well-built, sullen-featured girl, and in most of the pictures, her face has a resentful expression. An underground hippie newspaper refers to her as Manson's Judas Iscariot. And it seems a reasonable assumption that she confessed out of some obscure desire for publicity and revenge. Manson built up his hippie empire, his castle in the desert, like Hasan bin Sabbah, the grand master of the Assassins. With a few casual remarks, Susan Atkins made the whole thing topple like a child's sand castle.

But in fairness to Manson, we have to admit that there *was* an element of justice in the counter-charges he brought against the judges. For the real mystery of the case is the psychological mystery. How could a sincere, fairly intelligent, well-meaning little man who gave out an aura of love turn into a dictator obsessed with murder? The answer is that a lifetime in jail, of being pushed around by authority, could destroy the potential of a Saint Francis or Shakespeare. There *must* be psychological tests to enable us to recognize the potentialities of a Manson before his hatred of society becomes the permanent foundation of his consciousness. The sympathy shown for Manson by American youth was basically a recognition that good, creative human potential was here allowed to stagnate and turn rotten: for anyone under twenty, it is too easy to put yourself in his shoes. If Manson is guilty of criminal violence, society is guilty of criminal negligence. And unlike Manson, society is in the position of being able to learn from its mistakes.

At the time Manson came to Haight-Ashbury, a serial killer called Albert DeSalvo was beginning a life sentence for a number of rapes and burglaries. Oddly enough, he was never charged with the series of sex murders that earned him the label "the Boston Strangler". The first six victims of the Strangler, killed between 14 June 1962 and 20 August 1962, were elderly women, one of them eighty-five. Then, after murdering a twenty-five-year-old black girl, Sophie Clark, DeSalvo began killing younger women. The last victim – number thirteen – was nineteen-year-old Mary Sullivan, killed and raped on 4 January 1964. After that murder, DeSalvo did something completely untypical of the serial killer, and returned to raping but not killing his victims. His sexual appetite was apparently immense – on one occasion he raped four women in one day. Yet he was often curiously gentle with his victims, sometimes even apologising. He became known as the Green Man because he dressed in green clothes and wore green glasses. It was when police realised that descriptions of the Green Man sounded remarkably like descriptions of an earlier offender, known as the Measuring Man, that they arrested Albert DeSalvo. In 1959 and 1960, a polite young man had knocked on doors and told young women that he was from a modelling agency. If they expressed an interest in becoming models, he would measure them with a tape, and note down their vital statistics. He never made any attempt to commit sexual assault, but many of the girls offered themselves to him, presumably hoping this would ensure the job. When they failed to hear from the agency, some of the girls became annoyed and reported him to the police. In March 1960, DeSalvo was arrested, and served eleven months in jail. It was after he came out that the murders of the Boston Strangler began. And the identity of the Strangler was still unknown when

Albert DeSalvo was sent to the Bridgewater mental institution in 1965 for "observation" before being charged with the Green Man rapes. It was there that he told a fellow prisoner that he was the Boston Strangler, and the prisoner – a killer named George Nassar – reported it to his lawyer, F. Lee Bailey. It was Bailey who finally induced De Salvo to confess in detail to the thirteen Boston murders.

Why *did* DeSalvo stop killing? The conclusion of Dr James Brussel, who examined him, was that he had finally outgrown the need to kill. DeSalvo had always been sexually insatiable – he told Brussel that during his late childhood and teens, he had an almost perpetual erection, and that within ten minutes of orgasm, he was ready to make love again. In Germany, during US army service, he married a German girl, but she found his sexual demands excessive. After he came out of prison in 1961, she refused to allow him sexual intercourse. It was then that DeSalvo began to kill and rape. Brussel concluded that he had at first chosen elderly victims because he had received little affection from his mother as a child, and was expressing resentment. After killing and raping Sophie Clark, he discovered that he preferred younger women. Yet he never ceased to feel intensely guilty (he was a good Catholic) and after the murder of Mary Sullivan, finally experienced such revulsion that he decided never to kill again. He had come close to sparing another victim because, he said, she "treated him like a man".

DeSalvo was stabbed to death in jail in November 1973. His killer was never identified.

The Boston Strangler case throws an interesting light on the psychology of the serial killer. The Manson case demonstrates how someone can kill out of resentment, a feeling that certain members of society are "pigs" who do not deserve to live. Killers of this type are cut off from reality by a shell of resentment. DeSalvo's childhood was hard and brutal – his father once broke his mother's fingers one by one – yet he never developed the resentment that is so typical of the serial killer. The driving force behind the murders was his immense sexual obsession. Yet – as Brussel noted – he was a man of considerable personal charm, who found it easy to talk his way into the homes of his victims. It was because he found himself entering into personal relations with his victims that he found it increasingly difficult to kill. His last victim, Mary Sullivan, tried to talk him out of rape, and her words struck home. He also admitted that she reminded him of his own daughter.

It is precisely because most serial killers are incapable of entering into close relations that they are capable of murder. Some, like the California killer Ed Kemper, are so mentally disturbed that the killing is an act of pure destruction, like an angry child smashing a toy. Kemper was a necrophiliac who was obsessed with cutting up bodies. He killed and dissected six girls in 1972 and 1973; and finally he killed his mother and one of her elderly friends, removing the heads. Yet he also described how he had picked up two girl students, and – deciding that he had to stop this rampage of murder – took them to where they wanted to go and let them out. Like DeSalvo, Kemper was still capable of normal personal relationships. On the other hand, Herb Mullin, who killed thirteen people in California at the same time that Kemper was operating, was a full-blown schizophrenic whose murders were committed in a delusional state. He heard voices ordering him to kill, and told a minister to whom he went for advice that "Satan gets into people and makes them do things they don't want to". (Many serial killers have expressed the same view. Peter Sutcliffe, the "Yorkshire Ripper", declared that he felt he was possessed by the devil, and we have seen that H.H. Holmes came to entertain a similar belief.)

In considering the psychology of the serial killer, this is the crucial question: the nature of his relation to other people. Killers like Panzram and Ian Brady build up a feeling of resentment, based on self-pity, that makes it easy to kill. Killers like the Yorkshire Ripper, and probably Jack the Ripper himself, avoid the problem of the personal relation by attacking the victims from behind. (Sutcliffe struck them on the head with a hammer.) Others are forced to deliberately suppress their "human" side. Most of this type have recognised clearly that that are virtually dual personalities, Jekyll and Hydes, and that they have allowed Mr Hyde to gain control. One twenty-two-year-old sex murderer, Steven Judy, who admitted that he had "left a string" of murdered women across America, begged the jury to sentence him to death in case future victims were their wives or daughters. (He was electrocuted in March 1981.)

One of the best-documented examples of the "Jekyll and Hyde" syndrome is the case of Ted Bundy, perhaps the most notorious of modern serial killers. In 1978, before he had been sentenced to death, Bundy made it known that he would be willing to talk to a professional writer, with a view to telling his story. Two journalists, Stephen Michaud and Hugh Aynesworth, went to talk to him in jail, and the result was a book called *The Only Living Witness*, which affords some remarkable insights into the mind of a serial killer.

Early in the morning of Saturday 16 August 1975, Police Sergeant Bob Hayward was driving through a quiet neighbourhood of Salt Lake City, on the lookout for drunken drivers, when a Volkswagen suddenly accelerated away from the pavement and drove off at high speed. Hayward chased it across two stop lights (which the driver ignored), and finally caught up with it in a vacant gas station. The tall good-looking young man who climbed out was dressed entirely in black clothes; his driver's license showed him to be Theodore Robert Bundy, of 565 First Avenue. When Hayward looked in his car, he discovered a pantyhose mask with eye holes cut in it, and a pair of handcuffs. Deciding that Bundy was probably a burglar, Hayward placed him under arrest. He was booked at the local police station, then released on his own recognisances. But when the case was mentioned at a detective conference a few days later, one detective thought be recognised the name Bundy. He checked in his file, and discovered that Ted Bundy had been a suspect in a series of sex murders that had taken place in Seattle in the previous year – a series that had, in fact, become known as "the Ted Murders".

On 4 January 1974, a bizarre sex crime had occurred in a students' rooming house in Seattle. Sharon Clarke shared the house with a number of students. Her bedroom was in the basement. When she failed to appear by mid-afternoon on 5 January, friends went down to see if she had overslept. Sharon was unconscious, and her face was covered with blood. The weapon was a metal bar that had been wrenched from the bed frame. The attacker had not raped her, but the metal bar had been thrust into her vagina, causing lacerations. After more than a week in a coma, Sharon recovered, but she was unable to provide any useful information. The attack left her with brain damage.

The lesson of this case seemed to be that basement doors should never be left unlocked. The police theorised that the attacker had watched her undressing through her bedroom window, then found the unlocked door and made his way into her bedroom.

The same method, apparently, was used in the case of twenty-one-year-old Lynda Ann Healy. But Lynda was no longer in her bed when a fellow student went in to find out why the alarm was still buzzing at half-past-eight in the morning. Since the bed had been neatly made up, the girl assumed that Lynda had gone to classes. It was not until that evening, when Lynda's parents arrived for dinner, that someone pulled back the bedclothes and found that the sheets and pillowcase were stained with blood. In the closet, Lynda's nightgown, also stained with blood, hung on a peg. It looked as if the attacker had entered the basement, possibly by using the spare key kept in the mailbox, and knocked her unconscious with a blow that had probably cracked her skull. Then, for some reason, he had removed the nightgown, probably to dress her, and remade the bed. If the intention had simply been rape, it could have been accomplished there and then. The inference seemed to be that this man wanted to take his time, to enjoy in full the pleasure of possession.

A few days later, an unknown man rang the police, and told them that Sharon Clarke's attacker was the same person who had abducted Lynda Healey. According to the caller, the man had been seen outside both houses.

Two weeks later, nineteen-year-old Donna Gail Manson left her dormitory on the Evergreen campus, southwest of Olympia, on her way to a jazz concert. When she failed to return, her friends were not too concerned – Donna was prone to take off on spur-of-the-moment hitchhiking trips – and her disappearance was not reported for six days. Police learned that she had been obsessed with magic and the occult, and had been prone to depression. By the time they were called in, the trail was cold.

Susan Rancourt was a student at Central Washington State College in Ellensburg, on the other side of the Cascade Mountains. She was a pretty, shy blonde girl who was afraid of the dark. On 17 April 1974, she agreed to meet a girl friend to attend a German film, but failed to arrive. Like Lynda and Donna, she simply disappeared. Investigating officers asked whether any suspicious characters had been seen around the campus recently, and one girl was able to tell them a peculiar story. She had been coming out of the library five days before Susan had disappeared, and noticed a tall, good-looking man with his arm in a sling. He had dropped some books, and asked the girl if she would help him carry them to his car. This proved to be a tan Volkswagen, parked a few hundred yards away and as she came closer, she noticed that the passenger seat was missing. Some curious intuition of danger made her dump the books on the hood the car and run away.

On the day of Susan Rancourt's disappearance, the same man had accosted another girl and asked her to help him carry some packages to his car. He then asked her if she would get inside and try the ignition while he adjusted something under the hood. The girl had no desire to enter a strange car, so she made an excuse and hurried away.

Susan's route to the cinema would have taken her past the student parking lot . . .

The next disappearance took place on 6 May 1974. Roberta Kathleen Parks left her room on the Oregon State University campus at Corvallis, en route for the Student Union Building. She never arrived. This time no one had seen anything suspicious – no brown Volkswagen, no man with his arm in a sling. Kathy's abductor had left no clues.

This was not the case when twenty-two-year old Brenda Carol Ball vanished on 1 June 1974. Brenda shared lodgings with two student room-mates near Highline Community College. On the night of her disappearance, she had spent some time in the Flame Tavern near Seattle Airport, and when she left at 2 am she was hoping to find a lift home to Burien. Because Brenda was also an impulse-traveller, her room-mates waited for almost three weeks before reporting her disappearance. By that time, the only thing the police could discover was that she had last been seen in the car park talking to a handsome man with his arm in a sling . . .

Nine days later, eighteen-year-old University of Washington co-ed Georgann Hawkins left the Beta House on campus where her boyfriend lived to walk the hundred yards back to her own hall of residence. When she failed to arrive, her room-mate notified the police. Several students reported seeing a stranger on crutches, carrying a briefcase, in the area around the Beta House. One girl student had seen the man dropping his briefcase several times and had offered to help. But first she had to make a call at one of the students' residences. This took longer than expected, and when she came out, the man had gone.

Lynda, Donna, Susan, Kathy, Brenda and Georgann – six abductions in as many months. As July started, police were wondering who would be the seventh victim.

That question was answered in a manner that would cause nationwide headlines. On 14 July 1974, the handsome man with his arm in a sling had abducted two girls from the Lake Sammamish State Park – and, moreover, had done it openly and brazenly in front of a crowd of witnesses. The park, twelve miles east of Seattle, is a favourite picnic spot. At about 12.15, a girl named Doris Grayling was approached by a wavy-haired man with his arm in a sling, who asked her if she would help him lift his boat on to his car. She accompanied him to the car – a brown VW – but he then told her the boat was further up the hill. Unwilling to go further with a stranger, she excused herself and left. The man smiled politely and apologised. Next he approached a pretty blonde named Janice Ott, who was lying alone by the lake. When he asked her to help him with his boat, she invited him to sit down and talk. People sitting only a few yards away heard him introduce himself as "Ted", and noted that he had an accent that might have been Canadian or even British. Finally, after talking for ten minutes, Janice accompanied him to the car. She did not return to her place on the beach.

At mid-afternoon, eighteen-year-old Denise Naslund left a group of friends, which included her boyfriend, and went to the ladies' lavatory. Four hours later, when she had still failed to return, they reported her disappearance to the park ranger. Police investigating the case the next day learned that the young man with his arm in a sling had approached several girls with the same story about needing help with a boat. One of them had been approached, and had refused, only a few minutes before Denise Naslund disappeared.

Because "Ted" had been seen – and heard – by so many people, the Seattle newspapers were able to publish descriptions and artists' impressions of the suspect. As a result, the police received many tip-offs that the man sounded like the University of Washington law student Ted Bundy. One of those to make this suggestion was an old friend of Bundy, the crime reporter Anne Rule. Another was a girlfriend of four years' standing. But Bundy was only one of hundreds of suspects – the number soon swelled to 3,500 – and at first he seemed perhaps one of the least likely. He was apparently a decent, friendly young man who had been a political canvasser and worked for the Crime Commission and the Department of Justice Planning. Besides, would a sex-maniac abductor give his real name within the hearing of several other people? The Bundy file soon sank close to the bottom of the long list of suspects.

On 6 September 1974, grouse hunters two miles east of Lake Sammamish Park found human bones in the undergrowth. Dental charts identified them as those of Janice Ott and Denise Naslund. There was also a thigh bone belonging to a third body, but this defied identification.

In any case, as the months went by, it began to look as if the "Seattle murders" were now at an end. And, by an odd coincidence, a similar series was about to begin in Salt Lake City, where Ted Bundy had moved to become a law student at the University of Utah.

The good-looking, well-dressed young man aproached eighteen-year old Carol DaRonch in the shopping mall in Murray, a suburb of Salt Lake City, on a damp November evening in 1974.

"Excuse me, miss. I am a police officer. Did you leave your car in the Sears car park?"

"Yes".

"What is its licence number?"

"KAD 032".

"We have apprehended a man who was trying to break into it. Would you mind coming with me to see if anything has been stolen?"

The parking lot was some distance, and as they walked towards it through the drizzle, Carol noticed that the "police officer" was allowing her to lead the way. She asked:

"Could I see your identification?"

The man drew a wallet from his inside pocket, and opened it. In the semi-darkness, she could see something that looked like a police badge. This reassured her.

She was also relieved to see that her car seemed to be undamaged, and that it was still locked. She opened the driver's door, and told him that nothing was missing. As the man bent over to try the passenger door, she noticed a pair of shiny handcuffs in the inside pocket of his green sports jacket.

"My partner has taken the suspect to the sub-office on the other side of the mall. Would you mind coming with me?"

By now she was beginning to feel suspicious. But the man – who was about ten years her senior – seemed so serious and self-assured that she lacked the confidence to ask further questions. On the far side of the mall they approached a small building which the man identified as the "sub-office". Carol was unaware that it was a laundromat. The man tried the side-door, announced that his partner must have taken the suspect back to police headquarters, and told Carol that he would drive her there to sign a complaint.

"What's your name?" she asked, as they approached a battered-looking Volkswagen.

"Officer Roseland of the Murray Police Department."

The vehicle certainly did not look like a police car. It was scratched and dented, and as she climbed in, she observed a tear in the back seat.

In the enclosed space, she noticed alcohol on the man's breath. And when he made a U-turn and went in the opposite direction to the police station, vague anxiety suddenly turned to alarm. Minutes later, the VW turned into a dark side street and screeched to a stop outside a darkened high school, the front wheel bouncing up the pavement. It had taken Carol a long time to realise that she was being kidnapped, but as soon as she did, she made a grab for the handle and threw open the door. With terrifying speed, the man seized her wrist and snapped a handcuff on it. But as he tried to grab the other wrist of the screaming, struggling girl, he made a mistake and closed the handcuff on the same one. Then he pulled out a gun, pointed it at her head, and threatened to blow her brains out. Too terrified to care, Carol grabbed the handle, opened the door again, and fell out. The man was following her, a metal bar in his hand, when they were illuminated by the headlights of an oncoming car. As Carol ran towards it, screaming, the VW accelerated away.

Half an hour later, the hysterical girl told her story to a sergeant in police headquarters. He noticed a few spots of blood on the white fur trim of her coat – blood from scratches that Carol had inflicted on the face of her would-be abductor – and clipped them off for forensic examination.

In Viewmont High School, a few miles north of Murray, an audience of students and parents prepared to watch a comedy called *The Redhead*, presented by the school drama society. The drama teacher, Jean Graham, was of much the same type as Carol DaRonch – tall, pretty, with long brown hair parted in the middle. Just before the curtain was due to rise, she was walking towards the dressing-rooms when she was approached by a tall, good-looking young man who asked if if she would go to the car park and identify a car for him. Jean Graham was in a hurry, so she told him firmly that she did not have time. But, being less shy than Carol DaRonch, she took a good look at him, and observed that he had brown wavy hair and a moustache, and that in addition to the well-cut sports jacket he wore dress slacks and patent leather shoes. Moreover, he was persistent—in the first intermission, he was still there, and half an hour later, he again asked her to go with him to the parking lot. "It will only take a few seconds." Luckily for her, she was still in a hurry and declined.

In the audience sat seventeen-year-old Debbie Kent, together with her parents. Debbie was not entirely happy. She had left her brother Blair at a skating rink, promising to pick him up after the play. Now the play was overrunning, and Blair would be wondering what had happened to them. Debbie's father was just recovering from a heart attack, and she was anxious not to worry him. This is why, half-an-hour before the end, she decided to skip the rest of the play, and fetch her brother.

Jean Graham was seated on the back row, glad the play was drawing to a close, when the door opened and the handsome young man came in and sat down in the seat opposite. He was breathing heavily, as though he had been running, and the people in front of him looked round irritably. When the curtain finally came down, he stood up and hurried out.

As the school slowly emptied, Debbie's parents waited nervously for her to return. Eventually, they decided to walk to the home of friends who lived nearby. And it was as they were crossing the parking lot that they saw their car was still there, and realised that their daughter had not made the trip to the skating rink.

The following morning, police investigating Debbie's disappearance searched the school grounds. Just outside the south door, not far from the parking lot, they found a handcuff key. Residents in a nearby block of apartments described hearing two piercing screams coming from the parking lot some time after ten the previous evening. And it was when the police discovered that the handcuff key fitted the cuffs taken from the wrist of Carol DaRonch that they began to piece together what had probably happened. Carol's description of the "policeman" and Jean Graham's description of the persistent young man were too close for coincidence. After the failure to seize Carol, he had tried again. Debbie Kent had been grabbed as she walked into the car park. She had time to scream before she was rendered unconscious, probably with the iron bar. Why then did her attacker return to the auditorium? Probably because he knew that her screams had been overheard, and did not want to be seen driving away in his easily identifiable VW. If he stayed where he was, any watchers in the apartment building would lose interest. So he went back into the school, waited until the play was over, then drove off with his unconscious victim. All this indicated exceptional coolness – the coolness of a man who was no amateur in this game of deceit and abduction . . .

In fact, Debbie Kent was the fourth girl to disappear in the Salt Lake City area in five weeks. The first had been a sixteen-year-old High School cheerleader, Nancy Wilcox. On 2 October 1974, Nancy had quarrelled with her parents, and apparently accepted a lift in a Volkswagen. She had not been seen since. On October 18, Melissa Smith, the seventeen-year-old daughter of the Midvale police chief, left a pizza restaurant late at night with the intention of hitching a lift. She failed to return home. Nine days later, her naked body was found in Summit Park, violated and strangled, her face so battered that even her father failed to identify her at first.

On 3 October, another teenager, Laura Aime, set out for a Halloween party. She was six feet tall, an excellent horsewoman, and had a reputation of being able to take care of herself. Around midnight, she seems to have accepted a lift. Her body, beaten and violated, was discovered in the mountains four weeks later, on 27 November 1974.

The disappearances now ceased – at least, in the Salt Lake City area. In nearby Colorado a number of girls vanished in 1975, but there was nothing to connect these cases with the Utah abductions. On Saturday 16 August 1975, Police Sergeant Bob Hayward arrested Theodore Bundy after a car chase in Salt Lake City, and charged him with intent to commit a felony. Three days later, Detective Jerry Thompson realised that he had a file on Bundy in his office – sent to him by a Seattle detective, Bob Keppel – and that Bundy was a leading suspect in the "Ted murders" of the previous year. In fact, Keppel had finally decided that Bundy was "clean" – a hard-working law student with a degree in psychology from the University of Washington simply did not seem the sex maniac type. The iron bar, the handcuffs and the pantyhose mask seemed to cast doubt on that diagnosis. And at that point, Thompson remembered something else: the attempted kidnapping of Carol DaRonch. She had also been handcuffed and threatened with an iron bar. And her abductor, like Bundy, drove a battered VW.

When Bundy was re-arrested two days later, he showed no sign of concern. He knew enough about the law to realise that the burgling-tool charge was no more than a vague misdemeanour that could not made to stick. And under questioning, he showed the coolness and casual self-confidence that would become so familiar to the detectives trying to prove him guilty of murder. The pantyhose mask was something he wore when skiing to keep his face warm. He had found the handcuffs in a garbage can. The ice pick and the iron bar were merely part of his car toolkit . . . As to searching his apartment, he gave his permission freely.

Naturally, they found nothing suspicious – Ted had had almost a week to clear up. But when Thompson noticed a number of holiday brochures about Colorado, he recalled that several girls had vanished there during the past year. Asked if he had ever been in Colorado, Bundy flatly denied it. The brochures and a map had been left in his apartment by friends. In a drawer Thompson noticed a bunch of credit card receipts, and slipped one into his pocket.

Back in his office, Thompson talked to the Colorado police about the disappearances there. The map, he told them, looked new and unused. But one of the ski brochures had a cross next to a hotel called The Wildwood in Snowmass.

There was an exclamation at the other end of the line. "A girl called Caryn Campbell disappeared from there in January. Her body was found a month later. She'd been raped and battered to death."

Suddenly, it was all looking far more promising. And if Carol DaRonch identified Bundy as her abductor, they would have a case. But here Thompson met an unexpected setback. Carol had been so shatterd by her experience that her memory was poor. Looking through a pile of mugshots, she agreed that the one of Bundy looked a little like her abductor, but that is as far as she would go. And when they took her to see Bundy's Volkswagen, it was to discover that it had been recently resprayed.

On October 1, Thompson's luck began to improve. Bundy was taken to the Hall of Justice for a line-up. The women who were there to identify the abductor were Carol DaRonch, Jean Graham – the drama teacher – and a student from the Viewmont High School. And although Bundy had shaved off his moustache, had his hair cut short, and changed the parting to the other side, all three identified him. Later that day, Judge Cowans signed a complaint charging Bundy with kidnap and attempted homicide.

Within twenty-four hours, the name of Ted Bundy was known to headline writers across the United States. By now, the bones of four more of the Seattle victims – Lynda Healey, Susan Rancourt, Kathy Parks and Brenda Ball – had been discovered on Taylor Mountain, twenty miles from Seattle. The implications were horrible. Their abductor could have had only one purpose in taking them there – to be able to take as much time as he liked with the sexual assaults, before strangling or battering them to death. The implications of the double-disappearance from Lake Sammamish Park were just as bad. A man who abducts and rapes a girl would hardly be expected to abduct another girl a few hours later. "Ted" had wanted to experience the pleasure of violating two girls at the same time, possibly in front of one another. Clearly, he was more than an ordinary sex killer; he was an almost inhuman monster. This is why the news that Bundy had been charged was worthy of nationwide headlines.

Within eight weeks, he was out on bail – his mother had borrowed the money. $15,000. She, of course, had no doubt of his innocence. Neither had his student friends in Salt Lake City – they were convinced that the cops were out to frame him. Two ex-girlfriends were less certain. For the past five years he had been more or less engaged to a girl in Seattle, but she had started to experience doubts when she saw the artist's impressions of "Ted" in the newspapers. When she found plaster of Paris in his drawer, she had finally telephoned the police to relay her suspicions. And a more recent girlfriend described how Ted liked to tie her up with nylon stockings before having sex.

That, of course, was no proof that he was a killer. What *did* look more like proof was the fact that Bundy's blood group was the same as that of the blood found on Carol DaRonch after her struggle with her abductor, and that strands of hair found in his car were virtually identical with those of Carol DaRonch and Melissa Smith. A decade later, after the discovery of "genetic fingerprinting", the blood alone would have established Bundy's guilt or innocence. But in 1975, neither the blood nor hair evidence was conclusive. Neither was the fact that the credit card receipts proved that Bundy *had* been in Colorado around the dates when girls had disappeared.

When Bundy finally walked into court in Salt Lake City on 23 February 1976, another thing became immediately evident: that most of the spectators assumed the police had made a mistake. This decent-looking, clean-cut, obviously articulate young man could not possibly be the monster "Ted". He looked more like a young executive.

In spite of Carol DaRonch's identification, the case against Bundy looked thin and circumstantial. His main line of defence was that he had been the victim of a series of incredible coincidences. Bundy's case continued to look convincing until he himself stepped into the witness box on the fourth day. It was not that there was anything wrong with the way he presented himself – just that he seemed *too* plausible, too clever. Explaining why he had driven away from the police car, he told the court that he had been smoking pot, and had thrown it out of the car as he drove. He seemed a little too smart and confident to be innocent. In his closing arguments, the prosecutor admitted that the evidence was circumstantial. But when he went on to point out the odds against such a body of evidence pointing to the wrong person, everyone in court recognised the power of his argument. Even so, the prosecutor felt that the verdict was likely to go against him. It was not until the following Monday, when the Judge Stewart Hanson declared: "I find Theodore Robert Bundy guilty of aggravated kidnapping" that he knew he had won. Before being sentenced, Bundy sobbed and pleaded not to be sent to prison. The judge was unmoved, and sentenced him to between one and fifteen years in prison.

One thing was now obvious: that if Bundy was the man who had abducted Carol DaRonch, then he was also the man who had kidnapped Debbie Kent from the Viewmont High School. That in turn meant he was a leading suspect in the other Salt Lake City abductions. And since his credit card receipts revealed that he *had* been in Colorado several times in 1975 – when five young women had vanished – it began to seem highly likely that Bundy was a mass sex-murderer.

In January 1977, Bundy was moved to Aspen, Colorado. The Colorado authorities were beginning to build up a convincing case that he had been responsible for the abduction of Caryn Campbell – a man answering to Bundy's description had been seen in the hotel on the evening of her disappearance. And a third lot of hair found in Bundy's VW matched Caryn Campbell's. The crowbar found in Bundy's car matched the depression found in Caryn's skull. A credit card receipt showed he had been in the area when a girl named Julie Cunningham had vanished, and a gas station attendant had identified him. Altogether, the new case against Bundy looked rather more convincing than the previous one in Salt Lake City.

In the Colorado jail, Bundy was a popular prisoner. His charm, intelligence and sense of humour convinced many of his fellow prisoners of his innocence. He had decided to act as his own defence counsel, and this led to the decision to allow him in court without manacles. The District Attorney described him as "the most cocky person I have ever faced". Bundy was certainly becoming increasingly bitter, aggressive and dispirited as the time of his trial approached.

On the morning of 7 June 1977, Bundy appeared in court in Aspen, and listened to the public defender arguing against the death penalty. During the lunch hour, he strolled into the library on the second floor. Minutes later, a woman saw a man land on the grass verge below the window and limp off down the street. She asked a policeman: "Is it normal for people to jump out of windows around here?" Cursing, the officer rushed up to the library. As he had expected, Bundy was no longer there.

He was, in fact, already in a nearby river gorge, stripping down to his shirt and shorts to make himself look like a hiker. Then, with his clothes stuffed into his sweater and tied in a bundle, he strolled off along the road to Aspen Mountain. People and cars passed without giving him a second glance. Further up the mountain he found a refuge in an unoccupied cabin, where he hid for two days. But when he set out again, he somehow managed to retrace his steps and wander in a circle. After stealing a Cadillac, he was spotted by the police, and rearrested only blocks from where he had escaped eight days earlier. He looked thin and exhausted.

For the next six months, legal arguments dragged on about what evidence was admissible. The prosecution wanted to introduce evidence about other girls who had vanished in Utah. Bundy fought back, using endless delaying tactics.

At 7 am on the morning of 31 December 1976, a guard in the Garfield County Jail left the breakfast tray outside Bundy's cell and saw a figure asleep in the bunk. At lunchtime the tray was still there, and the figure had still not moved. On investigation, it proved to be a pile of books and pillows. A hole in the ceiling round the light fitting showed how, with the aid of a hacksaw blade, Bundy had made his second escape from prison. By the time the alarm was raised, Bundy was already in Chicago.

Tallahassee, the state capital of Florida, has certain things in common with Seattle – among them, a relaxed atmosphere and a pleasant university campus.

It was two weeks since Ted Bundy had escaped from Colorado, but the news had hardly penetrated this far south. And in the students' lodging house known as the Oaks, no one paid much attention to a new arrival called Chris Hagen, who had taken a small, shabby room for $80 a month. The few who talked to him found him intelligent and charming, but he seemed to prefer to keep himself to himself. What no one guessed was that Chris Hagen was almost out of money, and was stealing from supermarkets to keep himself alive.

At 3 am on the morning of Sunday 15 January 1978, Nita Neary said goodnight to her boyfriend and let herself into the Chi Omega sorority house on the edge of the campus. Someone had left lights on, and she turned them off. Then she heard the sound of footsteps on the stairs, and saw a man hurrying towards the front door. As he opened it she saw that he was wearing a dark knit cap, and was carrying some sort of wooden club.

Her first assumption was that one of the students had sneaked a man into her room. But there was something furtive about this man's bearing that worried her. She ran upstairs and roused her room mate, then the two of them went to waken the sorority president. As they were talking, a door opened and a girl staggered out, clutching her head. They recognised Karen Chandler, and a moment later saw that her hair was soaked with blood. They rushed into the room Karen shared with Kathy Kleiner, and found Kathy sitting up groggily in bed, blood streaming down her face.

The police were there within minutes. They quickly discovered that two more girls – Margaret Bowman and Lisa Levy – had been attacked, and that Margaret was dead, strangled with pantyhose; Lisa Levy died on her way to hospital. Margaret Bowman's knickers had been torn off so violently that her skin had been grazed, one of Lisa Levy's nipples had almost been bitten off, and blood was running from the anus and vagina. The medical examiner also discovered a bite mark on her left buttock.

An hour and a half later, in a small frame house six blocks away, Debbie Cicarelli was aroused by loud bangs apparently coming from the next room, occupied by Cheryl Thomas. Minutes later, she heard whimpering noises. She roused her room-mate, and they both listened to the sounds. Then Debbie tried dialling Cheryl's phone number. As the telephone rang, there was a bumping noise and a sound of running feet. Minutes later, the house was swarming with police who had rushed over from the Chi Omega house. Cheryl Thomas was semi-conscious, and the bloodstained bedclothes had been pulled from the bed. A wooden club lay on the floor nearby. Cheryl, like Karen and Kathy, would survive the brutal beating, although only after coming close to death.

The Chi Omega murders made nationwide headlines – although, oddly enough, no one thought of suggesting that Bundy might be in Florida. And in the Oaks, Christ Hagen continued to keep himself to himself. He often seemed to be drunk late at night.

In fact, he was now living mainly on theft – of credit cards and items from supermarkets. He was also becoming an expert at stealing women's purses. Then, on 5 February 1978, he stole a white Dodge van from a parking lot, and drove off in the direction of Jacksonville. Two days later, on Wednesday 8 February, a "sloppily dressed" man with a two-day growth of beard approached fourteen-year-old Leslie Parmenter in a Jacksonville street and tried to engage her in conversation but he seemed confused and unsure of himself. At that moment, her twenty-year-old brother drove up—he intended giving her a lift home – and asked the stranger what he wanted. The man mumbled something and wandered off towards his white van. Danny Parmenter followed him and, as he drove off, noted down the number of the van.

The following morning "Chris Hagen" left the local Holiday Inn without even bothering to pay with a stolen credit card, and drove around aimlessly until he found himself near the Lake City Junior High School.

Minutes into her first period gym class, twelve-year-old Kimberly Leach realised she had left her purse in another room, and asked to be excused to go and fetch it. But it was not until two o'clock that afternoon that someone noticed she had not returned, and rang her mother. By then, Kim Leach had vanished.

That same afternoon, Chris Hagen was back in Tallahassee. The following evening, he took a girl out to dinner, using a stolen credit card, and behaved impeccably. But later that night, after a policeman had looked searchingly at the stolen Dodge van, he left the apartment by means of the fire escape, stole an orange Volkswagen in which the owner had left the keys, and headed west towards Pensacola.

In the early hours of the morning of Wednesday 15 February 1978, Patrolman David Lee saw an orange VW driving erratically out of an alleyway. He radioed the license number, and moments later, was told that it was stolen. When he flashed his lights, the car accelerated for a moment, then pulled over. He ordered the driver to get out and lie down, but as the suspect obeyed, he kicked the policeman's legs from under him, and took to his heels. Lee pulled out his gun and fired. The man collapsed on the pavement. But as Lee bent over him and tried to turn him over, the man hit him on the jaw. They struggled grimly for a few moments, then Lee snapped the handcuffs on the man's wrists.

As they drove off towards the police station, the handcuffed man remarked gloomily: "I wish you'd killed me".

Back at the station, the suspect insisted that his name was Kenneth Misner and supported his story with identification papers and a birth certificate. The police soon learned that the papers had been stolen from a real Kenneth Misner in Tallahassee. It was another twenty-four hours before the Pensacola interrogators discovered – through overhearing the prisoner's phone conversations – that they had arrested a man named Ted Bundy. Absurdly enough, the name meant nothing to them.

In the early hours of the morning, a demoralised and exhausted Bundy talked into a tape recorder. His aim, he explained, was to try to make interrogators understand his problem. It had all started, he said, when he had seen a girl riding a bicycle. "I knew I had to have her." And although she had escaped, his future course was now determined. "Sometimes I feel like a vampire." But he denied being responsible for the sorority house attacks.

It was nearly two months later, on 7 April 1978, that a highway patrolman looked into an old shed near Suwannee River State Park, and saw a foot wearing a sneaker. Inside was the naked, decomposing body of Kimberly Leach. Injuries to the pelvic region suggested sexual assault. The cause of death was "homicidal violence to the neck region". One sickened lawman declared: "We're gonna send that Bundy to the electric chair".

But Bundy's hour of weakness had passed. He was once again insisting on his total innocence, and that his apparent connection with a chain of sex murders was pure coincidence.

Bundy was right about one thing: all the evidence against him was circumstantial – all, at any rate, except for one thing: the bite mark on Lisa Levy's left buttock.

Three weeks after Kimberly Leach's body had been found, policemen held the struggling Bundy down and took an impression of his teeth. That impression, more than any other piece of evidence, would finally convict him.

Once again, Bundy had decided to act as his own defence lawyer, and his delaying tactics succeeded in getting the trial delayed from October 1978 to June 1979. At one point he changed his mind, and decided to accept a defence team from the public defender's office. But when they made it clear that they wanted him to enter into "plea bargaining" – agreeing to plead guilty to the murders of Lisa Levy, Margaret Bowman and Kimberly Leach in exchange for a guarantee that he would not receive the death sentence – Bundy sacked them. It was the third major mistake of his criminal career. The first two had been the careless driving offences that had led to his two arrests. This third mistake would prove, eventually, to be the most serious of the three.

The trial began on 25 June 1979, and Bundy scored an initial success when his objections succeeded on having it moved from Tallahassee to Miami, on the grounds that Tallahassee jurors would be prejudiced. But from then on, it was clear that Bundy was losing ground fast. The evidence against him was damning: the girl Nira Neary who had seen him leave the sorority house, the pantyhose mask found in the room of Cheryl Thomas, which was virtually identical with the one found earlier in Bundy's car; but above all, the bite marks found on Lisa Levy's left buttock, which dental experts testified to be those of Bundy's own teeth. Bundy scored another success when the judge ruled that the tapes of his "confessions" to the Pensacola police were inadmissible because his lawyer had not been present. But while Bundy himself continued to believe he was doing well, no one else in court could doubt that the case against him was overwhelming. Public defender Margaret Good made a powerful speech in Bundy's defence, underlining every possible doubt. It was all to no purpose. On 23 July 1979, the jury took only seven hours to find him guilty on a long list of indictments. Asked if he had anything to say, Bundy put on another of his displays of injured innocence, and replied with tears in his voice: "I find it somewhat absurd to ask for mercy for something I did not do". After that, Judge Edward D. Cowart sentenced him to die by electrocution. The judge concluded: "I bear you no animosity, believe me. But you went the wrong way, pardner. Take care of yourself".

The first of many books on Bundy concluded with these words. But the Ted Bundy story was by no means over. From the Raiford Penitentiary, where he was placed on Death Row, Bundy continued to fight for his life. On 7 January 1980, he was tried in Orlando for the murder of Kimberly Leach. Colour slides of the body were shown, and the medical evidence seemed to indicate that the girl had been raped in the van, dressed again, then taken to the hut and stripped and possibly sodomised. On 7 February 1980, Bundy was again found guilty. Once again he burst into tears. Two days later he married a girl named Carole Boone, a divorce with a teenage son. She continued to believe in his innocence. And Bundy continued with his appeals.

Even before his trial in Miami, Bundy had decided to take "his case to the public". In 1978 that he made it known that he would be willing to talk to a professional writer, and Stephen Michaud and Hugh Aynesworth began to take it in turns to interview him in jail. As the best-known prisoner in the penitentiary, he apparently felt that he deserved a full-scale biography such as other celebrities like Frank Sinatra. He apparently envisaged a sympathetic, gossipy book that would start from the assumption of his innocence. Michaud and Aynesworth would have been perfectly willing to write such a book, but the more they studied the case, the more certain they became of his guilt. Both found that his chief characteristics were emotional immaturity and an apparently infinite capacity for self-deception. "So extreme was his childishness that his pleas of innocence were of a character very similar to that of the little boy who'll deny wrong-doing in the face of overwhelming evidence to the contrary." Bundy proved to be highly skilled in lying, hedging, self-justification and pleas of faulty memory. Gradually, he reached the decision to "speculate freely" about the motives and character of the murderer, and launched himself so enthusiastically into ambiguous speculation that he spoke for hours into a tape recorder.

What emerges in the book *The Only Living Witness* (1983) is the story of a "loner" who became totally obsessed by sex, and who advanced step by step into sex murder, like a man wading into a murky pool.

For Michaud and Aynesworth, the most baffling thing about Bundy was the normality of his background – no severe childhood deprivation, no sexual or physical abuse, no obvious traumas.

Theodore Robert Bundy was an illegitimate child, born to a respectable and religious young secretary – Louise Cowell – in a home for unmarried mothers near Philadelphia on 24 November 1946. His mother chose the name Theodore because it means "gift of God". The identity of the father is unknown, and Louise Bundy herself has always refused to discuss it. (Bundy himself once told an interviewer that it was his grandfather, a retired market gardener of tyrannical temper.) Louise continued to live at home, and her parents told neighbours that Ted was their adopted child. His grandparents certainly treated him as if he was their own child. When Ted was four, his mother decided to make a fresh start and went to stay with relatives in Tacoma (virtually a suburb of Seattle.) At a church social, she met a mild, easy-going southerner, John Bundy, who had just left the navy. He found a job as a cook in a veterans' hospital, and remained there for the rest of his working life. Ted found his new father dull and uncultured, but seems to have had nothing else against him. Neither did he show any resentment towards his new brothers and sisters.

Ted was an over-sensitive and self-conscious child who had all the usual daydreams of fame and wealth. He fantasised about being adopted by the cowboy star Roy Rogers, and actually asked his uncle Jack, a professor of music in Tacoma, to adopt him. At an early stage he became a thief and a habitual liar – as many imaginative children do. But he got fairly good grades at school, became an enthusiastic boy scout, and was a natural athlete. He later became an excellent skier, although the expensive equipment on which he learned was almost certainly stolen.

As a first-year student at college he was lonely, silent and shy. The desire to be "different" led him to decide to study Chinese. In his late teens he became heavily infatuated with a fellow student, Stephanie Brooks, who was beautiful, sophisticated, and came of a wealthy family. By now Ted had already developed something of that charm and air of sophistication that made him attractive to women, and they became engaged. To impress Stephanie and her family he went to Stanford University to study Chinese, but he was lonely, emotionally immature, and his grades were poor. "I found myself thinking of standards of success that I didn't seem to be living up to." Stephanie, weary of his immaturity, threw him over. He was shattered and deeply resentful. His brother commented: "Stephanie screwed him up . . . I'd never seen him like this before." He took a menial job in a hotel dining-room, and became friendly with a drug addict. One night they entered an abandoned cliffside house and stole whatever could be carried. He found it a strangely exciting experience. He began shoplifting and stealing for "thrills" – on one occasion he walked openly into someone's greenhouse, removed an eight-foot palm, and drove off with it sticking out of the sunroof of his car.

He also became a full-time volunteer for Art Fletcher, the black Republican candidate for Lieutenant Governor, and enjoyed the sense of being a "somebody" and mixing with interesting people. Later he took a job working for the Crime Commission and Department of Justice Planning – other males in the office envied his easy charm and good looks. When, seven years after throwing him over, Stephanie Brooks met him again, she was deeply impressed by the new, high-powered Ted, and once more agreed to marry him – they spent the Christmas of 1973 together. Then, having achieved his object and got his "revenge", Bundy "dumped" her as she had dumped him. When she rang him to ask why he had not contacted her since their weekend together, he said coldly: "I have no idea what you're talking about", and hung up on her. Stephanie wrote to a friend: "I escaped by the skin of my teeth. When I think of his cold and calculating manner, I shudder".

A few weeks later, as if his "revenge" had somehow broken some inner dam and inspired him with a sense of ruthless power and confidence, he became a rapist and murderer . . . But the craving for sexual violence had developed long before he committed his first murder. In his early twenties, Bundy developed into a Peeping Tom as a result of catching an accidental glimpse of a girl removing her clothes through a lighted window. From then on he began to prowl the streets around the University of Washington at night, looking for bedroom windows to spy through. "He approached it almost like a project", says Michaud, "throwing himself into it literally, for years." Then, "like an addiction, the need for a more powerful experience was coming over him". He made clumsy attempts to disable women's cars, but since these were parked in the university district, they usually found help without any difficulty. Bundy regarded this as a kind of game, a flirtation with danger, "but the habit grew perceptibly more insistent, just as Ted had become a bolder and bolder thief over the years". One evening in the summer of 1973, after drinking heavily, Bundy saw a woman leaving a bar and walking up a dark side street. He found a heavy piece of wood in a vacant lot, and stalked her. "There was really no control at this point. The situation is novel", said Bundy (speaking of himself in the third person), "because while he may have toyed around with fantasies before, and made several abortive attempts to act out a fantasy, it never had reached the point where actually he was confronted with harming another individual." "Nevertheless, he got ahead of the girl and lay in wait for her. But before she reached the point where he was hiding, she stopped and went into a house. Bundy told his interviewers: "The revelation of the experience and the frenzied desire that seized him really seemed to usher in a new dimension to that part of him that was obsessed with violence and women". (Like so many other serial killers, Bundy saw himself as a dual-personality, a Jekyll and Hyde; he referred to Mr Hyde as "the Hunchback.") "What he had done terrified him, purely terrified him. Full of remorse and remonstrating with himself for the suicidal nature of that activity" – Bundy also recognised murder as a form of suicide – ". . . he quickly sobered up. He was horrified by the recognition that he had the capacity to do such a thing".

The craving to watch girls undressing was too strong to be resisted. One night he was peering through a basement window at a girl preparing for bed when he discovered that the door had been left open. He sneaked into her room and leapt on her, but when she screamed, he fled. "Then he was siezed with the same kind of disgust and repulsion and fear and wonder at why he was allowing himself to attempt such extraordinary violence". He was so upset that he gave up his voyeuristic activities for three months. But on 4 January 1974, he again crept into a basement after he had watched a girl undressing. He wrenched a metal bar from the bed frame and struck her repeatedly on the head. Then, apparently finding himself impotent, he rammed the bar into her vagina. The girl recovered after a week in a coma. It took Bundy a month to recover from the trauma of what he had done. This time he carried his fantasy through to the end. On 31 January 1974, he entered a students' lodging house and tried bedroom doors until he found one that was unlocked. It was that of of twenty-one-year-old Lynda Ann Healy. This time he seized her by the throat and ordered her to remain silent. Then, either at knifepoint of gunpoint – it never became clear which – he forced her to dress, then bound and gagged her, and made her walk out of the house with him. He drove her out to Taylor Mountain, twenty miles from Seattle, then spent hours acting out his sexual fantasies. The interviewers asked him whether there had been any conversation with his victim. "There'd be some. Since this girl in front of him represented not a person, but again the image, or something desirable, the last thing we would expect him to want to do would be to personalise this person". Finally, he bludgeoned her to death and left the body on the mountain. Lynda Ann Healy would be the first of four girls he raped and murdered in the same place.

Perhaps the most frightening thing about Bundy's account of himself is the description of how he descended into sex murder by a series of almost infinitesimal steps. Any normal male might experience sexual excitement at a casual glimpse of a woman taking off her clothes near a lighted window. Any normal male might return to a place where he knew he could watch a girl undressing. Any normal male might become increasingly obsessed by watching girls undress until he had turned it into a "project". At what point *would* the normal male draw the line? Possibly at actually harming another human being. But then, Bundy also drew the line there – until his craving pushed him the inevitable step further . . . By the time he moved to Salt Lake City, Bundy knew that he would never be able to stop committing sex murders.

Time finally ran out for Bundy on 24 January 1989 when his final appeal was turned down, and the date set for his execution; he tried to bargain for his life by offering confessions in exchange for a reprieve. This attempt to "trade over the victims' bodies" caused violent hostility among the law officers. And the confessions themselves hardly created sympathy: for example, he told how Georgann Hawkins had offered to help him carry his briefcase when he was walking on crutches, and how, as she bent to put it down, he picked up an iron bar from the ground, knocked her unconscious, then bundled her into the car . . .

At 7 am on 24 January 1989, Bundy was led into the execution chamber at Starke Prison, Florida. Behind a plexiglass wall, an invited audience of forty-eight people were waiting. Bundy's head had already been shaved. As his arms were strapped to the electric chair, he recognised his attorney among the watching face and nodded. Straps were placed around his chest and over his mouth, and a steel cap fastened on his head with screws. At 7.07 the executioner threw the switch, and Bundy's body strained upwards in the chair. A minute later, the current was switched off, and Bundy was pronounced dead. Outside, a crowd carrying "Fry Bundy!" banners cheered as the execution was announced.

We return to the question raised earlier in this book: why has the serial killer emerged at this point in history? But this study of the development of crime over the centuries should have suggested the answer. It was when men came together in cities that they began to make war, and that they began to rob and murder one another. We can see what happened by looking at "primitive" peoples of today. They live in small villages and they subsist by hunting and agriculture. There is virtually no crime within such a small community because there is no need for it: everybody knows everybody else. They may occasionally mount a raid on another tribal community, but such occasional forays may be regarded as an extension of hunting rather than as war. Little by little, our remote ancestors saw their mud villages expanding into large communities with a temple and a priesthood. They became the first cities (often no larger than a modern village). A city needs agricultural land to supply it with food and if the city next door tries to expand its boundaries, the result is a "territorial" dispute. (It was not until the early 1960s that writers like Konrad Lorenz and Robert Ardrey made the general public aware of the importance of "territory" – the basic urge of all creatures to establish an area that belongs to them, and from which all invaders are repelled). The birth of the city made warfare inevitable, and because an anonymous mass of human beings were now crowded together, many of them close to starvation, robbery and murder also became a commonplace. "Dominant" individuals grabbed what they wanted. The successful ones became kings and generals. The unsuccessful ones became outlaws.

Even so, there is evidence that the early city builders were fairly peaceful and humane – after all, they had come together into communities for their own protection. But civilisation brings its own pressures. The more human beings who are collaborating to make their lives more fruitful, the easier it becomes to achieve "success", to become rich or powerful. The easier it also becomes to fail and "go to the wall". Society slowly turns into something like the modern "rat race".

Yet even this has its positive side. In a primitive society, no one has much time to relax; everyone has to work. The new city states, with their priests and merchants, could offer a small percentage of their citizens an astonishing new commodity called leisure. One of the tasks of the priesthood was to observe the movements of the heavenly bodies, so they could advise the farmers on the best times for planting. In ancient Babylon, these priests began making "star maps" – an activity that would have struck their ancestors of a few generations ago as tiresome and pointless. Yet these star maps enabled their sailors to navigate the seas with a new confidence. Moreover, some successful men had time to devote themselves to an altogether stranger exercise: thinking for the sake of thinking. Primitive man is inclined to explain things in terms of myth. Philosophers like Thales and Pythagoras were more interested in practical causes, and Thales is said to have known enough about astronomy to predict an eclipse of the sun. A mere century later, thinkers like Socrates, Plato and Aristotle were creating a body of knowledge and speculation that still strikes us as one of the greatest achievements of mankind. All this was a direct outcome of that change in the balance of society that also created poverty and crime. Piracy and brigandage were the unfortunate by-products of the evolution of civilisation. Science and philosophy were its positive achievements.

Two thousand years later, the Industrial Revolution created an immense reservoir of leisure, and this again gave rise to a revolution in science and philosophy. Yet, as we have seen, the Industrial Revolution also gave birth to "the age of sex crime". The life of the Marquis de Sade offers us an insight into how this came about. Before he was sent to prison – and confronted with a dreary wilderness of enforced leisure – Sade was fairly ordinary sexual pervert with a taste for blasphemy and flogging. Twelve years in jail – with nothing to do except develop his lurid fantasies – turned him into the arch-sadist and patron saint of all serial killers. This I believe, explains how the leisure of the nineteenth century gave birth to the age of sex crime. The Victorians placed Woman on a pedestal, but there were many unrefined individuals who were unable to resist the temptation to peer up her skirts.

The serial killer, like the sexual criminal, is an unsavoury by-product of the evolution of civilisation. He has been brought into existence by a culture that offers the rest of us the highest level of prosperity and security in human history. Like the human monsters we considered in an earlier chapter of this book, he is a misshapen symbol of our capacity for freedom and evolution. I venture to prophesy that our descendants will not feel that the price is too high.

16.
Conclusion

WE MUST now return to the question raised at the end of the first chapter: does the human race somehow *need* robbery and rape and murder? Man has achieved his present position as lord of the earth by sheer ruthlessness, his ability to survive. That struggle has been going on for the past fifteen million years. And then, in a mere two hundred years, he has achieved an unprecendented level of security and comfort. He firmly believes that his deepest desire is for peace and prosperity, but the wars of the twentieth century,, and the steady rise in levels of social violence, make it look like wishful thinking. Freud expressed the same view in a book called *Civilisation and Its Discontents*: that man's most basic impulses are aggressive, and that therefore civilisation is bound to be full of unhappy neurotics. If civilisation becomes too 'peaceful', it will end by exploding like a bomb.

If we accept Freud's pessimistic assessment of human nature, then we may as well agree that nothing can save us. But this book has suggested that Freud may not be wholly correct. Maslow believed that Freud had 'sold human nature short', and that there are 'higher ceilings' that psychoanalysts never even suspected. Even the emergence of the serial killer supports Maslow's theory of the 'hierarchy of needs'. In 1800, virtually all crime was 'economic' – connected with man's most basic needs. The Victorian age was the age of 'domestic murder', in which crime became connected with the next level of need: security. The late nineteenth century saw the emergence of sex crime, connected with Maslow's next level of need. The 1960s saw the emergence of the next level: the crime of 'self-esteem', the criminal whose basic craving was to '*be* somebody'.

But it is important to remember that, in talking about these levels of 'need', we are not talking only about criminals. They apply to the *whole* society. in the Victorian age, everyone became preoccupied with domestic security. By the middle of the twentieth century, everyone wasmuch more preoccupied by sex. The second half of the twentieth century has seen an increasing preoccupation with status. (For example, the whole 'anti-Establishment' revolt of the 1960s was a challenge to the notion that 'respectability' conferred status; young people with torn jeans and green hair were insisting that they had just as much right to be 'noticed'.) And the post-sixties era also saw an increasing preoccupation with the fifth level of Maslow's hierarchy: self-actualisation, the craving for deeper and more satisfying levels of consciousness, for a more meaningful and purposeful existence.

Once we begin to think in terms of an evolution of the whole society, Freud's pessimistic conclusions begin to seem altogether less inevitable. He thought of human nature as fixed and unchangeable; but evolutionary pressures can change anything. For example, the 'average man' of today can cope with a degree of complexity that would have driven the average Elizabethan – or Victorian – to nervous breakdown or suicide. Our bodies may remain more or less the same, but our minds are changing. Even the phenomenon of the 'high I.Q. killer' demonstrates this. It is disturbing, because we are shocked at the notion that an intelligent person should commit murder. Yet there is an obvious sense in which the high I.Q. killer is preferable to the kind of brutal sadists described in the journal of Franz Schmidt, the Nuremberg Hangman, who disembowelled pregnant women and made a housewife eat a fried egg off the corpse of her murdered husband. He is preferable because an intelligent man is a step further away from murder than a mindless brute. And if the whole society is evolving in the direction of intelligence, there seems a reasonable chance that man will outgrow his aggressions, and find new outlets for his craving for adventure, freedom and creativity.

One thing is certain: that from the evolutionary point of view, the criminal is at a disadvantage. In 1982, I expressed the basis of my optimism in a paragraph in the introduction to *A Criminal History of Mankind*:

'Crime is renewed in every generation because human beings *are* children; very few of us achieve anything like adulthood. But at least it is not self-perpetuating, as human creativity is. Shakespeare learns from Marlow, and in turn inspires Goethe. Beethoven learns from Haydn and in turn inspires Wagner. Newton learns from Kepler and in turn inspires Einstein. But Vlad the Impaler, Jack the Ripper and Al Capone leave no progeny. Their 'achievement' is negative, and dies with them. The criminal also tends to be the victim of natural selection – of his own lack of self-control. Man has achieved his present level of civilisation because creativity 'snowballs' while crime, fortunately, remains static.'

That is why, in spite of three thousand years of cruelty and slaughter, there is still hope for the human race.